Inclusive Learning and Educational Equity

Volume 3

This book series reflects on the challenges of inclusive education as a strategy for improving educational equity, and includes in-depth analyses of disparities in education and the mechanisms by which they operate. It studies the development of educational processes and pedagogical interventions that respond to the tensions between education policies that promote competition and those designed to promote inclusion at individual, classroom, school, district, national, and international levels. Finally, it presents research and development activities in teacher education that respond to the challenges of preparing teachers for the changing demographic of schooling. Increasingly throughout the world, a broad concept of inclusive education has begun to emerge as a strategy for achieving basic education for all learners regardless of cultural, developmental or linguistic differences. Although considered an important aspect of a global human rights agenda supported by the multilateral Global Partnership for Education, basic education is a complex endeavour that is subject to the forces of globalization, and the exclusionary pressures associated with migration, mobility, language, ethnicity, disability, and intergenerational poverty. The reciprocal links between these factors and educational underachievement has led to an increasing interest in the development of inclusive education as a strategy for improving educational equity. By addressing these and related issues, this series contributes important advances in knowledge about the enactment of inclusive education. This series: Offers a critical perspective on current practice Stimulates and challenges further developments for the field Explores global disparities in educational provision and compares developments Provides a welcome addition to the literature on inclusive education.

More information about this series at http://www.springer.com/series/13450

Santoshi Halder • Lori Czop Assaf
Editors

Inclusion, Disability and Culture

An Ethnographic Perspective Traversing
Abilities and Challenges

 Springer

Editors
Santoshi Halder
Department of Education
University of Calcutta
Kolkata, West Bengal, India

Lori Czop Assaf
Department of Curriculum and Instruction
Texas State University
San Marcos, TX, USA

Inclusive Learning and Educational Equity
ISBN 978-3-319-55223-1   ISBN 978-3-319-55224-8   (eBook)
DOI 10.1007/978-3-319-55224-8

Library of Congress Control Number: 2017940487

Printed on acid-free paper

This Springer imprint is published by Springer Nature
The registered company is Springer International Publishing AG
The registered company address is: Gewerbestrasse 11, 6330 Cham, Switzerland

Dedicated to all children, parents and families of the world for inclusion, access and equity.

–S.H

For all those willing to reconceptualize and deconstruct what it means to be abled human beings in a global world

–L.C.A

Foreword: *Nihil De Nobis, Sine Nobis*

Despite over a century of activism by advocates for equal access to society regardless of sociocultural factors, these irrelevant factors still result in the marginalization of billions worldwide. For example, although the number of people who work to facilitate racial equality has increased tremendously over the last century, subtle prejudices that limit opportunity remain common everywhere, and even egregious discrimination can still be found. Given the longstanding struggle for equality experienced by people who differ only in terms of sociocultural or racial factors, it is not surprising that the relatively recent struggle for equal access to society's benefits (inclusion) by people with physical, intellectual and developmental differences is understudied, daunting and sometimes controversial. Additionally, the obvious fact that ability and developmental diversity exists in tandem with sociocultural and racial differences adds further complexity.

The title of this foreword, 'Nihil De Nobis, Sine Nobis' or 'nothing about us without us', expresses a sentiment that often arises when marginalized populations self-advocate for improved societal access and opportunity. I believe it is suitable in this foreword as an acknowledgement to the seminal book by James Charlton (1998). Charlton eloquently argued against the not uncommon conceptualization of individuals with diverse abilities as dependent and powerless while also providing a cross-cultural perspective through his interviews with disability activists from ten countries. Charlton's landmark contribution was necessarily polemic and accessible and thus intentionally omitted descriptions of interview methodology and other similar details (Lazar, 1999).

The book, *Inclusion, Disability and Culture: An Ethnographic Perspective Traversing Abilities and Challenges*, is similar to Charlton's in that empowerment and participation of people with a range of abilities are central themes and cross-cultural discussion is interwoven throughout. However, the current text adds the voices of researchers representing many fields (e.g. education, public policy, psychology and sociology) alongside those of individuals with diverse abilities and their families to create a transdisciplinary and culturally anchored perspective for the reader while maintaining an academic tone. The result is an edited text that inspires advocacy as well as practical translation to directions for future research and current practice.

Families, clinicians, teachers, scientists and others who work to improve the quality of life of people with disability must operate from paradigms constructed from our own learning histories and experiences. This book aims, I believe successfully, to expand paradigms regardless of one's role in the field and adds meaningfully to the vital and ongoing conversation on disability and inclusion taking place worldwide.

Russell Lang

References

Charlton, J. I. (1998). *Nothing about us without us: Disability oppression and empowerment.* Los Angeles: University of California Press. doi:10.1525/9780520207950

Lazar, S. (1999). Nothing about us without us: Disability oppression and empowerment: Book review. *Disability and Rehabilitation, 21*(8), 400. doi:10.1080/096382899297558

Series Editor's Preface

The Sustainable Development Goals (SDGs) adopted by the UN in September 2015 set the global education agenda for 2030 in SDG 4: Ensure inclusive and quality education for all and promote lifelong learning. Inclusive education is a rights-based approach to education intended to reduce exclusion and marginalization in education that gained prominence in the 1990s as a strategy to achieve 'education for all', the global commitment to ensure that everyone has access to quality basic education. In May 2015, the World Forum on Education reaffirmed its commitment to this approach with the *Incheon Declaration* and the Education 2030 Framework for Action. The Incheon Declaration notes that 'inclusion and equity in and through education is the cornerstone of a transformative education agenda' and that 'no education target should be considered met unless met by all'.[1]

Issues of inclusion in education are of relevance for people with disabilities who remain among the most excluded of all marginalized groups in educational systems throughout the world. The *World Report on Disability*[2] found that children with disabilities are less likely to start school, do well in school and complete school than children without disabilities (p. 206). This inequality of opportunity has long-term consequences not only for educational outcomes but for quality of life after school.

In a world where 10% of the estimated one billion people living with disabilities are children,[3] it is more essential than ever that their voices and those of their families and caregivers become part of the discussion on how to improve access and ensure better quality educational opportunities for all. Combing the multidisciplinary voices of professionals with those of caregivers and people with disabilities from different world regions helps to establish a more integrated approach to the literature on inclusion for the twenty-first century. It is fitting therefore that this

---

[1] Unesco (2015) Education 2030: Incheon Declaration and Framework for Action, http://www.uis.unesco.org/Education/Documents/incheon-framework-for-action-en.pdf

[2] WHO/World Bank, (2011) World Report on Disability http://www.who.int/disabilities/world_report/2011/en/

[3] Global Partnership for Education, http://www.globalpartnership.org/focus-areas/children-with-disabilities

timely volume on disability and inclusion is published now when there is so much to learn from hearing these voices as part of one narrative rather than as fragments. While many books have addressed issues of inclusion and disability, this one takes a sociocultural perspective that permits an exploration of disability identities in different national and cultural contexts, along with insights from caregivers, and the communication issues that can arise between differently abled persons. A consideration of inclusive policies, practices and interventions complements these discussions leading to a critical reflection on future directions for research and practice.

University of Edinburgh   Lani Florian
Edinburgh, UK

Preface

Being engaged in disability research for so many years across multiple countries, we feel strongly about creating a space for researchers, teachers, practitioners and parents to discuss, compare and challenge how disability is culturally defined and played out around the world. Current global population predictions estimate that more than a billion people (15% of the world population) will live with some form of disability in the next 10 years. Alarmingly, these individuals have a higher risk of discrimination, exploitation, violence and abuse because of a disability. Yet, the term disability is a relative and subjective concept that varies throughout the world not because of an individual's functional or intellectual abilities but because of environmental and cultural barriers imposed upon them by societal norms and unchallenged histories. Such barriers can influence one's mobility, identity and social standing. The significance of the environment and the cultural context is evident from the Convention on the Rights of Persons with Disabilities (CRPD) definition of disability which clearly marks a paradigm shift by utilizing a 'social model of disability' as an evolving concept resulting from the interaction between persons with disabilities and the attitudinal and environmental barriers existing in society.

This book provides a unique perspective on the notion of disability across cultures and countries by describing and challenging cultural norms and limitations. The authors of this edited volume employed either ethnographic or mixed-methods approaches to explore and systematically analyse their personal experiences and cultural influences on disability. They utilized self-observations and reflexive investigative methods in order to understand disability from a specific cultural space while critically reflecting upon their personal and professional identities. Authors represent a variety of stakeholders including parents, special educators, researchers and clinical practitioners and provide cross-disciplinary perspectives on disability and inclusion across many disciplines such as special education, early childhood, curriculum and instruction, architecture and interior design, psychology, science education, sociology, comparative education, international initiatives and relations, English language, disability studies, literacy and language education, city and regional planning and economics. They share cross-cultural perspectives within and across a variety of countries such as India, Australia, the USA, Sri Lanka, the UK,

Croatia, Brazil, South Africa and Qatar and provide expert and personal knowledge in disability studies and comparative analyses – provoking symptomatic and critical analysis of each country and issue. This book will help all readers (scholars, teachers, parents and community members) develop a deeper awareness of how disability is culturally conceptualized.

The book is categorized into four parts:

Part I: Deconstructing Disability Identities

In this part, the authors explore the concepts of disability and identity from a variety of sociocultural perspectives. Using auto-ethnographic methods, the authors provide thoughtful portrayals of how their lives have been shaped by their disability. They describe how inequities can prevent people with disabilities from living normal lives and how they became advocates for themselves and others.

Part II: Exploring the Complexities of Communication with Differently Abled Persons

The chapters in Part II highlight the research on communication disabilities and the communication patterns, barriers and interactions between individuals with and without disabilities. Relevant practices and new technologies are discussed.

Part III: Inclusive Policies, Practices and Interventions

In Part III, the authors provide personal insights and research-based practices and interventions from a variety of disciplines. The authors argue for integrated, inclusive approaches that empower persons with disabilities in order to create an equal and just society.

Part IV: Insights from Caregivers

In this last part, the authors describe their experiences as caregivers to children with disabilities. They draw on their unique perspectives as mothers to highlight the complexities and challenges of navigating a variety of social systems that don't always meet their child's needs.

   The book is designed to be of use to a wide range of professionals; researchers, practitioners, advocates, special educators and parents providing information and/or discussions on educational needs, healthcare provisions and social services which may be beneficial to all irrespective of country and culture who are working or are associated with the field of disability in various ways.

Kolkata, India   Santoshi Halder
San Marcos, TX, USA   Lori Czop Assaf

Acknowledgements

The initiation and the idea to bring out a book as an edited volume were conceived while meeting several people and experts from various aspects of disability and working very closely in some way for the people with disabilities. The definite structure of the book started crystalizing while sharing knowledge and information in various national and international forums like those conducted in India, Malaysia, the United States of America (USA), Thailand, Singapore, the United Kingdom (UK), South Africa and Australia.

I'm extremely thankful to the University of Calcutta for providing me the platform and support to flourish my research endeavour.

I would like to thank the United States-India Educational Foundation (USIEF) which provided the opportunity and scope as a Fulbright-Nehru Senior Research Scholar (2011–2012) to get connected with so many academicians and researchers of the world. In fact the whole idea of compiling this book initiated during the interviews, meetings and discussions with so many dedicated, versatile and amazing people as a Fulbright Scholar in the USA. My sincere thanks go to the whole team of the United States-India Educational Foundation (USIEF) and Council for International Exchange of Scholars (*CIES*) for their constant support.

I would like to acknowledge the Australian Government Department of Education and Training for providing the scope again to get connected to the world of scholars in various universities in Australia as an Endeavour Australia India Education Council Research Fellow (2015–2016).

My sincere acknowledgement goes to the Indian Council of Social Science Research (ICSSR), National Institute for the Humanities and Social Sciences (NIHSS) and University Grants Commission (UGC) for continuously supporting me financially to carry out multiple research projects on the various aspects of disability.

I would also like to thank all my research scholars and students who are my constant source of enthusiasm, energy and passion, directly or indirectly driving and energizing me towards significant and contributory work for the society and community. Special mention would be to my Ph.D. scholar Sanju Saha.

Transforming all the transcripts in the form of a book was only possible due to the publishing team at Springer International, who provided the scope and guided us through their step-by-step process in making this book in the current form.

My sincere thanks to my research colleague and friend Prof Lori Czop Assaf, Texas State University, the co-editor of this book, for all her assistance and valuable suggestions in all phases and stages of this book.

Finally, I would also like to thank my husband Dr. Arindam Talukdar, daughter Mihika, son Kiaan, mother in-law and parents for providing me the inspiration and throughout support, without which the book would not have been possible.

The book is the product of the cumulative efforts of so many people around the world in various countries who trusted to share their own experience and stories and agreed to extend their experiences of abilities and challenges to the world as a book chapter. Special thanks are due to all those people whom I may have missed out.

Santoshi Halder, Editor

Collaborating with Dr. Santoshi Halder and the authors of this edited book has provided me the opportunity to better understand the complexities and cultural influences of how we view and treat individuals with disability around the world and how important it is to gather these stories in one edited volume. I want to thank Dr. Halder for her patience and willingness to include me on this project as well as the Department of Curriculum and Instruction at Texas State University along with the Fulbright Scholar Program for funding Dr. Halder's visit to San Marcos allowing us to develop a friendship and professional relationship.

Lori Czop Assaf, Co-editor

Contents

Contributors

Alison F. Eardley Department of Psychology, University of Westminster, London, UK

Anjali J. Forber-Pratt Department of Human & Organizational Development, Vanderbilt University, Nashville, TN, USA

Bernardo Carlos Spaulonci Chiachia Matos de Oliveira Columbia University, New York, NY, USA

Pontificia Universidade Católica de Sao Paulo, Sao Paulo, Brazil

Beth Lewis Samuelson Literacy, Culture and Language Education, Indiana University, Bloomington, IN, USA

Caroline Muster Texas State University, San Marcos, TX, USA

Chandani Liyanage Department of Sociology, University of Colombo, Colombo, Sri Lanka

Christine Grima-Farrell School of Education, University of New South Wales, Kensington, NSW, Australia

Christopher J. Johnstone Assistant Professor, Department of Organizational Leadership, Policy, and Development, University of Minnesota, USA

Darren Hedley Olga Tennison Autism Research Centre, La Trobe University, Melbourne, Australia

David F.E. Hedley Independent Economic Consultant, Melbourne, Australia

Elizabeth M. Anderson Graduate School of Education, Binghamton University, Binghamton, NY, USA

Erna Alant School of Education, Indiana University, Bloomington, IN, USA

Flávia Affonso Mayer Fulbright Visiting Scholar, Department of Cognitive Science, Case Western Reserve University, Cleveland, OH, USA

Post-Doctoral Associate, Department of Communication and Arts, Pontificia Universidade Católica de Minas Gerais, Belo Horizonte, Brazil

Harsha Kathard Communication Sciences and Disorders, University of Cape Town, Cape Town, South Africa

Department of Health and Rehabilitation Sciences, University of Cape Town, Cape Town, South Africa

Ivana Bilić Faculty of Economic, University of Split, Split, Croatia

Joselia Neves College of Humanities and Social Sciences, Hamad bin Khalifa University, Ar-Rayyan, Qatar

Kerstin Tönsing Centre for Augmentative and Alternative Communication, University of Pretoria, Pretoria, South Africa

Lily Chakraborty Aarohan Welfare Society for Differently Abled Children, Kolkata, West Bengal, India

Lindsey Ogle School of Education, Indiana University, Bloomington, IN, USA

Lori Czop Assaf Department of Curriculum and Instruction, Texas State University, San Marcos, TX, USA

Louise Fryer Centre for Translation Studies (CenTraS), University College London, London, UK

VocalEyes, London, UK

Mary Keeffe Department of Education, La Trobe University, Melbourne, VIC, Australia

Matthew Cock VocalEyes, London, UK

Michal Harty Communication Sciences and Disorders, University of Cape Town, Cape Town, South Africa

Mirko Uljarević Olga Tennison Autism Research Centre, La Trobe University, Melbourne, Australia

Misa Kayama Department of Social Work, University of Mississippi, Oxford, MS, USA

Mitchell Graeme Coates School of Education, Australian Catholic University, Brisbane, QLD, Australia

Natalya Panteleyeva Mother (Parent) Greater Denver Area, Denver, CO, USA

Chromosome 18 Registry, San Antonio, TX, USA

Norma Isa Figueroa School of Architecture, Interior Design Program, University of Texas at Arlington, Arlington, TX, USA

Partha Pratim Roy South Point High School, Kolkata, West Bengal, India
Physics Education Research Group, University of Maryland, College Park, USA

Peter Ride Department of English, Linguistics and Cultural Studies, University of Westminster, London, UK

Poulomee Datta School of Education, Australian Catholic University, Brisbane, QLD, Australia

Rachel Hutchinson Department of Psychology, University of Westminster, London, UK

Rittika Ghosh La Trobe University, Melbourne, Australia

Samidha Shikha Goverment College for Women, Rewari, Haryana, India

Sandhya Limaye Center for Disability Studies and Action, School of Social Work, Tata Institute of Social Sciences, Mumbai, India

Santoshi Halder Department of Education, University of Calcutta, Kolkata, West Bengal, India

Satendra Singh Associate Professor of Physiology; Medical Humanities Group; Enabling Unit (for Persons with Disabilities), University College of Medical Sciences (University of Delhi) & GTB Hospital, Delhi, India

Shakila Dada Centre for Augmentative and Alternative Communication, University of Pretoria, Pretoria, South Africa

Simon Hayhoe Lecturer, Department of Education, University of Bath, Bath, UK

About the Editor, Co-editor and Authors

About the Editor

Santoshi Halder, Ph.D., is an associate professor in the Department of Education, University of Calcutta, India. She completed postgraduate studies in education with specialization in special education and educational technology and Ph.D. in applied psychology from University of Calcutta. She is recipient of the prestigious Fulbright-Nehru Senior Research Fellowship, United States (2011–2012), Endeavour Australia-India Education Council Research Fellowship, Australia (2015–2016), and Indian Council of Social Science Research (ICSSR)-National Institute of Humanities and Social Sciences (NIHSS) grant (2016–2018) for conducting research in USA, Australia, South Africa and India. Her research interest includes special education, educational technology, educational psychology, gender studies, comparative studies, cultural studies, etc. She has more than 16 years of teaching and research experience working with people with various categories of disabilities especially people with locomotor disabilities, visual impairment, hearing impairment, intellectual disabilities and autism spectrum disorder. The importance of her work is evident with more than 70 international publications in peer-reviewed international and national journals and more than 60 paper presentations or invited talks in national and international forums in the USA, Australia, South Africa, Malaysia, Singapore, the UK, India and Europe. Dr. Halder has been awarded various national and international funding to carry on independent projects by the *University Grants Commission* (*UGC*), ICSSR and *NIHSS grants*. She is also consultant and co-investigators for various international projects. She received the Governor's Medal (West Bengal) for her contribution towards the community and people as a National Cadet Corps (N.C.C) 2001. Four Ph.D.'s and 12 M.Phil. dissertations have been awarded under her supervision. She has been an *Honorary Visiting Fellow at Olga Tennison Autism Research Centre (OTARC)*, *La Trobe University*, Australia.

She hails from an army family background, thus following a strict disciplinarian way of life since childhood midst exploring various geographical corners of India together with its culture, adventure and challenge. Being a regular in scout and guide activities during schools years and as an N.C.C cadet during college and University years has taught her the basic goal of human existence – 'life for all'. She has been formally trained in Basic and Advance Mountaineering from Himalian Mountaineering Institute (WHMI), Manali and National Institute of Mountaineering (NIM), Uttarkashi, India and also been selected for the All India Women Mountaineering expedition, West Bengal. Rather than being called a typical Indian she would love to see her-self as a Global citizen in a Global world. She is trying in all her capacity for working towards inclusion, equity and access for all.

For more information click on the link: http://www.caluniv.ac.in/academic/department/Education/Santoshi-Halder.pdf.

About the Co-editor

Lori Czop Assaf, Ph.D., serves many roles in her work as a full professor at Texas State University. She teaches both undergraduate and graduate courses in language and literacy, reading and writing connections, teacher research and cultural and linguistic diversity. As the director of the Central Texas Writing Project, Dr. Assaf directs multiple grants focused on professional development and writing instruction and facilitates numerous professional development institutes for over 450 teachers in Central Texas. Dr. Assaf runs the South African Study Abroad Programme where she and a group of teachers work in local schools on the Eastern Cape. Dr. Assaf's research is on literacy learning in the linguistically diverse classrooms, teacher learning, teacher identity and international service learning. In addition, she has worked on a variety of projects with teachers and students in countries such as Pakistan, South Africa and Chile. Visit her website for more information: http://loriczopassaf.wp.txstate.edu.

About the Authors

Alison F. Eardley, Ph.D., is a cognitive psychologist at the University of Westminster, whose work has explored the nature of non-visual mental representation in the sighted people and those with a visual impairment. Her work has suggested that the mechanisms underlying spatial mental representation and imagery function are not reliant on vision. Her current work is extending theoretical understanding into applied domains, exploring how multisensory processing and imagery (including audio description) can be applied within museums and heritage environments to create inclusive design protocols which would benefit *all* visitors.

Anjali J. Forber-Pratt, Ph.D., is assistant professor at the Department of Human and Organizational Development at Vanderbilt University, USA. Her research agenda adopts a social-ecological framework and looks at issues surrounding identity, equity and empowerment through methodology for individuals who are different in some way, with a large focus on disability. Dr. Forber-Pratt was also a member of Team USA at the 2008 and 2012 Paralympic Games. She has been actively involved to help create inclusive sport opportunities for individuals with disabilities in Bermuda, India and Ghana. She is recipient of the prestigious 2013 Paul G. Hearne Leadership Award by the American Association of People with Disabilities (AAPD), given to emerging leaders within the national disability community. Dr. Forber-Pratt has appeared on several television programmes and radio shows including *NPR*, *The Stream* and *Sesame Street* and has been quoted in the national print press, including *The Boston Globe*, *The New York Times*, *The Huffington Post*, *USA Today* and *Runner's World*. She was honoured by the White House as a Champion of Change in 2013 and had an opportunity to participate in a roundtable discussion with President Obama about disability policy issues.

Bernardo Carlos Spaulonci Chiachia Matos de Oliveira is a Ph.D. candidate in social sciences at the Pontifical Catholic University of Sao Paulo (Capes Fellow). He is a recipient of the Fulbright Visiting Scholarship in 2014–2015 at Teachers College, Columbia University, Department of International and Transcultural Studies, USA. Currently, he is research fellow at Complexus – Complexity Studies Center at PUC-SP and research associate at World Enabled/ Pineda Foundation. His research expertise is in organization and sustainability issues, alternative and social economy, disability culture and society, inclusive cities and disability rights.

Beth Lewis Samuelson, Ph.D., is an associate professor of literacy, culture and language education at the Indiana University School of Education, USA, where she teaches classes in literacy theory and in the English as a second language and world languages teacher education programmes.

Caroline Muster, M.S.W., born in Ontario, Canada, to European parents, graduated summa cum laude with a bachelor of arts (B.A.) degree in psychology from Texas State University in 2010. Ms. Muster went on to earn her master of social work (MSW) degree from Texas State University in 2012, along with her master's level social work license. Since then, she has worked in the field of mental health, providing a variety of therapeutic services to individuals diagnosed with severe mental illness and myriad other psychosocial challenges. Currently, she is employed as a social worker for two prestigious Florida hospitals and is pursuing her clinical social work license. As a woman living with osteogenesis imperfecta (OI), commonly known as brittle bone disease, Ms. Muster has dedicated her personal and professional life to advocating for the equality and inclusion of the differently abled community. In addition to advocacy, her professional passions include research, public speaking and cultural competence training. She was a presenter at the 2015 NASW Florida Conference in Orlando and has been selected to speak again at the 2016 NASW Florida Conference and for the first time at the 2016 National NASW Conference in Washington, D.C.

Chandani Liyanage, Ph.D., is a senior lecturer in sociology in addition to being the head of the Department of Sociology, University of Colombo, Sri Lanka. She has been a Fulbright Research Fellow, specializing in medical sociology/medical anthropology. She is also the reigning director of the Centre for Disability Research, Education and Practice (CDREP), Department of Sociology, Faculty of Arts, University of Colombo. In this role she has organized many discussions on disability and symposiums bringing together experts from varying disciplines. She has further participated in the 'Professional Fellows On-Demand' programme in the USA, sponsored by the U.S. Department of State Bureau of Citizen Exchanges, designed by World Learning in honour of the 25th anniversary of the Americans with Disabilities Act (ADA). She is currently involved with advocacy and awareness-raising activities to enhance and to promote inclusive education within Sri Lanka's higher education framework.

Christine Grima-Farrell, Ph.D., has taught in schools in various capacities and currently lecturers in the School of Education, at the University of New South Wales. Chris' work has been honoured with a number of awards including an Australian Government Citation for Outstanding Contribution to Student Learning, and she holds University Excellence in Teaching Awards. Chris lives her scholarly work as she strives to raise awareness of ways to merge research and practice initiatives to support the diverse needs of students and enhance their well-being and resilience through promoting collaborative partnerships.

Christopher J. Johnstone, Ph.D., is an assistant professor of comparative and international development education, University of Minnesota, USA. In his research he explores operationalizations of inclusiveness as they relate to international development, education and campus internationalization. He has worked on education or development-related projects on every continent except Antarctica, but has primarily focused his research in sub-Saharan Africa and South Asia. His current projects include studies of livelihoods (Kenya and Tanzania), disability identity (India) and equity issues in internationalization (University of Minnesota).

Darren Hedley, Ph.D., is a research fellow at the Olga Tennison Autism Research Centre, La Trobe University, Melbourne, Australia. He completed postgraduate studies in psychology at Flinders University, South Australia, and clinical training in neurodevelopmental paediatric psychology at The Ohio State University and Nationwide Children's Hospital where he specialized in the assessment and diagnosis of children with intellectual and developmental disability. Dr. Hedley's current research examines the psychosocial impact of engagement in employment on individuals with autism. He is also involved in cross-cultural research associated with early screening for autism and other developmental disabilities.

David F.E. Hedley is an independent economic consultant from Melbourne, Australia. Mr. Hedley completed degrees in both international business and economics at Flinders University, South Australia. He spent 15 years as a senior economist and advisor to the Australian Federal Government in the Department of Treasury and the Department of the Prime Minister and Cabinet and also worked as a consultant for Access Economics, Australia. Mr. Hedley has extensive experience in micro- and macroeconomics, worked in the field of health economics preparing disease cost burden analysis reports as a consultant, and was a director of economic policy in the Prime Minister's G20 Taskforce during Australia's G20 Presidency in 2014. He is particularly interested in enhancing the social and economic well-being of all Australians through the delivery of innovative policy interventions.

Elizabeth M. Anderson, Ed.D., is an early childhood special education teacher, child development specialist, administrator, teacher educator and researcher. Dr. Elizabeth M. Anderson has been interested in better understanding the intersections of academics, mental health and physical health for over 25 years. She is currently an assistant professor in the Graduate School of Education at Binghamton University/SUNY in Binghamton, New York. She is a parent to four adult children, one of whom has experienced complex academic, mental health and health issues.

Erna Alant, Ph.D., is professor and Otting Chair in Special Education at the Indiana University School of Education. She teaches in augmentative and alternative communication, assistive technology and language learning.

Flávia Affonso Mayer is a Fulbright/CAPES Visiting Scholar in the Department of Cognitive Science at Case Western Reserve University, 2014–2015, and a Ph.D. candidate in the Department of Linguistics at Pontifícia Universidade Católica de Minas Gerais, Brazil (CNPq Fellow). Mayer has two books published in the field of semiotics and audio description. Her current research is focused on human conceptual creativity and congenitally blind constructions of colours.

Harsha Kathard, Ph.D., is a professor in communication sciences and disorders at the University of Cape Town. She has been lecturing at the university for 11 years. She is interested in generating knowledge which will serve in the interests of developing and transforming the professions of speech-language therapy and audiology. She has many years of experience in educating speech-language pathologists and audiologists and has participated in projects on service delivery with emphasis on population-based approaches, disability and enhancing classroom communication. Prof Kathard has taught across speech-language therapy and audiology in the areas of fluency disorders, primary healthcare, disability, research methodology, occupational audiology and professional management issues. Prof Kathard is involved in fluency research focusing on life history research, identity formation with stuttering and school-age learners who stutter.

Ivana Bilić, Ph.D., is an Assistant Professor at the Department of Management of the Faculty of Economics, University of. She is an alumna of the JFDP exchange programme financed by the U.S. Department of State. Her main scientific interests are public relations, corporate communications, community management, crisis management, entrepreneurship and reputation management. Dr. Bilić is a member of national public relations associations and currently serves as the president of the U.S. Alumni Community of Croatia and 3PSPLIT. In scientific area she has published two book chapters and more than 20 articles in international peer-reviewed journals or international scientific conference. One of her special professional interests is inclusion of persons with disabilities in higher education and society, and she was leader, coleader and team member in many related projects. Also, she is member of the national board for students with disabilities.

Joselia Neves, Ph.D., is associate professor at Hamad Bin Khalifa University, Qatar, where she teaches audiovisual translation. In her career as a university teacher and researcher, she has led a number of collaborative projects for the provision of subtitling – subtitling for deaf and hard of hearing viewers and audio description for blind audiences on television, the cinema, museums and cultural venues – the performing arts and education. She is a member of the TransMedia Research Group (transmediaresearchgroup.com) and a board member of the European Association for Studies in Screen Translation (http://www.esist.org/).

Kerstin Tönsing, Ph.D., is a speech-language pathologist and a senior lecturer at the Centre for Augmentative and Alternative Communication at the University of Pretoria. Her area of interest is promoting language development in children with severe communication disorders using augmentative and alternative communication (AAC). She has taught courses in severe disability, AAC and research methodology. Her current research focuses on the implementation of AAC in multilingual settings.

Lily Chakraborty is a mother of a child with autism and a special education teacher who is a versatile and dedicated child advocate with experience on the individual needs of identified and special education students. She is an empathetic professional who is flexible and accommodating in the design and implementation of inspiring hands-on training to parents and excellent interpersonal and communication skills to develop excellent rapport with all members of the school community. She is currently working as a special educator in Aarohan Welfare Society for Differently Abled Children. Her past experience includes working as a founder teacher in 'Blossom' in Bangalore; trainer in Amrit Somani Memorial Centre, affiliated with Behavior Momentum India; and visiting faculty at Manovikas Kendra, Kolkata.

Lindsey Ogle completed her master's degree in psychology focusing on social skills interventions for children with autism and is currently studying for a Ph.D. degree in special education at Indiana University. Her area of interest is supported decision making with adults with severe communication problems.

Lori Czop Assaf, Ph.D., serves many roles in her work as a full professor at Texas State University. A former elementary teacher and reading specialist in Dallas, Austin and Houston, Dr. Assaf now teaches both undergraduate and graduate courses in literacy methods, reading and writing connections, teacher research and cultural and linguistic diversity. As the director of the Central Texas Writing Project, Dr. Assaf leads a variety of professional development for local teachers in Central Texas and teaches at the Invitational Summer Institute. **Dr. Assaf** directs the South African Study Abroad Programme where she and ten preservice teachers work in schools in an underserved community on the Eastern Cape. Much of Dr. Assaf's research and publication have been related to literacy learning in the diverse classroom, teacher learning, teacher identity and international service learning. In addition, she has worked on a variety of projects with teachers and students in countries such as Pakistan, South Africa and Chile. Visit her website for more information: http://loriczopassaf.wp.txstate.edu/.

Louise Fryer, Ph.D., is one of the UK's most experienced audio describers, working regularly at the National Theatre and for VocalEyes, in both theatres and museums. Most recently, she provided the AD and worked as the accessibility consultant for the film Notes on Blindness (dirs. Middleton and Spinney, 2016). She is a teaching fellow at UCL, teaching the accessibility module of the M.A. course in audiovisual translation. She has published widely, and her book, An Introduction to Audio Description: A Practical Guide, was published by Routledge in May 2016.

Mary Keeffe, Ph.D., is an associate professor in inclusive education at La Trobe University, Australia. She develops and teaches postgraduate programmes in inclusive education to build teacher capacity. Her research areas include learning for students with autism, learning disabilities and trauma, and her pedagogical expertise is in the area of educational neuroscience.

Matthew Cock is chief executive of VocalEyes, a UK charity that champions the right of blind and partially sighted people to access arts and heritage. VocalEyes works with venues and sector organizations to remove barriers to access and provides audio description services and training. Before joining VocalEyes, Matthew was head of web at the British Museum, where he was responsible for the museum's web and digital projects. He is also on the board of the Jodi Mattes Trust that runs the Jodi Awards, for museums, libraries and archives that demonstrate best practice in digital access and inclusion.

Michal Harty, Ph.D., is a speech-language pathologist and a senior lecturer in the Division of Communication Sciences and Disorders at the University of Cape Town, South Africa. She lectures in the areas of augmentative and alternative communication (AAC), language development and family-focussed intervention practices. She has published several articles in local and international accredited journals and has presented conference papers at both local and international conferences.

Mirko Uljarević, M.D., Ph.D., completed his Ph.D. in the Wales Autism Research Centre, Cardiff University, and is now an Autism CRC Postdoctoral Research Fellow based in the Olga Tennison Autism Research Centre, La Trobe University, Melbourne, Australia. He is currently working on a large, Autism CRC-funded longitudinal study of Australian school-leavers with autism that aims to describe the outcomes and identify risk and resilience factors for these young people and their families during the transition from secondary school into adult life. His other research interests include a strong focus on repetitive behaviours and co-morbid conditions in individuals with autism as well as focus on well-being in parents of children with autism, particularly exploring stress, anxiety and depression, and factors contributing to individual differences in parental outcomes.

Misa Kayama, Ph.D., is a assistant professor in the Department of Social Work, University of Missippi. She is an international scholar from Japan. She received her Ph.D. and master of social work in the USA. She has been involved in several research projects examining cultural understandings of disability. Her dissertation research, a combination of disability policy analysis and ethnography of a Japanese elementary school focusing on children with disabilities, has been published as a book by Oxford University Press and as four journal articles in Social Work, Children and Youth Services Review, and Qualitative Social Work. She is currently codirecting a cross-cultural project on stigma experienced by children with disabilities, their parents and educators at public schools in the USA, Japan, South Korea and Taiwan. This project in India and the USA is her third cross-cultural project.

Mitchell Graeme Coates, Ph.D., is a lecturer in the School of Education at Australian Catholic University and a special education teacher within mainstream schools in Brisbane, Australia. Mitchell's Ph.D. thesis is in the final stages of completion. His research interests lie in the area of inclusive education and ASD, with a focus on improving the quality of education that preservice teachers receive prior to entering the profession.

Natalya Panteleyeya, Ph.D., is a parent of a ward with disability in the USA. She is a single parent and a passionate researcher of computational bioscience at the University of Colorado Denver, focusing on text mining from clinical records. She is currently working on postsecondary transition of her eldest daughter as well as her own transition into the workforce after completion of her training. While she did not opt for a career in a field that supports disabilities, she acquired knowledge and expertise in evaluating professional opinions and extensive experience in obtaining services from various supporting agencies. She will continue advocating for her daughter with a disability and working on improving outcomes for her and hopefully others.

Norma Isa Figueroa, Ph.D., is an assistant professor at the School of Architecture, University of Texas at Arlington, where she teaches interior design studio, architectural graphics and research methodologies. She obtained a B.S. in environmental design and a Ph.D. in history from the University of Puerto Rico and did her master's studies in architecture at the University of Wisconsin in Milwaukee. Before joining UTA, Figueroa taught at Gulf University in Kuwait and led the Community Design Studio at the School of Architecture in Puerto Rico, developing service-learning projects that helped non-profits in the acquisition of building permits and funding for their projects. Her most recent work deals with evidence-based research as it relates to healthcare environments and the well-being of patients. Figueroa has over 25 years of experience as an architect and interior designer in the Middle East and Puerto Rico.

Partha Pratim Roy is the head of the Physics Department of South Point High School, Kolkata, India. He is also the founder-head of the Center for Physics Education Research, a centre he started in Kolkata in 2012. He obtained his B.Sc. and M.Sc. in physics from the University of Calcutta, India. In 2011, he was a Fulbright Teaching Fellow at the Physics Education Research Group of the University of Maryland, College Park, USA, and he had won the Distinguished Fulbright Award in Teaching. Partha Pratim Roy is a lifetime member of the Indian Physical Society and the American Association of Physics Teachers. He has been a participant in PHYSWARE, an initiative of the Abdus Salam International Centre for Theoretical Physics, Trieste, Italy, for the improvement of physics teaching throughout the developing world. He conducts discovery learning programmes in Indian National Television channels regularly and is actively associated with the Jagadis Bose National Science Talent Search (JBNSTS), the oldest talent search programme of India.

Peter Ride is the course leader for the master's in museums, galleries and contemporary culture at the University of Westminster. He has worked in a wide range of museums and arts organizations in the UK with a particular emphasis on photography and digital media, and he was one of the first curators in the UK to produce exhibitions of Internet artworks in the 1990s.

Poulomee Datta, Ph.D., is working as a lecturer in special and inclusive education at the School of Education, Australian Catholic University (ACU). She has worked in several research projects designed to improve the self-concept, test anxiety and the educational outcomes for children and adolescents with disabilities in Australia and internationally. She was the recipient of four prestigious awards that shaped her career, the 'Dr. Neelu Singhvi Sancheti Memorial Gold Medal' for excellence in academics at the University of Calcutta, India; the 'Outstanding Student Publication Award' at the University of Adelaide, Australia; the 'Graduate Scholar Award' at the University of California, USA; and the 'Research Capacity Building Award' at the Australian Catholic University, Australia.

Rachel Hutchinson holds degrees in modern languages and English literature and is interested in access to the arts for people with a visual impairment. Her Ph.D. research at the University of Westminster focuses on audio description in museums and its potential to provide both access for visitors with a visual impairment and guided looking for sighted visitors as part of an inclusive design approach. She is particularly interested in multisensory audio description and its potential impact on enjoyment, learning and memorability for all visitors.

Rittika Ghosh was born in Kolkata, India. She always wanted to work with special children; so after schooling in La Martiniere for Girls and her bachelor's degree in education honours from Loreto College, she volunteered as a teacher's assistant in special institutions like IICP (Indian Institute of Cerebral Palsy), Kolkata; the Spastics Society of Karnataka, Bengaluru; REACH (Remedial Education Assessment Counselling Handicapped); and Mentaid. She also worked with adults with special needs in vocational centres. She did her teacher's training and B.Ed. in special education from IICP in affiliation with Jadavpur University and worked as a full-time teacher in REACH. Rittika did her master's degree in special education from La Trobe University, Australia, under Dr. Mary Keeffe. She is now working for 'i.can.fly', the special education and vocational centre for young adults with disabilities, a section of Caring Minds, a psychological and cognitive wellness centre in Kolkata.

Samidha Shikha, Ph.D., is an associate professor of English and Principal in Dronacharya Government College, Gurgaon, India. She has made literature her passion and profession. As a versatile teacher in service for the past 32 years (with 10 years of postgraduate teaching), her interests range from literature and environment to poetry/drama enactment, women empowerment, gender sensitization, legal literacy, Indian aesthetics and philosophy. She has participated in many social and academic workshops and has been ardently presenting papers in numerous seminars and conferences in India and abroad. Her Ph.D. research has been in the field of 'eco-criticism', a relatively new entrant in literature.

Sandhya Limaye, Ph.D., is a former Rockefeller, Fulbright and Erasmus Mundus Fellow and has experiences working with the disabled population for the last 30 years in India. She is a qualified social worker in the field of disability and has an M.Phil. and Ph.D. in the field of disability social work. From 1984 to 1996, Dr. Limaye was the social welfare officer in the National Institute for the Hearing Handicapped. In 1996, she joined as associate professor of the Centre for Disability Studies and Action, School of Social Work, Tata Institute of Social Sciences, Mumbai. She has experience working with different types of disabled people across her lifespan, especially teenagers with disabilities and their families. She works with them at individual and family intervention level and conducted many community education programmes and workshops such as sensitization about disability, awareness about disability among railway commuters and inclusive education practice in regular schools. She has an opportunity to work with different stakeholders who work in the field of disability and work on policy issues and implementation of programmes. She has published multiple articles based on her research on various issues related to disability.

Santoshi Halder, Ph.D., is an associate professor in the Department of Education, University of Calcutta, India. She has completed postgraduate studies in education with specialization in special education and educational technology and a Ph.D. in applied psychology. She is recipient of the Fulbright-Nehru Senior Research Fellowship (2011–2012), Endeavour Australia India Education Council Research Fellowship (2015–2016) and ICSSR-NIHSS grant (2016–2018) for conducting research in the USA, Australia and South Africa. She has more than 16 years of research experience working with people with various categories of disabilities, especially people with locomotor disabilities, visual impairment, hearing impairment, intellectual disabilities and autism spectrum disorder. The importance of her work is evident with more than 50 international publications in peer-reviewed international and national journals and more than 60 paper presentations or invited talks in national and international forums like those conducted in the USA, Australia, South Africa, Malaysia, Singapore, the UK, Europe and India. Dr. Halder has been awarded various national and international funding to carry on independent projects by the University Grants Commission (UGC), Indian Council of Social Science Research (ICSSR) and NIHSS grants apart from acting as a consultant to various international projects. She received the Governor's Medal (West Bengal) for her contribution towards the community and people as a National Cadet Corps (N.C.C). 4 Ph.D.'s and 12 M.Phil. dissertations have been awarded under her supervision with many more currently pursuing. She has been awarded an honorary visiting fellow at Olga Tennison Autism Research Centre (OTARC), La Trobe University, Australia.

Satendra Singh, M.D., M.B.B.S., is an associate professor of physiology at University College of Medical Sciences & GTB Hospital, Delhi. He is the coordinator of the Enabling Unit (for persons with disabilities) and founder of Infinite Ability – a medical humanities group on disability. These are first such bodies in any medical institution in India. Dr. Singh is associate editor of *Research and Humanities in Medical Education*; member of the statutory body of Delhi Medical Council; adjunct faculty at the Medical Education Unit, UCMS; and FAIMER (*Foundation for Advancement of International Medical Education and Research*) Faculty at CMC Ludhiana. He is a disability rights activist and was awarded the NCPEDP MphasiS *Universal Design Award 2013* for his disability initiatives.

Shakila Dada, Ph.D., is an associate professor at the Centre for Augmentative and Alternative Communication at the University of Pretoria. She is a speech-language pathologist and has many years of experience in training and implementing AAC in the South African context as well as student training in AAC implementation. Her research and publications concern augmentative and alternative communication interventions with a particular focus on the role of graphic symbols in language learning.

 **Simon Hayhoe, Ph.D.,** is a lecturer, and the admissions tutor for the M.A. in education and B.A. education with psychology at the University of Bath, and a centre research associate at the London School of Economics. His Ph.D. is from Birmingham University and his M.Ed. is from Leicester University. During his school teaching career in the UK, Simon taught design, information technology and computing, key-worked students with special needs and implemented inclusive courses for students from schools for the blind. In intervening years, he has also researched educational attainment with London University and Toronto University and was a fellow of the Metropolitan Museum of Art, New York – the latter sponsored by a Fulbright Award. His single-authored articles also appear in journals and books such as special issues of the *Harvard Educational Review*, *British Journal of Visual Impairment*, *Social Inclusion* and *Disability Studies Quarterly*. He is also one of the series editors of the last two volumes of *e-Learning in Action* and the editor of a special issue of the *International Journal of Christianity & Education* on disability and Christianity.

Chapter 1
Disability and Inclusion: Current Challenges

Santoshi Halder, Lori Czop Assaf, and Mary Keeffe

Abstract This text creates the rationale for the various sections and chapters of the book, thus laying the foundation for flourishing the purpose and objectives of the book. The idea is to lay down possible link up intersecting disability, inclusion, and culture as explored through the interdisciplinary and cross-cultural lens of the authors from various origins. This text establishes the rationale for various sections of the book, beginning with the voices of people with disabilities as they explore the evolution or shaping of their identities through the barriers and abilities in the way diversity is understood in various cultural contexts to see how our communities are progressing toward an inclusive society. Through a socio-cultural lens from which the structures within society all contribute to inform the attitudes and beliefs that are held about persons with a disability and how they may access services such as education, employment, and social engagement/independent living or a life of inclusion is laid down. Communication is a fundamental human expression that allows access to choice, voice, and personal understandings and expressions of value and worth. Communication is the link, in this text, to a more strategic decision-making with regard to inclusive policies and practices. The discourse brings in how the legislation, policies, and processes work together to lead community expectations so that cultural and personal barriers may be overcome and all individuals with disabilities feel they are an integral part of the social fabric of society. Finally, it culminates the concept of inclusion through the voice of parents and caregivers to make explicit the complex issues that surround living with a disability in any culture.

S. Halder (✉)
Department of Education, University of Calcutta,
Alipore Campus, Kolkata, West Bengal, India
e-mail: santoshi_halder@yahoo.com

L.C. Assaf
Department of Curriculum and Instruction, Texas State University, San Marcos, TX, USA

M. Keeffe
Department of Education, La Trobe University, Melbourne, VIC, Australia

© Springer International Publishing AG 2017
S. Halder, L.C. Assaf (eds.), *Inclusion, Disability and Culture*, Inclusive
Learning and Educational Equity 3, DOI 10.1007/978-3-319-55224-8_1

Introduction

In every society, the unequal status of individuals with disabilities causes enormous losses to the community. At any given time, people with special needs experience tremendous hindrances often due to a variety of structural, psychological, and sociocultural barriers (Halder 2008, 2009). These constraints are prevalent in developing nations as poverty, class structures, employment opportunities, and social expectations impinge directly on the quality of life for people with disabilities and their families. Our immediate objective for this book is to explore various global, social, and personal perspectives about disability so that we can gain insight into emergent trends and practices in inclusion and diversity. We begin with narratives from people with disabilities as they describe some of the social challenges they have experienced. Included in these stories are reflections on issues of culture and inclusion and how these core constructs are shaped and manipulated by social influences.

Attitudes, values, and beliefs about the nature of disability vary around the globe and are largely determined and shaped by the society in which people live. While developed countries have entrenched social standards and policies designed to reduce or limit discrimination, many developing countries tend to rely on the values established in religious, cultural, or social practices. In these situations, the lack of inclusive policies along with values and beliefs associated with social exclusion, impairment, and a reduced quality of life negatively influence social practices. In educational contexts, an emergent understanding of inclusion relates to the notions of access and participation while a more developed understanding includes all aspects that are responsive to the needs of each individual and quality experiences for all (Barton and Armstrong 2001). It is important to listen to the voices of people with a disability, promote the importance of communication, and reflect on inclusive practices in order to understand the various sociocultural influences that may be specific to each country. Such a stance will help gain insights into the quality and availability of services for the successful inclusion of people with disabilities around the globe (Rees et al. 1991). This book aims to provide a cross section of perspectives from developed and developing countries to describe and identify effective and cohesive trajectories toward inclusive practices.

According to the World Report on Disability (2011), the World Health Organisation (WHO), and the more than one billion people have a disability. The WHO and World Bank argue that inclusion or 'a sense of belonging' is a universal human right where the aim is to embrace, value, and give equal access and participation to all individuals irrespective of any sort of differences (Minkowitz 2006). Miller and Katz (2002) and others (see for example: Ainscow et al. 2013; Keeffe 2008) expand on a human rights approach to claim that inclusion is a sense of belonging by: (a) feeling respected and valued for who you are; (b) feeling a level of supportive energy and commitment from others so that one can participate actively in social, community, and employment opportunities; (c) actively consult and make decisions on all issues that influence life; and (d) to depend on social structures and relationships to identify one's own strengths, interests, and abilities.

As a fundamental premise, inclusive practices value diversity (Kunc 1992), yet progress toward an inclusive society cannot be established if a significant part of the population is treated unfairly and discriminated against due to disability. The global trend toward a raised awareness of disability issues, however, reveals significant inequalities across cultures (Barton and Armstrong 2001), ethnic groups, and nationalities (Crystal et al. 1999). There is evidence that individuals with a disability experience higher risks of discrimination, exploitation, violence, and abuse (Ghai 2001; Halder 2009) particularly in developing world contexts. These aspects need to be explored along with their various contextual factors and multifaceted issues for possible explanations and a better understanding of their consequences.

Although various legislations and policies in every society aim to determine social expectations and practices that reduce discrimination, the unequal status of individuals with disabilities is a current and lived reality in many countries. The WHO describes barriers as being more than just physical obstacles including factors in a person's environment that, through their absence or presence, limits functioning and creates disability. These include aspects such as a physical environment that is not accessible; lack of relevant assistive, adaptive, and rehabilitative devices; and negative attitudes of people toward disability, services, systems, and policies that are either nonexistent or that hinder the involvement of all people with a health condition in all areas of life (WHO 2001). These factors may become more complicated when interacting with cultural, religious, and historic contexts thereby making the inclusion of individuals with disabilities a complex phenomenon that is unique to each case. The immediate concern and challenge is to explore various global and social perspectives and contexts to listen to the voices of persons with disabilities and examine their life experiences to evaluate how the various policies, processes, and services are experienced and/or practiced worldwide in any context. Together, we reference multiple perspectives and insights into ways that topics such as disability, society, and culture interact.

Sociocultural Factors for Inclusion

In its broadest sense, a sociocultural system includes all interactions between society and culture to include culture, class, education, ethnicity, and religious systems based on sociocultural perspectives, and we are joined in our common endeavor to learn about policies, practices, and processes that improve the lot of people with disabilities so that the quality of the interactions between society and people with disabilities can be improved. Some developed communities will not have the pressures of poverty and class distinction that people with disabilities may experience and developing countries will not have the first-hand experience of protective policies and organized support services that may exist in developed countries. It is important to make reference to Coleridge's (1993) distinction between developed and developing countries. Each will have unique perspectives on the cultural influences that impinge on a person with a disability, yet all countries are grappling with the basic issues of how to improve the quality of life and autonomy for persons with disabilities. In this book, authors describe perspectives and life stories from developed and developing countries and how they engage in inclusive practices.

Various researchers have examined the influence of sociocultural variables on the life experiences of people with disabilities (e.g., Dalal and Pande 1999; Greenwell and Hough 2008; Ross-Gordo 2002).

Barona and Faykus (2006) indicated that sociocultural factors (ethnicity, socioeconomic status, family characteristics) made a significant influence on the population with special needs and suggested that legislative mandates have the capacity to influence sociocultural factors in the determination of special education and the most inclusive practices they're in. Groce (2000) proposed that sociocultural approaches were important in the understanding of disability as much as other social issues or diversity. Rehman (1999) also described how cultural factors influenced the outcome of rehabilitation of special populations in Pakistan and explained how certain modifications were introduced to overcome these barriers. It is evident from these and similar studies (Halder 2008, 2009) that sociocultural factors are influential in the conduct and success of inclusive policies and practices and that these factors will vary in different cultural contexts.

 ## Current Challenges and Barriers in Education

In many developing countries people with disabilities remain underprivileged and are unable to access or participate in mainstream education and development programs. There is a scarcity of needs based support services available for the welfare of people with disabilities, and services remain beyond the reach of most people (Halder 2008, 2009). Yet, even in the more developed countries, the voice of people with disabilities is rarely heard in issues that relate to equality in education and employment or how services should be distributed or accessed. The level of autonomy in making decisions about issues that are of a direct concern to the individual with the disability is regularly transferred to parents, caregivers, schools, organizations, or government departments, thus making the individual passive in the control of their own lives. This lack of autonomy and passivity in decision-making only serves to increase dependence and limit social or employment initiatives.

Social exclusion is not only experienced by the person with the disability. Research by Halder (2008, 2009) demonstrates how public and negative stereotypes may disenfranchise and isolate some family members. Halder also found that educators who were inexperienced or untrained in the educational needs of students with disabilities struggled to provide appropriate modifications to facilitate learning. In some contexts, teachers are unable to access expertise or advice to differentiate the curriculum or to keep students with disabilities safe and encourage learning in a way that suits the student. The boundaries of inclusive education are often redefined when the student has challenging behaviors or is diagnosed with a disability.

Parents are also challenged in the way they accept and address the complex needs of the whole family when there is a child with a disability. Balancing work and home duties becomes a balance of loyalties and resources as well as time management. According to one mother in Halder's (2009) research,

> ...Every morning I have to prepare her for school and go with her from Chandan Nagar Kolkata (faraway Sub urban location to the cities) by train, bus, and then auto. It is really a hard task for me to take her along every day to school for education. We had to spend most of our time in vehicles and roads.

In a society dominated by negative misrepresentations or stereotypes of persons with a disability, the potential to lead a productive life may be reduced and social inclusion will be conditional on overcoming numerous barriers. Identity and dignity may be compromised as lowered expectations and a lack of support and understanding limit possibilities.

This is particularly the case for women with disabilities in developing countries like India (around 42% of the total disabled population) (Census 2011) who may experience a double and triple jeopardy. Discrimination against a woman on the grounds of gender, disability, and poverty will challenge her rights to belong to community and receive advantages from inclusion in social, educational, and employment. Research highlights that women with disabilities living in India are significantly less likely to marry than women without disabilities (Nagata 2003) and many of those who do marry are vulnerable to psychological abuse and exploitation (Monahan and Lurie 2003; Young et al. 1997). Successful experiences, policies, and strategies that reduce discrimination for women with disabilities can help to inform inclusive practices in developing countries and provide strategies and frameworks to approach complex problems with an improved possibility of success.

In the previous section, we discussed community attitudes, values, and beliefs that inform inclusive practice. Yet, many countries in the world still lack the resources and the good will required to address the problem of physical access to buildings. Community and public places are still characterized by architectural barriers such as steps and small doorways. For example, the absence of ramps in public places (Halder 2008, 2009) creates a barrier to access that is physical as well as sociocultural. The values that underpin community inclusion for people with disabilities in the low-resource countries and regions still remain, as theoretical concepts due to the lack of access and participation within the society for people with disabilities. This means that people with disabilities are unseen in schools, social venues, and employment yet highly visible in street poverty.

In addition, a vast disparity occurs as developing countries struggle to provide basic amenities such as water, electricity, and toilets while people with disabilities in developed countries may enjoy an improved quality of life through the ability to access major scientific and technological developments. The combined impact of the barriers that people with disabilities face at every stage of their lives in developing countries creates a challenge that extends beyond a local community to impact on social and economic acceptance within the global community.

It is from this perspective that authors of this text share knowledge and experience between developed and developing countries. By listening to the voices of people with disabilities in the first section of the text, we find that there are numerous similarities in our expectations of basic human dignity and identity. Although the aim to lead a quality and valued life for people with a disability is consistent for all countries, the pathway to achieve that is different in each context. A mirror to the practices in developed countries, for example, will not necessarily provide developing countries the answers to the best practices in their own contexts. Instead, the metaphor of the mirror referred to in this section of the text reflects more progress to be made in all countries, more stereotypes to be challenged, and more respect and dignity to be gained.

Significant Legislation Supporting Rights of Individuals with Disabilities

The United Nations Convention on the Rights of Persons with Disabilities (2006) provides a framework for countries to change attitudes and beliefs about the potential of people with disabilities and their active participation in the society. Legislative changes to reduce discrimination are the strongest statements a society can make to change entrenched or negative cultural values and beliefs and to enforce a change in practice. Though the influence of cultural factors is individualistic and unique to each society, legislation and policies on disability in some developing countries remains unclear and evasive (Miles 2006; Thomas and Thomas 1998). In those countries, the legal requirements to reduce discrimination are at a higher risk of failure because they tend to conflict with various cultural factors within the host country. So while it is important to look toward the developed nations for examples of current equitable practice in the strategies adopted, laws framed, and policies in practice, it is from this base that developing countries must reflect on their own cultural influences and address those within the relevant legislative framework.

The Convention on the Rights of the Person with Disabilities (CRPD 2006) is the first general United Nations Human Rights convention that was introduced to protect the rights of persons with disabilities. The CRPD adopted a nonradical social model and introduced a new disability rights paradigm that was aimed to assist persons with disabilities in every aspect of their lives. With the rapid ratification and commencement of this convention in 2008, a new disability rights paradigm emerged that was built upon a nonradical understanding of the social model of inclusion. Disability was recognized as an evolving concept that resulted in collaborative and organizational approaches designed to reduce attitudinal and environmental barriers for persons with a disability. At the time, the new disability rights discourse created a unique opportunity to drive change and provide disability scholarship and politics as a common focus. Yet, the pace of change has slowed, and the expected responsiveness from all aspects of society has not yet materialized to make substantial improvements in the quality of life for a person with a disability worldwide.

On a global scale, there are still inconsistencies in the way services are offered to those with a disability. Questions surround who is eligible for support services and why. The quality and relevance of facilities and support programs have to be personalized to suit individual needs. Technology is still expensive and inaccessible in many regions. Schools and teachers need high-level skills and abilities to be responsive to individual needs. Employers rely heavily on economic accountability to minimize social responsibility. Improvements, development, and resourcefulness are required in all aspects of life for a person with a disability. There are countries where the very nature of a disability is still questioned and inconsistencies prevail in information, attitude, resourcefulness, and strategic approaches. The general population will only respond more effectively when leaders in governments, the media, schools, and employers accept diversity and model decision-making for greater inclusion. Even in the embryonic stage in terms of inclusion, developing countries can depend on the fundamental aspects of respect for the individual and a democratic appreciation for diversity.

It is from this appreciation of diversity that a more complex understanding of disability will emerge. A person will be treated with respect as a person first and then a person with a disability next. The use of inclusive language teaches us there are students with special needs (the student first), and they are not just those kids where the challenges of the disability extinguish their unique capacity for being an individual. When such values are made explicit in legislation, policy, and process, then the general public will learn to communicate inclusively.

There are still countries with few statistics on the prevalence of various disabilities. The lack of record-keeping may serve to make the problem of service delivery invisible, but denial of the educational, social, and employment needs of a large part of the population is not sustainable. Prevalence studies of individuals with disabilities are a foremost challenge in national reporting, and services are unable to be provided when the community needs are not identified. For instance, the National Data on Disability for India provides an estimate for only 8 types of disability. Children with autism do not have a category and are documented in home and school care as 'other disability' or within 'multiple disability' where the prevalence is as high as 18% and 8% respectively (India Census 2011). The data is unable to inform policies and equitable services. Possible inaccuracies or lack of information makes the national data confusing and can mislead parents, caregivers, schools, employers, and government departments. Clear guidelines and services to address the difficulties experienced by each category of disability may not be realized and with the disabilities and their range of complex needs remain invisible.

Still numerous children in many parts of the world remain unidentified, misdiagnosed, and without any support services throughout their lives. There is a huge global imbalance in the knowledge of various aspects of the management of

disability issues, particularly with regard to identification, assessment, lack of qualified specialized professionals trained to provide services, and lack of skills needed
for teachers to address challenges for students with various categories of disabilities, including lack of parental support groups (Barbaro and Halder 2016). All these
issues impose additional barriers in low-resource settings. National and international voices and professional networks are essentially needed in order to extend
and disseminate the knowledge required to address complex difficulties in service
provision and thereby lead toward exploring the real challenges of coping with an
improved quality of life for persons with a disability (Elsabbagh et al. 2012; Grinker
et al. 2015). Most importantly, the lack of data collection on prevalence and etiology
reduces any accountability for environmental risk exposure (Adak and Halder
2017). The potential health and well-being risks from environmental hazards remain
a hidden problem where social responsibility is reduced (Hilton et al. 2010).

Countries that experience high rates of community poverty are vulnerable to
complex difficulties (Brown and Guralnick 2012). Access to relevant information
about effective and equitable practices should be considered one of the priority
issues as 80% of individuals with disabilities live in developing countries (Barbaro
and Halder 2016; UN Enable 2012). It is indeed a most challenging task for governments in developing countries who may choose priorities for their populations, such
as clean water, environmental degradation, business, and transport. Modelling best
practices from a range of country contexts may induce action and reduce the complexity of suitable responses a government may choose. With the CRPD (2006)
being ratified and signed by so many countries, one can hope for a better outcome
worldwide. However action is needed on a strategic and global level so that a range
of recommendations can be implemented at a grass-roots level.

The rights-based approach underlying CRPD contends that individuals with disabilities should not be denied the opportunity of a meaningful educational experience on the grounds of disability (CRPD 2006; Marshall and Goodall 2015). While
every nation continues to struggle with accessibility, employment (Hedley et al.
2016), and housing rights, etc., there are countries who are just struggling in the
initial stages of acceptance of diversity and implementation of inclusive practice.
Henceforth, it can be argued that a paradigm shift toward a 'social model' of disability, though necessary for all our communities, very clearly has quite a long way
to go before it reaches equality for people with disabilities. A matter of great concern is that societies need to think strategically about accessibility and reasonable
accommodation for persons with disabilities for the implementation of the CRPD
(Melish 2007). To achieve such social change and access the benefits of inclusion,
organizations need to ensure that the dynamic paradigm change in disability policies begins with an awareness of human rights for people with a disability (Quinn
2009a, b). Strategic planning through legislation will filter through to policies and
practices in schools and industry (Lord and Stein 2008; Harpur 2015). In this text,
we look to a variety of effective practices in order to learn from each other in the
global challenge of inclusion.

Henceforth, the broad sections of the book provide instances of current issues
and trends for individuals with disabilities and describes how strategic and

operational perspectives and processes may be similar yet unique in developed or developing countries. Thus the book is categorized into four sections.

In Part I: Deconstructing Disability Identities, the authors explore the concepts of disability and identity from a variety of sociocultural perspectives. Using auto-ethnographic methods, the authors provide thoughtful portrayals of how their lives have been shaped by their disability. They describe how inequities can prevent people with disabilities from living normal lives and how they become advocates for themselves and others.

In Part II: Exploring the Complexities of Communication with Differently Abled Persons, the authors highlight the importance of communication and report on the research on communication disabilities and the communication patterns, barriers, and interactions between individuals with and without disabilities. Relevant practices and new technologies are discussed.

Part III: Inclusive Policies, Practices and Interventions, provide personal insights and research-based practices and interventions from a variety of disciplines. The authors argue for integrated, inclusive approaches that empower persons with disabilities in order to create an equal and just society.

Part IV: Insights from Caregivers, returns to the personal voice of caregivers. The authors describe their experiences as caregivers to children with disabilities. They draw on their unique perspectives to highlight the complexities and challenges of navigating through a variety of social systems that don't always meet their child's needs.

Conclusion

Being engaged in disability research for so many years across multiple countries, we feel strongly about creating a space for self-advocates, researchers, teachers, practioners, and parents to discuss, compare, and challenge how disability is culturally defined and understood around the world. The term disability is a relative and subjective concept that varies throughout the world not because of an individual's functional or intellectual abilities but because of environmental and cultural barriers imposed upon them by societal norms and unchallenged histories. This book provides a unique perspective on the notion of disability across cultures and countries by identifying and challenging cultural norms and limitations. The authors of this edited volume employed either autoethnographic or mixed-methods approaches to explore and systematically analyze their personal experiences and cultural influences on disability. They utilized self-observations and reflexive investigative methods in order to understand disability from a specific cultural space while critically reflecting upon their personal and professional identities. Authors represent a variety of stakeholders, including parents, special educators, researchers, and clinical practitioners, and provide cross-disciplinary perspectives on disability and inclusion across many disciplines.

References

Adak, B., & Halder, S. (2017). Systematic review on prevalence of autism spectrum disorder with respect to gender and socio-economic status. *Journal of Mental Disorders and Treatment, 3*(1), 133.

Ainscow, M., Dyson, A., & Weiner, S. (2013). From exclusion to inclusion: A review of international literature on ways of responding to students with special educational needs in schools. *En-clave pedagogica: Revists International de investigacion e Innovacion Educativa, 13*, 13–30.

Barbaro, J., & Halder, S. (2016). Early identification of autism spectrum disorder: Current challenges and future global directions. *Current Development Disorder Report, 3*(1), 1–8.

Barona, A., & Faykus, S. P. (2006). Differential effects of socio-cultural variables on special education eligibility categories. *Psychology in the Schools, 9*(4), 313–320.

Barton, L., & Armstrong, F. (2001). In G. L. Albrecht, K. D. Seelman, & M. Bury (Eds.), *Disability, education, and inclusion. Handbook of disability studies*. Thousand Oaks: Sage Publications.

Brown, S. E., & Guralnick, M. J. (2012). Infants & young children, international human rights to early intervention for infants and young children with disabilities. *Infants & Young Children, 25*(4), 270–228.

Census. (2011). The Registrar General & Census Commissioner, India, New Delhi, Ministry of Home Affairs, Government of India.

Coleridge, P. (1993). *Disability, liberation and development*. Oxford: Oxfam.

Crystal, D. S., Watanabe, H., & Chen, R. (1999). Children's reactions to physical disability: A cross national and developmental study. *International Journal of Behavioral Development, 23*(1), 91 111.

Dalal, A. K., & Pande, N. (1999). Socio-sultural perspectives on learning and learning disabilities. *Psychology & Developing Societies, 11*(1), 55–75.

Elsabbagh, M., Divan, G., Koh, Y. J., Kim, Y. S., Kauchali, S., Marcin, C., Montiel-Nava, C., Patel, V., Paula, C. S., Wang, C., Yasamy, M. T., & Fombonne, E. (2012). Global prevalence of autism and other pervasive developmental disorders. *Autism Research, 5*, 160–179 . This systematic review reports the prevalence of autism across the globe, and highlights the incredibly limited data in low-income countries. It is stressed that there is a critical need for further research and services in these low-resourced settings.

Ghai, A. (2001). Mothering a child of disability. *The Journal Hyptia, 2*(1), 20–22.

Greenwell, A., & Hough, S. (2008). Culture and disability in sexuality studies: A methodological and content. *Sexuality and Disability, 26*(4), 189–196.

Grinker, R. R., Kang-Yi, C. D., Ahmann, C., Beidas, R. S., Lagman, A., & Mandell, D. S. (2015). Cultural adaptation and translation of outreach materials on autism spectrum disorder. *Journal of Autism and Developmental Disorders, 45*(8), 2329–2336. doi:10.1007/s10803-015-2397-6.

Groce, N. E. (2000). Framing disability issues in local concepts and beliefs. *Asia Pacific Disability Rehabilitation Journal, 10*(1), 4–7.

Halder, S. (2008). Rehabilitation of women with physical disabilities in India: A huge gap. *Australian Journal of Rehabilitation Counseling, 14*(1), 1–15.

Halder, S. (2009). Prospects of higher education of the challenged women in India. *International Journal of Inclusive Education (IJIE), 13*(6), 633–646.

Harpur, P. (2015). Embracing the new disability rights paradigm: The importance of the convention on the rights of persons with disabilities. *Disability and Society, 27*(1), 1–14.

Hedley, D., Uljarevic, M., Cameron, L., Halder, S., Richdale, A, & Dissanayake, C. (2016). Employment programs and interventions targeting adults with autism spectrum disorder: A systematic review of the literature. *Journal of Autism*, 1–13.

Hilton, C. L., Fitzgerald, R. T., Jackson, K. M., Maxim, R. A., Bosworth, C. C., Shattuck, P. T., & Constantino, J. N. (2010). Brief report: Under-representation of African Americans in autism genetic research: A rationale for inclusion of subjects representing diverse family structures. *Journal of Autism and Developmental Disorders, 40*(5), 633–639.

Keeffe, M. (2008). The inclusive society. In M. Keeffe & S. Carrington (Eds.), *Schools and diversity* (2nd ed., pp. 17–30). Frenchs Forest: Pearson Education.

Kunc, N. (1992). The need to belong: Rediscovering Maslow's hierarchy. In R. A. Villa, J. S. Thousand, W. Stainback, & S. Stainback (Eds.), *Restructuring for caring and effective education: An administrative guide to creating heterogeneous schools* (pp. 25–39). Baltimore: Paul H. Brookes Publishing.

Lord, J., & Stein, M. (2008). Symposium: Framing legal and human rights strategies for change: A case study of disability rights in Asia. Article: The domestic incorporation of human rights law and the United Nations convention on the rights of persons with disabilities. *Washington Law Review, 83*, 449–489.

Lord, C., Shulman, C., & DiLavore, P. (2004). Regression and word loss in autism spectrum disorder spectrum disorder. *Journal of Child Psychology and Psychiatry, 45*, 1–21.

Marshall, D., & Goodall, C. (2015). The right to appropriate and meaningful education for children with ASD. *Journal of Autism and Developmental Disorders, 45*, 3159–3167.

Melish, T. J. (2007). The UN disability convention: Historic process, strong prospects, and why the U.S. *Should Ratify, Human Rights Brief, 14*(2), 1–12.

Miles, M. (2006). *Social Responses to Disability & Poverty in Economically Weaker Countries.* Research, Trends, Critique, and Lessons Usually Not Learnt. Annotated bibliography of modern and historical material.

Miller F. A., & Katz, J. H. (2002). *Unleashing the real power of diversity.* In The Inclusion Breakthrough, Berrett-Koehler Publishers.

Minkowitz, T. (2006). United Nations convention on the rights of persons with disabilities and the right to be free from nonconsensual psychiatric interventions. *Syracuse Journal of International Law and Commerce., 34*, 405–428.

Monahan, K., & Lurie, A. (2003). Disabled women sexually abused in childhood: Treatment consideration. *Clinical Social Work Journal, 31*, 407–418.

Nagata, K. K. (2003). Gender and disability in the Arab region: The challenges in the new millennium. *Asia Pacific Disability Rehabilitation Journal, 14*(1), 10–17.

Quinn, G. (2009a). Resisting the 'temptation of elegance': Can the convention on the rights of persons with disabilities socialise states to right behaviour? In O. Arnardottir & G. Quinn (Eds.), *The UN convention on the rights of persons with disabilities: European and scandinavian perspectives.* Boston: Martinus Nijhoff.

Quinn, G. (2009b). The United Nations convention on the rights of persons with disabilities: Toward a new international politics of disability. *Texas Journal on Civil Liberties & Civil Rights, 15*, 33–53.

Rees, L. M., Spreen, O., & Harnadek, M. (1991). Do attitudes towards persons with handicaps really shift over time? Comparison between 1975 and 1988. *Mental Retardation, 29*(2), 8186.

Rehman, F. (1999). Influence of cultural factors on the practice of CBR in north west frontier province of Pakistan. *Asia Pacific Disability Rehabilitation Journal., 10*(1), 32–33.

Ross-Gordon, J. M. (2002). Socio-cultural contexts of learning among adults with disabilities. *New Directions for Adult and Continuing Education, 96*, 47–57.

Thomas, M. J., & Thomas, M. J. (1998). Influence of cultural factors on disability and rehabilitation in developing countries. *Asia Pacific Disability Rehabilitation Journal., 9*(1), 20–24.

UN Enable. (2012). *United Nations Enable factsheet on persons with disabilities.* Retrieved March 24, 2012, from http://www.un.org/disabilities/default.asp?id=18

United Nations. (2006). *Convention on the rights of person's with disabilities and optional protocol, office of the high commissioner.* Geneva: United Nations.

World Health Organization. (2001). *International classification of functioning, disability and health* (p. 214). Geneva: WHO.

World Report on Disability. (2011). *World Health Organization and World Bank, 28.*

Young, M. E., Nosek, M. A., Howland, C. A., Chanpong, G., & Rintala, D. H. (1997). Prevalence of abuse of women with physical disabilities. *Archives of Physical Medicine and Rehabilitation Special Issue, 78*(12, Suppl 5), S34–S38.

Part I
Deconstructing Disability Identities

Chapter 2
Disability, Culture, and Identity in India and USA

Christopher J. Johnstone, Sandhya Limaye, and Misa Kayama

Abstract In 1963, Erving Goffman was one of the first scholars in the world to identify the concept of identity as it relates to disability. In his *Stigma: Notes on the Management of Spoiled Identity*, Goffman theorized that persons with disability often have "spoiled" identity formation related to the construction of disability stigma and the negative social impact of overt physical, sensory, and cognitive differences. He focuses on the relationship between an individual who has potentially stigmatizing conditions and the agents of social control, such as people in the community, who define stigma in their context. Friedson (1965) expanded Goffman's stigma theory, specifically in terms of the field of rehabilitation. Research on disability and identity has since considered a wider range of possibilities. Rosalyn Benjamin Darling published her 2013 book, *Disability and Identity: Negotiating Self in a Changing Society*. In conducting research for this book, Darling found that there is a taxonomy of identities that may exist among persons with disabilities, including: (a) Resignation (passive focus on the challenges that are brought about by disability); (b) Normative typicality (a desire to hide disability and "pass" in the non-disabled world); (c) Personal activism (acceptance or pride for disability and orientation toward struggling for personal rights); (d) Affirmative activism (acceptance and pride for disability and orientation toward societal change and reform related to disability); and (e) Affirmative typicality (an acceptance of disability but the desire to live and work in mainstream environments).

In this chapter we then discuss the beginnings of a collaborative research project in India. The aim of the project is to better understand and characterize disability identity in India. We, as authors, came to this work from very different perspectives.

C.J. Johnstone (✉)
Assistant Professor, Department of Organizational Leadership, Policy, and Development, University of Minnesota, Minneapolis, MN 55455, USA
e-mail: john4810@umn.edu

S. Limaye
Center for Disability Studies and Action, School of Social Work, Tata Institute of Social Sciences, Mumbai, India

M. Kayama
Department of Social Work, University of Mississippi, Oxford, MS, USA

© Springer International Publishing AG 2017
S. Halder, L.C. Assaf (eds.), *Inclusion, Disability and Culture*, Inclusive Learning and Educational Equity 3, DOI 10.1007/978-3-319-55224-8_2

Each of these perspectives informed the design and implementation of the study. In the pages that follow we describe how we came to our interests in this topic, what we hope to achieve, and the study's preliminary findings. Through this project (and preliminary discussion in this chapter) we seek to place identity as a phenomenon that is highly contextualized through highlighting two national examples (India and US), thus reinforcing that identity intersects with a wide variety of contextual factors including (but not limited to) national context.

Introduction

This chapter focuses on the concept of disability and identity in the USA and India. Through a review of the literature, authors' past publications, and preliminary data from a current study funded by the University of Minnesota's Global Spotlight program (2014), the authors characterize the diversity and complexity of disability identities in two countries that have distinct cultural and historical backgrounds, and then conclude by finding common and explanatory themes across the two countries.

Both disability and identity are complex issues that have been examined and discussed over the past decades. Identity formation is one of the developmental challenges adolescents have to go through to become productive adult members of the society to which they belong (Steinberg 2011). Disabilities add complexity for their identity formation. Individuals with disabilities may have to manage even more difficult tasks to balance their self-identity with socially imposed identity. Such societally imposed identities often reflect biased ideas about disability in a larger society, which affects their self-identity and self-perception (e.g., Goffman 1963). Disability generally is associated with stigma across cultures around the world, yet its impact on the everyday experiences of individuals with disabilities varies across cultures (e.g., Rao and Valencia-Garcia 2013). Until recently, most research on disability and identity was conducted from Western perspectives. Diverse perspectives from non-Western countries provide us with new insights into understanding the complexity of disability and identity, especially in this increasingly globalizing and diverse society, even within Western countries (e.g., Kayama and Haight 2014). By contrasting two distinct sociocultural contexts, the USA and India, this chapter provides an overview of cultural variations in how disability interacts with culture as part of identity formation.

Disability Identity in the USA: A Review of Literature

The intersection of disability and identity in the USA was historically characterized as a stigmatizing phenomenon. In 1963, Erving Goffman was one of the first scholars in the world to identify the concept of identity as it relates to disability. In his *Stigma: Notes on the Management of Spoiled Identity*, Goffman theorized that persons with disability often have "spoiled" identity formation. Due to the stigma of disability and the negative social impact of overt physical, sensory, and cognitive differences, individuals with disabilities may have a limited opportunity for full identity development. Goffman focused on the relationship between an individual who has potentially stigmatizing conditions and the agents of social control, such as people in the community, who define stigma in their context. Friedson (1965) expanded Goffman's stigma theory, specifically in terms of the field of rehabilitation. According to Friedson, rehabilitation agencies often consider themselves to be acting in the best interest of their clients. The very notion of "being a client" or a person with a professionally designated condition, is stigmatizing in and of itself. Friedson noted that agencies and professionals working with individuals who have stigmatizing conditions must define stigma and what needs to be "fixed" in their clients in order to remain viable and conscious about potential stigma. Minow (1990) described this "dilemma of difference" when examining disability and identity formation. Individuals with disabilities may become a target of stigma due to their differences. Yet providing formalized supports may also have a stigmatizing effect. Only recently has this dilemma of difference been questioned. Over the past two decades, individuals with disabilities themselves have advocated for new models and understandings of disabilities in their communities.

As in all sociological fields, increased research activity often leads to increased recognition of complexity about the phenomenon of stigma and its impact on identity development of individuals with disabilities. Johnstone (2004) found that disability identity research in the 1980s, 1990s, and early 2000s addressed a variety of identities associated with disability. According to his review of the literature, disability identity could be defined as: (a) an externally ascribed, disempowering identity; (b) identities that shift focus away from disability; (c) overcompensating identities; (d) empowered identities; and (e) common identities.

First, *externally ascribed identities* are those which are legacies of Goffman's initial stigmatized identities. According to Riddell, Baron, and Wilson (2001), social participation by individuals with disabilities is often limited because of others' understandings and beliefs about disability, which may not necessarily be correct. Individuals with disabilities also may internalize such limited range of societal understandings. This, according to Seale (2001), may be a result of the predominant medical model that was used to understand disability until interrogations of the medical model began in the field of disability studies. Without such interrogations, feelings of shame may be more present (Murphy 1990) and may be reinforced by unfavorable representations of people with disabilities in the media (Garland-Thomson 2001).

Second, some persons with disabilities choose to identify with other parts of their whole selves and shift focus away from disabilities because of the stigma and shame introduced by societal forces. Goffman (1963) noted this phenomenon using concepts of "discreditable" and "discredited." Individuals with discreditable conditions, including disabilities, may avoid being labeled as discredited. If they can conceal their discreditable conditions, they can pass as "normal" persons. For example, Szivos-Bach (1993) and Epp (2001) found that North Americans with learning or cognitive disabilities preferred to either not disclose or hide their medically ascribed labels. In many ways, the minimization of disability as a primary identifier is both a personal and political decision. The political approach to person-first thinking in the USA can be tied to its independent living movement, which focused on people-centered policies (Lifchez and Winslow 1979).

A third mechanism for managing stigma is to overcompensate in an effort to contrast the appearance or external conception of disability. Maintaining a status as "normal" requires ongoing effort. For example, by managing information one reveals with others over time during social interactions, one can control perceptions of others (Goffman 1963). Stocker (2001) noted that her personal identity was heavily focused on overcoming impairments to appear more "normal." To this end, she spent a great deal of her childhood working to achieve normative success among her peers and at school and minimizing the visibility of her impairment. Both Gabel (2001) and Cook (2001) also describe qualitative events where their research participants work to hide impairments (especially invisible ones) in order to embrace a more normative identity.

Fourth, empowered identity has been gradually emerging in the USA since the 1970s. Fleisher and Zames (2001) have described a process of reclaiming disability as a term of power and political identity. By "owning" the term disability, persons with empowered identities embrace the notion of disability as a personal attribute. The notion of ownership and power provides a platform for pushing back against societal stereotypes, stigma, and policy decisions. By claiming disability identity (Linton 1998), persons with disabilities have been able to claim rights to housing (Lifchez and Winslow 1979), civil rights (Fleisher and Zames 2001), and personal freedoms to enjoy the same private and public opportunities as non-disabled persons (Cook 2001).

Last, the pathway to political power is often through a process of finding common identity. Fine and Asch (1988), Albrecht, Seelman and Bury, and Fleischer and Zames (2001) have all found evidence of common identities among persons with disabilities. Although not all persons claim a common identity, Barnes and Mercer (2001) describe this identity as related to the above-mentioned political motivations, calling common identity "membership of an oppressed or marginalized group extolling its virtues" (p. 525). Ware (2001), however, notes that common identity may emerge from such simple reasons as common experience. Whether through common experience or politically motivated, there is historical evidence of common disability identities forming among people across geographic, socioeconomic, and gender differences.

As shown above, the notion of disability identity has been present in North American literature since Goffman. Johnstone's (2004) categorization of literature on disability identities in the late 1990s and early 2000s is consistent with a sociological taxonomy presented by Darling in 2013 in her book, *Disability and Identity: Negotiating Self in a Changing Society.* While conducting research for this book, Darling found that there is a taxonomy of identities that may exist among persons with disabilities, including: (a) Resignation (passive focus on the challenges that are brought about by disability); (b) Normative typicality (a desire to hide disability and "pass" in the non-disabled world); (c) Personal activism (acceptance or pride for disability and orientation toward struggling for personal rights); (d) Affirmative activism (acceptance and pride for disability and orientation toward societal change and reform related to disability); and (e) Affirmative typicality (an acceptance of disability but the desire to live and work in mainstream environments).

Through quantitative and qualitative inquiry, Darling was able to identify both the incidence of particular identities (via self-reporting in surveys) as well as mediating factors (such as access to media, age, etc.). In general, Darling found that older adults were more likely to identify in ways which aligned with the literature themes during the time of their formative years. Specifically, older adults with disabilities are more likely to feel stigma and shame about their disability and have a sense of resignation. Professional adults were more likely to have normative typicality identities. More activist identities were often characterized by access to either on-line or personal networks of affiliation (Darling 2013).

Limaye's (2013) interviews with 14 US adults with different disabilities, completed during a Fulbright experience, produced similar findings to Darling's. Older males with disabilities using wheelchairs felt they had stigmatized life. It was not easy for them to accept their own disability as it affected their construction of masculinity and male sexuality and that reflects their behavior. Many older females with disabilities strongly felt that they needed more family supports than they were, but also generally accepted their disability. Gender difference also was indicated among younger participants. Young males participants preferred to hide their disabilities whereas young women were more open about their disability as they have everything including a "normal" boyfriend.

Yet, disability identity is more complex than one can simply label using a taxonomy of identities. Frequently, individuals with disabilities have experienced mixed feelings. For example, these young women who presented normative identities were also confused about their identities when their boyfriends treated them as if they were "normal." Further, one woman with disability was excluded by her family and friends because of her additional identity as lesbian. Overall, the types of support these individuals received depend on how they identified themselves, but many of them still hoped to have some miracle to become "non-disabled."

In summary, the evolution in literature in the USA (and, to an extent, Canada) has demonstrated a slow progression in understanding of the phenomenon of disability and identity. Original conceptions of spoiled identities have given way to more nuanced understandings of how disability and identity interact. Darling's taxonomy and Limaye's findings build on an emerging literature from the 1970s to early 2000s which identified specific identities. Darling took advantage by presenting them across a taxonomy, while Limaye noted that identities are often too complex to easily characterize. The development of taxonomies and recognition of complexity have contributed to the evolution of our understanding of disability and identity, and facilitated the process to move out from a medically modeled deficit perspective (1960s) to one that challenged the assumptions of such a model (1970s through 2000s) to one that seeks to understand the great complexity of disability identities (present).

Disability Identity in India: An Overview

Unlike the USA, research on disability and identity is just at the beginning stage in India, and a taxonomy, like the one Darling presented in the USA has not yet been available to use in an Indian sociocultural context. Further, it is likely that a taxonomy of disability identities exists in India, but the contextual factors of India lead us to believe that the taxonomy may look different than Darling's. In this section, we first review Indian literature from sociocultural perspectives, and then attempt to examine to which extent Darling's taxonomy is relevant in studies in India. The review of Indian studies illustrates how social and cultural contexts in India have influenced individuals' understanding of disabilities and identity, which are distinct from and often more negatively framed than those in the USA. For example, these studies suggest that not only individuals' understanding of identity, as we assumed, but also the concept of identity itself is understood differently in India and the USA.

In India, much attention has not yet been paid to the issue of identity and disability. Disability in India is not a singular marker, as it is embedded within a matrix of poverty, caste politics, class struggles, types of impairments, and above all, patriarchy (Ghai 2003). Identity as a concept may not be something readily discussed or considered in India. Friedner (2013) found in her study with deaf women in Delhi, India that identity as a concept did not resonate among deaf women and she had to explain the deaf women about the meaning of identities and intersection of deaf with gender, religion, caste, family background, and geographic place of origin.

Leading a stigmatized life, a person with a disability in India may belong to a marginalized and invisible category. Because the lives of many people with disabilities in India tend to revolve around their disability rather than their abilities, their self-concept is often unrealistically low. Consequently, self-expectation, level of aspiration, and general motivational level are unnecessarily diminished (Murickan and Kareparampil 1995).

Establishing a sense of identity and belonging is a lifelong process. Our environment and the experiences with which we interact provide us with the knowledge base and skills to cope with life's daily challenges. It also helps us to gain insight into who we are and explores what we want to become. Self-concept is developed on the basis of evaluation by self and by others during interpersonal interactions at home, school, and in the community. Once established, this self-concept will exert its influence on every behavior for the rest of its owner's life (Combs et al. 1979).

For example, pilot interviews for a current collaboration between authors in India revealed that persons with congenital disabilities may not be aware about their disabilities at an early age. When they enter school, they meet other children and see themselves "mirrored" in everyday responses that their peers and adults make to them. These interactions make them aware of their differences from others. When they grow up, they begin to realize the meaning and implication of disability. Disability in a sociocultural context is explained by Booth (2000) as an interaction between a personal impairment or illness with societal factors such as attitudes, cultures, policies, and institutional practices.

Such interactions can be challenging for persons with disabilities. In Indian society, family ties remain throughout life. As a person with a disability ages, stress may be induced by the role of parents, peers, and teachers who may have their own understandings of disability. Social discrimination may be a lifelong factor influencing identity. Ideas about disability and about ourselves are generally formed by those who are not "disabled" (Morris 1991).

Cultural meanings of imperfect bodies also exert a great influence on the formation of gendered identities. Many women with disabilities have recognized the centrality of the body and impairment in their personal experiences and social reactions to disability. The more visible and severe their disabilities are, the more they develop negative identity, and thereby affect their self-esteem. Such negative perceptions of impairment and disability are internalized by persons with disabilities and influence their behavior and self-concepts (Addlakha 2013).

Individuals with disabilities in Indian mythology as well as history have been depicted as cruel and spiteful (Bhambani 2003). Such language and images can produce stereotypes. In a country like India, where many are illiterate, visual media such as films can facilitate these negative images toward disability and make a powerful and lasting impact on their attitudes and perceptions (Bhambani 2003).

Parents of children with disabilities know that societal views of people with disabilities are often deemed less acceptable and that people with disabilities have difficulties in establishing satisfying social relationships and obtaining jobs (Wright 1983 cited in Weinberg and Sterritt 1991). Further, the birth of children with disabilities tends to be seen in the Indian society as the result of Karma or a family's past deeds (see Antony 2013). Some parents may make efforts to hide their children's disabilities or even deny that they exist. In stressing the importance of "passing" as able-bodied, parents may also communicate to the child, that being "able-bodied" is good and being "disabled" is bad (Weinberg and Sterritt 1991). Thus, disability has become the central feature, and the issue of personhood assumes secondary significance (Ghai 2003). In such a case, parents help their children with disabilities to mold themselves into what they feel is an "ideal young adult." As a result, people with disabilities have to struggle to live with their own "true self" and "forced self" when they grow up.

In the Indian context, the family's activities and contacts in the community lead to the broadening of its members' interests and experiences and help the members to develop a sense of their place in the community through participation as responsible adults and develop different social relations within the community. Society expects a person with a disability to fit into societal structures, rather than structures fitting into the persons with disability needs. The images of women with disabilities in Bollywood films in contrast to men with disabilities may be an indicator of the way society responds to men and women with disabilities (Bhambani 2003). This attitude may have influenced their personal self related to the social environment. Shahnasarian (2001) argues that the implications might lead to experiences of underachievement and inadequate fulfillment. This lack of self-actualization may lead to low self-esteem, poor self-image, and negative self-concept. A study by Irungu on the nature of guidance and counseling that learners with disabilities receive at school found that a majority of learners who fall in the 17–18 age range find it difficult to discover their self-identity and assert independence, or search for goals that would give meaning to their lives (cited in Murugami 2009). Anita Ghai, an activist with a disability from India, noted in Hershey (2001) that her negative feelings toward her disability eventually gave way to an acceptance because there was no alternative. At that point, Ghai began to move forward with disability as a part of her complex identity.

Indian culture and society unlike in the West, encourage dependence and subjugation and this dependent culture is a direct result of a society dominated by patriarchal attitudes (Bhambani 2003). Therefore, an important aspect of understanding disability and identity in India is to focus on the implications of economic independence of people with disabilities, especially women with disabilities, from social and cultural perspectives.

Friedner (2013) discussed deaf identity as both gendered and culturally embedded. She found while taking interviews of deaf women in Delhi, India that culture plays a critical role in their construction of selfhood and the culture and gender modify the experiences and articulations of deaf identity in a non-Western setting.

Limaye's (2013) study in Mumbai illustrates how individuals with disabilities navigate challenges associated with their disabilities and formulated disability identity in Indian cultural context. Specifically, she focused on deaf adolescents' perception of their lives, their identities and the world around them, and the ways in which they learn to adjust to the disability and suggest means of intervention. It was found that while struggling to discover their own identity and making an effort to be part of a hearing world, youth who are deaf realize that they can never become nondisabled members of society. It was found that these youth are still victims of "normalization" as their parents and society expected them to use oral means for communication to be a part of hearing world. Their insights into themselves, coupled with their perceptions of how society views their disability, have a significant impact on their identity. The types of supports they received are strongly correlated with their deaf identity. Some parents and professionals try to help deaf adolescents in accepting their impairment as a reality that they live with without losing a sense of self. Self-esteem and emotional support from family and deaf friends/deaf club played important roles in deaf adolescents' adjustment to their deafness.

Three Researchers, Three Paths to Research

I, Christopher, likely came to my research interests on disability unconsciously. As a young child I grew up within close proximity of a "State School" in New York State (USA). In the 1970s in the US, State Schools were a euphemism for institutions for children with complex and significant disabilities. Although I never entered the institution (such opportunities were not afforded to the general public), I remember clearly the special carnival days at the State School that I attended as a child. As a child with little exposure to disability, I remember being overwhelmed by seeing hundreds of children with complex physical and sensory needs all in a very small space participating in carnival-like events.

I was raised Catholic, and instilled with a strong sense of service to humanity. This service orientation led me to major in special education, and choose to spend my first year after graduating with a Bachelor's degree in India. Part of that year in India was spent at a "Home for the Dying" run by a mission organization. My job was clear-cut – provide service to the homeless men who needed basic food, shelter, and clothing. At this point in my life I had many more encounters with persons with disabilities and was no longer overwhelmed when I discovered the men with whom I worked had a variety of what might be considered disabling conditions. As I got to know the men of the home better, I saw a variety of impairments that may have hindered them in their daily activities. At the same time, I began to see (and critique) what appeared to be artificial barriers to the men's participation in daily activities, self-care opportunities, informal education, and recreation. I became very upset at what Darling (2013) would call "Resignation." In fact, I began to see the home as a place that was creating and reproducing a culture of resignation.

It was at that point in my life that my mindset switched from a service to social justice mentality in relation to the phenomenon of disability. Several years later I had the good fortune of pursuing a PhD, which allowed me to conduct independent research on the various identities (from social justice orientation to resignation) assumed by persons with disabilities. It was through this preliminary research that I encountered my colleague Sandhya Limaye. As we began to talk about issues of identity, I realized I longed to return to India to gain a better sense of how identity works in a context for which I have reasonable experience and understanding. Sandhya's insider knowledge has been at the center of our work as we have developed research protocols and conducted interviews. In these conversations we also added Misa Kayama to our team. Misa's understanding of the phenomenon of stigma along with her own research and experiences has added fresh perspectives to our study.

As we enter into analyzing a complex data set, we have three distinct lenses. We represent three countries of birth, two sexes, diverse impairment narratives, differing professional training (education and social work), and two different institutions. Despite this, our interest to learn more about identities drives this work.

I, Sandhya Limaye from Mumbai, India, am qualified as a social worker from Tata Institute of Social Sciences and I am working in the field of disability as an academia and as a practitioner for the last 30 years. While working with a population with different types of disabilities, many youth with disabilities were upset and were confused about their own identities and they shared it with me. I also conducted a workshop for the women with disabilities from slums to share many issues including identity. It was found that majority of them were confused about their own identities irrespective of caste, class, education, and gender as society has a negative attitude toward disability and people with disabilities.

In Indian society, people strongly believe that the birth of child with a disability is the result of a family's past deeds and it reflected on youth with disabilities. One woman with muscular dystrophy said, "Who has seen the previous birth? But people labeled us as bad, useless and we were brought up with this idea that 'we are bad people and therefore our identity is bad and useless person.' It is difficult for us to think that we have identity like other non-disabled people." One youth said, "I was so angry with my mother as she is responsible for my deafness. Once I realized the causes of deafness, I felt that it is no one fault for my deafness but the damage is there. I am making an effort to be proud of myself but people around me make constant remarks and ask a no. of questions. It is very tiring for me to answer the questions and explains the implications of deafness."

Many people with disabilities also made very clear that their parents' concept of "normalization" affected the idea of their own identities. One girl with locomotor disability, who used a stick and wheelchair, said, "My parents asked me not to use stick or wheelchair while attending family function and they asked me to practice walking without assistance. I do not understand why my parents want to make me as normal? What is wrong with having a disability? I am comfortable with my disability as an identity but at the same time I have to please them...It is difficult for me to adopt two kinds of identities." One post-graduate woman who has acquired low vision said,

My parents were shocked to know about my sudden vision problems. They did not support me and they asked me to pretend to be normal in front of society. This is because I am a girl from south of India and it would be difficult to get married because of my vision needs. They wanted to present me as a 'normal' identity to society for my marriage but they did not feel that they are cheating the people and they are not concerned about my feeling. I have no choice but to listen to my parents. This is painful for me to live with two different identities. Pretending to be normal also affects my performance as an individual professional.

The quote above demonstrated how the push to hide disability because of social stigma may have a negative impact on persons with disabilities and their families.

There are many families who support people with disabilities and work hard for their overall rehabilitation. But the kind of intervention can also create problems for them. One youth with a hearing impairment said, "I am oral deaf and studied in a regular educational system. But the people from hearing world do not accept me because according to them, I am disabled. So I tried to contact the Deaf community but the Deaf community did not accept me because of my oral language needs. To Whom I belong? Neither hearing world, nor deaf world, I am hanging between both worlds. What kind of identity I have? Oral Deaf identity? We are few oral deaf people and we do not have a lobby to support each other." One woman with polio said, "I introduced myself with my name and designation as I am proud of my achievement but people called me 'crippled'. I get furious hearing it. My identity is not disabled as I strongly feel that I have my identity based on my name and achievement like other non-disabled people."

A majority of people with disabilities felt that everyone talks too much about stigma but no action is taken to reduce this stigma! They demanded to take such actions that make them adopt their identity as they want to be and not to have forced identity. I can understand their feelings as they have to struggle to establish their own identity. The fact is that very few professionals offer services for developing positive self-concept and confidence. In our (Indian) society, many professionals in the field of disability talk about education and livelihood as an important issue whereas sexuality, identity, parenthood, etc. are overlooked (Raja and Boyce 2003). The major reason is likely due to lack of counseling, lack of awareness of disability issues among people, and lack of adequate intervention plan. Parents do not have many options other than consulting such professionals for professional advice. Thus, the professionals get the authority or control to decide the future of the people with disabilities. In my experience there is a disconnect between the desire of people with disabilities to explore issues such as identity development and sexuality and NGOs' focus on services.

Therefore, I have conducted many sessions such as facilitating them to ventilate their feelings, discussing the ways to deal with their feelings, providing role models to them at individual level, and conducted awareness program on different disabilities among the community. These programs were conducted in Mumbai and there is need to focus more on it. Through this project with Chris and Misa, we are hopeful to find need-based intervention plans for people with disabilities to develop positive self-concept.

Misa Kayama: As part of our work on disability identity, Chris and I visited Sandhya in India in 2014. My visit to India gave me new insight into the experiences of individuals with disabilities. I experienced a series of challenges in handling attitudes toward my wheelchair and inaccessibility of public facilities and transportation, which reminded me that I took for granted my independence in the USA and Japan where most public facilities are accessible for people with disabilities. As an international student and scholar from Japan, I have seen cultural differences between the USA and Japan in addressing and communicating about disability and how they impact individuals' understandings of their disabilities and identity development. My thoughts about my "disability" shifted as I moved to new places and got to know new peoples. Before visiting India, therefore, I expected that I would have a whole new experience through my wheelchair. Yet, the challenges I faced in India were much more than I expected. After briefly describing a "trajectory" of what I understand my wheelchair in Japan and the USA, I will reflect on my experiences in India.

In my everyday experiences in the USA and Japan, my wheelchair is only one of many things I have to deal with, which, I believe, are similar to what other people are dealing with on a daily basis, such as at work and home. The only time I seriously think about my wheelchair, or disability, is when I face a problem, for example, when an elevator is out of order for maintenance, or when I feel I am not treated respectfully. As long as things I have set up for my wheelchair work, for example, my apartment and office that are accessible to my wheelchair, and my colleagues and friends understand what I need, my wheelchair is not a primary issue I have to think about. How I handle such accessibility and other people's attitudes is, however, somehow different in Japan and the USA. Until I found that I had to use a wheelchair for the rest of my life when I was a graduate student in Japan, disability was a problem of someone else, not mine. Therefore, I initially did not feel comfortable with going out in a wheelchair because of the way other people looked at and talked about my wheelchair, such as, "I'm sorry for you." Over time, I have witnessed changes in attitudes of Japanese people and society toward my wheelchair. Public facilities also have become accessible gradually. In a situation in which an issue of accessibility comes up, people are empathetic and pay close attention to my needs. Such reactions still remind me of my "difference," but I feel that it has become less negative recently, in part, due to the increased public awareness and acceptance. In contrast, when I came to the USA 12 years ago, I enjoyed accessibility and freedom from other people's "eyes," which made me think more positively about my wheelchair than when I was in Japan. I liked many people's reactions, such as "you are brave," instead of "I'm sorry." Yet I began to notice and experience discriminations and exclusion behind such positive attitudes as well as accessible facilities. I experienced public's ignorance to my needs, for example, when I found a pile of snow blocking the accessible curb and sidewalk, that made me realize my "differences" and feel frustrated. Such situations, however, occur only once in a while, and I tend to forget about my "disability" in Japan and the USA.

From the first day in India, however, I realized that my wheelchair was the primary issue I had to handle. My first encounter was that my wheelchair was lost on the way to India. Until it was delivered 2 days later, I had to survive in a heavy wheelchair I borrowed at the airport, which was too large to get into the elevator of a guesthouse I stayed. I realized that my "independence" was possible only because I had a wheelchair that helped me perform everyday activities. When I lost my wheelchair, I did not know how I could survive or even do simple things such as going to a rest room to wash my hands. Furthermore, staff members at the airport did not take it seriously. After explaining for more than 1 h why I needed a wheelchair, I was finally able to borrow that oversized wheelchair. Later, I was able to connect the staff members' attitudes to everyday experiences of people with disabilities in India. When we discussed with several people with disabilities, many of them described that other peoples' "mentality," such as the one I experienced at the airport, was an issue that had to be changed and affected how they understood their "disabilities."

I also found immediately that even in my own wheelchair, going out and exploring the town was challenging for me. I had to be accompanied by other people who could push me to climb on a sidewalk, which had a small step, and carry my wheelchair to go upstairs. At the beginning, I tried to take it as a challenge that I could manage, and I went out with other people's help. Gradually, however, I started feeling that my wheelchair was giving them extra work. I gave up to go outside by myself, and began to rely on other people, for example, when I needed to buy even a bottle of water. This also affected how I thought about myself, including something that was not directly related to my "disability," for example, motivation and confidence in my work. After I came back to the USA, I felt "free," and noticed how I was affected by these environmental issues.

Other people's reactions to my wheelchair was another challenge I had to handle. In many places, I noticed people who looked or pointed their fingers at my wheelchair. Initially, I thought that such reactions were because the wheelchair I was using, which is adjusted to my needs, might not be typical yet in India. Later, I realized that it was much more than that. The social status of someone in a wheelchair was not very high. For example, I saw several people sitting in their old wheelchairs who were begging on the street.

I also noticed that such social status plays an important role in marginalizing people with disabilities. Back at the airport, I again faced another challenge to advocate for myself. When I checked in at the counter, a staff member cautioned me that I was not allowed to go through the security check in my wheelchair. I did not take it seriously and thought that I would be able to negotiate. It was not that easy after all. The staff members insisted that it was a rule and I was not allowed to go through the security check in my wheelchair. Unlike other airports I ever visited, mostly, in Japan and Western countries though, they did not offer me a choice to be checked by a person. I had to go through a metal detector in an airport equipped wheelchair. While we were arguing, someone in military uniform came and joined us. At this point, I felt scared, and began to think that I had to give up. Fortunately, they finally agreed that I would be able to have my wheelchair back immediately after the security check. If I were living in India and knew about the cultural and societal norms better, I would have been frightened and never thought about negotiating with them.

Through all these experiences of handling situations that are emotionally difficult, I also noticed that individuals with disabilities in India were exposed to such discrimination on a daily basis. My experience was just a glimpse of challenges they were facing every day. My interpretations of the Indian culture are also based on my experiences in Japan and the USA and may not be correct. Yet my first-hand experiences of these challenges gave me deeper understandings of the personal narratives people with disabilities shared with us in India.

Conclusions

In conclusion, identity intersects with a wide variety of contextual factors including (but not limited to) national context. In our early empirical work, we have learned that there are a host of factors which influence the identity of persons with disabilities in the US and Indian context. However, different cultural expectations of what it means to have a disability, different social support systems, and different levels of importance on concepts like independence, marriage, and family heavily influence how we think about identity.

Further, agencies that aim to support persons with disabilities approach identity in different ways. US agencies vary, focusing on a wide range of identity outcomes. The Indian agency representatives we interviewed seemed quite focused on "normalizing" the person with a disability so they could better fit within the existing societal norms. Through this exploration of theory, preliminary empirical work, and self, we have come to learn that personal identity is dynamic as each person with disability has a way of thinking about disability and themselves as having disability, and is affected by personal traits and characteristics, life experience, attitude of the society around us, and availability of the supports. If positive self-identities are the goal for persons with and without disabilities, a careful approach to disentangling the societal barriers that promote exclusion, as well as personal services such as counseling, building the self-concept, and vocational supports appears to be the most appropriate path forward in both countries.

References

Addlakha, R. (2013). Body politics and disabled femininity: Perspectives of adolescent girls from Delhi. In R. Addlakha (Ed.), *Disability studies in India.* New Delhi: Routledge.

Antony, P. J. (2013). *Segregation hurts: Voices of youth with disabilities and their families in India.* Rotterdam: Sense Publishers.

Barnes, C., & Mercer, G. (2001). Disability culture: Assimilation or inclusion? In G. L. Albrecht, K. D. Seelman, & M. Bury (Eds.), *Handbook of disability studies* (pp. 515–524). Thousand Oaks: Sage.

Bhambani, M. (2003). Societal responses to women with disabilities in India. In A. Hans & A. Patri (Eds.), *Women, disability and identity.* New Delhi: Sage Publications.

Booth, T. (2000). *Progress in Inclusive Education.* Paper presented at "Meeting Diverse Educational Needs: Making Inclusion a Reality," World Education Forum, Dakar, 26–28 April 2000.

Combs, A., Avila, D., & Purkey, W. (1979). Self-concept: Product and producer of experience. In D. Elkins (Ed.), *Self concept sourcebook: Ideas and activities for building self-esteem.* New Jersey: Growth Associates.

Cook, J. A. (2001). Sexuality and people with psychiatric disaibilities. *SIECUS Report, 29*(1), 20–25.

Darling, R. B. (2013). *Disability and identity: Negotiating self in a changing society.* Boulder: Lynne Rienner Publishers.

Epp, T. (2001). Disability: Discourse, experience and identity. *Disability Studies Quarterly, 20*(2), 134–144.

Fine, M., & Asch, A. (1988). Disability beyond stigma: Social interaction, discrimination, and activism. *Journal of Social Issues, 44*(1), 3–21.

Fleisher, D. Z., & Zames, F. (2001). *The disability rights movement: From charity to confrontation.* Philadelphia: Temple University Press.

Friedner, M. (2013). Identity formation and transnational discourse: Thinking beyond identity politics. In R. Addlakha (Ed.), *Disability studies in India.* New Delhi: Routledge.

Friedson, E. (1965). Disability as deviance. In M. B. Sussman (Ed.), *Sociology and rehabilitation* (pp. 71–99). Washington, DC: American Sociological Association.

Gabel, S. (2001). I wash my face with dirty water. Narratives of disability and pedagogy. *Journal of Teacher Education, 52*(1), 31–47.

Garland-Thomson, R. (2001). Seeing the disabled: Popular rhetorics of popular photography. In P. K. Longmore & L. Umanski (Eds.), *The new disability history: American perspectives.* New York: New York University Press.

Ghai, A. (2003). *(Dis)embodied form: Issues of disabled women.* New Delhi: Shakti Books.

Goffman, E. (1963). *Stigma* (pp. 1–40). Englewood Cliffs: Prentice-Hall.

Hershey, L. (2001) An interview with Dr. Anita Ghai, one of India's advocates for rights of disabled women. *Disability News (8)*, May–June.

Johnstone, C.J. (2004). Disability and identity: Personal constructions and formalized supports. *Disability Studies Quarterly,* 24 (4), http://www.dsq-sds.org/_articles_html/2004/fall/dsq_fall04_johnstone.html

Kayama, M., & Haight, W. (2014). *Disability, culture and development: A case study of Japanese children at school.* New York: Oxford University Press.

Lifchez, R., & Winslow, B. (1979). *Design for independent living.* New York: Whitney Library of Design.

Limaye, S (2013, April 16–17). *Constructing disability as an identity: A study of Indian adolescents.* Presented at 13th Annual Multiple Perspectives on Access, Inclusion, and Disability Annual Conference, Columbus.

Linton, S. (1998). *Claiming disability.* New York: New York University Press.

Minow, M. (1990). *Making all the difference: Inclusion, exclusion, and American law.* Ithaca: Cornell University Press.

Morris, J. (1991). *Pride against prejudice.* London: Women's Press.

Murickan, J., & Kareparampil, G. (1995). *Persons with disability in society.* Trivendrum: Kerala Federation of the Blind.

Murphy, R. (1990). *The body silent.* New York: Holt.

Murugami, M. W. (2009). Disability and identity. *Disability Studies Quarterly, 29,* 4.

Raja, S., & Boyce, W. (2003). Standing on our own feet. In A. Hans & A. Patri (Eds.), *Women, disability and identity.* New Delhi: Sage Publications.

Rao, D., & Valencia-Garcia, D. (2013). Stigma across cultures. In P. W. Corrigan (Ed.), *The stigma of disease and disability: Understanding causes and overcoming injustices* (pp. 283–296). Washington, DC: American Psychological Association.

Riddell, S., Baron, S., & Wilson, A. (2001). The significance of the learning society for women and men with learning difficulties. *Gender and Education, 13*(1), 57–73.

Seale, J. K. (2001). The same but different: The use of the personal home page by adults with Down Syndrome as a tool for self-presentation. *British Journal of Educational Technology, 32*(3), 343–352.

Shahnasarian, M. (2001). Career rehabilitation: Integration of vocational rehabilitation and career development in the twenty first century. *Career Development Quarterly, 49*(3), 275–283.

Steinberg, L. (2011). *Adolescence* (9th ed.). New York: McGraw-Hill.

Stocker, S. S. (2001). Disability and identity: Overcoming perfectionism. *Frontiers, 21*(2), 154–173.

Szivos-Bach, S. E. (1993). Social comparisons, stigma and mainstreaming: The self esteem of young adults with mild mental handicap. *Mental Handicap Research, 6*(3), 217–236.

Ware, L. (2001). Writing, identity, and the other dare we do disability studies? *Journal of Teacher Education, 52*(2), 107–123.

Weinberg, N., & Sterritt, M. (1991). Disability and identity: A study of identity patterns in adolescents with hearing impairment. In M. Eisenberg & R. Glueckaut (Eds.), *Empirical approaches to the psychosocial aspects of disability.* New York: Springer.

Chapter 3
Disability: A Result of Cultural Ostracism

Samidha Shikha

Abstract After reading some of these travails of heroic courage and resilience of disabled people, my problem seemed to be too trivial to share. Yet, I know that it has drastically impacted me. One can't imagine how a drooping eyelid, they call it ptosis, could cause so much pain and give me an inferiority complex that has been so hard to shrug off. This problem was so personal that a reticent person like me could share it with none. Perhaps, now I am bereft of those complexes, which were really gnawing at my entrails as a child. Here, I try to untangle the web of my life to reveal how I came out of my shell. In the course of this journey my academic learning also came in handy. Delving deep into literature and theosophy, I looked at myself with renewed vigor and understanding. I also went further ahead to discuss with some of my colleagues about the nature and reasons of a variety of psychological and physical disabilities that occur both in the human and non-human world due to the interference of culture. As a culmination to my odyssey, I would say that an all-inclusive growth pattern needs to be recognized and adhered to for a symbiotic relationship. This chapter asserts the need to recognize those mental and physical handicaps as disabilities which are the results of social and cultural disregard or unwarranted intrusions that are often overlooked and therefore cause permanent damage to the affected persons.

Self-Reflection

I have not experienced "disability" as it is commonly understood but have had its impact on an entirely different plane. For me it became a state of my mind that had deep roots in not only my psyche but also the socio-cultural environment to which I belong. There was a time when this slight drooping of my left eye gave me an "inferiority complex" which has been very tough to shed. Even though all the functions of my eye are absolutely normal, when I look at myself in pictures I see that half-opened eye staring back at me. How ugly it seems to me, how unbearable. While in school, one day, a classmate jeered at me with spiteful remarks about this eye. I

S. Shikha (✉)
Goverment College for Women, Rewari, Haryana, India
e-mail: shikha.samidha@gmail.com

© Springer International Publishing AG 2017   31
S. Halder, L.C. Assaf (eds.), *Inclusion, Disability and Culture*, Inclusive
Learning and Educational Equity 3, DOI 10.1007/978-3-319-55224-8_3

shrank into a cocoon severing all attempts to relate with people around. Not being able to communicate easily with classmates, my reticence was often subdued by vociferousness of others. I therefore became an introvert, a recluse. There were no friends to share my woes. My parents, perhaps, had more important issues to bother about. However, for me it has eaten into my psyche well beyond complete repair. Somehow I managed to study enough to be employed as a regular college lecturer. Then the question of my marriage arose. No one could fall in love with a "recluse" who had a half-opened eye. Not that "Love marriages" were easily accepted in our society during that time, but that was what my father lamented when he was unable to find a match for me due to this ill begotten eye. He finally came across a person who found beauty beyond that wretched eyelid and I was married off. This story might appear weird to some who may not be familiar with the Indian social setup of our times. Non-acceptance of anything unusual is a trait of our society. What a wreck it made of me was hardly ever noticed. I am reminded of the American poet W.H. Auden's poem *The Unknown Citizen* where this person is absolutely normal according to biological and statistical records but "…Was he free? Was he happy? The question is absurd." The sarcasm in these questions is very evident. American society has its own pitfalls as the poet here conveys, but the point I am making here is that physiological disability is not the only impediment in a person's life. Societal and cultural dictates also lead to complexes that disable the affected person. They may be even unsurmountable because of their latent, termite-like infestation.

The question now is how, if at all, I have been able to overcome it. I was sent to one of the best English medium convent schools in our town and I must have unknowingly imbibed a lot there which was revealed to me later. We used to have poetic recitations and inter-class elocution competitions and I was generally a part of the chorus or background. Our English recitation was thoroughly polished by our teachers. However, while I was there I felt stifled in my own cocoon of "self-degradation" which became my greatest impediment. Sitting all by myself, even during recess hours I did not experience the joy of eating or playing with friends. So, my mind dragged me into an unfathomable dungeon of loneliness. I felt no one could either like or accept me. My father was a strict disciplinarian and my mother kept emotions at bay. Hugs and kisses were unheard of in our house and I longed for a loving home, a lap where I could bury my head and relate all my woes. Also, I was not as good as my younger brother in studies and so he managed to get all the attention and have his way around, whereas I was a non-entity. Somehow, I passed school and entered a professional institute. Here I found that my fellow students could not speak English as fluently as I could (credit to my convent education) and also that I was actually good at studies. The director of the college admired my potential and soon I became a student leader fighting for the recognition of our college. I'll leave out the politics that ensued later on due to this. However, in the ordeal, my inner being started flowering and my confidence rose. No one mentioned my drooping eyelid and I too forgot all about it. My parents disapproved my entering student politics so I was made to drop the regular homeopathic medical studies in order to join M.A. English and then continued further to get an M.Phil. The only friend I made here was a disabled girl not out of sympathy for her but for me since I believed that a normal person could not befriend me. My father would often rebuke me saying, "You are head to foot dependent upon me!!" After my post-graduation I desperately wanted to be financially independent and I did manage to become so. This was an attempt to improve my self-worth, which by itself was not an easy proposition in our culture during those days. I moved out of my secure environment to work at a far-off place. I started living in a hostel, managing things all by myself. I was still a recluse though, attempting to befriend but not entirely successful. Then "marriage" happened; "happened" because I was not the chooser. Next came two lovely children who adored me and I basked in the joy that I got in nurturing them. When my son was 10 and daughter just 6 years old, the government decided to transfer me and my husband to Bhiwani, a remote place far away from Gurgaon, our workplace for the past 10 years or so. We had to leave our children behind with my parents. In Bhiwani, my husband and I had ample time to spare after duty hours. Osho became our spiritual comfort and to me his discourses started unwinding my inner knots. Then I learnt about a month-long workshop on "Women Empowerment" to be held in Chennai, which is in the south of India. I convinced my husband to let me go for it. I boarded the train to freedom. I simply enjoyed being all by myself. In Chennai, I listened to eminent speakers, interacted with them and also with other participants; I undoubtedly had an engaging time. Surprisingly, my colleagues there didn't seem to be as happy and satisfied as I was. I wondered why. Soon I realized that many of them were doing this only to fulfill a requirement in their teaching career. They were mentally trapped in their daily domestic routines and so their minds were elsewhere during the workshop. I realized that compulsion seldom results in real learning or joy. However, I was confidently expressing myself throughout the month-long workshop and it was received very well. The "Inferiority complex" was gradually loosening its grip on me and at the end when I was judged as a "cyclone" from the North, it left me dumbfounded. I felt accomplished. Now there was no turning back, I kept looking for opportunities to go and refresh my mind time and again to distant places, be it a seminar on oral examination, a "Legal Literacy workshop," a workshop on "Promoting Women Leadership," Indian and film aesthetics, an "Art of Living" course, a Gurdjieff (a mystic) work group, an Osho camp, a literature conference, or a multidisciplinary seminar on eco-cultural ethics. My whole emphasis was to leave my routine far behind for some time every year. I went to Delhi, Faridabad, Rohtak, Hisar, Kurukshetra, Simla, Goa, Chennai, Thiruvarur, Tiruchirapalli, and even to Paris. There was nothing to stop me in my adventures. I felt fulfilled in such retreats and I loved them. No longer did my childhood complexes trouble me. This was not a conscious therapeutic training but a natural consequence of my need to find my worth. On one such sojourn, I went to NIAS Bangalore for a 3-week orientation program on "An Integrated Approach to Knowledge and Information." We were a group of enthusiastic learners and researchers. The evenings were all ours to enjoy and know about each other. I made friends for the first time and was no longer fighting self-pity.

Literature and Me

Teaching literature, besides being my profession, also has an enlivening value for me. My journey with literature as a student and as a teacher chiseled out my self-confidence. I came across so many inspiring anecdotes that became instrumental in self-empowerment. John Milton's poem "On His Blindness" was one such. Even blindness could not deter this poet from his path. How could I complain about that significant nothing that I was living with? Indian literature written in English has often captured my interest. It has a lot to offer in terms of social and cultural beliefs. At times, it has been literature of the English people that echoes my Indian ethos too since humanity is basically the same everywhere. Literature reflects "Culture" in its myriad diversities. What intrigues me most, however, is that "Culture" instead of enhancing could disable one's natural prowess also. In the course of one such reading, I came across AK Ramanujan's poem "At Forty" in *Collected Poems* (1995).

> '…Jatti, the Wrestler, our teacher at the gym,
> is now in top form, our state's very best',
> and so they trim his hair, give him all-body shaves…
> Eggs and meat for breakfast, massages
> of iguana fat…
> No sex, they whisper, for even
> a look at your wife or that rumored Muslim mistress
> will drain/your power, loosen your grip. They weigh him,
> measure his chest, his belly, his thigh,
> and they pat his treasure. One April day,
> they take him out
> in a procession/…to market square
> to the white ropes of the red arena
> in the Town Hall, where he is thrown
> round after round, rolled over, jeered at
> by rowdies/and sat upon by a nobody from nowhere,
> …Jatti, the Wrestler, / our teacher at the gym, walks away….

This is the story of natural ability being thwarted by culture, resulting in disability of the wrestler. Had "Jatti" continued to practice as before, he would have maintained his strength and easily vanquished the "rowdies." Physical disability, thus, may also be caused by unnatural interference of human culture. Jatti is no longer allowed to live his normal life. Culture misguides and overtakes him. Soon he loses his caliber and is ostracized from his position of being a formidable wrestler. This example shows how a person who had proved his prowess in society became handicapped due to the meddlesome "culture." It is not mere fiction that Ramanujan is writing about. Human society and culture are responsible to a large extent for many a disability caused by following the unnatural path.

A Meeting of Minds

When I broached the issue of "Cultural Disability" with my colleagues, we all agreed that before one realizes one's potential, often culture undoes the person. Psychological disabilities often occur due to the intrusion of culture. At other times, it may be a state of established "helplessness" that appears as a disability. However, before coming to these conclusions we decided to ascertain our parameters of "culture" and disability. We restricted ourselves to disability arising due to discrimination, inferiority complexes leading to functional inability, and simply culture-specific norms that inhibit expression. The diverse group of colleagues, with whom I interacted, put forth a variety of viewpoints since they belonged not only to different ethnic and religious groups but also because their views were gender specific.

We all agreed that "diversity" is part of existence but mankind imposes its own dictates therein, placing one at a higher pedestal than the other or simply decrying the other. This drives a wedge between or raises walls to separate disparate identities resulting in discrimination. It is human pride that leads one to self-glorification and eulogizing and placing the other in a meaner or disabled position. I was, here, reminded of my own challenges in dealing with discrimination and complexes as a child. The ensuing "Disability" may be physical, mental, or psychological. Surprisingly, even the attitude of society toward a handicapped person varies from culture to culture. One culture accepts the same physical handicap or deformity in its stride, laying more emphasis on the person's abilities whereas the other culture focusses on his disability to undermine or isolate the disabled. In this context, I am reminded of the story of my colleague whose brother has a hunch back. He decided to go away from India so that he could lead a normal life. Now, he is in the USA with a good job and family without having to suffer the mental torture of being subjugated due to his unseemly body. Nowadays, many people are suffering from hair loss. Specifically, some men have a tendency to lose the hair on their head from their youth onwards. A receding hairline or a thinning crown in many cases becomes an object of ridicule in families and society. The affected people try desperate methods for regrowth of their hair, more often than not without any success. Lack of confidence ensues that affects the personality of the individual. Yet again, it is the attitude of family, society, and culture that is responsible for the mental fiasco. In my own understanding, treating the person as normal makes one adjust better with society. It was observed that the West judges such persons actually as "differently abled" (not simply a euphemism). In our discussion we agreed that the East generally shows less of this sort of magnanimity and inclusiveness. Therefore, an insignificant disfigurement or an imperfection of the individual is translated into a mental block or handicap due to cultural seclusion, denigration, and ostracism.

In the group was Meera, an ecology lover. She pointed out that the present "culture" has also tried to restrain or incapacitate natural tendencies, which in turn has adverse consequences. She brought our attention to animals that mankind has domesticated. Dog breeders do not allow the dogs in their captivity to breed normally instead use artificial insemination to get the breed that sells most or is extremely expensive. Thus they render them incapable in many aspects. The pet dog is also incompetent to search for food or even defend herself like the stray ones because she doesn't need to. The owners are there to look after her needs. Haven't we disabled the pet animal? Genetically modified plants may produce better looking tomatoes and oranges but they are unable to retain the same food value. Cows and buffaloes are milked to the extent that they are unable to feed their own calves. Thus, mankind has raised its own selfish world in opposition to the natural one. We have devised walls and barriers between disparate beings and made hazardous intrusions into nature to the extent of establishing discriminating ideologies that govern societies. These ideologies then become mental blocks for both the victim and the perpetrator that haunt the society for ages with various forms of "disability" attributed to one or the other. Else it may all be a power game where the one who is powerless or has less power is disabled in one way or the other. Meera insisted that a divisive approach to existence is a cultural issue that is the cause of the resultant disabled mind. This tends to make hierarchical divisions rather than attribute complementary inclusiveness and growth to separate identities. A vividly rampant power game is on play between humans and non-humans. Human beings wield the baton and are generally not inclined to either empathize with or "hear" the latter. The speech of the "non-human" world is thus muted and disabled due to the impact of human culture. People tend to listen to the more powerful. As Christopher Manes says in "Nature and Silence" (*The Ecocriticism Reader* 1996):

> The words of these speakers are taken seriously (as opposed to the discourse of "meaningless" and often silenced speakers such as women, minorities, children, prisoners, and the insane) p.17.

The inhumanity and apathy of mankind in general toward the non-humans and other less privileged beings makes natural symbiosis impossible. The green cover of trees and plants is removed in order to construct cultural havens for humans. Such mindless actions of mankind expose the disunity with the rest of existence and as a consequence inability of the human species to live in coordination with nature.

Jagdambe, the feminist among us was most vocal and also hailed by all. She picked the lead there to reflect upon the cause of "Women folk" who have generally been at the receiving end across countries and ages. Their undermining is so complete that they themselves assume to be disabled in many respects, say for example my mother would often harp upon her incompetency to write a cheque till after my father expired. When tears flow out easily from the eyes of women, it is attributed as their weakness and we hear the oft-quoted statement of the master: "Frailty thy name is woman." Women themselves believe it and weakness becomes their nature. It makes them vulnerable in society in spite of their innate mental tenacity. Similarly, it is assumed that the men folk need to show a tough exterior and so have to subdue the tears welling up inside them rendering them "disabled" to respond emotionally.

> Men have been discouraged from feeling emotional. We have been mocked, attacked, and belittled when showing emotions. Big boys don't cry, toughen up, and bite the bullet are all

phrases men grow up with. So when we are faced with emotional situations, we are total novices. (Elephant Journal 2014)

This male-female hierarchical or emotional divide has created an unbridgeable chasm. It has created untenable expectations from each other. As a consequence, they are generally unable to understand each other. Further, the male folk helping in the kitchen are still looked down upon in India, as is a woman not interested in household chores. With such a bent of mind, the woman is thought to be a lesser being meant only for the hearth (which is considered lowly). Men are automatically considered to be more capable in the outside world while women have to prove themselves. There are disadvantages for men too. It is assumed that men are not capable of managing household affairs. In this way men are culturally disabled in one respect and the women in another. It may be pointed out that the scenario has changed since we find more and more women at enviable altars in society. However, such women are in decimal proportions. The vast mass of women feels powerless and helpless, which is a form of mental disability, when it comes to spearheading significant projects or being self-initiated. This is not because they are really incompetent but because family/society has rendered them so. The deeper we go and explore the realities, we find that even the apparently powerful women face gender bias and therefore feel disabled in many a situations. One mistake by a woman driver and a cultural judgment is echoed "I told you women can't drive!" One has to be very strong to counter such an attitude. Else, the woman herself is demoralized to incompetency and loses her confidence to drive.

We also find that unnecessary caesarean sections, performed due to the vested interests of many of the doctors, have disabled the mothers to deliver normally. The women are not allowed to listen to their own bodies. The mother is considered incompetent because of lack of medical knowledge. Vandana Shiva's own courageous example was quoted: "In spite of a normal pregnancy… and having prepared myself for a natural childbirth…As a mother, however, I was denied the status of 'expert' in child-bearing; that status was restricted to the doctor…But I preferred to listen to my own good sense and walked out of the delivery room. My father drove me to a more modest hospital where they were willing to give my baby and me a chance to be natural. As expected, I had a smooth, un-traumatic delivery."(Shiva and Mies 1993) The use of diapers may be convenient for parents but regular use of such like aids may inhibit normal, gradual bladder control of the infant. Natural instinct has often been disabled by advancing technology, which is most detrimental to society. The present generation, depending more and more on calculators and computers is disabled to calculate mentally. This is advanced culture showing its true effects. Even among women, the working ones have an added edge over the ones not working. The ones who are exclusively home makers many a times may suffer from lack of self-worth and incompetency. Incompetency is also a type of disability. I pointed out that the relationship of parents and children is also a kind of power game. Children are considered incompetent to choose their course of higher studies. This also has a detrimental effect on the psyche of the child. This may not be so common in the Western world where children are more or less on one's own financially after the basic school education. Other problems might be there due to this structure.

Whereas "Interdependence and group solidarity" are the positives in Asian Indian societies, they have their down side too. "Humility" is one such attribute that has strange forms of expression in society. During those days, in my country, if you looked into a person's eyes, while talking, it was considered to be rude. So I learnt to evade my eyes in all communication such that I have been unable to recognize people's faces easily. Even public figures, movie stars, politicians, I fail to recognize. Such disability that arises due to societal dictates stunts natural development and growth. Here in India, parents need to give more freedom to their children. Else, Kamala Das, the famous Indian poet, talking about her father in the poem "Next to Indira Gandhi," wouldn't have painfully cried out:

"You chose my clothes for me
My tutors, my hobbies, my friends,
And at fifteen with my first saree you picked me a husband..."
(*Only the Soul Knows...* p.148). (Das 1996)

How well I could relate to Das' assertion that reminded me of my own past. I have been unable to decide about the choice of my dress or a particular hair style since that freedom to choose was not given at the formative stages. It is not that I was incapable of having my own views about things but the society collectively and family individually placed me in a state of choice-less debilitation.

Sally, our colleague from the States insisted that cultural inhibitions and covert behavior are another kind of "disability" that one becomes conscious of only on interaction with a different culture. Show of affection in public is normal in the West, she asserted, but is not considered proper in India. So a "couple" "kissing" openly in public may have to face averting eyes and disparagement in India because the Indian mind considers this indecent behavior whereas it is quite normal in the West. In India, women wearing shorts or noodle straps in public have been considered as indecent and hence the general disability of Indian women to don the bikini model. The comfort level of an individual when dictated by culture is sure to cause various forms of disabilities. I agreed and gave my input that men comfortably moved without their shirts in public areas in Hong Kong whereas this would be quite unseemly here in North India. In South India, however, it is not uncommon to see men roam about in their dhotis (loin-cloth) without covering their upper body. Body consciousness is very obvious in the north of India and probably more so in cultures where women are required to wear a burqua (a cloak that covers from head to toe). Inhibitions, such as these also affect the mind-set of the people concerned and so whole cultures may be victims of certain "inferiority complex." It is often assumed in India that whatever comes from abroad (foreign countries) is better than indigenous stuff. This is self-cultural denigration which makes one look down upon oneself with respect to the other. For example, it is assumed that for creativity to be at its best it has to be borrowed from the West. So, even T.V. programs or movies are at times replicas of the West reflecting a self-inflicted incompetency. However, one cannot deny that the freedom to adopt and adapt needs to be there even though "diversity" is the basis of all creation. Culture need not create problems when it comes to creativity. Debilitating cultures should be universally condemned. This summed up the whole discussion.

Societal and Cultural Disabilities

The other day, our maid was telling me of her inability to wear sun glasses because of her social status. She could afford it but because of the tag of being in the menial job category she felt dissuaded to wear the same. Such kinds of economic and cultural debilities tend to pigeonhole people/culture groups into un-traversable slots. Another area of disparity is about the concept of beauty. Beauty is considered to be color dependent which is again a cultural fallacy leading to isolation of the dark colored ones. Dark-skinned women being considered less beautiful than the fair-skinned ones may not only be ethically and factually wrong but this also creates a mental hang-up or "complex" in the concerned individuals, especially in countries where fair skin is synonymous with beauty. All such instances are cultural obsessions that lead to stunted mental and emotional growth of an individual or a particular society. The yesteryear "slavery" of Afro-Americans in the USA. was defined by the color of the skin. It may not be legally possible to discriminate on this count now but it is doubtful whether the fixations have totally been routed out. This tends to create some sort of obsessive compulsive disorder (OCD) leading toward lack of confidence and self-worth in the affected parties. Language barriers are another significant cause of disparity and discrimination in society that results in cultural ostracism. In India, a person fluent in speaking English garners more respect than those who can't. The incapacity of the latter generally makes one diffident. This is a type of disability which is the consequence of a cultural dictate. Then there is the example of the older generation that is at times less infirm than they are considered to be. I remember my grandfather telling me that people in the US would stop their car to offer him a lift while he was on his regular walk. Hence, assumption of disability is also another cultural snag. Thus, there are innumerable latent abilities that have been overlooked and disabilities that have been over-projected that cause pain and embarrassment to the persons concerned.

Insensitivity toward others is so much rampant in society that it is not easy to gauge the extent of harm it perpetrates. It is the family, culture, and society that are both the cause and answer to the entire incompetency rampant in the so-called able society. It needs a very strong mind to counter imposed disabilities. This chapter is an attempt to think about the nameless prodigies and "would be" achievers that may appear normal but actually need tender concern to return to normalcy. In other words, the apparently "able" people may actually be suffering from unrecognized disabilities or mental handicaps which establish themselves on the physique and personality of the individual. One needs a discerning attitude to fathom the scale of cultural ostracism that leads to conquerable incapacities.

References

Das, K. (1996). *Only the soul knows how to sing.* Kottayam: D C Books.

Manes, C. (1996). Nature and silence. In *The Eco criticism reader: Landmarks in literary ecology.* Athens: University of Georgia Press.

Mies, M., & Shiva, V. (1993). *Ecofeminism.* Jaipur: Rawat Publications.

Ramanujan, A. K. (1995). *The collected poems of A.K. Ramanujan.* Oxford: Oxford University Press.

http://www.elephantjournal.com/2014/02/why-men-withdraw-emotionally

Chapter 4
Perseverance Pays

Satendra Singh

Abstract I have experienced life as a person with a disability, as a specialist medical doctor, a teacher, a family person, and as a disability rights activist. The varied experiences and notable discrimination forced me to "react" as well as "respond." Being a staunch proponent of health humanities, I paused, wondered, and reflected on these experiences as per Kolbe's experiential model, and later transitioned into Gibbs iterative model of self-reflection. The journey has been exhilarating as I unearthed hidden layers of my own capacity. In this chapter, my transition from a sufferer to an activist is presented in evocative autoethnography with narratives from my life offering an understanding into the larger political, social, and cultural scenario of living in India with disabilities.

Early Days: From School to Medical College

I am holding my favorite drink, a hot cup of tea, as I walk across my bedroom, on dual crutches, and step out on to the balcony. An early morning breeze and lush greenery greet me. As usual, the water flows unperturbed in the canal across the road – it never fails to inspire me to push ahead. My gaze shifts to a child who is skipping along to her school bus, holding one hand each of a young man and a woman. The sight takes me back to when my journey began.

One of the most vivid memories of my childhood is how my elder brother, Devender, and his classmate, Ambrish (I still remember his name), used to walk me from my class to the school bus and vice versa. I used to wear an iron-rod caliper with a pelvic belt at that time, and my brother would hold my right hand and Ambrish the left. With them by my side, I even dared to hop over minor obstacles that came my way. This trust in their support made me look forward each day to the trip to school.

S. Singh (✉)
Associate Professor of Physiology; Medical Humanities Group; Enabling Unit (for Persons with Disabilities), University College of Medical Sciences (University of Delhi) & GTB Hospital, Delhi 110095, India
e-mail: dr.satendra@gmail.com

© Springer International Publishing AG 2017
S. Halder, L.C. Assaf (eds.), *Inclusion, Disability and Culture*, Inclusive Learning and Educational Equity 3, DOI 10.1007/978-3-319-55224-8_4

I was born in a village in the state of Haryana, India. My father was serving in the Indian army at that time and I was the youngest of four children, and also the plumpest of them all. At 9 months of age, I developed a high-grade fever which persisted despite treatment. I never stood on my own after that. I was diagnosed as having post-polio residual paralysis, 70%, of both lower limbs. In the late 1970s there was limited awareness about the disease and most village children with a disability simply languished; however, since my father was in the army, my supportive parents took me all over the country and tried all sorts of treatment – allopathic, homeopathic, acupuncture, even hearsay. One gentleman in Amritsar swore that he would shave off his mustaches if he could not cure me. I don't remember what happened to his mustaches but I am still riding through life on crutches. I have faint memories of my parents taking me on long journeys in over-crowded buses; they went wherever anybody suggested that something could help – something that could get me to walk again – I recall being massaged with pigeon's blood too, but it was all in vain.

As therapy continued, I started exploring my surroundings crawling with the help of my arms. When the time came to join formal schooling, I was entrapped in an iron-rod caliper with a pelvic belt. It was a nightmare to wear those calipers every day. The bigger horror was when the caliper broke either at the ankle or the pelvic region. It was a frequent problem; even now, government aided assistive devices are still not of very good quality. That is why the support of my brother during those early days was so comforting.

Ironically, polio turned out to be a blessing in disguise; it forced my father to take the whole family out of the village. The transition meant better education for us; his frequent transfers all over India occasioned a wider cultural perspective, a broader worldview, and better opportunities. As it turned out, my eldest brother is now a personal manager, the second is a vascular surgeon, the third an army colonel, and yours truly is a medical doctor at a premier institute in Delhi.

At school, I was exempted from the morning prayer assembly. Whether that was exclusion or reasonable accommodation was too early for me to determine. I was a laborious child and was the apple of most teachers' eyes – of the science teacher the most. Her constant support was very helpful but I think there was a hint of sympathy as well. I remember once when we were taking a science test that I wasn't adequately prepared for; I deposited my answer sheet well before the scheduled time. My ardent supporter, my sweet teacher, took it for granted that I had answered everything. She praised me, telling the class to follow my example – he studies and so he has finished before everyone, she said. I was uncomfortable – the praise, something I ordinarily craved, hurt because it was undeserved this time. Years later, I see it for what it was – the disabled are seen as superheroes even when their achievements are of a "normal" degree.

By the time I got to class XI, better rehabilitation services were available to me at the Allahabad Medical College where the orthotic, Mr. Bharat Gupta, worked with me and rid me of my pelvic belt. He also devised a lightweight polypropylene caliper that enhanced my morale and self-confidence considerably.

I experienced both delight and anguish during my school years. I remember watching my friends play football while I was assigned to take care of their belongings. One day, they were a player short when the skipper asked if I would keep goal. The request was so unexpected, I was flummoxed; regaining composure, I said, "If you think I can do it, I will certainly try." Indeed, my classmates never teased me for my disability, though it was routine for strangers to look at me with pity. *Inhe kya hua hai?* (What has happened to him?) or *pair dekho iske* (Look at his leg) were routine comments. Not only did they treat me as an object, they also had no disability etiquette, choosing to address my caregiver instead of me.

I changed several schools because of my father's transfers. At each, I would skip the morning assembly, as it was difficult for me to keep up with the student queue, or climb up and down stairs in time for the 30-min ritual. At one school, a senior teacher on rounds found me in the classroom during assembly. Irritated, he dragged me out by my collar. Continuing to ignore my pleas, he took me all the way to the assembly. I toppled a few times on the stairs but the teacher was hell bent on teaching me a lesson. He forced me to stand facing my schoolmates and sing the national anthem with everyone. I did it, but with moisture in my eyes. My classmates gathered around me after the horror show to show their support, but I wanted to be alone. I learned later that the other teachers had not approved of the "scene"; as a result, the principal formally relieved me from attending the mandatory assembly. I never encountered that "gentleman" again as he taught senior students, but even now I wonder about him. Why was he so agitated that he dragged me to the assembly? Was he normally so hostile? Instances like this give us, the people with disabilities, an additional immune system – a thick skin!

My elder brother cracked the medical entrance test and I followed, soon joining medical school in Kanpur, Uttar Pradesh. It was a very big occasion for my mother who had worked tirelessly behind the scenes so that we fulfilled our aspirations. The time had now come for the boy to face the real world. From the comfort of home, a protective environment, I stepped straight into a boys' hostel. The fear of hazing was paramount. Past media reports of hazing-induced medical student suicide, eardrum perforations, and bony fractures were bothering me. New students never dared to join the hostel in the first year because of this fear.

Of the 190 first-year medical students, only four had no recourse but to join the hostel and I was one of them. Vikrant Sirohi, a tall boy who also had polio, was another, and we became best friends. All four of us opted to share rooms with senior boys whom we knew already; this saved us from the more physical forms of hazing – in any case, Vikrant and I were usually, mercifully, spared.

Coming from an army background, secularism was second nature to me; however, in Kanpur Medical College, the caste system, or social stratification, mattered to people. Traditionally, the Hindu society is organized into four social orders – Brahmins, Kshatriyas, Vaishyas, and Shudras. One day, a group of seniors stopped us and one of them asked my caste. I said, general category. There was an ominous silence and then a stinging explosion in my right ear – I had been slapped! He asked again and this time I said, Kshatriya. Another tight slap, this time over the other ear. That night, I learned the gory details of social stratification in India. Nobody had ever asked me my caste in my 12 years of schooling, perhaps because they were spent in predominantly army schools. But here, the social divide was clearly visible – a deeply inculcated traditional culture. I was a Jaat! I realized for the first time that caste politics played a very important role in the political scenario.

Medical life is stressful. One has to cope with the anxiety of separation from home, with a new, challenging, environment, with ragging, and with an arduous curriculum. For a student with disability, there are additional stressors. Accessibility can be a problem. My lecture theatre was in the college building and Hallet hospital was across the road. Our clinical postings ended at 12 pm and we were expected to be in the lecture theatre in time for the 12–1 pm lecture. I could never make it in time – fortunately there were two entrances to the classroom and I would quietly slip in from the back door at about the middle of the lecture and was spared public humiliation. Instead of focusing on what was taught in the clinics, my mind would be busy trying to figure out how to get to the lecture on time. People with disabilities are forced to start early because of inaccessibility issues; but here it was a lose-lose situation – miss a part of the clinical posting to make the lecture on time, or miss a bit of the lecture so as not to lose out on clinical teaching. I was forced to compromise.

At that time, the "medical model of disability" was in vogue and I accepted my fate thinking that my problems were entirely my responsibility. The "medical model" (Singh and Gupta 2016) views disability as a problem of the person. It focuses on the diagnosis and tries to "fix" the disability as the management is aimed at "curing" the disability. Since I could not afford to be late for every class, I requested that my father get me a kinetic scooter. Fortunately for me, the two-wheeler was easily modified at Ahmedabad, Gujarat; the two extra wheels gave me stability. I learned to drive it in just a day and my maroon colored Kinetic Honda began to be called "Gigantic – that which never sinks" as its arrival coincided with the theatrical release of Titanic.

Gigantic gave me wings; I was more independent, and life was fun, fast, and fabulous. I even raced the pretty girls of my batch on their scooters. My college days engendered my biggest learning, both good and bad – courtesy of fabulous seniors and peers, my first crush, my first and last cigarette, a plethora of medical cases, exceptional teachers, great physicians, brawls with the police, serious clashes between seniors and juniors, strikes, and last but not the least, the murder of a dear senior on campus.

After graduating, I went on to do my Masters in Physiology from Rohtak, Haryana. This was another critical phase in my life; I earned my MD, got married to my sweetheart, Ranjita, lost my biggest pillar of strength – my mother, and was blessed with a daughter.

My mother always worried about me. I was her one-point agenda and she dedicated her life completely to me. She was not educated but she was my best teacher. She taught me to focus my energies not to curing one life but to bringing about change that would affect the life of millions. Today, when all four of her children are well settled and doing what she advocated, she is not here to see it.

It was the longest night, and my worst nightmare, wh' leukemia. I rushed to Delhi, short weeks later, when she ' against hope, touching her, wanting her to clasp my hand behind the biggest void. I discovered that the doctor who was a batch mate; it was a sad reunion with an old frienc reality of her passing, and my walk toward her final ritu my struggles combined.

My daughter Shambhavi was born the next year. When I broke the new. father from the labor room, my voice was choked – "Dad, mom has come back." In the same year, I joined the University College of Medical Sciences (UCMS), University of Delhi, as Assistant Professor of Physiology. Academically, this was my rebirth as the college gave me a new lease on life. I found mentors here, who nurtured my passion for medical education, and I dived into medical humanities and disability activism.

My mentor, Professor Navjeevan Singh, introduced me to the medical humanities. He encouraged me to start a disability subgroup under the Medical Humanities Group that led to the formation of "Infinite Ability" (Singh 2012). Our earliest ventures were a Theatre of the Oppressed workshop for medical students and a Blind with Camera workshop for visually impaired students of the University of Delhi (Times of India 2012a). Beholding dreams, I embraced life diligently!

From Facing Discrimination to Fighting It

I was waiting outside the radiology department of a prestigious private hospital in the capital city of India (East Delhi to be precise). I had recurrent renal colic and had been advised an ultrasound of the kidneys. To avoid having to remove my calipers and then put them on again, I took my crutches along instead. When my name was called, I rose with the help of the crutches. The lady sitting next to me rushed to help me. I thanked her saying, "I can manage." Still sympathetic, and adamant to share her pearls of wisdom, she said, "You must sit at home and take care of yourself. Have you ever been to school?" Without waiting for an answer, she advised, "You must open a PCO (Public Call Office); at least you will earn something."

It is the twenty-first century, and people with disabilities are still considered cases for charity, asexual objects, and too incompetent to complete even basic education. Thus, when we do achieve something, we are glorified as if we have scaled Mount Everest. There are just these two extremes and nothing in the middle. Add to such a mindset fear of the unknown – of disability – and you have the perfect plot for discrimination of the marginalized.

In another example I was returning to college after the holidays, when I decided to travel alone as I craved independence. Indian railways provide concessions to the orthopedically disabled and to one escort. Even though I was traveling alone, I had to buy the second concessional ticket because of archaic rules. On my way back from Ahmedabad to Kanpur, the train ticket examiner (TTE) came to check the

He noticed that I had two berths and asked, "Where is your escort?" I _ly announced, "I don't have an escort so you can give the berth to somebody _o needs it." With a sneer he responded, "No! That is against the rules. If you can _ravel without an escort, your concessional berths are invalid."

My disability was clearly visible because of the caliper and the crutches; nevertheless, I showed him my disability certificate. The TTE took advantage of my obvious anxiety, my youth, and my helplessness. Smacking his lips at the chance to make a few bucks, he ignored my pleas and ordered me to vacate both berths. "Where will I go?" With a stony face he said, "I don't care." Shocked and scared, I vacated my berth and watched as he "sold" the berths to two other travelers.

Despite _two_ valid, reserved tickets in my hand and a disability certificate in my bag, I was thrown out of the compartment on a cold winter's night. I never imagined that I could have sought help from other passengers; it was only my second time traveling a long distance on a train. The TTE benevolently claimed that ordinarily he would have thrown me – an invalid ticket holder – out of his compartment, but because of my disability he was going to allow me space in the corridor. I spent the next day and a half, chilled and weepy, outside the toilet. There were no mobile phones in those days so I could not speak to anybody at home. The TTE passed by me many times but felt no remorse. He was my single-man welcome party to the real world – an insensitive and cruel place!

During my postgraduate studies at Rohtak, I would go home to Rewari every weekend by bus. It was 2007, a day before Holi, the festival of colors. Because of the festival there was a huge rush; however, I managed to get two tickets for seats on the last row for my pregnant wife and myself from the Rohtak bus stand. When we got to our seats, rowdy university boys already occupied them; their clothes were soiled with Holi colors. I asked the conductor to get our seats vacated. He responded rudely and said, "This is not my job." I replied, "We have tickets. Whose job is it?" When he did not react, I pointed towards a seat reserved for the disabled, which was occupied by an able-bodied man. The conductor sneered, "There are umpteen regulations in our country. Should I leave my conductor's job and become a judge or policeman? Find yourselves a place to sit." We stood for the most part of the 2 h that it took us from Rohtak to Rewari.

At our destination, we got off and I noted down the bus number – HR46B 7246. Before leaving, I warned the conductor, "I am Dr. Satendra. Remember my name and face. We will meet again." He laughed and told me to do whatever I wanted to do.

I immediately reported the matter to both the bus depots. Nothing happened despite repeated reminders, until 6 months later, when I was told that they could not pursue the complaint as the conductor had been transferred (routine transfer) to Jhajjar; the case was considered closed. I could not leave it at that; I imagined other people with disabilities suffering as I had, and knew that for their sakes I couldn't give up. I wrote to the Jhajjar bus depot that called me 3 months later. There, I saw him, the conductor, going about his business with the same gloating insensitivity as ever. Nothing concrete happened in that meeting. I was advised to leave the matter be, but the need to make a lasting difference to how public servants dealt with persons with disabilities fueled my determination to carry on.

I then wrote to the Transport Commissioner, to the Director General, State Transport, and to the Transport Minister. One and a half years after the incident, my departmental contact told me that a bus conductor wished to meet me. As I expected, it was he and he was almost in tears as he rushed to touch my feet. Apparently, he had received letters from the ministry and his job was at stake, even his pension. From being discriminated against, my transformation into an advocate against discrimination had begun, but was horrified – it had never been my intention to get him sacked. There was no vengeance in my heart, more a doggedness to make him realize that, as a public servant, it wasn't all right for him to mistreat people. He apologized so profusely and with such conviction, that I immediately gave him a letter withdrawing my complaint.

I was on permanent post, as Assistant Professor in Physiology, at UCMS and GTB Hospital, University of Delhi, when the Union Public Service Commission (UPSC) announced openings for Assistant Professors in the Teaching Specialist Sub-cadre of the Central Health Service. UPSC posts offer a time-bound promotion, which was not the case in my university job, so I decided to apply. Everybody else who had applied got a call letter for the next stage – the interview – except me. I kept waiting until a week before the scheduled interview, when I contacted UPSC. Their response was shocking – since I was a person with disability (I had accepted as such against a mandatory question in their application form), I was considered ineligible to teach in a medical college. Shocked, I explained that I was already working on the same post in a government medical college; and that I had successfully completed both undergraduate and postgraduate studies with the disability. They said that they couldn't do anything, they were just a recruiting agency and were following the rules. I was advised to talk to the Health Ministry.

Not knowing where to go, I contacted Mr. Javed Abidi, a leading disability activist at the National Centre for Promotion of Employmentfor Disabled People (Disability News and Information Service 2011). He spoke to the additional secretary at the Health Ministry but feared the order might come too late to help me since the interviews were scheduled in 2 days. I then contacted Human Rights Law Network, who filed a case on my behalf in the High Court of Delhi. The matter was referred to the Central Administrative Tribunal on the same day; they passed an interim order to allow me to appear for the interview. I took the order and rushed to the UPSC, where nobody was willing to receive the order. Apparently, the seal of the judge was not legible. Frustrated, I went away and faxed the order to the Chairman of the UPSC. In the evening, I received a call from the UPSC that I could appear for the interview the next day. After a few weeks, I also received a fax from the Health ministry stating, "It has been decided that Dr. Singh and other similarly placed candidates, if any, may be called for the interview. A detailed clarification in this regard will follow shortly."

Sadly, neither court judgments nor ministerial orders were able to avert future alleged discrimination against the disabled by the UPSC (The Hindu 2013a). Lightning does strike twice and at the same place when it comes to the plight of doctors with disabilities (India Medical Times 2013). Two years after the incident that involved me, the UPSC advertised the same posts again. Buoyed by the previous court judgments and ministerial orders in my favor, I applied again. This time it was an online form and I thought nothing of it when the website asked for my disability type and percentage. Within seconds, however, my hopes came crashing down when the website refused to allow me to complete my application. It flashed, "Sorry you are not suitable for this post." I wrote to the Chief Commissioner for Persons with Disabilities (CCPD) as well as to the Ministry of Health. Immediately, I got a fax saying that I could apply for the said posts; however, the relaxation applied only to me probably because of my nuisance value, while other colleagues with disability were still being denied. I wrote again that all doctors with disability who are eligible for these posts should be allowed to apply (The Hindu 2013b).

It is shocking to see such rampant prejudice. I completed 5 years of a tough medical course – attending outpatients, wards, operation theatres, and emergency rooms – and then went on to do my internship. I successfully completed postgraduate training. Nobody ever questioned my ability; yet, here was the UPSC and the Health Ministry, clinging to the view that we were incompetent. I wonder if they have heard of Dr. Suresh Advani – a wheelchair user, and a doctor who pioneered the bone marrow transplant program in India. We, as polio survivors, have a physical impairment, but discriminatory societal attitudes make us completely disabled.

To add salt to the wound, the UPSC insists on submission of a disability certificate in their own signature that asks candidates to photograph their disability (Times of India 2013a). They do not accept a permanent disability certificate issued by government hospitals. This is not only discriminatory but also violates human rights – our right to respect, equality, and dignity. My written objection caused UPSC to withdraw the discriminatory preformat eventually (*IBN Live*2014a).

Through repeated right to information (RTI) petitions to the Ministry of Health, I opened a Pandora's box. My question was simple: which posts did the UPSC consider as suitable for doctors with disabilities? The response was an eye-opener: not only the post that I had applied for, but all specialist posts in the Central Health Services (CHS) were not suitable for doctors with disabilities. This not only exposed the disabled mindset but also highlighted how many people were silently facing discrimination. Single-legged, I fought a lengthy 4-year battle and finally the war was won when the Ministry of Health unlocked 1674 central posts in the CHS (teaching, non-teaching, and public health posts; Times of India 2015c).

By this time, I was well versed with disability issues, with the Persons with Disabilities (PWD) Act, and the United Nations Convention on the Rights of Persons with Disabilities (UN CRPD). Unlike the previous occasions, this time I flagged the issue in leading newspapers that created mass awareness. From fighting individual discrimination, I transited to flagging issues for advocacy and for unifying individual effort. I was charting into unknown territory but I was passionate and pertinacious.

In February 2014, I was invited to speak at the *International Conference on Evidence in Global Disability and Health* jointly organized by the London School of Hygiene and Tropical Medicine and the Public Health Foundation of India, in

Hyderabad. Ironically, on my return the security officials at Hyderabad airport asked me to remove my calipers. I explained gently to them that I was not saying no to the security check but it was difficult for me to remove the caliper. I asked them to do a thorough checking, even physical frisking, but the chap was adamant on removing it and passing it through an X-ray scanner (Times of India 2014a). My appeal that I am a government officer, a medical specialist doctor, and a disability rights activist left him unmoved. The IndiGo operator also failed to convince him. I finally put my "foot" down, refusing to remove it as it was against my dignity. I asked my wheelchair assistant to take a picture but she got scared and abandoned me. People around me were staring; I noticed some elderly citizens whizzing by in their wheelchairs – apparently they did not want to be part of this ugly confrontation.

In the heated atmosphere, I could well picture their plight if it had been a senior citizen or a woman instead of me wearing an orthosis. I had heard of incidents where people were asked to strip and remove their appliances. I was also aware of the Bureau of Civil Aviation Security (BCAS) guidelines so I asked the security officer to call his senior. The senior officer came and I repeated the whole story politely and firmly. He reiterated that he had to follow orders. I asked them to scan me with their Explosive Trace Detector, whereupon they finally gave in, scanned me in my wheelchair, and certified me as "harmless." The confrontation lasted 20 min (The Hindu 2014a). I was the last person to board the flight, but I did so with my head held high.

On my return to Delhi, I petitioned the Director General of *Central Industrial Security Force* (CISF) attaching the media reports. CISF is in charge of airport security in India and they are also the largest industrial security force in the world. The complaint created a ripple effect; a training program in soft skills was organized for the CISF staff and I was invited to share my "harrowing Hyderabad" incident, interact with, and provide feedback to the CISF staff. I asked the participants how many of them had interacted with a person with autism or Down syndrome. Only one hand rose in the gathering of 200 people. My point was made – you cannot train people about disabled people without involving disabled people. Unfortunately, on the same day the BCAS released an updated Standard Operating Procedures (SOP) manual that did not include suggestions of the disability sector (Deccan Chronicle 2014a). It was time to take the BCAS head on.

Other disability activists and I wrote of our concerns with the new SOP to the Joint Commissioner of BCAS who met with us. We pointed out that while the SOP mandates screening of prostheses by an x-ray, even in the US the Transport Security Administration that is responsible for security at US airports stipulates that passengers with prostheses can be screened without removing them and those with prostheses can be screened using imaging technology, metal detector, or thorough a pat down (Transport Security Administration, 2014). Our delegation reiterated that we were not seeking relaxation of security standards that would put aviation travelers at risk; however, it was important that we, passengers with disability, were handled with dignity and respect and did not feel humiliated (India Post 2014).

I was aware of the use of two new screening technologies – millimeter wave and backscatter (Deccan Chronicle 2014b). The former being non-ionizing is considered safe. BCAS shared that they were experimenting with modifications that would be acceptable in the Indian scenario and we left it at that.

Meanwhile, my Hyderabad incident was shared along with other similar incidents in the Supreme Court of India in the case of Jeeja Ghosh versus Union of India. The airline staff forcibly removed Jeeja, as they could not understand her disability (cerebral palsy). The Apex Court directed the Directorate General of Civil Aviation to meet with the disability sector in an effort to plug loopholes and be more sensitive to the needs of disabled passengers. We gave our inputs covering all disabilities and hope now that both BCAS and CISF will come up with revised guidelines that compromise neither national security nor the dignity of disabled flyers.

Giving Back: Charity Begins at Home

I was entering my office when I saw Poonam, a fifth-semester medical student who has locomotion disability. She stood outside the lecture theatre while the lecture was going on. This was the third such instance in the past week. I asked her *why she wasn't inside the classroom*. She said, "Sir, our clinical posting in the hospital ends around 12 o'clock and the teacher *doesn't let students in if they are more than ten minutes late.*" Poonam is a bright student but she has to face numerous barriers on her way from the hospital building to the college building.

I completed my MBBS without realizing that structural barriers that prevented me from displaying my ability were the root cause of my disability. It was only when I came to Delhi that I learned about the social model of disability as opposed to the medical model. Poonam's impairment disables her only because our college lacks accessible infrastructure. The UGC mandates all colleges to have an Enabling Unit exclusively for students with disabilities. In line with the worldwide mantra "Nothing about us, without us," staff, faculty, and students with disabilities run our Enabling Unit. Remembering my own difficulties with accessibility during my MBBS days, I immediately wrote to the head of the institution in my capacity as Coordinator, Enabling Unit. I requested leniency for students with disability; a circular was issued based on my recommendation giving them some leeway (Deccan Herald 2013a).

The Enabling Unit meets often; during one such meeting, one of our student members with disability told me that the boys' hostel was not accessible. For 3 years he had been struggling every day to enter the building. This became our first major task – to make all hostels in the campus accessible.

Letters and reminders were sent to the Public Works Department but nothing moved for 6 months. The Medical Superintendent (MS) of the hospital, who was in charge of real estate, also remained aloof. Feeling frustrated, I decided to protest subtly in my individual capacity on World Disability Day. I wrote to the MS and wore a black armband in silent protest (Millennium Post 2012a).

The very next day, I received an order from the Additional MS that sanctioned INR 12, 73, 300/– for construction of ramps in all the hostels, in the bank premises and at the college entrance. In the next few months, all the hostels were made accessible; however, the big question still remained – how many medical institutions in India are accessible to persons with disabilities?

I am not aware of any medical institution using sign language interpreters for hearing impaired patients. What if a deaf person were to land up in an emergency unaided? The majority of hospital websites are inaccessible to persons with visual impairment. Don't they have any right to use the web to locate hospitals or doctors? Hospitals may be accessible, but are the toilets accessible to wheelchair users?

> "Is any medical institution in the country accessible enough to invite the famous theoretical physicist Stephen Hawking to deliver a lecture?" I asked the nation through a leading daily (Deccan Herald, 2013b).

Sadly, the answer is a big NO.

I first ran into trouble when I went to the Delhi Medical Council (DMC) at Maulana Azad Medical College (MAMC) in Delhi to renew my registration certificate. Two steps greeted me, without a grab rail, at the entrance to the administrative block. I had to ask the guard to lend support. By law, it's obligatory for institutions to give us reasonable accommodation; however, the concept of Universal Design seems alien to hospital authorities.

MAMC constructed a ramp eventually but it was in stark contrast to what had been proposed by the access consultant and was termed "dangerous." Their lack of intent was visible when they constructed the ramp where I had faced difficulty, but did not make accessible the nearby auditorium.

Aggrieved and disheartened at not finding a single medical institution in India completely accessible, I sent a strong representation to the Court of the CCPD, who asked the Medical Council of India (MCI) to issue directions to the Deans/Principals of all medical colleges/institutions in India to comply with and submit compliance report on access facilities for persons with disabilities (Times of India 2013b). Many hailed the move as a historic one, not only in India but in America as well (India America Today 2013).

Though I had specifically requested mandatory "access audits" to be completed during inspections by the MCI, with de-recognition of all such institutions that failed the audit, and for inclusion of persons with disabilities in the inspection team (The Hindu 2013c), the MCI chose to ask only for a compliance report.

More frustration was in store for me; only 32 out of around 355 medical colleges/institutions in India submitted their compliance reports. Some of the responses showed utter disregard toward creating a barrier-free environment. The Principal of Medical College, Kolkata, said: "There are 21 students with disabilities and they do not require any special access for their disability" (The Hindu, 2013d).

Many institutions claimed that they were accessible without realizing what accessibility meant – for example, hospital toilets were inaccessible to wheelchair users. A few wrote that as persons with visual and hearing impairment were not allowed to study medicine, they did not have appropriate signage for them. This effectively shut the doors on patients with visual or hearing impairment. The prestigious All India Institute of Medical Sciences (AIIMS), in Delhi, constituted a committee of engineers to look into the matter (Times of India 2013c). What they lacked was vision as they did not include any person with disabilities in the committee. It is more than a year now and their library is still without a lift. The six new AIIMS-like institutes set up in various parts of the country did not even respond to the MCI.

The government provides financial assistance under the Scheme for Implementation of Persons with Disabilities Act, so there should be no excuse for government medical colleges to not make their campuses barrier-free. The scheme offers up to Rs 50,000 to make a building accessible and up to Rs 15 lakh for making websites accessible (Deccan Herald 2013c). Information sought under RTI revealed that none of the medical institutions in India has availed this grant in the last 5 years. Only a few district hospitals have applied for it.

Rehabilitation is another important aspect for persons with disability, yet only a few hospitals in India have a full-fledged department of physical medicine and rehabilitation (PMR). MCI circulars mandate PMR departments in colleges as well as a 15-day posting in one during internship; however, compliance is non-existent as a result of which treatable, temporary impairments get neglected and run the risk of becoming permanent disabilities.

Strangely, the CCPD did not take any further action. I wrote to the Department of Disability Affairs, the Ministry of Social Justice and Empowerment, the MCI, and the Delhi Government but nothing happened. The watchdogs ignored my pleas but the NCPEDP awarded me the Universal Design Award last year on my initiatives to promote accessibility in medical institutions (Times of India. 2013d). I have approached the National Human Rights Commission; let's see how that goes.

Medical, banking, and postal services are termed essential services. The two automated teller machines (ATMs) within our hospital campus both had stairs and no ramp. I wrote to both banks' managers to make the ATMs disabled-friendly. After a chain of letters, I approached the Court of the CCPD who sent notices to the managers; within a month both banks constructed ramps outside the ATMs (Statesman 2013a). This prompted me to look at the overall state of affairs. I filed an RTI against the Reserve Bank of India and asked about the details of all the ATMs made accessible to the disabled. Sadly, they didn't have any record (Times of India 2012b). Their master circulars were exposed, as they were not following the implementation part. Thankfully, the new master circulars have more teeth.

My RTI against the Department of Posts in the capital of India opened another Pandora's box (Hindustan Times 2012). The replies were worrying as many first-floor post offices had no lifts and many of those declared "barrier-free" had stairs leading to them. In the first question, I had sought "accessibility status" and explained what I meant by adding parenthetically, "whether accessible/barrier-free or not to persons with disabilities." In reply to this query, the office of the director, General Post Office, informed, "The General Post Office is centrally located and it is, therefore, accessible for all" (Times of India 2012c). This was their awareness about accessibility! Inaccessibility affects not only the disabled but also elderly people. The follow-up with the Senior Superintendent of Posts shows promise but actual implementation has to be done in letter and spirit.

Article 9 of the UNCRPD concerns accessibility and we ratified it in 2007. It became mandatory for India to harmonize all its domestic laws and policies in line with CRPD. The office of CCPD had already written to all the states and union territories to change their policies. I filed an RTI in 2012 to see what changes had been brought about. Sadly, nothing concrete had been done and the reply only indicated that it was one item on the agenda of one meeting (Millennium Post 2012b). On contacting the people with disability who were invited for this meeting, they said they had received the letter only after the date of the meeting.

My independence depends upon my caliper and crutches, but I am wary of their quality. I could not find an appropriate appliance for a long time and had to use whatever was available. I can afford the costlier auto-lock calipers but what about the poor people? In many states, free appliances are provided to poor people but there is a price to be paid – one has to prove again and again that he is disabled. I contacted the Red Cross Society in my State of Haryana and found that they have a proforma that needs to be filled.

Despite having a valid disability certificate, a person seeking aid has to paste a photograph of his disability in part A, has to get it signed from Tahsildar in part B, and has to come back to the doctor who certifies again that he is disabled. I highlighted it to the state headquarters adding that these devices are not "special needs" but are a part of our lives. These are not luxuries, but necessities. This discrimination is denying us our fundamental right to live (Article 21 of the Indian Constitution). My plea was to use the disability certificate alone for all the benefits. The secretary of the state branch responded to me and admitted "the procedure is difficult and causes further discomfort and delay to the beneficiary" (Dainik Jagran 2012). He directed the district secretary to simplify it.

Moving from Activism to Advocacy

There was a huge buzz. The entire nation was buzzing at the prospect of participating in the world's largest election. People in the world's largest democracy were gearing up for an unfettered chance to exercise their choice, their say. It was a huge opportunity for voters with disability to enfranchise their basic right. But were they treated equally and with dignity?

The assembly elections in Delhi (Dec 2013) and the general elections (Apr 2014) made the citizens frantic to exercise their rights. I use this experience to convey to our readers how systematic and planned advocacy can bring change. The first step in any advocacy is problem identification. Despite Article 329 of the Constitution of India and Article 29 of UNCRPD in place, voters with disabilities face numerous problems during elections. Elderly citizens, pregnant women, and those with transient injuries all can benefit from accessible polling booths.

With the overall goal of making the General Elections-2014 accessible to voters with disabilities, I decided that a test run was in order. I would pilot the process in December 2013, during the assembly elections in Delhi.

I wrote to the Election Commission of India (ECI) as well as to the Chief Electoral Officer (CEO), Delhi, to pay attention to the rights of voters with disability in November 2013 (Bottom-up approach). The news was carried in a Hindi newspaper on World Disability Day (Hindustan 2013). The CEO, Delhi assured that they were prepared to safeguard the rights of electors with disability. As it turned out, many people with disabilities could not vote and all claims of preparedness fell flat. We vented our frustration through social media (Times of India 2013e). Leading newspapers carried my story on how people with disabilities could not vote either due to lack of ramps or due to sheer attitudinal barriers (The Hindu 2013e; Statesman 2013b). Complaint was also made to the ECI and the CCPD.

The judiciary had been responsible in the past in making the electoral process easier for persons with disabilities (Top-down approach). The difficulty of dignified access to the electoral process ultimately led to the Supreme Court (SC) taking cognizance of a letter written by the Disability Rights Group; interim orders were passed in 2007 for the Election Commission to provide ramps for wheelchairs and Braille facilities on electronic voting machines (EVM), and to ensure training and sensitization of election officials.

I used this SC order as the basis of an RTI that I filed against the ECI and the CEO, Delhi. The results were shocking – the ECI had done nothing to safeguard the rights of voters with disability. There was no sensitization, no training, no special media drive, practically nothing. These revelations were carefully released on key days like National Voters Day and Republic Day and received much media coverage (Times of India 2014b; Punjab Kesari 2014). With January over and general elections scheduled for April, I focused on "developing messages" and the "framing" phase of my advocacy effort. I employed "social math" to simplify the enormous information gathered from 70 Assembly Constituencies in Delhi. The second set of RTI in March created further furor in media (Statesman 2014; Deccan Herald 2014; Times of India 2014c) and drew the attention of the CEO, Delhi, who met with me to chart the future course of action.

Success is the result of like-minded people coming together. The CEO, Delhi called a meeting of NGOs working in the disability sector, and persons with disabilities (yours truly). He admitted frankly that there had been lapses and vowed to rectify them before the general elections in Delhi. Though time was short, I had come prepared with a checklist for access audits at polling booths that, if implemented, would make this the most inclusive election ever (The Hindu. 2014b). It was immediately circulated to all constituencies. Along with an NGO, *AADI* (Action for Ability Development and Inclusion), we were called for another high-level meeting with top officials from the Ministry of Social Justice and Empowerment (MSJE), Department of Disability Affairs, CCPD, CEO Delhi, all municipality commissioners, and nodal officers. The primary and secondary target audience was systematically approached in this advocacy effort and results were showing.

MSJE volunteered to provide wheelchairs at all the booths. AADI prepared a video as well as a pictorial booklet for booth officers. I conducted sensitization workshops for all nodal officers of the CEO, Delhi, on disability etiquette and how to make booths accessible to persons with mobility, visual, hearing, and speech impairment.

I further insisted on broadening the scope of Rule 49 N of the Conduct of Election Rules, 1961. The rule allows a companion for visually challenged voters and those with "infirmity." I gave an example of persons with cerebral palsy who, based on the severity of their spasticity of hands, may not be able to press the ballot. The suggestion was accepted by the CEO, Delhi (Times of India 2014d).

Since the CEO, Delhi, did not have any data on voters with disability, I proposed that a registration link be set up where voters with disability could register before polls, enter their type of disability and ask for specific assistance on polling day. The CEO, Delhi set up a link on the website and many voters with disabilities registered and took advantage of the service (Times of India 2014e).

On polling day, voters with disability and elderly citizens were given preference in a separate queue, there was reserved parking close to the booths, wheelchairs were available with volunteers, at all places, all EVMs were Braille enabled, and many booths had sign language interpreters. I myself checked 40 polling booths on the D-day and the media also highlighted the positive response where voters with disability enfranchised their right with dignity (IBN Live 2014b; Times of India 2014f).

One of the key issues in any advocacy is evaluation that involves formative, process, outcome, and summative evaluation. The mixed approach of bottom-up and top-down proved successful as the process moved from pre-campaign RTI info gathering (formative) to building support among stakeholders (process), positive media report post-poll (outcome) and request from other states to replicate the model (summative). The overall impact was that the ECI also made its website disabled-friendly. In a nice gesture, Mr. Vijay Dev, CEO Delhi, personally thanked me via text message in contributing toward the national duty.

"Dr Satendra (please correct me if spellings are not ok)! Just wanted to convey my heartiest gratitude to you for undertaking this first-ever historic journey together with us towards bringing smiles on the faces of PwDs. The journey is long but as they say first steps break the inertia. Thanks a lot for handholding us, guiding us and being with us at all times as we undertook this noble cause. There has been widespread applause of our endeavors and resultant demands from PwDs from other States to follow suit. It has been a pleasure interacting with you. My best wishes." Vijay Dev, IAS

I used to react earlier to discrimination but time and experience taught me to respond in order to be more effective. I was featured among the top 15 craziest cricket fans in India on ESPN-Star because of my obsession with the Zimbabwe cricket team. Unfortunately, I could watch only one match featuring them in a cricket stadium simply because stadiums were not accessible. Then, I reacted angrily on the state of affairs, but now I have filed a complaint to a quasi-judicial civil court to make Kotla stadium in the capital of India accessible to spectators with disabilities in a given time frame (Times of India 2015a). I highlighted the missing voices of PwDs from India's National HIV response and now my suggestion has been taken up by the nodal department on AIDS (The Hindu 2015). I am continuing with my dream of making all medical institutions in India disabled-friendly. As a second step, all hospitals in Delhi have been told to make the websites accessible within a time frame. The Central Government nodal ministry on disability has also taken me up in its ambitious nation-wide campaign, Accessible India Campaign (Times of India 2015b).

This was my transition from a sufferer to an activist with narratives from my life offering an understanding into the larger political, social, and cultural scenario of living in India with a disability. For inclusion to happen in higher education, we have to embrace the ethos of "Nothing about us, without us." This is the reason why I am persuading MCI to introduce disability studies in the medical curriculum and, doctors with disabilities in the committee on "Identification of posts." The journey is long but if you are passionate and pertinacious, perseverance certainly pays!

References

Dainik Jagran. (2012, June 21). *Prove your disability time and again to get assistive device.* Retrieved from http://infiniteability.yolasite.com/blog/p
Deccan Chronicle. (2014a, April 7). *Airport security riles differently abled.* P 3.
Deccan Chronicle. (2014b, April 8). *BCAS plans imaging technology at airports.* p 3.
Deccan Herald. (2013a, June 22). *Hospitals waking up to the disabled's needs, but slowly.* Retrieved from http://www.deccanherald.com/content/340497/hospitals-waking-up-disabled039s-needs.html
Deccan Herald. (2013b, June 10). *Disabled medicos face hurdles.* Retrieved from http://www.deccanherald.com/content/337999/disabled-medicos-face-hurdles.html
Deccan Herald. (2013c, June 22). *Every step is a struggle.* Retrieved from http://www.deccanherald.com/content/340490/every-step-struggle.html
Deccan Herald. (2014, March 14). *Election offices lack complete data on disabled voters.* Retrieved from http://www.deccanherald.com/content/391919/election-offices-lack-complete-data.html
Disability News and Information Service. (2011, March 1). M.S.J.E. doesn't consider disabled doctors fit for teaching jobs. *8*(5). Retrieved from http://www.dnis.org/news.php?issue_id=5&volume_id=8&news_id=1142&i=6
Hindustan. (2013, December 4). *Matdankendro par viklangokeliyejaroorisuvidhaokaabhaav.* Retrieved from http://theenablist.blogspot.in/2013/12/blog-post.html
Hindustan Times. (2012, December 2). *Access denied: Delhi not for disabled.* Retrieved from http://www.hindustantimes.com/India-news/NewDelhi/Access-denied-Delhi-not-for-disabled/Article1-967459.aspx
IBN Live. (2014a, Oct 14). *UPSC asked to withdraw proforma that demands photographs showing disability from applicants.* Retrieved from http://www.ibnlive.com/videos/india/disability-gfxdisability-upsc-meenakshiguest-live-720098.html
IBN Live. (2014b, April 10). *LokSabha polls: Spirited disabled voters throng well-equipped poll booths.* Retrieved from http://ibnlive.in.com/news/lok-sabha-polls-spirited-disabled-voters-throng-wellequipped-poll-booths/464145-3.html
India America Today. (2013, June 8). *Hope in India as mandatory access for people with disability takes shape.* Retrieved from http://www.indiaamericatoday.com/article/hope-india-mandatory-access-people-disability-takes-shape

India Medial Times. (2013, November 14). *Success for Dr. Singh, but other physically challenged doctors still in lurch*. Retrieved from http://www.indiamedicaltimes.com/2013/11/14/success-for-dr-singh-but-other-physically-challenged-doctors-still-in-lurch/

India Post. (2014, April 7). *NPRD members meet Bureau of Civil Aviation Security*. Retrieved from http://www.theindiapost.com/nation/nprd-members-meet-bureau-of-civil-aviation-security/

Millennium Post. (2012a, December 4). *Black armband silent protest against GTB hospital*. Retrieved from http://www.millenniumpost.in/NewsContent.aspx?NID=14990

Millennium Post. (2012b, August 7). *Delhi's policy for disabled has a long way to go*. Retrieved from http://millenniumpost.in/NewsContent.aspx?NID=6556

Punjab Kesari. (2014, January 26). Viklangokeliyegambhinahichunavaayog.p 3

Singh, S. (2012). Broadening horizons: Looking beyond disability. *Medical Education, 46*(5), 522.

Singh, S., & Gupta, P. (2016). Persons with disabilities. In P. Gupta & A. M. Khan (Eds.), *Textbook of community medicine (chapter 13, p 546)*. New Delhi: CBS publishers.

Statesman. (2013a, April 24). *Doctor's efforts bring disabled-friendly ATMs at GTB Hospital*. p 3.

Statesman. (2013b, December 4). *Raw deal for physically challenged voters*. Retrieved from http://theenablist.blogspot.in/2013/12/raw-deal-for-physically-challanged.html

Statesman. (2014, March 13). *Most polling booths not disabled-friendly*. Retrieved from http://www.thestatesman.net/news/44248-most-polling-booths-not-disabled-friendly.html

The Hindu. (2013a, November 10). *UPSC discriminating against me, alleges differently-abled doctor*. Retrieved from http://www.thehindu.com/todays-paper/tp-national/tp-newdelhi/upsc-discriminating-against-me-alleges-differentlyabled-doctor/article5334572.ece

The Hindu. (2013b, November 16). *Doctor with disability alleges discrimination by UPSC*. Retrieved from http://www.thehindu.com/todays-paper/tp-national/tp-newdelhi/doctor-with-disability-alleges-discrimination-by-upsc/article5356631.ece

The Hindu. (2013c, April 18). *MCI asks all medical institutions to be 'accessible'*. Retrieved from http://www.thehindu.com/todays-paper/tp-national/tp-newdelhi/mci-asks-all-medical-institutions-to-be-accessible/article4628862.ece

The Hindu. (2013d, August 12). *Most medical colleges ignore directive on facilities for disabled*. Retrieved from http://www.thehindu.com/todays-paper/tp-national/tp-newdelhi/most-medical-colleges-ignore-directive-on-facilities-for-disabled/article5014252.ece?textsize=large&test=1

The Hindu. (2013e, December 5). *Not a disabled friendly electoral system*. Retrieved from http://www.thehindu.com/news/cities/Delhi/not-a-disabled-friendly-electoral-system/article5424837.ece

The Hindu. (2014a, February 26). *Harassed at Hyderabad airport, says disability activist*. Retrieved from http://www.thehindu.com/news/cities/Hyderabad/harassed-at-hyderabad-airport-says-disability-activist/article5726938.ece

The Hindu. (2014b, March 20). *Call for inclusive elections*. Retrieved from http://www.thehindu.com/todays-paper/tp-national/tp-newdelhi/call-for-inclusive-elections/article5807757.ece

The Hindu. (2015, May 10). *No national data on HIV/AIDS among differently-abled, reveals RTI*. Retrieved from http://www.thehindu.com/news/cities/Delhi/no-national-data-on-hivaids--among-differentlyabled-reveals-rti/article7189456.ece

Times of India. (2012a, October 8). *They capture the world in their mind's eye*. Retrieved from http://timesofindia.indiatimes.com/city/delhi/They-capture-the-world-in-their-minds-eye/articleshow/16716938.cms?referral=PM

Times of India. (2012b, December 3). *Few ATMs disabled-friendly*. Retrieved from http://timesofindia.indiatimes.com/city/delhi/Few-ATMs-disabled-friendly/articleshow/17457342.cms?referral=PM

Times of India. (2012c, October 29). *No ease of access for disabled to post offices*. Retrieved from http://epaper.timesofindia.com/Repository/ml.asp?Ref=Q0FQLzIwMTIvMTAvMjkjQXIwMDcwMA%3D%3D

Times of India. (2013a, November 16). *UPSC flouts govt's job criteria for disabled*. Retrieved from http://timesofindia.indiatimes.com/city/delhi/UPSC-flouts-govts-job-criteria-for-disabled/articleshow/25854018.cms

Times of India. (2013b, February 26). *Demand for barrier-free buildings*. Retrieved from http://timesofindia.indiatimes.com/city/delhi/Demand-for-barrier-free-buildings/articleshow/18683893.cms?referral=PM

Times of India. (2013c, August 12). *AIIMS plans access to disabled, others silent*. Retrieved from http://timesofindia.indiatimes.com/city/delhi/AIIMS-plans-access-to-disabled-others-silent/articleshow/21768471.cms

Times of India. (2013d, August 15). *They innovate to e-enable*. Retrieved from http://timesofindia.indiatimes.com/city/delhi/They-innovate-to-e-nable/articleshow/21837337.cms

Times of India. (2013e, December 6). *Delhi election 2013: Disabled voters rip apart system on web*. Retrieved from http://timesofindia.indiatimes.com/city/delhi/Delhi-assembly-polls-Disabled-voters-rip-apart-system-on-web/articleshow/26922114.cms

Times of India. (2014a, February 25). *DU professor with disability harassed at Hyderabad airport*. Retrieved from http://timesofindia.indiatimes.com/india/DU-professor-with-disability-harassed-at-Hyderabad-airport/articleshow/30971043.cms

Times of India. (2014b, January 27). *Polls near, but no data of voters with disabilities*. Retrieved from http://timesofindia.indiatimes.com/india/Polls-near-but-no-data-of-voters-with-disabilities/articleshow/29432418.cms

Times of India. (2014c, March 12). *SC order on disabled voters not implemented*. Retrieved from http://timesofindia.indiatimes.com/city/delhi/SC-order-on-disabled-voters-not-implemented/articleshow/31863281.cms

Times of India. (2014d, March 23). *Voting to be made easier for disabled*. Retrieved from http://timesofindia.indiatimes.com/home/specials/lok-sabha-elections-2014/news/Voting-to-be-made-easier-for-disabled/articleshow/32517091.cms?

Times of India. (2014e, March 27). *Voters with disability can register online*. Retrieved from http://timesofindia.indiatimes.com/news/Voters-with-disability-can-register-online/articleshow/32751952.cms?

Times of India. (2014f, April 11). *Less last-mile pain for disabled, but some not so lucky*. Retrieved from http://mobiletoi.timesofindia.com/mobile.aspx?article=yes&pageid=3&sectid=edid=&edlabel=CAP&mydateHid=11-04-2014&pubname=Times+of+India+-+Delhi&edname=&articleid=Ar00300&publabel=TOI

Times of India. (2015a, May 12). *Disabled cricket lovers want equal access to Kotla*. Retrieved from http://timesofindia.indiatimes.com/city/delhi/Disabled-cricket-lovers-want-equal-access-to-Kotla/articleshow/47240825.cms

Times of India. (2015b, May 12). *Gov. plans app for the disabled*. Retrieved from http://timesofindia.indiatimes.com/india/Govt-plans-app-for-the-disabled/articleshow/47116331.cms

Times of India. (2015c, June 14). *One man's crusade opens up CHS jobs for disabled docs*. Retrieved from http://timesofindia.indiatimes.com/india/One-mans-crusade-opens-up-CHS-jobs-for-disabled-doctors/articleshow/47661044.cms

Transport Security Administration. 2014. *Department of homeland security. Disabilities and medical conditions*. Retrieved from https://www.tsa.gov/tra

Chapter 5
"Not Everybody Can Take Trips Like This": A Paralympian's Perspective on Educating About Disability Around the World

Anjali J. Forber-Pratt

Abstract This chapter presents an autoethnographic account of my experiences living with multiple identities as a disabled adopted woman of color and reflections from my travels to poverty-stricken areas helping to advance disability policies and promoting awareness. The stories presented allow readers to interrogate, or question the world, where we've come from, where we are today. The significance of this chapter rests in what Ellis (The ethnographic I: a methodological novel about autoethnography. Altamira Press, Walnut Creek, 2004), a well-known autoethnographer, describes as producing survivor tales that open up a moral and ethical conversation. The two stories being told are about my experiences returning to India, my place of birth, and the moment of shifting from being an outsider looking in at the culture to becoming an insider looking out. This story is about the intersection of disability, race, and my perspectives on poverty pertaining to my own identity development. The second story, building on these experiences, is about work I've completed in Ghana to help develop opportunities for persons with disabilities in the realm of sport. In this nation, I learned the power sport has to serve as a catalyst for social change in improving the lives and opportunities for persons with disabilities. Key policy makers and decision makers for the country of Ghana interested in disability affairs who had previously never met each other came together to improve lives for persons with disabilities. Collectively, these experiences of oppression and facing stigmas strengthened and enhanced my own identity development, and may serve as a catalyst for others' reframing of their own experiences.

A.J. Forber-Pratt (✉)
Department of Human & Organizational Development, Vanderbilt University,
230 Appleton Place, Nashville, TN 37203-5721, USA
e-mail: anjali.forber.pratt@vanderbilt.edu

© Springer International Publishing AG 2017   59
S. Halder, L.C. Assaf (eds.), *Inclusion, Disability and Culture*, Inclusive
Learning and Educational Equity 3, DOI 10.1007/978-3-319-55224-8_5

Introduction

These essays present an autoethnographic account of my experiences living with multiple identities as a disabled adopted woman of color and reflections from my travels to poverty-stricken areas helping to advance disability policies and promoting awareness. The stories presented allow us to interrogate, or question the world, where we've come from, where we are today. The significance of this rests in what Ellis (2004), a well-known autoethnographer, describes as producing survivor tales that open up a moral and ethical conversation.

The two stories being told are about my experiences returning to India, my place of birth, and the moment of shifting from being an outsider looking in at the culture to becoming an insider looking out. This story is about the intersection of disability, race, and my perspectives on poverty pertaining to my own identity development. The examples of this were numerous; some would have been enough for many to cancel the trip, to run back home to a lawyer, or to break down. I remember panicking at times, but also reveling in the opportunities to lead by example.

The second story, building on these experiences, is about work I have completed in Ghana to help develop opportunities for persons with disabilities in the realm of sport. In this nation, I learned the power sport has to serve as a catalyst for social change in improving the lives and opportunities for persons with disabilities. This story was, in part, about getting people to talk to each other, to talk about Paralympic sport, to talk about disability in the context of education and work. We were the connectors in a giant life-size game of connect the dots. Key policy makers and decision makers for the country interested in disability affairs who had previously never met each other came together to improve lives for persons with disabilities.

Why Autoethnography?

Stories allow us to organize and share our experiences as they connect to the political, social, historical constructs in which we live. They allow us to interrogate, or question the very world in which we live, where we've come from, where we are today. I like to think of our personal stories as the underlying foundation or structure of reality—it's something that shapes our very existence and provides rationale for our own perceptions. Through the telling of story, this deeper exploration and reflection can lead to the generation of new knowledge and meaning. I hope readers become informed about how I see the worlds which I live in—including the realms of disability, interracial adoption, athletics, education, privilege, and discrimination. I do not want the readers to feel discouraged by my experiences, or to feel belittled by my accomplishments; rather, as Ellis (2004) explains, I see this as a survivor's tale. I want others to leave feeling motivated to take control over their own lives, to think differently about the notion of diversity and to feel empowered in their own lives.

India: The Journey

How do you begin to describe something that is so indescribable? The journey alone to India would be enough for some people. How do you prepare yourself for having to check your dignity and independence at the door? These are two values that prevail in American disability culture. I knew getting on the airplane was a feat in and of itself. You can never have too much patience when traveling to a foreign country, being a woman in a very male-dominant culture, and having a visible disability. I suddenly was very aware of these facets of my identity. Facing oppression and discrimination square on is something I will never see the end of. Nothing can ever fully prepare you for these moments. But, knowing that you will need every ounce of patience you have and then some, and knowing in your heart of hearts that this is the right thing for you to be doing, is sometimes enough. Sometimes you just have to keep your perspective in check and make the most of the situation.

I do not know where this courage comes from, I asked myself every day before leading up to this trip why I was going and whether I had it in me to do it or not. I doubted myself every single day, and yet, there was this gut-wrenching thing keeping me up at night for 7 months that I had to do it, even though I had no clue why. This is something that is so hard to explain about with others, very few people can relate, and that's okay. It is not a Bahamas vacation, it's a real trip—a transformational experience, one that gets at your core whether you want it to or not. One that forces questions of identity, of existence, of purpose in life, one that just has to happen.

I travel a lot, as an international competitive athlete, and there are certain procedures having a disability that we are all used to. You convince the ticket agent that you should take your own wheelchair to the gate, not an airport wheelchair that you cannot even push yourself. You arrive at the gate and get a gate delivery ticket for your wheelchair, say a little prayer that the country you are traveling to is not going to have a labor strike, that your independence and life as you know it actually makes it to your connection, and ultimately to your destination in one piece. If all goes as planned, I can travel independently around the world. But, when does anything ever go as planned?

There are little things, such as forgetting the fact that an aisle chair works better if the plane is not full of people. Or, asking to use the aisle chair to use the bathroom, but being told that there is a line. And then, having to explain that unless I get up and into the aisle chair and in the same line as everybody else, there will always be a line and I may never get to use the bathroom. Educating the world. That is what I'm talking about.

I arrived in Mumbai, a totally foreign airport to me. Actually landing in Mumbai, it was like the scene from *Slumdog Millionaire* where you see the tent city up close, pan out, see more of it, and pan out again, more. For as long as you can see, the slums, with the airplanes zooming right overhead. I was there, living that moment. The deplaning process goes relatively smoothly until I am in the aisle chair on the jet bridge and my wheelchair is not there. I inquire. I am told, it is raining. That is the reason for not having my own wheelchair, is because it is raining a bit. It is times like this when you make the decision to rely on all those ounces of patience, and to just go with the flow. I inquire as to when I will see my wheelchair, will it be at baggage claim? Will I get it before customs? When will I have my independence back? I get an answer in Hindi that I do not fully understand, but I think it means that maybe it will be at luggage, to not worry and that this chair is fine…this chair that I cannot push myself. So I get lined up with the other elders and pregnant women who are also using wheelchairs and I am just left to wait for an appropriate person to come to push me through this foreign airport.

After some time goes by, I notice I am the only one left in the terminal building, sitting in a chair that I cannot propel myself. This is about the time when you start to wonder, have I been forgotten about? What now? All the other passengers are off the plane and on their way; it is now about midnight in Mumbai international airport and I am sitting in a wheelchair I cannot propel myself with my carry-on luggage decoratively placed like a Christmas tree. Great! Wow, what an opportunity! I just sit patiently, what else is there to do?

After some time goes by, a man comes over speaking in Hindi, I presume, and wants to know why nobody has come for me. I wish I knew the answer. He gets a bit irritated, then keeps rapid fire asking me questions I don't understand. I show him my boarding pass and tell him *saamaan?* (meaning, "luggage/baggage claim") Thinking to myself, "If I got this far, I can figure it out." We start on a long journey through the halls of the deserted airport, go through customs. I spot one of my favorite signs, "unaccompanied women, pregnant women, and handicapped." It is in this moment I am keenly aware I am very low in the social stratosphere here.

I then go through customs, even though I am not even the one to hand my passport over or to interact with the customs agent at all. I am parked in a corner while this man handles this. We then go to collect luggage. I see my two checked luggage bags circling on the carousel, but no sign of a wheelchair yet. I keep asking, will it be here or somewhere different? Nobody really knows, but I trust it will appear eventually. Sure enough, the last thing to the belt, wheelchair just thrown on the conveyor belt, rear wheels spinning, at least I can relax a little now.

We then go through the process of checking in our bags again. I am stopped because the domestic terminal is not connected to the international terminal. The security guard tells me, no wheelchairs allowed. Too many stairs on the bus. I volunteer to crawl up the stairs. I hand my bags to someone and bring my chair with me. *Nahin, Nahin* ("no, no"). Of course not, that would be too easy. My options are to go to the street at 1 AM in Mumbai and find a taxi to the international terminal or to have physical assistance to board, meaning accepting help from others. After some negotiating, I explained having help would be a good option. I successfully boarded the bus and drove to the other terminal.

However, they forgot to give my wheelchair security clearance at Mumbai with a special tag with a stamp on it. We went through security, and I asked if my wheelchair needed a tag since every carry-on item was getting a purple tag with a stamp. I was told no. I waited overnight at the Mumbai airport sleeping in airport chairs. The hustle and bustle of the airport was beginning to pick up around 5 am.

When trying to get on the bus to go find our plane, I was told I needed to wait for someone to come to help. For what, I was still unclear, but I went with it. I went to go through security and it became a problem that my wheelchair did not have the appropriately stamped tag. The lady ran back to security to get clearance for my wheelchair; she was mad they did not give it to me earlier. I board this bus, with assistance of course, packed in like sardines and commence the ride to the plane. I get to the plane; there is an aisle chair, and of course men to carry me on board. In America, we balk at the overprotection of people with disabilities when getting on and off airplanes. Having yourself strapped in at least five ways, across your lap, crisscross over your shoulders, around your legs and feet is an ordeal every time, and typically you do not win that battle; you just suck it up and get strapped in, or crawl on board the plane. In India, there are no straps on these aisle chairs, and sometimes the people lifting you are not the same height, meaning it is a little off balance. It was another experience.

Educating Everywhere

No rest for the weary! When you are in Udaipur only for a few days, and Ian Anand is your brother (also an Indian adoptee), you better believe that you are going to have lots to do and people to meet and things to see starting immediately upon leaving the airport. So exciting! We got a tour of Udaipur, learned about the history of the city. The city has ~600,000 people. Marble is in abundance. It is desert-like but there are also beautiful mountains, perhaps the oldest in the world. On the car ride back, I'm relatively emotionless, just taking it all in, letting it sink in that I have actually arrived in India. The traveling part is in my past, now it's taking in the invasion of the senses, the smells of spices, of street life, the radiant colors, the honking, and the sounds of the city. Udaipur is different from Kolkata; it is beautiful, has more landscapes than Kolkata, and is more touristy of an area in parts. We drove through the old city, saw the water palaces. Udaipur is a blend of old and new, modern and ancient. The old city has narrow streets and ancient walls; you just know you are in the old part of the city. The streets are filled with people, rickshaws, camels, elephants, cows, goats, fruit, vegetables, kids, bikes; the city is alive.

After the tour of the old city, we stopped by the local school for the Deaf and school for the Blind. I always make a point to connect with disability schools, hospitals, and community groups in the places I travel to. School had just started for the kids again, and so this was their first trip there to begin to figure out what they will be doing with them for the next few months. The program coordinator was thrilled to hear my passion for this population and was ecstatic to have me come for this site visit and to share any ideas I may have for future programming and activities.

I was excited that I still remembered how to introduce myself in Indian Sign Language (ISL) from my first trip to India. I remembered the last time I was here that many of the schools are a hodgepodge of languages, because many foreigners and ministry groups come in; oftentimes these kids are learning more American

Sign Language (ASL) than they are ISL. Regardless, they get so excited when a visitor comes in who can sign even a little bit. You better believe it. I had the whole school surrounding me introducing themselves, asking questions, wanting to know more about me. "Was I Deaf? Where did I learn sign? How did I know sign? Were my parents Deaf? What are schools for the Deaf like in America? Did I live at a school for the Deaf?"

When communicating was a challenge, no problem, just write it in the dirt on the ground or on your arm and then teach each other the different signs, both in ASL and ISL. In this school they learn both ASL and ISL. We brought a book my brother found written in ISL. I believe it was the first time these kids had ever seen a book with signs represented as pictures with the Hindi and English word written.

To some of you, that may not sound like a big deal. But, if you could have seen the scene that it caused. Everybody wanted in on this book. The older students immediately took charge; they were the ones who could read Hindi and English, so they should be the ones to handle the book. They were so proud that they knew the signs that were in it! They flipped open to the address of the publisher and asked me if I could go there and get more books to bring back to them. They asked how much it cost; on the front page it said, Rs 100. That's about $2. Let me reiterate this scene, the first time ever seeing a book in their language. It was better than kids picking up candy at a party after the piñata is broken; they were equally enthusiastic about learning. We told them we would try to find more books like it to bring back. I saw the dormitories, the dining hall, and the cricket area. The kids showed me their school books. We took lots of pictures. The excitement was overwhelming. The I-LOVE-YOUs (ILY, made with ASL hand shape) were everywhere. And of course, there was sadness when it was time to leave. Every kid in the school rushed to the rooftops and windows to wave goodbye and to share a last ILY or a story as we were leaving. It truly was an incredible afternoon.

On the rickshaw drive back, it was just so peaceful to take in all the sounds and just to know that I was here in India with my brother Ian Anand. I finally got to meet everybody who he had been talking about for so long, see the life he had built for himself, and be a part of it.

My brother Ian Anand lives there. He is at home there. You can see it in his face. I have never seen him so happy, so at peace, so much like himself. I am so proud of him and all the wonderful things he is doing in the world. He has done some amazing things, literally changing people's lives for the better. He continues to do incredible things. Secretly, or perhaps not so secretly, I am jealous of him and all that he has done and will continue to do here. Accessibility is scarce. This is always a constant struggle of mine coming here and being a part of India. As an adoptee, many always feel a little bit on the outside in America, and a little on the outside in their home country too. Though Ian Anand may feel some of that here in India, he is very much an integral part of this community. That is something I am envious of; as a person with a disability and as a woman, it is not as practical for me to just come and live here. However, I am beginning to think it is not impossible, just certainly not easy. It is hard to explain to others why I would even want to come and live here for a year. It is invigorating to meet all these people from all over who share the same passion for living each moment and doing good. There are always possibilities.

After a whirlwind of 48 h of traveling and visiting and meeting people, I crawled into bed last night just taking in the sounds of the dogs barking, the horns in the background and fell fast asleep. I am not sure whether it was the long traveling or just being here, but I slept sounder than I have ever slept and cannot wait for what more is to come.

Tourist Attempts

After a morning of volunteer work, we had a wonderful rooftop lunch looking over the Monsoon Palaces and hundreds and hundreds of years of history. As we were up there admiring the view, you just have this realization that pictures can give no justice to the beauty of Udaipur. Every place you look is like a full page spread in National Geographic rich with history, colors, and life.

We then decided to put our tourist hats on and go to City Palace to experience some of the history firsthand. City Palace was incredible. Getting in to City Palace, well that was a little bit more interesting. We arrived via rickshaw and the officials took one look at my wheelchair and said, "No. Too many stairs, not possible." We told them, "no problem, be carried." The first guy agreed and said, "Okay, free for her, handicapped, others pay." Well, in order for handicapped to get free ticket you have to show proof of disability with a government-issued disability card. I do not have one of those, so we were told to go talk to the man who signs off on the papers. Ian Anand went in to negotiate with the man, but he did not believe that I had a disability; he thought Ian Anand was trying to scam him. So he said he needed to see me, Ian Anand pointed down the stairs to where I was, he wanted me to come meet him. I began crawling up the stairs with my brother's assistance. The short version of the argument was that he would sign off for me to go but not my wheelchair.

Other individuals with disabilities began to form a line to also get signed off, the paperwork that they had come from the hospital and it counted as their physiotherapy for the day. One man tried to help me, to show me his papers and to ask why I didn't have any. I explained I was from America, born in India, but had no papers. The man was getting quite angry at this point, arguing back and forth with Ian Anand and giving many unhappy looks to me. At one point he said, "Handicapped cannot travel from abroad!" It was a brand new thing for him to ever have a person with a disability there at City Palace who was a tourist, even though it is one of the busiest tourist areas around. He tried convincing us that it was not worth going up; it was a bad view, and no fun. After about 15 min of arguing and negotiating, Ian Anand, miraculously got a ticket for my wheelchair and me to enter.

This place was filled with security guards and workers, none of whom had ever seen such a spectacle. Ian Anand reported one security guard who was following me around a little bit and then looked at me and my wheelchair, looked around at the stairs, the palace around us, and just shook his head. He was completely dumbfounded at how I had made it up to that level and just could not wrap his mind around it. Interestingly, as we reached the top, one of the last rulers in the palace in 1955 was "an invalid" and he used a wheelchair, which was on display there, along with an explanation of how because of him ruling, an elevator was installed in the palace, also there on display. Too bad it was on display only. This concept is so interesting that an area that is so anti-disability was able to accept a ruler who was disabled, made accommodations without question, and yet people with disabilities may never know that if they can't get in the door. Irony. This is just a taste of the challenges. And, I am so grateful that Ian Anand was a negotiator because the palace truly was breathtaking.

Insider Looking Out

Insider looking out. Take a moment to think about that statement. Insider looking out. What does that even mean? What does that look like? We took an amazing day trip to Kumbhalgar and Ranakpur. For under Rs 9000 total, we rented a bus for 24 people, traveled to these two areas of India, went up the fortress at Kumbhalgar in the monsoons and into the Jain temple in Ranakpur, had plenty of chai stops along the way, and ate a buffet lunch at a restaurant on the way back. For 12 *bachchas* (children), it was their first time ever seeing these sights, this culture, and history of India.

In our group, only two were foreigners, meaning only two non-Indians. To go see these sights would be amazing in itself, but to do it as a group of locals, wow. The bus ride was filled with laughter and hand games and picture taking. The children were so content just entertaining themselves, no iPods, no radio playing, no movies to watch, just the company of each other. We do not do that often enough elsewhere. It is easy to become so self-absorbed that you miss out on these wondrous opportunities…opportunities to be a kid again, to play dress-up and hairstylist, to play hand games, to simply enjoy each other's company.

In Ranakpur, we visited a gorgeous Jain temple that has 1444 unique hand-carved marble columns. The architecture and the presence of such a sight is breathtaking, not to mention the history. When we arrived, we encountered some more wild monkeys. Eventually, we made our way on to the temple.

Again, we were met with resistance for my entering the temple with my wheelchair. I was beginning to sense a theme of this trip. Because this was a religious temple, we decided it was not worth fighting. For any visitors entering the temple, you are requested to remove your shoes, any leather (belts etc.) and for women, if you are on your menstrual cycle you are asked not to enter. There was a sign outside explaining all of this. So, we left my wheelchair with the sea of shoes and I climbed onto Ian Anand's back for the climb into the Jain temple.

Remember what I said about being an insider looking out? This was the moment. This temple is world renowned, so it is a popular tourist spot. We were a spectacle, because we were the locals. Foreigners were stopping to take pictures of *us* because we were Indian. I was finally, on the other side, and truly an integral part of this other side. I do not really know how to explain this, but, I am truly Indian. It was in this moment when that realization occurred. Part of me wonders too whether leaving my wheelchair outside contributed to this, because just sitting with the children or others on the stairs of the temple, there was no line of demarcation between us, we just were a group of Indians visiting the Jain temple, which the Americans, French, Germans, Swiss were simply in awe of.

The temple itself was so peaceful, so powerful, so serene; regardless of your religious or spiritual beliefs, I firmly believe there is something in there for everybody.

When Ian Anand and I were looking at our pictures, we had to both laugh when there were pictures of little white kids taken by some of the members of our group. This is the whole concept of being intrigued by those different from you, natural human curiosity. Neither Ian Anand nor I felt like we needed to have pictures of random white children; we felt like we knew them already and that it was a little bit creepy. Nonetheless, it goes to show what it truly is like being an insider looking out, as opposed to an outsider looking in as we so often are. Ian Anand summed it up nicely, "Kind of cool to be on the other side, huh?"

Ghana

In the middle of Accra, you do the best you can with what you've got. It is a good thing that I'm a person with a disability with a natural tendency to adapt. Without this mentality and attitude, this sense of adventure, engineering, and ingenuity, very little can get accomplished. I ventured in Ghana with a team of four other individuals, three of whom have physical disabilities and also use wheelchairs. We were there to teach a wheelchair track clinic, have meetings with government officials, and help to advance the needs of persons with disabilities.

Teachable Moment

Accra, Ghana is more modern than I had anticipated, and that is because we were in the capital city and not in the outskirts or rural areas. I know that we are in the more developed, wealthier part of the city, but just from the drive to the airport to our lodging, I was taken aback, in a good way, by the scene. There are paved roads, actual construction, English billboards, with a splash of "other." We were warmly greeted at the airport including athletes with disabilities who were so genuinely excited for the week. It's less intense than India—by that I mean, it's not the same invasion of the senses, chaotic beauty that defines India, but it's more subtle, you have to be looking for things. For example, there were at least five individuals I spotted on our drive from the airport who presumably had polio and had makeshift scooter boards using flip flops on their hands to maneuver around. And of course there was the street-side vendor who had an array of walkers, crutches and even a pretty decent-looking wheelchair for someone with more severe disabilities.

We arrived at our fairly newly constructed hotel. We were impressed with some aspects. The interior had ramps built right in to go from the main lobby through the hallways, to the adjacent dining room and to the courtyard, etc. However, a small oversight was an actual ramp into the main door of the hotel! This was a topic of discussion upon our arrival, because naturally, yes, we could rely on the assistance of the two able-bodied individuals who had accompanied us on this journey, or on the helpful assistance from the security guards or receptionists themselves; however, if the goal and the point is to improve access and awareness about disability in Ghana, then this seemed like a very teachable moment to all of us. And so, it was.

We discussed options for how to build a ramp. The workers scrounged around and found some temporary solutions, though some of the first prototypes were a bit sketchy, to say the least. Like the piece of wood that was meticulously balanced, with no support in the center…we were slightly concerned that one use of this early prototype and it would snap in half. We explained the benefits of a permanent ramp instead of getting assistance each time, so that the hotel could do business with other guests with disabilities, that workers with disabilities might come to work here too. You had to put everything in terms of what people can relate to. For example, if working with a business manager or a hotel manager, we put it in terms of how access can help them to improve their business. We discussed, and then were off to scope out the track where our training camp was to be hosted. We figured that we could revisit this issue later, but we had begun the process of educating. To our pleasant surprise, after about an hour of being gone at the track, we came back to find two beautifully constructed, perfectly fit, ramps there at our disposal! Unbelievable. If only it were that easy with certain places in the U.S.! We thanked everybody, took pictures and considered our first teachable moment a success. We do hope that in future months or years to come that these ramps to the main entrance still exist. But, for now, small victory number one was accomplished.

Spirit of Adventure

We had a welcoming meeting with some dignitaries and officials who came to greet us, along with local media outlets who came for the occasion. The positive energy at this meeting was absolutely incredible. The tone was truly set for the week, as one that is very open, receptive, welcoming, and collaborative. The three guests who were there in the morning to officially welcome us included the President of the National Center for Persons with Disabilities, the President of the Ghana National Paralympic Committee and the President of the Ghana Society for the Physically Disabled. The message of this meeting was one of hope and one of commitment from the top officials who see the potential of the disabled athletes of Ghana, and of the hard work that Jean Driscoll, one of our team members, and Joni and Friends, an organization Jean had worked with in the past, put in for the past 9 years. It brought tears of joy to the room.

As we piled into their van to drive through the nightlife of Accra, it struck me, where does this spirit of adventure come from? I know it is not for everybody, there are some people who would literally be unable to function coming to a place like this, a place that is perhaps far out of their comfort zone, a place where the process is so hard to understand, because it is constantly changing. And yet, this same place, is the one that excites something deep within us who are here, a place where you can see hope, a place where you can make a difference every minute of every day, a place where human potential is oozing out of every corner if your eyes are open, a place where there are no complaints because all you have to do is look down the street and you will see five or more people significantly worse off than you. It is risky, it is adventurous, but it is wondrous. I get that not everybody can take trips like this. It's not for the faint of heart. I was grateful to be surrounded by people who could though, and this common bond is something that has strengthened our friendships to this day.

Where does this spirit of adventure come from? Are we born with it? Is it something we learn along the way from our parents, our upbringing, and our own experiences? Why is it that some people have it, and others do not? For me, I like to think that perhaps it was a survival tool. When life gives you lemons, you make lemonade, you make fun out of even the worst situation, look at it as a learning adventure or an expedition. As an adoptee, perhaps this was something that I just learned from that early age in order to make it in the big scary world. I have had numerous examples of this: Being abandoned at birth, leaving India at 2.5 months of age to come to the United States of America, getting sick with transverse myelitis at 4 months, and being left paralyzed from the waist down, dying during surgery not once but twice in my life, taking on my school district in federal court due to inaccessibility and discrimination, or becoming an incomplete quadriplegic for an unknown reason for 9 months. However, the sugar added to the lemonade also abounds: Becoming a Ph.D. scholar, representing my country at two Paralympic Games, and making a difference in the lives of others around the world. I also think that credit ought to be given where credit is due. My parents encouraged and nurtured that sense of adventure in all of us. Had they not, I may not be where I am today.

Adaptability

For the athletes, the impact of our trip was felt on many levels. Whether it was the athlete who got to feel the wind in their face for their very first time as they whizzed around the track on a handcycle, or the athlete who had never previously seen an airplane other than a small speck in the sky (the track was located quite close to the airport, so we had some low-flying planes overhead while training), or the athlete whose family now talks to them because of her athletic success, it was clear we made an impact. There was the athlete who received a used everyday wheelchair who came up to me and said, thank you for one of the happiest days of my life.

 It is in these unique moments of ingenious adaptability when you have this out-of-mind, out-of-body experience and for me, I just start laughing in my head thinking to myself, "Gosh, if only people back home in the U.S. could *see* what we are doing right now," or examples of how we fixed a wheelchair with a rock or how I made a pair of hard racing gloves with boiling water that was carried on someone's head from a local village restaurant.

 In the moment, it is sometimes hard to appreciate these times. The other part of the culture is that nothing is absolute. There is no predictable process or order to how things get done. I know that sounds vague, perhaps hard to comprehend, but it is true. As humans, particularly as Americans, I feel we naturally look for patterns and predictable ways of being. Guess what, that doesn't exist in other cultures. For example, even something as simple as ordering a meal at the hotel restaurant, you would think that if the menu says "vegetarian pizza" and lists all the ingredients that if you order for one meal and perhaps order later that same day, or even the next day, that it would be somewhat similar. Nope. Not a chance! That vegetarian pizza came out the first time with a spicy sauce, some veggies on it…the next time it came out with some sweet sauce, some cabbage, other vegetables…the third time it came out with hardly any sauce, some potatoes and onions. Perhaps some of it is an artifact of unique cooks, but this prevailing lack-of-consistent-process permeates all of daily life and business. And so, it becomes a lesson in patience. It is just the way of life.

 The athletes were broken into an elite group and a newbie group, and let me tell you, the potential these athletes have is incredible. Their sheer strength is impressive, largely from having to crawl around, push on rough terrain just to get around—there's your built-in strength and conditioning component! But, broader than that, training at this facility, Ghanaians took notice of what we were doing—able-bodied athletes, coaches, military and the general public. The interest was there, people would gather to just watch us training, to ask questions, to come and see it for themselves. We created a Paralympic buzz! Even that scene itself was chaotic—I was training with the elite racers, dodging runners, coaches, discuses, javelins, and soccer balls or curious onlookers who were in a dazed state of amazement that they just happened to wander onto the track without looking!

 We packed our days like it was a can of sardines. There was not a single moment of the day where we weren't doing something—even if it was just processing or thinking about the next meeting or thinking about how to fix that wheel with what we had with us. In between the 6 am and 3 pm training sessions, we had meetings with various government and local officials, organizations, and representatives. I cannot even begin to describe the power these meetings had. First of all, it was getting people to talk to each other, to talk about Paralympic sport, to talk about disability, to talk about the Olympics and Paralympics. We used this analogy a lot within our own group—we were the connectors in a giant life-size game of connect the dots. We are not the answer for a sustainable Paralympic sport program, and we knew that going into it. And, to be honest, we can't be—it would be wrong and unethical to walk into a country and just create what I want. It has to come from within; it has to have roots and a foundation there.

Our diverse team of expertise was able to fill this void, however, and to really be helpful connectors for these organizations serving people with disabilities in Ghana, for the government, for the National Sports Council, for various athletic associations. We had Jean Driscoll, an extraordinarily accomplished Paralympic athlete, successful business woman, a truly exceptional leader, and ambassador for sport and for disability. We had Marissa Siebel who is a trained athletic trainer with exceptional knowledge of additional Paralympic sports, a passion for life that you could just taste in the air. We had Jennifer Scott, a former dual sport University of Illinois wheelchair athlete herself who also has the ability to help us all to think a bit more out of the box. We had Tom Cameron, former wheelchair race organizer for the Bloomsday 12km in Spokane, WA, an engineer with a keen eye and tremendous skill in fixing anything. And, while Jean Driscoll was involved with Paralympic sport in the past, I was able to provide some clarity and guidance to current operations within the International Paralympic Committee, the nitty gritty nuts and bolts for how to move on to the next stage and ultimately to the world stage. Together, our team was a unique blend of talents, expertise all uniting around the same passion with a shared spirit of adventure.

Sport as a Catalyst for Social Change

These endeavors had the power to change Ghana. By having meetings with government officials, sport and disability organizations, we got the general population with and without disabilities excited about Paralympic sport. One of our last meetings was with the Board from the National Council on Persons with Disability, and it was in that meeting where I felt everybody realize what the power of sport truly is. Sport unifies us all. Sport provides an opportunity for individuals to come together regardless of race, political background, ability, status, and gender. Sport is unique in that it transcends these boundaries and barriers imposed by society and allows for the focus to be on the activity itself, the sportsmanship, the finish line, or the end of the match. Sport can be a catalyst for social change. Deeper than that is the honor of representing one's country that sport can also provide. For people with disabilities in Ghana, who have previously been excluded from many affordances of society such as an education or pursuing a career, sport is one way where this can change (Forber-Pratt 2015).

The two main takeaways I had from this trip are the power of the ripple effect and the importance of being true to oneself. The power of the ripple effect, was something my Ph.D. advisor had to help to point out to me. The most memorable moments of this trip were being able to ignite a fire within people—athletes with disabilities to realize they have athletic potential in sport and in life. It is absolutely, indescribably cool when you are there to witness that fire igniting deep within somebody or to even be that fire-starter. And that's what I get to do so naturally in a disability sport setting just by being me. However, there is an element of not wanting to sell myself short by working *only* with disabled athletes around the world—this is something that I feel is true for me personally. Though this is certainly not true for all, and I admire very much those who are able to work with one population every day, it's just not something I would be able to do. I learned that in fact the effect of our work is so much bigger than just that. It is the power of the ripple effect at work. It was something we talked about when we were there, even this Ghana project evolved from something bigger than just Jean to include our team being there. The power of one person's dream becoming bigger than any one person is overwhelming. But, the truth is that we all need people to help to point out our impact sometimes, the effect of the fire that is started, or of that ripple effect is often hard to fathom or even recognize ourselves. Looking back, I realize now that the impact of what we were doing in Ghana was so much bigger than just helping athletes with disabilities. We were changing the world by changing perceptions and educating others about disability and about Paralympic sport.

Lastly, intertwined with all of these amazing experiences in Accra, is the reminder of being true to oneself. This goes without much explanation, as I feel this message comes through just by being able to articulate and describe these experiences. But it is something that is important to be reminded of!

Reflection and Implications

It is rare in life that we get a true glimpse of how life could have panned out if a different trajectory had been taken. I was adopted from India when I was 2.5 months old. Two months after arriving in the United States, I got sick with transverse myelitis which left me paralyzed from the waist down. I wholeheartedly believe that acquiring my disability was just in my deck of cards, so to speak; that it would have happened regardless of whether I was adopted or not. However, had I acquired my disability as an orphan in India, I would not be the person who I am today, or may not even be alive. Traveling to these two countries, I needed that glimpse into what my life could have been like in India in order to recognize the wins that I have had in my own life. These trips reaffirmed my own sense of self and sense of belonging. Pieces of these reflections and connections to the broader disability literature come from my dissertation work (Forber-Pratt 2012).

Traveling to these locations gave me that perspective in multiple ways. I witnessed and had my own everyday struggles and battles every moment that I was in India. I describe it to others as being a challenging trip to take, not just emotionally, but also challenging in the sense of having to go from being completely independent here in American culture to completely dependent. For example, I had to plan out my entire day for when I would have access to a somewhat usable, preferably Western-style restroom and when somebody would be available to help me up the stairs to use it.

I saw firsthand the lack of educational opportunities and meaningful work experiences for people with disabilities. I would sit in a manually pulled rickshaw taking in the scene of the dirty street, extreme heat, the invasion of the senses by the smell of spices, bright colors, honking of horns and lack of traffic rules, and the man with polio caught my eye. Amid the chaos and sensory overload, I wondered, why this man with the classic dropped-foot gait due to polio would be working at least 20 times harder than a normal able-bodied person to walk infinitely slower up the street carrying that bucket, when to me, a wheelchair would be so much more enabling? And then I did a scan of my surroundings and realized, that man has a job and he does the best he can to hide his disability to be given the chance to be a contributing member to society. To him, on these streets, a wheelchair would be disabling.

While culture in its purest sense can take on a variety of forms around the world depending on the unique elements of that region, disability culture is a cross-cultural phenomenon. Disability impacts individuals of all ages, races, geographic background, religion, gender, socioeconomic status, etc. Human beings interact with the society around them, therefore the potential to identify with more than one culture is extremely high. Mindess (2000) uses a metaphor of an iceberg to describe culture. Only one tenth is visible, such as what one may quickly notice if visiting a foreign country such as differences in clothing, language, food, or music versus the deeper unseen values of culture that may be overlooked. These are the norms, values, and beliefs that comprise the very essence of that culture—perhaps particular notions of friendship, family, justice, and independence.

Steven E. Brown (2002), the founder of the Institute on Disability Culture describes disability culture as a forged group identity that people with disabilities have, based on the common history of oppression and bond of resilience. I drew parallels between my own experiences of oppression faced in high school with those the people with disabilities in India were struggling with daily. I discovered that roots of resilience were the common tie between our experiences, and my resilience came largely from my Indianness! These journeys started to fill in some of the missing holes in my identity. I had always previously only defined myself as a person with a disability, and I now realized I was also a woman, a person of color, and an adoptee.

It was the first time I entertained the idea of allowing these multiple identities to truly develop. It may sound silly to some, but up to this point my identity development had been very sequential; I would spend a period of time in my life developing my identity as a person with a disability and set that aside, then there were rare times that I would dabble in developing my identity as a person of color, but I usually would just forget about it and resort to my white ways of living that came from my surroundings. These trips allowed me to finally develop these multiple identities simultaneously.

Marcia (1966, 1980, 2002) expanded on Erikson's ideas on identity development by suggesting that it is not quite as simple as the discrete sequential stages proposed by Erikson. Marcia proposes that individuals go through identity development cycles including diffusion, foreclosure, moratorium, and achievement. Individuals who are in a state of ongoing crisis and have not made a commitment to an identity may not be ready to address these issues, let alone be able to assist others in achieving commitment to their identity.

Thinking about multiple identities, Jones and McEwen (2000) examined how dimensions of identity interact with each other among college women of varying race and ethnicity. Others have looked at the intersection of an individual's African-American identity with their gay identity or lesbian identity and college student identity (Crawford et al. 2002; Abes and Kasch 2007). The findings consistently show that there are multiple layers of identity and that depending on contextual or situational factors, certain aspects of one's identities may prove to be more salient than others. One trend in the literature is about how various social stigmas can influence identity development. This trend draws from Goffman's (1963) early work that describes how social stigmas—attributes, behaviors, or reputations—can cause an individual to be outcast by the greater society, thereby negatively impacting one's identity development. If, or when, these negative stigmas turn into an act of oppression, racism or any other type of "-ism" against an individual, this also has the potential to profoundly affect one's identity development (Edwards and Jones 2009; Hipolito-Delgado 2007, 2010; Jones 2009; Talburt 2004). For people with disabilities, one such stigma is ableism, or discrimination against people based on physical ability in favor of those without disabilities, greatly influences identity development.

A healthy, intact identity provides a stronger sense of self and ability to face ableism by reaffirming desired goals and personal worth (Albrecht and Devlieger 1999; Campbell 2008; Forber-Pratt & Zape 2017; Mpofu and Harley 2006; Noonan et al. 2004). Just as in the non-disabled population, individuals with disabilities, like myself, often have multiple competing or complementing identities. Research has shown how individuals with disabilities must integrate what it means to be a woman or a man, and develop or re-develop, that identity in congruence with their disabled identity (Asch 2001; Barron 1997; Charmaz 1994, 1995; Najarian 2008; Yoshido 1993). My journeys to these countries were about achieving, as Marcia put it, congruence across all of my identities and reframing the potential negative impact of the stigmas I had faced into a positive and healthy identity.

As part of a program evaluation report, Ferreyra explained the heightened risk that adolescent females with physical disabilities have for developing and maintaining their sense of self because of stigmas and oppression (2001). Several empirical studies related to women with disabilities have concluded that stigma and experiences of oppression jeopardize one's development of identity (Anderson 2009; Barron 1997; Najarian 2008; Noonan et al. 2004; Wendell 1989). Yet, I believe that these experiences of oppression and facing stigmas can actually strengthen and enhance one's development of identity, rather than jeopardize it. These experiences made me who I am today. I am able now to connect to others on this level and give them hope that by embracing these experiences and allowing it to shape their identity rather than destroy it, they too can develop a strong sense of self and find their purpose in life.

References

Abes, E. S., & Kasch, D. (2007). Using queer theory to explore lesbian college students' multiple dimensions of identity. *Journal of College Student Development, 48*(6), 619–636. doi:10.1353/csd.2007.0069.

Albrecht, G. L., & Devlieger, P. (1999). The disability paradox: High quality of life against all odds. *Social Science & Medicine, 48*(1967), 977–988. doi:10.1016/S0277-9536(98)00411-0.

Anderson, D. (2009). Adolescent girls' involvement in disability sport: Implications for identity development. *Journal of Sport & Social Issues, 33*(4), 427–449. doi:10.1177/0193723509350608.

Asch, A. (2001). Critical race theory, feminism and disability: Reflections on social justice and personal identity. *Ohio State Law Journal, 62*, 1–17.

Barron, K. (1997). The bumpy road to womanhood. *Disability & Society, 12*(2), 223–239. doi:10.1080/09687599727344.

Brown, S. E. (2002). What is disability culture? *Disability Studies Quarterly, 22*, 34–50.

Campbell, F. A. K. (2008). Exploring internalized ableism using critical race theory. *Disability & Society, 23*(2), 151–162. doi:10.1080/09687590701841190.

Charmaz, K. (1994). Identity dilemmas of chronically ill men. *The Sociological Quarterly, 35*(2), 269–288.

Charmaz, K. (1995). The body, identity, and self: Adapting to impairment. *The Sociological Quarterly, 36*(4), 657–680. doi:10.1111/j.1533-8525.1995.tb00459.x.

Crawford, I., Allison, K. W., Zamboni, B. D., & Soto, T. (2002). The influence of dual-identity development on the psychosocial functioning of African-American gay and bisexual men. *The Journal of Sex Research, 39*(3), 179–189. doi:10.1080/00224490209552140.

Edwards, K. E., & Jones, S. R. (2009). "Putting my man face on": A grounded theory of college men's gender identity development. *Journal of College Student Development, 50*(2), 210–228.

Ellis, C. (2004). *The ethnographic I: A methodological novel about autoethnography*. Walnut Creek: Altamira Press.

Forber-Pratt, A. (2012). *Dream. Drive. Do: becoming that 'someone like me'*. Doctoral dissertation, University of Illinois at Urbana-Champaign.

Forber-Pratt, A. J. (2015). Paralympic sport as a vehicle for social change in Bermuda and Ghana. *Journal of Sport for Development, 3*(5), 35–49.

Forber-Pratt, A. J. & Zape, M. P. (2017). Disability identity development model: Voices from the ADA-generation. *Disability and Health Journal*. Advanced Online Publication. doi:10.1016/j.dhjo.2016.12.013

Goffman, E. (1963). *Stigma: Notes on the management of a spoiled identity*. New York: Simon & Schuster.

Hipolito-Delgado, C. F. (2007). *Internalized racism and ethnic identity in Chicana/o and Latina/o college students*. Doctoral dissertation. Available from ProQuest Dissertations and Theses database (UMI No. AAT 3277390).

Hipolito-Delgado, C. F. (2010). Exploring the etiology of ethnic self-hatred: Internalized racism in Chicana/o and Latina/o college students. *Journal of College Student Development, 51*(3), 319–331. doi:10.1353/csd.0.0133.

Jones, S. R. (2009). Constructing identities at the intersections: An autoethnographic exploration of multiple dimensions of identity. *Journal of College Student Development, 50*(3), 287–304.

Jones, S. R., & McEwen, M. K. (2000). A conceptual model of multiple dimensions of identity. *Journal of College Student Development, 41*, 405–414.

Marcia, J. E. (1966). Development and validation of ego-identity status. *Journal of Personality and Social Psychology, 3*(5), 551–558. doi:10.1037/h0023281.

Marcia, J. E. (1980). Identity in adolescence. In J. Andelson (Ed.), *Handbook of adolescent psychology*. New York: Wiley.

Marcia, J. E. (2002). Identity and psychosocial development in adulthood. *Identity: An International Journal of Theory and Research, 2*, 7–28. doi:10.1207/S1532706XID0201_02.

Mindess, A. (2000). *Reading between the signs: Intercultural communication for sign language interpreters*. Yarmouth: Intercultural Press.

Mpofu, E., & Harley, D. A. (2006). Racial and disability identity: Implications for the career counseling of African Americans with disabilities. *Rehabilitation Counseling Bulletin, 50*(1), 14–23. doi:10.1177/00343552060500010301.

Najarian, C. G. (2008). Deaf women: Educational experiences and self-identity. *Disability & Society, 23*(2), 117–128. doi:10.1080/09687590701841141.

Noonan, B. M., Gallor, S. M., Hensler-McGinnis, N. F., Fassinger, R. E., Wang, S., & Goodman, J. (2004). Challenge and success: A qualitative study of the career development of highly achieving women with physical and sensory disabilities. *Journal of Counseling Psychology, 51*(1), 68–80. doi:10.1037/0022-0167.51.1.68.

Talburt, S. (2004). Constructions of LGBT youth: Opening up subject positions. *Theory into Practice, 43*(2, Sexual Identities and Schooling), 116–121. doi: 10.1207/s15430421tip4302_4

Wendell, S. (1989). Toward a feminist theory of disability. *Hypatia, 4*(2), 104–124. doi:10.1111/j.1527-2001.1989.tb00576.x.

Yoshido, K. K. (1993). Reshaping of self: A pendular reconstruction of self and identity among adults with traumatic spinal injury. *Sociology of Health & Illness, 15*(2), 217–245. doi:10.1111/1467-9566.ep11346888.

Chapter 6
When Gucci Make Hearing Aids, I'll Be Deaf: Sensory Impairment in Later Life and a Need to Define it According to Identity

Simon Hayhoe

Abstract This chapter examines my experience of late deafness – becoming impaired, being diagnosed as such and then living with this new identity. The analysis considers this experience of impairment from the point of view of subjective and objective disability. I argue that I am currently less impaired now that I have been diagnosed as being hearing impaired than I was when I was not. The chapter concludes that impairment is subjective and should be considered so. It also concludes that context and form of impairment should be considered when understanding disability.

Introduction

Are legal definitions of perceptual impairments always effective? Are the words *deaf* and *blind* merely descriptions, individual identities or are they practical problems that need to be overcome?

Many people I interviewed who became sensory impaired later in life, particularly people who lost their perceptions in old age, often find it difficult to adjust to an impaired identity (Hayhoe 2008, 2013a, 2014). These people mix more with sighted and hearing people. They maintain their old habits. They communicate and understand the world through their previous identity. Many of these people also express confusion about why they are seen in a similar way to other people with other forms of disability. These others' experiences of life have little relevance to their own.

General models trying to describe disability as a single concept have been forthcoming in the literature (Pfeiffer 2002). Yet there are few that accurately define disability as it relates to individuals from all walks of life (Hayhoe 2016a). There are

S. Hayhoe (✉)
Lecturer, Department of Education, University of Bath, Bath, UK
e-mail: s.hayhoe@lse.ac.uk

© Springer International Publishing AG 2017　　　　　　　　　　　　　　　　77
S. Halder, L.C. Assaf (eds.), *Inclusion, Disability and Culture*, Inclusive
Learning and Educational Equity 3, DOI 10.1007/978-3-319-55224-8_6

even fewer that define how we can identify and classify disabled people who acquire their impairments later in life. There is also little attempt to measure aspects of the antonym of disability, 'ability', as a universal concept (Hayhoe 2012). Hence, such issues remain entirely subjective in the context of method and study.

Perhaps a reason for holding with an idea of a whole disabled identity is the need for institutional convenience. It is also the inability of science to overcome reductionist aspects of the mind-body problem (Nagel 2012). Importantly, beyond social scientific models and definitions, government organisations have had to introduce workable, holistic definitions of disability. This allows them to perform operations such as the distribution of funds and practical support. It also allows these organisations to provide a workable explanation that can be used as the basis of legislation (Tibble 2004).

Similarly, over the past 35 years, the World Health Organisation has attempted to define a holistic intra-cultural notion of disability in relation to terms such as 'normalisation', 'impairment' and 'handicap' (World Health Organisation 1980, 2014; Barbotte et al. 2001). However, these brief definitions appeared less clear than the imperfect academic models they were informed by.

Criticism of cultural norms and the difficulty of imposing a social identity on another person make such terms especially meaningless at best and dangerous and undemocratic at worst. This was illustrated clearly in research I conducted on blindness and computer programming. During this study, for example, I observed that blind programmers who became impaired later in life had a conception of programming that mirrored their previous sighted life. By contrast, those who had been born blind had a conception of technology according to their experiences in schools for the blind or inclusive mainstream education (Hayhoe 2011).

So how can we best understand what it is to be sensory impaired in the context of social scientific and philosophical study? Furthermore, how can such concepts ever be defined in a capacity that gives meaning to disparate cultures with different ideals of social and cultural identity?

This chapter explores these questions through an analysis of the social identity of disability, impairment and thus an implied definition of ability. It also examines the broader social-philosophical notions of subjective and objective cultural identity. This chapter begins this task with an exemplar problem of my own late deafness and the anomalies that this has caused. This case is designed to illustrate this problem using an auto-ethnographic approach, with my own experiences being examined qualitatively (Ellis et al. 2011). My reason for using this methodology was that I felt it reflected my own experiences and the process of developing ambiguous cultural identity. In addition, it lessened any ethical issues of constructing a case study of experiences of impairment.

A Problem of Late Deafness

I can define my problem thus: I am 48 years old. Tinnitus runs in my mother's family. My mother has it; my uncle had it; my grandmother had it for as long as I can remember. When I was in my mid-twenties, I began to notice my hearing deteriorating. Because this problem was in my family, doctors monitored my progress.

Early tests revealed that this problem wasn't so great. I resisted further hearing tests until my mid-thirties, when it became too much of a problem to ignore. At this point, I had a further hearing test and discovered I had lost enough high frequencies to be classified hearing impaired. I now have to wear an ugly National Health Service hearing aid, until I earn enough to afford a high tech Danish hearing aid that can sit in my ear (virtually) invisibly.

Am I disabled by my perceptual impairment? I would argue, not.

There could have been a case for me being slightly disabled between my mid-twenties and the time the hearing therapist put a harsh plastic earpiece in my ear and asked me whether it was comfortable or not. After that moment, my problem was more manageable. Despite the pain, his was the clearest voice I had heard for ages. Then when he plugged the chord into his computer to adjust its settings and rang a small bell, it felt unlike anything I had felt or heard for a long while – the sound was too loud and sharp. It was completely the opposite problem to the one I had had before. Before this test, I had to rely solely on staring at my family, students and friends, hoping to see their voices as accurately as possible.

The initial answer to *my* problem then is that I have never felt disabled although I could have been said to be once. I grew up in a community where I was treated as an able-bodied person. I managed to handle what was felt to be my impairment in my own way, something to be controlled. In fact, I now overcompensate for it. Like some closet gay men who desperately bed women to preserve their manhood, I try to become super able, super normal. I wear Paul Smith jeans, Burberry socks, and dress for work with Jaeger suits and Hawes and Curtis shirts; I buy Gucci sunglasses; I have taken degree upon degree; I have to think that my health, blood pressure, heart rate and waistline always have to be in good form; I write, draw and photograph as if my life depends on it.

I am trying to move away from the life and the disability that I have seen in others. It was something they fought and hated, and it is something I feel I do not want to be a part of now. So, who does feel disabled by sensory impairment, and how do we take account of whether a person wants to legally define himself or herself as disabled or impaired (Barbotte et al. 2001)?

In order to build a workable definition of what sensory impairment and any subsequent disability[1] 'is', it is arguable that disability should be regarded as a description of how a person is excluded from behaving in a comfortable or *normal* fashion by their society. However, this understanding of *the normal* has been found to be

---

[1] For brevity, in this chapter, I refer to disability alone in many circumstances where disability and impairment are seen as being similar social concepts.

dependent on two dimensions of the historical era and the social and cultural environment in which a disabled person resides (Hayhoe 2000, 2012, 2016a). In addition, disability can be visible or invisible, and it can also depend on individuals' circumstances, such as their social class or occupation (Hayhoe 2016a, b).

Medically, disability is not an illness. It most often is, however, the outcome of an illness. Practically, it can be regarded as an injury to the functioning of culturally defined tasks (Crow 1996). In this chapter, it is this last aspect of this definition that is of particular importance; and in the discussion that now follows, this concept shall be broken into two further sub-concepts: subjective and objective aspects of disability.

Subjective and Objective Aspects of Disability

In order to simplify the 'definition problem' of disability, it is necessary to see these conceptualisations in the context of social and cultural phenomenology. Firstly, the individual can define disability given particular circumstances: what an individual can do in those circumstances. In this chapter, I refer to this as Subjective Disability.

Subjective disability is so-called because it examines each person's trait according to its context and subject: the environment, the task, the man, the woman, the girl or the boy, *not* the disabled identity of the person. For instance, I have no hearing impairment whilst I am reading a book, but I have a walking impairment when I am carrying heavy shopping bags.

Thus, my identification as a hearing-impaired person by others is based on many different concepts to those of a perception of my lived reality in many situations, i.e. although my hearing problem only takes up a little of my life and its degree of annoyance or disability is dependent on individual circumstances, this is felt to control enough of my *normal* existence to constitute disadvantage, suffering or discomfort.

In a social context, however, subjective disability is related to the social and cultural consequences of its medical causes, such as whether a person can still make money or participate in the broader economy (Oliver 1996, 2001, 2013), whether they can present themselves in a way that is felt to be acceptable by their society or whether they can perform other social tasks as expected by their society (Goffman 1990; Hayhoe 2008). For instance, subjectively a person is never blind or an amputee never paralyzed when they are on the telephone, they are only felt to be disabled when they are presented with visual information or asked to walk or lift objects.

Secondly, disability can be seen as what a society tells a person they can or cannot do in particular circumstances. In this chapter, I call this concept Objective Disability. It is so-called because it classifies a group of people with similar traits as an object, a group or a sub-culture (Oliver 1996, 2001, 2013; Hayhoe 2012). It is then thought of as an identity, and symbols such as hearing aids, white canes and walking sticks – implements which are designed to help its common subjective traits, such as the amplification of sound, the information gained from the vibrations of a cane or the control of balance when walking – tell the greater society that the person possessing the symbol has a disability – hence the white of the white cane or the brown plastic of many modern functionalist hearing aids from the British NHS, which is for the purpose of the viewer and not the deaf or blind user.

Similarly, social scientific models of examining the constrictions and classifications of what are regarded as the deviant traits inherent in disability are discussed and framed by authors such as Foucault (1989) and Goffman (1990, 1991) in terms of disadvantage or social labelling; although their mode of describing these concepts and their conclusions differ radically according to their separate political conceptualisation. Foucault takes a radical approach to explaining this problem through a whole-society epistemology (Steinmetz 1994). By contrast, Goffman offers a more liberal and contextual symbolic interactionist interpretation, in which the individual is seen in the almost theatrical setting of his or her greater society (Goffman and Best 2005).

In terms of the cognitive sciences, the paradoxes and problems of crossing from one identity to another is particularly apparent in the sudden change from a sensorially impaired identity to a non-impaired identity (Berkeley 1899; Gregory 1974; Sacks 1993), or unimpaired to impaired (Hull 1990). The most extreme phenomenon associated with this latter change of identity is illustrated by Merleau-Ponty (2002) in his description of the phantom limb. In this instance, patients who have had a limb amputated consciously believe it is still present, and in this way the new objectively disabled human has a subconscious denial of his or her new condition.

Thus, there are many conditions that need to be fulfilled for a man to be considered Objectively Disabled (Hayhoe 2004). For instance, if a person has injured legs he or she will be considered objectively disabled. He or she will not be able to walk to his or her local shops without severe discomfort. He or she can use a wheelchair. However, this would also make him or her less agile or fast on most pavements/sidewalks than people walking normally.

Whilst walking or in his or her wheelchair, he or she will look very different and travel more slowly. His or her wheelchair is also associated with others with paralyzed legs. The man or woman cannot do anything to change his or her paralyzed legs, even with strengthening exercises. His or her legs will not heal themselves. His or her condition is also rare and extreme enough to be different from a great number of people in society.

In terms of a more esoteric example, considered to be on the edge of social reasoning since the Enlightenment (Hopkins 2005), we can define blindness as referring to a range of symptoms that affect the optical information required to fulfil many visually determined tasks – it must again be made clear at this point that blindness itself is not a disease, it is the outcome of a disease, a trait it leaves behind. It can also have a range of forms, and blindness can cause Subjective Disability, although in its social context it can also be considered an Objective Disability.

For instance, for individuals to draw a realistic picture, it is assumed that they require some degree of visual acuity. They must picture their subject as a whole. They must know that they are drawing correctly shaped and shaded areas on paper.

An individual must have feedback from the lines that he or she has drawn. This allows a person to know where to put further lines.

However, these difficulties can be overcome to a large extent, allowing an artist with no sight to touch. Persons can also be educated about what they are touching, and they can be taught to use tactile media such as German film, which rises as soon as it is scribed with a pen (Hayhoe 2008). Blindness in this case is not such a grave Subjective Disability.

Thus, to be considered blind in terms of a visual arts culture, an Objective Disability, a man or woman must not be able to perform what society deems to be most normal tasks without great assistance. For instance, even though blind people can read Braille or large print with residual vision, their relative speed of reading is severely restricted and thus more time should be given to allow for this in controlled situations (Warren 1994). The extra technology needed also requires more storage space. This is less efficiently produced (Hayhoe 2013b).

Blind people often have eyes that look different to people who are considered to be sighted. They wear glasses and carry white canes. If they are congenitally or early blind, they also often move their heads when talking. Blind or deaf people often have little chance of reversing their impairments in the short term. If their condition is operable, it usually takes a while for healing to take place. Their sight, hearing and bodies must also adjust or readjust. Some permanent conditions that cause impairments, such as cataracts, glaucoma or my tinnitus, can be reversed or at least controlled as a result of diet, exercise, relaxation techniques or therapy. This takes a long time, however.

Furthermore, small sensory impairments that require regular prescription glasses for correction are frequent. This is because these are relatively common implements that do not symbolise rare physical or psychological conditions or impairments and can be used by many members of the public temporarily or impermanently – this is particularly true of walking sticks and clear glasses as the strength of the impairment is not denoted by the objects themselves; for example, the difference between glasses for permanent, serious sight problems and weak reading glasses is not apparent until they are examined closely and the difference between the lenses becomes apparent.

Yet conditions that do not necessarily lead to normal dysfunctioning of the body apart from the limited ability to move, see or hear at a particular speed and in certain lighting or environmental conditions, such as amputation, paraplegia, multiple sclerosis, photophobia, achromatism and conductive hearing loss, are rarer and thus regarded as disabilities.

Cultural Anomalies and Disability

Most cultures have formalised their rules of defining disabilities such as blindness or deafness as objective disabilities. Legislation in many Western countries in particular has taken this a stage further. Such countries legally classify the level at which this weakness of optical functioning disables most social tasks. For instance, legal blindness is measured at 20° visual field or $^{20}/_{200}$ visual acuity or less, and with similar definitions being available for decades (Coakes and Holmes Sellors 1992).

This reductionist definition is too simplistic, however. For example, in the case of traits such as achromatism, visual acuity can increase through the lack of *normal* light perception (Sacks 2001; Hayhoe 2008). The testing of this visual acuity must therefore take place in what are considered to be normal lighting conditions. As a consequence, the whole of the person is not judged according to a rigid scientific test at a particular point in time, under culturally defined conditions.

Aside from people who have no light or sound recognition whatsoever, each person's visual impairment is perceptually unique. Scientifically, however, the range of symptoms can be classified as: blurred vision, tunnel vision (where peripheral vision is missing), peripheral vision only, tinnitus, spots in vision, achromatism (lack of certain or all colours), loss of low frequencies, loss or high frequencies, or a combination of all these symptoms. It is also very rare for someone to be totally blind or deaf. It is much more common for them to have a small amount of light or sound perception. However, in many circumstances, policies are often targeted at the rarest rather than the most common strengths of impairment (Hayhoe 2013c).

Therefore, psychologically and sociologically, blindness and deafness can be classified in three further ways – I acknowledge help from Lowenfeld's (1981) psychological definition of blindness for this classification:

1. *Congenital blindness/deafness*: When a man or woman is born impaired. The consequence of congenital impairment is that a person will have no sensory memory, or his or her sensory memory will be based solely on his or her highly restricted perception.
2. *Early blindness/deafness*: When a man or woman has become impaired in childhood. People who have early impairment often have sensory memories and can often understand sensory reference.
3. *Late blindness/deafness*: When a man or woman becomes impaired in adulthood. For example, at the turn of the millennium around 70% of all blind people in England and Wales were over 75 (Department of Health 2001). This number is still increasing as the older population increases. Much of this population's perceptual reference is still related to vision.

Thus, we find that all of these attempts to classify even a subset of disability can hold no single, measurable or firm answer, or workable definition in the context of academic scientific study.

What We Can Learn from Subjective and Objective Disability

What implications do these findings have for the process of identifying disability in modern democratic societies? Moreover, how does this help us to understand real abilities and social challenges that disabled people face?

In order to address these questions, I cite the case in the UK of the so-called Warnock Commission, and the issues of definition and identification that arose from it (Hayhoe 2016b). The Warnock Commission was a committee of inquiry appointed by the UK government in the 1970s, in order to recommend a system of inclusion for disabled school children – or as they were referred to in that era, handicapped children – who were educated in separate schools.

The report of the Warnock Commission attempted to redefine individual impairments, such as blindness or what we now call learning disabilities, as Special Needs – or in this context, Special Educational Needs (DoE 1978). There were three main reasons for this redefinition: (a) many children had a number of impairments – for instance, children with Down syndrome had learning difficulties and a number of physical impairments, (b) access to the school curriculum rather than impairment was the primary focus of inclusion and (c) it was important that social as well as physical impairments became the focus of inclusion. As Warnock recalled later in an interview:

> We wanted to bring home the message that, in the context specifically of education [emphasis added by Warnock], it did not matter so much about the nature of a child's disability, but on what steps could be taken to ensure that he (sic.) had access, as far as possible, to the curriculum...
>
> There are numerous children with multiple handicaps, and some have disabilities not even classified. (Hayhoe 2016b: P. 126)

These aims were laudable, and led to the introduction of an education bill, the 1981 Education Act of England and Wales. This act stipulated that children with Special Needs should, where possible, be included in mainstream education. In turn, this led to the inclusion of many disabled students in mainstream schools and, as a consequence, an increase in the number of disabled students going on to higher education (Hayhoe et al. 2015).

However, despite this step forward, there was a further problem with the attempt to get away from terms such as blind, deaf, impaired, handicap, etc. that could have been avoided. The problem was that institutions that were including disabled students still needed to define and describe these students in order to plan the support that they needed. As a senior member of the Warnock Commission, the former Deputy Chief Inspector of Schools, John Fish, recalled on this issue in 2000:

> [It] has to be remembered that prior to the Warnock Committee Report there were 10 statutory categories of handicap. Children ascertained as handicapped (considered a form of certification at the time) were placed in one of the 10 categories.
>
> The Warnock Report (Chapter 3) was anti-classification by category. Its evidence showed that there were very few children with a single disability. Most of the children deemed to have special educational needs had a variety of needs: hence the Report's stress on the need for an individual statement [of Special Needs]. Children were not considered to be part of a single category. Subsequently, a different form of labelling arose from administrative practices.
>
> **Postal interview with John Fish, Deputy Chief Inspector of Schools involved with the Warnock Report and the 1981 Special Education Needs Act. Interview answers supplied on 19 June 2001.**

Consequently, after the Warnock Report and the 1981 Education Act, students were still defined by their disability, but this time they were called 'a Special Educational Need', rather than after their impairment, such as 'blind' or 'deaf' – although British society still often considered these students as having these impairments too (Hayhoe 2016a). Thus, a new more reduced and less accurate name was developed to describe a highly complex, individual trait and many children received inadequate support as a consequence (Hayhoe 2016b). A further consequence was that a number of students also found themselves excluded by teachers and peers in mainstream settings (see e.g. the case study of Emile in Hayhoe 2008).

What is the solution to this problem?

Unfortunately, the solution to this problem is not easy. What we now need to do is take a step back from defining disability in the standard way and come up with a new system of classifying humans. More particularly, we must find a method that relies more on supporting ability in tasks, and not disability as identity. We also need to develop a system that encompasses all human communities, not simply fractured ones. This will need to allow disabled people to define their own identities, either as disabled people, able people or other, in fluid and evolving settings rather than as a settled character that we are assumed to be born and die with.

For this solution to work, I would suggest that philosophers, social theorists and policy makers need to learn from the design principle of universal design. Universal design began as the theory that all human-technology interactions can be designed to be flexible enough to adapt to all human shapes and sizes (Story et al. 1998) – an early example of universal design was the adjustable car seat, which could adapt to the driver's leg length. More recently, this concept has been applied in social and educational settings inhabited by disabled people, in an attempt to adapt mainstream buildings, technologies and information to their needs, in line with those of non-disabled people. For instance, in education this has led to the redefinition of instructional design to the term universal instructional design (Burgstahler and Cory 2009).

If universal design can be integrated into models of defining and identifying human performance, we can potentially develop a more flexible way of identifying people's needs according to adaptable subjective tasks – much as I have defined Subjective Disability. This would allow for the person for whom support could be arranged in mainstream settings to define their own identity, whether that identifies themself as a wholly disabled person, or as a person with an impairment, or even one that identifies themself as neither. This would allow for support to be arranged by the individual according to their needs at a given time and place, through adaptation of flexible policies, environments, objects and social settings. If this could occur, identification would move from a political context more to one of practical support for independent living.

Conclusion

When academics and institutions attempt to understand the concept of disability and impairment, the personal histories of people they are trying to define or identify are rarely taken into account. In truth, some people who are objectively classified as impaired or disabled later in life will still want to be associated with an able-bodied culture, and if they are disabled later in life, they will want to relate their identities with their previous experiences and culture. These people, as Merleau-Ponty found, will even subconsciously want to physically feel they are that same person that they used to be.

Therefore, the experience that older sensorially impaired people are now legally entitled to is largely an adapted version of their able-bodied experiences. Hence, the language used to describe such people is more often than not the same as an able-bodied person. The social and cultural references are those you would give to any other person because, in their mind, there is no difference.

The person who has sensory impairment from a very young age, for example, can often be said to have a different sensory culture from those impaired later on. They often want to feel that they are of the class, gender, ethnicity or religion they were born into, but the cultural medium they have to refer to this culture will be different, because of their early institutional experiences. This means that certain technologies and objects, such as walking sticks, canes, dark glasses or hearing aids that are associated with disability may have a greater symbolic meaning to the person with the sensory impairment than the person without it.

To use the metaphor of art, for instance, I like the works of Klimt, Bacon, Freud, Gilbert and George, Mozart, Puccini and Debussy. However, do their pieces mean the same to a person who has never seen or heard their works of art as I have? Or do these art works mean nothing to anyone who has never heard of these artists?

It does not matter whether we see or hear, touch or smell as everyone else does, we can still engage culturally and emotionally in any subject matter uniquely according to our personal histories. These emotions come from different life experiences. Therefore, the different experiences of educational, medical, governmental or cultural institutionalisation, and the exclusion that is derived from this institutionalisation, in relation to the early impaired person must be considered when communicating or developing policies and support for them; just as the need to feel as a person did when they were physically abler should be to the person who develops a later sensory impairment.

Moreover, in this process perhaps the phrase *unique context* should be emphasised. When Gucci makes a National Health Service hearing aid or white cane, just as they make fashionable glasses, many more people will be happy to call themselves deaf. But until institutions and the greater society they say that they represent accept that such people want to be considered equal in the culture they were raised in, yet preserve a unique sense of identity and self-expression, they will often continue to keep their deafness or blindness as close to the closet as their physically and socially painful hearing aids and white canes will allow them to.

Acknowledgments To my family, John Kennedy, and the memories of John Hull and Oliver Sacks. All of their conversations and correspondence have been invaluable.

References

Barbotte, E., Guillemin, F., & Chau, N. (2001). Prevalence of impairments, disabilities, handicaps and quality of life in the general population: A review of recent literature. *Bulletin of the World Health Organization, 79*(11), 1047–1055.

Berkeley, G. (1899). *Selections from Berkley* (A. C. Fraser, Ed., 5th ed. amended). Oxford: Clarendon Press.

Burgstahler, S. E., & Cory, R. C. (Eds.). (2009). *Universal design in higher education.* Cambridge, MA: Higher Education Press.

Coakes, R. L., & Holmes Sellors, P. J. (1992). *An outline of ophthalmology.* London: Butterworth-Heinemann.

Crow, L. (1996). Including all of our lives: Renewing the social model of disability. In C. Barnes & G. Mercer (Eds.), *Exploring the divide: Illness and disability.* Leeds: Disability Press.

Department of Health. (2001). *Registered blind and partially sighted people year ending 31 March 2000, England.* London: HMSO.

DoE (Department of Education). (1978). Special educational needs: Report of the Committee of Inquiry into the Education of Handicapped Children and Young People (The Warnock Report). London: HMSO.

Ellis, C., Adams, T. E., & Bochner, A. P. (2011). Autoethnography: An overview. *Historical Social Research, 36*(4), 273–290.

Foucault, M. (1989). *Madness and civilisation* (R. Howard, Trans.). London: Routledge Classics.

Goffman, E. (1990). *Stigma: Notes on the management of spoiled identity.* London: Penguin.

Goffman, E. (1991). *Asylums.* London: Penguin.

Goffman, E., & Best, J. (2005). *Interaction ritual: Essays in face-to-face behaviour.* Piscataway: Aldine Transaction.

Gregory, R. L. (1974). *Concepts and mechanisms of perception.* London: Duckworth.

Hayhoe, S. (2000). The effects of late arts education on adults with early visual disabilities. *Educational Research and Evaluation, 6*(3), 229–249.

Hayhoe, S. (2004). *The development of an epistemological model of disability: The enlightenment, scientific theories on blindness and arts/crafts education in the US.* Guest lecture presented at Toronto University in March, 2004.

Hayhoe, S. (2008). *Arts, culture and blindness: Studies of blind students in the visual arts.* Youngstown: Teneo Press.

Hayhoe, S. (2011). Non-visual programming, perceptual culture and mulsemedia: Case studies of five blind computer programmers. In G. Ghinea, F. Andres, & S. R. Gulliver (Eds.), *Multiple sensorial media advances and applications: New developments in MulSeMedia.* Hershey: IGI.

Hayhoe, S. (2012). *Grounded theory and disability studies: Researching legacies of blindness.* Amherst: Cambria Press.

Hayhoe, S. (2013a). Expanding our vision of museum education and perception: An analysis of three case studies of independent, blind, arts learners. *Harvard Educational Review, 83*(1), 67–86.

Hayhoe, S. (2013b). A review of the literature on the use of mobile tablet computing as inclusive devises for students with disabilities. In *Proceedings of the current trends in information technology 2013 conference*, Dubai, 11–12 December 2013, IEEE, New Jersey.

Hayhoe, S. (2013c). The philosophical, political and religious roots of touch exhibitions in 20th century British Museums. *Disability Studies Quarterly, 33*(3), http://dsq-sds.org/article/view/3760/3273

Hayhoe, S. (2014). An enquiry into passive and active exclusion from sensory aesthetics in muse-
    ums and on the web: Two case studies of final year students at California School for the Blind
    studying art works through galleries and on the web. *British Journal of Visual Impairment,
    32*(1), 44–58.
Hayhoe, S. (2016a). The epistemological model of disability, and its role in understanding passive
    exclusion in eighteenth and nineteenth century Protestant educational asylums. *International
    Journal of Christianity and Education, 20*(1), 49–66.
Hayhoe, S. (2016b). *Philosophy as disability and exclusion: The development of theories on blind-
    ness, touch and the arts in England, 1688–2010*. Charlotte: IAP.
Hayhoe, S., Roger, K., Eldritch-Boersen, S., & Kelland, L. (2015). Developing inclusive technical
    capital beyond the disabled students' allowance in England. *Social Inclusion, 3*(6), 29–41.
Hopkins, R. (2005). Thomas Reid on Molyneux's question. *Pacific Philosophical Quarterly, 86*(3),
    340–364.
Hull, J. (1990). *Touching the rock: An experience of blindness*. London: SPCK.
Lowenfeld, B. (1981). Effects of blindness on the cognitive functioning of children. In B. Lowenfeld
    (Ed.), *On blindness and blind people: Selected papers*. New York: American Federation for the
    Blind.
Merleau-Ponty, M. (2002). *Phenomenology of perception* (C. Smith, Trans.). London: Routledge
    Classics.
Nagel, T. (2012). *Mind and cosmos: Why the materialist neo-Darwinian conception of nature is
    almost certainly false*. New York: Oxford University Press.
Oliver, M. (1996). *Understanding disability: From theory to practice*. Basingstoke: Macmillan.
Oliver, M. (2001). Disability issues in a postmodern world. In L. Barton (Ed.), *Disability, politics
    and the struggle for change*. London: David Fulton.
Oliver, M. (2013). The social model: A victim of criticism. *Disability Now*. Retrieved from http://
    www.disabilitynow.org.uk/article/social-model-victim-criticism
Pfeiffer, D. (2002). The philosophical foundations of disability studies. *Disability Studies
    Quarterly, 22*(2), 2–23.
Sacks, O. (1993). *A neurologist's notebook: To see and not to see*. New York: The New Yorker
    Magazine.
Sacks, O. (2001). *The island of the colour blind*. London: Picador.
Steinmetz, G. (1994). Regulation theory, post-Marxism, and the new social movements.
    Comparative Studies in Society and History, 36, 176–212.
Story, M. F., Mueller, J. L., & Mace, R. (1998). *The universal design file: Designing for people of
    all ages and abilities*. Raleigh: Center for Universal Design.
Tibble, M. (2004). *User's guide to disability estimates and definitions*. London: Department of
    Work and Pensions.
Warren, D. H. (1994). *Blindness and children: An individual differences approach*. Cambridge:
    Cambridge University Press.
World Health Organization. (1980). *International classification of impairments, disabilities, and
    handicaps: A manual of classification relating to the consequences of disease*. Geneva: World
    Health Organisation.
World Health Organisation. (2014). *Disabilities*. Retrieved from http://www.who.int/topics/dis-
    abilities/en/. On the 1 Apr 2014.

Chapter 7
Looking Back Over My Shoulder: Through The Disability's Mirror

Bernardo Carlos Spaulonci Chiachia Matos de Oliveira

Abstract In a conference celebrating the 25 years of American Disability Rights (ADA) I was invited to write about my story as a person with a disability. A friend suggested, "You should share your personal achievements and how you became a Fulbright fellow." At the time, I was reluctant about it. I didn't want to expose my life and I was really scared at the beginning when they asked me to write it. However, I accepted the challenge of telling my story, and even worse for me, talking about my disability. After 1 week of reflecting, I embraced this mission. I decided that after being exposed to wonderful stories of people using wheelchairs to visit faraway places, their stories inspired me to start thinking that my story could do the same for others. Thus, people can better understand how it is to be a person with a disability in Brazil by tracing my path. The reason I didn't readily accept the chance to write was very personal. In my life, I've never wanted to use my illness as an excuse for anything. But now, after all the barriers that I have faced and accomplished, I have decided to expose my story and show how I have overcome my difficulties. My intention is to expose my educational and professional trajectory through the disability lens by showing in a linear base three interconnected phases: my childhood and school, disability law and jobs, and eventually going back to the university to get my doctorate.

Childhood and School

In this section I will show how I began to see myself as being a person with a disability. The negation and acceptance of my disability are processes that are in constant movement. I have always wondered, is this disease mine? Does she belong to me? I have Larsen syndrome (LS). According to Mitra et al. (2012), LS is a congenital disorder discovered in 1950 by Larsen and associates when they observed dislocation of the large joints and face anomalies in six of their patients. Liang and Hang (2001) describe that patients suffering from Larsen syndrome normally

B.C.S.C.M. de Oliveira (✉)
Columbia University, New York, NY, USA

Pontificia Universidade Católica de Sao Paulo, Sao Paulo, Brazil
e-mail: oliveira.bernardo@gmail.com

© Springer International Publishing AG 2017
S. Halder, L.C. Assaf (eds.), *Inclusion, Disability and Culture*, Inclusive
Learning and Educational Equity 3, DOI 10.1007/978-3-319-55224-8_7

Fig. 7.1 My life cycle
experience

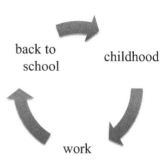

back to   childhood
school

work

present a variety of symptoms, including congenital anterior dislocation of the
knees, dislocation of the hips and elbows, flattened facial appearance, prominent
foreheads, and depressed nasal bridges. Because it is too complex to describe it as
we read above, my doctor usually defines it as a widespread multiple dysplasia,
which is a simple and gentle way to say that the illness spreads all over my skeleton.
Every joint in my body has some anomaly, or does not work normally.

"Normal," "average," "regular": these words will be recurrent in the text; as long
as I have pursued a normal life and a regular job, I have fought hard to be considered
"average." The concept of what is normal varies greatly from one individual to
another, but when the balance is affected, it becomes clear that there has been a
break with "normal," which might cause pain and suffering. These moments of
unbalance have been very important for my personal growth. From these moments,
I have realized that although I have struggled, so far I am a unique person.

I would like to invite you to visualize a circle. Imagine you are at the top of the
circle, facing the clockwise rotation. Now, turn all the way around, so that you're
facing counter-clockwise. At this point you will find this text, a description of my
life story through the disability lens, the denial of the disease at the beginning and
overcoming the stigma with acceptance at the end (Fig. 7.1).

My disease is not mine, she just follows me. Like heavy luggage, it has been difficult to carry her; I have wanted to leave her aside, hidden in the corner, until someone sees her and asks me to explain: What is this burden doing in the middle of the
room? Yes. That's how I used to feel most of the time when someone asked about
my disability. According to the Brazilian census of 2010, I am part of a group composed of 45.6 million people having some disability. People with disabilities represent 23.9% of the total Brazilian population. I am part of the second most represented
group (7%) of those with some motor difficulty.

I'd like to describe how I came into the world, beginning with the story my
grandfather told me: "You were born very small, you looked like a mouse; a tiny
ball. We could not see your little legs. But you were very hairy." My mother had a
complicated pregnancy because she had fallen during her 7th month of gestation,
giving birth to me after 8 months of pregnancy. Everyone, according to my father,
was rather perplexed when they saw me for the first time. Even the medical staff
were surprised. One nurse told my father, "it seems like his knee is bending
backwards."

Afterward, various treatments and surgeries were made. When I was 3 months old, they unsuccessfully attempted to fix my knees using a nonsurgical method. So 6 months later, my first surgery was completed in my knees. According to my mother, I've passed through 67 surgical operations and dozens of hospitalizations. An image illustrates the ending of this phase: imagine a little chubby child with legs stretched and slightly elevated with a painful facial expression. That little child is me. I do believe that this is the most striking image I have in my photo album.

Walking was a real challenge for me. I started walking when I was 4 years old, with a lot of difficulty. Yet, I could only stand up using orthopedic boots. I hated them deeply. To this day, every time I watch *Forrest Gump* I remember those boots. I feel like Forrest Gump every time I watch the opening scenes of this film: Run Forrest! Run! My boots were very similar to his. Unlike the movie, my use of those boots was long and did not magically stop one day. I wore those boots feeling embarrassed for 4 years.

I first experienced prejudice as a result of those boots. Even though I was a child, I'd learned early that I always would be noticed because of my disability, whether I wanted it or not. People stared from afar and pointed their fingers at me, their expressions saying: What a pity, does it hurt? "What does he have in his legs?" was one of the most recurrent questions asked about me in my presence, to my mom. This might be an explanation for why I don't like to be seen as a disabled person. I thought I'd never be anything other than a poor person with a disability during that time in my life. My saddest memories can be summarized in two specific moments: going to school for the first time, and the day I couldn't wear jeans because of my knee injury.

I remember it like it was yesterday: on the first day of class, the institutionalized segregation in the school slapped me in the face. At that time, I could not walk up stairs easily. My classroom was on the fourth floor, the last and most distant building. I vividly remember my mother arguing with (almost screaming at) the director of the public school: "Really? The 4th floor? The very last building? It cannot be true."

And this matter was not solved until months later, when my mother went to the secretary of education requesting special services. Then, my classroom was moved to the nearest building and next to the school administration office. I still had to go up a small stairway, but as I was special (that's what they used to call me) they allowed me to use the teacher's entrance where there weren't any stairs. I wanted to be normal, a regular student. But I turned out to be further differentiated: the special one.

Some years later, I was studying in a private school. Yes, my family dared to dream about my graduation, so I needed a good high school. Dreaming of my pursuing a college career was very daring, considering that almost 61% of disabled people in Brazil have only a basic education. In high school, I was no longer using the boots, only limping, but because of that people still looked at me. All students of the college had to wear a student uniform, which at the time could be any type of dark blue pants except loose ones. On that particular day I did not have uniform pants, and I had only loose pants. The cleaning lady was not at home, and my mother was working in the bank. Like any teenager, I thought I was an adult and wanted to handle the situation by myself, so I decided to go to school wearing the loose pants. I didn't want to bother my mother with issues like a uniform.

I was stopped at the school gate because I was not wearing the proper uniform. Then the employee of the college said "you could have worn jeans and a shirt from high school, but loose pants is too much!" Unable to react, I felt humiliated because I could not wear jeans as a regular student because they were too tight, and of course, self-esteem wasn't my strength back then. I felt embarrassed; I turned around and went toward my house. When she got home, my mother asked me why I had not gone to school that day. I explained the situation and she angrily told me "let me talk to this director." She spoke to the principal and after clarifying my situation, they gave a special authorization to use loose pants: again, I was the special one.

I attended high school in the same college where I was barred because of my improper uniform. At the end of the third year, I took vocational tests to determine my future career. From the vocational tests, the best options for me were medicine, advertising, and administration. I chose the course of administration, believing in better chances of employment. Two years after this resolution, I moved to Londrina, a city with about 500,000 inhabitants 4 h by car from the city where I used to live. I began taking courses in administration in 2003 at the State University of Londrina. The dream of freedom and financial independence was becoming closer at that time, and a new phase of my life had just begun.

Working

Independence and freedom are targets for many young adults. Most of them fulfill the social expectation of growing up by being accepted into college and entering the labor market which functions as a passage into adult life. However, for a person with disability, this journey can be overwhelming. Being independent for a disabled person is first and foremost a daily struggle, which includes the planning of all steps to be taken for each day, considering the distance, the possible routes, possibilities of walking around, and the distance between the places. It's a daily forethought. It is a constant calculating exercise. Always, balancing the things I want to do, and things I might be able to do, and things I might be able to do; most of the time, it's a lottery. I celebrate when an elevator or escalator is found in an unexpected space.

In this pursuit of freedom, working plays a very important role. According to the Brazilian Institute of Geography and Statistics (IBGE), Brazil has more than 45 million people with a disability. Of this total, almost 13 million have severe disabilities. The number, however, is not reflected in the labor market. Approximately 325,000 or less than 1% of the 44 million workers with employment are disabled (IBGE 2010).

During my second year in college, I decided to apply for a job. I was hired as a bank teller in a major Brazilian bank. Since 1991, Brazil has had a law known as the Quota Law (Article 93 of LOAS - Organic Law of Social Welfare), which requires companies with more than one hundred employees to set aside 2–5% of vacancies for people with disabilities.

Working as a bank teller was a very enriching experience. I learned how a bank works from the inside, how to treat the customers, and what a boss expects from his/her employees in terms of behavior. Although I was ensured by disability labor laws, I had problems getting my working hours flexible. As a bank teller, only a 15 min break is allowed, which means working in the same sitting position for more than 3 h straight. Then, because of that, I needed to visit my physiotherapist more often, however; it wasn't easy to do that. In the end I was forced to try my last alternative: the Union. Sadly, most of the companies who hire people with disabilities are not prepared to accommodate us, so after 3 months I had to quit the job.

Even though I achieved financial security, this postion taught me that education is more important. This somehow explains why I studied so hard during college, and it was 4 years of great experiences. I started by deceiving myself during the first month by overusing my knee attempting to walk around the city, trying to have a "regular" life. But the public transportation was horrible. The difficulty was to get a cheaper, automatic car in the beginning of my college. Unlike the USA, cars in Brazil are mostly equipped with stick shift, and automatic ones are expensive and the only kind I can drive. At that moment I couldn't afford a new car or even cover the expenses of having an old car. However, in order to go to university, in other words, to have a "normal," independent life, I didn't have many choices: I had to buy a car.

I have always exceeded in everything academic, for good and for bad. I've sought the best grades, I've always wanted more. An inner voice always compelled me, "You need to keep going. Don't look for excuses, you'll get it." I got involved in various activities during my first year in college: I was the vice president of the academic directory, student's representative to the collegiate course of administration, and also a junior businessman. Finishing my term paper in 2007, I received a job invitation to be a commercial assistant in the fashion industry. Again, I was excited about being productive. The job required that I travel 100 km all week long. Despite my building not having an elevator, I was feeling glad to work. I used to work from Monday to Saturday. I was happy. I overworked myself, always giving my best to the customers and to my boss. Nothing and no one could take away my willpower: I finally had achieved the normal life.

Unluckily, I ended up paralyzed for 3 months. This was the worst moment of my life, because I was paralyzed at the time that I felt the most fulfilled. Because of a pain in my back, I called my family asking for help. After medical exams, my physician said to me, "you will need to be on sick leave for a while. I do not know what you have in your spinal column yet. I do not know what will happen from now on." Because my bones are very specific, he took a longer time researching and talking to his peers. That period was horrible, I cried almost every day. The uncertainty of my future, all my fear and weakness was clearly facing me every moment that I wanted to move my body and I couldn't. Therefore, I realized that I am neither normal nor special; I am a different person who requires specific arrangements to have freedom in life.

Fortunately, after a long-awaited medical diagnosis, I no longer had to worry about my spinal column because after that I was allowed to move and return to a social life again. After that I would return to society, but what should I do? Work, after that trauma? I had passed through many months of recovering. As a consequence, insecurity was dominant in my mind. How to get back to work and be productive? I had only questions and no answers at that time. I couldn't work 9–5, I needed to find something feasible where I could put my energy and my skills, and play to my strengths without overstressing my body.

Going Back to School

Talking to friends who were completing their master's programs, I was convinced of the possibility of having a productive and nice life going back to school. After that recent temptation of working and then being paralyzed, this time I was really worried, and taking care of my health has been a priority since then. So I reflected a lot about an academic career and the future seemed to be very optimistic. Then I decided to apply for my master's in 2009.

In Brazil, a "mestrado" is a preparation for research and lasts 2 years. Similar to master's programs in other countries, it includes a teaching component and a research project resulting in a dissertation. The selection process normally consists of reviewing qualifications, professional experience, and the relevance of the course chosen for the future career. Because I didn't have any research experience or academic publication to my name, I needed to achieve the best score in the Test ANPAD similar to Graduate Record Examination (GRE) in the USA. Then, I prepared a syllabus to study, and in order to facilitate my preparation I chose to move closer to the same university where I went to college.

In the meantime, I searched for a job opportunity and I got one as a financial assistant in a multinational pharmaceutical company. I worked and studied hard for the test, and after the second time, in December 2009, I was accepted into the Master's program in Management at the State University of Londrina.

Despite the fact that I had the quota law on my side and that I was working at a large, international company which could have helped me, I still was not receiving the basic rights I needed in order to go to physiotherapy and rest my body. Unfortunately, I was soon on sick leave again, but now it was my feet. This time I tried not to push too much. But the bus trips and the walking inside the company between the buildings had killed me. As a result, my body again gave me a sign: I must slow down. The reality shows me that although being hired under the quota law, my mobility rights didn't reach me. For the second time, I had to reduce my pace. However, I did not lose hope, because this time I had my master's degree to hold on to.

It was love at first sight: a master's degree in management and sustainability. I finally saw a real opportunity to change the world. I discovered that my wanting to help people could be done. By studying social and environmental issues, I could understand and prepare myself to act in these matters. It was 2 years of intense study and dedication. From beginning as a bad writer to having a book published, I finished my master's program facing all the adversities, and I wasn't looking for a "normal" life. I accepted my singularity, and for the first time I understood that going against the mainstream could be fruitful. I also discovered that having a different background, with a complex, personal life story as well as professional work experience, could be my strength. As business people used to say, I had found my competitive advantage.

Conclusion

Now I understand what resilience means, and it makes me feel stronger. I have endured my illness with great fortitude. So in 2012 after graduating from my master's program I started to teach for undergraduate and Master of Business Administration (MBA) programs. However, teachers are not well remunerated in the beginning of their careers. To get a good position as a professor in Brazil, one must obtain a PhD. I tried five different doctoral programs in the best Brazilian universities. In March of 2012, I was accepted into the social sciences postgraduate program at the Catholic University of Sao Paulo, a very well-recognized university in Brazil and the best private school in Sao Paulo. I was really amazed. Doing a PhD at this university would be the highest achievement of my academic life.

I took several classes. Basically, I did a full master's in social sciences, which was wonderful for me, because while doing that I almost overcame the feeling of being behind compared to other students. But something still lacked in my basket of desires: an international experience. Once again I reflected a lot. How I could reach that? Where could I find the money for that?

Luckily, I found the Fulbright scholarship. After a year searching for grants and sponsorships, I ended up writing a very good proposal. So in 2012, I tried the Fulbright process for the first time: I failed. If this happened before my sick leave I might have given up, but after that experience I became more confident. So I didn't give up and in 2013; I tried another time and received the acceptance letter in January of 2014. Fully boosted with great energy and happiness, I finally achieved my dream: Columbia University in New York City, specifically Teachers College, would be my home for 9 months.

Living in New York City (NYC) compared to Sao Paulo was pretty easy for my disability. Here in NYC I can walk, and I can go wherever I want! Being a person who demands special requirements is very complicated in Sao Paulo, but NYC seems better structured for this purpose. As I said at the beginning of this text, I have strived to be a "normal" person and to be one more in the crowd. But all the experiences that I have passed through have changed me, and I don't want to be a normal person anymore. All the barriers made me realize that I am different. Not special, just different.

It was a very hard exercise to share this with you, dear reader. I didn't realize how much I had fought against my disability before writing this. I accepted the challenge of writing about my life. Some would say how wonderful, how inspiring it is. Yes, I've squeezed my heart and brought up the memories. Out of all the moments that drove me here to the USA, NYC is at the top of the hill. Now, looking back, I can see how the path was torturous and sloping. I know it's only the beginning. Nonetheless, it's still not the easiest part. Now my life is really open and fulfilled with hope and willingness to impact others' lives. I have learned that I have to fight to change the inequality and the injustice that prevents people from living in their personal normality, whatever their normality might be.

Looking back over my shoulder now brings me a great learning and an inner new understanding of the stigma. It is clear now what the concept of stigma is. The concept was well developed by Ervin Goffman in *Stigma: Notes on the Management of Spoiled Identity*, first published in 1963. For me, being stigmatized as a special one in my childhood interfered in my social skills later. This turned social relations more complicated, making it difficult to express that I really was a human, complete in my disabilities. Now the luggage that I used to hide is over my back. A backpack fulfilled with personal experiences and self-knowledge. The adjectives "special" and "normal" have turned in the concept of social justice in my perspective a democratic society is reached only through an inclusive education, a frequent dialogue between different and diverse. A cross-cultural and cross-disciplinary encounter is extremely necessary to enhance the debate about disability and inclusion.

Acknowledgments I would like to thank my sponsors Brazilian Federal Agency for the Support and Evaluation of Graduate Education (Capes) and the Fulbright Commission in Brazil and North America. Without their support, I could not have this enhancing experience. I extend my gratitude to Sabina Simon for her patience in guiding me to write this manuscript, Prof. Juliette de Wolfe and Cynthia Fields for their suggestions and comments about this paper, and Victor Pineda – a true inspiration since our first meeting.

References

Brazilian Institute of Geography and Statistics (IBGE). (2010). *Census 2010*. http://censo2010. ibge.gov.br/en/censo-2010. Accessed 4 Nov 2015.

Goffman, E. (1963). *Stigma, notes on the management of spoiled identity*. London: Penguin.

Liang, C. D., & Hang, C. L. (2001). Elongation of the aorta and multiple cardiovascular abnormalities associated with larsen syndrome. *Pediatric Cardiology, 22*, 245–246.

Mitra, N., Kannan, N., Kumar, V. S., & Kavita, G. (2012). Larsen syndrome: A case report. *Journal of Nepal Paediatric Society, 32*, 85–87.

Chapter 8
From Stigma to Empowerment – A Journey to Reframe Disability

Flávia Affonso Mayer

Abstract Much has been written about the way society misinterprets impairment and how important it is to promote a new discussion framework on this issue. However, what should happen when people with disabilities don't believe in their own capabilities? Working with the blind and their relationship with visual images, I have faced situations in which visually impaired individuals were so influenced by misleading ideas about their impairment that those stigmatized viewpoints became entrenched in their own experiences. By discussing some experiences I have had in my research and describing the scenarios of social mobilization and accessibility rights in Brazil and in the United States, I argue how social barriers and the lack of information can reinforce the stigma on people with disabilities. This historical and cultural context of prejudice can lead to a low self-perception and contribute to the loss of opportunities and important social interactions. I claim that education and the articulation of the organization and social movements are key to strengthening the identity construction of these impaired individuals and promote a more inclusive society.

Starting Point

As a doctorial candidate, my entrance into the field of disabilities was through educational research. In 2009, Luiza Sá and I started to work on a social mobilization investigation on the issue of audio description (Mayer and Sá 2011). Broadly speaking, audio description is a mediation operation where visual information is presented in a braille alphabet or in an auditory way, seeking to increase the interaction of people with visual impairment with the visual information. Important visual details such as scenery, costumes, indication of time and space, movements, and

F.A. Mayer (✉)
Fulbright Visiting Scholar, Department of Cognitive Science, Case Western Reserve University, Cleveland, OH, USA

Post-Doctoral Associate, Department of Communication and Arts, Pontifícia Universidade Católica de Minas Gerais, Belo Horizonte, Brazil
e-mail: flavia.mayer@gmail.com

© Springer International Publishing AG 2017   97
S. Halder, L.C. Assaf (eds.), *Inclusion, Disability and Culture*, Inclusive Learning and Educational Equity 3, DOI 10.1007/978-3-319-55224-8_8

facial expressions are presented. In an audiovisual product audio description is inserted between the source product's dialogues and important sound tracks, so as not to interfere with its comprehension. Taking this issue as a starting point and after an extensive literature review, interviews with people with disabilities, researchers, representatives of organizations and social and political movements, I was thoroughly immersed into the disability rights movement agenda, and as an extension, to the laws related to it.

In Brazil, Law 10.098 (BRAZIL 2000), known as "the Brazilian law of accessibility," regulates the rights of people with disabilities and establishes general standards and basic criteria in different sectors, such as urbanism, communication, and public transportation. Regarding the media, this law made audio description a right guaranteed by Brazilian legislation, obligating that TV stations offer 2 h of audio description programming by June 2008. According to the law, the number of hours of audio description was expected to gradually increase until the entire program schedule was accessible in 2016. However, the battle between communication companies and movements for the rights of disabled people eventually resulted in the suspension of this mandatory feature. This change in accessibility led to protests by institutions for people with disabilities who demanded the implementation of measures that had already been discussed and approved at a public consultation.

It should be emphasized, however, that despite all this important articulation from social organizations, it became clear during our research interviews that the vast majority of people with disabilities were significantly misinformed – although the law existed, people with disabilities were not always aware of it. Consequently, they weren't taking action and fighting for their rights, making it easy for communication companies to slow the audio description implementation.

This disconnection between beneficiaries and individuals' rights intrigued me deeply. It was hard to understand why, despite all the social organization's movements and their fight for more accessible conditions. Yet, those who were supposed to be on the front line of the discussions were so apart of it. After all, how could people with visual disabilities have so little knowledge about an issue so important to them? Were they not interested? I couldn't believe people weren't interested, so I went back to my investigations and started to put it in a historical perspective.

From the reports of researchers as Sassaki (1997), Mazzotta (2005), Jannuzzi (2006), and Glat and Blanco (2007), and representatives of organizations for the visually impaired, it was revealed that by the end of the seventeenth century, impairment was practically an abandoned topic in Brazil. It was only after this period that special institutions for the impaired were created and they started to be viewed differently in Brazil, especially in the matter of education and labor. However, the remnants of years of negative perceptions about their capacities continue to make the welfare policies perspective strong.

After years of deadlock and discussions, on July 1, 2011, audio description was finally implemented in Brazil, through Decree n. 188/2010. It is now mandatory for public broadcast television stations with a digital signal to provide part of its programming with audio description. It started with 2 h weekly and now is required to have a minimum of 6 h per week. Besides the Portuguese programming, movies, documentaries, and programs broadcast in different languages also have to be fully adapted, with dubbed dialogue.

By the time this happened, I had already started my Masters research and had decided to investigate how audio description could be developed in Brazil. The implementation of the law increased my interest in the ways in which people with visual impairments engage in discussions about audio description and how they perceive and relate to visual images. Thus, during my studies, the idea of creating a socio-cultural space to integrate people with visual impairments and, at the same time, provide empirical data for research on audio description emerged.

The Project Cinema on the Ear

Based on my research interests, the scant bibliography about audio description and the incipient status of Decree n. 188/2010, an interdisciplinary team of researchers was created in 2011 at the Pontifícia Universidade Católica de Minas Gerais to investigate the importance of audio description in a more in-depth way. This team comprised of researchers in the fields of social communication, psychology, linguistics, and pedagogy. It was the beginning of the Project Cinema on the Ear, which continues to work actively (Mayer 2014; Mayer et al. 2015).

Looking to better understand the process of audio description in an experimental and exploratory way, the project scope was structured with the following steps: form a group of visually impaired volunteers, analyze their profile, and select movies to be audio described. Then, make an audio description script of each movie, record respective audio description tracks, show the film with audio description to the group of volunteers, promote a debate about it with the audience, and analyze their perceptions. The central idea of the project's activities is to interact with the target audience of audio description, so that they inform the development of the project.

Although it seems obvious, the participation of visually impaired people in the production and evaluation of audio description does not happen very frequently in Brazil. For many years, there was (and still exists in certain segments) a thought that as people with visual impairment cannot see images, they had no knowledge of them. Therefore, their only role was to sit, watch, and assimilate what audio description described to them.

With the objective to change this point of view, in 2014 one of our volunteers with visual impairment, graduated from the department of pedagogy, joined our research group as our consultant. Thus, participants were not restricted to just making comments on post production but were invited to fully engage in the whole process of audio description – contradicting all the stigmatized points of view and becoming co-creators of the audio description.

This change in participants' engagement has brought a great positive impact on our investigations. The discussions of the scripts, which were based on an inference of researchers and then ratified (or not) by the audience, have become more intense since the very beginning of production. Questions such as "How to describe this particular scene?" and "Which important elements should be highlighted?" to "How to describe them?" were not answered by inference anymore. Instead, a representative of individuals with visual impairments described how the images apply to him and how we, as a research team, can make the movies more accessible for the visually impaired community.

To our surprise, the project has had a great impact on the audience of our screenings too. Once the participants knew that there was a visually impaired consultant on our team, they understood that their own experiences were relevant and thus the project became important – not just for the researchers conducting the study, but also for the volunteers as the co-builders of audio description. Consequently, the participants became more willing to debate and more involved with the project. It is important to emphasize that all this movement in the project wasn't based only on the desire to improve our internal processes and research. It was also an attempt to better articulate our conceptual model of impairment.

According to Enfield and Harris (2003), there are four main models to comprehend impairment. The Charitable Model understands disability as a deficit. The person is seen as a victim of his inability, so he needs our help, sympathy, and charity. The second model is the Medical Model. According to it, people with disabilities have problems that need to be healed, assigning them the passive role of patients. This leaves them with the exclusive responsibility to overcome their physical, sensory, or intellectual limits. The society is exempt from any liability. In the Social Model, disability is seen as a result of the way society is organized – it depends not only on the subject but also on the conditions which the social environment offers to the person to be independent (Enfield and Harris 2003). Finally, the Rights-based Model is similar to the Social Model, but they are distinguished on an important emphasis: on the Rights-based Model, accessibility can't be understood as a humanitarian action or charity – it is the fulfillment of a basic human right that any person can claim. That is, as a democratic society, and in our case, as a research group, it is our duty to promote the inclusion of people with impairments in all sectors. We deeply agreed with this perspective, not just because it reinforces the Social Model's discussion, which put into the scene the role of society, but also because it reinforces the status of the impaired as a citizen, who like all of us, has the right to have access to information and culture. Thus, to be coherent on what we stand for, we changed our way of working – and the results of this effort couldn't be better.

The Role of Color

As expected, the participation of a visually impaired consultant did not mean finding answers to all questions in our investigation. One of the topics that caught my attention was the audio describers' and the audio description's audience resistance to approach the issue of colors. In the process of writing the scripts, audio describing the color information is a very tricky topic. After all, how can colors be audio described to an audience that can't see them (or in the case of the congenitally blind, never saw them at all)? Even the audio describers who demonstrated an openness to include colors in their scripts experienced difficulties in approaching color and because of that, most of time, they give up. Likewise, every time we discussed this issue at our screenings, we realized that we were not the only ones who were having difficulties in approaching this topic. The participants with visual impairment avoided the issue too. For most of them, color is "not important" since they can't see it. This statement left me quite puzzled. Could it be possible that colors are not an important piece of information for the blind? This is definitely not a case of advocating a visual experience of colors for the congenitally blind. My hope was to understand why the social, the symbolic, and the aesthetic values of color, negotiated in personal interactions, weren't considered important issues by these participants. Why do they think that color is not important, since it has more than a visual relevance?

This issue intrigued me so deeply that I decided to dedicate my PhD research to this topic. I've conducted interviews, experiments, and discussed the topic with people with visual disabilities. However, the participants' resistance in regard to color has proved bigger than I imagined – and even unleashed situations where some of the visually impaired participants felt offended with my approach to colors. Nevertheless, when I discussed the issue in an indirect way – e.g., talking about clothes for a party, the purchase of food (to see if the fruit is good enough to be consumed) or even in the joy of giving or receiving red roses on Valentine's Day – most participants were perfectly comfortable discussing the subject. Colors are sensory information (visual), which has a strong symbolic meaning, constructed and negotiated by social interactions. In this sense, even if the blind don't have a visual experience of colors, they still have the symbol and their personal experiences with the symbol. Then, why did they avoid talking about colors when I asked them directly about it?

Stigma

As we mentioned before, the relationship between the visually impaired and Brazilian society was mostly marked by welfare policies. The stance in favor of accessibility is fairly recent (Mazzotta 2005; Jannuzzi 2006). As a result, one of the barriers still to overcome is the family's lack of information of the capacities and potentials of their relatives with disabilities. Because of prejudice, it can be very difficult for families to publicly accept their relatives, contributing to the perpetuation of stereotypes and poor access to education. This deficit-minded context contributed to endorsing a negative social stigma surrounding people with disabilities in Brazil.

The term "stigma" was coined in ancient Greece to refer to bodily signs that evidenced something extraordinary or bad about the moral status of those who had them. However, Goffman (1963) shifted the concept of stigma to be understood as a social process. According to Goffman (1963), society establishes the means of categorizing people and the attributes considered as common and natural features for its members. Thus, a man who could easily be welcomed in everyday social interactions has a trait that can distract attention from his other attributes.

Martin (1986) argues that stigma is created, preserved, and perpetuated through social learning. Therefore, people who have attributes that make them different from the logic of that social categorization are labeled negatively. According to Link and Phelan (2001), these social labels provide the existence of two hierarchy groups in the society: "us" and "them." The "us" is the symbol of the dominant ideology – their members "fit" the standardized stereotype. The label "them" is characterized by people who are different from the characteristics said to be "normal." This social difference provides the loss of status in the community, becoming the basis for discrimination.

In this same line of thought, Jones et al. (1984) work with the idea of stigma in relation to the individual's self-concept. According to the authors, the stigma alters the social process of development of the self, since it can alter the interpersonal relationships that are vital for self-knowledge and self-assessment. However, as Crocker and Major (1989) advocate, stigmatized people do not always have lower self-esteem, since this process is dependent on the subject's personality and stigmatization conditions. Ainlay et al. (1986) argue that stigma is a process directly linked to the cultural and historical moment in time – that is, a specific attribute or behavior is analyzed according to the meaning of that specific culture and the historical context. Thus, as cultural patterns change over time, so the understanding and perception of stigma changes.

After I started to familiarize myself with this discussion about stigma, I better understood my research participants. The historical condition of impaired people in Brazil has always been focused on the limits, the lack of perspective, and the pity instead of offering opportunities. Mostly they were seen as unable to understand, unable to work, unable to improve or to be independent. This stigma is so ingrained in families and institutions that the participants appear to assimilate this stigma through social learning. If we examine movements like the one related to Law 10.098, we can begin to better understand changes and shifts in the way we frame impairment in Brazil. However, as in any other process of cultural change, this is a slow process, which continues to perpetuate prejudices toward the individuals with visual impairments and leaves them deeply scarred.

In my research I argue that thinking that color is not important for those who cannot see color is a consequence of cultural stigma. The importance of color is not only related to the eyes but it is also connected to the social and semiotic dimensions, as well as the human capacity to imagine things that go beyond our senses and direct experiences.

If we ask anyone with visual impairment what is the flag of his country, he will know how to differentiate the flag of his homeland by the shapes and designs in it but also by its colors. He would be perfectly capable of describing what each color represents and the reason why the colors are on the flag. This is because people with visual impairment, like all of us, have learned and negotiated these meanings in social interactions. Living in society, we cannot avoid the social learning process. In these interactions, we use our previous experiences, and social and cultural motivations, to exchange experiences and build on our own concepts. Thus, although they cannot see colors, people with visual impairment are able to construct their own meanings about it and negotiate these constructions in their interactions, like any other human being. Focusing on the capabilities of these citizens, this frame implies that it is not necessary caution to the audio describer, families, friends, and institutions to address colors to the visually impaired. Moreover, it is a society's duty to create more equal opportunities that promote the inclusion of people with visual impairment, offering them the conditions to build meaningful experiences for themselves, whether by audio description or other accessibility devices.

Some Experiences in the United States

As part of my PhD, I went to the United States as a Fulbright visiting scholar in the Cognitive Science department at Case Western Reserve University. Throughout this period, I developed my research in theoretical terms and studied some organizations that work for the accessibility for people with visual impairments, such as the American Council of the Blind and the Audio Description Coalition.

Seeking information on how the country defended the rights of people with disabilities, I found great material on the Americans with Disabilities Act (ADA). The ADA itself is a very important written document that legally guarantees the access of disabled people to public spaces, ensuring their status of citizens, and enabling them to exercise their rights and duties the same as everyone else. However, what stood out the most to me was the joint effort of the different movements to fight for the rights of all individuals with impairments. More than pointing to the particularities of each sector, they all focus on defending a broad definition of disability. This focus is on the way society relates to a disability experience, the barriers in society that prevent full participation, the discrimination, prejudice and exclusion of those that are common to all kinds of people with impairments.

Furthermore, I had the great opportunity to attend the Fulbright Enrichment Seminar on the theme US Disability Rights: 25 Years of the ADA and Beyond. In the seminar, I had the chance to learn more about the Americans with Disabilities Act and to actually meet some of its most important activists, such as Arlene Mayerson, Pat Wright, Judith Heumann, and Victor Pineda. During the panel discussion, it was clear that the movement in America is based on a basic assumption that people with disabilities want to be active members of their communities and are perfectly capable of doing so.

As in many places in the world, the ADA has many issues in its implementation, but the main idea is that segregation will not be tolerated.

Even after many struggles to fight against prejudice in the United States, it is now possible to see that people with impairments have built a self-image of possibilities and opportunities. Interestingly, a significant proportion of individuals with impairments in the USA are "war heroes." They are soldiers who fought for their country and when they returned home with the scars of battle, society gave them a more prestigious and respected place than the population in Brazil. This does not decrease the great merit of all the struggles of the American social movements for accessibility. The continual work of these organizations to guarantee the rights for people with disabilities, such as the ADA, has led the country to a level that, while it is still not the ideal scenario, gave individuals with impairments their deserved status as active citizens. This fact reinforces the ideas of Ainlay et al. (1986), when they argue that stigma is a process directly linked to the cultural and historical moment in time – despite my very brief experience in the USA, I noticed that the American society's view toward people with disabilities is different from Brazil. Overwhelmingly, in Brazil people with disabilities belong to lower social classes, those who have less access to education, health, and culture. This context contributed to endorsing a strong social stigma surrounding people with disabilities.

Still a Long Way to Go

Although the social movements for accessibility stand for the Model Based on Rights, the Medical Model still continues to be the most widespread position in most societies. This continues because most societies, including Brazil, focus on what the disability prevents the impaired from doing, instead of concentrate on their capabilities or on the community's accountability. We do not think about how our society is preventing the full access of these citizens with all the barriers we have, and because of that, not rarely these citizens remain with no access to information and culture. This is a very difficult frame to change, but urgent to be discussed when it comes to a democratic society.

Besides the gaze of society on individuals with disabilities, it is also important to consider the way stigma influences one's self-perception regarding individual abilities. The lack of access to information makes this population even more vulnerable to this kind of misconstruction, contributing to the stigmata resonate in social learning. However, it became clear in the ADA's movement that when different social groups build an extensive network where everyone faces discrimination together and supports the development of a positive self-perception, it challenges the stigma of being incapable and reinforces the idea that the problem is in the social barrier and lack of inclusion. Thus, the first step to change this cycle is to promote greater articulation among all social movements in order to strengthen the identity construction of individuals with impairments. Only then, I believe, people with impairments will be able to change their own ideas about their conditions and fight for their citizenship, their rights, social participation, and access to culture and education.

Acknowledgments I would like to express my appreciation for the financial support of the Fulbright Commission and the Brazilian agencies CAPES and CNPq. I am grateful to Mark Turner for his guidance during my internship in the Department of Cognitive Science at Case Western Reserve University. I extend my gratitude to Milton do Nascimento, Sandra Cavalcante and Julio Pinto for their contributions.

References

Ainlay, S. C., Becker, G., & Coleman, L. M. A. (1986). Stigma reconsidered. In S. C. Ainlay, G. Becker, & L. M. A. Coleman (Eds.), *The dilemma of difference* (pp. 1–13). New York: Plenum.

Americans With Disabilities Act of 1990. (1990). Pub. L. No. 101–336, 104 Stat. 328.

Audio Description Coalition. (2009). *Standards for audio description and code of professional conduct for describers: Based on the training and experience of audio describers and trainers from across the United States*. [S.L.]: Audio Description Coalition. Available in: http://audio-descriptioncoalition.org

Brazil. Decree n° 5.296, 2nd of December, 2004. (2004). *It lays down general rules and basic criteria for promoting accessibility for people with disabilities or reduced mobility*. Official Diary of the Union, Brasília, 3 of December, 2004.

Brazil. Decree n° 5.645, 28th of December, 2005. (2005). *New wording of Decree N° 5.296, which establishes general rules and basic criteria for promoting accessibility for people with disabilities or reduced mobility*. Official Diary of the Union, Brasília, 30th December, 2005.

Brazil. Law n° 10.098, 19th of December, 2000. (2000). *Establishes general rules and basic criteria for promoting accessibility for people with disabilities or reduced mobility*. Official Diary of the Union, Brasília, 20th of December, 2000.

Brazil. Ordinance n° 403, 27th of June, 2008. (2008). *Provides for the suspension of the obligation to display on the TV programming*. Official Diary of the Union, Brasília, 30th of June, 2008.

Brazil. Ordinance n° 466, de 30 de julho de 2008 (2008). *Awards within ninety days, so that the radio and television companies start to show accessibility features*. Official Diary of the Union, Brasília, 31st of July, 2008.

Brazil. Ordinance n° 661, 14th October, 2008. (2008). *Suspension of the application of audio description of scenes in television programs*. Official Diary of the Union, Brasília, 15th of October, 2008.

Crocker, J., & Major, B. (1989). Social stigma and self-esteem: The self-protective properties of stigma. *Psychological Review, 96*, 608–630.

Enfield, S., & Harris, A. (2003). *Disability, equality and human rights: A training manual for development and humanitarian organizations*. Oxford: Oxfam. Retrieved from http://hpod.org/pdf/disability-equality-oxfam.pdf.

Glat, R., & Blanco, L. (2007). Educação especial no contexto de uma educação inclusiva. In R. Glat (Org), *Educação inclusiva: cultura e cotidiano escolar*. Rio de Janeiro, Brazil, 7 Letras.

Goffman, E. (1963). *Stigma: Notes on the management of spoiled identity*. Prentice-Hall: Englewood Cliffs.

Jannuzzi, G. (2006). *A educação do deficiente no Brasil: dos proportios ao século XXI*. Campinas: Autores Associados.

Jones, E., Farina, A., Hastof, A., Markus, H., Miller, D. T., & Scott, R. A. (1984). Stigma and the self-concept. In E. Jones, A. Farina, A. Hastof, H. Markus, D. T. Miller, & R. A. Scott (Eds.), *Social stigma: The psychology of marked relationships* (pp. 111–154). New York: Freeman and Company.

Link, B. G., & Phelan, J. C. (2001). Conceptualizing stigma. *Annual Review of Sociology, 27*, 363–385.

Martin, L. G. (1986). Stigma: A social learning perspective. In S. C. Ainlay, G. Becker, & L. M. A. Colman (Eds.), *The dilemma of difference* (pp. 145–161). New York: Plenum.

Mayer, F. (2014). *Imagem como símbolo Acústico: A semiótica aplicada a prática da audiodescrição*. Saarbrucken: Novas Edições Académicas.

Mayer, F., & Sá, L. (2011). *Diagnóstico de comunicação para a mobilização social: Promover autonomia por meio da audiodescrição*. Belo Horizonte: PROEX/UFMG.

Mayer, F., Xavier, A., Rezende, A., Anacleto, B., Moreira, W., Aquino, G., Pacheco, R., & Guimarães, M. (2015). A importância do consultor com deficiência visual no processo audiodescritivo: grupo SVOA/Cinema ao Pé do Ouvido. In *Revista Brasileira de Tradução Visual* (Vol. 18). Recife: Universidade Federal de Pernambuco.

Mazzotta, M. (2005). *Educação especial no Brasil: história e políticas públicas*. São Paulo: Cortez.

Sassaki, R. (1997). *Inclusão: construindo uma sociedade para todos*. Rio de Janeiro: WVA.

Chapter 9
There is No "Dis" in our Abilities: Acknowledging the Experience of the Differently-Abled Community

Caroline Muster

Abstract Living with a disability, or *different ability*, is undeniably challenging. Not only are individuals with different abilities challenged to overcome the physical trails associated with their respective medical conditions, they must also persevere through the life-long process of reconciling their personal views of themselves with the negative perceptions and prejudices of society. The psychological consequences of this task are complex and often indelible. In addition to combating social stigma, the *differently-abled* community is confronted with numerous physical barriers, political restrictions, and a history plagued with inferior status. Fortunately, the world has progressed in its acceptance, and is continuing to improve its treatment of individuals with different abilities. Nevertheless, there is still great progress to be made in the movement toward equality and full inclusion. Differently-abled women, for example, are continuously faced with the trials of *intersectionality*, the results of being both female and differently abled, which primarily includes sexual oppression. Thus, individuals with different abilities are encouraged to be more engaged in the practice of self-advocacy. Family, friends, and allies must also maintain their support of individuals with different abilities, an element that is critical to the community's success. Helping professionals who serve the differently-abled community are urged to educate themselves on the adversity experienced by the community, to acknowledge how other cultural identities intersect with the differently abled culture, and to employ strengths-based theoretical paradigms that will produce the most empowering results for their clients. Helping professionals with different abilities, furthermore, are called upon to lead the identity and civil rights movement of the differently-abled community.

C. Muster (✉)
Texas State University, San Marcos, TX, USA
e-mail: caroline.muster@gmail.com

© Springer International Publishing AG 2017   107
S. Halder, L.C. Assaf (eds.), *Inclusion, Disability and Culture*, Inclusive
Learning and Educational Equity 3, DOI 10.1007/978-3-319-55224-8_9

Introduction: The Challenges of Being Different

The existential process of overcoming adversity is understood by many cultural groups, whether these groups are defined by gender, race, ethnicity, sexual identity, age, socioeconomic status (SES), education, spirituality, political affiliation, or any of the myriad traits that are used to distinguish individuals from each other. Moreover, the trials presented by adversity are the experiences that test individuals' resolve and influence identity. How each trial is perceived, furthermore, is highly subjective: A difficult circumstance for one individual may be a routine occurrence for another. Yet life's trials are not simply manifestations of personal perceptions. Adversity is often generated by the perceptions of others, by those who view certain individuals or groups as inferior or defective in their being, behavior, or beliefs. Thus, life is especially challenging when personal characteristics are identified as different from what is "normal".

Indeed, for individuals who possess multiple deviations in any of the personal characteristics noted above that could and often do lead the majority to deem them as lesser, such as being female and Muslim or a person of color who identifies as queer, the quantity of life's challenges is significant. To describe the experiences of these individuals more effectively, particularly African American women, an intervention framework termed *intersectionality* was developed to highlight the overlap, or *intersection*, among multiple facets or cultures of an individual's identity (Crenshaw 1989). Discrimination and other forms of oppression are principally addressed in this analysis. Yet the challenges that accompany cultural overlap can be ameliorated though education and the promotion of social justice. It is also noteworthy that the compounded difficulties experienced by individuals living in the crosshairs of intersectionality produce a resilience that cannot be matched or measured (Shontz 1977).

Throughout history, philosophers, psychologists, researchers, and countless other academics have dedicated their careers to investigating human nature and the variable paths individuals take to overcome trials and navigate the complexities of life. These investigations have revealed intrinsic inclinations common to all people, such as the pursuit of relationships spurred by a need to belong (e.g., Baumeister and Leary 1995; Glasser 1998; Maslow 1943), as well as individual and group differences, such as those defined by culture (e.g., Ogbu 1993). Further research has narrowed the scope of this inquiry to focus on the challenges experienced by particular cultural groups, including women (e.g., Moradi and Huang 2008), people of color (e.g., Hochschild and Weaver 2007), the LGBTQ community (e.g., Tilcsik 2011), children and youth in foster care (e.g., Bass et al. 2004), and families living in poverty (e.g., Small et al. 2010).

Much less attention, however, has been directed to individuals with disabilities, or to use a more empowering term: individuals with *different abilities*. Consequently, even fewer efforts have been made to investigate the effects of intersectionality within the *differently-abled* community. For example, the quantity and quality of challenges faced by a woman who is differently abled vary significantly from those faced by a man who is not differently abled (Nosek and Hughes 2003). Moreover, the life of such a woman is arguably vastly different from another woman who is not differently abled (Schriempf 2001). Still, the challenges faced by a woman of color who is differently abled are undoubtedly different – and likely greater – than those faced by an Anglo woman who is also differently abled. With each facet of identity that deviates from the majority come additional challenges to acknowledge and conquer.

To address this empirical deficit, the following is a reflection on several profound challenges facing individuals with different abilities as a specific cultural group. The present chapter was developed from both a historical and theoretical context, as well as from my personal experiences and unique observations as a young woman living with a rare genetic bone disease, which has made me a distinctly discernible member of the differently-abled community. Commentary on samples of the limited existing research on the differently-abled community is also included in this exposition to promote understanding of the community's culture, and to advocate for the community's equality and full inclusion, not merely integration. In addition, suggestions for helping professionals who work with and on behalf of the differently-abled community will be offered. Furthermore, while this chapter focuses on individuals with physical conditions, it must be recognized that individuals diagnosed with psychiatric, cognitive, and other developmental challenges are also valuable members of the differently-abled community.

History of Discrimination

Euthanasia, experimentation, and extermination are practices noted in the histories of numerous cultural groups. Whether directly or indirectly, these oppressive methods have been used to assert power and superiority by the perpetrating forces over their targets. Assisted suicide among older adults remains a controversial form of euthanasia (Rosenfeld 2000). Many argue that this practice, in addition to being immoral, reinforces the devaluation of older adults in society and the influence of *ageism* (e.g., Nelson 2005). The Tuskegee Syphilis Study, an experiment with which White researchers deceptively dominated and denigrated Black participants, is a prominent example of the many tragic events in the history of the African American community (Gray 1998). The genocide of approximately six million individuals belonging to the Jewish community during the Holocaust is arguably the most horrendous and infamous practice of extermination against a particular group (United States Holocaust Memorial Museum 2013). Nonetheless, there are countless more incidences of euthanasia, experimentation, and extermination affecting various cultural groups that have occurred throughout the history of the world, and regrettably more to follow. Moreover, it can be argued that all of these acts of terror are, at their core, motivated by a lack of acceptance for cultural diversity.

In contrast to the historical events cited above, what is not nearly as well known are the numerous acts of euthanasia, experimentation, extermination, and other forms of overt control that have been and continue to be committed against the differently-abled community, including forced sterilization, revocation of parental rights, and various methods of abuse. Furthermore, these acts of oppression are so easily perpetrated because of the community's persistent – albeit unwanted – state of vulnerability and dependence on others, as its members continue to live in a world that is slow to promote their equal rights and independent functioning.

As an abhorrent illustration, Adolf Hitler included individuals with different abilities among the cultural groups he targeted with his extermination practices, considering them definitively subhuman (USHMM 2013). Prior to World War II, however, the biosocial movement known as *eugenics* had already begun in the United States. Through the experimental measures of *selective breeding* and *sterilization*, this ostensibly progressive practice sought to eliminate what were deemed undesirable genetic traits in humans by promoting the production of desirable features, which certainly would not have included any form of different ability. Indeed, the goal was to eradicate the differently-abled community. It was the eugenics programs in America, in fact, that inspired Hitler to pursue his goal of creating a perfect Aryan race in Europe (Kühl 1994).

Fortunately, not every member of the differently-abled community has faced death or torture at the hands of an injudicious politician or scientific leader. Nevertheless, the freedom of countless differently-abled children, youth, and adults capable of living happy, productive, self-sufficient lives has been seized by institutionalization and other methods of oppression. What is more, the freedom of these individuals was restricted simply because someone with the power of authority decided they were abnormal, mentally ill, or born with genetic defects that allegedly made them incapable of living freely in society. Consequently, the resources and supports that would enable independent living were not afforded. An example of more overt oppression occurred during the first few decades of the twentieth century, when individuals diagnosed with Schizophrenia were institutionalized in asylums – another questionable practice – and used as test subjects for that period's novel forms of psychiatric treatment, namely *electroconvulsive therapy* (*ECT*), or *shock therapy* (Shorter and Healy 2007). In the modern era, the differently-abled community is still struggling to enforce its right to self-determination and equity.

Another notable means by which the unequal status of the differently-abled community is perpetuated today is public media. Most cinematic productions featuring an actor who is differently abled, or that depict the life story of someone with a different ability, regardless of the historical context, portray the protagonist's experience with experimentation, exploitation, or exile. At the very least, the differently-abled character is the target of every joke, mocked and demeaned with each punch line. Rarely do films, shows, or other theatrical performances feature a powerful hero, engaging main character, or beautiful love interest played by an actor who is differently abled, and that are not classified in the comedy genre. Dare I ask how many fashion magazines have ever featured a woman or man sitting in a wheelchair on the front cover? If members of the differently-abled community are granted such spotlight, it is most often a charitable act. The evolution of what society perceives as naturally beautiful does not yet include different abilities; nor are different abilities considered assets for social capital.

Evolution of Theory

While numerous acts of discrimination have been and continue to be committed against members of the differently-abled community, over the course of the last century, several theological frameworks have been proposed to explain the causes of this oppression, and to facilitate society's understanding of the community's experience. The efficacy of these sociological models is arguably ambiguous; however, each paradigm shift represents progress in the civil rights movement for individuals with different abilities.

The first of these models to develop was the *medical model*, which upholds that members of the differently-abled community have physical, cognitive, or psychiatric deficits requiring correction. If these medical errors are not corrected, furthermore, the individuals who possess them are doomed to suffer the cessation of financial or even medical assistance, ruptures within the family system, or judgments from professionals that the individuals have not come to terms with their conditions (Pfeiffer 2000).

Likewise, the *rehabilitation model* views different abilities as a problem with independent functioning. The defect is located in the individual, and there is an onus imposed upon professionals to cure the community by eliminating what is viewed as disease (Lutz and Bowers 2003). Paradoxically, while my diagnosis is classified as a bone *disease*, I have never considered myself as having an ailment, or being in need of a cure.

Another major theoretical paradigm used to address issues affecting individuals who are differently abled is the *social constructivist model* (Pfeiffer 2000). This model asserts that the experience of being "disabled" is the result of society's negative perceptions of the differently-abled community, rather than medical symptomatology. Under this model, individuals with different abilities are viewed by those outside of the community as dependent, deficient, and even tragic because of what are deemed to be abnormalities that cause an inability to function properly in society. Inequality, therefore, is the result of discriminatory cognitive schemas.

Complementing the theory of social constructivism, the *oppressed minority model* suggests that the differently-abled community is oppressed by those who are not differently abled through the denial of common resources and lack of cultural understanding, which consequently reduces individuals with different abilities to second-class citizenship (Pfeiffer 2000). Members of other cultural groups, primarily African Americans, have also been connected with this model (Balcazar et al. 2010).

Developed during the 1960s, the *social model* is a combination of social constructivism and the oppressed minority model, and it explains that the psychosocial experiences associated with "disability" are the consequences of sociopolitical and physical – that is, environmental – barriers (Lutz and Bowers 2003). Simply put, the social model asserts that the differently-abled community is discriminated against, marginalized, and oppressed because society fails to uphold the community's full inclusion. To combat this discrimination, proponents of the social model support equal rights, autonomy, and responsibilities for all members of the differently-abled community, which is achieved through empowerment, self-determination, and activism (Lutz and Bowers 2003). In opposition to the medical model, the social model does not identify the challenges faced by individuals with different abilities as symptoms of their medical conditions, but rather as products of restrictive social environments (Swain et al. 1993). Thus, complete accommodation and not medical treatment would eliminate inequality.

Despite any validity that may be found in these paradigms, none of the models is exclusively sufficient to capture the comprehensive experiences of the differently-abled community, including the *feminist theory* (Nosek and Hughes 2003). For example, the medical model does not consider the psychological and social implications of being differently abled. The social model does not adequately address the importance of advances in medical technology. Consequently, to address the gaps in these models, additional theoretical frameworks have been proposed – paradigms that attribute the challenges associated with being differently abled to various forms of discrimination, such as *handicapism* and *ableism* (Pfeiffer 2000). These models propose that when members of the differently-abled community are treated justly and equally, psychosocial challenges are minimized and physical challenges are more easily overcome.

Indeed, when I am treated as I prefer to be, my experience supports these theories; given that it is in these moments I do not *feel* different. I emphasize the effect on my emotional experience because, while just and equitable treatment from society greatly reduces the psychological and social implications of my diagnosis, the physical symptomatology of my medical condition will always remain. Nevertheless, being embraced by society as a unique rather than deficient individual greatly ameliorates the challenges associated with the physical symptomatology of my diagnosis. Moreover, along with identifying that different abilities manifest physically, psychiatrically, and cognitively, and that each subgroup has its own history of discrimination, it is important to acknowledge that the conditions classified under each subgroup can be categorized as either *congenital* or *acquired* – that is, conditions present at birth or conditions that develop as a result of injury or illness, respectively. This division is helpful for understanding the extent of the challenges faced by the differently-abled community. Furthermore, there are numerous diagnoses classified under each subgroup.

Living with a Congenital Condition

Individuals living with physical different abilities are challenged daily to overcome the variable trials associated with their respective medical conditions. For me, like many others, this process began in utero. My postpartum diagnosis was preceded by my excessive crying, which could not be quelled by food, a clean diaper, or any of the usual treatments for an apparently unhappy newborn. Only when a pediatric orthopedist was consulted was the major fracture in my leg discovered – an injury that likely occurred at the hands of a nurse who was innocently unaware of my remarkably fragile condition. Several smaller or "hairline" fractures were also present, signifying the trauma that resulted from the physical pressure I was exposed to during the birthing process. After just a few days of life in the world, I was diagnosed with *Type III* of a rare congenital condition called *Osteogenesis Imperfecta*, abbreviated as *OI* and commonly known in the medical field as *brittle bone disease*.

In addition to producing low bone density, OI has limited my growth. As an adult, I stand at about 4 ft, which is actually quite tall for the OI community, and a feature I do not take for granted. Throughout my childhood, I used a manual wheelchair and later a walker and forearm crutches for mobility. I now typically ambulate independently; however, for relatively long distances and in crowded public settings, I opt for the assistance of either my crutches or my wheelchair, to reduce physical exertion and increase safety.

As suggested by my ability to choose whether or not to use a mobility aid on most occasions, Type III is not the most severe form of OI. Nevertheless, in less than 30 years of life, I have endured more than a dozen fractures and undergone numerous surgical procedures, all of which resulted in additional fractures. Each of these fractures, furthermore, was as painful as the last, despite the theory of diminishing trauma once dubiously purported to my mother by a pediatric orthopedist. The recovery process after each operation was also painful and emotionally taxing. Moreover, the physical trials I experience daily as a result of living with OI are notably difficult, including pain and stiffness in my joints, deterioration in my acetabula (hip sockets), and a "progressively deforming" skeleton, as physicians have described.

Yet my experience with physical pain is certainly not unique. Indeed, there are millions of individuals living with countless types of different abilities who are challenged with overcoming this burden every day; and for many, their pain is extreme. I have met individuals who have endured painful, debilitating, and often repeated operations on their arms, legs, backs, and other areas, resulting in far more physical trauma than I have experienced. Furthermore, there are other individuals with short stature who have even elected to undergo excruciating limb-lengthening procedures in the pursuit of adding just inches to their height, or to extend the reach of their arms. I would argue that these elective procedures serve as evidence that the challenges of being differently abled extend beyond the physical.

That an individual with a different ability would choose to endure additional physical pain as an antidote for the negative psychological ramifications of ableism is one of many profound indications of the dire need for change in society's thinking and behavior toward the differently-abled community. Moreover, in developing nations, where advanced and elective medical procedures like the aforementioned are unknown, let alone available, most individuals who are differently abled are tragically cast aside. Thus, whether it is the physical, political, or psychosocial barriers that are most prominent in each individual's nation of residence, the members of the differently-abled community find themselves living in a world that was not built for them, that typically does not fight for them, and that – even if inadvertently – does not welcome them. There could be no greater reason for change.

Living with an Acquired Condition

While the physical and psychological trails encountered by individuals with congenital conditions such as OI are notable, the adversity facing individuals with acquired conditions is uniquely challenging. Individuals with acquired conditions are not only faced with adjusting – whether gradually or abruptly – to the symptomatology of their altered physical conditions, they are also confronted with the harsh stigma and discrimination that surrounds the differently-abled community. Moreover, individuals with acquired conditions are challenged to reconcile their new status as a member of the differently-abled community while trying to maintain a connection to their original communities. Thus, the stages of grief are also commonly experienced by individuals with acquired conditions – grief for the loss of their former physical ability and their former identities, as new identities must be formed because of a change in functioning. The families of individuals with acquired conditions are often challenged by the processes of grief, acceptance, and adjustment as well (Livneh and Antonak 2005). If an individual with an acquired condition is also a woman, a person of color, and identifies as gay, for instance, the trails associated with forming a new identity are multiplied.

To illustrate: A soldier whose primary identity was founded on his ability to perform highly physical tasks in military combat, and who has now returned from overseas after losing his leg, will likely experience sadness, frustration, and even anger as he navigates the process of redefining his identity. A single mother who develops multiple sclerosis (MS), and consequently observes her physical ability progressively declining, may experience grief and fear as she is forced to redefine her role in the lives of her young children while learning to manage her increasing physical pain. A man from the Congo whose ability to walk was a casualty of civil war must now develop the resilience needed to find alternative means of securing his family's basic needs, in a region where wheelchairs and other needed resources are scarce, and where jobs are reserved for those with no physical limitations. An older lesbian woman who recently lost her sight to diabetic retinopathy must now learn to navigate through a world she can no longer see, in a rural city where public transportation is not available, with her partner and gay peers living miles away. In the lives of these individuals, the marginalizing effects of intersectionality manifest tremendously.

Hence, whether the origin of an individual's different ability is congenital or acquired, several additional factors challenge the process of identity formation and adjustment to life roles for members of the differently-abled community. One of these factors is the degree to which independent daily functioning is challenged, which may gradually worsen or improve (Livneh and Antonak 2005). Accordingly, although OI causes progressive deformity of the skeleton, though what is considered deformed is highly subjective, it would be blatantly misleading to suggest that my daily functioning is not remarkably independent. While I may not, for example, be able to access half of the items on the shelves of grocery stores or fit into most age-appropriate clothing, most of my daily activities are unhindered. For many other members of the differently-abled community, this is not the case. Being able to lie down, sit up, stand, walk, bathe, dress, eat, speak, hear, and see are invaluable abilities that not everyone can perform without assistance, if at all.

Furthermore, I must acknowledge the relative infrequency in which I require painful medical treatment, or simply any form of medical care. Indeed, medical care is yet another factor that challenges identity formation and causes psychological stress for many members of the differently-abled community. In addition, medical care is often exacerbated by a costly financial burden (Livneh and Antonak 2005). While many individuals with different abilities living in the United States have some form of health insurance, there are millions more who do not (Brault 2012). Moreover, for members of the differently-abled community living around the world whose conditions and therefore lives would be greatly improved with even simple medical treatment, health care is a foreign concept, and thus often never received.

The Impact of Stigma

In addition to the degree to which independent functioning is challenged, social stigma significantly increases the complexity of life for individuals with different abilities (Phemister and Crewe 2004). The severity of a differently-abled individual's psychological challenges, therefore, is not necessarily equivalent to the degree of the individual's physical limitations. Moreover, the psychological challenges are typically greater and often indelible, as both the pain resulting from physical symptoms and the harm created by society's responses, or lack thereof, to what is observed create compounding negative effects on the psyche of each community member. Fittingly, I do not feel challenged when I require costly modifications to be added to my vehicle or my clothing to be altered, in order for these items to accommodate my size; or when I remain on the sidelines while watching friends play sports; or even when I am lying in a hospital bed after a painful operation or accidental injury. Rather, I feel challenged – that is, psychologically – by the negative thoughts and resulting uninformed actions of those who do not embrace the differently-abled community.

Furthermore, it is arguable that the negative perceptions espoused by those who are not differently abled not only harm the personal identities of individuals with different abilities, they also foster deleterious effects on the collective identity of the differently-abled community, similar to the effect a hate crime perpetrated on a person of color or a person who identifies as transgender has on the entire community with which the individual identifies. Yet interestingly, the harmful misperceptions upheld and perpetuated by society, and the consequential exclusionary behavior, are often unintended consequences caused by limited awareness of the true capabilities of the differently-abled community. To that effect, until each member of society is educated on the culture and value of the differently-abled community, the community's members will continue to encounter acts of discrimination, including denial of available resources, reduced social status, and segregation through environmental barriers. The on-going advocacy efforts for individuals with different abilities, therefore, must continue.

As qualitative evidence of the differently-abled community's exposure to discrimination, several of my peers who also use the assistance of wheelchairs have echoed my experience with being treated by those outside of the community as though we cannot think intelligibly – as if our physical exceptionalities indicate a lack of passion, pursuit, and profession, or even basic brain function. For example, a friend I met at my alma mater who is living with cerebral palsy (CP) was once denied the offer of a menu upon entering a restaurant with her mother, who was provided a menu. This friend has a degree in technical writing; her current profession involves editing business contracts. Needless to say, she is more than capable of ordering food from a menu. The hostess more than likely did not intend to offend or oppress my friend. She was merely operating from her experience, which her behavior suggested includes limited interaction with members of the differently-abled community. Nevertheless, while this isolated event may not appear significant on the surface, it represents a common, long-standing perception of the differently-abled community: that its members are incapable.

Yet why should members of the community who do experience difficulty with cognitive processing, psychiatric functioning, or activities of daily living (ADLs) be treated as though they are less valuable or deserving than any other person? The answer: They absolutely should not! Moreover, a lack of positive conceptions and attitudes that espouse this truth can be just as oppressive to the differently-abled community as overt ableism. In other words, passive disregard for the adversity encountered by individuals with different abilities is debatably parallel to active discrimination. Thus, advocacy is a paramount practice, not an elective endeavor. How can the oppression endured by the differently-abled community be eliminated unless the oppressive perceptions of the community are challenged and corrected?

Resilience and Reconciling

One of the most demanding trials for individuals with different abilities is the task of persevering through the life-long process of reconciling personal views of themselves with the narrow perceptions of society, which are manifested socially, politically, and economically. Stated differently, the community is challenged with overcoming the prevalence of negative attitudes and the scarcity of positive attitudes, in order to develop and maintain an affirming identity and achieve life goals. Teaching others to acknowledge that being a member of the differently-abled community is not the only – or even primary – component of each member's individual identity is also challenging, especially when the different ability is visible. For instance, being short is not who I am; it simply determines my clothing sizes. I would sooner identify myself as a woman, a daughter, an aunt, a friend, a spiritual being, a lover of people, a professional, a writer, an advocate, and a public speaker than as a "little person". Truthfully, I do not identify at all as a "little person"; because, while I would not ever change the part of my tangible being that is often the object of scrutiny, I do not define myself by it. Just as a person with green eyes is not likely to define her whole self by the color of her eyes, I perceive my short stature and low bone density simply as physical features of my body, not tangible representations of my being.

Nevertheless, experiences with discrimination make forming and maintaining a positive self-image and identity difficult for the differently-abled community, especially for differently-abled women (Nosek and Hughes 2003). These encounters, furthermore, test the community's resilience far beyond what can be tested by physical challenges. Over the years I have developed much resilience to the uninformed responses of the majority; however, at times, the maintenance of my self-esteem and identity is still thoroughly challenged. Yet I have also developed an understanding that the negative responses I encounter are more often than not the result of society's perpetuated unfamiliarity with the differently-abled community, rather than pure hatred, bigotry, or a blatant desire to offend. (Unfortunately, though, that is not always the case.)

Furthermore, throughout my life thus far, I have received myriad compliments and praises from others – men and women, peers and elders, discreetly and boldly – regarding my character, my personal achievements in academics and occupation, and even parts of my physical appearance. Nevertheless, the enduring dichotomy between positive and negative responses creates an interesting interaction and another unique challenge to my identity formation and maintenance, with which other members of the differently-abled community can very likely empathize.

Reconciling the common negative assessments of my physical appearance from the majority with the whole-hearted affirmations of my personhood from a close few is a complicated process. To that effect, research has indicated that the combination of stigma and objective self-awareness often results in intense self-criticism, and reduces the likelihood of forming of a positive identity (Phemister and Crewe 2004). Considering the negative influence of stigma, it is therefore understandable that, throughout the process of my identity formation, I have pondered: Why do some reject me based on traits that have only positive influences on my character while others seem to accept me openly? Do others compliment me out of pity, guilt, or genuine admiration? Are others truly able to know me, or does my appearance serve as a silent and fixed impediment to uninhibited relationship? Where am I safe to be myself? Can I share my unique experiences with others without causing them emotional discomfort?

While the answers to these questions remain fluid and somewhat elusive, I have deduced conclusions that satisfactorily support an overall positive identity by dissecting the sources of the positive and negative information: Those who encourage me have close relationships with me; those who ridicule me do not. I choose, therefore, to accept and internalize the responses of those who encourage me, in order to promote a positive self-image and my ability to encourage others, both within and outside of the differently-abled community. Thus, I also diligently monitor my reactions to those who reject me, in order to assure that I display behavior that encourages them to be more accepting of the community I proudly represent – another challenging endeavor.

The Value of Allies

The psychological challenges that accompany different abilities are not limited to the individuals who possess them; family members and friends are also affected. In addition to the overwhelming emotional pain my parents experience when I suffer a broken bone or am wheeled into an operating room on a gurney, they continue to be frustrated by the stigma attached to their daughter's condition. Similarly, my friends have verbalized their feelings of anger and annoyance when they have observed unkind glances from strangers aimed in my direction, especially during the beginning of our friendships. My older brother is also deeply affected when he witnesses acts of discrimination committed against me.

I recall a memorable incident that occurred a few years ago when my brother and I went out with a group of friends to have a few drinks and shoot a few games of pool. My brother was the only man in the group; so he held the door for the ladies as we entered the bar. I entered first, with my mission to secure the prime pool table; my friends followed. Not realizing my brother was part of the group of women for whom he had just held the door, the bouncer caught my brother's attention as he entered the bar and whispered something like, "Hey, did you see that *midget* who just walked in?" My brother's response was, "Yeah, my *sister!*" By this time in our lives, being in our early twenties, my brother was well aware that "midget" is the label that vexes me most. Needless to say, he was now terribly vexed by the bouncer's question.

Not long after that brief albeit impactful dialog, of which I was initially oblivious, the group and I received a free round of drinks from the bar manager, with his sincerest apologies for the behavior of his staff member. We were also informed that the bouncer was sent home without recompense that night. I later learned that these reparations were the result of my brother having a respectful yet assertive conversation with the manager on my behalf. Realizing how upsetting the incident was for my brother, because of his love for me, while the free drinks were appreciated, I certainly would have preferred that the incident had not occurred. Nevertheless, my brother's unwavering defense of my dignity strengthened our bond; and, as his actions have continued to show, I know he will always be one of my most formidable advocates.

Though memorable, the recounted incident is merely one of numerous occasions during which my brother, parents, and other close allies have supported my life's value. Moreover, while I could have taken offense to the bouncer's ignorant question, I was instead hurt by the effect of his words on my brother. Indeed, I am typically more disheartened by the negative consequences that acts of discrimination create for my family and friends than they do for me. As the target, I have developed a greater immunity. Yet during the encounter at the bar, I was encouraged by my brother's passionate support. His commitment to advocating for me not only makes me proud of him, it also reminds me that the fight for advocacy and full inclusion is not over. My brother's actions also symbolize the importance and efficacy of peer support for promoting the psychosocial well-being of the differently-abled community.

I once asked my mother to identify the most challenging aspect of having and raising a daughter who is differently abled. Her response was feeling alone. Not long after my birth, my mother was connected with a support group for parents of children with different abilities. Despite the obvious psychosocial benefits of this group, my mother still felt challenged by caring for such a fragile infant, whose condition was entirely foreign to her prior to my birth. When I asked my father the same question, his response was that he constantly worried about me being hurt, physically and emotionally – a sentiment my mother shared.

Conversely, when I asked my mother what the best aspect of having and raising a daughter who is differently abled was, she replied that it was and still is the joy of having a wonderful daughter. When I asked my father this question, his response was that my uniqueness helped create a closer connection between us. Both my mother's and father's responses identify my uniqueness as a strength, wonderfully reminiscent of the *strengths perspective* upheld by the social work profession. Moreover, while my parents' responses were developed from their personal experiences, their feelings are notably common to many parents of children with different abilities (Berry 2009; Burke 2008). My parents desire the best for me; yet they maintain a conscious understanding that the world sees me through a highly distorted and prejudiced view.

I asked my brother, who is just 15 months older yet over 2 ft taller than me, a modified version of the question I asked my parents – that is, what was or is the most challenging aspect and the best aspect about having a sister who is differently abled? With credit to his honesty, my brother shared that the most challenging experience for him was observing and adjusting to the additional attention I received from our parents during our childhood, due to my fragile condition, which at times made my brother feel as though our parents loved me more than they loved him. My brother's experience is very common for siblings of children with different abilities (Berry 2009; Burke 2008). Still, my brother clarified that this was his perception only before he fully understood why our parents gave additional attention to my unique needs.

My brother now appreciates the person I have become, how my experiences – both positive and negative – have fostered great resilience. Furthermore, my brother also believes I could have used my different ability as an excuse to be dependent on others; and thus conformed to one of society's misconstrued and generalized perceptions of the differently-abled community. On the contrary, the community seeks greater independence, not dependence.

My parents' and brother's statements and actions strongly reinforce my gratitude for the love and support of my family. Their encouragement has been and is vital for the on-going fulfillment of my potential, as a woman, daughter, sister, aunt, and professional. Their practical and emotional support has also spurred my motivation to continue advocating for the differently-abled community, in both public and private settings. They have shown me how impactful love and encouragement is for successfully overcoming the challenges associated with my medical condition and society's reactions to it. In other words, because my family has such deep and genuine affection for me, they have helped teach me how to love and support other members of the differently-abled community. In addition, as I did not have a differently-abled family member, friend, or public figure to model after during my childhood and adolescent years, the love and support of my family and friends who embraced my difference spurred my ability to accept and value myself, to strive to become my own exemplar, and to value cultural diversity.

As my experience attests, *social connectedness* has been shown to significantly alleviate the deleterious effects of stigma by supporting and validating self-worth (e.g., Crisp 1996, as cited in Dell Orto and Power 2007). Accordingly, support from those outside of the differently-abled community is instrumental for improving the status of individuals with different abilities; and thus for advancing the community's full inclusion. Not every member of the differently-abled community, however, experiences social connectedness with allies, which is why promoting advocacy and advancing social justice is so crucial. In order for individuals with different abilities to thrive and achieve, relationships must exist. To that effect, I am truly grateful for and highly value the connections I have developed with peers, professors, and colleagues. As an expression of that gratitude, I dedicate this chapter to them, and to all allies of the differently-abled community, those who look beyond the physical. Thank you for seeing a person, not a body.

Intersectionality and the Power of Empathy

As suggested in the initial comments on intersectionality, a number of cultural groups have been identified by society as having divergent physical appearance, diminished overall ability, and reduced social status. Consequently, the members of these groups, which include women, people of color, and the LGBTQ community, are often treated as though they possess lesser human value because of their gender, ethnicity, sexual identity or expression, and so on. These groups can therefore empathize with the differently-abled community, as they have also historically been omitted from descriptions of who is worthy and deserving of equality (Balcazar et al. 2010). Indeed, throughout my life I have been able to form relationships with members of these groups with much less effort than with members of the majority, which I attribute to a shared – albeit mostly unspoken – understanding of stigma and discrimination. Furthermore, it is possible that individuals who identify with these cultural groups and who are differently abled are the most familiar with stigma, oppression, and marginalization, especially those living in developing nations where the full inclusion of the differently-abled community is not as easily advanced, due to resource limitations and a priority for meeting basic needs.

While it is deducible that women, people of color, members of the LGBTQ community, and other historically persecuted cultural groups share more than one common experience with members of the differently-abled community, some researchers argue against drawing such between-group comparisons (e.g., Henderson and Bryan 2011). Among other arguments, these academics assert that individuals who are differently abled are so different from each other that even making within-group comparisons is impractical. Conversely, proponents of intersectionality favor these comparisons (Balcazar et al. 2010). A counterargument could indeed be made for engaging between-group and within-group comparisons when researching the differently-abled community, as well as a third approach.

Between-group comparisons can promote social support among the members of varying groups by promoting empathy. Within-group comparisons can help researchers identify how to cultivate social justice for an entire group – that is, by identifying gaps in research in order to promote the group's social status and improve its functioning. Thirdly, a *person-in-environment* (*PIE*) approach enables helping professionals to acknowledge and address the unique challenges facing each individual client; in this case, individuals with different abilities (Engel 1977, as cited in Dell Orto and Power 2007). Moreover, a PIE orientation to the helping process facilitates the implementation of best practice methods to employ with each client, pursuant to the individual's needs, cultural identification, and environment (Bishop 2005).

The experiences of women with different abilities can be used to illustrate the application of between-group and within-group comparisons and PIE, along with the challenges associated with intersectionality. Women who are differently abled share experiences with women in general. They also share experiences with the differently-abled community as a whole. Moreover, differently-abled women with the same diagnosis will have additional common experiences. Every woman with a different ability, however, has her own unique life story – one that is unlike any other woman with a different ability, regardless of any similarities. Therefore, when advocating for women who are differently abled, their experiences as women, their experiences as members of the differently-abled community, their experiences as unique individuals, and how all of these factors intersect must be considered (Nosek and Hughes 2003).

Expanding on the experiences of this subgroup, a major challenge for women with different abilities is that they are primarily viewed as *asexual*, or genderless. This largely explains why the sexuality of differently-abled women, which includes sexual identity and expression, is rarely acknowledged let alone supported (Esmail et al. 2010; Schriempf 2001). Women with different abilities are mostly regarded as having no sexual passions, abilities, or rights; to think otherwise is considered perverse, inappropriate at the least. This prejudice is the primary catalyst for sexual oppression and other social barriers that inhibit the establishment of romantic partnerships (Esmail et al. 2010). Consequently, differently-abled women are inconvenienced with the ridiculous task of enlightening others to the fact that they do desire intimate relationships, as the average person does. This imposition, furthermore, typically causes women with different abilities to feel compelled either to prove that they are capable of participating in romantic partnerships or, conversely, to hide their sexuality; thus, inadvertently supporting society's inaccurate perception that they are asexual.

Differently-abled women are then faced with another challenging task: finding a romantic partner who perceives them as genuinely desirable – a partner who can accept what are deemed to be socially unacceptable differences. As part of this process, differently-abled women must overcome potential partners' hindering self-reflective questions: Can a woman who uses a wheelchair have sex? Do I want to date a girl who cannot walk? What will people think if I marry a woman who is that short? How am I supposed to be intimate with a girl who cannot see? What am I supposed to do if she has a seizure while we are on a date?

Queries like these allude to the reality that the relational needs and sexual identities of differently-abled women are not only significantly affected by physical challenges, but also by society's prejudiced view of their functional capabilities (Nosek and Hughes 2003). Fortunately, the latter can be eliminated through advocacy and education (Esmail et al. 2010). Nevertheless, the overall life experience of women with different abilities remains influenced by the intersection of gender, membership in the differently-abled community, and the common misconceptions of individuals with different abilities in general. Women with different abilities, therefore, also encounter the challenges faced by the entire differently-abled community, which include environmental, sociopolitical, and economic barriers.

Eliminating Barriers to Promote Inclusion and Equality

I am both a woman and differently abled; therefore, I am personally familiar with many of the challenges faced by differently-abled women. Yet I am also a young professional with two university degrees, a burgeoning career as a Masters level social worker, access to a variety of economic and sociopolitical resources, seemingly limitless opportunities to continue advocating for social justice, and highly independent overall functioning. Thus, my life is far less challenged than the lives of most individuals with different abilities living outside of North America, women and men, and undoubtedly many living within North America.

I recount my successes and prosperity not for self-adulation, but rather as a testament to the truth that being differently abled is not an automatic indicator of an inherent inability to achieve excellence. On the contrary, having significant challenges in one or more facets of life often produces relative brilliance in another. Nevertheless, in order for members of the differently-abled community to accomplish goals, various accommodations and resources specific to each individual's physical, psychiatric, or cognitive abilities are often required, along with cultural understanding – considerations many nations cannot or, worse, choose not to afford.

To illustrate the above statements, hundreds of thousands, possibly millions of young people with physical different abilities living in developing nations – India, for example – who have just as much potential for occupational success and valuable contribution to their nation's economy and society as I do, will never see the inside of a university classroom or secure gainful employment. While the resources to do so are available, universities and businesses are not built to accommodate individuals with different abilities, such as with ramp access, simply because those who construct the buildings are not conscious of the importance of these modifications (Halder 2008). Furthermore, laws that mandate such accommodations, like the *Americans with Disabilities Act (ADA) of 1990* (United States Code 2008), are still being developed.

Thus, even the differently-abled students who may be able to secure transportation (yet another challenge) to their local universities cannot attend classes because they cannot physically enter the campus. Consequently, so many exceptional minds filled with limitless potential are neglected; and the upward social mobility that is significantly advanced with a degree in higher education is thwarted. These individuals, therefore, are at an even greater disadvantage for securing their basic needs independently in a nation with a vast population and unrelenting competition for employment. Moreover, as further evidence of the deleterious impact of intersectionality, this disadvantage is exponentially greater for female students living in highly patriarchal societies (Halder 2008).

The environmental or structural barriers found on university campuses and other public facilities all over the world are not the only impediment to full independence and self-sufficiency for the differently-abled community. Caste systems that place the differently-abled community at the bottom are still widely enforced, designating individuals with different abilities as the *untouchables* (Anant 1972). These hierarchies of social status are likely the antecedents of environmental barriers; and the diminished status assigned to the differently-abled community appears to be present in some form – whether consciously or not – in every nation. Indeed, certain cultures even consider the medical conditions of individuals with different abilities to be consequences of familial sin, or manifestations of evil spirits (Munyi 2012). These beliefs are not exclusive to developing nations. An American colleague once shared with me that a client of his informed him I must have behaved very poorly in my past life, as my current corporal vessel is the resulting consequence of my justly karma.

Furthermore, millions of members of the differently-abled community living in Africa, South America, and elsewhere cannot leave their homes because they do not have wheelchairs and there is no one to carry them, nor any other appropriate means of transport, indicating a dire lack of necessary resources. Still, countless individuals with different abilities do not even have a home because they have been rejected by their families and geographic communities, due solely to the notion that being "abnormal" is unacceptable. The rejection of individuals with different abilities around the world, therefore, is not always the result of economic limitations. Rather, members of the differently-abled community are often exiled and even killed because of lasting cultural mores that classify the community as helpless and hopeless (Munyi 2012).

From the above descriptions, it is evident that the physical, psychological, and social challenges individuals with different abilities face are augmented by the environmental and political restrictions imposed on the differently-abled community as a result of society's negative reception of the community members' differences. Moreover, those in power often lack the understanding or desire to allocate resources to accommodate the community – that is, to help individuals with different abilities fulfill their potential. These barriers, again, are why advocacy and education are the pinnacle and foundational efforts to achieving full inclusion for the differently-abled community. Moreover, the lack of complete accommodation in public transportation, schools, businesses, and other public settings threatens the community with the unwelcomed constraints of dependence.

What is more, when individuals with different abilities and the community's allies come to learn of the procedures and protocols that must be navigated – the proverbial political hoops that must be jumped through – in order to eliminate these and other barriers, effecting change can seem like an insurmountable challenge. Yet there is hope for progress. Indeed, I have witnessed others effecting change on my behalf and for other members of the differently-abled community, with no evidence of bureaucratic obstructions or resource limitations; thus, signifying that inclusion is possible. We must continue the movement.

Advocacy in Action

A poignant first-hand example of how change can be effected for the differently-abled community occurred in the summer of 2009 during a study abroad program I completed in Monterrey, Mexico. Every weekday morning for the 2-month duration of the program, my classmates and I walked from our apartment complex to the campus of the Mexican university where our Spanish classes were held. The side entrance of the university we were instructed to use had a very steep curb, about 18 inches high – quite an obstacle for a young woman who stands 4 ft tall.

One morning toward the end of my time in Monterrey, I turned the corner to face the monstrous curb leading into the campus, only to find that overnight the curb had transformed into two stairs. I was stunned. As I looked up, I saw the two university employees who checked the students' identification cards every morning. They were awaiting my reaction with restrained anticipation. I immediately smiled as brightly as I could and thanked the men enthusiastically in their native language. Not only did the actions of those men advocate for my needs, but as the stairs are a permanent modification to the physical environment, they forever improved the accessibility of the campus for future students and faculty.

I made no form of request to the Mexican university to modify the curb I initially struggled to maneuver during my study abroad program; however, much of the limited research on policies affecting the differently-abled community supports the idea that these policies are best developed and most effectively implemented when members of the community collaborate and utilize the knowledge acquired from personal experiences to achieve the needed change. Moreover, this practice, founded on the principles of *participatory action research* (*PAR*), promotes the community's self-determination (Tate and Pledger 2003). The utility of PAR is not only valuable for helping professionals who work directly with members of the differently-abled community, but for all allies whose work is intended to advance the rights of the community.

Indeed, in order for individuals living with different abilities to achieve full participation in the policy-making process, they must be fully heard. The differently-abled community's challenges, experiences, concerns, hopes, and goals must be acknowledged and advanced to develop the most efficient and effective policies to promote the rights of the community – rights that are equally important to those of any other community.

Motivated by the tenets of PAR, I wrote a letter to my alma mater's School of Social Work as a project for one of the policy courses I completed during my graduate program. In the letter, I proposed that all occurrences of the words "disability/ies" and "disabled" in the School's curriculum and administrative documentation be replaced with the terms "different ability/ies" and "differently-abled," respectively. My intention with this proposal was to advocate for the differently-abled community by upholding the importance of using *person-centered* or *person-first language* that is empowering, rather than perpetuating normative terminology. It was and still is my perspective that the current universal terms used to reference the differently-abled community are highly stigmatizing, as they maintain the medical model's standard of emphasizing what is deemed deficient; they foster a negative context.

In other words, individuals with different abilities are categorized as "*dis*abled" because there is something "*dys*functional" with their bodies or minds. Accordingly, I felt eliminating this terminology was especially appropriate for an academic program that is founded on the strengths perspective. Most importantly, I believed this proposal, whether or not it was accepted, would create opportunities for students and faculty to examine their personal perceptions of the differently-abled community. More specifically, it would prompt an examination of the automatic thoughts that are generated by the words "disability" and "disabled."

My individual advocacy efforts as a graduate student and emerging professional may not yet have extended far beyond the confines of my alma mater's School of Social Work, or the audiences I have spoken to at NASW Conferences. Nevertheless, history has shown how the synthesis of small efforts by many individuals often collectively produces large advancements in social justice, especially when these efforts are performed by members of the community for which they are intended.

It is not widely known that during the Civil Rights Movement of the 1960s, which produced historical sociopolitical advancements for the African American community, the differently-abled community had begun its own civil rights movement (Balcazar et al. 2010). Accordingly, while greater political advancement is still needed for the differently-abled community, if the self-advocates and allies had not pursued greater political presence and social justice than the community was afforded in 1960, the ADA and subsequent ground-breaking legislation would likely never have developed.

Advancing the Civil Rights Movement

Notwithstanding the indelible familiarity of the differently-abled community with discrimination, stigma, and marginalization, the community's civil rights movement has made and is making significant progress. As with other civil rights movements, adversity, conflict, legislation, protests, research, technology, and many other elements have influenced this progress. From the passing of the ADA in 1990, to the establishment of countless non-profit organizations, to individual acts of advocacy – like my brother's passionate defense of my dignity – all of these measures serve to advance the community's equality; and they are occurring all over the world.

Therefore, as agents of change pursuing the utopian goal of social justice, it is vital for social workers and other helping professionals to continue addressing the needs and promoting the rights of individuals with different abilities. Utilizing direct practice, community organizing, public policy, and other interventional methods, professionals in various fields can engage their skills in order to advance the differently-abled community's attainment of full inclusion in society – that is, to eliminate segregation and achieve equity. The prejudiced and stigmatizing attitudes still upheld by society that equate different abilities with weakness, dysfunction, and inferiority must be challenged and eradicated. What is more, individuals with different abilities must be empowered to engage in more self-advocacy. Who better to represent and educate others on the community's abilities, needs, and rights than its members?

In order to effectively eliminate prejudiced perspectives of the differently-abled community, it is advantageous for helping professionals and members of the community to first understand why prejudice against individuals with different abilities exists. Research aimed at answering this question has identified three causes: ethnocentrism, lack of significant interaction with members of the community, and preference for categorization. According to this research, *ethnocentrism* refers to the belief that a particular culture is superior to all others. Furthermore, manifestations of ethnocentrism often occur unconsciously, such as when individuals with different abilities are institutionalized based on the argument that institutionalization is for their benefit, whether or not those being institutionalized agree. Lack of interaction with members of the differently-abled community, understandably, is often a secondary consequence of ethnocentrism (Henderson and Bryan 2011). How can people come to appreciate the differently-abled community if they do not develop relationships with anyone from the community?

When individuals who are differently abled are institutionalized, they are not able to remain in their respective geographic, familial, and other natural communities. As a result, those who are not differently abled are denied opportunities to become familiar with the differently-abled culture, and to develop relationships with members of the differently-abled community. They are also, therefore, prevented from learning to appreciate the individual challenges and strengths of the community. This segregation consequently fosters prejudice and leads to discrimination, such as the sexual oppression commonly experienced by differently-abled women. Preference for categorization also cultivates prejudice by contributing to the association of negative labels with individuals who are differently abled, labels such "dependent," "inferior," and – as I would argue – "*dis*abled" (Henderson and Bryan 2011).

The fact that further research has identified correlations between negative attitudes toward specific groups of people and how those groups are treated is not surprising; nor that how groups are treated, in turn, significantly influences the identify formation of the groups' members. Accordingly, several forms of treatment frequently imposed by society upon individuals who are differently abled include avoidance, pity, and overprotection. In addition, society often projects a *suffering role* on the differently-abled community (Henderson and Bryan 2011). Interestingly, while OI has presented me with numerous physical and psychosocial challenges throughout my life, with certainly more to follow, I have never perceived my brittle bones, short stature, physical pain, or any other symptom of my diagnosis as an indication of suffering. What I suffer, actually, is prejudice from those who think I am suffering and who consequently pity me, avoid me, try to segregate me, or patronize me, whether with helpful or hurtful intent.

Related to suffering the insufferable, Schilder's (1935) notion of *body image* relates to the discomfort others feel when they see a member of the differently-abled community whose difference is physically apparent, because the individual's body is not congruent with what a body is expected to look like (as cited in Henderson and Bryan 2011). Furthermore, the common curious reactions my physical appearance elicits from children suggests that individuals develop an understanding of body image at a very early age. To that effect, I struggle more often to accept my body for how it looks when I observe others responding adversely to my physical composition than when my composition creates challenges with, for example, finding appropriately fitting clothing. To make matters worse, reinforcements from the media on what idealized bodies look like – that is, those permitted to grace magazine covers – only contribute to the perpetuation of prejudice and discrimination against all people with visible different abilities. The bodies of individuals who are differently abled are seldom depicted as beautiful.

To combat the effects of this and the many other challenges faced by the differently-abled community, social workers and other helping professionals must be sensitive to and understanding of this adversity. They must also consider how clients' multiple cultural identities intersect to create their personal experience of the world, such as how a client's experience as a woman is affected by her medical condition and vice versa. Moreover, they must observe how integrated and salient clients' different abilities are in their personal identities. For example, I have been asked numerous times how I would like to be referenced – that is, because of my petite build. My response is always my first name. I have no desire to be characterized by my height or any other physical feature. (Unless, of course, someone wants to call me beautiful!) Yet another individual with OI may proudly identify as a "little person" and prefer to be referenced with that term.

Helping professionals must understand, therefore, that while the cultural groups familiar with discrimination share similar experiences, such as a diagnosis, each client will respond to those experiences uniquely, as an individual. Ultimately, the primary goal of helping professionals should be to empower differently-abled clients to be as self-determining and autonomous as they can be by establishing partnerships rather than dictatorships; and by engaging in a strengths-based perspective (Henderson and Bryan 2011). Additionally, helping professionals must continue to eradicate the prejudices and stigma that surround the differently-abled community through advocacy, education, inclusive practices, and positive language.

Conclusion: Striving for an Inclusive World

The adversity faced by individuals with physical, psychiatric, and cognitive different abilities is undeniably challenging. Moreover, these challenges will only be maintained by the effects of discrimination and oppression until helping professionals, policy makers, and social leaders who work with and on behalf of the differently-abled community adopt a theoretical model and personal mindset that is founded on empowerment, self-determination, and acceptance of the community, just as the community's allies have done. Individual differences of the community's members must not be seen as ailments and deficiencies to be cured, but rather as unique characteristics and strengths that add to the diversity of society, to "the spice of life." Yet the work cannot end there. Helping professionals must apply their new strengths perspective to effect practical change for the differently-abled community, such as through policy, and promote their paradigm shift throughout society – that is, so that the differently-abled community will be viewed globally as a community of unique, capable individuals. Only then will real change be achieved.

To support this change, members of the differently-abled community are encouraged to continue teaching the world about the community's culture and how to respond to it. Furthermore, the community must be given equal access to the environmental, sociopolitical, and economic resources available to those who are not differently abled, in order to achieve this goal and the full inclusion the community ultimately seeks. This is where helping professionals and other leaders can support the equality of the differently-abled community through practices such as legislative action. Only when this is accomplished will individuals with different abilities be able to contribute to society in the greatest capacity, fulfill their potential as citizens of the human race, and create a future for the differently-abled community that is markedly different from its history. Indeed, previous environmental, political, and social advancements have proven that it is possible for society to replace its distorted view of individuals with different abilities as abnormal, deficient, and helpless with an understanding, inclusive, and empowering perspective.

So, in sum, what is to be taken from the present chapter? The objectives of this piece and the research discussed herein were intended to facilitate readers' understanding of the variable factors that affect the personal and political identities of the differently-abled community, in both historical and modern contexts. In addition, the author aimed to provide insights for helping professionals – namely, social workers – that can be utilized to affect positive change for the differently-abled community on the micro, meso, and macro levels of practice. These insights, furthermore, were also intended to spur members of the differently-abled community to be more active in their civil rights movement. Accordingly, it is important to remember that it will require the efforts of social leaders, both differently abled and not, who have skills in the areas of advocacy, policy practice, research, community organizing, education, technology, and social engagement to effectively promote complete equity for the differently-abled community.

Understanding the past, present, and desired future of individuals with different abilities is significant because it facilitates the identification of the community's goals, which are: (1) To promote self-determination, empowerment, and inclusion, not merely integration; (2) To eradicate stigmatizing attitudes that equate differences with weakness, dysfunction, and inferiority (i.e., the elimination of ethnocentrism); (3) To advance self-advocacy and cultural competence; (4) To achieve social, political, and economic equality; and (5) To remove the remaining barriers to education, employment, medical care, recreation, and relationships. Furthermore, the achievement of these goals – that is, the full inclusion of the differently-abled community – is beneficial to society as a whole.

Some poignant examples of this positive impact include: (1) improvement of economic functioning through the addition of more people (both differently abled individuals and those creating inclusive environments) to the global workforce; (2) elevation of the mental and physical well-being of society through the promotion of interconnectedness and personal relationships; (3) increased gains from social capital as various individual traits meet identified needs in personal and professional settings; (4) reduced stigma and discrimination for other communities that are often treated as inferior; and (5) fewer resources expended on predetermined interventions historically employed to address the needs of the differently-abled community, interventions that are often more costly, less timely, and neutrally effective than interventions founded on independence, inclusion, and integration. Thus, through the application of *grounded theory*, it is understood that the consequences resulting from the current experiences of the differently-abled community result in the inverse of the desired phenomenon noted here.

As further guidance for change, the following is an abridging list of suggestions for helping professionals and others outside of the differently-abled community that will promote inclusion for individuals with different abilities: (1) Avoid feelings of pity toward members of the differently-abled community; (2) Create alliances and partnerships, not hierarchies, during personal and professional encounters with members of the community; (3) Ask questions regarding members' experiences respectfully and listen actively; (4) Consider the intersections of multiple identities and cultures for each member, as identification with the differently-abled community is not the sole essence of each member's being; (5) Educate others on the experience of the community, especially children, in order to promote future positive encounters for members; (6) Challenge traditional notions of physical beauty and assumptions about functioning; (7) Implement person-centered approaches to the helping process; (8) Engage strengths-based perspectives; (9) Support more advocacy efforts, both on local and global levels; and (10) Value all life experiences by avoiding comparisons of individuals' functioning.

In closing, being a member of the differently-abled community, having identification with the community, is most often a source of pride for members. Among other accomplishments, our daily challenges make us resilient. Our unique traits contribute to a sense of identity. Our physical scars serve as reminders of the pain we have endured and overcome. Our moments of rejection foster more authentic relationships with our allies. Our encounters with barriers to personal and political freedom engender creativity and perseverance. Inclusion, however, full participation in all that life has to offer, is still our goal. Inclusion would mean having unlimited opportunity to engage our individuality in personal and professional endeavors, not despite functional limitations, but in ways that celebrate our differences. May that dream one day become our reality.

> Until the great mass of the people shall be filled with the sense of responsibility for each other's welfare, social justice can never be attained. – Helen Keller

References

Anant, S. S. (1972). *The changing concept of caste in India*. New Delhi: Vikas Publications.

Balcazar, F. E., Suarez-Balcazar, Y., Taylor-Ritzler, T., & Keys, C. B. (2010). *Race, culture, and disability: Rehabilitation science and practice*. Sudbury: Jones and Bartlett Publishers.

Bass, S., Shield, M. K., & Behrman, R. E. (2004). Addressing the needs of children in foster care. *Children, Families, and Foster Care: Analysis and Recommendations, 14*(1), 5–29.

Baumeister, R. F., & Leary, M. R. (1995). The need to belong: Desire for interpersonal attachments as a fundamental human motivation. *Psychological Bulletin, 117*(3), 497–529.

Berry, J. O. (2009). *Lifespan perspectives on the family and disability* (2nd ed.). Austin: PRO-ED, Inc..

Bishop, M. (2005). Quality of life and psychosocial adaptation to chronic illness and disability: Preliminary analysis of a conceptual and theoretical synthesis. *Rehabilitation Counseling Bulletin, 48*(4), 219–231.

Brault, M. W. (2012). Current population reports. In *Americans with disabilities: 2010 household economic studies*. Retrieved from http://www.census.gov/prod/2012pubs/p70-131.pdf

Burke, P. (2008). *Disability and impairment: Working with children and families*. London: Jessica Kingsley Publishers.

Crenshaw, K. (1989). Demarginalizing the intersection of race and sex: A black feminist critique of antidiscrimination doctrine, feminist theory, and antiracist politics. *University of Chicago Legal Forum, 1989*, 139–167.

Dell Orto, A. E., & Power, P. W. (Eds.). (2007). *The psychological and social impact of illness and disability* (5th ed.). New York: Springer Publishing Company.

Dilmah Australia. (2012, September 5). *Helping the differently abled*. [Video file]. Retrieved from http://youtu.be/l0XswXRY8jQ

Esmail, S., Darry, K., Walter, A., & Knupp, H. (2010). Attitudes and perceptions towards disability and sexuality. *Disability Rehabilitation, 32*(14), 1148–1155.

Glasser, W. (1998). *Choice theory: A new psychology on personal freedom*. New York: HarperCollins Publishers, Inc..

Gray, F. D. (1998). *The Tuskegee syphilis study: An insider's account of the shocking medical experiment conducted by government doctors against African American men*. Montgomery: NewSouth, Inc..

Halder, S. (2008). Rehabilitation of women with physical disabilities in India: A huge gap. *The Australian Journal of Rehabilitation Counseling, 14*(1), 1–15.

Henderson, G., & Bryan, W. V. (2011). *Psychosocial aspects of disability* (4th ed.). Springfield: Charles C. Thomas Publisher, Ltd..

Hochschild, J. L., & Weaver, V. (2007). The skin color paradox and the American racial order. *Social Forces, 86*(2), 643–670.

Kühl, S. (1994). *The Nazi connection: Eugenics, American racism, and German national socialism*. New York: Oxford University Press, Inc..

Livneh, H., & Antonak, R. F. (2005). Psychological adaptation to chronic illness and disability: A primer for counselors. *Journal of Counseling & Development, 83*(1), 12–20.

Lutz, B., & Bowers, B. (2003). Understanding how disability is defined and conceptualized in the literature. *Rehabilitation Nursing, 28*(3), 74–78.

Maslow, A. H. (1943). A theory of human motivation. *Psychological Review, 50*, 370–396.

Moradi, B., & Huang, Y. (2008). Objectification theory and psychology of women: A decade of advances and future directions. *Psychology of Women Quarterly, 32*(4), 377–398.

Munyi, C. W. (2012). Past and present perceptions towards disability: A historical perspective. *Disability Studies Quarterly, 32*(2). Retrieved from http://dsq-sds.org/article/view/3197/3068

Nelson, T. (2005). Ageism: Prejudice against our feared future self. *Journal of Social Issues, 61*(2), 207–221.

Nosek, M. A., & Hughes, R. B. (2003). Psychosocial issues of women with physical disabilities: The continuing gender debate. *Rehabilitation Counseling Bulletin, 46*(4), 224–233.

Ogbu, J. U. (1993). Differences in cultural frame of reference. *International Journal of Behavioral Development, 16*(3), 483–506.

Pfeiffer, D. (2000). The disability paradigm. *Journal of Disability and Policy Studies, 11*, 98–99.

Phemister, A. A., & Crewe, N. M. (2004). Objective self-awareness and stigma: Implications for persons with visible disabilities. *The Journal of Rehabilitation, 70*(2), 33–37.

Rosenfeld, B. (2000). Assisted suicide, depression, and the right to die. *Psychology, Public Policy, and Law, 6*(2), 467–488.

Schriempf, A. (2001). (Re)fusing the amputated body: An interactionist bridge for feminism and disability. *Hypatia, 16*(4), 53–79.

Shontz, F. C. (1977). Six principles relating disability and psychological adjustment. *Rehabilitation Psychology, 24*(4), 207–210.

Shorter, E., & Healy, D. (2007). *Shock therapy: A history of electroconvulsive treatment in mental illness*. New Brunswick: Rutgers University Press.

Small, M. L., Harding, D. J., & Lamont, M. (2010). Reconsidering culture and poverty. *The ANNALS of the American Academy, 629*, 6–27.

Swain, J., Finkelstein, V., French, S., & Oliver, M. (Eds.). (1993). *Towards a psychology of disability: Disabling barriers – Enabling environments*. Thousand Oaks: Sage Publications, Inc..

Tate, D. G., & Pledger, C. (2003). An integrative conceptual framework of disability: New directions for research. *The American Psychologist, 58*(4), 289–295.

Tilcsik, A. (2011). Pride and prejudice: Employment discrimination against openly gay men in the United States. *American Journal of Sociology, 117*(2), 586–626.

United States Code. (2008). *Americans with disabilities act of 1990 (ADA)*. Retrieved from http://www.ada.gov/pubs/adastatute08.pdf

United States Holocaust Memorial Museum. "The Holocaust." (2013). In *Holocaust encyclopedia*. Retrieved from http://www.ushmm.org/wlc/en/?ModuleId=10005143

Part II
Exploring the Complexities of Communication with Differently Abled Persons

Chapter 10
Communication with Persons with Disabilities vs. Communication with Differently Abled Persons

Ivana Bilić

Abstract My efforts regarding persons with disabilities have so far been mainly focused on economic, more precisely on communication aspects of their inclusion. In this chapter, my main research focus is in; first, to present cornerstones of any communication in an extensive theoretical research on attitudes and communication with persons with disabilities. Secondly, to present attitudes toward communication from different perspectives, communication of other survey participants, with or without previous contact with persons with disabilities, and finally other research where persons with disabilities perception of communication with others will be in focus. Empirical part of this study was conducted at the Faculty of Economics, University of Split as a part of the thesis of two undergraduate students. The study was designed as a part of participation in the project "Equal Access to Higher Education for Persons with Disabilities" where the author of this paper served as a project partner.

Introduction

According to the last available data (http://www.dzs.hr/Hrv_Eng/menandwomen/men_and_women_2014.pdf: 2013), in Croatian population there are 11.9% (510,274) persons with disabilities out of which 9.1% are female (202,214), and 14.9% are male (308,060) (War of Independence has had an impact there). Out of the total 11.9%, 9.7% are younger than 19 years, 10.2% are 20–64 years old, and 26.3% are older than 65. Living in Croatia, a small country in Eastern Europe, which was faced with the persons with disabilities through the history with war victims in World War 1, World War 2, and Croatian War of Independence in the 1990s, it was expected that in our culture and tradition we would have a developed system of inclusion of persons with disabilities. Our culture and tradition is

I. Bilić (✉)
Faculty of Economics, University of Split, Split, Croatia
e-mail: ibilic@efst.hr

© Springer International Publishing AG 2017
S. Halder, L.C. Assaf (eds.), *Inclusion, Disability and Culture*, Inclusive Learning and Educational Equity 3, DOI 10.1007/978-3-319-55224-8_10

dominantly non-supportive and is moreover filled with shame about disabilities. In some parts of the country, some families used to hide persons with disabilities from other people.

The situation is slowly but continuously improving. When I started teaching at the University of Split, Faculty of Economics I realized that some of my students are persons with certain disabilities, and I realized that I did not have appropriate knowledge or education regarding teaching persons with specific disabilities. During my American experience (within the Junior Faculty Development Program on a Scholarship provided by the U.S. Department of State), and academic stay and living in Long Beach, California I learned that persons with disabilities (veterans and others) are completely included in society, particularly in my U.S. city Long Beach.

Soon upon my arrival home, my friend who was part of the same program organized the first conference on the inclusion of persons with disabilities in higher education. I took part in the conference and prepared my first paper on the topic. Since then I have been intensively looking for information on what I should do in certain situations and how to adjust my lectures or exams to persons with specific disabilities. At the same time big TEMPUS – EU project EduQuality was started in Croatia. I got the chance to participate in lectures, met colleagues from other universities and had a chance to continuously exchange experience with them. Since that period I have been involved in three projects aimed at helping persons with disabilities meet their needs. It has even enabled me to become the most educated person at my faculty regarding adjusting classes and exams to persons with disabilities.

As a professor of economics, with major in communications, I see communication, particularly interpersonal one as a major problem in modern society, even more so because of high usage of online communication tools. Being a professor, I have had the opportunity to teach many students with disabilities, which made me realize that I needed to raise my knowledge on the topic, and moreover, teach my students about that, through the Business Communication courses, their seminars and final thesis. Furthermore, communication with persons with disabilities could be even more challenging because, most people do not have the necessary knowledge or previous experience on how to behave and communicate with a person with disabilities in class or at workplace, since they lack any training or course on that topic in most educational systems in Balkan countries and in even wider area. They used to start communication from their own perceptions and prejudices before acquiring any experience and sometimes with and sometimes without good intentions so they make mistakes, which is the other side of the medal.

Communication as a Basic Human Need

Communication is a fundamental social process, a basic human need used by every human being on a daily basis in any society. As a complex and multidimensional phenomenon communication was in the focus of many academics, and numerous definitions are available. One of them which encompasses the purpose of this chapter is cited here:

> Communication is concerned with sending and receiving knowledge, ideas, facts, figures, goals, emotions and values. *Communication is the interpersonal event which is the building block of the society* (Smith et al. 2002).

Communication in its nature is a process that consists of at least five phases (Bovee and Thill 1992): sender has an idea, the idea becomes a message, the message is transmitted, the receiver gets the message, and the receiver reacts and sends feedback to the sender.

A communication message needs to be conveyed via appropriate media, to be noticed in the crowded communication environment. Messages are usually covered or disturbed with other messages, receptiveness of the receiver, receiver's current emotional state, external noise, lack of interest, and so on; these are together called communication barriers. Communication barriers have a variety of forms and may arise in any type or form of communication such as interpersonal, intrapersonal, cross-cultural, face-to-face, distance, media, social media, and so on.

Communication feedback is very important for the sender, at least to ensure that the message has reached the receiver and that the communication goal is reached, i.e., the communication results in the desired understanding or actions.

Communication needs and goals for all persons, with or without any type of disabilities are similar, i.e., understand others and be understood by others whoever they are, be they family, friends, business partners, colleagues, teachers, coworkers, a nurse, and so forth.

A lack of comfort in communication with others, which is a characteristic of individual's personality, more than of any disorder or (dis)ability, could be an inhibitor to success in any domain (Blume et al. 2013). Blume et al. (2013) also point out that some individuals can have good communication skills when interacting with others, but if they are introverts, they may hesitate to step in and miss to show their full potential. When people need to communicate with persons with disabilities, driven by their own prejudice, lack of knowledge or fear, they can make this communication even more complicated or unpleasant. Considering all my knowledge about the topic, I see communication as a key driver of inclusion of persons with disabilities in various domains of social life, and more importantly at workplace.

Furthermore, it is very important to highlight that a person with disabilities, as any other person may be affected by their personality and personal communication style. Thus, a person may be an introvert and personal communication style may not necessarily be connected to disabilities. Some of them may even be extremely social people, such as persons with Down syndrome usually are.

In this chapter, communication will be analyzed as a potential medium and prerequisite for deeper inclusion of persons with disabilities in the observed societies, in all aspects of inclusion, with an accent of attitudes of business students, future coworkers, and employers of persons with disabilities.

Literature Review of Communication and Appropriate Title in the Field of Research

In most of the available literature about persons with disabilities, the same term is used – **persons with disabilities**[1]. However, in some literature other terms are used with mandatory involvement of impolite words such as *disabled or handicapped*. It is therefore important to clarify the roots and meaning of the basic term. The most used terms by many academics are: **"Persons/People/Children with disabilities"** (Sharma et al. 2006; Iezzoni 2006; Findler et al. 2007; Järvikoski et al. 2013; Yan et al. 2014 etc.) to refer to people with disabilities of different age; or depending on the type of disabilities, **"Type (intellectual, physical etc.) disabilities"** with or without prefix, the word "person or children" is used (Klooster et al. 2009; Buchholz et al. 2013; Morin et al. 2013 etc.).

It is obvious that when the first group of terms is used, people/persons are being discussed and that those persons have some kind of disability or handicap. Thus, from the first term it is clearly stated that the discussion is about persons and when we use the second group of terms, it may be hidden. After all, it is clear that the discussion is about the persons and there is no need or reason to treat that person/those persons differently in any aspect of their life, particularly in communication, and to, for example, talk to the accompanying person instead of talking to the blind person or to the person who uses mobility assistance device, and so on.

Finally, in more recent researches appears one more suitable term: **differently abled** (Schriempf 2001). Even though this term is an old one, it can be found very rarely in academic literature or everyday use. According to Oxford Dictionaries (2014): *Differently abled was first proposed (in the 1980s) as an alternative to disabled, handicapped, etc. on the grounds that it gave a more positive message and so avoided discrimination towards people with disabilities. The term has gained little currency, however, and has been criticized as both over-euphemistic and condescending. The accepted term in general use is still disabled.*

According to suggestions from the literature review and with the aim to promote a more suitable term, the term "differently abled" (abbreviated to DA) will be used in further text, without replacing other terms from the beginning of this text as a reminder for readers and future researchers in this field about the importance of using this term, of showing kindness, raising awareness, and promoting this more appropriate term.

According to the Maslow's Hierarchy of Needs, human needs are classified into five categories, which act as a motivation (Maslow 1954; in Berl et al. 1984): *physiological needs; safety and security needs; social and belongingness needs; ego, status and self-esteem needs; and self-actualization needs.* There is no reason to even think that differently abled persons have different needs, but still use the same

---

[1] In some research it is possible to find usage of the term disabled, without even using the word "person," which marks an evident lack of knowledge on this topic. Thus, it will not be discussed in this chapter.

motivators for inclusion in any aspect of social life as others do. Thus, communication can be observed as a basic need, a medium, and a motivator to accomplish those needs, especially the higher ones.   *Hungry - food*

Furthermore, the lower needs are more powerful than the higher needs, and the more these basic needs are satisfied, the better the psychological health of the individual will be (Lester 2013). Communication is a basic human need, and is complex in its nature and process. Through the communication process we not only send our words, but also consciously or unconsciously send our emotions and attitudes toward each other.

Types of Communication

Face-to-face communication is even more sensitive, which is regularly named as interpersonal communication which may be observed through the complexity of its verbal, nonverbal, and preverbal elements. For two or more persons, communication could be even more complicated if communication is conducted with people who are different in terms of their knowledge, attitudes, experiences, communication styles, communication skills, cultures, citizenship, and so on.

Interpersonal Communication is communication between two or more persons. For that purpose, some interpersonal skills such as listening and dealing with conflict are used in one-to-one interchanges. Possessing these skills will make any person more successful in the job, and in social groups (Locker 2000) as it will clearly make any inclusion in any aspect of social life much smoother.

Interpersonal interaction involves exchange of verbal and nonverbal messages. Communication systems use two kinds of signals (Krauss 2014): signs and symbols. Signs are signals that are causally related to the message they convey. We say that blushing means someone is embarrassed because we know that embarrassment is a cause of blushing. Symbols, on the other hand, are products of social conventions.

Used words, facials expressions, eye contacts, dressing, or body posture are ways of sending messages to the receiver. According to many authors in the field of communication, there is a widespread belief that the overall communication, more precisely understanding of communication, is divided (for example: Mehrabian 2009; Pease and Pease 2004 etc.) into three parts: 55% nonverbal communication; 38% preverbal (vocal) communication, and only 7% words.

Nonverbal Communication is communication that does not use words, and can be expressed without any intention to send a message occasionally, or can be used very intentionally in some cases, professions, or when somebody faces hearing problems (sing language). It can be quite complex, confusing, or unfriendly if the participants in the communication process are not aware of the message they are sending. Smiles, frowns, who sits where (Locker 2000:317), eye contact, handshake, and many other signs may be more relevant for making an impression in particular communication than anything told verbally.

Preverbal or Vocal Communication is a powerful tool in communication, although people are not aware of that all the time. Speaker's voice expresses emotions more transparently than spoken words. Paraverbal communication consists (Papa et al. 2008:27) of nonverbal speech sounds such as tone, pitch, volume, inflection, rhythm, and rate.

Verbal Communication is the main preoccupation of any speaker, or a person who wants to achieve successful communication. As it was explained above, it is only a small proportion in the overall communication process and a small part in mutual understanding, as the more important part is listening without talking, in order to understand the other party, which is one of the best characteristics developed by excellent speakers.

Words, attitudes, and emotions are transmitted through the communication process and more of its understanding from the receiver's perspective is finding the way the receiver interprets it. Emotions or energy is transmitted even with unspoken words. According to my previous knowledge, in communication with the differently abled it is crucial to be aware of other signals; high voices can disturb persons with hearing impairments, body language/body gestures are a mystery for the visually impaired, and they do not like it at all.

When attitudes toward the differently abled are negative, they can seriously hamper inclusion in any aspect of social life (Vilchinsky and Findler 2004), especially when sent occasionally they can lead the receiver to reaching completely wrong conclusions.

Literature Review of Previous Researches on the Attitudes and Communication with Differently Abled Persons

Previous researches are mostly preoccupied with communication of medical and rehabilitation staffs and the differently abled, and very few of them take into consideration other participants, such as colleagues, friends, families, partners, employers, and so on. Moreover, some researchers are focused on particular types of different abilities. In the following paragraphs, some interesting results from previous researches will be presented with reversible chronology.

Morin et al. (2013) researched public attitudes toward persons with different intellectual abilities, with the aim to explore their possibilities of integration in community life in Quebec. The Attitude toward Intellectual Disability Questionnaire was administered by phone to 1605 randomly selected respondents. Five factors were considered: discomfort, sensibility of tenderness, knowledge of causes, knowledge of capacity and rights, and interaction. Some interesting results from that study reveal that male participants had a more negative attitude toward discomfort, while females had more negative attitudes regarding knowledge of capacity and rights factor. Also, younger and more educated participants had more positive attitudes, while income status was generally irrelevant to their attitudes.

Buchholz et al. (2013) surveyed text messaging with pictures and speech synthesis as usage of assistive technologies for the adolescent and adults with cognitive and communicative disabilities. Seven professionals, who worked with the seven users, participated in the project, and were interviewed about the effects of that assistive technology. Research results showed that texting with picture symbols and speech is useful for remote communication of that population.

Smeltzer et al. (2012) also surveyed communication and attitudes between differently abled and nursing staff. The study identified four items: poor communication on the part of the nursing staff, compromised care, negative attitudes among staff, and participants' fear related to the quality of care.

Ten Klooster et al. (2009) researched students' attitudes toward the differently abled. A questionnaire based on ATDP-Form A[2], SADP[3], and CLAS-MR[4] was used. Research participants were Dutch nursing and non-nursing students. They found out that nursing students had a more positive attitude than their non-nursing peers. Another significant conclusion was that contact with the differently abled, e.g., having friends or family members with different abilities, was connected with more positive attitude. Furthermore, ATDPS[5] and SATDP[6] showed very similar results.

Findler et al. (2006) developed a new instrument, the Multidimensional Attitudes Scale toward Persons with Disabilities (MAS), based on three dimensions: affect, cognition, and behavior. Research results confirmed previously mentioned research that female participants in the survey held more positive behavioral attitudes than males. Also, a relevant factor was personal level of self-esteem, and male participants with higher level held more positive cognition than others.

Iezzoni (2006) researched communication between the differently abled and clinicians, using interview, from the perspective of differently abled persons. Research results revealed that a lack of the communication knowledge of the observed clinicians, resulted in confusing differently abled and sick, particularly lack of communication with the differently abled regarding their preferences in communication or in the treatment.

Communication with persons with different abilities could be even more challenging because of insufficient knowledge or lack of previous experience on how to behave and communicate with them. People usually start communicating with their own perceptions and prejudices when they meet the differently abled for the first time and, either with or without malicious intentions, make mistakes. From other

---

[2] Yukker et al. (1960). A Scale to Measure Attitudes Toward Disabled Persons. Human Resources Centre, Albertson, NY.

[3] Antonak, R. F. (1982). Development and psychometric analysis of the Scale of Attitudes Toward Disabled Persons. Journal of Applied Rehabilitation Counseling, 13 (2), 22–29.

[4] Henry, D. et al. (1998). The Community Living Attitudes Scale – Mental Retardation Version Reference Manual. University of Illinois at Chicago, Chicago, IL.

[5] Attitude Toward Disabled Persons Scale.

[6] Scale of Attitudes Toward Disabled Persons.

point of view, persons with different abilities usually have plenty of unpleasant experience with others, so they sometimes simply expect unpleasant experience, notice more than they wish to say through the nonverbal and paraverbal communication, and may react in an embarrassing or inappropriate way. One of the potential issues in perceptions of the differently abled is in the deficiency of understanding of the condition caused by it. Persons with different abilities do not necessarily feel ill or need acute medical attention, and for all the interested parties in communication it is important to differentiate:

disability ≠ sickness (Iezzoni 2006).

The impetus for this research was awareness of all this misunderstanding in a very sensitive field of communication with the differently abled and vice versa, and evident lack of surveys that include more than just medical or rehabilitation staff. The research was conducted with business students and teaching and non-teaching staffs at faculties of business in Croatia and Bosnia and Herzegovina. In this chapter, some descriptive research results are presented, with the primary goal to help understand the topic, and serve as a kind of first aid help for all those interested to improve their communication skills or knowledge in the field.

Survey Design and Methodology

For this purpose, the primary research goals were to reveal the respondents' attitudes in communication of the general adult population toward communication with the differently abled, and to reveal attitudes and perceptions of communication from the point of view of the differently abled with others.

The research focus was to present attitudes toward communication from different perspectives, communication with differently abled persons regarding respondents' previous knowledge, contacts, and experience. Empirical part of this study was conducted at the Faculty of Economics, University of Split as a part of thesis of two undergraduate students.[7] The study was designed as a part of author's participation in the project "Equal Access to Higher Education for Persons with Disabilities" where the author served as country project leader for Croatia and three of my students as volunteers. The study was motivated by discussion on project workshops, where differently abled persons, teaching and non-teaching staff participated, and where communication problems were identified as important ones. Attitudes and

---

[7] Undergraduate students, Andrea Raguž (project team member - http://www.equalaccess4pwds. org/) and Franka Vrkić under the mentorship of Assistant professor Ivana Bilić, PhD (who was the project leader. US Alumni Community of Croatia www.usaccroatia.com was project partner. Ivana Bilić currently serves as the President of the association) prepared these topics as their final thesis, course Business Communication. Andrea Raguž: Communication with Persons with Disabilities from Their Point of View, and Franka Vrkić: Communication with Persons with Disabilities from Others Point of View. Both students agree that the results of their research can be used by the author of this chapter.

knowledge about the differently abled and a lack of communication knowledge were identified as key obstacles to successful inclusion of differently abled persons in higher education, workplace, and social life in general. The main goal of the study was to gain new knowledge regarding the topic, and then to use the survey to raise awareness of the respondents and general public regarding the topic.

So, the author decided to develop a questionnaire and conduct a survey among the teaching staff (University of Split, Faculty of Economics), business students, and differently abled community. The questions used in this survey were agreed upon by the participants of two focus groups conducted in Split, Croatia in the early stage of the research design. The author of this chapter served as a moderator to both focus groups, used the topic guide, and followed focus group protocols to encourage participants to express their observation about communication between the differently abled and others. Two focus groups were organized: one in the office of local network of differently abled associations (Split-Dalmatia County), with 7 participants. It took more than 2 h to identify key issues and concerns of differently abled persons in mutual communication. Another focus group was organized at the University of Split, Faculty of Economics University of Split with other participants (students and professors, 7 in total). It also took 2 h. At the beginning, the participants were introduced to the purpose of the study, and I encouraged them to express their observations and concerns which they faced in communication with differently abled persons. As a mitigating factor we used the fact that the Faculty of Economics is accessible for differently abled students, so the participants in this focus group, both professors and students had plenty of experience in communication with the differently abled. Both focus groups had the same purpose, i.e., to develop a representative questionnaire for assessing attitudes toward communication with the differently abled from both perspectives.

In the academic literature, there are many available instruments for measuring attitudes toward the differently abled. Some of them have in focus particular disabilities, some observe the differently abled as one group and in that way measure different perspective of attitudes toward the differently abled (See more in, Findler et al. 2007). Most of the results mentioned above highlight attitudes and perception of the communication process from the point of view of the medical/rehabilitation professionals or others who plan to become one. It is very hard to find a study with participants from different professions (particularly economy or management) than the above mentioned. Thus, the aim of this research was to explore attitudes of professors and students from different fields. With the aim to make differently abled persons more comfortable, the survey was designed in a manner to skip questions regarding the group of disabilities they can be classified into according to their medical record.

In academic research it is possible to use two main methods, indirect or direct. In the indirect method participants are not aware of the purpose of the survey, while in the direct one they know what the purpose of the study is. In this survey, the direct method was used intentionally, i.e., with the purpose to raise awareness about the topic.

In two parallel researches, previously developed, same questionnaires were used with the aim to explore attitudes toward communication in both groups of respondents, the differently abled and the others. However, some questions were different, with the aim to discover the roots of the attitudes in a particular group. In two separate surveys, we tried to find out the basic demographic characteristics of both groups in terms of gender, age, residence, and educational level. Surveys were available online, and disseminated via e-mail too. In surveys for others we used the mailing list of the University of Split, with the aim to involve teaching and non-teaching staff and students from different faculties. The survey was also distributed to a neighboring country, Bosnia and Herzegovina, via informal student associations and networks.

Our second survey was administered to the differently abled (as declared by themselves, as no medical documents were checked), to research communication from their point of view. The survey was distributed via formal and informal groups of the differently abled in Croatia and Bosnia and Herzegovina with the aim to involve respondents who preferred to be a part of differently abled associations, and other individuals, who found out that they would be happier if they did not observe themselves as a part of the differently abled group. This decision was the outcome of extensive discussions conducted before the survey was launched with several differently abled individuals in Croatia and Macedonia. Some of the participants thought that their inclusion in a social life was much more successful if they did not observe themselves as a part of the differently abled community or associations, and they lived without using any of the benefits related to such kind of membership. With the aim to reach respondents for this survey, the questionnaire was distributed though the network of formal associations of the differently abled and via informal communication channels, e.g., social network, with the purpose to reach both groups of the differently abled.

As we can see from the results presented in Table 10.1, most of the respondents were female, over 60% in both groups, dominantly aged between 21–30 and 31–40, with the exception of higher proportion of the differently abled aged over 51, which can be interpreted in many ways: they are more independent from family and feel more comfortable to discuss the topic, have realized that they are more comfortable if they maintain good relations with the association, or are more aware of the importance of research in this field. Finally, the respondents' overall attitudes toward life are dominantly or mostly optimistic in both observed groups.

We also tried to find out some other basic information about our samples. First, we tried to find out more about their employment status, especially bearing in mind the current high unemployment rates in the observed countries. Most employed respondents were in group of "others," 67%, while 43% of the differently abled were employed. In terms of marital status, we did not find significant differences between the two observed groups. Research results show that more people from Croatia participated in this survey as compared to other countries, which means that the results presented here are better in explaining current situation of the researched topic in Croatia than in other previously mentioned participating countries. The reason is rather simple; more people in Croatia were familiar with the project,

Table 10.1 Some basic demographic characteristics about participants

Item	Values	Frequency (DA)	Frequency others	Percent (DA)	Percent others
Gender	Male	24	115	39.3	31.5
	Female	37	53	60.7	68.5
	Total	61	168	100.0	100.0
Age	– 20	2	14	3.3	8.0
	21–30	17	61	27.9	36.0
	31–40	16	57	26.2	34.0
	41–50	11	28	18.0	17.0
	51 –	15	8	24.6	5.0
	Total	61	168	100.0	100
Attitudes	Optimistic	27	74	44.3	44
	Mostly optimistic	18	56	29.5	33
	Flexible	13	33	21.3	20
	Pessimistic	2	5	3.3	3
	Mostly pessimistic	1	0	1.6	0

All survey results for the groups of "Other" dominantly represent attitudes of business professors and business students, from the Faculty of Economics, University of Split

researchers, and survey. To the best knowledge, all aspects of inclusion of the differently abled are less developed in the rest of former Yugoslavia than in Croatia, which has been the 28th member of the European Union since July 1, 2013, which resulted in the improvement of supporting legislation for inclusion of the differently abled in all aspects of social life. The bottom of Table 10.2 shows the survey results regarding participants' current educational status.

The results of attitudes about the differently abled and communication (common questions) will be presented in parallel with the perspective of both groups. The respondents showed their agreement on a 5-point Likert scale, from 1 – totally disagree to 5 – totally agree.

The first interesting insight was respondents' perceptions of the level of knowledge about the differently abled in their societies. According to the results presented in Table 10.3, it is more than obvious that both groups of respondents showed the same perceptions about the level of knowledge about the differently abled in their societies. The percentages are almost the same, and they show a great amount of dissatisfaction as, more than 75% of the respondents in both groups marked answers "strongly disagree" or "not agree" about the statement on the level of information and knowledge is developed enough.

Answers in Table 10.3 show that many respondents thought that their societies are driven by prejudices about communication with differently abled persons. According to the research results, it is evident that the level of prejudice is extremely high, and both groups found that the level of prejudice-free society is less than 10%. Furthermore, 16.4% of the differently abled and 25% of others choose the answer "moderate." Finally, the rest of the respondents, which means around 70% of the

Table 10.2 Some parallel statistics for survey participants

Item	Differently abled (%)	Others(%)
Employed		
Yes	43	67
No	57	33
Marital status		
Single	44	42
In a relationship	49	57
Separated[a]	6	1
Country		
Croatia	70	85
Bosnia and Herzegovina	30	8
Macedonia	–	7
Educational level		
Primary school	5	1
Secondary school	54	19
Undergraduate	13	24
Graduate	25	32
Master	2	7
PhD	2	28

[a]The participant could choose between divorced or widowed

Table 10.3 Level of knowledge about differently abled in your society is excellent

Values	Frequency (DA)	Frequency – others	Percent (DA)	Percent – others	Cumulative percent – DA	Cumulative percent – others
1.00	10	30	16.4	17.9	16.4	17.9
2.00	36	99	59.0	58.9	75.4	76.8
3.00	12	29	19.7	17.3	95.1	94.0
4.00	3	9	4.9	5.4	100.0	99.4
5.00	0	1	0	.6		100.0
Total	61	168	100.0	100.0	–	–

In further text for the differently abled, abbreviation DA will be used

differently abled and 64% of others "agree" and "strongly agree" that in their societies people are full of prejudice regarding communication with the differently abled.

In Table 10.4 we can see the results of respondents' attitudes toward fear in communication with each other. Only 13.1% of the differently abled, and 9.1% of others think that they are not afraid to communicate with each other, and the rest of both groups mostly agree with the fact they feel fear when they need to communicate with each other (Table 10.5).

According to research results, it is more than obvious that a small proportion of the respondents agrees or strongly agrees on equal treatment of the differently abled from others in communication. From the perspective of the differently abled group,

Table 10.4 Society showed prejudices about communication with the differently abled

Values	Frequency (DA)	Frequency – others	Percent (DA)	Percent others	Cumulative percent – DA	Cumulative percent – Others
1.00	0	3	0.00	1.8	0.0	1.8
2.00	6	14	9.8	8.3	9.8	10.2
3.00	10	42	16.4	25.0	26.2	35.5
4.00	33	84	54.1	50.0	80.3	86.1
5.00	12	23	19.7	13.7	100.0	100.0
Total	61	166	100.0	98.8	–	

Table 10.5 Communication between society and the differently abled is full of fear from both sides

Values	Frequency (DA)	Frequency others	Percent (DA)	Percent – others	Cumulative percent – DA	Cumulative percent – others
1.00	1	2	1.6	1.2	1.6	1.2
2.00	7	13	11.5	7.7	13.1	9.1
3.00	20	39	32.8	23.2	45.9	32.7
4.00	27	100	44.3	59.5	90.2	93.3
5.00	6	11	9.8	6.5	100.0	100.0
Total	61	165	100.0	98.2	–	–

Table 10.6 Other people treat the differently abled equal in communication

Values	Frequency (DA)	Frequency – others	Percent (DA)	Percent – others	Cumulative percent – DA	Cumulative percent – others
1.00	3	11	4.9	6.5	4.9	6.5
2.00	19	84	31.1	50.0	36.1	56.5
3.00	29	49	47.5	29.2	83.6	85.7
4.00	9	21	14.8	12.5	98.4	98.2
5.00	1	3	1.6	1.8	100.0	100.0
Total	61	168	100.0	100.0	–	–

the highest score is recognized from a maximum of 16.4% respondents, while others see the highest scores even lower, up to 14.3% (Table 10.6).

In Table 10.7 we can see attitudes toward communication without barriers between the differently abled and the society. The results are very close in both groups, and definitely not very encouraging. Differently abled persons reached 68.9% with answers "totally disagree" and "disagree," while the other group reached 79.5%, as the expression of attitudes toward a barrier-free society in the communication between differently abled persons and the society. We found only three persons (in the group of others) in a total of 227 respondents, who agreed that the observed societies are completely barrier-free.

The results presented in Table 10.8 represent respondents' attitudes that weak communication is the result of prejudice that persons who have different physical abilities also have mental disorders. Most of our differently abled participants chose

Table 10.7 Communication between society and the differently abled is excellent, without barriers

Values	Frequency (DA)	Frequency – others	Percent (DA)	Percent – others	Cumulative percent – DA	Cumulative percent – others
1.00	13	42	21.3	25.0	21.3	25.3
2.00	29	90	47.5	53.6	68.9	79.5
3.00	15	26	24.6	15.5	93.4	95.2
4.00	4	5	6.6	3.0	100.0	98.2
5.00	0	3	0	1.8	–	100.0
Total	61	166	100	98.8	–	

Table 10.8 Reason for weak communication is prejudice that persons who have different physical abilities also have mental disorders

Values	Frequency (DA)	Frequency – others	Percent (DA)	Percent – others	Cumulative percent – DA	Cumulative percent – others
1.00	3	14	4.9	8.3	4.9	8.3
2.00	12	57	19.7	33.9	24.6	42.3
3.00	11	30	18.0	17.9	42.6	60.1
4.00	29	58	47.5	34.5	90.2	94.6
5.00	6	9	9.8	5.4	100.0	100.0
Total	61	168	100.0	100.0	–	–

answer 4 – agree, while others dispersed their answers within all five picks, with a central tendency – more like normal distribution.

Before starting this research, we assumed that lack of knowledge about the differently abled is the crucial cause of unsuccessful communication between the observed groups. According to the survey results we can see that both groups agree that lack of knowledge is the main problem in communication between each other. Only a small proportion in both groups sees knowledge as unimportant (Table 10.9).

More experience and familiarity with the differently abled change the perspective of the observer by making it more open (Sharma et al. 2006). The level of knowledge about communication is considered very important by both observed groups, i.e., for more than 80% respondents in the both groups (Table 10.10).

Previous contact with differently abled persons was examined using the question about having a friend or family member with any type of disability. According to research results, 62% (104 participants) have had previous experience, and 38% (64) have not. This fact can thus be used to examine the correlation between the experience and attitudes toward communication with the differently abled. We assume that survey results will show a positive correlation between the respondents' familiarity with the differently abled, and previously mentioned observations, but according to the correlation analysis there is no evidence to support this hypothesis, at least in the observed country at this moment.

Table 10.9 For successful communication, the level of knowledge about the differently abled is important

Values	Frequency (DA)	Frequency – others	Percent (DA)	Percent – others	Cumulative percent – DA	Cumulative percent – others
1.00	2	0	3.3	0.0	3.3	0.0
2.00	2	13	3.3	7.7	6.6	7.7
3.00	7	21	11.5	12.5	18.0	20.2
4.00	33	94	54.1	56.0	72.1	76.2
5.00	17	40	27.9	23.8	100.0	100.0
Total	61	168	100.0	100.0	–	

Table 10.10 For successful communication, level of knowledge about communication is important

Values	Frequency (DA)	Frequency – others	Percent (DA)	Percent – others	Cumulative percent – DA	Cumulative percent – others
1.00	1	1	1.6	.6	1.6	.6
2.00	0	7	1.6	4.2	1.6	4.8
3.00	8	22	13.1	13.1	14.8	17.9
4.00	39	92	63.9	54.8	78.7	72.6
5.00	13	46	21.3	27.4	100.0	100.0
Total	61	168	100.0	100.0	–	

Discussion and Directions for Future Researches

At the end of this chapter it is important to emphasize for readers some desirable learning outcomes. First, it is important to be aware of the term differently abled person/s as a more appropriate one when discussing or mentioning person/s with any kind of disability. Second, differently abled persons have the same communication needs as everybody else. Third, they are persons with different characters and communication preferences as everybody else.

Croatian academia and business sector is still insufficiently informed about the importance of proper inclusion of differently abled persons in society, which may be the result of absence of learning outcomes about differently abled persons at all education levels, for non-professionals in the field, as it is obviously the case in many other countries. For future directions, it is more than obvious that some basic education about communication and inclusion of differently abled persons needs to be offered during primary education, as a first step for both observed groups.

Furthermore, future research could be directed in a way to explore attitudes and knowledge about communication and inclusion from the perspective of different groups of people, than the usually surveyed medical or related students/staffs or business students as it was in this research.

Conclusion

This research has been motivated by many personal and professional reasons. First, I personally wanted to enrich my personal knowledge regarding the researched topic, and my professional curiosity was to explore one insufficiently researched topic. Also, I am definitely aware that survey in itself is a good promotional tool, so I am sure that all survey participants will rethink their communication habits with the differently abled, after participation in this survey.

Secondly, I was curious to find out attitudes of the differently abled and others in terms of mutual, interpersonal communication, which serves as the main medium of correspondence in numerous situations, particularly among business students, future coworkers, and employers of differently abled persons. The third reason was even more enthusiastic, as some participants, especially from the group of other do not have a clue how to communicate with the differently abled. After passing through the survey questions they will at least get some necessary insights. And last but not least, to write down some of the new facts gained through the research and make them available to others, both practitioners and academics.

In this research, the respondents were dominantly females, aged between 21 and 40, with the exception in the group of the differently abled, where we found a significant number of participants aged 51 and above. Most of the survey participants have optimistic or mostly optimistic attitudes toward life that can be considered as a plus in the context of this survey, and as a presumption to have positive attitudes about the observed topic.

According to the main research, I can conclude that the observed societies are full of prejudice regarding communication with the differently abled, with an evident lack of knowledge about that population in their societies. Equal treatment of the differently abled in communication does not exist according to the research results, and people approach communication without basic knowledge about it. Other observed phenomena, such as barrier-free communication, or knowledge about the differently abled, etc. is insufficiently developed at this moment. As was assumed before this research was conducted, our society and our neighbor societies need to invest more time in formal and informal education about the differently abled so as to establish prerequisites for their complete inclusion in societies around the globe. In the pre-accession period, Croatia signed many useful documents, accepted many encouraging laws; nevertheless, all of this is still work in progress.

References

Berl, R. L., Williamson, N. C., & Powell, T. (1984). Industrial salesforce motivation: A critique and test of Maslow's hierarchy of need. *Journal of Personal Selling and Sales Management, 4*(1), 33.

Blume, B. D., Baldwin, T. T., & Ryan, K. C. (2013). Communication apprehension: A barrier to students' leadership, adaptability and multicultural appreciation. *Academy of Management Learning & Education, 12*(2), 158–172.

Bovee, C. L., & Thill, J. V. (1992). *Business communication today* (3rd ed.). New York: McGraw Hill.

Buchholz, M., Mattsson Müller, I., & Ferm, U. (2013). Text messaging with pictures and speech synthesis for adolescents and adults with cognitive and communicative disabilities – Professionals' view about user satisfaction and participation. *Technology and Disability, 25*(87), 98.

Findler, L., Vilchinsky, N., & Werner, S. (2007). The multidimensional attitudes scale toward persons with disabilities (MAS): Construction and validation. *Rehabilitation Counseling Bulletin, 50*(3), 166–176.

Iezzoni, L. I. (2006). Make no assumptions: Communication between persons with disabilities and clinicians. *Assistive Technology, 18*(2), 212–219.

Järvikoski, A., Martin, M., Autti-Rämö, I., & Härkäpää, K. (2013). Shared agency and collaboration between the family and professionals in medical rehabilitation of children with severe disabilities. *International Journal of Rehabilitation Research, 36*(1), 30–37.

Klooster, T., et al. (2009). Attitudes towards people with physical or intellectual disabilities: Nursing students and non-nursing peers. *Journal of Advanced Nursing, 65*(12), 2562–2573.

Krauss, R. M. (2014). The psychology of verbal communication. In N. Smelser & P. Baltes (Eds.), *International encyclopedia of the social and behavioral* sciences. London: Elsevier. Retrieved from http://www.dpcdsb.org/NR/rdonlyres/138975AC-B110-4D1E-902F81C8E69BF9A0/124798/PsychologyofVerbalCommunicationKrauss.pdf. September 6. 2014

Lester, D. (2013). Measuring Maslow's hierarchy of needs. *Psychological Reports: Mental & Physical Health, 113*(1), 15–17.

Locker, K. O. (2000). *Business and administrative communication* (5th ed.). New York: US Irwin McGraw-Hill.

Mehrabian, A. (2009). *Nonverbal communication* (3rd ed.). New Brunswick/London: Aldine Transaction A Division of Transaction Publishers.

Morin, D., Rivard, M., Crocker, A. G., Boursier, C. P., & Caron, J. (2013). Public attitudes towards intellectual disability: A multidimensional perspective. *Journal of Intellectual Disability Research, 57*(3), 279–292.

Oxford Dictionaries. (2014). Retrieved from http://www.oxforddictionaries.com/definition/english/differently-abled. (August 27, 2014).

Papa, M. J., Daniels, T. D., & Spiker, B. K. (2008). *Organizational communications: Perspective and trends*. Thousand Oaks: Sage publications.

Pease, A., & Pease, B. (2004). *The definite book of body language*. Buderim: Pease International.

Schriempf, A. (2001). (Re)fusing the amputated body: An interactionist bridge for feminism and disability. *Hypatia, 16*(4), 53–79.

Sharma, N., Lalinde, P. S., & Brosco, J. P. (2006). What do residents learn by meeting with families of children with disabilities?: A qualitative analysis of an experiential learning module. *Pediatric Rehabilitation, 9*(3), 185–189.

Smeltzer, S. C., et al. (2012). Interaction of people with disabilities and nursing staff during hospitalization: A qualitative study finds that people with disabilities often feel unsafe and poorly communicate with in hospitals. *American Journal of Nursing, 112*(4), 30–37.

Smith, P. R., Berry, P., & Pulford, A. (2002). *Strategic marketing communications: New ways to build and integrate communications*. London: Kogan Page.

Vilchinsky, N., & Findler, L. (2004). Attitudes towards Israel's equal rights for people with disabilities law: A multi-perspective approach. *Rehabilitation Psychology, 49*, 309–316.

Women and Men in Croatia 2014. (2014). http://www.dzs.hr/Hrv_Eng/menandwomen/men_and_women_2014.pdf. Accessed 4 June 2014.

Yan, M., Go, S., Tamura, H., & Tanno, K. (2014). Communication system using EOG for persons with disabilities and its judgment by EEG. *Artificial Life and Robotics, 19*(1), 89–94.

Chapter 11
Empathetic Communication: Bridging Differences in a Global Context

Erna Alant, Beth Lewis Samuelson, and Lindsey Ogle

Abstract The aim of this chapter is to describe the concept of empathetic communication and its relevance in facilitating communication between people with communication disabilities and typical communicators. After a description of the concept of empathetic communication, we will discuss different examples of interactions to enhance understanding of manifestations of empathetic communication. These examples include an interaction between a caregiver and an adult with disabilities as well as a cross-cultural interaction between a therapist and a mother of a child with disabilities. Finally, some conclusive comments are made.

Introduction

We live in a global, mobile, and super-diverse world made possible by easy travel, digital communications, and the commodification of culture. As a result, language learners are not locked into static and standard cultural identities, and postnational perspectives on diversity and difference have rejected the notion of the intercultural speaker who mediates between cultures or travels across cultures. Many individuals today possess multiple, complex cultural and linguistic alliances. These "cosmopolitan speakers" (Ros i Solé 2013) may be members of a diaspora or heritage language learners, e.g., or they may be migrants or immigrants or language learners who inhabit many identities and affiliations. They are super-diverse, in that they are not easily categorized by their national identity or by their language or ability status.

E. Alant (✉)
School of Education, Indiana University, Bloomington, IN, USA
e-mail: ealant@indiana.edu

B.L. Samuelson
Literacy, Culture and Language Education, Indiana University, Bloomington, IN, USA

L. Ogle
School of Education, Indiana University, Bloomington, IN, USA

© Springer International Publishing AG 2017   153
S. Halder, L.C. Assaf (eds.), *Inclusion, Disability and Culture*, Inclusive
Learning and Educational Equity 3, DOI 10.1007/978-3-319-55224-8_11

Many in academia and elsewhere assume that exposure to all kinds of diversity and difference will result in empathy (Bollinger 2002), but in many cases, the idea of empathy, whether cognitive or affective, is simply seen as a given. In much of the research on multilingual or multicultural development, it is not operationalized as a variable or coded directly as an aspect of development to be studied. Beck (2006), for instance, posits that cosmopolitan speakers develop "cosmopolitan empathy" that enables them to critically assess and feel empathy for the historical, social, and cultural circumstances of the new cultures and languages that they encounter. Some recent work has shown a small positive correlation between cognitive empathy and multilingualism in persons with advanced proficiency who made frequent use of several languages and often code-switch (Dewaele and Wei 2012). And some work has suggested that emotional intelligence traits, including empathy, may be connected to self-reported personality changes while speaking other languages, but the relationships are not strong (Ozanska-Ponikwia 2012). These studies are uncommon, though. More common is the inclusion of empathy as a side note, as in Pratt-Johnson's (2006) recommendations for helping teachers to develop more intercultural competence in their classrooms. She suggests that teachers "listen empathetically," further explaining that this means listening actively and carefully. Empathy is recommended but rarely included as an object of study. It seems to be treated as an inevitable outcome of the experience.

The ability to feel and be with another form an integral part of being socially included in our society. Being emotionally responsive to others enables us to not only understand others better but also allows us to act towards others in ways that are meaningful and constructive. As the world we live in becomes more global and diverse, our ability to be with another, however, become more challenging. We are confronted with people who think differently from us and/or grew up in different cultural contexts or circumstances, and we also have to interact with those who have different types of abilities. Insecurities about how to talk to or interact with those we perceive as different greatly impact the way in which we interact. The more we perceive others in terms of socially exclusive categories ("us" and "them"), the higher the likelihood of acts of exclusion, aggression, or hostility toward them.

The opportunities for inclusion of people with disabilities in mainstream societies have significantly improved over the past decades as governments develop policies (e.g., Americans with Disabilities Act [ADA], the Individuals with Disabilities Education Act [IDEA]) to facilitate these practices (Pinker 2011). However, physical proximity of people with disabilities to others does not guarantee social inclusion. Although frequency of contact between people with disabilities and typical people do provide more opportunities for interaction, it is not surprising to still find frequent reference to the barriers experienced by people with disabilities in integrating into society. Physically appearing different from others often remains a major barrier in facilitating interaction. Similarly, however, sharing a similar appearance to others but having a disability that is less obvious (e.g., severe communication problem) could be equally challenging as typical people make false assumptions about these individuals in daily interactions. People with severe communication problems can therefore have multiple layers of challenges in interacting with typical communicators. Parents of children with disabilities also often experience challenges communicating with professionals that can be exaggerated by existing linguistic, cultural, and socioeconomic differences between communication partners.

Although the trend toward social inclusion of people with disabilities is prevalent in many countries around the world, the challenges in developing countries can be significant, as attitudes and perceptions of people with disabilities vary based on socioeconomic, religious, and cultural contexts. In spite of 114 countries signing the United Nations' *Convention on the Rights of People with Disabilities* (UN General Assembly 2006), the human rights of people with disabilities are still violated on a daily basis (Devi 2013; Drew et al. 2011). These violations reflect the need for more consistent efforts to increase mutual understanding and empathy between those with and those without disabilities within a global environment.

This chapter grew from a project that all three authors were involved in which focused on the development of a graduate course on the Art and Science of Empathetic Communication. Although the concept of "empathy" is well entrenched in clinical practice, it is only within recent years that researchers and practitioners have started to reflect on the importance of empathy in daily interactions. The more we are able to "put ourselves in the shoes of the other," i.e., take the perspective of the other and be in emotional resonance with them, the more likely it is that our interactions and learning efforts will be more effective and sustained (Decety and Ickes 2009).

Both Erna Alant and Beth Samuelson have extensive international experience having worked in South Africa and various other African countries before working at Indiana University, USA. Erna Alant founded the Centre for Augmentative and Alternative Communication at the University of Pretoria in 1990 to provide training and conduct research in the field of augmentative and alternative communication (i.e., strategies that can be used to facilitate communication of people with severe communication problems who have little or no speech).

Beth Samuelson has been an English teacher and teacher trainer since 1992. Her experience includes working with teachers in China, Taiwan, Sudan, Rwanda, and Afghanistan. She has also provided professional development for teachers from South Korea, Turkey, Armenia, South Sudan, and Saudi Arabia. She spent several of her teenage years in Zaire, now known as the Democratic Republic of Congo, and has been pursuing research lines of inquiry in Congo and Rwanda. She is interested in engaged learning and service learning, hence her interest in empathetic communication.

The third author, Lindsey Ogle, is a doctoral student with an interest in people with severe disabilities. This interest stems in large part from her personal experience as a sibling to her brother who has severe autism and intellectual disability. Her brother is currently 24 years old, primarily nonverbal with limited communication skills, and receiving day respite care through Medicaid while living at home. This experience has profoundly influenced her interest in individuals with disabilities and the challenges families and professional caregivers face in caring for people with severe disabilities. Her primary interest is in how caregivers interact with adults with severe disabilities and their ability to demonstrate empathy as part of daily interactions.

The Concept of "Empathy"

Empathy can be defined as "feeling with another," a concept derived from a German word *einfuhling* (Titchener 1909). Carl Rogers (1975) further elaborated on the clinical definition of empathy in his therapeutic work with clients who received psychotherapy. He emphasized the ability to feel what the other is feeling without becoming the other. To be empathetic requires an awareness of self that differentiates oneself from the other but, at the same time, allows one to imagine how the other is feeling. This emotional being-together with another is different from the ability to understand the other, or perspective-taking. Perspective-taking is the ability to take the position of the other, i.e., to put oneself in the shoes of another but does not necessarily imply being effectively with the other. The term "empathetic accuracy" (Ickes 1993) emphasizes the level of accuracy with which one individual is able to feel or be with another.

Empathy is distinctly different from "sympathy" as it requires a self-other awareness that allows the individual to feel with another without becoming the other or acting on behalf of the other. It allows one to feel with another while recognizing the other as a distinct entity apart from oneself. The relevance of the concept "empathy" and the ability to feel with another in activities of daily life—e.g., in teaching—becomes evident from the following example.

Cindy is an 8-year-old girl who has autism and severe communication problems. She gets upset every time she is required to change from one activity to the next during daily classroom routines. As a result, the teacher developed a visual aid, i.e., an activity schedule to facilitate transitions between different activities. This schedule board consists of graphic symbols of activities Cindy engages in for each day of the week. When Cindy finishes the one activity—e.g., circle time—the teacher would point to the next symbol representing "maths" to facilitate Cindy's transition to the next classroom activity. Cindy would become visibly upset, hit her hand on the table, and scream to indicate her displeasure in needing to change activities. The two classroom assistants who work with Cindy tend to have very different approaches in dealing with this behavior: the first classroom aide, Sara, tends to get very upset when Cindy responds in this way and consequently tries to avoid confrontation. She is committed to assist Cindy in completing all the scheduled activities each day. She, therefore, immediately tries to distract Cindy by doing something Cindy generally enjoys doing: drawing. More often than not, this will calm Cindy down. After about 5 minutes of drawing, Sara reintroduces the graphic symbol representing "maths" to alert Cindy that they should move on to do another activity. The transition to maths generally is easier at this stage although Cindy would often only pay attention after significant external rewards (tangible reinforcement).

In this example, Sara has difficulty in separating her own emotional state (i.e., her level of upsetness) from that of Cindy. She, therefore, prefers to distract Cindy by introducing another activity rather than acknowledging her emotional state. However, Mary, the other classroom assistant, has a different approach. After finishing circle time, Mary would engage Cindy in talking about what they did during circle time that morning. She would emphasize Cindy's responses to what others said as a means to enhance Cindy's awareness of herself as part of the group activity. She would acknowledge Cindy's emotional state during the activity—e.g., "you laughed, you thought that was funny"—before encouraging Cindy to think about what they will do next. When Cindy looks at the maths symbol, however, she would shake her head or start screaming. Mary, who is accepting of Cindy's behavior, typically acknowledges that this is difficult for Cindy and that Cindy finds it upsetting to change to a new activity. She then provides Cindy with two choices: Cindy could choose to take a bit of a break first or proceed to do maths by taking the first turn to draw a math card. After some discussion, Cindy decides to take a break first. She walks to the free play section in the room. Mary follows her and reminds her that they can only play for a short time—then they need to get back. After the break, Cindy sits down to start with the maths.

Both classroom assistants have developed their own way of working with Cindy. Sara tends to be more directive than Mary (more task-oriented), while Mary seems more interaction-oriented. Although Sara demonstrates some understanding of Cindy's difficulties, she tends to interact less with Cindy and focus on activities. Mary encourages Cindy to reflect on her own behavior and provide choices to allow for Cindy's growth in self-determination (i.e., making her own choices). Although both these approaches can be effective in the short term, one has to reflect on the long-term impact of each of these approaches. Mary's approach is focused on self-awareness and communication with Cindy to allow for personal growth and self-understanding, while Sara prefers to focus on the tasks that need to be completed. This difference between a task-oriented and relation-oriented teaching approach is very common in teaching of students with severe communication problems. Although a combination of both task- and relation-oriented approaches in the classroom is desirable, the real challenge relates to a clear understanding of what we are working for in providing education and training to these students. Are we working to teach skills in a segregated way (a direct focus on drill and practice) or are we focused on integrating skills within the personal and social development of the student to enhance the meaning that these skills have for the student? One way of approaching this question is by highlighting the importance of empathetic communication within the teaching context. Mary in the above example was more oriented to interact with (i.e., be with) Cindy on an empathetic level as a basis for engaging in skill training.

Empathetic Communication

Empathetic communication can be defined as the process of meaning-making between people that includes both affective as well as cognitive aspects of interaction (Alant 2005). Communication therefore goes beyond the exchange of messages (turn-taking between two people) to synthesize what one observes and hears in interaction to facilitate mutual understanding through two integrated processes:

(a) a cognitive sense of where the other is coming from (i.e., perspective-taking) to build common ground between the communicators, and (b) emotional resonance (i.e., being with the other on an affective level). Apart from understanding what another is communicating on a cognitive level, it is the ability to be together on an emotive level that makes it possible to develop friendships and social closeness. Being emotionally distant while sharing information with others might be acceptable in some contexts; however, it is the level of emotional resonance between people that facilitates interpersonal relationships and social closeness. Feeling emotionally close to someone significantly increases the likelihood of meaningful and sustainable interactions between the communication partners.

Empathetic communication, therefore, basically revolves around three interlinked concepts, which will be elaborated on in this chapter: being emotionally resonant with another, perspective-taking, and self-other awareness as integral to this intersubjective process.

Emotional Resonance

To be emotionally resonant with another implies that one is able to be with another in an emotional sense (i.e., in emotional harmony with the other). It is often also referred to as emotional contagion: the ability to "catch" or mirror (Iacoboni 2008) the emotion of the other. In the above example, Mary was able to acknowledge Cindy's emotional state by making statements about how Cindy experienced the circle activities as a basis for further interaction. The ability to imitate or experience the emotion of another, however, does not necessarily imply that one will act on the experience. For example, one can feel with another during a specific situation while feeling quite distant from the other after the interaction. Mary, however, acted on her experience of emotional resonance with Cindy by providing her with choices in relation to what she wanted to do. She acknowledged Cindy's emotions and allowed Cindy a bit more freedom in terms of what she wanted to do next as a means of engaging Cindy. Mary was therefore able to integrate the empathy she felt into actions in working with Cindy.

Sara, on the other hand, chose not to acknowledge Cindy's emotional state but rather used the introduction of a favorite activity to try and sidestep Cindy's emotional experience. Although the use of distraction strategies can be useful at times, these are generally not very effective in the long-term as they tend to avoid rather than deal with an integration of the affective and cognitive learning experiences of students.

Perspective-Taking

Perspective-taking is often defined in terms of theory of mind (Korkmaz 2011), which relates to the ability to attribute mental states (e.g., beliefs, intents, desires) to oneself and to others and to understand that others have beliefs, desires, intentions, and perspectives that are different from one's own. The Sally–Anne Test is one strategy that has been used to investigate children's ability to understand reality from more than one perspective (Mitchell 2011).

Perspective-taking is primarily oriented to understanding the other's point of view and interpretation of reality in an effort to develop common ground (Clark 1996) for mutual understanding and interaction. Dixon and Moore (1990) described two aspects of perspective-taking: the information effect and the weighting effect. The information effect refers to the quality and quantity of information available to the person to gain understanding of the other. The ability to take the perspective of the other is, therefore, dependent on the availability of sufficient information about the other. The frequency of opportunities to interact with others as well as the quality of interactions thus largely facilitates the process of perspective-taking. Talking to children and allowing them to explain or expand on how they experience reality is one strategy that can be used to facilitate teachers' understanding of a child's perspective. This process is more difficult in young children and those who have severe communication problems as they are less able to express themselves to others. Perhaps one of the most limiting aspects of Sara's approach to Cindy (in the above example) relates to this aspect of perspective-taking. As Sara tends not to discuss Cindy's actions and responses with her, the quantity and quality of information available to Sara about how Cindy experiences reality could be limited. It would, therefore, be more difficult for Sara to develop a better, more in-depth understanding of how Cindy experiences and interpret the world around her as a basis for effective teaching and learning.

The weighting effect refers to the ability to compare the similarities and differences between one's own perspective and that of the other. In our example, Sara might be less able to see how the information obtained from Cindy differs from her own as the information available for comparison is limited. Sara therefore needs to make assumptions (e.g., introduce drawing based on past experiences with Cindy) about what Cindy might consent to (which might either be accurate or inaccurate) rather than engaging with Cindy in making the decision. The weighting of the information (i.e., understanding the child's perspective as different from her own) could therefore be more challenging. Empathetic communication is, therefore, an intersubjective process based upon self-other awareness. Meaning-making with another includes not only the ability to understand the other from your own perspective but also the ability to imagine how the other feels.

Fig. 11.1 Empathetic
communication

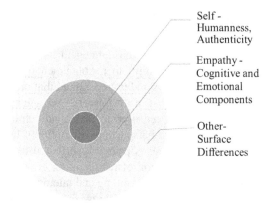

Self -
Humanness,
Authenticity

Empathy -
Cognitive and
Emotional
Components

Other-
Surface
Differences

Intersubjectivity

In developmental psychology, intersubjectivity is often defined as a deliberate sharing of experiences about objects and events (Stern 1985; Trevarthen and Hubley 1978). It is this intention to share that is the driving force behind people's interactions with each other (Brinck 2008). Sharing of experiences is, however, not necessarily deliberate but can occur unintentionally. The communication partner observes the actions of the other and interprets these on a conscious and unconscious level. Also, the expressive behavior of each communication partner can provoke inadvertent emotional reactions in the other (Gallese et al. 2004) as part of the intersubjective process of meaning-making.

Communication is therefore a process of symbolic interaction (Alant 2005; Alant et al. 2009) whereby both partners are able to interpret and use verbal and nonverbal symbols to develop joint meaning. Inherent to this process is the ability to differentiate between self and other, as both partners respond to the other's messages in an effort to facilitate mutual understanding. Figure 11.1 visually represents the role of empathy in bridging self-other awareness, understanding, and meaning-making. Although symbolic interaction is at the core of the communication process, it is the interpretation and use of symbols between individuals that constitute the level of meaning developed in interaction. The bigger the differences (e.g., in terms of abilities, cultural, linguistic, and socioeconomic backgrounds) between the two individuals communicating, the more effort and skill it requires to develop shared meaning.

Empathetic communication is rooted in interest in the other (i.e., the motivation to watch and listen as a means to gain a better understanding of the perspective and emotional state of the other), while being self-aware. Figure 11.1 represents empathetic communication as the bridge between self and other by not only enhancing mutual understanding (cognitive process), but also being emotionally resonant (affective process). This process of interpreting and using symbols in interaction enables individuals to develop constructive relationships and social closeness.

The next section of this chapter will focus on two interactions as a basis for exploring empathetic communication.

Two Interactions for Understanding Empathetic Communication

The first interaction occurred between an adult with disabilities and their caregiver; the second is an intercultural interaction that took place between a therapist and a mother during an assessment interview of a child with severe communication problems. Challenges imposed by limited shared experiences and understanding will be highlighted and suggestions identified to address these in an effort to enhance the process of empathetic communication.

Interaction 1: Between a Caregiver and an Adult with Moderate Intellectual Disabilities

The participants were asked to interact in general conversation on a topic of their choice. J is W's caregiver in a group home for adults with intellectual disabilities. J is 28 and W is 34. They've known one another for around a year. W has a moderate intellectual disability. This spontaneous conversation is about W's dream to be a race-car driver (like Jeff Gordon) and J helping him plan for it. Staff are trained not to discourage their client's dreams, but rather use them as motivation for developing skills.

W: I'm getting ready to learn to drive like Jeff Gordon.
J: You want to be a race-car driver? … I know. When did we talk about it?
W: During my annual [meeting] … Remember?
J: Yeah … I was thinking about it … Do you remember the steps?
W: No, I don't.
J: … that we talked about?
W: About me getting a job?
J: What do you have to have to drive?
W: A license.
J: And how do you get a license?
W: Going through the actual test.
J: Right, and what do you have to do before the test?
W: Get my permit.
J: You've got to take the license exam, right? … and a driver's ed [education] course?
W: Right, that's what I'm going to take—drivers ed [education].
J: … and getting a permit, and getting a license, and having a car costs … money, right?
W: Yeah. Yeah, it does.
J: Where are you going to get that money?
W: Well, I don't know, J!
J: You don't know?!

W: I need to get a job first. I've been wanting to get a job down at the workshop.
J: I know. We talked about that too, didn't we?
W: A job in the greenhouse.

From the above interaction, it is evident that the caregiver, J, is focused on supporting W to understand the process that is needed for W to become a race driver. The interaction between J and W is therefore task-oriented; J asks questions to encourage W to think about the process. The approach of supporting W in following his dreams is commendable as it allows W to grow on a personal–emotional level to develop insights to fine-tune his aspirations. What was intended to be a spontaneous interaction, however, developed into a structured question–answer interaction focused on recalling steps that needed to be followed to help W become a race driver. Even though J and W interact on a daily basis, they felt more comfortable conversing in a way that was focused on understanding steps of the task-oriented process. This interaction pattern, however, allows for very little opportunity to explore relational-oriented interaction. Although J invested some effort in understanding the perspective of W in terms of his interest in becoming a race driver, the interaction offers little in terms of emotional engagement between the two.

There is significant evidence to support the structured (stereotypical) nature of interactions between people with disabilities and their caregivers in institutional settings (Antaki et al. 2006; Morse et al. 2006). Morse et al. (2006) developed a model of empathetic communication in caregiving focused on the level of engagement regarding the degree the caregiver is focused on himself or herself or the patient and the degree of professionalism. These dimensions determine the degree of engagement and relatedly empathetic insight with patients. Using this model, J is "pseudo-engaged" with W's emotional state in this interaction due to the high degree of learned professional behavior and thus misses an opportunity to engage with W in a more genuine, reflexive way (Morse et al. 2006). For adults in residential settings who interact almost exclusively with professionals, these professional, pseudo-engaged interactions deny them genuine connection with others and may negatively impact quality of life for both the adult with a disability and his or her caregivers.

Interventions focused on exposing caregivers and their clients to interaction experiences based on emotional resonance in addition to perspective-taking could enhance their interactional experiences. It might, therefore, be beneficial to engage the caregiver in some discussion about how interactions between J and him can be varied to become less task-driven to allow for more openness in the development of conversation. One way of doing this might be to allow J to experience interactions that are more empathetic to allow him to contrast the difference between task-driven and empathetic interactions. Having experienced a different type of interaction might facilitate self-other awareness as part of the interaction process. In addition, W will also need guidance in experiencing what it means to spontaneously interact with another, i.e., observe and listen as part of engaging in dialogue with another rather than just responding to questions. Creating some level of awareness of how to facilitate a different experience, however, needs to be conducted from the basis of acceptance of the current status of their interaction. This is not about evaluating people in interaction but rather assisting them in finding ways to become more aware and sensitive to themselves and others as they engage in interactions.

The second case describes an interaction between a mother and a therapist who come from different cultural backgrounds to further our insights into the challenges of self-other awareness in these types of interactions.

Interaction 2: Between a Therapist and a Mother of a Child with Severe Communication Problems in an Intercultural Context

B is the mother of a child with a severe communication problem. Their home language is an African language (Zulu), but B is fluent in English. She brought her child (a little girl, A) in for an assessment as A has a severe communication problem. A is 8 years old and has cerebral palsy. The mother and father are both working, and A stays with the grandmother during the day. This interaction is part of an interview conducted between a speech-language therapist and the mother during the initial assessment meeting. The segment is selected as it presented a significant challenge to the professional, who anticipated that the mother would at least share a common perspective on the purpose of her visit to the center, i.e., to assess her child's communication ability.

T: Good morning—nice to meet you.
B: Yes …
T: Can you tell us why you came to the center today?
B: Yes, it is because of A … she is not doing so well …
T: Can you tell me about it?
B: She does not play with the other children. The children play with the balls and toys, but A cannot do that …
T: … she cannot do that?
B: Yes … she just sits and looks around … she doesn't play with them.
T: Have you tried to play with her?
B: … mostly she just plays by herself … We put her in the walking ring and then she moves herself forward … she likes that! She smiles and moves her legs … she is very happy …

The rest of the interview supported this initial exchange between the mother and the therapist. The mother clearly had not thought about communication and its importance for the child. She was concerned about the overt behavior of her child and how the child's mobility issues impacted on the child's ability to be included in interactions with other children. She was referred for a communication assessment by a physician without having a clear understanding of the role of communication in the development of her child.

A was brought in for a communication assessment, but the mother's main concern was that A was not able to play with other children. Although it was quite evident to the therapists that A has some serious communication problems (she had severe cerebral palsy), this was not the primary concern verbalized by the mother. The way in which the mother therefore defined the problem was very different from the perspective of the professional. The second point of interest related to the mother's understanding of the concept of play. She described A's play as trying to propel herself forward while in a baby walker, which suggests a more physical orientation to play. This orientation is also congruent with her tendency to focus on the more observable (play behavior) of the child rather than on the child's ability to communicate even though she is bringing her child for a communication assessment.

For a therapist, particularly for one trained in a Western context, this type of intercultural interaction can be very challenging—not only because the parent (in this case the mother) can have very different perspectives on her child's difficulties, but also because it is difficult for the therapist to understand the perspective of the mother and be emotionally resonant with her. The challenge here is for the therapist not to impose a specific perspective, but to allow for a spontaneous interaction between therapist and mother to encourage the development of common ground in terms of the purpose of the visit and the outcomes of the assessment. Similar to the previous example, it is pertinent that professionals have the skill to engage with parents to facilitate deeper understanding of each other's perspectives without judgment or evaluation. Empathetic communication is only possible in a context of acceptance and genuine interest.

Creating common ground with the mother could involve a discussion of various topics for the purpose of (a) exploring the importance of play with the mother and asking her about the role that she thinks communication plays in participating in play activities, (b) inquiring why she decided to bring A for a communication assessment to better understand her expectations of the process, and (c) exploring her perspective on parenting and the role of different family members in the child's life. Spending time to develop common ground in this way not only serves to increase the relevance of the interaction, but also builds a more solid basis for sustainable intervention.

Providing the parent with information about the importance of communication skills in a child's development becomes relevant only once some level of mutual trust has been established. Common ground, the ability to be emotionally resonant (i.e., acceptance and harmony), and shared understanding of a problem are at the basis of empathetic communication. It is the ability to create meaning with the parent on both cognitive and affective levels that provides the best guarantee for positive long-term outcomes.

Although this example represents an "in-your-face" scenario of how different perspectives can manifest in interaction, misunderstandings of a less-obvious nature can be equally, if not more, challenging to deal with. Accepting differences in perspectives in interactions without feeling pressurized to come to a predefined consensus constitutes a pivotal basis for empathetic communication.

Conclusion

The above discussion identifies two main issues of note that impact the process of empathetic communication: (a) the level of task-orientedness or purposeful structure imposed on the interaction and (b) the experiential and conceptual differences between communication partners. Although being task-oriented within some contexts can be beneficial and probably necessary, the first example clearly describes the difficulties associated with becoming "set" in a task-driven mode of interaction even when the purpose of the get-together is to spontaneously interact. The ability to engage with a person with disabilities can be significantly compromised when caregivers feel pressure to "accomplish" something every time they interact with one of their clients. Caregivers who define their roles in terms of "caring for" rather than "communicating with" people with disabilities largely take responsibility for their clients and often times fail to "see" the true nature of the clients they are working with. Moreover, as caregivers gain experience, they learn to better control their reflexive emotional reactions with the people they care for and become more and more detached and disengaged further exacerbating the distance between caregivers and clients (Morse et al. 2006). While it may be true that in some cases emotional distancing can be a protective measure for caregivers, the pressure to maintain a professional demeanor with clients imposes significant stress on the caregiver, who must exhibit tremendous emotional self-control. This may inadvertently contribute to the high levels of burnout experienced by professional caregivers (Skirrow and Hatton 2007).

Disengaged or pseudo-engaged professional interactions are also detrimental to the relationship between caregiver and clients, and potentially clients' quality of life. Particularly for adults in residential settings, such as W who interacts almost exclusively with professional caregivers, denying genuine emotional connection in favor of clinical, professional interaction is a violation of their human rights. Creating an awareness of the importance of self-other awareness in these types of interactions could go a long way in empowering caregivers to explore different ways of interacting with their clients. In both interactions presented here, the professional caregiver or therapist has a specific goal that ultimately presents difficulties for empathetic communication when their interlocutors express different perspectives on the reasons for the conversation.

Each of our examples highlights the need for building common ground in interactions where communication partners clearly have very different perspectives. We have also suggested some ways in which a greater degree of empathetic communication can be promoted. Self-other awareness—awareness of one's agenda and one's perspective—and willingness to make an effort to ask further questions and to take time to understand the other is a communicative strategy that can be learned through observation, practice, and reflection. The ability to communicate empathetically is at the foundation of promoting inclusion of people with disabilities in our society. Communication is not just a cognitive process that requires exchanging messages with someone; it is also a process based on emotional resonance with another. As we move towards more inclusive societies, our awareness of emotional understanding and our acceptance of others play a significant role in promoting authentic communication with people with disabilities. This chapter highlights the importance of self-other awareness as part of the intersubjective process of meaning-making to facilitate inclusion of people with disabilities in our society. Only by understanding the need for self-other awareness as part of the communication process can we move towards sustainable intervention processes.

References

Alant, E. (2005). Intervention issues. In E. Alant & L. Lloyd (Eds.), *Augmentative and alternative communication: Beyond poverty* (pp. 9–29). London: Whurr Publications.

Alant, E., Uys, K., & Tonsing, K. (2009). Communication, language and literacy learning in children with developmental disabilities. In J. Matson, F. Andrasik, & M. Matson (Eds.), *Treating childhood psychopathology and developmental disabilities* (pp. 373–402). New York: Springer.

Antaki, C., Finlay, W. M. L., Sheridan, E., Jingree, T., & Walton, C. (2006). Producing decisions in service-user groups for people with an intellectual disability: Two contrasting facilitator styles. *Mental Retardation, 44*(5), 322–343.

Beck, U. (2006). *The cosmopolitan vision*. Cambridge: Polity Press.

Bollinger, L. (2002, July 12). Debate over the SAT masks perilous trends in college admissions. *Chronicle of Higher Education*, p. B11. Retrieved from http://chronicle.com

Brinck, I. (2008). The role of intersubjectivity in the development of intentional communication. In J. Zlatev, T. P. Racine, C. Sinha, & E. Itkonen (Eds.), *The shared mind: Perspectives on intersubjectivity* (pp. 115–140). Amsterdam: John Benjamins.

Clark, H. H. (1996). *Using language*. Cambridge: Cambridge University Press.

Decety, J., & Ickes, W. (Eds.). (2009). *The social neuroscience of empathy*. Cambridge, MA: MIT Press.

Devi, N. (2013). Supported decision-making and personal autonomy for persons with intellectual disabilities: Article 12 of the UN convention on the rights of persons with disabilities. *Journal of Law, Medicine & Ethics, 41*(4), 792–806.

Dewaele, J. M., & Wei, L. (2012). Multilingualism, empathy and multicompetence. *International Journal of Multilingualism, 9*(4), 352–366.

Dixon, J. A., & Moore, C. F. (1990). The development of perspective taking: Understanding differences in information and weighting. *Child Development, 61*(5), 1502–1513.

Drew, N., Funk, M., Tang, S., Lamichhane, J., Chávez, E., Katontoka, S., et al. (2011). Human rights violations of people with mental and psychosocial disabilities: An unresolved global crisis. *The Lancet, 378*(9803), 1664–1675.

Gallese, V., Keysers, C., & Rizzolatti, G. (2004). A unifying view of the basis of social cognition. *Trends in Cognitive Sciences, 8*(9), 396–403.

Iacoboni, M. (2008). *Mirroring people: The new science of how we connect with others*. New York: Farrar.

Ickes, W. (1993). Empathic accuracy. *Journal of Personality, 61*(4), 587–610.

Korkmaz, B. (2011). Theory of mind and neurodevelopmental disorders of childhood. *Pediatric Research, 69*(5), 101R–108R.

Mitchell, P. (2011). Acquiring a theory of mind. In A. Slater & G. Bremner (Eds.), *An introduction to developmental psychology* (2nd ed., pp. 357–384). New York: BPS Blackwell.

Morse, J. M., Bottorff, J., Anderson, G., O'Brien, B., & Solberg, S. (2006). Beyond empathy: Expanding expressions of caring. *Journal of Advanced Nursing, 53*(1), 75–87.

Ozanska-Ponikwia, K. (2012). What has personality and emotional intelligence to do with "feeling different" while using a foreign language? *International Journal of Bilingual Education and Bilingualism, 15*(2), 217–234.

Pinker, S. (2011). *The better angels of our nature: Why violence has declined.* New York: Viking.

Pratt-Johnson, Y. (2006). Communicating cross-culturally: What teachers should know. *The Internet TESL Journal, 12*(2). Retrieved from http://iteslj.org/Articles/Pratt-Johnson-CrossCultural.html

Rogers, C. (1975). Empathic: An unappreciated way of being. *The Counseling Psychologist, 5*(2), 2–10.

Ros i Solé, C. (2013). Cosmopolitan speakers and their cultural cartographies. *Language Learning Journal, 41*(3), 326–339.

Skirrow, P., & Hatton, C. (2007). Burnout amongst direct care workers in services for adults with intellectual disabilities: A systematic review of the research findings and initial normative data. *Journal of Applied Research in Intellectual Disabilities, 20*(2), 131–144.

Stern, D. N. (1985). *The interpersonal world of the infant.* New York: Basic Books.

Titchener, E. B. (1909). *Lectures on the experimental psychology of the thought processes.* New York: Macmillan.

Trevarthen, C., & Hubley, P. (1978). Secondary intersubjectivity: Confidence, confiding, and acts of meaning in the first year. In A. Lock (Ed.), *Action, gesture, and symbol: The emergence of language* (pp. 183–229). New York: Academic.

UN General Assembly. (2006, December 13). *Convention on the rights of persons with disabilities.* Retrieved from http://www.un.org/disabilities/d

Chapter 12
Severe Communication Disabilities in South Africa: Challenges and Enablers

Shakila Dada, Harsha Kathard, Kerstin Tönsing, and Michal Harty

Abstract Persons with severe communication disabilities in South Africa experience many barriers to their inclusion in society. These barriers occur across contexts and within all levels of the individual's family and community life. Congruent with the current models of disability, effective and sustainable communication intervention requires a broad systemic and context-relevant approach that addresses the interaction between individual and environment. This chapter will identify the enablers and barriers to inclusion of people with severe communication disabilities in the South African context within different levels of the ecology. Augmentative and Alternative Communication (AAC) intervention as one method to increase levels of engagement and participation for this group of individuals will be discussed. Reflection on the context-relevant practices and considerations for change across different levels of the ecology to ensure feasible, versatile, and sustainable AAC intervention will be highlighted. These include, but are not limited to, adaptations, the cultural appropriateness of graphic symbols used, the cultural and linguistic competence of the professionals who work with families from diverse backgrounds, as well as availability and provision of technology (in particular speech-generating devices).

S. Dada (✉) • K. Tönsing
Centre for Augmentative and Alternative Communication, University of Pretoria,
Pretoria, South Africa
e-mail: shakila.dada@up.ac.za

H. Kathard
Communication Sciences and Disorders, University of Cape Town, Cape Town, South Africa

Department of Health and Rehabilitation Sciences, University of Cape Town,
Cape Town, South Africa

M. Harty
Communication Sciences and Disorders, University of Cape Town, Cape Town, South Africa

© Springer International Publishing AG 2017   169
S. Halder, L.C. Assaf (eds.), *Inclusion, Disability and Culture*, Inclusive
Learning and Educational Equity 3, DOI 10.1007/978-3-319-55224-8_12

Introduction

South Africa (SA) provides a unique setting in which to understand inclusion of persons with disability from cross-cultural and cross-disciplinary perspectives. South Africa is a diverse country, with a population of more than 51 million people (Statistics South Africa 2011). The country is divided into 9 provinces with 11 official languages, a variety of cultures and religions. The disability discourse in South Africa is influenced not only by international developments but also by numerous contextual factors specific to itself. The impact of South African political history and the effect of a constitutional democracy in 1994 on the lives of persons with disability in South Africa should not be undervalued (Grobbelaar-du Plesis and van Eck 2011).

The aim of the chapter is to explore the role of various policies and legislation on the inclusion of persons with disability, particularly those with little functional speech who require augmentative and alternative communication (AAC) intervention, in South Africa. The chapter provides a case study to highlight the limitations and benefits of AAC with a specific focus on the influence of multicultural and environmental factors that affect the inclusion of people who use AAC.

Legal Framework

The postapartheid South African Constitution is considered to be one of the most inclusive and progressive constitutions in the world, with specific attention being paid to protecting the rights of vulnerable populations including women, children, persons with disabilities, and those without adequate access to nutrition, security, housing, health care, and education (South African Government 1996). The South African Constitution is complemented by the South African Bill of Rights, which promises the rights to nondiscrimination, education, information, safety, and housing (African National Congress 1993).

Disability rights in South Africa should be understood within the broader context of the development of human rights (Biegon 2011). South Africa has come a long way in terms of promoting and protecting rights of those with disabilities, and there has been a steady movement toward disability rights being framed within a human rights perspective. However, the challenges in terms of changing attitudes, traditions, and beliefs about persons with disability remain (Beigon 2011). In recent years there has been global increased awareness of the impact of disability on social development which has resulted in various policies. Governing bodies such as the United Nations (UN) and the World Health Organization (WHO) have advocated for universal human rights. The most widely accepted human rights convention in history, and the key authoritative international instrument governing rights of persons with disability, is the United Nations Convention on the Rights of Persons with Disability (CRPD), ratified by South Africa in 2007. For children in general and also for children with disabilities, the United Nations Convention on the Rights of a Child (CRC) (United Nations General Assembly 1989) represents a key complementary document. South Africa was one of the first countries to ratify the CRC in 1995.

Within the health-care sphere, the focus on disability and its impact on the lives of persons with disability have largely been driven by the World Health Organization. The International Classification of Functioning, Disability and Health (ICF), developed by the WHO, is a classification of health and health-related domains (World Health Organization 2001). The ICF as a "common language" about disability has attempted to initiate an international dialogue on disability, and the relevance of this classification framework for the local context will be considered in this section. The ICF (World Health Organization 2001) for children and youth (ICF-CY) was created to provide a universal framework for classifying and documenting disability (Simeonsson 2009). The ICF has been an endorsement of a social rather than a medical model of disability. The social model of disability emphasizes that disability is not primarily due to biological conditions inherent in the person with a disability, but rather is determined by the arrangement of the physical and social environment in which one has to operate. Disability has been defined as a dynamic multidimensional interaction between the key domains of impairment of body structure, function, activity limitations, participation restrictions, and contextual factors (WHO 2001). In this framework, disability has further been described as the outcome or result of a complex relationship between an individual's health condition and personal factors, and the external factors that represent the circumstances in which the individual lives (UNESCO 2006).

The ICF has its foundations in the concept of person – environmental interactions. The environmental factors include physical, social, and attitudinal. Environmental factors such as physical barriers, attitudes, or social policies can act either as supports or as barriers to activity and participation for persons with disability (McCauley et al. 2013). The ICF/ICF-CY can document the limitations and environmental barriers that can limit the rights to protection, care, and access (Simeonsson 2006). Environmental factors add information about how the context affects a person's functioning (WHO 2007). However, the influence of environmental factors such as poverty and unequal societies receive less emphasis. The ICF also describes the participation of each individual within the context of environmental and personal factors, rather than classifying the individual according to his/her health or health-related conditions only (UNESCO 2006). This has resulted in a placement of a culture of rights within numerous policies and conventions developed to protect people with disability.

Carlhed et al. (2003) are of the opinion that, although such rights are often implicit in the legislation of various countries, the ICF may provide the basis for the explicit documentation of rights. The ICF may thus serve as a source of evidence to identify, in particular, the lack of rights at the level of the individual child or a population (Simeonsson 2006). The ICF framework is congruent with the consideration of disability as being the result of the combination of a person's functional ability, the adaptability, and inclusivity of the environment in which they live, as proposed by the social model of disability. While the environment is considered as a dimension in the ICF, the "unpleasant realities" of the environment are not sufficiently captured or mentioned. For example, Helander (2003) states that the disabling context of poverty, which is relevant to countries like South Africa, is not fully considered. Further critiques include the lack of political clout (Kathard and Pillay 2013), the lack of links to existing disability-related national legislation, as well as the lack of positive views of persons with disability and a concentration on the negative aspects of disability (Helander 2003). The "realities" of abuse of persons with disability, use of alcohol and illicit drugs, children living without parents (living on streets), exploitation and oppression, and other common problems which are realities of persons with disability in some environments are not fully considered (Helander 2003).

Despite these progressive policies and guiding frameworks as well as international momentum to improve the lives of persons with disability, progress to date has been limited and slow. The contextual and other factors that have impeded progress are varied and contribute significantly to the experiences of persons with disability living in South Africa. While South Africa, according to the World Bank, is regarded as an upper middle-income country (World Bank 2015a), its distribution of wealth is uneven (Tregenna 2012) perpetuating poverty and inequalities. The GINI coefficient (a measure of income disparity) rates South Africa as one of the top four countries in terms of income inequality, with a coefficient of 64 (100 implies perfect inequality). This is evident in the health and education systems of South Africa. It is estimated that 38% of the South African population are living in rural areas (World Bank 2015b). These rural areas are defined by the poor infrastructure, lack of services, low levels of literacy and education, limited access to education and health care, a high incidence of communicable diseases, and high mortality rates. The country continues to face enormous challenges imposed by the legacy of apartheid policy poverty, limited access to services, poor literacy levels, high levels of unemployment, and many people living below the poverty line (Statistics SA 2011).

The Role of Environmental Factors in Inclusion of Persons with Disability

The understanding of the mechanisms of poverty has been deepening over the years, with a move away from describing poverty purely in terms of limited income. In addition, influence of poverty on disability has been explored (Emmett 2005). Currently, poverty is both a cause and a consequence of disability (Emmett 2005) due, in part, to the mutual reinforcement of these two conditions. The heightened exposure to risks and environmental hazards related to poverty can increase the likelihood for congenital or acquired disabilities. Likewise, disability can reinforce poverty through its negative association with education and employment. Poverty is reported to be ubiquitous in developing countries where up to 50% of the population can exhibit stunted growth from a lack of proper nutrition (Walker et al. 2007). Emmett (2005) argues that poverty requires an understanding from multiple dimensions including impoverishment in terms of education, literacy, health and nutrition, vulnerability and risk, isolation and powerlessness, capabilities and freedoms, and social exclusion. The relationship between poverty and disability has been demonstrated, and in South Africa, there is a disproportionate representation of persons with disability among the poor. Hence, the impoverishments experienced by person within these contexts result in further disadvantage.

The quadruple burden of disease in South Africa has also been identified to create a major context for disability (Statistics South Africa 2011). This disease burden refers to (1) maternal, newborn, and childhood illness; (2) chronic noncommunicable diseases, such as diabetes and cardiovascular diseases; (3) communicable diseases such as human immunodeficiency virus (HIV) and tuberculosis; and (4) violence and injury in the population. These conditions are all associated with disabilities of communication and affect a large proportion of the black South African population, particularly women and children who continue to live in poverty (Kathard and Pillay 2013; Sanders and Chopra 2006).

Persons with disabilities account for approximately 15% of the world's population (WHO 2001). It is further estimated that sub-Saharan Africa has the highest incidence of disability in the world with almost 66% of persons with disability (McLahan and Schwarts 2009). It is estimated that the prevalence of disability in South Africa is approximately 13% with the prevalence of severe disability at approximately 5% (Statistics South Africa 2013). The prevalence of communication disabilities for South Africa is estimated to be 6–12% in children over the age of 5 years, although accurate statistics are lacking.

Current research suggests that the experience of living with disability (in South Africa) is dominated by stigma and discrimination (Mall and Swartz 2012; Mueller-Johnson et al. 2014) and social exclusion (Kijak 2011; Mpofu et al. 2011). A recent report (Human Rights Watch 2015) found that many children with disabilities in schools face discriminatory practices which serve as barriers to receiving a quality education. The barriers include access to education, access to the same curriculum as children without disabilities, costs of education, increased vulnerability to violence and abusive practices, low quality of education, and inadequately trained teachers. These barriers have resulted in youth with disabilities leaving school with a lack of basic life skills which are needed to find employment or continue with further education (Human Rights Watch 2015). Despite political freedom gained by South Africans, economic access to health services and education continues to be challenging for the majority of people in the country, and persons with disability face added challenges. Despite progressive policies, the majority of people continue to struggle with inequality. These challenges are particularly pronounced in persons with severe communication disabilities.

Communication Disabilities

Communication is considered to be intrinsic to our humanity and is considered a basic human right. Human beings need communication to socialize, to learn and to work, and to participate in society. Communication "is the essence of human life" (Article II, Section 1, USSAAC Bylaws cited in Koppenhaver 2000, p. 270). Communication can be defined as an interpersonal process which occurs between two or more people in a context. It has to comply with a set of rules of discourse, interaction, social roles, understanding, and use of language, additionally involving implementation of individual styles and strategies. Being unable to communicate can be seen as one of the most extreme forms of exclusion and disempowerment. A well-functioning democracy presupposes active citizens who not only know their rights, but also are able to claim them by "speaking up."

When individuals have a communication impairment – and particularly for those unable to communicate using speech – the very act of making meaning together is threatened. Potential communication partners often perceive the process of attempting to engage meaningfully or co-creating meaning with such a person as too difficult and uncomfortable, as the normative rules for this process cannot be complied with. Fast efficient communication with both partners sharing the responsibility of making meaning is typically what is required. During communication, all participants play a role in the meaning-making process. However, when this process is compromised, then the strain created requires that each participant makes additional effort (Watermeyer and Kathard 2015). People with a severe communication disability – who have minimal resources to add to this process – may find that they are excluded because their partners often do not know what to do to negotiate meaning making. AAC therefore may be a way to reduce the strain in the communication process because the person with severe communication disability has the opportunity to contribute actively. Ideally the power relationships between the communication partners are equal (Watermeyer and Kathard 2015). However, when partners feel uncomfortable and unsure of what to do, they may minimize communication opportunities or even exclude the persons with limited speech or speak on behalf of or for them. Hence, as communication partners, they become complicit in the exclusion of people with communication impairments. The ICF has played a role in the slow shift from thinking of impaired communication as an individual's condition to viewing it as a condition which is lived in a social context with relational consequences. Hence, it has enhanced a more human and social understanding of communication (Watermeyer and Kathard 2015) highlighting the role of the environment in the inclusion of people who have communication disabilities.

Augmentative and Alternative Communication

Augmentative and alternative communication (AAC) encompasses any form of communication used to supplement or replace oral speech that is not functional (ASHA 2015). The word *augmentative communication* is important to the definition; it describes facilitative or supportive strategies that are used by a person to enhance their spoken communication abilities. *Alternative communication* however refers to strategies that serve as an alternate way of communicating, in the absence of natural speech. Hence, depending on the person with severe communication disabilities, AAC strategies can be provided either to augment their communication or as an alternative way for them to communicate. These forms comprise aided methods (such as the use of alphabet boards, picture communication boards, or speech-generating devices [SGDs]) as well as unaided methods (e.g., the use of gestures and signs from sign language). Access to appropriate forms of AAC can play a pivotal role in mediating communication and promoting the participation and inclusion of persons with no functional speech in society (Beukelman and Mirenda 2013).

In the language of the ICF, AAC systems (comprising of aids, symbols, techniques, and strategies) can be seen as environmental adaptations intended to compensate for limited or absent functional speech. In order for such adaptations to foster inclusion meaningfully, however, they need not only be available, accessible, and affordable, but also acceptable to, and appropriate for, the person and his/her communication partners and the greater physical and sociocultural context (see Maxwell and Granlund 2011, for a discussion of these five dimensions of the environment). The potential of AAC systems to support social inclusion can be realized only when these individuals gain access to meaningful communication contexts and interactions with willing communication partners.

When considering availability, accessibility, and affordability of AAC systems in the South African context, access to training and rehabilitation services as well as provision of assistive technology (AT) needs to be taken into account. The provision of AAC services, although still limited in South Africa (Maguvhe 2014), has received support in official policy documents, both from the Department of Health (2000) and from the Department of Education (2005, 2007, 2010). However, all health and educational service provision in South Africa is still characterized by gross inequalities, linked not only to a poor distribution of resources, but also to models of service provision that marginalize the majority of persons with disability – those who are poor and not from Western cultural and language backgrounds (Pillay and Kathard 2015). AAC service provision is additionally hampered by a lack of indigenous models of communication intervention to guide service providers (Alant 2005b). Formal training (if provided) regarding the implementation of AAC is typically based on a narrow view of what AAC entails (as it typically excludes informal methods of communication as well as interactions that are not synchronous and face-to-face) and is rooted in Western models of service delivery. Current ways of ensuring cultural sensitivity between health-care providers and persons with disability and their families are addressed in a subsequent section of this chapter. The need for cultural sensitivity in service delivery is another factor which is discussed in more detail in the section following.

Although policies exist regarding the provision of assistive technology (AT) through public health and educational services, lack of coordinated implementation, uneven distribution of resources, and high levels of fund mismanagement and corruption significantly hamper AT provision. Consequently, the availability varies significantly from one institution to the next. AAC technology in particular, as a relative "novelty" in the AT and rehabilitation field in South Africa, is still rarely provided through public funding, and reliance on private funding or sponsorship is the norm rather than the exception. Since the majority of people with severe communication disabilities have neither the financial means to acquire the systems themselves nor the social capital to access sponsorships, acquisition of dedicated AAC technology (i.e., technology that is developed to function solely as an AAC system) remains largely unrealized. An ironic corollary of this situation is that knowledge and availability of such specialized technology remain limited with very few vendors/companies importing AAC devices and associated AT due to a small market – and these factors in turn keep technology prices high.

The rapid developments in mobile technologies over the past years have resulted in more available and affordable mainstream technologies being used as AAC systems – making the acquisition of AAC technology possible for a greater group of people (McNaughton and Light 2013). Uptake of mobile technologies such as cell phones is high in many developing countries, including South Africa (Phew Research Centre 2015), and the move toward so-called nondedicated AAC systems is a particularly positive one for many people from resource-limited environments who need AAC. At the same time, challenges such as limited solutions for alternative access for people with physical disabilities as well as lack of durability and sturdiness are currently still notable drawbacks of this technology (McNaughton and Light 2013).

Case Example The case example of Mpho aims to highlight the role of the environment in shaping disability, engagement, and the incorporation of the voices of the "voiceless" (i.e., those who use AAC and their families). The case highlights the importance of having a more human and social understanding of persons that use AAC. It also highlights that rehabilitation professionals need to consider outcomes broader than their specific disciplines toward environmental interventions for a more holistic approach. The need for rehabilitation professionals to be agents of social change in contexts such as South Africa is also highlighted in this case.

Mpho is a 25-year-old male who has a cerebral palsy. He lives in the Valley of a Thousand Hills in a rural area of Kwa-Zulu Natal, one of the poorest provinces in South Africa. He lives with his unemployed mother in a one-bedroom house along with other family members. He attended a special school in Durban that catered to children with disabilities. He lived at the boarding school and only went home every fortnight for a weekend. He obtained a grade 12 qualification and passed the national exams and his results would have provided him entry into a tertiary training college.

He was the first person in the family to complete a grade 12 education. His parents had limited educational opportunities and his siblings dropped out of school as tertiary education seemed impossible. Mpho also did not attend college as the cost of tertiary education was beyond what his family could afford. In addition, he had not received any career guidance while at school and was not sure about what he would be able to study.

He is dependent in most activities of daily living like dressing. However, he is able to propel his wheelchair independently for short distances on smooth surfaces. His speech is limited to a few vocalizations and some words that are intelligible to familiar communication partners. He uses a few gestures as well. His AAC system is a laptop computer with text-to-speech software. This software produces English synthetic speech only, which limits his communication partners in the isiZulu-speaking community. In addition, he uses his mobile phone to text and communicates with friends on Facebook and other social media. He also uses the phone as a quick way to communicate his message when he is in the community as he is not always able to take his laptop computer with him. He uses a low-technology alphabet board to communicate some of his messages which he spells out. He is, however, able to use the phone and communication board only with literate communication partners. He is able to benefit from his extended family networks and attends weddings, prayer groups, and other communal gatherings where he is able to socialize albeit in a limited way with gestures, limited spoken abilities, and his English voice. In his social circle, literate communication partners are limited. He was also provided with a picture-based system in the hope that it would help him communicate with nonliterate partners. But he does not like using graphic symbols on his communication board because he perceives the pictures to be childish. Also, the messages he is able to communicate in this way are so limited that they do not meet his communication needs.

The house he lives in has indoor sanitation, running water, and electricity. His closest neighbors live on the next hill approximately 3 km from him. The closest town is approximately 45 km from his house. In order to travel to town (e.g., to visit the hospital), he needs to go to the main tarred road 5 km away to hail a minibus taxi. He has to be accompanied by a family member to communicate his messages and assist with getting on and off the taxi. He is charged a surcharge for taking his wheelchair on the taxi.

Unemployment in his area is extremely high. Government policies promote employment of persons with disability, and it has benefits for business. Through the help of an occupational therapist working at the school he attended, Mpho was able to secure part-time employment doing some office work for a local nursery for a short time after leaving school. He enjoyed the work, although he wanted to do more computer-based work. Mpho, however, found that the cost of getting to work by minibus taxi resulted in his transport costs being higher than his earnings. He is now unemployed and stays at home. He receives a monthly disability grant from the state for the equivalent of 80 USD. He attends a monthly advocacy meeting in the city center where he is part of a support group on using AAC. His ability to make friends, be part of community activities, and live independently in society are limited not only by the disability but also by his environment.

Mpho benefited from the nondedicated AAC devices as he was able to use a text-to speech software on his laptop. His laptop has always been sponsored via his school or more recently via Interface (nongovernmental organization). The difficulties with these sponsored laptops are that they are usually "hand-me-downs" and therefore have older, slower hardware. The text-to-speech software also has limited capacity in terms of organizing prestored messages for more efficient and quicker spontaneous conversations. In addition, the laptop frequently has problems and leaves Mpho without his "voice" for weeks when it is in need of repair. He gets by with his low-technology communication board, which is limiting.

Mpho is able to communicate with his literate peers and "old school friends" with his AAC device as well as mobile phone. He does, however, express frustration at being unable to communicate with friends from the neighborhood in isiZulu. He laments that his social circle consists primarily of professionals and students that he has come into contact with but that he has very limited friends outside of that.

Appropriate Assistive Technology

It must be acknowledged that technology, despite its inevitable "lure," is not the ultimate solution to all severe communication challenges (Hershberger 2011). First, technology provision that is not accompanied by context-relevant training and support for implementation typically leads to underuse or abandonment (Alant 2005a; Baxter et al. 2012; Johnson et al. 2006). Such training needs to be family-led in order to ensure meaningful outcomes (Anderson et al. 2016). According to Alant (2005a), successful use of AT is influenced by factors beyond the person and the family, including the orientation toward and infrastructure for general and assistive technology use within communities. Second, various forms of more affordable nonelectronic-aided or unaided AAC systems may be equally effective in promoting various aspects of communicative competence in individuals (see Gevarter et al. 2013 for a review; see also Tönsing 2015). Such less expensive systems nevertheless also require training and support for both the person using the system and communication partners, and consideration of community orientation toward and acceptance of such AAC methods.

Besides barriers restricting availability, accessibility, and affordability of AAC systems, lack of appropriateness and acceptability of such systems may be factors restricting AAC use. When AAC systems have been made available, yet are not implemented, one should ask whether the aids, symbols, techniques, and strategies proposed are appropriate for and acceptable to the person in need of AAC, his/her partners, as well as the physical, linguistic, and sociocultural context within which they are to be used (Alant 2005a).

In many instances, less formalized methods of communication, developed between people with severe communication disabilities and their close communication partners, may be perceived as more effective and more congruent with expectations and values around communicative exchanges in specific contexts than formal AAC systems such as communication boards and SGDs. Cultures valuing interdependence rather than independence may place less emphasis on communicative autonomy of individuals and be very comfortable with a co-constructive process of meaning making (for further reading on these terms, please see Brekke and Von Tetzchner 2003; Von Tetzchner and Grove 2003). Mexican American families, for example, reported that their children's use of SGDs negatively impacted on rate and breadth of content (due to preprogrammed messages), and intimacy in conversational exchanges decreased (McCord and Soto 2004). As a result, families preferred to use other methods of communication in the home context, such as "reading the child's eyes" (McCord and Soto 2004). Partner-dependent methods of communication do, of course, raise interesting questions about authorship and censorship, and can easily be misused to deny a person his/her own voice. In view of high rates of violence against and abuse of persons with disability committed by caregivers and family members (Milberger et al. 2003), authorship questions are pertinent to ask. While more formal AAC systems may not always be the method of choice in all contexts, they may serve an important function in giving access to an independent method of communication. Findings by Smith and Connolly (2008) suggest that, even when used infrequently for specific communication situations, AAC devices were highly valued and regarded as important methods of communication by the adults using them.

Language Considerations in AAC Implementation

With its 11 official languages, South Africa is a context of great linguistic diversity. One aspect that needs consideration is the design and customization of aided AAC systems appropriate for this multilingual context. As indicated, such systems include electronic options, such as SGDs and nonelectronic options such as communication books and boards. Typically, meaning is represented on these systems using text (orthography), icon sequences (e.g., Minspeak™), or single-meaning graphic symbols (e.g., Picture Communication Symbols or PCS™).

Commercially available graphic symbol libraries (e.g., PCS) are often chosen as a method of representation for persons in need of AAC who are nonliterate, especially if physical disabilities limit the use of unaided systems. These libraries have almost exclusively been developed from within Western contexts. Not only are typically South African vocabulary items (such as "pap") not represented in these libraries, but the attempts by (most) developers to depict vocabulary in a way that visually represents the referent or at least an easily learnable association with the referent result in context- and culture-specific images, such as a yellow sedan car to represent "taxi" (while the most common South African taxi is a minibus) or a snowman to represent "January." It follows that many symbols may not be congruent to South African cultures and contexts. The views of the persons who will use these graphic symbols in terms of their appropriateness and ability to enhance meaning making within a particular culture are vital.

Haupt and Alant (2002) investigated the iconicity ("guessability") of selected PCS symbols for Setswana-speaking 10–11-year-old children from rural contexts and found it to be low. One explanation proposed by the authors was the lack of access to printed materials resulting in the tasks of picture recognition being unfamiliar. Children particularly struggled, for example, with interpreting the meaning of arrows in graphic symbols, suggesting that they were not familiar with this abstract yet relatively widespread convention. Basson and Alant (2005) found similar results for Afrikaans-speaking 6-year-olds. Dada et al. (2013) found higher iconicity of PCS symbols among South African adolescents with English as a second language and mild intellectual disability. The children participating in this study were from urban contexts and had been included in a well-resourced school following the adapted national curriculum. They may therefore have had extensive print exposure. De Klerk et al. (2014) found differences in the graphic symbols which children from Setswana- versus Afrikaans-speaking backgrounds selected to depict basic emotions, suggesting that language background influences the way a person relates to graphic symbols. Taken together, these studies illustrate that learning demands of graphic-symbol-based systems may be high for people with limited print exposure and for those from contexts that differ culturally and linguistically from those in which the symbols were developed. These learning demands would extend even to nonliterate partners when picture symbols without speech generation are used for communication.

The inability of most SGDs to "speak" more than one language has been found to be a factor hindering their implementation in multilingual contexts (Baxter et al. 2012; McCord and Soto 2004). Most South Africans are multilingual and are required to use different languages each day as they move between contexts such as home, school, and work (Davis 2013). AAC in South Africa therefore must inherently be multilingual due to the diverse languages spoken and the population and multilingual context. Code switching (using different languages in one sentence) is a relatively common phenomenon (Slabbert and Finlayson 2000). The lack of text-to-speech engines (synthetic voice produced by a device from the conversion of text entries) in African languages is one barrier (Van Niekerk and Tönsing 2015). Lack of knowledge and skill in customizing graphic-symbol-based SGDs in ways that provide relevant access to two languages while minimizing learning demands may be another. Even when provided to give access to one language, such systems require a number of design and customization decisions for which little guidance exists (Thistle and Wilkinson 2015). Decisions about vocabulary selection, layout, and organization for systems that are to be used for two or more languages will require good knowledge not only of user and partner preferences and expectations, but also of the vocabulary and grammar of the target languages (Soto and Yu 2014).

Infrastructure and Partner Considerations in AAC Implementation

The acceptance of and infrastructure for technology use also need careful consideration (Alant 2005a). Access to electricity is, for example, not a given in rural areas. High crime rates make many of the young adults using AAC whom we work with reluctant to take their nondedicated SGDs to community settings. One young man received sponsorship through his school for an AAC device, and the system eventually chosen for him was a desktop computer securely bolted to a large desk in his home due to the high-risk area he lived in and poor security of his home. Although it has proven an excellent tool for access to social media and Windows-based programs, it is impossible to use for social conversations in locations other than in this particular room of the house. Since family members have often found ways to communicate without the use of formal AAC systems, such systems are often more necessary in situations outside of the home.

The use of AAC systems influences communication exchanges in unique ways (Tönsing et al. 2005). Face-to-face conversational exchanges follow subconscious yet very much conventionalized patterns (see, for example, Grice's [1975] cooperative principle), although these may differ between cultures to some extent. Departures from these conventions are typically noticeable. They often result in discomfort on the side of the communication partner and may lead to abandonment of the exchange and rejection of the communication methods employed. As illustrated by McCord and Soto (2004), cultural expectations of certain types of exchanges may be incongruent with the restrictions AAC system use may impose on such exchanges. At the same time, it has been noted that "(AAC) is not …within anybody's culture" (Binger et al. 2008 p. 326, quoting a Latino parent). Nevertheless, open and continued dialogue with partners and community members forms an important cornerstone of AAC intervention (Alant 2005c; McCord and Soto 2004) as service providers together with family and community members explore effective and sustainable AAC intervention options.

Partners (e.g., parents and teachers) may be intimidated by the demands of technology, perceiving the task of supporting its use by the person in need of AAC as challenging (van Niekerk and Tönsing 2015). In a pilot investigation, Tönsing and Dada (2015) found that, in a sample of 26 educators from special schools who taught children using aided AAC, 77% wanted further training in the use of electronic devices, while 38% felt that they needed training on nonelectronic-aided AAC systems, suggesting that the former may have been perceived as more complicated. However, Dada and Alant (2002) and Horn (2014) found that South African teachers and peers generally had positive attitudes toward SGDs. Peers were in general significantly more positive about an iPad-based application than a nonelectronic alphabet board. Dada and Alant (2001) did not identify a significant difference in inclusive teachers' preference for using voice output technology over low technology (a communication board) for children with complex communication needs in a rural special school setting. Similarly, teachers in mainstream urban schools were more positive in their attitudes toward a dedicated, graphic-symbol-based SGD versus a graphic-symbol-based communication board (Dada and Alant 2002).

In summary, AAC systems need to be available, accessible, and affordable, but also acceptable and appropriate for the person, partners, and environment in order to foster meaningful inclusion. A broad view of communication and AAC needs to acknowledge existing "informal" communication methods and strengthen and support these, while introducing more formal systems where needed in a way that articulates with rather than disrupts the existing patterns. Limitations of formal systems need to be acknowledged and addressed through participatory research and design (Blackstone et al. 2007). The need for relevant AAC service delivery was also highlighted, and importance of health-care providers' commitment to becoming culturally competent will be addressed in the section following.

The Role of Cultural Competence in Culturally Sensitive Service Delivery

Leavitt (2002) describes cultural competence as "a set of behaviours, attitudes and policies that come together in a continuum to enable a health care system, agency or individual practitioner to function effectively in trans-cultural interactions, (p. 1)." Families and professionals are likely to have differing values, beliefs, and practices relating to disability, intervention, and participation in family and community activities. Culture has had a long standing of being a proxy for advantage (or disadvantage) in South Africa. Access to quality health care and education in South Africa has historically been reserved for members of the White middle and upper class (Kathard and Pillay 2013). In 2011, investigation into the distribution of speech-language therapy (SLT) services indicated that more than 50% of registered clinicians were in private practice and in urban areas (Kathard and Pillay 2013). However, the General Household Survey (Statistics South Africa 2013) indicates that 87% of the population does not have access to private health care (as determined by active membership of a medical-aid scheme). Therefore, the majority of the population is serviced by the public health-care system. This is problematic since the population needs relating to communication are diverse and range from preventative and development opportunities through to the tertiary level care discussed in the previous section relating to the provision of AT-related services. However, the concern is not restricted to the number of therapists employed to provide services in government facilities. Another pressing concern is that the majority of rehabilitation professionals working in state-run health and education systems come from backgrounds which are vastly different from the cultural background of the individuals/families they serve. In order for professionals to navigate these differences and provide services which are perceived as beneficial by the consumers of these services, Campinha-Bacote (2002) argues that professionals need to nurture "cultural desire."

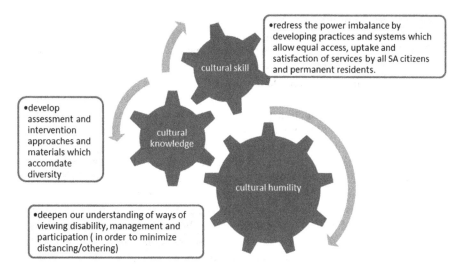

Fig. 10.1 Schematic of the components of cultural competence

Cultural desire encompasses the desire to learn more about another person's cultural beliefs and practices and has also been termed "cultural humility" (Tervalon and Murray-Garcia 1998). Cultural humility, although an important foundation, is only one component of cultural competence. Other components regularly included in models of cultural competence include cognitive (knowledge) and behaviors (skills) components (Balcazar et al. 2009). These three components have been schematically represented in Fig. 10.1.

According to Bettancourt et al. (2003), a "culturally competent" health-care system acknowledges and incorporates – at all levels – the *importance* of culture, assessment of cross-cultural relations, vigilance toward the *dynamics* that result from cultural differences, expansion of cultural *knowledge*, and *adaptation* of services to meet culturally unique needs (p. 294). Balcazar et al. (2009) propose that this process starts with critical awareness, which leads to an expansion in the knowledge of other cultures and eventually advances to include the development of skills. These components in combination promote engagement in culturally sensitive practices. However, it is important to acknowledge that the degree of organizations/systems support for engaging in these practices can either be a barrier or be a facilitator. These definitions suggest that cultural competence is not present solely at an individual level, but crosses all the ecological levels from microsystem (individual), meso-level (transcultural interactions), to macro-level (policy issues).

At an individual (microsystem) level, cultural competence is present on a continuum which, Hanley (1999) proposes, runs from cultural blindness (lack of understanding of differences that exist between cultures) to cultural proficiency (which encompasses the ability to tailor service delivery offerings to ensure the best possible outcomes for families and communities). The professional needs to obtain information about each of the following aspects before service delivery are likely to be viewed as successful from the person with a little or no functional speech perspective. These include, but are not limited to, the clinician's own cultural concept of disability, intervention, and meaningful participation; the person with little or no functional speech cultural concept of disability, intervention, and meaningful participation; determining shared definitions of successful outcomes; determining appropriate assessment and intervention settings; as well as determining appropriate assessment and intervention protocols (materials, equipment, products, etc.) (adapted from Kagawa Singer and Chung 1987).

Engagement with people with little or no functional speech, their families, and the communities that they are part of should be emphasized in order to determine the health outcomes that *they* value. Throughout this process, it is important to take cognizance of the inherent power dynamic and to ensure that knowledge brought by the consumer is viewed as being as valuable as the knowledge brought by the therapist. In order to achieve this, the authors would like to use four of the challenges previously highlighted in this section and describe some key research findings within the South African context. These include the communities' views of disability; restricted participation for people with little or no functional speech; the choice of symbols to represent language concepts; and the acceptability of AT within different cultural contexts. Using the concept of "professional humility," we will then identify the knowledge gaps which still exist which are hampering our ability to provide relevant and accessible services to people with little or no functional speech.

Community Considerations in AAC Implementation

The first contextual issue we highlighted related to community's and family's cultural perceptions of health and disability shapes their willingness to interact with persons with disability. Consider what this example might suggest of a community's view of disability: "a woman is accused of cheating on her husband with a young adult with Downs Syndrome in the community, because her child is born with Down syndrome." Or this example of a teacher's perception of what it means to have a disability: "'Mpho' means gift – but this gift is broken" [pointing to a child with athetoid cerebral palsy]. South African research has focused on perceptions of teachers (Dada and Alant 2001, 2002), community nurses (Bornman and Alant 2002) peers (Lilienfeld and Alant 2005), parents (Harty et al. 2007; Stobbart and Alant 2008; Joseph and Alant 2000), and siblings (Opperman and Alant 2003; Harty et al. 2002). However, as pointed out by de Villiers (2015), very little research has been conducted with the persons with disability themselves, and reports of the lived experiences of people with little or no functional speech in the South African context is limited.

The second contextual issue we have highlighted is that people with severe disabilities have restricted access to participation in community and civic life. According to Beukelman and Mirenda (2013), opportunity barriers (such as other people's knowledge, attitude, and skills toward persons with disability) shape the quality and frequency of the participation opportunities a child has. Within a South African context, results from a study by Bornman and Donohue (2013) indicate that although teachers reported that the learner with attention deficit hyperactivity disorder (ADHD) would be more disruptive in class and have a more negative effect on the classroom climate, they overwhelmingly favored including a learner with ADHD over the learner with limited functional speech. The studies highlight the power that teachers have in providing participatory learning opportunities for children with complex communication needs within their classrooms. De Villiers (2015) reported that the general education teachers interviewed in her study themselves had an overwhelming sense of not being supported in their attempts to reintegrate children with traumatic brain injury back into the school context. This suggests that additional insights and information are needed to understand how best to enable teachers, within different school contexts, to support children with little or no functional speech within their classrooms. This is an important element which needs to be given attention if we are to provide truly inclusive education services to this population in the future.

The third contextual issue we have highlighted is the cultural appropriateness of the choice of specific symbols used to represent language concepts and the impact this has on symbol learning and use. This aspect has received substantial attention within the South African context, with studies which investigated Setswana-speaking (Bornman et al. 2009), Sepedi-speaking (De Klerk et al. 2014), Zulu-speaking (Haupt and Alant 2002), and Afrikaans-speaking (Basson and Alant 2005) participants' perceptions of various aspects of common graphic symbol systems which are frequently used in the South African context. However, future research endeavors should focus on the investigation of the appropriateness of symbols across all of the languages and cultures presented in our "rainbow nation."

The final contextual issue is the levels of acceptability of AAC systems and characteristics for different cultures and communities. Awareness of user and family's cultural perceptions of assistive technologies are not uniform. The authors have heard family members of people requiring AAC systems' say "an AAC device which talks will make my child lazy to talk," as well as acceptability issues "I won't have that American voice sitting around my dinner table." Research within the South African context has primarily focused on the operational issues clinicians face when designing aided AAC systems such as color-coding (Alant et al. 2010), symbol layout (Alant et al. 2007), the use of word prediction (Herold et al. 2008), as well as modes of delivery (AiLgS) (Dada and Alant 2009). However, the understanding of what factors affect the acceptability of AAC systems from the perspective of families and communities is still lacking. The authors feel that this body of research is critical for the development, selection, and implementation of culturally appropriate AAC systems, and future research within the South African context should prioritize this issue.

An important aspect of cultural knowledge (and cultural humility) is acknowledging that there are areas where knowledge gaps still exist. We would like to suggest the following areas that haven't yet received adequate attention within the SA context. Future research should seek to define what meaningful communication participation looks like within different cultures. The work of Mary Blake Huer and colleagues explored perspectives of African American families (Parette et al. 2002) and Mexican American families (Blake et al. 2001) regarding the use of AAC by their children with disabilities. To the best of our knowledge, no such evidence exists with reference to families from diverse background in South Africa. Using Parette et al. (2002; p. 204) and Pickl (2011, figure 1: p. 233) as a basis, we would like to suggest the following questions as a starting point in addressing Mpho's case:

- How does the community see itself?
- How is meaning co-created within the community?
- How is communication defined within the community?
- What are the community's and family members' views on disabilities, intervention, and the role of different health experts (e.g., health-care professionals and traditional healers)?
- What are Mpho's needs during everyday activities?
- What specific capabilities, knowledge, and skills does he demonstrate?
- With whom does he use AAC systems to communicate on a regular basis?
- What is the impact of AAC technology/systems on the process of meaning making (and communication) within different South African communities?
- What is the level of acceptance of AAC by important members of the family and the community?

We as health-care providers are participation brokers. In essence, we negotiate and arrange a communication system for people with little or no functional speech that is intended to assist them to participate more independently within the different contexts they inhabit. If this is true, then we cannot talk about disability without highlighting the need to revisit the fact that the clinician is often the one who is viewed by the family as having all the power (due to specialized knowledge and skills). For this reason, establishing channels of interaction/engagement with families and key community stakeholder is a critical part of the intervention dialogue. Negotiating roles which initially acknowledge the power imbalance and actively seek to gradually cede over control to communities and families is an important element of the sustainability of our services (Alant 2005b). The element of control is just as important for persons with disability themselves as for their families and the communities in which they live. For this reason, we would like to suggest that professional humility is an important element of the quality and sustainability of our services.

Conclusion

This chapter is written from a point of accepting diversity and promoting social inclusion within society. The social model of disability reminds us that a person is often made to feel more or less disabled by environmental factors such as poverty,

Fig. 10.2 Image of Dan Ncobo

unequal societies, the view from which AAC systems are developed, communication partners, multilingual and multicultural contexts, people, and resources. For this reason, the role of rehabilitation professionals as advocates for change and in empowering individuals with significant communication disabilities and their families cannot be overlooked.

The chapter highlights the importance of accessible communication through AAC as a key strategy for inclusion of persons with communication disability. Communication is a shared meaning-making process – that which we do together. AAC affords persons with severe communication disability an opportunity to participate meaningfully in everyday communication – a fundamentally humanizing process. An integrated approach is required in order to facilitate inclusion of persons that use AAC. While the needs of the persons that use AAC need to remain central, integration is also required at policy level as well as at the level of rehabilitation professionals, manufacturers of AAC systems, as well as families and communities in which persons that use AAC live. The chapter highlights the need to use an asset-based approach toward cultural diversity, and this is celebrated as a means of creating more inclusive strategies for persons that use AAC. It promotes at the outset an integrated approach across disciplines and stakeholders to create an inclusive society for persons that use AAC.

The chapter argues that creating opportunities for persons that use AAC implies also creating opportunities for the marginalized within that society. The voices of those who use AAC are essential, as are the voices of families and communities in which they live, in creating inclusive environments. Thus inclusion should be based on the voices of the marginalized within unequal societies. The solutions to providing inclusive environments should be pursued from the views of the marginalized rather than only from the perspective of the empowered.

Dan Ncobo, a South African activist for AAC, confronted people's perceptions about the role that individuals with significant communication disabilities can play in society. During a speech given at the Centre for AAC, in 2011, Dan challenged the audience to view persons with disability as having knowledge and skills, which enables them to become meaningful contributors to society. He shared a powerful visual image of himself beside a statue (see Fig. 10.2) and commented as follows: "This is a picture of two heads. One of them has nothing inside… guess which one!"

References

African National Congress. (1993). *A bill of rights for a new South Africa*. Retrieved from http://www.anc.org.za/show.php?id=231

Alant, E. (2005a). AAC technology for development. In E. Alant & L. L. Lloyd (Eds.), *Augmentative and alternative communication and severe disabilities: Beyond poverty* (pp. 192–220). London: Whurr.

Alant, E. (2005b). Intervention issues. In E. Alant & L. L. Lloyd (Eds.), *Augmentative and alternative communication and severe disabilities: Beyond poverty* (pp. 2–9). London: Whurr.

Alant, E. (2005c). Support-based AAC intervention. In E. Alant & L. L. Lloyd (Eds.), *Augmentative and alternative communication and severe disabilities: Beyond poverty* (pp. 155–191). London: Whurr.

Alant, E., Du Plooy, A., & Dada, S. (2007). The impact of visual sequencing of graphic symbols on the sentence construction of children who have acquired language. *The South African Journal of Communication Disorders, 54*, 105–110.

Alant, E., Kolatsis, A., & Lilienfeld, M. (2010). The effect of sequential exposure of colour conditions on time and accuracy of graphic symbol location. *Augmentative and Alternative Communication, 26*, 41–47.

American Speech-Language-Hearing Association. (2015). *AAC: More than three decades of growth and development*. Retrieved from http://www.asha.org/public/speech/disorders/AACThreeDecades/

Anderson, K. L., Balandin, S., & Stancliffe, R. J. (2016). "It's got to be more than that". Parents and speech-language pathologists discuss training content for families with a new speech generating device. *Disability and Rehabilitation. Assistive Technology, 11*(5), 375–384. doi:10.3109/17483107.2014.967314.

Balcazar, F. E., Suarez-Balcazar, Y., & Taylor-Ritzler, T. (2009). Cultural competence: Development of a conceptual framework. *Disability and Rehabilitation, 31*(14), 1153–1160.

Basson, M., & Alant, E. (2005). The iconicity and ease of learning of picture communication symbols: A study with Afrikaans-speaking children. *South African Journal of Communication Disorders, 52*, 4–12.

Baxter, S., Enderby, P., Evans, P., & Judge, S. (2012). Barriers and facilitators to the use of high-technology augmentative and alternative communication devices: A systematic review and qualitative synthesis. *International Journal of Communication Disorders, 47*(2), 115–129. doi:10.1111/j.1460-6984.2011.00090.x.

Betancourt, J. R., Green, A. R., Carrillo, J. E., & Annaneh-Firembong, O. (2003). Defining cultural competence: A practical framework for addressing racial/ethnic disparities in health and health care. *Public Health Reports, 118*(4), 293–302.

Beukelman, D. R., & Mirenda, P. (2013). *Augmentative and alternative communication: Supporting children and adults with complex communication needs* (4th ed.). Baltimore: Paul H. Brookes.

Biegon, J. (2011). The promotion and protection of disability rights in the African human rights system. In I. Grobbelaar-du Plessis & T. van Reenen (Eds.), *Aspects of disability law in Africa* (pp. 231–260). Pretoria: Pretoria University Law Press.

Binger, C., Kent-Walsh, J., Berens, J., Del Campo, S., & Rivera, D. (2008). Teaching Latino parents to support the multi-symbol message productions of their children who require AAC. *Augmentative   and   Alternative   Communication,   24*(4),   323–338. doi:10.1080/07434610802130978.

Blackstone, S. W., Williams, M. B., & Wilkins, D. P. (2007). Key principles underlying research and practice in AAC. *Augmentative and Alternative Communication, 23*(3), 191–203. doi:10.1080/07434610701553684.

Blake Huer, M., Parette, H. P., & Saenz, T. I. (2001). Conversations with Mexican Americans regarding children with disabilities and augmentative and alternative communication. *Communication Disorders Quarterly, 22*(4), 197–205.

Bornman, J., & Alant, E. (2002). Community nurses' perceptions of and exposure to children with severe disabilities and their primary caregivers. *Health SA, 7*(3), 32–55.

Bornman, J., & Donohue, D. K. (2013). South African teachers' attitudes toward learners with barriers to learning: Attention-deficit and hyperactivity disorder and little or no functional speech. *International Journal of Disability, Development and Education, 60*(2), 85–104.

Bornman, J., Alant, E., & Du Preez, A. (2009). Translucency and learnability of Blissymbols in Setswana-speaking children: An exploration. *Augmentative and Alternative Communication, 25*(4), 287–298.

Brekke, K. M., & Von Tetzchner, S. (2003). Co-construction in graphic language development. In S. Von Tetzchner & N. Grove (Eds.), *Augmentative and alternative communication: Developmental issues* (pp. 176–210). London: Whurr.

Camphina-Bacote, J. (2002). The process of cultural competence in the delivery of healthcare services: A model of care. *Journal of Transcultural Nursing, 13*(3), 181–184.

Carlhed, C., Björck-Åkesson, E., & Granlund, M. (2003). Parent perspectives on early intervention: The paradox of needs and rights. *The British Journal of Developmental Disabilities, 49*, 69–80.

Dada, S., & Alant, E. (2001). Teachers' attitudes towards learners' with little or mo functional speech using two AAC devices. *South African Journal of Education, 21*(2), 199–203.

Dada, S., & Alant, E. (2002). A comparative study of the attitudes of teachers at special and educationally inclusive schools towards learners with little or no functional speech using communication devices. *South African Journal of Education, 22*(3), 213–218.

Dada, S., & Alant, E. (2009). The effect of aided language stimulation on vocabulary acquisition in children with little or no functional speech. *American Journal of Speech-Language Pathology, 18*(1), 50–64.

Dada, S., Huguet, A., & Bornman, J. (2013). The iconicity of picture communication symbols for children with English additional language and mild intellectual disability. *Augmentative and Alternative Communication, 29*(4), 360–373. doi:10.3109/07434618.2013.849753.

Davis, R. (2013). *SA's shifting language landscape*. Retrieved from http://www.dailymaverick.co.za/article/2013-04-24-sas-shifting-language-landscape/#.Ujv9KX_4KqD

De Klerk, H. M., Dada, S., & Alant, E. (2014). Children's identification of graphic symbols representing four basic emotions: Comparison of Afrikaans-speaking and Sepedi-speaking children. *Journal of Communication Disorders, 52*, 1–15. doi:10.1016/j.jcomdis.2014.05.006.

De Villiers, A. J. (2015). *Stories of being back at school following traumatic brain injury (TBI): The experiences of children, their parents and educators*. Unpublished master's thesis, University of Cape Town, South Africa.

Department of Education. (2005). Conceptual and operational guidelines for the implementation of inclusive education: Special schools as resource centres. Pretoria: Department of Education. Retrieved from http://www.education.gov.za/LinkClick.aspx?fileticket=wHOV7lRtQlA=

Department of Education. (2007). *Guidelines to ensure quality education and support in special schools and special school resource centres*. Pretoria: Department of Education. Retrieved

from http://www.google.co.za/url?sa=t&rct=j&q=&esrc=s&source=web&cd=1&ved=0CB8Q
FjAA&url=http://www.thutong.doe.gov.za/resourcedownload.aspx?id=37716&ei=NYaOVbj
WOOKa7gbF1YP4DA&usg=AFQjCNGnk392PP1WTa_kzhnTQzQC-VJavA&sig2=0s0vUo
9xbff2zgsIy7gs2Q

Department of Education. (2010). *Guidelines for inclusive teaching and learning*. Pretoria: Department of Education.

Department of Health. (2000). *Rehabilitation for all. National rehabilitation policy*. Pretoria: Department of Health.

Emmett, T. (2005). Disability and poverty. In E. Alant & L. L. Lloyd (Eds.), *Augmentative and alternative communication and severe disabilities: Beyond poverty* (pp. 68–94). London: Whurr.

Gevarter, C., O'Reilly, M. F., Rojeski, L., Sammarco, N., Lang, R., Lancioni, G. E., & Sigafoos, J. (2013). Comparing communication systems for individuals with developmental disabilities: A review of single-case research studies. *Research in Developmental Disabilities, 34*(12), 4415–4432. doi:10.1016/j.ridd.2013.09.017.

Grice, P. (1975). Logic and conversation. In P. Cole & J. Morgan (Eds.), *Syntax and semantics. 3: Speech acts* (pp. 41–58). New York: Academic.

Grobbelaar-du Plessis, I., & van Eck, S. (2011). Protection of disabled employees in South Africa: An analysis of the constitutions and labour legislation. In I. Grobbelaar-du Plessis & T. van Reenen (Eds.), *Aspects of disability law in Africa* (pp. 231–260). Pretoria: Pretoria University Law Press.

Hanley, J. (1999). Beyond the tip of the iceberg: Five stages toward cultural competence. *Reaching Today's Youth, 3*(2), 9–12.

Hanson, M. J., Wolfber, P., Zercher, C., Morgan, M., Gutlerrez, S., Barnwell, D., & Beckman, P. (1998). The culture of inclusion: Recognizing diversity at multiple levels. *Early Child Research Quarterly, 13*(1), 185–209.

Harty, M., Alant, E., & Opperman, S. (2002). Adolescents: Typically developing siblings and siblings with severe disabilities. *Social Work, 38*(1), 62–70.

Harty, M., Alant, E., & Uys, C. J. E. (2007). Maternal self-efficacy and maternal perception of child language competence in pre-school children with a communication disability. *Child: Care, Health and Development, 33*(2), 144–154.

Haupt, L., & Alant, E. (2002). The iconicity of picture communication symbols for rural Zulu children. *The South African Journal of Communication Disorders, 49*, 40–49.

Helander, E. (2003). A critical review of the international classification of functioning (ICF). Paper presented at Bucharest, Romania. Retrieved from http://www.einarhelander.com/critical-review

Herold, M., Alant, E., & Bornman, J. (2008). Typing speed, spelling accuracy and the use of word prediction. *South African Journal of Education, 28*, 117–134.

Hershberger, D. (2011). Mobile technology and AAC Apps from an AAC developer's perspective. *Perspectives on Augmentative and Alternative Communication, 20*(1), 28–33. doi:10.1044/aac20.1.28.

Horn, T. (2014). *Children's attitudes towards interaction with an unfamiliar peer with little or no functional speech: Comparing high- and low-technology devices*. Unpublished master's thesis, University of Pretoria, South Africa.

Human Rights Watch. (2015). "Complicit in exclusion": South Africa's failure to guarantee an inclusive education for children with disabilities. Retrieved from https://www.hrw.org/report/2015/08/18/complicit-exclusion/south-africas-failure-guarantee-inclusive-education-children

Johnson, J. M., Inglebret, E., Jones, C., & Ray, J. (2006). Perspectives of speech language pathologists regarding success versus abandonment of AAC. *Augmentative and Alternative Communication, 22*(2), 85–99. doi:10.1080/07434610500483588.

Joseph, L., & Alant, E. (2000). Strangers in the house? Communication between mothers and their hearing impaired children who sign. *The South African Journal of Communication Disorders, 47*, 15–24.

Kagawa-Singer, M., & Chung, X. (1987). Model for culturally-based care. *Journal of Medical Education, 55*, 200–203.

Kathard, H., & Pillay, M. (2013). Promoting change through political consciousness: A South African speech-language pathology response to the world report on disability. *International Journal of Speech-Language Pathology, 15*(1), 84–89.

Kijak, R. J. (2011). A desire for love: Considerations and sexuality and sexual education of people with intellectual disability in Poland. *Disability and Sexuality, 29*, 65–74.

Koppenhaver, D. A. (2000). Literacy in AAC: What should be written on the envelope we push? *Augmentative and Alternative Communication, 16*, 270–279.

Leavitt, R. L. (2002). Developing cultural competence in a multicultural world. Part I and 2. *Physical Therapy, 10*, 36–47.

Lilienfeld, M., & Alant, E. (2005). The social interaction of an adolescent who uses AAC: The evaluation of a peer-training program. *Augmentative and Alternative Communication, 21*(4), 278–294.

Maguvhe, M. O. (2014). Augmentative and alternative communication: Requirements for inclusive educational interventions. *International Journal of Educational Sciences, 7*(2), 253–260.

Mall, S., & Schawartz, L. (2012). Sexuality disability and human rights: Strengthening health care for disabled people. *South African Medical Journal, 112*, 792–790.

Maxwell, G., & Granlund, M. (2011). How are conditions for participation expressed in education policy documents? A review of documents in Scotland and Sweden. *European Journal of Special Needs., 26*(2), 251–272.

McCauley, D., Gorter, J. W., Russell, D. J., Rosenbaum, P., Law, M., & Kertoy, M. (2013). Assessment of environmental factors in disabled children 2–12 years: Development and reliability of the Craig Hospital inventory of environmental factors (CHIEF) for children-parent version. *Child: Care, Health and Development, 39*, 337–344.

McCord, M. S., & Soto, G. (2004). Perceptions of AAC: An ethnographic investigation of Mexican-American families. *Augmentative and Alternative Communication, 20*(4), 209–227.

McLachlan, M., & Schwartz, L. (2009). *Disability and international development: Towards inclusive global health*. New York: Springer.

McNaughton, D., & Light, J. (2013). The iPad and mobile technology revolution: Benefits and challenges for individuals who require augmentative and alternative communication. *Augmentative and Alternative Communication, 29*(2), 107–116.

Milberger, S., Israel, N., LeRoy, B., Martin, A., Potter, L., & Patchak-Schuster, P. (2003). Violence against women with physical disabilities. *Violence and Victims, 18*, 581–591.

Mpofu, E., Ukasoanya, G., Mupowase, A., Harley, D., Charema, J., & Nthinds, K. (2011). Counseling people with disabilities. In E. Mpofu (Ed.), *Counseling people of African ancestry* (pp. 294–309). Cambridge: Cambridge University Press.

Mueller-Johnson, K., Eisner, M., & Obsuth, I. (2014). Sexual victimisation of youth with a physical disability: An examination of prevalence rates and risk and protective factors. *Journal of Interpersonal Violence, 29*(17), 3180–3206.

Opperman, S., & Alant, E. (2003). The coping response of the adolescent siblings of children with severe disabilities. *Disability and Rehabilitation, 25*(9), 441–454.

Parette, P., Blake Huer, M., & Wyatt, T. A. (2002). Young African American children with disabilities and augmentative and alternative communication issues. *Early Childhood Special Education, 29*(3), 201–206.

Phew Research Centre. (2015). Cell phones in Africa: Communication lifeline. Retrieved from http://www.pewglobal.org/2015/04/15/cell-phones-in-africa-communication-lifeline/

Pickl, G. (2011). Communication intervention in children with severe disabilities and multilingual backgrounds: Perceptions of pedagogues and parents. *Augmentative and Alternative Communication, 27*(4), 229–244.

Pillay, M., & Kathard, H. (2015). Decolonizing health professionals' education. *African Journal of Rhetoric, 7*, 193–227.

Sanders, D., & Chopra, M. (2006). Key challenges to achieving health for all in a inequitable society: The case of South Africa. *American Journal of Public Health, 96*, 73–79.

Simeonsson, R. J. (2006). *Classification of communication disabilities in children: Contribution of the international classification of functioning, disability, and health.* Geneva: WHO.

Simeonsson, R. J. (2009). ICF-CY: A universal tool for documentation of disability. *Journal of Policy and Practice in Intellectual Disabilities, 6*(2), 70–72.

Slabbert, S., & Finlayson, R. (2000). "I'm a cleva!": The linguistic makeup of identity in a South African urban environment. *International Journal of the Sociology of Language, 144*(1), 119–135. doi:10.1515/ijsl.2000.144.119.

Smith, M. M., & Connolly, I. (2008). Roles of aided communication: Perspectives of adults who use AAC. *Disability and Rehabilitation, 3*(5), 260–273. doi:10.1080/17483100802338499.

Soto, G., & Yu, B. (2014). Considerations for the provision of services to bilingual children who use augmentative and alternative communication. *Augmentative and Alternative Communication, 30*(1), 83–92. doi:10.3109/07434618.2013.878751.

South African Goverment. (1996). *Constitution of the Republic of South Africa, Chapter 2: Bill of rights.* Retrieved from http://www.gov.za/documents/constitution/chapter-2-bill-rights, 28 August 2015.

Statistics South Africa. (2011). *Midyear population estimates.* Pretoria: Statistics South Africa.

Statistics South Africa. (2013). *Statistical release P0302: Midyear population estimates 2013.* Retrieved from http://www.statsa.gov.za/publications/P0302/P 0302 2013.pdf

Stobbart, C., & Alant, E. (2008). Home-based literacy experiences of severely to profoundly deaf preschoolers and their hearing parents. *Journal of Developmental and Physical Disabilities, 20*(2), 139–153.

Tervalon, M., & Murray-Garcia, J. (1998). Cultural humility versus cultural competence: A critical distinction in defining physician training outcomes in multicultural education. *Journal of Health Care for the Poor and Underserved, 9*(2), 117–125.

Thistle, J. J., & Wilkinson, K. M. (2015). Building evidence-based practice in AAC display design for young children: Current practices and future directions. *Augmentative and Alternative Communication, 31*(2), 124–136. doi:10.3109/07434618.2015.1035798.

Tönsing, K. M. (2015). Supporting the production of graphic symbol combinations by children with limited speech: A comparison of two AAC systems. *Journal of Developmental and Physical Disabilities.* Early Online, 1–25.

Tönsing, K. M., & Dada, S. (2015, November). *The implementation of augmentative and alternative communication aids in schools for learners with special educational needs.* Poster presented at the annual SASLHA/SAAA/ENT Conference, Durban, South Africa.

Tönsing, K. M., Alant, E., & Lloyd, L. L. (2005). Augmentative and alternative communication. In E. Alant & L. L. Lloyd (Eds.), *Augmentative and alternative communication and severe disabilities: Beyond poverty* (pp. 30–67). London: Whurr.

Tregenna, F. (2012). What are the distributional implications of halving poverty in South Africa when growth alone is not enough? *Applied Economics, 44*, 2577–2596.

United Nations. (1989). Convention on the rights of the child. *Annual Review of Population Law, 16*, 485–501.

United Nations Educational, Scientific and Cultural Organization (UNESCO). (2006). *EFA global monitoring report: Strong foundations: Early childhood care and education.* Paris: UNESCO.

Van Niekerk, K., & Tönsing, K. (2015). Eye gaze technology: A south African perspective. *Disability and Rehabilitation: Assistive Technology, 10*(4), 340–346. doi:10.3109/17483107.2014.974222.

Von Tetzchner, S., & Grove, N. (2003). The development of alternative language forms. In S. Von Tetzchner & N. Grove (Eds.), *Augmentative and alternative communication: European perspectives* (pp. 1–27). London: Whurr.

Walker, S. P., Wachs, T. D., Gardner, J. M., Lozoff, B., Wasserman, G. A., Pollitt, E., & Carter, J. A. (2007). International child development steering group child development: Risk factors for adverse outcomes in developing countries. *The Lancet, 369*(9556), 145–157.

Watermeyer, B., & Kathard, H. (2015). To be or not to be: stuttering and the human costs of being "un-disabled". *International Journal of Speech-Language Pathology*. Early Online, 1–9. doi:1 0.3109/17549507.2015.1060528

World Bank. (2015a). *World development indicators: Children environment and land use.* Retrieved from http://wdi.worldbank.org/table3.1

World Bank. (2015b). *South Africa.* Retrieved from http://data.worldbank.org/country/ south-africa

World Health Organization (WHO). (2001). *International classification of functioning, disability, and health.* Geneva: World Health Organization.

World Health Organization (WHO). (2007). *International classification of functioning, disability, and health for children and youth (ICF-CY).* Geneva: World Health Organization.

Chapter 13
Enriched Audio Description: Working Towards an Inclusive Museum Experience

Alison F. Eardley, Louise Fryer, Rachel Hutchinson, Matthew Cock, Peter Ride, and Joselia Neves

Abstract Within a museum context, audio description (AD) is generally thought to be a tool for enhancing access for people with a visual impairment, in other words, as a means of providing access, through verbal description, to visual details of an object or artwork. Taking evidence from researchers and practitioners, we argue that AD has a much broader potential scope and benefit. We consider AD in more established fields, such as film, and then explore the issues impacting on AD within museum environments. We also explore the literature on multisensory learning and memory, to create a rationale for the benefits of AD based on multisensory imagery, with or without perceptual experience. We conclude that, through the use of imagery, AD has the potential to guide people around a painting or object in a way which can enhance the 'seeing' ability of all people, whether or not they have sight. Further, multisensory experience, based on imagery or perceptual experience, combined with semantic or fact information, would enhance memorability. As such, taking AD from the niche audience of visual impairment, and projecting it into the

A.F. Eardley (✉) • R. Hutchinson
Department of Psychology, University of Westminster, London, UK
e-mail: a.eardley@westminster.ac.uk; r.hutchinson@my.westminster.ac.uk

L. Fryer
Centre for Translation Studies (CenTraS), University College London, London, UK

VocalEyes, London, UK
e-mail: louise@utopians.co.uk

M. Cock
VocalEyes, London, UK
e-mail: matthew@vocaleyes.co.uk

P. Ride
Department of English, Linguistics and Cultural Studies, University of Westminster, London, UK
e-mail: p.e.ride@westminster.ac.uk

J. Neves
College of Humanities and Social Sciences, Hamad bin Khalifa University, Ar-Rayyan, Qatar
e-mail: jneves@qf.org.qa

© Springer International Publishing AG 2017   195
S. Halder, L.C. Assaf (eds.), *Inclusion, Disability and Culture*, Inclusive
Learning and Educational Equity 3, DOI 10.1007/978-3-319-55224-8_13

mass market of the 'sighted', could have a revolutionary impact on the museum experience and our understanding of access and difference.

Introduction to Audio Description

Audio description (AD) is intrinsic to human communication. When we reference the world through words, we use descriptors including size, shape and colour. We add details on the basis of our perception of the world, the context in which we are communicating and/or knowledge of our conversational partners' needs or expectations. Audio description also comes as second nature to educators and parents, who 'describe' in order to direct attention to detail or to make explicit what may go unnoticed. In fact audio description can take place in apparently trivial contexts, such as when an adult guides a child through a picture book, somebody describes a scene to somebody else over the telephone, or when a sports reporter commentates on a football match. In yet another context, audio description is one means by which blind and visually impaired (VI) people can access information presented within the dominant visual culture. Family members, friends and educators, among others, create a verbal description to provide crucial or complementary information that provides access to visually coded messages.

In the early 1980s, the discipline of Audio Description (AD) was introduced in the USA as a form of audiovisual translation, starting in theatre, and often limited to small group experiences in blind clubs and local venues. AD has since been formally introduced in multiple contexts and has become a research topic for numerous scholars working not only in Audiovisual Translation for Access, amply referenced in this reflection, but also in fields including Education (Freire et al. 2010), Anthropology (Gerber 2007), Tourism (Small et al. 2012), Disability Studies (Alper et al. 2015) and Museum Studies (see Eardley et al. 2016). Indeed, it is AD within museums which is the collective interest of our team of researchers and practitioners. Through our various research backgrounds and applied experiences, the authors of this chapter illustrate the highly multidisciplinary and practice-based nature of this discipline. Here, we will consider AD within museums in a British cultural context, from a theoretical and practitioner perspective.

AD began to be used in the UK in the late 1980s. In the UK, legislation was introduced in the Disability Discrimination Act (1995) (now superseded by the Equality Act 2010), which stipulated that service providers (including museums, galleries and heritage sites) have a duty to make 'reasonable adjustments' for people with disabilities. VocalEyes, a UK charity that champions the right of blind and partially sighted people to access arts and heritage, was established not long after the 1995 Act, to provide AD for the arts and to support research and develop this emerging profession. VocalEyes' scope has grown as the discipline has grown in the UK. They now describe at museums, galleries, heritage sites as well as architecture and built environment. In the UK, AD currently addresses the needs of a population of 360,000 people registered blind or partially sighted (RNIB 2016). Driven by legislative change, which has strengthened the notion that access is a right, rather than a privilege, there has been a growth in organisations seeking support from VocalEyes to identify and remove other barriers to engagement. Given the needs of an aging population, the applications of AD seem set to increase.

Although the application of AD has expanded from theatre into TV and Cinema and into the visual arts, it is still seen largely as a form of audiovisual translation which is uniquely beneficial to visually impaired audiences. We aim to challenge this, firstly by exploring what has been learnt about AD as a communicative tool for people who are blind or partially sighted in established applications, such as film, and secondly exploring AD within museums to provide a case for AD within an Inclusive Design provision that would enhance the museum experience of vision impaired and sighted visitors alike. In fact, it is through trans-disciplinary development that the work on Descriptive Guides, presented within the context of the ADLAB project by Neves (2014), moves from the specific field of AVT and blindness to the context of some of the projects described in this article.

Telling the Story: The Challenges and Opportunities of Intermodal Translation

Much of the academic research on AD considers it a form of intermodal translation – taking a visual *source* element and translating it into a *target* element of verbal narrative. Indeed, the fundamental challenge facing AD is one that it shares with translation. Specifically, description does not involve simply replacing each visual element with a verbal one, but it must adhere to an internal logic, with AD needing to 'tell a story' above all else (Braun 2011). As with standard inter-lingual translation – where information is translated from one language to another – an intermodal translation that draws undue attention to itself can jar with the user and be ultimately unsatisfying. Anecdotal feedback from users suggests that AD is most effective when users are not consciously aware of it (Fryer and Freeman 2012).

How AD strives to tell a story, however, depends to a great extent on the task at hand. For example, film AD provides a supplement to the already accessible audio information (speech/sound/music effects). Within all types of dynamic AD (Braun 2011) including film, a primary challenge in the scripting of AD is timing. The practitioner must capture and transmit the visual aspects of the film that have narrative value. However, they must deliver it in the gaps between dialogue and other sound effects, or take the decision to lower the soundtrack for its own delivery. Related to the question of timing is one of rendering simultaneity. The audiovisual medium involves seeing multiple images simultaneously or in close proximity. The visual elements can stand in complex relation to one another, with one bringing meaning to another. The AD practitioner must try to preserve this meaning or risk the audience failing to comprehend the underlying narrative that the AD is trying to communicate. A simple example is the presence on screen of two characters, where the implied relation between them and our understanding of what action might follow may be depicted simultaneously through facial expression or bodily movements. For example, a couple lying back to back in bed are unlikely to be enjoying a harmonious relationship. AD, in contrast, is linear in construction, which means the describer must carefully select, order and prioritise which visual elements he or she wishes to address, and must ensure that each word of the description works to convey as much meaning as possible. For this reason, adjectives, verbs and adverbs must be carefully chosen.

However, it is not only the visual aspects of film that AD must translate. AD descriptions will typically involve a consideration of the interdependence of sound and image (Braun 2011). The meaning of sounds in film may be clear only alongside the visual context, as such researchers have called for sound to be 'analysed and considered as an element of image' (Maszerowska et al. 2014, pp.8–9). Sounds may be heard by visually impaired viewers but their implications or contexts might not be fully comprehended unless they are successfully contextualised by the AD. This puts the AD under pressure to deliver yet more information in its limited linear timeframe.

Telling a comprehensible story is one concern, keeping it as artistically close to the source as possible is another and various film genres present differing challenges. In their work on the 'cinema of attractions', Matamala and Remael (2014) raise the question of how to handle film that is particularly visual, where the emphasis is placed on 'spectacle versus storytelling'. When space, time and action are conveyed primarily visually rather than through verbal narrative, the AD must work harder to facilitate the visually impaired audience's comprehension of the film's developments. Careful use of language can help with issues such as focalisation, defined as 'what a character can "know" or "see" at a given point in the narrative' (Matamala and Remael 2014, p. 67).

A challenge related to focalisation is how filmic techniques, for example, moving from middle distance to close-up, panning across a scene or an abrupt edit, can be described since these all contribute to the meaning of the film. Guidelines for practitioners have typically discouraged description of, or reference to, filmic techniques in AD Ofcom (2016). Underlying this seems to be an assumption that VI people will not want or benefit from references to the cinematic technique of the film in AD. However, Fryer and Freeman (2013) found a correlation between age of onset of blindness and preference for the inclusion of cinematic techniques in AD, probably accounted for by the residual visual memory of films in those who became blind later in life. Congenitally blind participants found cinematic AD unnecessary. However, only 5 % of the UK population of blind people are in this category, raising the question of whether AD might address cinematic techniques for the comprehension and enjoyment of the rest of the visually impaired population.

AD for film, then, is a complex and challenging exercise. The focus is on providing as coherent and artistically faithful a translation of the visual elements as possible, within the timeframe available for the insertion of AD. This service is also developed primarily for the needs and enjoyment of visually impaired people. AD for the visual art and artefacts of museums, however, brings with it a range of different challenges and opportunities.

AD in Museums: Translation and Transcreation

Within the UK, many museums, galleries and heritage sites have access provision in place for blind and partially sighted visitors. A recent survey (March 2015, unpublished) by VocalEyes of the websites of 87 museums receiving funding from Arts Council England as Major Partner Museums found that 28 % offer large print versions of maps or gallery labels and 15 % offered AD tours or a recorded AD guide.

However, at this point, it is necessary to consider broader issues in terms of museum access, before we explore the role AD might have in facilitating access to collections. As an AD trainer, Louise's starting point illustrates this very well:

> As an audio describer, I am often asked to attend a museum to deliver training to their staff. Generally I work with a blind or partially sighted co-trainer. We see our job as highlighting what is already (in) accessible at the museum, raising staff awareness and offering them strategies on ways to improve. So the first step is simply seeing what the museum already provides in terms of interpretation and assessing how accessible it is for someone with a visual impairment. It may be as simple as asking a curator to reposition a bench that has been sited so as to prevent a blind person exploring a large object, such as a locomotive, through touch, or addressing competing audio from neighbouring exhibits to make it easier to concentrate on one or the other.

In other words, it is not just access to objects that is an issue for people with a visual impairment, but also the wider 'visitor experience'. These observations are reinforced by the opinions and experiences of blind and partially sighted museumgoers, 30 of whom were surveyed as part of a report commissioned by VocalEyes (Pereira 2009). This identified issues such as confidence; transport; companionship; information about events and resources; understanding the space; collaboration and feedback; confident, knowledgeable and enthusiastic staff; time management; non-segregation/inclusion; and personal attention, all had a significant impact on their museum visit. It is also important to mention the significant access issue in museums, which is the restriction on spontaneous visits. Where access services are delivered through interaction with museums staff, for example, combined AD and touch tours, they must generally be booked in advance, often with a lead time of several weeks. Pereira's (2009) survey concluded that 'even though events designed for the audience were popular, 50% said they did not like going to events and being segregated from the general public'. This sense of segregation is obviously an issue and suggests that museums should adopt both an inclusive approach to all their interpretation (i.e. larger print labels, tour guides able to include AD within all tours) and a policy of 'equality of choice' where access provision is offered, allowing for the preferences of the blind or partially sighted visitor that are not immediately connected with their visual impairment. For example, some people do not like audio guides as they find them isolating, instead preferring the opportunity for discussion and social interaction afforded by a guided tour. For others, the audio-described orientation information offered by an AD audio guide gives them the opportunity to make an independent visit that suits their preferences and/or needs. It is also important to note that AD, where it is pre-recorded, does not have to be presented in the form of an audio guide. It could be presented within a shared listening experience.

AD in museums emerged out of the same philosophy of access as AD for film or TV. Audio Descriptive Guide has become the preferred term that differentiates an audiovisual translation designed specifically for blind and visually impaired people from the more general audio guide, which is something that provides guided information to people with sight. It is worth considering too how the activities of the visually impaired audience may shift in emphasis depending on the source element. Whereas the visually impaired audience of a film AD may employ their cognitive effort primarily in following the film's progression, seeking coherence and anticipating action, and all in a timely fashion, accessing art through AD works within different time constraints. In theory, one might take as long as needed to contemplate the art piece. However, in practice, an audio description itself should not go beyond 3 min, a timespan that is seen in the media as ideal. This echoes Louise's perspective as a practitioner:

> The museum environment is distinct from other AD applications, as the describer is required to describe three-dimensional objects, and to include orientation information, to help a blind person find their way from one exhibit to the next. Purely descriptive information must be married with background factual information. Exhibits are generally (although not always) static and the only timing constraint on the description is how long a person can bear to devote to one object before wanting to move on. Similarities include the fact that all AD is delivered orally and received aurally. Passion in particular will be carried through the rhythms and intonations of the describer's voice. A curator's enthusiasm for an exhibit will often come shining through.

For someone without sight, 'contemplation' can then continue in a purely cognitive way, with no additional sensory or semantic experience, or it can continue through sensory 'exploration', perhaps through touch, or face-to-face human discussion with the enthusiastic curator. Louise points out that face to face is 'obviously more interactive. It offers the chance for the visitor to ask questions, allowing the describer to tailor their description around an individual's particular interests. As the writer of an audio description guide, I have to pre-empt such questions. In this case, structuring the description becomes all important.'

Although description of art has a long history and is to an extent inextricable from art history itself, translating the visual nature of an artwork into a verbal narrative is a complex and challenging task. The development of AD for visual art therefore brings with it a set of new questions and variables, very few of which have been explored in the literature to date. Verbal description of art dates back as early as Homer's *Iliad* (Book 18), where he describes the Shield of Achilles made by Hephaestus. Homer's description is one of the earliest examples of *ekphrasis*, a description of a work of art produced as a rhetorical exercise. A more recent example of a poet describing art can be found in Rilke's *Letters on Cezanne* of 1907. His description of *Madame Cézanne in a Red Armchair* (c. 1877, now in the Museum of Fine Arts, Boston) is as serene and harmonious as the painting itself.

> A red, upholstered low armchair has been placed in front of an earthy-green wall in which a cobalt-blue pattern (a cross with the centre left out) is very sparingly repeated...
>   Seated in this red armchair, which is a personality in its own right, is a woman, her hands in the lap of a dress with broad vertical stripes that are very lightly indicated by small

loosely distributed flecks of green yellows and yellow greens, up to the edge of the blue-grey jacket, which is held together by a blue, greenly scintillating silk bow (Rilke 1907).

However, while the poet is permitted to create description which is considered art in its own right, much modern AD seeks not to intrude or draw attention to itself, but rather aims to blend in/remain in the background so that, after the event, it is the experience of the artwork that is recalled, not the description itself. AD for visual art must address issues of interpretation, subjectivity and ambiguity. A useful framework, which draws once again upon theories of translation, is set out by de Coster and Muehleis (2007) in their discussion of AD for paintings and sculptures. Their approach rests on the notion that all artworks consist of signs. Clear signs, which give clear pieces of information, can be translated into verbal narrative with relative ease. Signs such as these might also be readily translated into a tactile relief, for example, Andy Warhol's *Brillo Boxes*. Ambivalent signs, that suggest multiple layers of meaning and interpretation, would not be translatable into a relief and require a different approach in the AD. They take the optical phenomenon of the duck/rabbit (Jastrow 1899) as example, which, depending on how you look at the image, could be a rabbit or a duck.

Where possible, the authors suggest attempting to convey this visual ambiguity 'by giving comparable examples of ambiguity in touch or hearing', or if this is problematic, introducing the 'whole object as a carrier of ambiguity' (Coster and Muehleis 2007, p. 193). The process of translation for artworks could also incorporate other modes in the AD, such as sound or touch in addition to verbal narrative. An example from Louise illustrates this point: 'I described a series of photos for an exhibition at the Cardiff Diffusion exhibition curated by Zoe Partington who is a partially sighted artist. One was of a woman whose hair is being whipped by the wind. Zoe mixed wind noise with the description to enhance the effect of the words.'

The ambiguity of artwork also reminds us that meaning is not held inherently in the work itself, waiting for a viewer to 'extract' it, but rather that viewers are themselves potential meaning-makers, bringing their own experiences, memories and emotions to their interpretation. AD for visual art may enable the visually impaired audience to reconstruct a series of visual images, although Fryer (2016) suggests that this is not what many listeners choose to do. The construction of a mental representation of an artwork *may* include visual imagery, but it might also include nonvisual or spatial imagery. A congenitally blind person, for example, may prioritise nonvisual imagery compared to someone who became blind later in life and therefore has access to a lifetime of visual memory (Eardley and Pring 2014). This is in line with Louise's practitioner experience which suggests 'the more evocative the language, the more powerful that trigger might be'. In these instances, the aim of AD for visual art may be to facilitate for the audience an *experience* of the artwork. Put differently, the approach of the AD may be to offer a kind of *transcreation*, the creation of a new artwork, rather than a translation.

AD that offers a transcreation of an artwork is consciously subjective and interpretative and can draw upon various modalities for an immersive, multisensory experience. Neves (2012) for example, proposes 'soundpainting' as a form of artistic transcreation where AD is enriched with music and sound effects and, where possible, touch. Artists develop soundscapes for paintings where carefully researched, authentic historical and contextual sound effects aim to tell the story of visual art through sound. Recent works such as those by Sonic Paintings (Sonic Paintings 2016) extend this by creating soundscapes that are responsive to the viewer's movements, permitting them to step into and out of layered zones of sound. More research is needed to evaluate the potential for these approaches to create enjoyable immersive AD experiences for museum visitors, compared to 'standard' AD. The creative potential for multisensory immersive AD in museums has many implications, not least the fact that it may enhance the experience of sighted people alongside their visually impaired peers.

AD, Multisensory Experiences and Inclusive Design

One of the principles behind the creation of AD was that people with a visual impairment should be able to access visuocentric culture, including film, TV, performing and visual arts and cultural heritage. Within film, theatre and TV, AD is able to provide access to visual information important to the understanding of the text by combining the description with the rest of the auditory messages – speech, sound effects and music – in the original audiovisual text. However, in situations where the 'original text' does not provide a platform to build over or work with, such as visual art, there are reasons why immersive AD may actually enrich the visitor experience, by creating a narrative structure that will engage blind and sighted museum visitors alike. Whereas the former will use the AD to create mental images, the latter will use it to make sense of the images that are seen but might not be adequately perceived or understood.

Studies in psychology and neuroscience show that direct multisensory perceptual experience enhance cognitive processing (e.g. Lehmann and Murray 2005, and imagery, e.g. Cornoldi et al. 1989; Jonides et al. 1975). It is suggested that this enhanced processing results from increased neural connections (Murray et al. 2005; Nyberg et al. 2000). However, not only does multisensory information play a significant role in learning semantic information or 'facts' but it also plays a significant role in our autobiographical memories. Autobiographical memory is memory for information related to the self (Brewer 1986) and it is generally agreed that we recall these memories by reconstructing them from a pool of sensory traces in the full wealth of modalities (Eardley and Pring 2006). An autobiographical memory can incorporate all aspects of the museum visit to include the personal, social and physical contexts of a visit and can be explored in the weeks or months following, or decades later (e.g. Falk and Dierking 2012). While the visitor to the museum may talk about wanting an experience, arguably what they are seeking is an autobiographical memory – a memory which feeds in to and enriches their notion of self and can linger throughout life. Thus, both memory of the factual information gathered during a museum visit, and the overall sense of 'experience', and the autobiographical memories associated with that, are enhanced by multisensory presentation.

The exhibition *Tate Sensorium* (2015) at Tate Britain is part of the emerging interest in a multisensory approach to display and interpretation in current museum practice in the UK and globally. It took four twentieth-century British paintings from Tate's collection of art and displayed them alongside aural, tactile and olfactory material. This is illustrated by the description given on the Tate Website about the experience: 'The taste of edible charcoal, sea salt, cacao nibs and smokey lapsang souchong tea bring out [Francis Bacon's Figure in a Landscape]'s dark nature, and the wartime era in which it was painted – while a hint of burnt orange connects to flashes of colour and blue sky.'

One could argue that Descriptive Guides are not necessary for the experience of sighted people; however, research on the way individuals and experts 'see' visual art suggests that AD could be beneficial to both sighted and visually impaired as an aid to 'seeing' visual images. The standard visuocentric presentation of works of art assumes not only that people can see but also that they know how to use that vision to 'look' at a piece of art or a historical artefact to be able to extract some part of the rich cultural heritage associated with it. Research suggests this is not the case. Artists seem to pay more attention to formal composition, textures, combinations of colours, whereas fixations of novice viewers are primary driven by distinguishable and easily recognisable elements, such as faces, objects and locations (Koide et al. 2015). If looking varies according to knowledge, experience and ability, then *guided* looking may enhance the non-expert visitor's experience.

Thus, drawing this evidence together, it seems that AD would enhance the museum experience of people with or without sight. As such, AD could be the basis for an Inclusive Design approach. Little empirical research exists so far to explore the impact of AD as a means of inclusive design, but anecdotal evidence is encouraging practitioners to implement it within a framework of inclusive or universal design. Louise extends this usefulness to those who may have a disability they are not aware of or willing to admit and to those with no recognised disability:

> Description is also an example of guided attention, from which any visitor might benefit, turning a swift glance into a lingering examination, appraising small details that are easy to overlook. Many visitors may not realize that they have a disability or may be in denial. In this case efforts to improve access for blind and partially sighted people can often assist others. An enlarged tactile image of tiny Anglo-Saxon coins may help many sighted visitors who would struggle to see the detail on an object the size of a fingertip; competing audio is tiring to many. A locomotive can be fun for anyone to explore without having to negotiate your way around a poorly-positioned bench.

Some museums are taking this on board and creating an inclusive AD provision for all (e.g. Benjamin Franklin Museum, Philadelphia; The Franklin Delano Roosevelt Presidential Library and Museum, New York; The Museum of Florida History, Florida and the Batalha Municipal Community Museum, Portugal). Practitioners argue that AD makes visual images more accessible for visitors with vision impairments and more meaningful for all visitors (Snyder 2014). Taking AD in museums from the 'niche' realm of disability access and into the mainstream of 'sighted' museum experience will require us to deepen our understanding of the potential for AD to impact on the visits of sighted people.

Initial research in film is encouraging. AD can be even more effective in stimulating emotions in sighted people than images in films (Ramos 2015) and more effective than simply listening to the soundtrack (Fryer and Freeman 2014). Similarly, sighted children watching film clips with and without AD show AD presentation resulted in better attentional focus and better memory for content for clips with AD, compared to those without (Krejtz et al. 2012). In fact, Louise's observations suggest that the scope of AD goes beyond the visitors to the curators:

> Often my role is to boost the trainees' confidence in addressing an audience or in reigniting their awareness of objects and spaces with which they have become so familiar, they have ceased to 'see' them...The benefits are not limited to visitors. A curator at the Natural History Museum recently mentioned that the powerfully emotive effect of an exhibit showing plaster casts of victims of the volcanic eruptions in Pompeii in 79 AD had been brought home to her more by listening to the audioguide than by looking at the exhibits. As the audio guide describes them: 'These plastercasts from Pompeii record the final positions of the unfortunate victims. On the left a large dog with a sturdy collar around its neck lies on its back, convulsed in agony, head contorted towards its tail, four legs stretched out.'

For museums where multisensory perceptual experience is possible, the potential impact of AD is even greater. In the same way that guided seeing can enhance people's ability to see (whether that be with or without vision), AD can be used to enhance people's ability to touch. Tactile drawings, models or other touchable materials that provide concrete form to the verbal description, enhance experience. However, when the AD guides touch, we would argue that the experience is no longer simply a 'substitute' for a lack of vision, but rather a multisensory experience that allows for easier, deeper, meaning making. It was this approach that was taken by Batalha Municipal Community Museum, Portugal. Here, the Enriched Multisensory Descriptive Guides employ sound effects, music and touch, to create a more immersive, embodied, memorable experience and one that visually impaired and sighted people can enjoy together. The success of this approach was recognised by the award of the prestigious Kenneth Hudson (EMYA) 2013 award.

If Enriched AD can offer more enjoyable and memorable museum visits for sighted as well as visually impaired people, then the picture looks bright for the future of using AD in museums. By providing access, translation, guided looking, or all of these simultaneously, AD can operate as a facilitator within a multisensory experience; thus, a fundamental element of an Inclusive Design approach to be enjoyed by all. Further research is needed to explore the potential of enriched AD and Enriched Multisensory Descriptive Guides.

Shared Museum Experience

Within this piece, we have explored research evidence and practitioner perspectives on AD, multisensory learning and museum experience to create an argument for the extension of use of AD in museums to blind and sighted audiences. Access strategies tend to focus on compensating for each type of sensory loss in isolation with the premise that they will benefit only individuals demonstrating that particular type of impairment. By maintaining separate strategies for different disabilities, we reinforce exclusion. We marginalise the minority audiences and create a conflict between the expenditure for 'minority' audiences and the majority audience. Audio Description, for example, is intended to aid people who are blind or partially sighted. Our research shows that AD has unseen benefits for other types of museum visitor (and staff) and that addressing access from a multisensory perspective can widen the pool of beneficiaries still further. Irrespective of your visual experience, the evidence suggests that AD can be used to enhance your ability to 'see'. However, it must be noted that we are not asking people to simply follow the visual form or create some form of spatial or visual image. The evidence from practitioners, as well as the evidence on multisensory memory and imagery suggest that the use of a rich range of multisensory imagery and metaphor would create a richer experience for the listener. We would argue further, that the strongest level of cognitive engagement will arise when the enriched audio description incorporates the invaluable semantic or factual details and highlights of a piece, which help the listener create a story about that piece. The story does not have to be prescribed by the audio describer, but rather there can be clues and hints. Thus, AD can enhance the perceptual experience at the same time as inspiring or evoking a deeper cognitive level of engagement. As such, AD could enhance the museum experience of everyone within a museum, including the staff. Seen in this way, AD becomes a crucial step towards creating a shared museum experience for those with and without sight, within which people of all levels of visual experience and visual ability can gain an enhanced experience of 'seeing' and perhaps also of 'touching', 'hearing', even 'smelling' and 'tasting'. At the same time, while AD may prove to be a valuable tool in the enhancement of a museum visit for all visitors, irrespective of their level of vision, museums have to be responsible for inclusive and accessible communication with their audiences before they are likely to make a visit at all, and that any number of accessible resources are of little worth without marketing and audience development to encourage attendance, and training staff in awareness and guiding and communication for visitors with and without a disability. Future research on the impact of multisensory AD on engagement, learning and memorability should consider its use for a variety of audiences who 'see' in a variety of ways. This may support museums in considering the full breadth of opportunities that AD has to offer, for all their visitors. Nevertheless, taking AD from the niche audience of visual impairment and projecting it to the mass market of the 'sighted' could have a revolutionary impact on the museum experience and our understanding of access and difference.

Access stops being a sidelined addition for a small group of visitors and becomes a shared inclusive approach which considers the needs of all visitors.

References

Alper, M., Ellcessor, E., Ellis, K., & Goggin. (2015). Reimagining the good life with disability: Communication, new technology, and humane connections. In H. Wang (Ed.), *Communication and the "good life"* (pp. 197–212). New York: Peter Lang.

Braun, S. (2011). Creating coherence in audio description. *Meta, 56*(3), 645–662.

Brewer, W. F. (1986). What is autobiographical memory? In D. C. Rubin (Ed.), *Autobiographical memory* (pp. 25–49). New York: Cambridge University Press.

Cornoldi, C., Beni, R. D., Roncari, S., & Romano, S. (1989). The effects of imagery instructions on total congenital blind recall. *European Journal of Cognitive Psychology, 1*(4), 321–331.

De Coster, K., & Mühleis, V. (2007). Intersensorial translation: Visual art made up by words. In J. Díaz Cintas, A. Remael, & P. Orero (Eds.), *Media for all* (pp. 189–200). Amsterdam: RODOPI.

Disability Discrimination Act 1995. http://www.legislation.gov.uk/ukpga/1995/50/section/21/ enacted. Accessed 10 Mar 2016.

Eardley, A. F., & Pring, L. (2006). Remembering the past and imagining the future: A role for nonvisual imagery in the everyday cognition of blind and sighted people. *Memory, 14*(8), 925–936.

Eardley, A. F., & Pring, L. (2014). Sensory imagery in individuals who are blind and sighted: Examining unimodal and multimodal forms. *Journal of Visual Impairment and Blindness., 108*(4), 323–334.

Eardley, A., Mineiro, C., Neves, J., & Ride, P. (2016). Redefining access: Embracing multimodality, memorability and shared experience in museums. *Curator: The Museum Journal, 59*, 263.

Equality Act. (2010). http://www.legislation.gov.uk/ukpga/2010/15/contents. Accessed 09 Mar 2016.

Falk, J. H., & Dierking, L. D. (2012). *Museum experience revisited*. Walnut Creek: Left Coast Press.

Freire, A., Linhalis, F., Bianchini, S., Fortes, R., & Pimentel, M. G. (2010). Revealing the whiteboard to blind students: An inclusive approach to provide mediation in synchronous e-learning activities. *Computers & Education, 54*(4), 866–876.

Fryer, L. (2016). *An introduction to audio description: A practical guide*. Oxford: Routledge.

Fryer, L., & Freeman, J. (2012). Presence in those with and without sight: Audio description and its potential for virtual reality applications. *Journal of CyberTherapy & Rehabilitation, 5*(1), 15–23.

Fryer, L., & Freeman, J. (2013). Cinematic language and the description of film: Keeping AD users in the frame. *Perspectives, 21*(3), 412–426.

Fryer, L., & Freeman, J. (2014, March). Can you feel what i'm saying? The impact of verbal information on emotion elicitation and presence in people with a visual impairment. In A. Felnhofer & O. D. Kothgassner (Eds.), *Challenging presence: Proceedings of the 15th International Conference on Presence* (pp. 99–107).

Gerber, E. (2007). Seeing isn't believing: Blindness, race, and cultural literacy. *The Senses and Society, 2*(1), 27–40.

Jastrow, J. (1899). The mind's eye. *Popular Science Monthly, 54*, 299–312.

Jonides, J., Kahn, R., & Rozin, P. (1975). Imagery instructions improve memory in blind subjects. *Bulletin of the Psychonomic Society, 5*(5), 424–426.

Koide, N., Kubo, T., Nishida, S., Shibata, T., & Ikeda, K. (2015). Art expertise reduces influence of visual salience on fixation in viewing abstract-paintings. *PloS one, 10*(2), e0117696.

Krejtz, I., Szarkowska, A., Krejtz, K., Walczak, A., & Duchowski, A. (2012). Audio description as an aural guide of children's visual attention. In *Proceedings of the symposium on eye tracking research and applications – ETRA '12* (pp. 99–106). New York: ACM Press.

Lehmann, S., & Murray, M. (2005). The role of multisensory memories in unisensory object discrimination. *Cognitive Brain Research, 24*, 326–334.

Matamala, A., & Remael, A. (2014). Audio-description reloaded: An analysis of visual scenes in 2012 and hero. *Translation Studies, 8*(1), 63–81.

Maszerowska, A., Matamala, A., Orero, P., & Reviers, N. (2014). Introduction: From source text to target text: The art of audio description. In A. Maszerowska, A. Matamala, & P. Orero, (Eds.), *Audio description: New perspectives illustrated* (pp. 8–9). Amsterdam: John Benjamins B.V.

Murray, M. M., Molholm, S., Michel, C. M., Heslenfeld, D. J., Ritter, W., Javitt, D. C., Schroeder, C. E., & Foxe, J. J. (2005). Grabbing your ear: Rapid auditory–somatosensory multisensory interactions in low-level sensory cortices are not constrained by stimulus alignment. *Cerebral Cortex, 15*, 963–974.

Neves, J. (2012). Multi-sensory approaches to (audio) describing the visual arts. *MonTi, 4*, 277–293.

Neves, J. (2014). Chapter 3.3.2 descriptive guides: Access to museums, cultural venues and heritage sites. In ADLAB, A. Remael, N. Reviers, & G. Vercauteren (Eds.), *Pictures painted in words. ADLAB audio description guidelines*. Trieste: Edizioni Università di Trieste. ebook: www.adlabproject.eu/Docs/adlab%20book/index.html. Accessed 7 Mar 2016.

Nyberg, L., Habib, R., & Herlitz, A. (2000). Brain activation during episodic memory retrieval: Sex differences. *Acta Psychologica, 105*(2–3), 181–194.

Ofcom, Audio Description. (2016). http://stakeholders.ofcom.org.uk/broadcasting/guidance/other-guidance/tv_access_serv/guidelines/. Accessed 09 Mar 2016.

Pereira, E. (2009). *Feasibility study into the potential contribution of VocalEyes' services for Museums, Galleries and Heritage sites*. http://www.vocaleyes.co.uk/core/core_picker/download.asp?id=2593&filetitle=Visual+Arts+Research+Study+PDF. Accessed 10 Mar 2016

Ramos, M. (2015). The emotional experience of films: Does audio description make a difference? *The Translator, 21*(1), 68–94.

Rainer Maria Rilke. (1907). In C. Rilke (ed) (2002). *Letters on Cezanne* (2nd ed., J. Agee, Trans.). New York: North Point Press.

RNIB. (2016). *Key information and statistics*. http://www.rnib.org.uk/knowledge-and-research-hub/key-informationand-statistics. Accessed 10 June 2016.

Small, J., Darcy, S., & Packer, T. (2012). The embodied tourist experiences of people with vision impairment: Management implications beyond the visual gaze. *Tourism Management, 33*(4), 941–950.

Snyder, J. (2014). *The visual made verbal: A comprehensive training manual and guide to the history and applications of audio description*. Arlington: American Council of the Blind, Inc..

Sonic Paintings. (2016) . www.sonicpaintings.com. Accessed 09 Mar 2016.

Part III
Inclusive Policies, Practices and Interventions

Chapter 14
Inclusive Practices in Mainstream Schools: An Australian Perspective

Poulomee Datta, Christine Grima-Farrell, and Mitchell Graeme Coates

Abstract The concept of inclusive education within the Australian context is portrayed. The autoethnographic experiences of the authors presented in the form of case studies provide vivid descriptions of how students with special educational needs and disabilities are supported within mainstream Australian classrooms. In particular, interesting inclusive strategies outline the ways in which students with disabilities are included in mainstream classrooms across the three states in Australia – South Australia, New South Wales and Queensland. The total education plan has been taken into consideration while providing deep insights into the inclusive practices undertaken for the case study of students.

Introduction

Over the last 20 years, Australian legislation and policies have strengthened and supported the rights of students with disabilities to be included in mainstream classrooms (Pearce et al. 2009). According to van Kraayenoord (2007), the term "inclusive education" has been differently defined, both in the literature and in practice. During the 1980s and 1990s in Australia, the term most usually referred to the integration of students with disabilities in regular or mainstream classrooms (Elkins 1994; Organization for Economic Co-operation and Development 1999). However, with the passage of time, the concept of inclusion was broadened and extended to include many other groups of students in Australian schools today. For example, tenets of the inclusion concept, according to Ashman and Elkins (2009, p. 41) are as follows: "complete acceptance of a student with a disability or other marginalized students in a regular class, with appropriate changes being made to ensure that the student is fully involved in all class activities. Thus, inclusion is characterized by the

P. Datta (✉) • M.G. Coates
School of Education, Australian Catholic University, Brisbane, QLD, Australia
e-mail: poulomee.datta@acu.edu.au

C. Grima-Farrell
School of Education, University of New South Wales, Kensington, NSW, Australia

© Springer International Publishing AG 2017
S. Halder, L.C. Assaf (eds.), *Inclusion, Disability and Culture*, Inclusive
Learning and Educational Equity 3, DOI 10.1007/978-3-319-55224-8_14

redesign of regular schools both physically and in curriculum, to provide for the complete education of all students who seek to attend" (Ashman and Elkins 2009). According to van Kraayenoord et al. (2000), inclusive education is "the practice of providing for students with a wide range of abilities, backgrounds and aspirations in regular school settings" (p. 9). Such definitions acknowledge the diversity of students who attend Australia's mainstream schools in the present-day context. This chapter describes recent practices in inclusive education in Australian mainstream classrooms.

Methodology

The qualitative narrative methodology known as autoethnography was employed for this chapter. According to Dyson (2007), autoethnographic writing links the personal within the culture in which the investigation, or experience, takes place. Raab (2013, p. 1) indicated that this research method "utilizes autobiographical writing in that it examines the personal experience of the researcher and participants." Mendez (2013) further substantiated autoethnography to be a valuable qualitative research method used to examine people's lives.

The following sections discuss the autoethnographic experiences of the authors of how students with disabilities are supported within mainstream classrooms across the three states of Australia – South Australia, New South Wales and Queensland. The indicative case examples included in this chapter have been identified in order to illustrate key features and potential approaches for supporting students with disabilities in mainstream Australian classrooms. The authors were fully immersed in the case studies they presented in their different roles (e.g., as a researcher, teacher and school special needs coordinator).

South Australia Context

Poulomee Datta presents an autoethnographic account of her experiences of how a student with vision impairment and another student with intellectual disability were supported in mainstream settings in two different schools in South Australia.

In South Australia, the Department for Education and Child Development (DECD) is responsible for providing children's services and public education. The DECD provides the Disabilities Support Program, wherein extra support is provided to support students with disabilities to work alongside students without disabilities in mainstream settings (DECD 2012). The DECD provides a variety of learning and teaching materials, resources and specialized services which support learners with disabilities in mainstream and specialist schools in South Australia (DECD 2012). My PhD in Special Education was conducted with two distinct cohorts, students with vision impairment and students with intellectual disability in

South Australia. I would like to present two elaborate case studies on how these students were included in mainstream classrooms and the impact of inclusion on their social and academic lives.

Vision Impairment

Iqbal, 15 years of age, is a student with vision impairment, completely blind in his right eye and low vision in his left eye. His parents migrated to South Australia 3 years back and he is enrolled in his local secondary school in one of the popular suburbs in South Australia. He has a genetic eye disease called "Retinitis Pigmentosa" which could progressively lead to blindness. His mother married one of her cousins and Iqbal believed that because her marriage was confined within the family, he was born with this genetic eye disorder.

Coming from a different country with different cultural expectations, Iqbal described his initial school days to be secluded, solitary and reticent. But soon, he found himself actively involved in most of the sports and other activities conducted in the school. I would like to take the readers through a transformative inclusion journey which Iqbal went through in the first few years of his secondary school. Since Iqbal hails from a different culture and is visually impaired, it was quite difficult for him to be social with his classmates. He was conscious about his vision loss and feared that he might be ridiculed by his peers. Iqbal said that he was never invited to parties organized by his classmates. He did not want to attend any gatherings with his peers as he did not want his friends to drop him home and be a burden on them. Iqbal believed that his ability to meet new people was restricted due to his lack of independence and mobility. This could potentially have an adverse impact on his social life. Halder and Datta (2012) substantiated that when the Piers-Harris Children's Self-Concept Scale was administered, adolescents with vision impairment scored low on the "Popularity" domain compared to their sighted counterparts as they were too shy to interact with their sighted peers. Lucy (1997) found that students with vision impairment preferred to remain isolated because they dreaded rejection by their sighted peers. Huurre and Aro (1998) indicated that adolescents with vision impairment experienced more often feelings of isolation and seclusion in making friendships. Fitts and Warren (2003) too believed that people with vision impairment experienced some degree of alienation from the mainstream society due to their disability.

Iqbal's teacher believed that he had enough vision to walk in the classroom, choose his seat, know who was in the classroom and learn names of students quickly. His support teacher claimed that Iqbal was not very chatty in between classes because he used all his concentration on moving. After Iqbal's teachers and other school staff had a Negotiated Education Plan (NEP) meeting to discuss Iqbal's strengths and needs, the team came up with a more structured plan to support him in a mainstream setting. In South Australia, students with special needs are supported within the mainstream Curriculum Framework through the NEP. The purpose of the

NEP is to support access, participation and achievement in the mandated curriculum for students with disabilities [Government of South Australia Department of Education and Children's Services (GSA DECS) 2001].

An outcome of the NEP meeting was that Iqbal's support teacher created social role-play situations and explicitly taught him everyday gestures, body language and movements needed to interact in a social situation. Iqbal was strategically involved in community work in the form of environmental cleanup with a few responsible peers in his school. This not only helped him to engage with people in the community but also strengthened his bond with some peers in the school. Fitness clubs and sessions were organized within the school environment where children like Iqbal could use this as a platform not only to stay healthy but to interact with other students with and without disabilities in the school. After visiting Iqbal a couple of times, I found that his support teacher organized some interactive lunch sessions between Iqbal and his sighted peers. Clearly, I could see Iqbal benefitting from the peer lunch sessions as this not only improved his social life but had an indirect positive influence on his academic life as well. After talking to his support and mainstream teachers, I found that Iqbal was demonstrating an increasing interest in academics.

All of Iqbal's subject teachers were making a conscious attempt to differentiate lessons and include accommodations that would support him. Iqbal was provided a handout in advance for every lesson, outlining the lesson steps and the content for that particular class. The handout would be on the enlarged print format and it was negotiated with Iqbal that he could read best if the font style was Tahoma and size 22 or more. His lessons were audio-recorded so that he could use these tapes as study aids at home. Some books on tape were ordered for Iqbal. Further, several resources like tactile equipment for science classes, special lighting equipment, magnifiers, closed-circuit televisions, typing stands, dark-lined stationary and graph paper, talking calculators and watches, sloping desk tops were purchased for Iqbal. He was allowed to examine any apparatus and materials before an experiment. Iqbal was provided with one-third extra time allocation to complete his work, assignments and tests in all subjects. Iqbal was also encouraged to use adaptive computer technology by his support teacher, for example, Jaws Speech software, screen magnification software, text-to-speech software, and so on. Iqbal could easily scan reference materials and listen to a computer with voice access to decrease the amount of reading required. I could clearly witness that this South Australian school had taken every possible measure to accommodate Iqbal in mainstream classes. This was not only achieved in the prioritized classes like Maths, Science and English but also in other classes like drama, dance and physical education. An example of inclusion in a dance class was during a dance exam, wherein Iqbal had to observe and then perform an extremely challenging sequence of dance steps. This was an incredibly difficult exam for Iqbal due to his restricted field vision. The format of the exam could not be changed because it was a group situation. Therefore, the result was that his grade had to be given for the dance steps that were done throughout the year because the exam format could not be changed to accommodate his vision needs. With the help of these auditory, tactile and general accommodations, Iqbal could effortlessly participate in his classes on the same basis as other students without disabilities and wanted to spend more time in school than home. Soon, Iqbal volunteered to participate in the Science Talent Competition being held in his school. I felt that this South Australian school had undertaken an inclusive approach in supporting Iqbal in his classes and helped him to easily transition to high school.

Intellectual Disability

I would like to share my experiences about Sally, a student with intellectual disability who I also met during the data collection process of my doctoral candidature. Sally, 15 years of age, was diagnosed with Down syndrome with an I.Q. of 50. Her rate of response was slower than the other children in her class. She had a short attention span and would get easily distracted. She often experienced dry mouth caused by mouth breathing associated with upper respiratory infections. Her mainstream and support teachers always ensured that she had access to a bottle of water/ juice to help her with the dry mouth. Sally's support team considered that routines, structure, and consistency were important in her case. A combination of visuals, demonstrations and ICT were used to teach new concepts to her and provide practice in existing skill areas. Sally was found to do particularly well in individual computer-based tasks. She was provided with additional repetitions and scaffolding of the same lesson in the mainstream classroom by the support teacher. At times when it became difficult for her to learn a particular skill in the mainstream classroom, she was withdrawn only for some parts of the day and put in a special setting to teach that particular skill.

A distinct characteristic of Sally was that she would burst into sudden explosions of anger and rage without any apparent reason and due to this it was becoming quite difficult to support her in the mainstream classroom. In most instances, it was found that these explosions were linked to stress or noise in the environment. Given such circumstances, Sally could not be included in group work in the classroom as group conversations could get very noisy. Additionally, frequent "time out" from the classroom was encouraged for Sally. Initially, her teachers arranged for a separate room for Sally's group to work in. But this did not prove very effective in the long run as she would get quite stressed with the usual chit-chat among the group members. Moreover, Sally experienced major difficulties in initiating a new conversation or sustaining any discussion in a group situation. Therefore, the result was that for a group activity, Sally had to do it individually with the help of the support teacher in a separate room. And this made me contemplate if Sally was excluded more often from the mainstream classroom as she had less time to spend with her peers. Sally's teachers reported that they found it quite challenging and stressful to support Sally in the mainstream classroom as she required constant supervision and monitoring. She had to be provided with a lot of individual attention and this meant substantial reduction in the teachers' teaching time. Sally was reported not to have many peers in the mainstream classroom. Zic and Igrić (2001) also found that students with intellectual disability were more often excluded by their peers. Research conducted by Abells et al. (2008) revealed that adolescents with intellectual disability could not interact well with their peers, the reasons mainly being their disability and lack of available supports. In fact, Sally's support teacher claimed that Sally had greater friends online through the social networking sites than in the mainstream classroom. This made me reflect on the fact that was Sally really included in the mainstream classroom? As a lecturer and researcher in the field of Special Inclusive Education, I felt that Sally was excluded on several occasions under the mask of inclusion.

New South Wales Context

Christine Grima-Farrell shares her experiences with students with special needs in mainstream classrooms in New South Wales (NSW) schools. Within NSW students with disabilities have access to special schools, classes within regular schools and funding to support them in regular classrooms (NSW Government 2012). A report compiled by the NSW Legislative Council (2010) highlights that supports to students with disabilities in mainstream schools should consist of "…the school learning support team, the Learning Assistance Program, the Integration Funding Support Program, the School Learning Support Coordinator, and the proposed School Learning Support Program" (p. 17). The aim of these supports is to "assist the classroom teacher to adapt and modify curriculum and environments to ensure they can be accessed appropriately by students with disability" (ARACY 2013, p. 22: Grima-Farrell 2017).

A collaborative whole-school approach is encouraged to ensure that all students experience a sense of belonging, mastery, independence, and courage. This section highlights my attempts (as a teacher and school special needs coordinator) to address the needs of two male students in inclusive school contexts.

DiGeorge Syndrome

Simon came to Trinity Primary School from a special school in year 3. He was the second son to healthy parents and started walking at 18 months, produced his first words at 23 months and was toilet trained at the age of 5. Simon had been diagnosed with DiGeorge syndrome shortly after his birth. DiGeorge syndrome is a genetic disorder that's usually visible at birth. Simon was born with heart defects, cognitive concerns and a cleft palate. These features resulted from a genetic fault, or mutation, called 22q11 deletion. Essentially it is a missing piece of chromosome that affects approximately one in every 4000 births; however, DiGeorge syndrome is generally considered one of the most serious types of 22q11 deletion (Simon et al. 2007). Typically the symptoms children display can vary widely. When I met Simon, his face was rather narrow and his eyes were almond shaped. His nose was broad and he had scars from cleft palate surgery. Simon was rather small for his age and his parents described this trait to be linked to his underactive thyroid gland and multiple seizures as a baby.

When Simon was introduced to his classmates he was rather shy, seemed quite floppy, and would not make any eye contact at all. He was 18 months to 2 years older than the other students in his class and remained reserved and reluctant to participate in class or playground activities.

The school special needs team (consisting of myself, another qualified teacher and a teacher aide), Simon's class teacher and his parents met on a monthly basis to conduct regular Individual Planning (IP) meetings to set, address and evaluate social and academic outcomes for Simon. This collaborative home and school approach proved to be beneficial for Simon, his parents and the school staff as it created an ongoing and responsive dialogue around Simon's specific strengths and challenges. It created opportunities for feedback, rich communication, shared support and responsibility as we worked together to provide learning opportunities for Simon to reach his full potential. We discussed and created ways to differentiate instruction, expectations and assessments that focused on reading, comprehension, time and money (key life skills).

Simon's feedback was often sought and he often expressed excitement when talking about social stories and the whole-school buddy program. Social stories would provide images of students engaging in socially encouraged behaviors including eye contact, smiles, and so on. These images were accompanied by short phrases and sentences that would guide appropriate behaviors in different social contexts. The whole-school buddy system allowed Simon and others to work with the same kindergarten student on a weekly basis. Everyone in the class has a pre-selected buddy and both classes would come together on a Thursday afternoon to play educational games and complete craft activities. By term 4 of Simon's first year at Trinity, his confidence had increased significantly and he volunteered to partici-pate in a basic dance sequence with his buddy for the school assembly.

His willingness to "have a go" at challenging academic and sporting tasks con-sistently strengthened. Although Simon did not reach stage- and age-appropriate outcomes in literacy and numeracy, he demonstrated consistent growth across all curriculum areas. During year 5 Simon's popularity had increased and he was selected (by the school staff and students) as one of the six Trinity student leaders. He wore his student leader badge daily with great pride and rarely missed a day of school.

Simon's parents often reported that they were pleased with the school's consis-tent and clear communication and ability to cater for their son's academic, emo-tional and social needs. They valued the use of assistive technology and voice-activated applications that were employed on a regular basis to enhance cur-riculum access, as Simon struggled with his fine motor control and his ability to write for extended periods.

Collectively we as a staff were also pleased with Simon's participation, academic growth and his increased independence, social skills and confidence. As Tomlinson (2012) highlights, special education is increasingly located in mainstream schools.

This was the case for Simon and we worked collaboratively with speech pathologists and Simon's medical team (via his parents) and his family to support Simon's significant growth in the mainstream primary school setting. Nevertheless this steady growth unexpectedly began to deteriorate at the start of year 6 with Simon's onset of puberty. From my perspective, DiGeorge syndrome swung into overdrive and Simon increasingly needed to be excused from class to visit the bathroom, he began to squint more often, he was often tired and his muscle tone and overall strength appeared to be weakening. I raised these concerns with his parents, who shared that they had noticed a similar degeneration in Simon's abilities at home.

Medical reports later confirmed that additional supports were required as Simon's condition was degenerative and the onset of puberty had negatively impacted on his kidney function, vision, hearing, gross and fine motor coordination and his ability to grow. Simon needed to be injected with a growth hormone daily and the physical accessibility of the school was improved due to increasing mobility concerns.

Practical accommodations were made to respond to the changes in Simon's circumstances. School bags were placed in bag racks rather than beside desks and Simon's parents were able to use the staff car park to avoid the steps at the school entrance. Adhesive florescent yellow strips were placed on poles and a card system was set up to allow Simon to rest on a beanbag or in the school bed if he became fatigued. Simon was able to use the toilet located in the school office area, as there was always somebody in close proximity during school hours. A spare school uniform and underwear were kept in the bathroom as a backup. These measures represented a flexible and proactive approach to overcoming possible barriers and obstacles to learning. Simon's condition gradually deteriorated and well-planned programs and supports remained flexible and responsive to ensure Simon could continue to be actively engaged in school life.

It is important to ensure we do not lose sight of the fact that like Simon, all students learn in a variety of ways and have different learning profiles. UNESCO (1994) advocates that developing a school ethos of trustworthiness and human reciprocity is based on the human rights of ALL students and teachers. In an effort to set high, realistic and attainable expectations for the behavior and work of all members of the school community, it is critical for staff to understand that all students are different and all should be supported. Tom was another student whose needs were very different to Simon's, yet a collaborative and responsive school-based approach was once again employed in an effort to maximize confidence, growth and development.

Asperger's Syndrome

Tom was a student with Asperger's syndrome. He was a very intelligent young man who had a fascination with trains and recycling. Tom experienced some difficulty controlling emotions and managing unplanned changes. Tom appeared disorganized and he processed things differently to his peers. He always displayed increased sensitivity to lights, sounds, smells and touch. He seemed to have an eye for details and a photographic memory. Tom's vocabulary was significantly advanced but his conversational skills were quite delayed. He often misread social cues and always strongly reinforced class rules with other students.

Various approaches were implemented by Tom's year 6 teachers and the Special Needs team to encourage access and participation for all the students in the class. Attwood (2006) suggests the use of visual cues, direct and simple language, explanation of jokes and avoidance of sarcasm. The whole class benefitted from these approaches and the use of color-coded books, labels and timetables to prepare them for secondary school and to assist with day-to-day organization. When the class teacher was away, a member of the special needs team (a familiar face) would introduce the casual teacher to explain the change.

Overall these approaches worked well during Tom's final year at primary school and transition into high school became a priority. A transition program including staged visits to the secondary school with Tom followed. During term 2 of year 6, I accompanied Tom to his new school and introduced him to the Special Needs Coordinator (SNC), year 7 Coordinator and the High School setting. The need for consistency and proactive supports were suggested prior to and during the visits. During term 2, Tom's classroom teacher, Tom and I visited the school and during term 3, his mother also joined us on our scheduled visit.

During these visits the SNC highlighted the changes that were occurring at the secondary school and stated that they would not offer professional development to the staff until Tom arrived the following year. Unfortunately, Tom struggled significantly at secondary school and he perceived situations differently to others. During a game of cricket in his first term of year 7, he was called "out" by a classmate. Tom believed the ball was in fact "not out," as he often gave considerable attention to specific detail. He attempted to explain his perspective to the classmate, whose opinion differed; however, the classmate (and many of his team) continued to yell "out" at Tom. Tom reacted by hitting the classmate in the head with the cricket bat. A string of other similar events followed until Tom was suspended from school due to behavioral concerns.

Simon, Tom and all students have various strengths and needs that contributed to significantly different learning profiles. A safe and supportive school climate is something that we as educators strive for. Within NSW and Australia, the inclusion of all students is now an element of the Australian Professional Standards for Teachers. Teachers are required to identify and use strategies which differentiate learning for students with disability (Standard 1.5), to understand the legislation in regard to students with disability (Standard 1.6), and to support the inclusive participation and engagement of students with disability (Standard 4.1) (Australian Institute for Teaching and School Leadership 2012).

Simon and Tom's stories serve to highlight the importance of knowing individual students and their learning profiles prior to implementing a proactive, flexible and collaborative whole-school approach to inclusion. They also provide an insight into the practical significance of state, national and global policies in the creation of inclusive cultures that "represent a whole-school concern that works to align special education with general education in a manner that most effectively and efficiently imparts quality education to all students" (Grima-Farrell et al. 2011, p. 118).

Queensland Context

Mitchell Graeme Coates shares his experiences with students with special needs in mainstream classrooms in schools in Queensland. "Queensland! Beautiful one day, perfect the next." This catchy little slogan was created by Tim Bond in 1985 and was immediately embraced by the Queensland Tourism Industry (QTI) in its attempt to arouse holidaymakers from all over the world. QTI's prime draw card was undoubtedly Queensland's tropical and sub-tropical climates where visitors were almost guaranteed to experience a holiday destination that would provide them with "the least restrictive environment."

Chance would have it that around the same period, educationalists worldwide had been suggesting that children with disabilities should be receiving their education in a similar setting, not as individuals on holiday of course, but as students who would learn in educational settings that would provide for them, at best, the "Least Restrictive Environment" (LRE). This implication was to be eventually adopted as a universally preferred practice, and the inclusion of children living with disabilities into regular classroom settings was to become the order of the day.

The etiology behind the adoption of an LRE is based on a theory that supports the rights of all people who live with a disability to equal educational opportunities within a regular classroom setting. However, if assessment data indicates that it is doubtful that prescribed goals will be met in any particular educational setting, other arrangements and avenues must be investigated for the applicant concerned. The Australian Education Union (AEU) has found that eight-out-of-ten principals in public schools do not have the resources required to educate the ever-growing number of students living with a disability, and that the learning opportunities for this increasing population are suffering as a result (Duncombe 2015).

The aphorism that a child's disability is often the only part of a person that many of us see, is still regrettably a reality among many within our general population. Do we not comprehend that the parents of children living with a disability are as ardent about the quality of their children's education as is any other parent? They also recognize that a sound education is absolutely crucial if their child is going to become an active and contributing participant within our society. As a society of the twenty-first century, we need to get this right!

At the beginning of my teaching career, I was indeed fortunate to be given the opportunity to undertake my internship at my old alma mater in Brisbane. It was during this position that I became alarmingly aware of the number of children attending my old school who were living with a range of disabilities, and who were receiving their education within regular classroom settings. Some years earlier, the school had extended its educational philosophy to include children who presented with special needs. Eventually a Special Education Program (SEP) was established in which there were 32 children living with one disability or another. These children with disabilities were interspersed throughout 11 classrooms, which was statistically more than a school of this size could cater for efficiently. Immediately I had some doubt as to whether these children were really being educated in an LRE.

Concerns raised from professional educators were unsettling to me as I could see with my own eyes that the education that these children with disabilities were receiving in the regular classroom setting, was not what was envisaged within the "Disability Standards for Education, 2005." The Standards were designed:

- To eliminate, as far as possible, discrimination against persons on the ground of disability in the area of education and training; and
- To ensure, as far as practicable, that persons with disabilities had the same rights to equality before the law in the area of education and training as the rest of the community; and
- To promote recognition and acceptance within the community of the principle that persons with disabilities have the same fundamental rights as the rest of the community (Disability Standards for Education 2005, paragraph 31).

The primary purpose of the standards was to make more explicit, the obligations of all education and training service providers under the Disability Discrimination Act of 1992, and to make even more explicit, the rights of all people with disabilities in relation to education and training. As a beginning teacher I could clearly see that these standards were not being met by our classroom teachers, and that little attempt was being made to professionally develop these educators in the area of successfully assimilating children with disabilities.

My initial PhD research revealed that in comparison to other areas of teacher education, our tertiary institutions allocate very little lecture time to this crucial area. As a result, many practicing teachers are severely lacking the skills required to equitably provide for children with disabilities. I was given the responsibility for a number of primary school children, all of whom had been diagnosed and were receiving funding from the Federal Government. A discussion pertaining to my experiences with two children for whom I was responsible are outlined below.

Down Syndrome

Kevin had been with the SEP for only a few weeks following his expulsion from another school for what the administration regarded as inappropriate behavior. He was 12 years of age, going on 13 and had very little coherent language, and no apparent interest in any type of formal instruction. As he was living with Down syndrome, his protective parents had decided to keep him domiciled in order to home educate him, but unfortunately their admirable intensions presented more difficulties than they could handle. Kevin's mother was an airhostess and her work took her away from home on frequent occasions leaving Kevin with his father who, while working from home, had little if any effect upon his ongoing education. It was as a result of this failed attempt to bridge the already widening gap in their son's education that they decided to enroll him at the school to work in our SEP.

It was my intention that Kevin should derive maximum benefits from his inherent and already acquired abilities, so it was imperative that I recognize both the strengths and weaknesses in his cognitive profiles and to utilize the former to compensate for the latter wherever possible. In my attempt to learn as much as I could about Down syndrome, I became aware that learning for children living with this disability is critically compromised by the disruption to normal developmental processes, caused specifically by the presence of an extra copy of chromosome 21. This seemed to imply that the differences in the structure and development of Kevin's brain meant that a number of basic information processing skills, central to the achievement of specific cognitive and linguistic milestones, had been, in his case, adversely affected.

I found this to be increasingly evident on the occasions when Kevin would choose to opt out of certain tasks that I had set up for him. He would refuse to engage for any more than a couple of minutes, and would sometimes use quite subtle social maneuvers to distract attention away to some less demanding activity. Then all of a sudden, he would pretend to be extremely interested in something else by producing some sort of digression, or by simply turning on his charismatic charm. It became apparent that Kevin preferred to avoid making errors than to attempt to solve any problem that he imagined might be potentially difficult.

Basic understandings in mathematical concepts were soon to be achieved as a result of playing board games. These games were clear and the rules easy to follow, and as a bonus, they were enhanced by colorful visual cues. Kevin's oral language was further defined through the repetitive words and short expressions used throughout each specific game played. It wasn't long before Kevin was able to interact verbally and relatively coherently with those he invited to share these board game experiences. Before many weeks had passed, Kevin became more positive toward his scheduled learning times, and he appeared to bask in the predictability of each and every hour. He had slowly but progressively become more comfortable in this learning environment that no longer restricted him from being able to express himself, an environment which encouraged him to interact with others in his own peer group.

Now fortified by the assertion that Kevin was working agreeably to his tight and structured schedule, I arranged with his classroom teacher that he spend one full period a day with his peers. Some days he would go directly to class in the morning, and on other days he would attend after morning tea or after the main lunch break. It was inspirational for me to see that his neuro-typical peers were willing to embrace his presence without any obvious signs of animosity, but unfortunately the same couldn't be said for the classroom teacher. It was evident that this teacher was extremely uncomfortable with Kevin being in the class. It could well have been that this teacher may have felt that he had temporarily lost control of his students as Kevin had, momentarily taken advantage of being the center of attention. I saw no problem with this personally, as I considered that very little attention had been paid to Kevin in the past. To be fair to the teacher though, it may just have been that his perception of his own competencies may have unintentionally revealed themselves, but I must admit, for me personally, it was professionally unsettling as it suddenly became clear that Kevin had, just moments before, left behind the security of his LRE to enter this much more restricted location.

As for the majority of students with whom we worked in the SEP, Kevin remained within the SEP during his lunch breaks. Free-time activities were always planned and supervised by the resident staff, and the children were able to chatter and socialize at will. However, we decided that it was time for Kevin to venture out into the playground during the lunch breaks. While these free-for-all play times are most anticipated by many students, they can be the most challenging time for those with a disability. "After all, here are two periods of the day where such students may experience sensory assault and social agony. These periods so often tend to be totally unstructured with no clear or fixed rules" (Boroson 2011, p. 145). No longer would it be just Kevin, myself and the other compassionate SEP staff with whom he felt comfortable. It was in this outdoor environment that Kevin's different facial features would become evident, and he may become extremely vulnerable against playground bullies. In such an environment where children such as Kevin need the most support, the least support is provided, and tragically such periods can became fraught with confusion, hurt and feelings of rejection. Here we may bear witness to an instance of gross sensory overload brought about by an occasion that should have been a joyous and harmonious time for all concerned.

During the fourth term, Kevin spent early mornings and late afternoons at the Outside School Hours Care (OSHC), and it was during this period that we noticed an appreciable downturn in his overall behavior. The Christmas holiday period was fast approaching, and even though we were all in agreement that much had been achieved academically as well as in the area of speech, he was, as were we all, ready for the 6-week summer break.

Kevin was welcomed back to the SEP in the New Year; however, we soon discovered that the progress that he had made over the previous three terms had almost vanished. The refreshing elements of independence that had appeared during the latter part of the previous year were no longer present, as he had become clingy, touchy-feely and totally reliant upon me throughout the day. His schedule had to be immediately re-designed in order to cater for this new set of circumstances, and it really was akin to starting all over again. Converging evidence from a number of studies has indicated that with increasing age and experience, a learning style may emerge in children with Down syndrome where there is an ever-increasing reliance on others, even when help is not really needed (Cebula and Wishart 2008; Williams et al. 2005; Wishart 2001, 2007). Unwittingly, this student was validating this evidence so it was back to the drawing board for both of us.

Autism Spectrum Disorder (ASD)

Liam, my second student, was a 10 year old, diagnosed with ASD. His parents were both very anxious people, having two sons with ASD, and often at a loss to know what to do. My initial introduction to Liam was preceded by information supplied to me through Children's Services. Because of the negative interaction between the two boys at home, and as a result of the uncontrollable noise and constant melt-downs from both of them, the parents took to locking them in their outdoor garage with the intention of settling them down. Of course, the neighbors were soon to report their actions, and the practice was quickly brought to a halt.

Liam initially presented as a child who would not, or possibly could not respond to normal conversation. He was totally reluctant to accept that I would be his main teacher for the rest of the year, and he became obstinately defiant and rebellious to any of my attempts to engage him in learning-based activities. Liam proved to be my biggest challenge, and to gain his trust was my immediate endeavor. As we had areas within the SEP where students could withdraw when their anxiety dictated, I decided to spend the first couple of days with Liam, in one of these defined spaces. I scattered age-appropriate toys on the floor, none of which were particularly gender specific, and my observational vigil began.

His choice of toy materials rested solely on books and any equipment associated with trains. He quickly assembled a comprehensive railway track, bridges, cross-ings and tunnels, and would become lost in the imagined adventures that lay before him. It was through these observations that I was to eventually develop a program that was to work, to some degree, for us both. Having to share my time with other children within the SEP was difficult for Liam to understand, and he would often terminate whatever he was doing, run wildly around the room, throw whatever he could lay his hands on, and scream and swear at the top of his voice. On one occa-sion, it took three adults to hold him down for his own safety while another teacher rang his mother to come to the school to take him home.

As the weeks progressed, so did Liam's attitude toward his work. I had finally gained his trust and he was now more prepared to share his "me-time" with other students in the SEP. He even became somewhat of a tutor to some of the other chil-dren with ASD, and would eagerly participate in group social games. His melt-downs gradually lessened, and he was able to spend more time in the classroom where the teacher welcomed him and the other students in the class enveloped him into their working groups. This particular classroom teacher was willing to accom-modate Liam and provide for him an LRE in which he could work comfortably and without stress. Liam was indeed a very intelligent student, and we were encouraged to hear that he has settled down to his secondary school studies, and is doing very well.

Critical Reflections

The critical reflections derived from the case studies provided within the Australian context in relation to achieving inclusion in mainstream classes are as follow:

There is no "one size fits all approach." The Individual Education Plans (named differently across the different states of Australia) are designed specifically to cater to an individual's unique needs, and play a critical role in supporting students with disabilities in Australian mainstream classes.

A collaborative whole-school approach is encouraged to ensure that all students experience a sense of belonging, mastery, independence and courage.

Australian schools are making an attempt to use more ICT and assistive technology for the benefit of students with disabilities.

Students with disabilities are strategically engaged beyond the classroom within the Australian community to provide real-life experiences required for them to succeed.

Mainstream classroom teachers are supported by teacher aides, and in more highly resourced schools, a team of specialist staff provides for full inclusion for students with disabilities.

Students with severe disabilities and highly diverse needs are often excluded from many class group activities under the disguise of inclusion.

Recent Australian Education Union (AEU) research has revealed that eight-out-of-ten public school principals do not have the resources required to equitably educate the ever-growing number of students living with a disability.

Alarmingly, tertiary institutions in Queensland provide very limited instruction in "inclusion" strategies for their pre-service teachers in the area of ASD.

Conclusion

It has been estimated that one-quarter of all new teaching graduates will leave the profession within 3 to 5 years (Buchanan et al. 2013). Reasons for teacher burnout and attrition among staff include a lack of effective preparation in pre-service courses, stress from lack of time to develop effective and consistent instructional approaches, and a lack of support during induction programs at individual schools (Liston et al. 2006). Can we afford such a loss? These findings and some of the case examples should set off alarms within education departments and universities globally. While all Australian teachers have undertaken the necessary tertiary studies to qualify them for their respective roles in education, the majority of them have received little or inadequate appropriate in-service, or pre-service training in order to enable them to embrace the practice of inclusion. There is indeed a glaring need for a total transformation in our professional attitudes toward the manner in which our future generations are going to be educated.

References

Abells, D., Burbidge, J., & Minnes, P. (2008). Involvement of adolescents with intellectual disabilities in social and recreational activities. *Journal on Developmental Disabilities, 14*(2), 88–94.

Ashman, A. F., & Elkins, J. (Eds.). (2009). *Educating for inclusion and diversity* (3rd ed.). Melbourne: Frenches Forest, NSW Pearson Education Australia.

Attwood, T. (2006). *The complete guide to Asperger's syndrome*. London/Philadelphia: Jessica Kingsley Publishers.

Australian Government. (2005). *Disability standards for education 2005*. Canberra: Attorney-General's Department, Department of Education, Science and Training.

Australian Institute for Teaching and School Leadership. (2012). *Australian professional standards for teachers*. http://www.teacherstandards.aitsl.edu.au/Standards/AllStandards. Accessed 1 May 2015.

Australian Research Alliance for Children & Youth. (2013). *Inclusive education for students with disability: A review of the best evidence in relation to theory and practice*. http://www.aracy. org.au/publications-resources/command/download_file/id/246/filename/Inclusive_education_ for_students_with_disability_-_A_review_of_the_best_evidence_in_relation_to_theory_and_ practice.pdf. Accessed 1 May 2015.

Boroson, B. (2011). *Autism spectrum disorders in the mainstream classroom*. New York: Scholastic Inc..

Buchanan, J., Prescott, A., Schuck, S., Aubusson, P., Burke, P., & Louviere, J. (2013). Teacher retention and attrition: Views of early career teachers. *Australian Journal of Teacher Education, 38*(3), 112–129.

Cebula, K. R., & Wishart, J. (2008). Social cognition in children with down syndrome. *International Review of Research in Mental Retardation, 35*, 43–86.

Department of Education and Child Development. (2012). On the same basis: Implementing the disability discrimination act standards for education. Adelaide: Government of South Australia. http://www.decd.sa.gov.au/speced/pages/specialneeds/OnthebamebasisDDAEducationStandar ds/?reFlag=1. Accessed 1 May 2015.

Duncombe, T. (2015). Disability must not stop children learning. *Queensland Teachers Journal, 120*(3), 16.

Dyson, M. (2007). My story in a profession of stories: Auto ethnography – An empowering methodology for educators. *Australian Journal of Teacher Education, 32*(1), 36–48.

Elkins, J. (1994). The school context. In A. Ashman & J. Elkins (Eds.), *Educating children with special needs* (pp. 71–103). Sydney: Prentice Hall.

Fitts, W. H., & Warren, W. L. (2003). *Tennessee self-concept scale (2nd ed.) manual*. Los Angeles: Western Psychological Services.

Government of South Australia, Department of Education and Children's Services. (2001). *South Australian curriculum standards and accountability framework*. http://www.sacsa.sa.edu.au. Accessed 1 May 2015.

Grima-Farrell, C. (2017). What matters in a research to practice cycle? Teachers as researchers. Singapore: Springer.

Grima-Farrell, C. R., Bain, A., & McDonagh, S. H. (2011). Bridging the research-to-practice gap: A review of the literature focusing on inclusive education. *Australasian Journal of Special Education, 35*(2), 117–136. doi:10.1375/ajse.35.2.117.

Halder, S., & Datta, P. (2012). An exploration into self concept: A comparative analysis between the adolescents who are sighted and blind in India. *British Journal of Visual Impairment, 30*(1), 31–41. doi:10.1177/0264619611428202.

Huurre, T. M., & Aro, H. M. (1998). Psychosocial development among adolescents with visual impairment. *European Child & Adolescent Psychiatry, 7*(2), 73–78. doi:10.1007/ s007870050050.

Liston, E., Whitcomb, J., & Borko, H. (2006). Too little or too much: Teacher preparation and the first years of teaching. *Journal of Teacher Education, 57*, 351–358.

Lucy, Y. S. W. (1997). *Self-concept of visually impaired students in a mainstream secondary school in Hong Kong* (Master's thesis, The University of Hong Kong [Pokfulam, Hong Kong], Hong Kong). Retrieved from http://hub.hku.hk/handle/10722/28678. Accessed 1 Jan 2013.

Mendez, M. (2013). Autoethnography as a research method: Advantages, limitations and criticisms. *Colombian Applied Linguistics Journal, 15*(2), 279.

NSW Government. (2012). *Educational services supporting students with disability*. http://www.schools.nsw.edu.au/media/downloads/schoolsweb/studentsupport/programs/disabilitypgrms/eduservices-studisability.pdf. Accessed 1 May 2015.

NSW Legislative Council. (2010). *The provision of education to students with a disability or special needs*. http://www.parliament.nsw.gov.au/Prod/parlment/committee.nsf/0/47 F51A782AEABBBCA25 767A000FABEC. Accessed 1 May 2015.

Organization for Economic Co-operation and Development (OECD). (1999). *Sustaining inclusive education: Including students with special educational needs in mainstream schools: Lessons from the case studies*. Paris: Author.

Pearce, M., Gray, J., & Campbell-Evans, G. (2009). The inclusive secondary teacher: The leaders' perspective. *Australian Journal of Teacher Education, 34*(6), 101–119. doi.org/10.14221/ajte.2009v34n6.7.

Raab, D. (2013). Transpersonal approaches to Autoethnographic research and writing. *The Qualitative Report, 18*(42), 1–18.

Simon, T. J., Burg-Malki, M., & Gothelf, D. (2007). Cognitive and behavioral characteristics of children with chromosome 22q11.2 deletion. In Mazzocco & J. L. Ross (Eds.), *Neurogenetic developmental disorders: Manifestation and identification in childhood*. Cambridge, MA: The MIT Press.

Tomlinson, S. (2012). The irresistible rise of the SEN industry. *Oxford Review of Education, 38*, 267.

UNESCO. (1994). *The world conference on special needs education: Access and quality. Final report*. Salamanca: Ministry of Education and Science, Madrid; UNESCO.

van Kraayenoord, C. E. (2007). School and classroom practices in inclusive education in Australia. *Childhood Education, 83*(6), 390–394. doi:10.1080/00094056.2007.10522957.

van Kraayenoord, C. E., Elkins, J., Palmer, C., & Rickards, F. (2000). *Literacy, numeracy and students with disabilities: The literature review*. Canberra: Department of Education, Training and Youth Affairs.

Williams, K. R., Wishart, J. G., Pitcairn, T. K., & Willis, D. S. (2005). Emotion recognition by children with Down syndrome: Investigation of specific impairments and error patterns. *American Journal on Mental Retardation, 110*, 378–392.

Wishart, J. G. (2001). Motivation and learning styles in young children with Down syndrome. *Down's Syndrome, Research and Practice, 7*, 47–51.

Wishart, J. G. (2007). Socio-cognitive understanding: A strength or weakness in Down's syndrome? *Journal of Intellectual Disability Research, 51*, 996–1005.

Zic, A., & Igrić, L. (2001). Self-assessment of relationships with peers in children with intellectual disability. *Journal of Intellectual Disability Research, 45*(3), 202–211. doi:10.1046/j.1365-2788.2001.00311.x.

Chapter 15
Gifted and Talented Students: A Review of the Concept from Indian Experience

Partha Pratim Roy

Abstract What is the meaning of giftedness? How special are the gifted and talented children? Is there any age for the development of giftedness? What kind of intervention is necessary for nurturing the gifted and talented? Should there be special 'gifted and talented' programs in our education system? An auto-ethnographic study of my experience of more than 20 years, in teaching 1500 high-performing adolescents of an Indian high school, suggests that 'discovery teaching and learning' can help not just in identifying the gifted minds but also in nurturing their abilities. My experience also shows how the conceptual primitives can be utilized to facilitate metacognitive abilities of the learners. By engaging students in innovative project works, I have seen how 'ordinary' students can turn creative to win accolades in prestigious science competitions. Any special emphasis on the 'gifted and talented' in an education system does not help the greater cause of education, but promotes elitism and racism in the system.

Introduction

I have been teaching physics in a city high school of Kolkata in eastern India for more than 20 years. It is a private co-educational school with a very moderate fees structure. The medium of instruction is English and the enrolled students are mostly from middle-class families. The school's name featured in the Guinness Book of World Records as the largest school in the world in terms of number of students enrolled. This school began in 1954 and since then has produced many toppers in different statewide, countrywide and worldwide examinations. Every year, more than 80% of the students of this school score among the top 1% of all the examinees of the statewide Board exam. Every state in India has its own Board of Secondary and Higher Secondary Education and these Boards conduct statewide school-leaving

P.P. Roy (✉)
South Point High School, Kolkata, West Bengal, India

Physics Education Research Group, University of Maryland, College Park, USA
e-mail: roy.parthapratim@gmail.com

© Springer International Publishing AG 2017
S. Halder, L.C. Assaf (eds.), *Inclusion, Disability and Culture*, Inclusive
Learning and Educational Equity 3, DOI 10.1007/978-3-319-55224-8_15

examinations. Our school is regarded as one of the very best schools of the state on the basis of the performance of our students in this examination. I joined this school in 1991 as a physics teacher and now I am the Head of the physics department. Since 1991, nearly 800 of my students got selected to the Indian Institutes of Technology (IIT) through the IIT entrance exam. The entrance examination for the Indian Institutes of Technology is considered a world-class talent search examination by many people around the world. 'For example, Zakaria (2011) described the admissions exams of the Indian Institutes of Technology (IIT) as follows: Their (IITs) greatest strength is that they administer one of the world's most ruthlessly competitive entrance exams. Three hundred thousand people take it, five thousand are admitted, an acceptance rate of 1.7 percent… The people who make the mark are the best and the brightest out of one billion. Place them in any education system and they will do well' (Kell et al. 2013). The IIT alumni are spread all over the world and are placed in many key positions in industry and academics. In 1999, the Department of Science and Technology of the Govt. of India initiated a highly competitive fellowship program for school students. The program is named Kishore Vaigyanik Protsahan Yojana (KVPY) and it means – young scientists' encouragement program. The KVPY is designed to search students especially talented in science through extremely competitive pen-paper tests and face-to-face interviews with scientists. KVPY is a symbol of prestige among science students in our country. About 80 of my students had been selected as KVPY fellows since the inception of the fellowship. My students also participated in the prestigious Intel International Science and Engineering Fair (ISEF) of the USA since 2009 and had won awards in 2009 (two students won the MIT Lincoln Lab Award), 2010 (four students won Grand Awards), 2011 (one student won MIT Lincoln Lab Award) and 2014 (one student won Special Award). Five of my students had been in the Indian contingent at the International Olympiads in Mathematics (IMO) and Physics, and two of them had won medals in IMO. The Jagadish Bose National Science Talent Search (JBNSTS), the oldest talent search initiative in India, has judged our school as the best school of the year consecutively for the last ten years as my students won the maximum number of scholarships awarded by them every year.

All these highly performing students sat in my classes, discussed with me about their difficulty in understanding concepts and I observed them to grow up like all other children. I was never aware of 'gifted and talented education' as a field of educational research until the JBNSTS invited me in 2013 to present my experience with 'gifted students' at an International Conference on Gifted and Talented Education they had organized. I not only discovered an interesting field of study but also learnt that my experience was regarded as important data for research in this field. In the last 20 years, I taught nearly 7000 students; 1500 of them performed exceptionally well in different exams and/or competitions, and the rest also performed well but not as good as mentioned above. I had always taught and mentored my students without caring about teaching-learning theories and jargons. My primary objective had always been to help my students self-discover their subject. The variety of cases that I had to deal with enriched my experience every year. I am now conscious about the issue of the 'gifted and talented' and have decided to write an auto-ethnography to search for answers to a number of questions. Does the conception of 'giftedness' have any real basis at all in terms of a scientific analysis of mind, or is it just a socio-cultural perception? Does the identification of students as 'gifted' and 'non-gifted' help advance the cause of inclusion in education and social development or not? Should there be any special provision for the 'gifted and talented' in schools as there are for the differently abled children? Should 'gifted and talented education' be considered a part of 'special' or 'inclusive' education? Do the students considered 'gifted' by one school perform better than others in all other schools? Also, there are students who remain unnoticed as they are silent in the class, but can delve deeper into a subject to think independently. Are the teachers able to identify such students as 'exceptional' or 'gifted'? Do the students identified as 'gifted' at school remain ahead of their peers throughout their life? My story will try to search for the answers to these questions.

As a Teacher

When I joined this school as a physics teacher, there was a system of distributing students in different graded sections of standard IX in terms of their performance in the year-end exam of standard VIII. Up to standard VIII, there was no segregation of pupils in terms of their performance in exams. It was from standard IX onwards that performance-based segregation was made and teachers were assigned classes in these graded sections depending on their experience and 'quality'. I was told to teach in the sections of the 'best' and the 'brightest' as well as in the sections of the 'moderate' and the 'bad'. I treated all the students equally in terms of the method of teaching adopted by me. I found that the students in the 'best' sections were more serious about studying for the exams, while the others used to take it casually as they appeared to have accepted that they are not good students. There was a kind of subtle discrimination in dealing of students by the teachers. I saw teachers being proud when allotted the 'best' sections to teach and also heard teachers telling students of the 'bad' sections that being a teacher for the 'best' sections it is less enjoyable to teach the 'bad'. But I later discovered that my students from both the 'best' and 'worst' sections were now CEOs of leading organizations, professors at well-known universities, reputed doctors and successful entrepreneurs. I was never happy with this kind of a 'discriminatory' culture in the school as I recalled my own experience as a student in my schooldays. When I was a student in a sub-urban school, my performance in exams were always among the best. So I was placed in a section earmarked for the best performing students. As exams are the only indicators of good education in our socio-cultural perspective, I started believing myself to be truly exceptional. My teachers had also helped me think like that. But as I was growing up, I discovered that there were students in other sections of my class who did not score very high in exams but had a much clearer understanding of the subjects than I had. In the annual science exhibitions of our school, some of my low-scoring classmates demonstrated their creative and innovative thinking in a way that I was unable to do. At that age, I was not mature enough to realize the difference these abilities make in life as the societal perception of education was entirely exam-oriented. I left school with exceptionally high percentage of marks in the Board exam, but gradually realized that those of my low-scoring classmates who were creative in thinking were destined to scale greater heights than I was. This realiza-tion helped me form a strong opinion about our perception of the 'best' and the 'brightest'. I therefore tried in my own way to make all students feel that it was the spirit of inquiry that could make a difference in achievement in life, not the ability to write good answers in exams. I had formed groups taking students from all the sections to take part in science fairs and investigative projects. I found that the stu-dents of the 'best' sections were the 'best' performers in almost all the examina-tions, but not always in Olympiads or Science Fairs. Ten years after I joined the school, the school had finally got rid of the system of segregating students in sec-tions in terms of their exam grades, but the school's performance remained the same. I saw that on being stamped as 'best' on the basis of exam score develops a feeling in some students that they are the best in all kinds of academic activities. I also found parents of such students prejudiced with the 'best' syndrome. Once such a student's parents moved the court when their son failed to win an award in a sci-ence project competition and a so-called 'bad' student won it. I felt that there was a subtle elitism and racism embedded in the socio-cultural perception of the 'best' and the 'brightest' and the students also started subscribing to this feeling if proper intervention was not made by parents and/or teachers.

I had never found any of the highly performing students as 'accelerated' learners, nor any one with 'supernormal' intelligence. I dealt with each of these students through a span of four years (standards IX, X, XI and XII) and could observe their abilities to grow over these years. In my classrooms, I always adopted the discovery learning approach. I first tried to create an ambience where the students could feel free to discuss and argue on an issue on the basis of their pre-existing knowledge. This helped me know the epistemological foundation of the knowledge the students carried into the classroom and also the pattern of their discourse. I then planned the course of my teaching to fit into this pattern of epistemology and discourse. I designed experiments for students to observe and asked them to explain what they saw. They always came up with several hypotheses. I then asked them to design experiments to test their hypotheses and helped them in doing that. At this stage, I could observe how a student's thinking progressed and how a student struggled in determining the right way of thinking. I assisted them at this stage in deciding or discovering the correct route of thinking, helping their metacognitive ability to grow. I found that some students were truly different in their attitude towards the whole process and also in their way of looking at things. I have always faced innu-merable questions from these students and the questions they asked were not often 'intelligent'. While I taught any principle or law of physics, I found these students searching for counter-arguments before they could accept the law for themselves. These students always tried to understand any topic from the first principle by self-construction. Most of them showed strong commitment towards the task of con-structing the knowledge by themselves. I could observe the enjoyment they were having in doing all these. I can classify these 'different' students into three groups on the basis of their performance in in-house school exams at standard IX: high scorers (scoring 80% and higher), moderate scorers (scoring between 80 and 60%) and low scorers (scoring between 60 and 40%). High scorers constituted nearly 50% of the population (N ≈ 900 every year) while the moderate and low scorers formed nearly 30 and 20% of the population, respectively. Nearly 80% of the IIT entrance crackers (N ≈ 20 every year) were from the high scorers, while nearly 90% of the KVPY (N ≈ 15 every year) and Intel ISEF awardees (N ≈ 10 in total) were from the moderate scorers. Surprisingly, more than 5% of the successful students (N ≈ 1500) having exceptional achievements of some kind after they leave school had been low scorers at standard IX level. Below I present examples of a few of the 'gifted' students belonging to different scorer categories.

Student 1 This student belonged to the low-scoring group. He failed to get through the IIT entrance test. He didn't score among the top 1% of the examinees in his school-leaving Board exam. No definition would have termed him 'gifted' or 'talented'. But he was successful in becoming a JBNSTS scholar, was selected for admission to the PhD program of TIFR (Tata Institute of Fundamental Research, Mumbai) through an extremely competitive selection process, to do research in Astrophysics. TIFR is the ivory tower of Indian scientific research. He is now at the Harvard–Smithsonian Center for Astrophysics as a postdoctoral fellow. He is a Junior Fellow of the prestigious Harvard Society of Fellows. He won the Best Thesis Award at TIFR, the Price Award in Astronomy and Astrophysics at Harvard and several other prizes.

Student 2 This student belonged to the high scorer category. He was successful in the IIT entrance test, scored among the top 1% in all exams he appeared. He was among the top 20 in the state in the school-leaving Board exam. He was selected for admission to the PhD program in Theoretical Physics at TIFR by a ruthlessly competitive selection process, but left TIFR after his M.S. to go to Ohio State University to complete his PhD in Theoretical Condensed Matter Physics. He got substantive postdoctoral appointments at Harvard University, and then at University of Maryland, College Park, and now got appointed as a Reader at TIFR, Mumbai.

Student 3 This student was in the moderate scorer category at standard IX. He was not successful at the IIT entrance test, but scored among the top 1% of the Board examinees in the school-leaving Board exam in 2002. He was a JBNSTS scholar and studied physics at the Bachelors level and was selected for admission to the Indian Institute of Science, Bangalore (IISc) through a very strong competition, for an integrated program towards MS-PhD. IISc is another symbol of excellence in India's scientific research in many fields ranging from Engineering to Biological Sciences. He completed his PhD in Theoretical Condensed Matter Physics in a very short time (in 3 years compared to an average time of 5–6 years) without any actual supervisor as the assigned supervisor left for MIT within 1 year of accepting him as his student. After PhD, he has completed a substantive postdoc term at the Perimeter Institute of Theoretical Physics, in Canada, and is now at the Max Planck Institute for Physics of Complex Systems at Dresden, Germany as a senior postdoctoral fellow. He is offered a permanent faculty position by the International Center for Theoretical Sciences, of the TIFR.

Student 4 This student's category fluctuated between high scorer and moderate scorer category during standard IX. He was selected for admission to the IIT through the IIT entrance test and was also placed among the top 1% of all examinees of the school-leaving Board exam in 2000. He was a KVPY fellow and also a JBNSTS scholar. He studied physics for B.Sc. and then joined the Theoretical Physics Group of TIFR after a ruthlessly competitive selection process. After his M.S., he was offered admission to Harvard University to complete his PhD in Theoretical Condensed Matter Physics. After his PhD, he was a postdoctoral fellow at the University of Illinois, Urbana-Champagne. Now he is at the Argonne National Laboratory, USA. He received several awards like the Purcell Fellowship, the J.M. Price Fellowship, etc. at Harvard.

Student 5 This student was consistently in the moderate scorer category. He did not get through the IIT entrance test, but was among the top 1% of all examinees in the school-leaving Board exam in 2011. He is a KVPY Fellow and is studying at the Indian Institute of Science Education and Research (IISER) for his Integrated BS-MS in Physics. IISER is an institution of National importance, set up by the Govt. of India to become a Center for Excellence in scientific research across disciplines. He has a patent for a device he designed for participating in the Intel ISEF. He received the Gold Award at the Initiative for Research and Innovation in Science (IRIS) National Fair in India and had also won the third Grand Award in Intel ISEF in San Jose, California.

Giftedness: My Findings

All such students present a variety of examples to study which factor should be regarded a true indicator of 'difference' or 'giftedness' in an adolescent. My experiences in mentoring all of them suggest that the only trait that creates a pre-condition for 'difference' or 'giftedness' in a person is the eagerness or interest (inspiration) for hard work in a field. Enormous hard work mixed with inspiration can turn a person into 'exceptional'. If we call all these students ($N \approx 1500$) 'gifted' on the basis of their achievements, my study of the growth of their abilities reveal that the development of the right epistemology and metacognitive skill should be considered as key factors behind 'giftedness'. On the practical side, 'discovery learning' methodology has contributed significantly in the development of independent and creative thinking. This helped even the most silent student of the class to participate and demonstrate thinking skills. The IIT entrance test performance of the 'high scorer' students reveal no special feature as scoring high in difficult exams has been the practice of this group. But, only a tenth of this high scorer group could become successful when creative and independent thinking is a requirement. On the mentoring or nurturing side, I discovered that there must be a continuous monitoring of the epistemological orientations of a student to understand how the metacognitive abilities are guiding him/her. I observed that every student developed some conceptual primitives through his/her developmental process. When they are forming hypotheses for explaining an observation or planning to design a testing experiment, their primitive concepts come out to play a decisive role in decision-making. These primitives organize themselves in the students' minds to give shape to their epistemological foundation and this foundation help in developing metacognitive abilities in them. As the teacher, I have to note these thinking structures and guide them in rejecting any primitive idea that is problematic. The classroom discussions provide scope for identification of the nature of the conceptual primitives they carry with them in the class. Then through individual discussions with them, I could know how they organize their logical system in arguing in favour of an answer. Epistemology of a learner guides the learner to decide what knowledge is, and how this knowledge can be learned, and also to decide the degree of certainty, determinants and criteria used to determine and define knowledge (Benedixen et al. 1994; Hofer and Pintrich 1997; Schommer 1990). Metacognitive ability, on the other hand, is the awareness and knowledge about the process of knowledge formation and the ability to organize, evaluate and control thinking (Bonds 1992; Wilson 1998). Metacognition is an important parameter that helps effective learning by enabling one to monitor and regulate one's cognitive activity (Bouffard-Bouchard et al. 1993). Most of the students showing 'exceptionality' at the end of their schooldays and beyond, exhibit an interplay of three important factors either existing or developing in them – conceptual primitives, epistemology and metacognitive ability. Although I have not done any formal study of the conceptual primitives – epistemology – metacognition interaction of my students, my experience with students agree with the research that reveals that gifted students use their metacognitive abilities more than the ordinary students (Carr and Borkowski 1987; Alexander 1995). As it is possible to develop metacognitive strategies in learners through metacognitive experience while solving difficult problems or answering critical questions during discovery learning sessions, I had always trained the students to approach any problem or any question from the first principle. If the students are inspired and agreeable to do hard work, it becomes possible to bring out the achiever in a student, whether the student is 'gifted' or 'non-gifted'. I have seen that if a student is asked to construct a new concept or knowledge from a minimal set of accepted principles, the interesting interplay of primitive knowledge, epistemology and metacognitive ability can be studied and necessary intervention can be effectively made. In the absence of any such practice during the learning process, there is hardly any difference observed between the 'gifted' and the 'non-gifted' (Muil et al. 2013).

Literature Review: Conceptions of 'Giftedness'

I had tried to study the basis of 'giftedness' in my students from my own experience. Whenever I wanted to know about the authenticity of my explanation and analysis, I started referring to the existing research in this field. But when I looked into the 'gifted and talented' research literature, I found that there was hardly any convergence of opinions in the conceptual understanding of giftedness by the educationists and psychologists. But the most important unity in this diversity of opinions is the recognition of context and environment in shaping minds to perform exceptionally. If at all 'giftedness' is a concept worthy for any serious scientific investigation is also an issue being raised. James H Borland of Teachers' College, Columbia University, presents a radical view on this issue. Himself being a renowned scholar of gifted and talented education, he says, 'I believe that the concept of the gifted student is incoherent and untenable on a number of grounds. The first of these is that the concept of the gifted child in American education is a social construct of questionable validity. The second is that educational practice predicated on the existence of the gifted child has been largely ineffective. The third is that this practice has exacerbated the inequitable allocation of educational resources in the country' (Borland 2005). According to this school, both 'giftedness' and 'intelligence' are socio-political constructs suitable to a particular time in history. The emergence of the 'empirical' and 'scientific' measurement of intelligence (the Stanford–Binet scale) in the twentieth century and the consequent 'invention' of 'giftedness' in children may be viewed as the 'technologies of power' that helped the modern state control the diverse population by creating 'scientific' differences among people, hence justifying inequity in distribution of resources (Foucault 1995). A study of the US Department of education about the gifted program for eighth grade (1991) revealed that students from the socio-economically weaker section are five times less likely to be included in any gifted and talented program. Borland believes that the proponents of gifted education do never support any gifted program that is racist, elitist, sexist or blighted by socio-economic inequalities, but such inequalities have historically been an obvious outcome of the gifted programs worldwide and persist even today (Borland and Wright 1994; Ford 1996; Ford and Harris 1999; Passow 1989).

However racist or elitist the conception of giftedness may be, educators and psychologists have tried their best to design programs for a better nurturing of minds, in spite of serious disagreements about the definition of giftedness. Joan Freeman (2005) writes, 'There are perhaps 100 definitions of giftedness around, almost all of which refer to children's precocity, either in psychological constructs, such as intelligence and creativity, but more usually in terms of high marks in school subjects (Hany 1993), although in formal school education, social or business talents are rarely considered. How teachers perceive and thus identify the gifted has been seen to vary considerably between different cultures.' A comparison of the teachers' perception about giftedness was done with nearly 400 secondary-level teachers of Germany, about 400 teachers of USA and 159 teachers of Indonesia (Dahme 1996).

In Germany, 3.5% of the students were found as gifted by the teachers, while in the USA 6.4% were recognized as gifted, and the teachers of Indonesia selected 17.4% students as gifted. Freeman found that there can be wide variation between teacher perceptions of giftedness and objective measures of the same. 'Individually, teachers' attitudes toward the very able vary greatly; some feel resentment, whereas others overestimate bright youngsters' all-round abilities, as was found in a Finnish-British survey (Ojanen and Freeman 1994).' According to Freeman 'A cross-cultural view picks up a wide variety of international templates for the identification and education of the gifted and talented, which are sometimes entirely opposing… Although cultural nuances are complex and their dynamics difficult to define, it is clear that excellence can come from widely differing special education provision or from no special education provision at all' (Freeman 2005).

Jonathan Plucker and Barab (2005) conceptualize giftedness not just as an individual trait but also as the outcome of a dynamic interaction between the individual and the diverse contexts (social, economic, cultural, home, school, etc.) the individual is embedded in, intertwined with the concepts of creativity, intelligence and talent. They think that 'creativity emerges from an interaction among aptitudes, cognitive processes, and influences from the environment in which an individual or group exists…..With respect to the construct of giftedness, it is also a construct shaped by multiple influences, and its existence is best determined by the presence of unambiguous evidence of extraordinary achievement (i.e., both novelty and usefulness) within a specific social context. With this definition in mind the question is not, who is gifted, but how can we match children to specific instructional contexts to help them realize their potential giftedness?' Nuessel et al. (2001) emphasized the role of social context not just for development of creativity but also for its recognition too. According to them, creativity 'fashions or defines new questions in a domain in a way that is initially considered novel, but ultimately becomes accepted in a particular cultural setting'. According to this school, giftedness should not be searched in small children as it is problematic to identify special abilities before their full potential develops through interactions with the environment for a substantive period of time.

The Russian approach to giftedness is very different from that of the west. While most of the Western concepts of giftedness begin with psychometric measurements or IQ tests of some kind and are based on classification of students on the basis of their 'measured' intelligence, the Russian approach is interested in utilizing the students' special abilities in science and mathematics for the 'common good' of the society at large. The 'gifted and talented' in Russia are trained in the same common homogeneous education system and are identified through everyday activities and evaluations in different achievement domains. After the Soviet era, special models have been proposed for dealing with the gifted and talented in an integrated manner. The 'systemic model of giftedness' based on the works of many Russian psychologists 'rests on two major notions: the notion of qualitative differences between processes and products involved in giftedness and the notion of congruence (internal and external)' (Jeltova and Grigorenko 2005). The cognitive, physiological, genetic, emotional and motivational factors are among the 'process' variables which determine a child's potential and the performance in a given domain is the 'product'. Whether a process variable is capable of generating an expected product (superior performance) is dependent both on the compatibility or the 'internal congruence' of several process variables (extreme anxiety vs. superior intellectual activity) and on the degree of 'external congruence' between the process variables and environmental factors. This model views giftedness as the result of dialectical interactions between genetic and environmental factors. General mental ability in a cluster of domains (e.g. mathematics, physics and music) was also considered as a 'prerequisite' for giftedness by many Russian psychologists. But, after the high level of fragmentation and specialization of human knowledge, it is unrealistic to expect someone to be 'globally gifted' alongside being gifted in a particular domain (Teplov 1985). The idea that display of exceptional ability in one domain is an indicator of possible exceptionality in other domains puts forward the notion of 'potential giftedness' (Babayeva and Voiskunovskiy 2003; Leitis 2000).

Joseph S. Renzulli (2005) takes a much broader view of giftedness to include a variety of students into its fold. His conception of giftedness is based on taxonomy of various types of behavioural manifestations of giftedness both inside and outside schools. Based on his taxonomy, he proposes the 'three ring conception of giftedness' composed of: (i) above average ability, (ii) task commitment and (iii) creativity, to be spread over 'schoolhouse giftedness' and 'creative-productive giftedness'. His conception of giftedness is more practical than theoretical and it goes beyond quantitative classification of individuals through IQ tests. He cites the example of basketball coaches who become flexible to include players not having the requisite height, into his team, and turn them into successful players (Fig. 15.1).

In *Conceptions of Giftedness* (eds. Sternberg and Davidson 2005), Renzulli quotes Sternberg (1982) to present his point about intelligence tests – 'tests only work for some of the people some of the time – not for all of the people all of the time – and that some of the assumptions we make in our use of tests are, at best, correct only for a segment of the tested population, and at worst, correct for none of it'. As a result, we fail to identify many gifted individuals for whom the assumptions underlying our use of tests are particularly inadequate. The problem, then, is not only that tests are of limited validity for everyone but that their validity varies across individuals. For some people, test scores may be quite informative, for others such scores may be worse than useless. Use of test score cut-offs and formulas result in a serious problem of under-identification of gifted children. Research on correlations between different subject areas and measured values of intelligence (Barron 1968, 1969; Campbell 1960; Guilford 1964, 1967) reveals that in physics and mathematics this correlation is quiet low, while in areas of painting, sculpting and designing this correlation is negative. Also it is observed that no exceptional intelligence is necessary for a high degree of creative achievement.

The Munich Model of Giftedness (MMG) (Heller et al. 2005) presents a very systematic multifactorial conception of giftedness incorporating both cognitive and non-cognitive factors. Through its extension to the Munich Dynamic Ability-Achievement Model of Giftedness (MDAAM), the MMG has included different research paradigms to design an effective multidimensional mechanism for

Fig. 15.1 The Three Ring conception of giftedness (*Note*: **Above average ability (general):* High levels of abstract thought, Adaptation to novel situations; Rapid and accurate retrieval of in forma-tions. *Above average ability (specific):* Application of general abilities to specific area of knowl-edge, capacity to acquire and use advanced knowledge and strategies while pursuing a problem. *** Creativity:* Flexibility and originality of thought, open to new experiences and ideas, curious, willing to take risks, sensitive to aesthetic characteristics. ****Task Commitment:* Capacity of high levels of interest, enthusiasm, hard work and determination in a particular area, ability to identify significant problems within an area of study)

understanding giftedness. Based mostly on cognitive studies, MMG and MDAAM present a synthetic approach for conceptualizing giftedness and expertise. Fig. 15.3 illustrates the MMG in detail and Fig. 15.2 shows the complex causal interactions of the cognitive and non-cognitive parameters. The extended MMG, i.e. the MDAAM, takes many more cognitive factors into account in bridging the gap between giftedness research and research in cognitive studies. 'Individual charac-teristics, such as aspects of attention and attention control, habituation, memory efficiency (speed of information processing) and working memory aspects, level of activation, and aspects of perception or motor skills, can all be seen as innate dispo-sitions or prerequisites of learning and achievement. Indeed, these characteristics represent the basic cognitive equipment of an individual' (Perleth et al. 2000; Heller et al. 2005).

Sternberg (2003) and colleagues have brought in the factor of 'wisdom' in devel-oping their conception of giftedness. They proposed the WICS model as a synthetic model in which Wisdom, Intelligence and Creativity are synthesized to make a per-son great. According to Sternberg 'Wisdom' is connected to one's understanding of 'good' and 'bad' in relation to society at large. A person may be intelligent and creative, but the person is never 'gifted' if the person is selfish and careless about the well-being of others. Thus, Sternberg has included a moral and ethical criterion into the conceptual understanding of giftedness. Sternberg (1998, 2001) has defined 'wisdom' as the application of intelligence and creativity guided by socio-moral

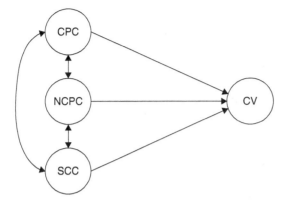

Legend: CPC= cognitive personality characteristics or traits of gifted individuals (predictors); NCPC = Non-cognitive personality characteristics or traits of gifted individuals (moderators); SCC = Socio-cultural condition variables (moderators); CV = Criterion variables (of achievement behavior in gifted individuals).

Fig. 15.2 The causal connectivity of the different factors in MMG and MDAAM (Heller et al. 2005)

values for achieving a common good by balancing: (i) intrapersonal, (ii) interpersonal and (iii) extra-personal interests over short term and long term for (i) adapting to existing environments, (ii) shaping of existing environments and (iii) selection of new environments. Sternberg (2005) writes, 'A person could be practically intelligent, but use his or her practical intelligence toward bad or selfish ends. In wisdom, one certainly may seek good ends for oneself, but one also seeks common good outcomes for others. If one's motivations are to seek certain people's interests and minimize other people's, wisdom is not involved. In wisdom, one seeks a common good, realizing that this common good may be better for some than for others.' But the question of measuring wisdom is a challenge for educators as the assessment tools for practical intelligence and wisdom may appear to be similar (Sternberg et al. 2000).

All these conceptions of giftedness have gone much beyond the Stanford–Binet scale and the so-called classification of 'normal', 'sub-normal' and 'super-normal' intelligence based on that scale. Local, cultural, economic and environmental contexts are considered as major factors over and above genetic-hereditary and biological determinants. Although some researchers have made distinctions among 'giftedness', 'talent', 'genius' etc. on the basis of subtle criteria like area of special ability (scholastic or performing arts) or nature of exceptionality (examination scores, or invention of some device, or solving a difficult problem, etc.), Howard Gardner (1983) has taken a differentiated view on this issue through his 'multiple intelligences theory' which presents a dynamic, flexible and pluralistic concept of 'intelligence'. According to Gardner, 'intelligence' decides if someone is 'gifted', or 'talented', or 'genius' and 'intelligence' can't be measured by asking one to answer some pen-paper questions. The principal question is to design an education

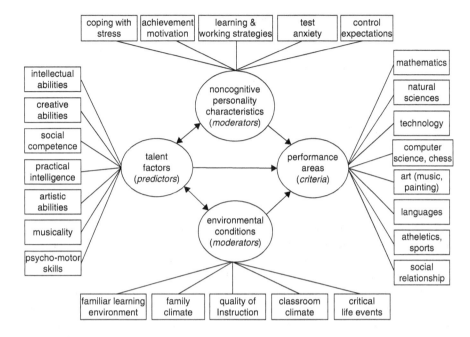

| coping with stress | achievement motivation | learning & working strategies | test anxiety | control expectations |

intellectual abilities

creative abilities

social competence

practical intelligence

artistic abilities

musicality

psycho-motor skills

mathematics

natural sciences

technology

computer science, chess

art (music, painting)

languages

atheletics, sports

social relationship

noncognitive personality characteristics (*moderators*)

talent factors (*predictors*)

performance areas (*criteria*)

environmental conditions (*moderators*)

| familiar learning environment | family climate | quality of Instruction | classroom climate | critical life events |

Legend:

Talent factors (predictors)
- intelligence (language, mathematical, technical abilities, etc.)
- creativity (language, mathematical, technical artistic, etc.)
- social competence
- musicality
- artistic abilities
- psycho-motor skills
- practical intelligence

(Noncognitive) personality characteristics (moderators)
- achievement motivation
- hope for success vs. fear of failure
- control expectations
- thirst for knowledge
- ability to deal well with stress (coping with stress)
- self-concept (general, scholastic, of talent, etc.)

Environmental conditions (moderators)
- home environmental stimulation ("creative" environment)
- educational style
- parental educational level
- demands on performance made at home
- social reactions to success and failure
- number of siblings and sibling position
- family climate
- quality of instruction
- school climate
- critical life events
- differentiated learning and instruction

Performance areas (criteria variables)
- mathematics, computer science, etc
- natural sciences
- technology, handicraft, trade, etc.
- languages
- music (musical-artistic area)
- social activities, leadership, etc.
- athletics/sports

Fig. 15.3 The Munich model of giftedness (Heller et al. 2005)

system that can identify and nurture individual characteristics of intelligence of a certain kind. Are these conceptions of giftedness applied equitably across all genders especially to women? Sally M. Reis (2005) have studied several women to understand the reason behind less representation of women among high-achievers in science, mathematics and other fields. She finds that most of the conceptions of giftedness are 'based on male indicators' as these concepts and also most of the assessment instruments are developed by men, especially white men. Several women expressed ambivalence when they confronted their responsibilities towards both their areas of special interest and their family and children (Antler 1987; Dash 1988; Winstone 1978; Gabor 1995). In developing any conception of giftedness, Reis argues that, diversities of several kinds especially those related to gender must be considered, and gender sensitivity of different cultures and societies must be taken into account (Fig. 15.3).

Gifted Education in India

In India, there is no gifted and talented program in schools. I have already mentioned that the entrance exams of the IITs are regarded by many as equivalent to a talent search exam in terms of the very low percentage of successful candidates. But how effective the entrance exam is in identifying true talents remains disputed even in Indian academia. A statistical survey of the results of this exam was done by the Indian Statistical Institute and it showed that the whole system has serious flaws in it so far as equity in the selection process is concerned. It is observed that students from cities and having parental income of more than 4.5 lakh rupees (about $7500) have a greater representation in the list of successful candidates (Table 15.1; Figs. 15.4, 15.5 and 15.6).

Table 15.1 The composition of candidates registered for the IIT entrance exam in 2012 and the success rates of different categories of candidates

Comparison of candidates in terms of	Criteria of classification	% of candidates appeared in the exam ($N = 479{,}651$)*	% of candidates successful in the exam (24112)
Parents' income (Per annum)	More than Rs. 4.5 lakh (6760 USD)	14.1 %	10.3 %
	Between Rs. 1 lakh and 4.5 lakh (1502 to 6760 USD)	49.3 %	4.8 %
	Less than Rs. 1 lakh (Less 1502 USD)	36.6 %	2.6 %
Place of dwelling	City	51.1 %	5.8 %
	Town	29.5 %	4.2 %
	Village	19.4 %	2.7 %
Board affiliation (XII)	CBSE	44.3 %	6.1 %
	ICSE	3.9 %	4.7 %
	Other boards	51.9 %	3.6 %

*Note: N indicates total number of candidates appeared
Total number of successful candidates is 24,112 i.e. 4.8% of N
Source: http://www.isicl.ac.in/~jeexiiscore_normal/JEE2012_analysis.htm;   http://www.isical.ac.in/~jeexiiscore_normal/JEE-2012Report.pdf

Fig. 15.4 Graphical representation of students' success rate as per parent's income

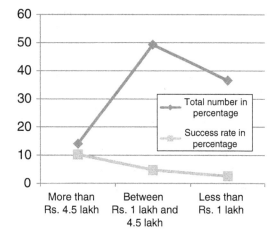

Fig. 15.5 Graphical representation of students' success rate as per place of dwelling

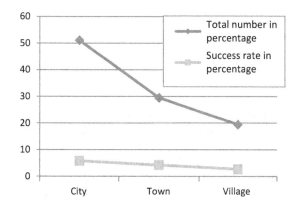

Fig. 15.6 Graphical representation of students' success rate as per Board affiliation

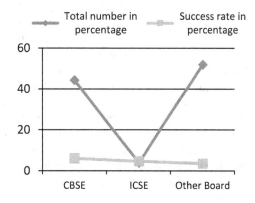

Out of the several boards of Secondary and Higher Secondary education, the share of CBSE (Central Board of Secondary Education) and ICSE (Indian Council of Secondary Education) have greater share in the list of selected candidates. The CBSE and the ICSE schools are considered 'elite' in Indian school education system. Many academicians believe that this disproportionate selection is due to the intensive training of the students of economically stronger families, in algorithmic problem solving by the highly priced coaching companies. So, there is serious doubt if the ability of the IIT entrance exam in selecting the gifted and talented is a myth or a reality.

The Department of Science and Technology of the Govt. of India has introduced several programs to identify 'exceptional' students from Indian high schools and attract them towards careers in scientific research. High-value scholarships are also given to such students until they complete their graduate studies. Dedicated institutions are set up to nurture these students throughout the country. Other than the IITs, five IISERs (Indian Institutes of Science Education and Research) have been established very recently with a mission of creating a culture of cutting-edge scientific research in India. Students are selected for admission to these new Institutes through multiple entry channels to ensure less error in selecting the 'exceptional'. The KVPY fellows are offered direct admission to these special institutions. The students who score among the top 1% of their final school-leaving exam are also offered admission after they perform well in a test designed especially for selecting talents in science. The INSPIRE (Initiative in Science Pursuit for Inspired Research) fellowship scheme is another initiative of the Indian government to attract talents in science. In this scheme, school students are inspired through specially arranged lectures alongside their usual regular classes, and if they score 99 percentile in their school-leaving Board exam they are awarded high-value scholarships. The famous IIT entrance test is also there and students selected through this test are also offered admission to these IISERs. IISERs are planned by the Indian government as their special universities for the scientifically gifted. The JBNSTS (Jagadish Bose National Science Talent Search) is the oldest non-government talent search initiative of India. Many JBNSTS scholars are spread throughout the world to hold key positions in industry and academia. JBNSTS scholars are automatically selected as INSPIRE fellows. Alongside all these initiatives, there is the training program for the international Olympiads in Mathematics, Physics, Chemistry, Biology and Junior Science. These programs are run by the Homi Bhaba Centre for Science Education of the Tata Institute of Fundamental Research. Students are selected for this program through nationwide examinations of very competitive nature and are trained rigorously in all these subjects to take part in the International Olympiads. How all these initiatives are succeeding in creating great minds has not yet been studied well. When studied over a period of nearly 20 years, we can get an idea about the efficacy of such programs. None of these programs are formal 'gifted and talented programs' according to international definitions, but the principal aim of such programs is to create a pool of creative and innovative scientists and engineers.

The National Institute of Advanced Studies (NIAS), Bangalore, has a research program on gifted and talented students. The project on 'Identification of Gifted Children in Math and Science in the Indian Context (3 to 15 years)' of the NIAS is the only gifted and talented education research project in India. In collaboration with the University of Delhi and Agastya International Foundation, NIAS planned to reach out to as many students as possible to identify the gifted and talented for case study. Focus of the Delhi University study is the urban population of 8–13 years studying in different government and private schools. The Agastya Foundation focused its attention on the children of rural areas and aged between 8–15 years. Between May 2010 and December 2011, only 12 case studies could be done by the NIAS.

The NIAS report by Maithreyi et al. (2013) summarily assessed this study as follows: 'While the case studies on the whole has indicated areas for research, and have provided important directions for a gifted education program, there are certain limitations to be overcome in order to make the study more effective. First, the number of children covered in the study is very small, and the findings from the study cannot be generalized. …Second, in the absence of appropriate mentoring mechanisms, the profiled children have received little help from the project, especially in cases where the children belonged to resource-poor homes, and had limited access to further education opportunities. Finally, information and interactions with the children and their families and schools has also been constrained by the available time.'

My Method: Auto-ethnography

In the beginning of this chapter, I have mentioned a few questions that I want to find answers to through an auto-ethnographic method. The questions I asked relate to the students' thinking abilities and patterns. Only personal interactions with students can help understand these abilities, and only interactions with a large number of students can help discover the patterns. No quantitative or statistical investigation is able to discover that as thinking patterns are not quantifiable and it is not possible for me to bring back my old students to test the thought process they had in their high school. Also no written multiple choice tests can be designed to detect and identify specific thinking routes of an individual. I have used a concept-survey test named 'Force Concept Inventory (FCI)' to measure the foundations of the concepts of force and motion of about 1000 high school students of the greater Kolkata region. The FCI is designed by a group at the Arizona State University, USA (Hestenes et al. 1992; and, Hestenes and Halloun 1995), and is a tool used widely throughout the world by the Physics Education Research groups. The FCI data could tell us about the overall situation prevailing among these students, but was unable to point to the reasons behind this situation. To identify the roots of the conceptual deficiency, we must interact personally with the students and that also for a substantive period of time. This experience has guided me to choose a qualitative method for studying the issue of the 'gifted and talented'. As I have personally interacted with so many highly performing students for so many years in a particular socio-cultural context, I have decided to use my rich experience as the source of first-hand data for my study. I have found that 'Auto-ethnography' or story of personal experience is now accepted as an important qualitative method of research (Struthers 2014; Denshire 2014). Being trained in physics and mathematics, I have a natural bias towards science as the only reliable method of investigation, because it gives deterministic results and accepts replicable data only. But, this kind of study of the 'gifted' minds involves so many parameters in a complex causal relationship, that my own experience of so many years, I think, can provide a better picture of the reality through a subjective analysis of the complexity than simple causal connection of objective scientific data. The narrative of my experience embedded in an Indian perception of being 'exceptional' is rooted in an affective involvement of both the teacher and the students in the task of knowing. Inclusion of all children into the process of learning being a challenge of present time, my experience of using the discovery method for so many years presents a first-person account of facing this challenge head on. In a system of 'education for all', the needs of the gifted and talented remain unaddressed and these children start feeling excluded from the process of learning as their demand of knowing more is mostly neglected by the teachers. On the other hand, any effort directed towards these specially abled ones is bound to ignore the demand of the majority in a classroom. This presents a practical challenge of implementing 'inclusion' in real-life classrooms. My experience of using the 'discovery learning' method especially by creating an 'Investigative Science Learning environment' (ISLE) (Etkina and Van Heuvelen 2007) has shown how all children having their specific abilities, both known and unknown to the teacher, can be included in the active learning process, ensuring a truly inclusive education.

Conclusion

The result of my study agrees with the statement that 'the concept of the gifted student is … a social construct of questionable validity' (Borland 2005). In a country like India where we are still far away from making education available to all children, any demand for special provisions for a few, because they are termed 'gifted' by some parameters, is untenable. My study has shown that the very idea of 'giftedness' is not at all independent of space and time. If a student is found 'ordinary' in one institution, in some other school the same student may demonstrate 'giftedness'. I have seen students who were unable to unleash their originality and creativity in my school as they were always scared of being compared with a good number of high-scoring classmates around them. When they were admitted to some other school where high scoring is not a usual practice, their 'giftedness' bloomed to the highest level to place them in key positions in their later lives. Also there were students who started demonstrating 'excellence' at the graduate degree level and beyond, but were termed as 'good for nothing' by their teachers at school. My study has revealed that if discovery learning method is adopted in teaching science for all students at the school level, the identification and nurturing of the 'gifted' students will be done automatically. My auto-ethnographic account of dealing with a large number of high school children (N ≈ 62,500) can provide teachers and researchers issues for further investigation and application. The role of collaborative and cooperative learning by peer-level interactions during a well-designed discovery learning activity can be studied for both 'gifted and talented' education and 'inclusive education'. The effectiveness of the ISLE not just for including and identifying both the 'gifted' and the 'ordinary' but also for the appropriate nurturing of the children of all kinds of abilities can be a topic for further investigation and research. The triangular interaction of the conceptual primitive, epistemology and metacognition gets conspicuously visible in a discovery learning situation and this interaction, as my experience shows, is the key to unleash the hidden ability in a student. So my account may provide important directions in identifying problems for newer research not only in the field of 'gifted and talented education' but also for 'inclusive education' and 'education' in general.

Although there is no 'gifted and talented' program in India, there are mechanisms of selecting 'exceptional' students of science and mathematics as they leave school. Also, there are under-graduate and graduate institutions for the 'best and the brightest'. Are all the high achievers in life products of these special institutions? Or, are all the products of these institutions doing something truly great in life? Obviously, the answer is 'no'. Finally, I can summarize the message of my study as that every human being is gifted with certain special abilities; our job as educators is to identify and nourish those abilities so that they can flourish at some point in life. We must work hard to discover the best way to do that job. Selecting only a few to be called as 'gifted and talented' not only disregards this duty of the educators and researchers but also promotes a kind of elitism and racism in education.

References

Alexander, J. M. (1995). Development of metacognition in gifted children: Directions for future research. *Developmental Review, 15*(1), 1–37.

Antler, J. (1987). *Lucy Sprague Mitchell*. New Haven: Yale University Press.

Barron, F. (1968). *Creativity and personal freedom*. New York: Van Nostrand.

Barron, F. (1969). *Creative persons and creative process*. New York: Holt, Rinehart, & Winston.

Babayeva, Yu. D. & Voiskunovskiy, A.E. (2003). *Odarennyi rebenok za komp'yuterom* [Gifted child behind the computer]. Ministry of Education of Russian Federation: Presidential program "Children of Russia".

Benedixen, L. D., Dunkle, M. E., & Schraw, G. (1994). Epistemological beliefs and reflective judgment. *Psychological Reports, 75*, 1595–1600.

Bonds, C. G. (1992). Metacognition: Developing independence in learning. *Clearing House, 66*(1), 56–59. New York: Macmillan.

Borland, J. H., & Wright, L. (1994). Identifying young, potentially gifted, economically disadvantaged students. *Gifted Child Quarterly, 38*, 164–171.

Borland, J. H. (2005). Gifted children without gifted education. In R. J. Stenberg & J. E. Davidson (Eds.), *Conceptions of giftedness* (2nd ed., pp. 1–19). New York: Cambridge University Press.

Bouffard-Bouchard, T., Parent, S., & Lavirée, S. (1993). Self-regulation on a concept formation task among average and gifted students. *Journal of Experimental Child Psychology, 56*(1), 115–134.

Campbell, D. T. (1960). Blind variation and selective retention in creative thought as in other knowledge processes. *Psychological Review, 67,* 380–400.

Carr, M., & Borkowski, J. G. (1987). Metamemory in gifted children. *Gifted Child Quarterly, 31*(1), 40–44.

Dahme, G. (1996, September). *Teachers' conceptions of gifted students in Indonesia (Java), Germany and U.S.A.* Paper presented at the 5th conference of the European Council of High Ability, Vienna, Austria.

Dash, J. (1988). *A life of one's own.* New York: Paragon.

Denshire, S. (2014). On auto-ethnography. *Current Sociology, 62*(6), 831–850.

Etkina, E. & Van Heuvelen, A. (2007). *Investigative science learning environment - A science process approach to learning physics.* In E. F. Redish and P. Cooney, (Eds.), Research Based Reform of University Physics, (AAPT), Online at http://per-central.org/per_reviews/media/volume1/ISLE-2007.pdf

Ford, D. Y. (1996). *Reversing underachievement among gifted black students.* New York: Teachers College Press.

Ford, D. Y., & Harris, J. J. (1999). *Multicultural gifted education.* New York: Teachers College Press.

Foucault, M. (1995). *Discipline and punish: The birth of the prison.* (A. Sheridan, Trans.) New York: Vantage.

Freeman, J. (2005). Permission to be gifted: How conceptions of giftedness can change lives. In R. J. Stenberg & J. E. Davidson (Eds.), *Conceptions of giftedness* (2nd ed., pp. 80–97). New York: Cambridge University Press.

Gabor, A. (1995). *Einstein's wife: Work and marriage in the lives of five great twenty first century women.* New York: Viking.

Gardner, H. (1983). *Frames of mind: The theory of multiple intelligences.* New York: Basic Books.

Guilford, J. P. (1964). Some new looks at the nature of creative processes. In M. Fredrickson & H. Gilliksen (Eds.), *Contributions to mathematical psychology* (pp. 42–66). New York: Holt, Rinehart, & Winston.

Guilford, J. P. (1967). *The nature of human intelligence.* New York: McGraw Hill.

Hany, E. A. (1993). How teachers identify gifted students: Feature processing or concept based classification. *European Journal of High Ability, 4,* 196–211.

Heller, K. A., Perleth, C., & Lim, T. K. (2005). The Munich model of giftedness designed to identify and promote gifted students. In R. J. Stenberg & J. E. Davidson (Eds.), *Conceptions of giftedness* (2nd ed., pp. 147–170). New York: Cambridge University Press.

Hestenes, D., Wells, M., and Swackhamer, G. (1992). Force concept inventory. *The Physics Teacher, 30,* 141–151.

Hestenes, D., and Halloun, I., (1995). Interpreting the force concept inventory. *The Physics Teacher, 33,* 502–506.

Hofer, B., & Pintrich, P. R. (1997). The development of epistemological theories: Beliefs about knowledge and knowing their relations to learning. *Review of Educational Research, 67*(1), 88–144.

Jeltova, I., & Grigorenko, E. L. (2005). Systemic approaches to giftedness: Contributions of Russian psychology. In R. J. Stenberg & J. E. Davidson (Eds.), *Conceptions of giftedness* (2nd ed., pp. 171–186). New York: Cambridge University Press.

Kell, H. J., Lubinski, D., & Benbow, C. P. (2013). Who rises to the top? Early indicators. *Psychological Science, 24*(5), 648–659.

Leitis, N.S. (2000). *Vozrastnya odarennost' shkolnikov* [Development of giftedness in school children]. Moscow: Academia.

Maithreyi, R., Basu, A., Jayan, P., Chandra, P. & Kurup, A. (2013) *Identification of gifted children in maths and science in the Indian context (3–15 years)*. National Institute f Advanced Studies, Bangalore, Publication.

Muil, W., Hussin, Z., Wan Mamat, W. H., Mohamed, M. F., & Zailani, M. A. (2013). The relationship between epistemological beliefs and metacognitive thinking of gifted and non-gifted students. *Journal of American Science, 9*(10), 313–319.

Nuessel, F. H., Stewart, A. V., & Cedeño. (2001). A course on humanistic creativity in later life: Literature review, case histories and recommendations. *Educational Gerontology, 27,* 697–715.

Ojanen, S., & Freeman, J. (1994). *The attitudes and experiences of head teachers, class teachers and highly able pupils towards the education of the highly able in Finland and Britain.* Savonlinna: University if Joensuu.

Passow, A. H. (1989). Needed research and development in educating high ability children. Roeper Review, 11, 223–229.

Perleth, Ch., Schatz, T. & Mönks, F.J. (2000). Early indicators of high ability. In K.A. Heller, F.J. Mönks, R.J. Sternberg & R.F. Subotnik (Hrsg), *International handbook of giftedness and talent* (2nd ed, pp 283–310). Oxford: Pergamon.

Plucker, J., & Barab, S. A. (2005). The importance of contexts in theories of giftedness. In R. J. Stenberg & J. E. Davidson (Eds.), *Conceptions of giftedness* (2nd ed., pp. 201–216). New York: Cambridge University Press.

Reis, S. M. (2005). Feminist perspectives on talent development. In R. J. Stenberg & J. E. Davidson (Eds.), *Conceptions of giftedness* (2nd ed., pp. 217–245). New York: Cambridge University Press.

Renzulli, J. S. (2005). The three ring conception of giftedness: A developmental model for promoting creative productivity. In R. J. Stenberg & J. E. Davidson (Eds.), *Conceptions of giftedness* (2nd ed., pp. 246–279). New York: Cambridge University Press.

Schommer, M. A. (1990). Effects of beliefs about the nature of knowledge on comprehension. *Journal of Educational Psychology, 82*(3), 498–504.

Sternberg, R. J. (1982). Lies we live by: Misapplication of tests in identifying the gifted. *Gifted child quarterly, 26*(4), 157–161.

Sternberg, R. J. (1998). Abilities are forms of developing expertise. *Educational Researcher, 27*(3), 11–20.

Sternberg, R. J. (2001). Giftedness as developing expertise: A theory of the interface between high abilities and achieved knowledge. *High Ability Studies, 12,* 159–179.

Sternberg, R. J. (2003). WICS as a model of giftedness. *High Ability Studies, 14,* 109–137.

Sternberg, R. J. (2005). The WICS model of giftedness. In R. J. Sternberg & J. E. Davidson (Eds.), *Conceptions of giftedness* (2nd ed., pp. 327–342). New York: Cambridge University Press.

Sternberg, R. J., & Davidson, J. E. (Eds.). (2005). *Conceptions of giftedness* (2nd ed.). New York: Cambridge University Press

Sternberg, R. J., Forsythe, G. B., Hedlund, J., Horvath, J., Snook, S., Williams, W. M., et al. (2000). *Practical intelligence in everyday life*. New York: Cambridge University Press.

Struthers, J. (2014). Analytic autoethnography: One story of the method. *Theory and Method in Higher Education Research II,* 183–202.

Teplov, B.M. (1985). Psykhophyziologiya individual'nykh razlitchiy [Psychophysiology of individual differences]. In B. M. Teplov (Ed.) *Izbrannye Trudy, tom 2* [Collected works, 2nd volume]. Moscow: Pedagogika

United States Department of Education (1991). *National educational longitudinal study 88*. Final report: Gifted and talented education programs for eighth grade public school students. Washington DC: United States Department of Education, Office of Planning, Budget, and Evaluation.

Wilson, J. (1998). Assessing metacognition: Legitimizing metacognition as a teaching goal. *Reflect, 4*(1), 14–20.

Winstone, H. V. F. (1978). *Gertrude Bell*. New York: Quartet.

Zakaria, F. (2011). *The post-American world* (2nd ed.). New York: W.W. Norton.

Chapter 16
Sociocultural Construction of Disability in Sri Lanka: Charity to Rights-based Approach

Chandani Liyanage

Abstract This chapter focuses on exploring the socio-cultural construction of disability in Sri Lanka and its impact on the everyday lives of persons with disability. The analysis is based on an ethnographic study in diverse social settings. As against context-specific characteristics, disability is defined merely as a physical or intellectual impairment of a person from a charity perspective where the ideology of karma plays a crucial role by providing a justification for the existence of inequality among human beings. The construction has adverse effects on all domains of the everyday lives of persons with disabilities. Discrimination against persons with disability originates from family itself that reinforces by other social institutions. Thus, not only the attitudes of lay people but also of service providers suggest no signs of moving from charity to a rights-based approach toward disability. Though Sri Lanka has a National Policy on Disability to promote rights of people with disability, there are huge gaps existing at the level of enforcement. While acknowledging the strengths of social mode, the chapter argues that disability demands an integrated approach toward empowering persons with disabilities and to mobilize the entire society to create an environment with reasonable accommodation for an inclusive society that accepts disability as part of the diversity. The government and civil society organizations have a crucial role in moving forward from a charity perspective to a rights-based approach toward disability.

Conceptualization of Disability in Sri Lanka

Conceptualization of disability varies across different socio-cultural contexts though it is considered as part of the universal human experience. The focus of this qualitative study is to explore the socio-cultural construction of disability in Sri Lanka and its impact on the everyday lives of persons with disabilities. Thus, the present

C. Liyanage (✉)
Department of Sociology, University of Colombo, Colombo, Sri Lanka
e-mail: chandanil82@hotmail.com

© Springer International Publishing AG 2017   251
S. Halder, L.C. Assaf (eds.), *Inclusion, Disability and Culture*, Inclusive
Learning and Educational Equity 3, DOI 10.1007/978-3-319-55224-8_16

ethnographic study attempts to explore the articulation of disability in diverse social settings in Sri Lanka that includes community in a village space; a total institution for persons with disabilities and incurable diseases; a special school for children with disability and higher educational institution. The empirical study adopted qualitative methods and techniques to grasp narratives of persons with disabilities, experience of their everyday life in particular social setting, perceptions and attitudes of parents, close relatives and community members of persons with disabilities, and attitudes and perceptions of service providers on the needs and rights of persons with disabilities. Each social setting has context-specific characteristics while sharing most of the common features in conceptualizing disability and responding toward it.

Disability conceptualizes within the Sri Lankan culture from a charity perspective. The local languages have rather unique vocabulary to distinguish "normal" from "disabled" such as *"arbadita"* – disabled, *"arbaditaya"* – a person with disability and also particular terms attributed to each impairment such as *andha* – blind, *golu* – deaf, *bihiri* – hearing difficulty, and so on. These expressions clearly differentiate the "able-body" from the "disabled-body," "normal" from "abnormal" and "ill-being" from the "well-being" where the fixed identity as disabled carries stigma and discrimination. Schools for special education are also named as "school of deaf and blind" that segregates from the ordinary school system in Sri Lanka.

The ideology of "karma" plays a vital role in not only conceptualizing disability but also responding toward persons with disability that promotes charity approach toward disability, justifying the existence of inequality among human beings. In the local context, the concept of karma is constantly used in order to explain the course of disability and many other incurable diseases. The theory of karma is a fundamental doctrine in Buddhism that embodies and reflects many of the ideas that motivate much of the Sri Lankans' attitude toward illness and misfortune and it's implicit in many aspects of the Sri Lankans' understanding. According to the doctrine of karma, individual experience and action is the result of previous volitional acts in their former lives (Rahula 1978:32).

The law of moral causation gives an explanation to understand the cause of inequality that exists among mankind. Why should one person be brought up in the lap of luxury, endowed with fine mental, moral and physical qualities, and another in absolute poverty, steeped in misery, or why should others be congenitally blind, deaf or deformed, and so on. According to Buddhism, this inequality is due not only to heredity, environment, nature and nurture, but also to karma. It is the result of one's own past actions and present doings. Individuals themselves are responsible for their own happiness or unhappiness. Thus, from a Buddhist point of view, our present mental, moral, intellectual and temperamental differences are, for the most part, due to our own actions and tendencies, both past and present (Sayadaw, www. free-ebooks.net/ebook/Insights-Into-Karma). It is the mind that is prominent in committing karma but not the action, not the word. If an individual does any good or bad action with a good or bad intention, the result will follow him/her accordingly. But in further clarification about karma, it says that karma alone is not decisive. There are five elements which can be called as *"niyaama dharma"*

Karma = 1 factor 253

kamma-niyama, beeja-niyama, utu-niyama, citta-niyama, and dhamma-niyama. So karma is only one factor. These are very important in deciding the karmic effect. Buddhism, however, doesn't prescribe fatalism and people are not supposed to submit themselves to karma alone and they can change karmic effect to a greater extent if they work out. However, in the local social context, disability is seen as an outcome of one's own past actions and present doings where the individual is responsible for his/her own happiness and misery (Sayadaw, www.free-ebooks.net/ebook/Insights-Into-Karma).

The fixed identity of disabled body has become a source of merit for majority of the able-bodied in the society, encouraging them to care for the disabled by simply providing survival needs such as food; clothing, shelter, and so forth while undermining or neglecting most of the civil rights of persons with disabilities as human beings. Thus, the above construction reinforces the identity of the disabled as dependents. The chapter argues that though the charity approach enhances social responsibility toward caring persons with disabilities, it denies equal accesses to education, health, employment, and many other domains of the everyday life of persons with disabilities. The empirical evidence of this study further verified the fact that most of the service providers who deliver various services for persons with disabilities in health, education and social services considered their official task in service delivery as charity while receiving monthly salary as employees. Thus, they assess their role of service delivery as one of the superior positions that allows them to accumulate further merit out of helping persons with disabilities.

Conventional approaches toward disability focus more attention on the challenges faced by persons with disability as an outcome of personal tragedy, locating impairments within the physical body of an individual where medical model plays a dominant role in defining disability, curing ill-health attached to it and rehabilitation of persons with disability. Accordingly, disability is considered as a loss to be compensated rather than a difference to be accommodated by the society (Addlakha 2013). In contrast to the above model, the social model has emerged in order to grasp socio-cultural barriers of disability that originates within the social context rather than identifying it as an individual tragedy (Oliver 1990, 1996). Thus, disability can be defined within the socio-cultural context as a barrier to participation of people with impairments or chronic illnesses arising from an interaction of the impairment or illness with discriminatory attitudes, cultures, policies or institutional practices (Booth 2000). In line with other societies in the world, disability is subjected to stigma and discrimination in Sri Lanka. In the past, there was a trend of hiding the disabled from the society while associating it with supernatural forces that totally excluded them from the mainstream society. However, though perceptions and attitudes toward disability have been slowly changing and persons with disabilities are gradually approaching their rights through self-advocacy movements, the social and physical environments are not adequately prepared with reasonable accommodation to integrate them into the mainstream society. It is evident that only a very limited number of persons with disabilities who come from upper or middle socio-economic backgrounds have been actively involved with disability movements, while the vast majority of lower socio-economic backgrounds remain the same with continuing charity perspective towards disability. Ethnographic reading of this study explores the articulation of disability in diverse social settings while identifying the challenge toward moving forward from charity to a rights-based approach.

Locating Disability in the Locus of a Village

A village is undoubtedly an embodiment of a cultural unit, a moral universe and coherent cultural order connected to the human body. Similarly, the village space is seen as wide open to both well-being and ill-being producing agents. Ethnographic reading of the village implies the fact that not only major impairments but also mild impairments are labeled with fixed identity as disabled that limits participation of persons with disability in most of the domains in their everyday life. The empirical evidence verified the fact that the villagers thoroughly maintain rigid dichotomies between "normal" and "abnormal." Accordingly, a woman with harelip has been labeled as a disabled throughout her life in the village. At the same time a family that includes a number of persons with minor impairments has been labeled "sick family." Participation in most of the activities in the everyday lives of those individuals has been strictly prohibited not due to their functional limitations but due to participation restrictions that are associated with fixed identity as disabled by other members of the family, close relatives, neighbors and the entire community. Pseudonyms are used to present the narratives of persons with disabilities from their voice as follows:

Experiencing Disability in Everyday Life

Karuna was 45 years old at the time she was interviewed. She was born with harelip and continuing with the same. Karuna is the youngest child among nine siblings in her family. As narrated by her mother "immediately after the delivery, I came to know that I had given birth to a disable child. That was the worst day in my life, initially it was very difficult for me to realize as why and how I got a disable child as I have already delivered eight very healthy children. Some of them were born at home without facing any difficulty. However, I prepared my mind with courage to face the situation as it was an outcome of our karma, not only the bad luck of the baby but also due to karma of our entire family."

The delivery took place at the nearest hospital where the baby was kept in the baby-room for few days due to the inability to be breast-fed with the impairment. The mother was informed that she had to stay at the hospital for few days until the baby is released from the hospital.

As Karuna's mother further pointed out "When Karuna was born, the other kids were also too small and therefore I couldn't help leaving her in the hospital for few days to attend the other children. Her father was not willing even to take this disable child home as we already had enough number of children, nevertheless I could not resist my own consciousness anymore and took the baby back home after one week. I was instructed to take the child to children's hospital in Colombo (100 Km away from the village) in a year's time for an operation to remove the impairment, but the domestic task and financial crisis never allowed us to do such a treatment for the new born baby. It was a big issue for the whole village. I struggled a lot to grow up this child even without getting a support from her father. All the other children are married and settled down but we haven't arrange a marriage for this girl because no use of giving a disabled to an outsider."

Along with the fixed identity as a disabled, Karuna was unable to continue her education. At present, the family has no regular income except for the little money that they get from a coconut garden. However, Karuna cultivates some vegetables for consumption and works as a wage laborer at the village. She takes care of her old mother, helps her sisters and brothers and also neighbors when they need her assistance, particularly for caring for the ill members when they are hospitalized, domestic work and agricultural tasks and so on. Though Karuna is an asset not only for her own family but also for the entire community, all of them were compelled to consider Karuna as a liability due to her mild impairment. Karuna's identity as a disabled maintains her position as a dependent though she is the breadwinner and works hard for the survival of the family. Her mother worries a lot about her uncertain future. As she pointed out "who is going to look after this disabled child after my death."

Labor shortage is one of the main problems in the village as there is a trend of the able youth to migrate to seek employment opportunities in the city. In such a context, there is a greater demand for her labor, but she does not receive a fixed wage for the labor, and receives some material supports in return. Evidence suggests that Karuna is exploited due to discriminatory attitudes toward disability both by her own family and the community while misusing her capabilities to the maximum.

The Sick Family in the Village

Wimal is labeled as a disabled due a slight intellectual defect and has physically not grown up to the standards of a "normal" person by the society. He is 40 years, has never gone to school, and is unmarried. Within the village space, the whole family of Wimal is labeled as "sick family" due to some reasons that include premature death of his mother; one of the sisters died due to leukemia; the other sister was separated from her husband; and father has a slight hearing problem. Only the younger brother is considered as normal by the community though he is also marginalized as being a member of the sick family.

At present Wimal lives with one of the relatives who is one of the main land owners in the village. He is responsible for domestic tasks that include bringing water from the well, finding fire wood, cleaning, animal husbandry, agricultural activities and so on. In return, he gets food, clothing and shelter. He doesn't get any salary for his work. Sometimes, he refuses to do certain tasks and there are few occasions when he ran away from this house. But he comes back after few days as he has no other alternatives in the village for survival. The land owner says "We take care of him while providing everything that he needs. Not only that, we will look after his future as well because there is nobody in his family to take that responsibility."

As narrated by the elder sister of Wimal, she was abused by her husband who did not even provide her the basic needs. She was aware that he has an affair with a lady who works at his workplace. Due to a victim of domestic violence, she decided to separate from her husband and came back to the village to live with her parents. However, the villagers compelled to consider the incident as a failure of Wimal's sister as she comes from a sick family and therefore she was unable to have a perfect family life. She has no other choice than a wage labor in the village. Karuna is her best friend; both of them work together and hardly get reasonable salary for their labor. The whole family of Wimal is marginalized in the village space due to the fixed identity as a sick family and they are subjected to exploitation by the able-bodied in the village.

The above construction of disability segregates the able-bodied from the disabled that leads to discrimination and exploitation. As mentioned earlier, disability conceptualizes as a position of dependency and caring for the disabled is considered as a social responsibility while taking it for granted as a source of merit. Both narratives highlight the fact that the above cultural construction of disability provides justification to maintain exploitative relationship between the able and disabled, creating social environment that is advantageous for the able-bodied while marginalizing the opposite.

Locating Disability in a Total Institution

Total institutions for caring for the disabled, those with incurable diseases and many other vulnerable groups were established in Sri Lanka during the British colonial period. This empirical study was conducted in one of the total institutions for the disabled and those with incurable diseases in Colombo district. This home was established in 1889 during the British Colonial Period. The institution is managed by a committee that comprises 16 members including the Government Agent of Colombo District, the Mayor, Director General of Health Services, Director-Social Services, and so forth. At present, the institution has 100 female and 75 male inmates. The medical model has played a great role in organizing the institution which is divided into 14 wards run by a medical staff that includes a matron, number of nursing sisters, and attendants for each ward who are responsible for caring for the disabled. Wards are arranged on gender basis, within that the type of disability and its severity has been taken into consideration. There are a number of criteria for admission. Accordingly, the inmates should be over 18 years and below 55 years old, physically handicapped by birth or accident with incurable nature. After getting admission, the inmates remain in the home for the rest of their lives. There is a great demand to get admission to the institution though a vacancy occurs only on the death of an inmate.

As the administrative officer of the institution pointed out, though the government provides annually 7 million to meet the running cost of this institution it is not sufficient enough for the purpose. However, 98% of the meal requirements are provided by the general public to commemorate their birthdays, wedding and death anniversaries. Institutions for the disabled are particularly attractive for Sri Lankans to celebrate death anniversaries of their close relatives as they consider the space as a source of merit. Most of the donors oblige to provide cash to the institution to cover the meal expenses due to their inability to provide prepared meals. However, the institution provides a regular menu for the inmates without much choice for the inmates and they are discontented. Though some of the inmates suffer from diabetes, they hardly get the diet that is suitable for the condition.

Most of the inmates are not satisfied with their life at the institution where they have lost the sense of "self" while adapting to the institutional setting as the situation goes beyond their control. This is an outcome of total institution as explained by Goffman in his Asylum (1961). The empirical evidence reveals that the institution provides only the minimum survival needs such as food, clothing and shelter for the inmates while neglecting most of their social, emotional and other needs. The space is organized according to the convenience of the service provider. Those with severe mobility impairments have been placed in commode-beds as it is convenient for the service provider, neglecting all the other needs of these people as human beings. Thus, the inmates with mobility challenge face a lot of difficulties as they have to totally depend upon the care given by the caretakers even for minor matters in their everyday life. Most of the inmates are not satisfied with the service that they receive from caregivers, particularly the attendants as they frequently enforce their power on the inmates while not giving sufficient attention to their duties. On the other hand, the attendants too are not satisfied with their employment as primary caregivers because their service is not adequately appreciated by the inmates and also they do not receive sufficient salary though they are involved in a tough task that requires both physical energy and a high level of tolerance to deal with the people with disability. However, the primary caregivers are satisfied with their task as they earn the merit of helping the disabled though they are not receiving sufficient salary for their service as caregivers. Not only the lay people who live in village but also the professionals who provide various services for persons with disability in an institution believe that disability is an outcome of karma and the responsibility of the able-bodied is to take care of them while accumulating merit for the future.

The charity approach encourages society to continue with discriminatory attitudes toward disability while neglecting the needs of persons with disability as human beings. Thus, there is a belief that one gains merit by showing charity toward people who have disability, who are considered to have sinned in the past. Charity is practiced in the belief that the giver is more fortunate than the recipient; it reinforces negative attitudes of inferiority in people who have disability and excludes them from the social mainstream. It is an affront to the self-esteem and dignity of individuals where charity practiced on the basis of sharing with others who have the same rights is to be encouraged. Sri Lanka has developed a National Policy on Disability (2003) in order to promote and protect the rights of people who have disability in the spirits of social justice. However, removing socio-cultural barriers is the main challenge to implement the above policy toward an inclusive society. Not only the lay people but also planners, architectures and different service providers are not sensitive enough to implement the above policy as they perceive disability from a charity perspective that reinforces exclusion and segregation.

Challenge Toward an Inclusive Education for Children with Disability

Sri Lanka has implemented compulsory education ordinance that applies equally to all children including the disabled between the ages of 5–14 years. Initially, more attention was given to provide education to children with disabilities under special schools. The first special school for deaf and blind was started in 1912 in Colombo district during the British colonial period and later on a number of special schools for children with different disabilities were established in other areas of the country. In the early 1970s, the Ministry of Education started increasing educational opportunities for children with disabilities through integration and more recently the emphasis has been given on inclusive education (National Policy on Disability 2003). As a result, children with disability now have an opportunity to obtain their education in government schools either through being included in the ordinary classrooms or in special education units attached to the schools. Though there is a provision in the National Policy to enhance equal opportunities in education, in reality access to inclusive education has become one of the main challenges for children with disability in Sri Lanka like in many other countries in the region due to social, cultural architecture and environmental barriers.

Access to transport facilities is one of the main problems faced by the vast majority of children with disabilities living in rural areas. Most of the children in rural areas have to walk several miles to reach even to the nearest school. At the same time there are no facilities in ordinary schools for children with disabilities such as toilets, wheel chair access, qualified teachers to handle specific issues related to different disabilities, residential facilities and so on. Therefore, most of the children with disabilities have to continue with their education in special schools though they have a right to study in ordinary schools.

Special schools are supported by both the Ministry of Education and the Ministry of Social Services. The teachers' salary is provided by the Ministry of Education and the daily expenses of children are provided by the Ministry of Social Services. Though the amount allocated is not sufficient to cover the daily expenses, nearly 90% of meal requirements and other expenditure are provided by the general public in commemoration of their birthdays, death anniversaries of close relatives etc. like in the total institution that helps the institutions to cover the expenditure. This is one of the reasons that encourage special schools and institutions to continue with the charity approach toward disability.

This empirical study was conducted in one of the special schools for deaf and blind in a remote area. The school was named as "school for deaf and blind" that started in 1978; at present there are 160 students and 25 teachers in this school. The narratives of children who study in this school reveal that special schools are quite convenient for students with disabilities due to some pragmatic factors. The students have an access to Braille and Sing languages with qualified teachers when they study at special school. At the same time, the students are comfortable at special school as they are treated equally with their fellow classmates. Both students and parents highlighted the point that they prefer special schools as they provide residential facilities, otherwise it would be impossible for them to educate their children as most of them come from rural, lower socio-economic backgrounds. Most of the students come from distant places and they go home only during their school vacations.

Special schools are segregated from the ordinary school system that leads to exclusion and discrimination from the mainstream society. Both parents of disabled children and the teachers believe that special school is the best option for disabled children. Some of the parents shared their past experience that they have encountered while their children were studying at ordinary schools with non-disabled students. Accordingly, there were some occasions where disabled students were treated differently by teachers and also some of the parents of non-disabled children did not allow their children to interact with disabled children in class rooms. Some of the children even refused to go to school as they were treated badly. Other than the above motivational factors of parents and children, the teachers at special schools encourage those students to continue their education at special school for their survival. Thus, the evidence suggests that most of the teachers at special schools lack the necessary competency to empower students to face the challenges, they rather socialize them simply to accept the existing disadvantaged position as normal. The evidence of special school also confirmed the fact that the charity approach toward disability is the main barrier for implementing a rights-based approach for inclusive education, though the government and civil society have already initiated some interventions to promote the equal rights that require more radical movements for attitudinal change in the society. Many children who have disability in rural areas are still not starting to go to school and the majority who started schooling are also not going up to the secondary level where gender disparity indicated. Children who have more severe degrees of multiple disability and intellectual disability have no opportunities at all. The education system in both state and private sector lacks expertise and the capacity to deal with these children (National policy on Disability 2003).

The evidence suggests that not only the children with disabilities, their parents and teachers but also the entire society should be mobilized for enhancing inclusive education system in the country. Though the Sri Lankan government has already taken necessary policy decisions toward an inclusive education, huge gaps exist at implementation level due to various social and attitudinal barriers with regard to disability. The following section explores the challenges faced by students with disabilities in higher educational setting.

Articulation of Disability in Higher Educational Setting

Meaningful participation and inclusion in education have become key concepts within the discourse of disability where higher educational institutions can play a significant role in enhancing integrated society with diversity. Entering state universities in Sri Lanka is highly competitive and only a very limited number of students get the opportunity to follow degree programs. State universities have opened the door for disabled students and the enrollment rate of students with disabilities during the last few years has shown an increasing trend (University Grants Commission 2013). However, inclusive education in universities is a greater challenge as academic, architecture, physical and social environments are not ready yet to integrate them with reasonable accommodation in higher educational institutions. According to the information by the University Gants Commission, only 8 out of 16 state universities accept disabled students for their degree programs (UGC 2014). This empirical study was carried out in one of the leading universities in Colombo focusing on understanding everyday experiences of students with disabilities in higher educational setting and the perception and sensitivity of non-disabled students, academic and non-academic staff on inclusive education for students with disability.

The findings suggest that not only the physical infrastructure but also the academic and social environment of the university is not ready yet with reasonable accommodation to integrate the undergraduates to provide an inclusive education. The experience of those students shows that they have very limited options in selecting study streams due to practical limitations. Most of them come from schools in remote areas of the country where there are no facilities to study science subjects. Even when they come to university they have barriers to follow some of the subjects that require more technical assistance. More than 90% of undergraduates with disability are visually impaired and only few students have auditory and mobility impairments. The experience of students with disabilities suggests that they face many difficulties due to both infrastructural and social barriers, particularly when they come to Colombo though it is the capital of the country. The physical barriers include transport difficulties, crossing roads without sound system, lack of wheel chair access, communication challenges and so on. Blind and deaf students have limited access to information as there are no facilities within the university to communicate in Braille or Sing languages. Most of them highlighted that lecturers are not sensitive enough toward them while delivering lectures, giving assignments, releasing results and so forth. They also have to face some difficulties related to administration due to lack of awareness among non-academic staff toward disability. The disabled students appreciated the support that they received from non-disabled students though they do not have enough sensitivity with regard to disability. It is interesting to note that, most of the time the partially blind students support the totally blind students than non-disabled students as they are more sensitive to the issue. Being the majority among disabled undergraduates, visually impaired students have organized themselves to face their challenges. Thus, the evidence reveals that self-advocacy movements among visually impaired undergraduates lead to segregation as they strengthen themselves and are well organized as a group to face specific challenges rather than ignoring interactions with other disabled and non-disabled students. However, few students with auditory and mobility impairments maintain a cordial relationship with non-disabled students while receiving their support for day-to-day activities. Thus, though there are advanced technologies that can be used to enhance accessibility of persons with disability toward knowledge and information, the educators are not well aware of them and also lack enough sensitivity to use them.

Finding employment opportunities for graduates with disabilities is also an issue due to discriminatory attitudes toward disability in the mainstream society. The charity perspective toward disability plays a crucial role even with the higher educational setting like in the above social settings. Evidence suggests that the students with disabilities in higher education need empowerment to face the challenges while mobilizing non-disabled students, academic and non-academic staff to create a favorable environment with reasonable accommodation for inclusive education. The university can play a crucial role in mobilizing not only the university community but also the entire society. However, it has not become a priority in higher education not only due the lack of resources but also due to lack of awareness and sensitivity toward disability.

Challenge to Move from Charity to a Rights-Based Approach

This chapter focuses on exploring the socio-cultural construction of disability in Sri Lanka which is predominantly based on charity perspective. Thus, the chapter highlighted some of the challenges toward shifting from charity perspective to a rights-based approach in order to address issues related to disability. In the Sri Lankan social context, the disabled body has become a source of merit for the non-disabled as it allows them to accumulate further merit while caring for the disabled. The evidence clarifies the fact that not only people with major disabilities but also the persons with mild impairments who have no functional limitations face a challenge due to fixed identity as disabled that has been re-enforced by socially and culturally constructed prejudices and obstacles that are equivalent to social oppression, which is further re-enforced by the doctrine of karma. The charity perspective encourages the society to take care of the persons with disability in the belief that the caregiver is more fortunate than the recipient, reinforces negative attitudes of inferiority in people who have disability and excludes them from the social mainstream. It is an affront to the self-esteem and dignity of individuals. Discrimination against persons with disabilities origins from his/her family to a large extent where they are socialized to acknowledge the disadvantaged position that is gradually reinforced by other social institutions such as religion, education, the economy, welfare system etc.

Though there are government and civil society initiatives to address issues related to disability, the empirical evidence highlights a number of common and context-specific challenges toward moving from a traditional approach based on charity perspective to a rights-based approach toward an inclusive society. The narratives of the locus of the village reveal that the above conceptualization leads persons with even mild impairments into exclusion and exploitation while utilizing their capabilities up to the maximum where there is labor shortage in agriculture. Thus, the findings suggest that the attitudes of not only lay people but also of service providers toward disability have no signs of moving from the charity approach to a rights-based approach. According to the perception of most of the service providers who contributed to this study, existing special schools and institutions for the disabled need to be continued for the well-being of persons with disabilities that requires further efforts to mobilize the society toward a rights-based approach.

The experience of persons with disabilities in the context of higher education where there is an access to inclusive education suggests that the challenges faced by undergraduates with disabilities are not only due to structural and socio-cultural barriers but also duc to lack of individual empowerment among the undergraduates with disabilities to fight against discrimination, as they have already been socialized to accept their disadvantaged position due to disability as part of everyday life. The socio-cultural construction of disability has many adverse effects on the everyday lives of people with disability that prevent both their social and physical access to various types of services and opportunities that enhance the quality of life.

How to Move Forward Toward a Disability-Inclusive Society?

Everyday life experience of persons with disabilities in diverse social settings narrated in this chapter clearly highlights some issues that require an urgent responsiveness to move forward toward a disability-inclusive society. The analysis of the present situation of disability inclusion reveals that persons with disabilities are quite marginalized from the mainstream not merely due to charity-based identity formation toward disability but also the shortcomings embedded in law enforcement and poor strategies adopted to implement the National Policy on Disability (2003), and the National Action Plan for Disability (2014) in Sri Lanka. Though there are various programs and activities by different ministries and departments of the government, the NGOs and Civil Society Organizations, the country lacks social and institutional cohesion and a multi-sectorial coordination body to implement interrelated and interdependent interventions from a holistic perspective. The situation leads to a number of drawbacks in the domains of education, health and rehabilitation, work and employment and mainstream enabling environment (Policy Outlines 2015).

The education policy fails to promote inclusive strategies and plans for children with disabilities. The attitudinal environment of school system segregates children with disabilities. Thus, the children with disabilities are left out of the preschool system and the primary and secondary schools are not equipped for students with disabilities where the school dropout rates are high. Children with disabilities are administratively under the special education branch of Ministry of Education and under the non-formal education department. Therefore, children with disabilities are immediately outside the mainstream education. Quality of secondary education limits opportunities for students with disabilities to access higher education.

There are a number of drawbacks in the domain of health and rehabilitation. Inadequate facilities for early detention and intervention; lack of assistive technologies and devices; poor access to health care facilities and specialized services; inadequate facilities and access to rehabilitation and inadequate knowledge and skills for disability work are some of the issues that need urgent interventions to ensure disability inclusion into mainstream.

There are also a number of issues that can be identified in the domain of work and employment. Attitudinal, physical and organizational barriers, inadequate opportunities for job preparation, carrier guidance and counseling, failure of mainstream vocational training system to adequately include youth, inadequate support for self-employment and micro finance, limited opportunities for mainstream employment and failure to provide reasonable accommodation in the work environment and lack of knowledge at the workplace on how to interact with persons with disabilities are some of the crucial issues in the domain of work and employment (Policy Outlines 2015).

The enabling environment has also a number of issues that require urgent attention. The public transport and the built environment are inaccessible. Also there is limited access to public accommodations and telecommunication services. There is no implementation, coordination, monitoring and evaluation mechanism to implement multi-sectorial approach toward disabilities in Sri Lanka. The country also lacks budgetary allocations for disability inclusion activities and lack of partnerships among state, NGOs and private Sector. There is also lack of professional standards and ethical guidelines in disability work.

Sri Lanka has a comprehensive national policy on disability and a national action plan for disability to give effect to the policy with the objective of promoting and protecting human rights of people with disabilities as equal citizens, taking into account the country's social, economic and cultural ethos while at the same time keeping in line with global trends and demands. However, the implementation of this policy has not kept pace with expectations and fails to have a significant impact on inclusion of disability into mainstream development. The drawback is mainly adhered to two fundamental issues. Firstly, the implementation of the national policy on disability is one of the main responsibilities of the Ministry of Social Empowerment and Social Welfare that reinforces charity perspective than a rights-based approach toward disability. Secondly, disability being a multi-ministerial policy, no one ministry can effectively bring other ministries together for disability work as each ministry is concerned with fulfilling the mandate assigned to the concerned ministry, thereby neglecting its interrelated and interdependent dimensions. Filling the gap requires a high level national commission for disability to be placed directly under the office of the executive which may be either the President or the Prime Minister of the country to implement the existing National Policy on Disability and the National Action Plan on Disability in order to promote and protect the rights of people who have disability in the spirits of social justice. Under the new setup of higher level national commission for disability, each ministry can continue the particular mandate with proper coordination where ministry of justice can play a crucial role in strengthening a rights-based approach to ensure disability inclusion in the mainstream development of the country. However, there are huge gaps existing at operational levels that require more social interventions not only to empower the persons with disabilities to exercise their own rights but also to mobilize the entire society to move forward from charity perspective to a rights-based approach to make disability a part of diversity. In order to move forward toward an inclusive society, the findings strongly suggest that strengthening a rights-based approach from top-to-bottom and mobilizing civil society organizations from bottom-to-up should drive simultaneously with appropriate strategies to enhance disability inclusion in the mainstream development. Thus, further research from a multidisciplinary approach is necessary for evidence-based practice as disability studies in Sri Lanka are located at the margin.

Summary

The chapter attempted to explore socio-cultural construction of disability in Sri Lanka and its impact on the everyday lives of persons with disabilities who come from diverse social settings. The study included a community setting, a home for people with disabilities and incurable diseases, a school for special education for children with disabilities and a higher education institution. Disability conceptualizes within the context of Sri Lankan society from a charity perspective. The findings suggest that not only lay people but also professional and different service providers have unfavorable attitudes toward moving from charity perspective to a rights-based approach. While acknowledging the strengths of social mode, the chapter argues that disability demands an integrated approach toward empowering persons with disabilities and also to mobilize the entire society to create an environment with reasonable accommodation for an inclusive society that accepts disability as part of the diversity. Evidence further suggests that there is no sign of emerging strong disability movements in Sri Lanka to fight against the discrimination due to disability as they have been organized in isolation with a narrow focus on addressing specific issues related to a particular disability than organizing them as a powerful group to fight against their rights as human beings with a common goal. However, Sri Lanka has a very comprehensive national policy on disability and national action plan for disability that requires an appropriate mechanisms to implement them. It is recommended to have a higher authority to deal with issues related to disability where the legal aspects should be further strengthened.

References

Addlakha, R. (2013). *Disability studies in India: Global discourses, local realities*. London: Routledge.

Annual Handbook. (2012). University Grants Commission, New Delhi.

Booth, T. (2000). *Index for inclusion: Developing learning and participation in schools*. Canterbury: Centre for Educational Research.

Compulsory Education Ordinance of Sri Lanka No. 1003/5 of 1997. (1997). Parliament of Sri Lanka.

Goffman, E. (1961). *Asylums; essays on the social situation of mental patients and other inmates*. Garden City: Anchor Books.

National Policy on Disability. (2003). Ministry of social services.

Oliver, M. (1990). *The politics of disablement*. London: Macmillan Education.

Oliver, M. (1996). *Understanding disability: From theory to practice*. New York: St. Martin's Press.

Policy Outlines. (2015). *These policy outlines were formulated by over 100 academics and professionals, through an inter-disciplinary workshop*. These outlines are an initial step in a 5 year programme for recommending sound national policy frameworks for Sri Lanka.

Rahula, W. (1978). *What the Buddha taught*. London: Gordon Fraser.

Sayadaw, Ven Mahasi. *Basic Buddhism: The theory of Karma*. Buddhist Studies: Buddha Dharma Education. Association & Buddhanet, 1996–2012. Sayadaw. www.free-ebooks.net/ebook/Insights-Into-Karma-The-Law-of.../313. Accessed 12 Nov 2014.

Chapter 17
Accessibility and Modernist Architecture: The Work of Oscar Niemeyer in Brazil

Norma Isa Figueroa

Abstract Mid-century Modern architecture represents a paradigm shift in the way society thought about the role of buildings. No longer exclusive to the rich or powerful, architecture became a utopian means including all of society, particularly the working class. This movement, originated in Europe, was adopted in the Americas, becoming influential not only in architecture but in other design professions as well. The quest for inclusion manifested in different forms, the most representative being the ramp as the primary means to enter a building. With the ramp, architecture opened its arms to the masses in a gesture welcoming everybody as equals. The ramp became an iconic element full of beauty and symbolism, even though at times it did not work technically. This chapter is about the way architects incorporated the use of the ramp in their buildings and the reasons behind their inclusion. The work of architect Oscar Niemeyer in Brazil will be highlighted in order to demonstrate that issues of inclusion were considered by architects decades before laws about accessibility were enacted.

Introduction

The way people approach, enter, and navigate a building, more than being the result of practical needs, is decided by factors such as the building's budget and purpose, the construction technology available, and equally, the discourse of the discipline at the time and the idea of the architects for its design. During the Modernist Movement in architecture, which originated in Europe between World Wars, the tendency was to create buildings without ornamentation, simple in design and with an honest expression of materials and structure. Buildings were conceived based on the premise that the resulting form was a reflection of its function in such a way that the integration of art and mass production seemed to blur the lines between architecture

Illustrations by Dustin Wheat

N.I. Figueroa (✉)
School of Architecture, Interior Design Program, University of Texas at Arlington, Arlington, TX, USA
e-mail: norma.isa@gmail.com

© Springer International Publishing AG 2017   267
S. Halder, L.C. Assaf (eds.), *Inclusion, Disability and Culture*, Inclusive
Learning and Educational Equity 3, DOI 10.1007/978-3-319-55224-8_17

and industrial design. But besides its technical and functional aspects, Modernist architecture had to do with social responsibility. With its ideal of a more democratic architecture, it made a commitment to the masses of creating buildings for the people: egalitarian buildings that would welcome everyone long before codes and standards of accessibility were established.

This chapter is about the Modern Movement of architecture and its ideal use of the ramp as the main pathway to the entrance of a building. Through examples of the work of Brazilian architect Oscar Niemeyer in Brazil, it will demonstrate that the democratic principles of Modern architecture inspired architects to use ramps in welcoming everybody to the interior of the building. The chapter's intent is to illustrate that modernist architects were aware of their responsibility in making their buildings accessible to everyone long before accessibility codes and regulations were considered and put into effect. The ramp, both as the viable means of accessibility and the iconic modernist element of design, will be the focus.

Background

I was born and raised in Ponce, the second most important city in the Caribbean island of Puerto Rico. A small city proud of its role in the economy of the Island during the eighteenth and nineteenth centuries, Ponce has a beautiful city square surrounded by majestic colonial buildings. My first recollection of Modernist architecture was during a visit to the Ponce Art Museum with my parents on a Sunday afternoon when I was just about 8 years old. Edward Durell Stone, an American architect who had also designed the Museum of Modern Art and the John F. Kennedy Center for the Performing Arts, both venues in New York City, designed the museum that opened in 1965. At that time, my limited understanding of architectural aesthetics derived from the arches and colorful tiles of my grandmother's house, which I would later identify as Spanish colonial style. But that day, the simple lines of the Modernist façade and the marble plaza just in front of the museum, made me feel we were approaching a place of compelling beauty.

The Ponce Art Museum is located in front of a boulevard lined up with tall trees that bloom with flowers of intense colors during different seasons. From the sidewalk, a series of steps flanked by a ramp, would rise to the top of the plaza, which acted as a prelude to its entrance; the ramp was as important, functional, and beautiful as the steps. I remember little of the artwork I saw that day, but the joy of eating ice cream with my parents in the plaza, and of playing with my siblings on the steps and on the ramp, created pleasurable memories of art, architecture, and community. Even though I did not realize it for a long time, my choice to become an architect might have originated that day.

The Ramp

The ramp is the iconic element of accessibility in the field of Architecture. Because of its required width and length, many times the ramp becomes difficult to incorporate in a building, especially in pre-existing ones. Nowadays, accessibility ramps are designed according to specifications found in governmental codes and standards, which can represent a challenge for architects as we struggle to integrate ramps in our buildings. Unfortunately, when the site or the budget is too small, the idea of a ramp is cancelled and replaced by an elevator, missing the opportunity of providing the mobility-impaired user with the sensory experience of circulating the building like everyone else. Architects working on the design of public buildings, which typically have bigger budgets, can effectively propose and integrate an accessibility ramp early on during the design process.

Although efforts to make more egalitarian accesses to buildings had started sometime with the work of Modernist architects, it was not until 1961 that organizations like the American National Standards Institute (ANSI) published specifications for making buildings and facilities accessible and usable by people with mobility disabilities (American National Standards Institute 1961). In a brief document of 11 pages, the ANSI presented accessibility recommendations in the design, construction, and retrofit of ramps in already existing buildings. It is important to note that practicing Modernist architects, when accessibility standards were not in effect, used the ramp as a state-of-the-art element with the intention of creating beautiful and inclusive buildings. Like the architects, the Institute believed that access for all was of utmost necessity and that it did not have the power to enforce any codes.

Changes came during the revolutionary years of the late 1960s. As a consequence of the Civil Rights Movement, many minority groups were able to fight for rights that society had never before considered a prerogative. In the United States, the Architectural Barrier Act of 1968, one of the first attempts to ensure building accessibility, was a result of this revolution. It mandated that all facilities funded partially or wholly by federal funds and intended for public use had to be designed and constructed in an accessible manner (https://www.access-board.gov).

In 1975, the American Institute of Architects published the *Syllabus for Barrier-Free Environment* with practical information regarding measurements and allowances needed to make a building accessible, but mostly for already existing buildings. It made information available about codes and spoke about the typical barrier problems in buildings, but the recommendation for accessibility ramps was insignificant. Under a section titled "Approaches to Building Entrance," the document advised against the use of ramps and specified that if these were inevitable, a maximum slope of a foot rise in 12 ft of length be used (Klimet 1975). This seemingly negative pronouncement toward the use of ramps articulates to this day the struggle professionals face when making old buildings accessible.

The Problem

Ramps are easier to incorporate during the design of new buildings rather than after the building has been completed. But even when architects are aware of the ramp's accessibility requirements, it is the availability of funds and the creativity of professionals that will determine the ramp's role as a main element or just a secondary one. In a building, ramps usually take more space and funds to build than stairs. If it was the other way around, we would have many more ramps everywhere and accessibility would not be a problem.

Because of regulations, older buildings that had limited accessibility have had to include a ramp in order to comply. Many of the unsightly and out-of-the-way ramps that we see in public buildings nowadays convey the idea that people with disabilities are not being considered by architects. But in reality, many of these ramps are created following regulations, and without the input of designers. Besides providing accessibility, the addition of a ramp to an already built structure can create problems with the aesthetics of the building and even with its circulation. Codes developed for integrating a ramp into historic buildings include suggestions like "place ramps to minimize their potential impact from the street" (http://www.naperville.il.us). Although these were conceived as an attempt to maintain the historic importance of the building, they fail to emphasize an egalitarian entrance for people with disabilities.

In order to comply with regulations, institutions have many times added a side ramp to existing buildings in an attempt to provide accessibility while maintaining the integrity of the façade. Even though the specifications of ramps guarantee a suitable entrance for people with disabilities, sometimes, if the ramp is not given the importance it deserves, it can be placed out of the main circulation creating two segregated ways of entering and navigating a building: the main one and the "special" one for people with disabilities. Since many institutionalized buildings around the world have been designed in some sort of neoclassical style, with lots of columns and steps at their main façade, adding ramps without affecting the historic appeal of buildings can be challenging.

Hiding a ramp can create problems for people with mobility issues when trying to get into a building. It also gives the impression that the more visible entrance is the main entrance while the "hidden" access provided by the ramp is a secondary entrance. Besides the complication created by the juxtaposition of styles and materials, ramps can bring about segregation of able and disabled users. A ramp built on the side and away from the main entrance of the building, besides creating confusion, causes inequality.

Take for example the addition of an accessibility ramp to the Teatro Solis, a neoclassical city theater in Montevideo, Uruguay. The whole neoclassic façade is composed of tall columns surrounded by steps all throughout the perimeter of the building and making it impossible to incorporate a ramp without impacting the façade. In this case, the designer responsible for making the building accessible decided not to segregate the entrances, and instead boldly positioned a ramp directly in front of the most important façade without blocking the main entrance, thus creating a subversive architectural statement. In terms of aesthetics, the designer created a beautiful ramp out of the latest construction materials and technology and made it look as important as the main entrance. By contrasting the new ramp to the old existing façade, it emphasized the building's historic importance. Yet, even though the ramp solution is daring and sculptural, at times its use is still secondary, like when the space is being utilized for an evening event. At night the red carpet guides the people toward the entrance while the ramp almost disappears as a side access, without the glamour of the cameras. Even though the accessibility ramp at the Teatro Solis is a successful case of integration between old architecture and new regulations, it is still at the margins. I believe the best way to guarantee accessibility in buildings is to include the ramp as the most important way of accessibility during the design phase executed by design professionals versed, not only in codes and regulations but also in human behavior and programmatic needs.

The Ramp as the Central Feature

Long before architectural barrier-free acts were implemented, Modernist architects had employed the ramp as a state-of-the-art inclusive way of moving through a building. Modernist architecture is generally characterized by simplification of form and absence of applied decoration. It developed as a result of social and political revolutions, technological developments, and new construction materials, as well as a reaction to the ornate neoclassical styles in architecture. The buildings constructed during this period by one of Modernism's most important figures, the Swiss architect Le Corbusier, made use of the ramp in his building designs, not only as a formal element but also for inclusion and accessibility. His influence traveled to Brazil when Oscar Niemeyer had the opportunity to work along Le Corbusier on several projects including the design of the nation's capital, Brasilia. For Oscar Niemeyer, architecture was about people's rights: the right to be treated decently, the right to experience pleasure, and the right to experience beauty (Goldberg 2013).

For one of his first projects, Niemeyer was commissioned to design the Grande Hotel in the eighteenth-century Portuguese city of Ouro Preto, a UNESCO world heritage-declared site. A four-story building of rectangular configuration completed in 1940, the hotel was situated on a hillside with its longer side oriented toward the view of the city. The reception on the first floor was accessed only through a ramp from the main parking lot located on the ground level. With no external stairs visible from the parking, a straight and simple ramp signaled the main circulation, ensuring that everybody had the same experience when entering the building. In the Grande Hotel, the stairs were placed inside the building in an inconspicuous way, subordinated to the importance of the ramp. From the beginning of his career, Niemeyer showed his sensitivity at creating an egalitarian architecture.

Niemeyer was granted international standing in architecture because of his design for the Brazilian Pavilion at the World Fair of 1939–1940 in New York, which showcased the architect's style of Brazilian Modernism. The main entrance to the pavilion featured a ramp with imposing dimensions and a central location on the façade. Upon entering the building, there is no segregation of users as all are equally greeted by the curved ramp, similar to an arm that embraces and gestures the way into and through the building. Influenced by Le Corbusier and his use of free-form ramps, Niemeyer used the curve not only as an expressive form but also as a flowing transition between interior and exterior spaces. This emphasis on the curve, and its successful application, defined his style early on in his career. The use of the ramp in this project was the concretization of a theme he had been working on for some time: the architectural pathway (Andreas and Flagge 2003). By using the ramp, Niemeyer manipulated the circulation into a path to make sure people did not just face empty walls or insignificant views when circulating, but that would actually face some kind of indoor activity or views of the outdoors, subtly determining the way a visitor experienced circulation, thus the term architectural pathway.

With the pathway concept, Niemeyer found the ramp to be the ideal means to provide an engaging circulatory experience while creating an accessible entrance. He went on to repeatedly use the ramp as an architectural element in the buildings he designed for Brasilia, which became the work he is most known for. There Niemeyer designed high-profile buildings like the National Congress, with its iconic concave and convex forms, several governmental buildings, the Cathedral, the residence of the president of the republic, and even the airport. In almost all of them, the ramp plays a significant part in accessing the building.

Although it might be easier to incorporate a ramp as an important element in a public building because of their higher construction funds, the ramp can also be incorporated in small-scale projects that are not particularly addressed for the masses. An example is the chapel at the Alvorada Palace in Brasilia (Fig. 17.1). Completed in 1958, the small chapel was designed for the use of the president and his family and sits on top of a platform accessed through a small ramp. A simple and beautiful composition, it reflects Niemeyer's desire to provide beauty and accessibility even at a smaller scale.

On a larger scale, in the Ibirapuera Auditorium in Sao Paolo, Niemeyer provided plenty of ramps for people to access the buildings from the exterior and to circulate the interior. The design of the concert hall, done in the 1950s as part of a complex of cultural buildings and completed in 2005, utilizes the ramp as the architectural pathway for large cultural gatherings. As he had done previously in other projects, the visitors access the building through the foyer on the ground floor and once inside, a central ramp of sculptural attributes lead to the interior of the hall (Fig. 17.2). The ramp was designed as a transition element where the visitor is able to watch other people and be watched as well. The ceiling, also displaying a sculptural quality, interacts with the movement of the ramp making for an iconic space that has become the brand of the complex. The way the access is treated and the importance it gives to the ramp, all speak of the architect's attempt at creating an egalitarian culture. There is no hierarchy, no side entrance, and no segregation. As evidenced by his other buildings as well, everybody has the same rights and privileges when inhabiting Niemeyer's architecture.

Fig. 17.1 Chapel at the Alvorada Palace in Brasilia

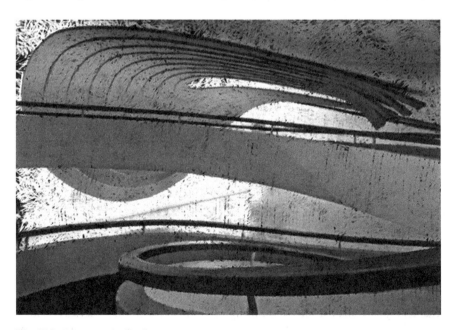

Fig. 17.2 Ibirapuera Auditorium

Fig. 17.3 Museum of contemporary art in Niterói

In 1996, Niemeyer designed the Museum of Contemporary Art in Niterói, Rio de Janeiro, Brazil. It is a saucer-shaped structure set on a cliff with beautiful views of the beach and the surrounding areas (Fig. 17.3). The ramp, in character with Niemeyer's style, marks the main entrance and wanders in several loops as a way to get visitors acquainted with the surroundings. Niemeyer consciously persuades visitors to admire the natural beauty of the place. In this case, nature itself is a museum.

Conclusion

I would like to emphasize that Niemeyer's ideals of social justice and egalitarian culture influenced his architecture. Like other Modernist architects, it was not his intention to design for people with disabilities but to create spaces to be enjoyed by all. The ramp always had a central role in his designs. The work presented in this chapter is just a small portion of the many buildings in which architects successfully created equality by the way the entrance receives people and the way the interior circulation is made accessible to everyone. Niemeyer demonstrates the proper use of the ramp as the main access to a building, providing everybody with the same welcoming experience.

Nowadays, the ideal utilization of the ramp as a main entrance element in public buildings has weaned, except for the work of several contemporary architects that understand the importance of inclusion. By creating spaces that embrace even what some would consider the weakest subjects, we take part in creating an egalitarian and just society. In order to achieve this, a recommendation in the design of new buildings would be to place ramps in a prominent location, equal to or more so than the stairs at the entrance of a building. In addition, buildings' budgets need to reconsider the importance of accessibility and its relationship to equality, and not use budget limitations as an excuse for creating a secondary, less desirable alternative. The architecture created by Oscar Niemeyer proves what many contemporary architects know too well, that creating a main entrance, without hierarchies and segregation, is not only possible but also beautiful.

References

American National Standards Institute. (1961). *Specifications for making buildings and facilities accessible to, and usable by, the physically handicapped*. New York: The Institute.

Andreas, P., & Flagge, I. (2003). *Oscar Niemeyer: A legend of modernism*. Frankfurt am Main/ Berlin: Deutsches Architektur Museum/Birkhäuser.

Goldberg, P. (2013). *A tribute to Oscar Niemeyer at the United Nations*. Retrieved September 27, 2014, from http://blog.espasso.com/category/niemeyer/

Historic Building Design and Resource Manual, Naperville, Illinois. Retrieved on September 27, 2014, from http://www.naperville.il.us/emplibrary/Boards_and_Commissions/HBDRM-July-revised.pdf

Klimet, S. A. (1975). *Into the mainstream: A syllabus for a barrier-free environment* (p. 16). Washington, DC: American Institute of Architects.

United States Access Board. *Architectural Barrier Act of* 1968. Retrieved on September 27, 2014, from http://www.access-board.gov/the-board/laws/architectural-barriers-act-aba

Chapter 18
Individualized Approach for Inclusion of Children with Diverse Behavioural Needs

Santoshi Halder

Abstract The foremost challenge for professionals and practitioners is to design the most suitable intervention programme to ameliorate the skill deficits in individuals with autism spectrum disorder (ASD). The significance of the implementation of effective intervention strategy for incorporating socially approved behaviour has been evidence-based practices worldwide. However, the implementation of the same in various countries and cultures is with mixed results, quite specifically in the low socioeconomic and less affluent countries. The author depicts and explores the significance of the strategies based on applied behaviour analyses and single-subject design research in shaping socially approved behaviour of the children with developmental delays in an Indian context. The chapter documents the application of three behaviour modification strategies based on the science of applied behaviour analyses (ABA) conducted in West Bengal (Eastern part of India). First is the application of trial-based functional analyses of self-injurious behaviour of a child with developmental disability. Second is the behavioural intervention through echoic and exemplar training in children having phonological disorder. Finally, third is effectiveness of video modelling to teach play skills (including both verbal and motor responses) to children with autism spectrum disorder. The findings of these three single-subject design research conducted on different subjects in different contexts applied individualized intervention approach for successful behaviour modification among the children with developmental disabilities. The author indicates a strong need for individualized intervention approach for shaping behaviours among the children with developmental disabilities with diverse behaviour needs. The author depicts how the intervention strategies can be individualized based on child-specific needs for successful behaviour modification and inclusion of the children.

S. Halder (✉)
Department of Education, University of Calcutta,
Alipore Campus, Kolkata, West Bengal, India
e-mail: santoshi_halder@yahoo.com

© Springer International Publishing AG 2017   277
S. Halder, L.C. Assaf (eds.), *Inclusion, Disability and Culture*, Inclusive
Learning and Educational Equity 3, DOI 10.1007/978-3-319-55224-8_18

Introduction

The author of the chapter is a scholar undergoing behaviour analysis course crrently affiliated and recognized by BCBA board, USA. She has successfully completed the BCBA course requirement and is currently completing her field work in an Autism Centre in Kolkata under a BCBA mentor as per norms. The experiments depicted in this chapter are the three experiments (documented as Case 1, 2 and 3) conducted as the course requirements and all the experiments have been conducted adhering to ethical requirements.

The idea of delving in ABA and understanding the science initiated while conducting research as a Fulbright Nehru Senior Research Fellow (2011–2012) at Indiana University, USA. The openness of Fulbright fellowship offered multiple avenues and scope to get engaged with significant people working closely with specific areas of disabilities. It was an excellent experience getting the scope to participate in many activities voluntarily with the children with disabilities at home and residential centres. The curiosity to understand and explore the diverse needs and challenges of the children with developmental delays and the possible ways for intervention was much evident. Returning to India after 8 months, the author could not resist getting enrolled for the behaviour analyst course for learning the science of applied behaviour analyses for positive behaviour modifications. Attending the course led to understanding of the science of ABA and the author noted that it was not only applicable for the individuals with disabilities but also for the typical average people for positive behaviour implementations, and it was equally interesting and significant to know that knowingly or unknowingly we all apply principles of ABA in our day-to-day lives. The author got attached to the centres offering services to children with autism and more specifically following ABA. The course and spirit of learning got shaped and extended while working as an honorary visiting fellow at Olga Tennison Autism Research Center (OTARC), La Trobe University, Melbourne, Australia, where she was placed as an Endeavour Australia-India education Council Research Fellow (2015–2016) and as Honorary Visiting Fellow at OTARC where she got multiple possibilities to explore various effective intervention strategies for the children with ASD and visited the various autism centres following the science of ABA during her stay as an International Fellow funded by the Department of Education, Australian Government.

The author clearly noted the scarcity of ABA for intervention and also the lack of specialized and trained professionals in India. It was surprising to note that there is complete invisibility of any work/findings being published or documented from an Indian context in spite of its effectiveness and implementation. Thus, the author finds it pertinent and quite necessary to write on the effectiveness of the science of ABA for individuals with developmental disabilities from her own practical experience and implementation including the conceptual understanding of the subject and extending forward through few snapshots of the three separate researches on varied areas with varied subject in an Indian context, highlighting the significance of the same for parents, teachers and stakeholders working in the field.

Early Intervention Strategies for Individuals with Developmental Disabilities including ASD

Autism, the fastest growing developmental disability is a lifelong neuro-developmental disorder characterized by deficits in multiple developmental areas, particularly social skills, communication and behaviours (Applied Psychological Association 2013). The prevalence of autism worldwide estimates 5.7–21.9 per 1000 (1 in 68) children aged 8 years (Centers for Disease Control, CDC 2014) and in India it is 1 in 250 (Ganaie and Bashir 2014). Recent statistics worldwide indicate the number of children diagnosed with autism has proliferated by leaps and bound as reports estimated 10 million children (one in every 50 school children) with autism in India (CDC 2014) indicating a 1/16% increase with 1–1.5% autistic children in India (International Clinical Epidemiology Network Trust (INCLEN). There is a similar incidence of increase in autism rates all over the world including the developing and developed counties (Stansberry-Brusnahan and Collet-Klingenberg 2010).

In an era when worldwide practitioners and researchers are facing tremendous challenges and struggling hard to provide effective interventions to cater the needs of individuals with ASD for making the best practices available for positive behavioural outcome, findings through evidence-based research imply the significance and implication of effective behaviour intervention to many challenging behaviours.

Challenges and Needs of Individuals with Autism Spectrum Disorder (ASD)

As the child with ASD may have normal intelligence level but scattered functions in various aspects, they face tremendous challenges starting from identification, diagnoses and implementing effective interventions for facilitating behavioural outcome. Whatever the degree of variation from average ability, every child has the potential to learn and progress, through an appropriate strategy (United Nations 2006). In spite of the UNCRPD recommendation on equal rights of educational for all, inclusion of the children with developmental disabilities including ASD remains the foremost challenge for educationists due to the diversities of the needs and challenges. There is also complete lack of trained and skilled personnel in the emerging intervention strategies in many developing countries including India. Special educators are often bound to struggle finding the best intervention to target the problem behaviour of the child which seems to be so different with respect to their problem behaviour, learning pattern, understanding, learning pace and so on. Although there is no ultimate cure for autism, if diagnosed early the symptoms of autism can be managed with intensive and appropriate intervention program at a young age. The possible solution to cater the needs of these children for inclusion would be to

incorporate the most individualized approaches to teaching-learning. Thus, diagnosing and analysing the behavioural challenges and implementation of appropriate
individualized interventions is of paramount importance if we need to include the
children with ASD.

Need for Research on Evidence-Based Practice

The literature depicts a significant gap between research and practice in the area of
autism research (Mayton et al. 2010). There is need of extensive research based on
consistent positive results through experimentation to establish the effectiveness of
a particular strategy/approach before implementing for intervention by special educators of professional standards for successful positive outcome and for further
implementation extension (Council for Exceptional Children 2009; Odom et al.
2010; No Child Left Behind 2002; Mesibov and Shea 2011; Boutot and Myles
2011).

The science of Applied Behaviour Analyses (ABA) is a commonly used for intervention for children with autism that is being applied throughout the world in an
effort to improve both short- and long-term outcomes (Thompson and Iwata 2007).
Evidence (Stansberry-Brusnahan and Collet-Klingenberg 2010) of ABA for effective interventions for children with autism has been much documented worldwide;
however, there is scarcity of such practices in developing countries like India and
also most of the research work done is not yet published. This chapter is an effort to
document snapshots (through three single-subject design researches) depicting the
effectiveness of the individualized intervention approach to target the problem
behaviour of the children with ASD, and generalizing results for global prospects.

Case 1: Implementation of Trial-Based Functional
Analyses (FA)

Children with ASD often engage in disruptive behaviour that negatively affects not
only their own lives but also the lives of others around them (Axelrod and Kates-
McElrath (2008, March), thus affecting their appropriate education, performance,
social interactions with peers, academic achievement and safety (Crone and Horner
2003). Identifying the function of problem behaviour before developing an intervention can increase the effectiveness of the intervention to a great extent as it
allows the teacher to manipulate the antecedents and consequences maintaining the
problem behaviour (Iwata and Dozier 2008; Iwata et al. 1982). The significance of
functional analyses for determining the function of problem behaviour has been
paramount.

The present study examines the application of trial-based functional analyses for determining the function of self injuriour behaviour (SIB) of a 8-year-old child with ASD with no vocal repertoire in a classroom setting. Findings indicate the effective way of determining the function of head hitting as target problem behaviour suggesting that the trial-based functional analysis may be an effective assessment mechanism for understanding the function of the behaviour. The study further establishes a function-based intervention reducing the problem behaviour of the child with autism.

Trial-Based Functional Analyses

The trial-based FA is broken down into different trials, such as attention, demand, alone, and tangible and occurs throughout the daily routine of the child. Each type of condition, i.e. tangible, demand etc., included for the child was conducted (both control and test segments of each trial) throughout a 1-week period. In order to shorten the length of the assessment, the study consisted of trials of 4-min each (2-min control condition and 2-min test condition). Data were graphically represented to identify the conditions under which the targeted behaviours occurred as a function of problem behaviour.

Function-Based Intervention

The function-based intervention was implemented based on evidence-based best practices and research in the field (Tiger et al. 2008). After baseline sessions were completed, treatment sessions ran until stable behaviour was reached to determine if the intervention was effective. If the problem behaviour did decrease during the intervention phase, based on the outcome of the trial-based FA, it was assumed that the trial-based FA conducted accurately determined the function of the problem behaviour. The function-based intervention comprised of functional communication training (FCT), differential reinforcement of alternative behaviour (DRA) and extinction (EXT). The intervention was designed in different phases.

Results from trial-based functional analyses comparing the percentages obtained during control segments to the percentages obtained during test segments (Fig. 18.1) clearly indicated the function of the target problem behaviour of the child. Result indicated that problem behaviour was high and stable. Subject's problem behaviour occurred in the demand and tangible conditions only. No problem behaviour occurred in the alone and attention conditions suggesting that the target behaviour was sensitive to demand and tangible as sources of reinforcement.

Result (Fig. 18.2) of the function-based interventions shows FCT responses and DRA for the subject in an hour. During intervention, the subject acquired the FCT response while differentially reinforcing alternative behaviour and the problem

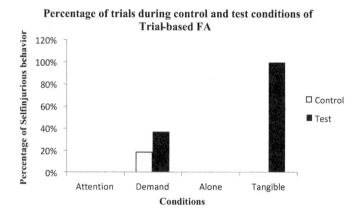

Fig. 18.1 Percentage of trials during control and test conditions of trial-based FA. The vertical axis shows the percentage of self-injurious behaviour (head hitting) of the child during the control and test conditions of the 4-min trials (2-min control and 2-min test segments of the trials) of the trial-based FA in classroom setting. The horizontal axis indicates the four conditions (attention, demand, alone and tangible) along with both the trials (control and test conditions)

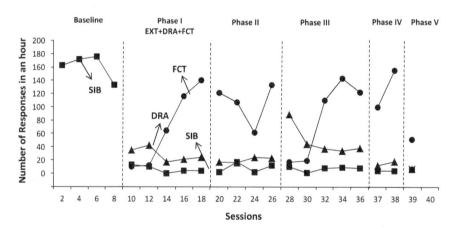

Fig. 18.2 Responses in an hour of problem behaviour and alternative responses during baseline for the participant. Note. *FCT* functional communication training, *EXT* extinction

behaviour decreased. The graph (Fig. 18.2) clearly demonstrates the increase in FCT and DRA, while substantial decrease in the self injuriour behaviour (SIB)-head hitting behaviour of the child may be noted. The head hitting behaviour in baseline was 161 which drastically decreased to 5 on average for an hour during intervention. The study demonstrated the efficacy of trial-based FA to establish the function of head hitting behaviour of a child with ASD in a classroom setting (Bloom et al. 2011).

Case 2: Behavioural Intervention Through Echoic and Exemplar Training in Children Having Phonological Disorder

Approximately 30–50% of individuals with autism fail to develop vocal imitation and remain minimally verbal throughout their lives, with little or no functional speech (National Institutes of Health and National Institute on Deafness and Other Communication Disorders 2010; Johnson 2004; Mirenda 2003). Research suggests that the inability to express in the socially approved or desired way of communication leads to various challenging behaviours in the individuals like tantrums, aggression and self-injury, thereby influencing performance. There has been strong evidence establishing substantial gains with applied behaviour analytic (ABA) interventions for children with developmental disabilities including autism (Eikeseth and Nesset 2003; Smith 1998; Horne and Lowe 1996).

The study examined the effectiveness of echoic and exemplar training to improve the vocal productions of two children with developmental disabilities. Two boys were selected for the present study who met the criteria for phonological disorders. The first participant was 5 years old with cats' eye syndrome having gross developmental delay and the second participant was 8 years old with autism. Both the participants were studying in a special school and had severe articulation/phonological needs in few single letters or phonemes causing difficulties and making speech unintelligible. These two boys were selected as they met the criteria for phonological disorder. An AB design was implemented to study the effect of echoic and exemplar training resulting in improved articulation. Pre- and post-intervention data were collected to determine whether improved articulation of target sounds was associated with improved articulation in related words with similar sounds and led to generalizations and transfer to other similar untrained words. The findings established significant progress in articulation up to 57 and 71% for the first and second participants respectively.

Final selection of the target phonemes was made after thorough analyses and baseline data for both the participants. Participant 1 (in Case 1) could not at all echo any of the words with the phonemes (/g/, /n/, /s/). Thus, a set of words was developed with these phonemes for participant 1. Participant 2 had difficulties with the phonemes (/j/, /r/, /h/), hence a set of words was developed with these phonemes for the intervention. A group of seven separate target words separately for each participant were finally selected for both the participants as they had severe difficulties in articulating them. Hence there were three sets of seven target words with each selected phoneme for both the participants. Word set 1 with phoneme (g/) and word set 1 with phoneme (/j) was selected as the first target for participants 1 and 2 (in case 1) respectively. Set 2 and Set 3 functioned as a control group (Table 18.1).

The dependent variable was vocal imitation of target words in a set of pre-selected words (Table 18.1). These were assessed through pre- and post-training tests. In the tests a correct response was defined as a correct imitation of the target word by the participant within 5 s. All other responses were marked as incorrect.

Table 18.1 List of target words for each participant

		Target sounds	Target words (a set of seven words)
Target words for participant 1	Target word set 1	/g/	**Gap**, Got, Gas, Gun, Gay, Gup, Gun
	Control group word Set 2	/n/	Net, Nit, Nut, Nap, Nib, Nod, Nob
	Control group word Set 3	/s/	Sun, Sat, Sit, Sip, Sag, Sub, Sad
Target words for participant 2	Target word set 1	/j/	**Jam**, Job, Jug, Joy, Jar, Jog, Jet
	Control group word set 2	/r/	Rat, Red, Rub, Rap, Rag, Rug, Rig
	Control group word set 3	/h/	Hat, Hit, Hip, Hop, His, Ham, Hot

Assessment for baseline data (pre-training test sessions) was taken for all of the above words (set 1, 2 and 3) for both the participants. Baseline assessment was made through vocal imitation of target words before training. After noting a stable data point the intervention was started. The intervention occurred for one word from set 1 for participants 1 and 2. After every four sessions of intervention, post-training data was collected again in baseline for all 3 sets. If less than 100% in the target set was achieved, then training continued for the target word. In addition, if this word was mastered then a new word would be selected. Testing after every four sessions would continue until the participant achieves 100% for the set.

Assessment was done through test sessions (both baseline and post-training). Each test session assessed all the three set of words in the target list in the same order they appeared in the list (Table 18.1). Hence each test session assessed the newly mastered target word, the remaining six words containing the same sound and also the other 14 target words of the other two word group in set 2 and 3. The need to assess the other group of target words was to establish experimental control. Articulation training began by having strong reinforcement available and visible to the learner to establish motivation for correct response. Before presenting any target 2–3 easy imitation and echoic were presented in quick succession. Then the full word was presented, e.g. "gap".

Figures 18.3 and 18.4 represent results from the test sessions conducted during the baseline and during training sessions in a one-and-half month span of the articulation intervention selected for the present study. The figures clearly depict that the number of correct articulation during the baseline was zero for both the participants. After the training sessions started both the participants irrespective of their varied nature of developmental disabilities showed significant improvement in the target words. For participant 1 the performance remained at zero for both the sets 2 and 3 throughout the study. For participant 2 the performance remained at zero or near to zero throughout the study, indicating strong effect of the articulation intervention under the study.

The present graphical data (Fig. 18.3) for participant 1 shows the performance or mastery of the target sound (more than 70%) with the training of only the first word (Gap). However, participant 1 took more training sessions for mastery of the target set words and the sound.

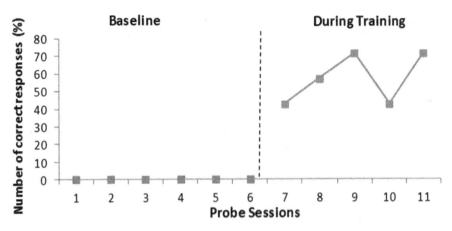

Fig. 18.3 Number of correct responses in the word group set 1 for participant 1 at baseline and during training of one-and-half month (45 days approx.)

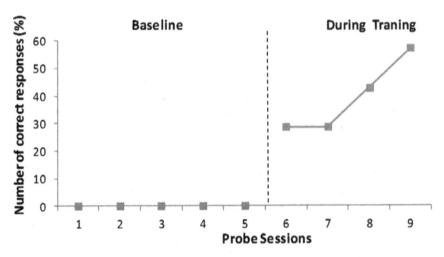

Fig. 18.4 Number of correct responses in the word group set 1 for participant 2 at baseline and during training of 1 month

For participant 1 (Fig. 18.3), the target was achieved in only 10 training sessions and the subject remained absent for two sessions in between due to sickness. Comparative analyses show that participant 1 performed better than participant 2 to achieve mastery of the target sound. However, for participant 2 (Fig. 18.4) the improvement was slow as depicted in the graphical representation. There were also few days of no training due to the participant's sickness and absence. The subject remained absent due to sickness for six sessions in between. Hence, training was interrupted for these reasons for participant 2. For participant 2 the training was conducted only for 6 days.

The study shows how the vocal imitation through echoic and exemplar training results in improved articulation in the children with developmental delays. The present study also clearly depicts the significance of response generalization or transfer in articulation intervention in applied behaviour analyses. The study shows how the training of only one word leads to correct articulation or mastery of untrained words. The same articulation intervention was successful with both the participants of different nature of developmental delays. This depicts the significance of echoic training and exemplar training for achieving mastery of the target sound and also transfer of the same to similar target word with the same target sound.

Case 3 Effectiveness of Video Modelling to Teach Play Skills Including both Verbal and Motor Responses to Children with Autism

Various legislations and policies have repeatedly stressed the need and necessity of implementing evidence-based intervention practices for individuals with disabilities (viz. No Child Left Behind Act of 2001; Government of India 1996; Individuals with Disabilities Education Act 1997; Simpson et al. 2004). There is strong support in the literature that visually based interventions support students' ability to shift attention (Quill 1995, 1997, 1998), make abstract concepts more concrete (Peeters 1997), and maintain and generalize newly learned skills (Krantz and McClannahan 1993, 1998).

Video modelling is a strategy involving the use of videos to provide modelling of targeted skills and has been found to be effective in teaching motor and verbal responses/communication to children with autism (Bellini et al. 2007; Delano 2007; Nikopoulos and Keenan 2004; Sigafoos et al. 2007). In video modelling a perosn imitates the behaviour after watching the video. This approach has wide utility and is appropriate for use with students of a range of ages and abilities, promotes independent functioning, and can be used to address numerous learner objectives, including behavioural, self-help, communication and social objectives.

The present study explores the effectiveness of video modelling to teach play skills including both verbal and motor responses to children with autism. Videotaped play sequence including verbal and motor responses was used for the study. Single-subject design was implemented separately for all three participants under the study to show the effectiveness of video modelling to teach play skills (including both verbal and motor responses) to three participants. Participant 1 aged 9 years, participant 2 aged 8 years and participant 3 aged 9 years were initially selected based on the following criteria: none of these three children had any severe behaviour problems and none of them had any issue of ADHD/inattention. All of the three children's age ranged from 7 to 10 years and all were diagnosed to have developmental delay. All of the three participants were enrolled in the same special school.

However, participant 3 was also enrolled in a mainstream school apart from the special school. All the three participants stayed in the special school in the post-lunch session so the experiment was also conducted on the same days and in the post-lunch sessions indicating similar setting. Participants 1 and 2 acquired 100% mastery in both scripted motor and verbal responses; however, participant 3 showed mastery acquisition above 73% in motor scripted responses and only 17% in verbal scripted responses. The intervention was implemented in one to three phases as and when required for the three subjects under the study. Results indicated that the video modelling intervention led to the rapid acquisition of both verbal and motor responses. This procedure was shown to be an efficient technique for teaching relatively long sequences of responses in relatively few teaching sessions in the absence of chaining procedures. In addition, the sequences of target verbal and motor responses were acquired with video modelling with individualized differential intervention for each participant.

Sessions were conducted in a separate room within in the special school. The dependent variable consisted of the responses described below. The participants had to demonstrate the responses (verbal and motor) as modelled within 2 min when asked "*Well this is a farm house and you may play with it*". The 2-min time requirement for the play responses was selected based on sample trials conducted by the experimenter. During these trials the experimenter measured the duration required for the responses as modelled. It was determined that all responses could be completed within 2 min, even accounting for variability in children's pace.

A single-subject design research was implemented separately with the three participants' design for the study. All the participants began in baseline at the same time and day but the training phase was implemented and progressed in individual pattern as per the criteria and mastery achieved to introduce the next stages of the intervention for each participant (Table 18.2).

In Figs. 18.5, 18.6 and 18.7 the primary y-axis displays the percentage of scripted motor and verbal responses of participants 1, 2 and 3 respectively. In Figs. 18.5, 18.6, 18.7 the secondary y-axis displays the number of unscripted motor and verbal responses of participants 1, 2, and 3 respectively. The baseline data projected stable, low trend data on the percentage of scripted responses for all of the three participants. For participants 1 and 2, it was noted that both of them followed the instruction given by the researcher to sit on the chair and play with the farm house. Both of them were totally interestingly engaged in the farm house toy items for the entire 2 min of the assessment. Participants 1 and 2 both were equally involved and not eager to leave the toy item when asked to and preferred to continue playing with it. In contrast, participant 3 did not show much interest initially to play with the items provided, rather he would prefer to be attentive to other things present in the room and would also try to escape in one session. No prompt, reinforcement or any other instruction was provided during the baseline sessions. Introduction of intervention clearly depicted the effectiveness of video modelling as an intervention strategy among the three participants. However, the progress of each participant showed differential effectiveness in the pattern of their progress in performance.

Table 18.2 Detail list of the modelled scripted responses (motor and verbal)

S.No	Motor responses	S.No	Verbal responses
1	The sheep indicating the *farm house*	1.	Sheep says: Wow! beautiful farm house
2.	Sheep on the *farm*	2.	Sheep says: Wow nice flowers!
3.	Sheep eat the *grass*.	3.	Sheep says: I am hungry
		4.	Sheep says: yummy grass!
4.	Cow near the farm.	5.	Cow says: Hey sheep… this is my grass, go away
5.	Cow pushes the sheep to go away on the farm.		
6.	Dog near the farm	6.	Dog says: bhow bhow… hey you both stop fighting bhow bhow
7.	*McDonald the Farmer* comes out near the farm.	7.	Farmer says: hey you both stop fighting. Time to go home.
8	Farmer on the farm to chase the animals.		
9.	McDonald goes near *wife-Merry* to call.	8.	Farmer says: Hey Merry let us go to the market.
10.	Farmer on the car	9.	Drives: Wooooooooooooooooooh
11.	Wife on the car		
12.	Both (farmer and wife) drives towards the *market*.		
13.	Wife *gets down* the car	10.	Merry says to seller: Give me some vegetables
14.	*Puts* the vegetables on the car	11.	Merry says: thank you
15.	Wife *on the car*		
16.	Both *drives back* home	12.	Drives: Wooooooh

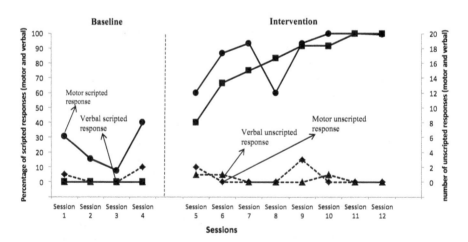

Fig. 18.5 Graphical representation of the percentage of responses (motor and verbal scripted) in the vertical y-axis (primary axis) and horizontal x-axis indicating the sessions. The secondary y-axis indicates the number of responses (motor and verbal unscripted) of participant 1

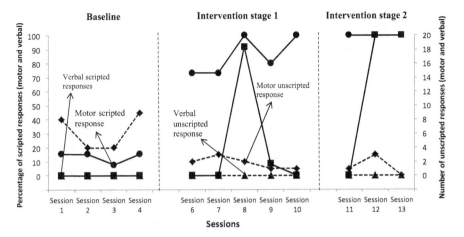

Fig. 18.6 Graphical representation of the percentage of responses (motor and verbal scripted) in the vertical y-axis (primary axis) and horizontal x-axis indicating the sessions. The secondary y-axis indicates the number of responses (motor and verbal unscripted) of participant 2

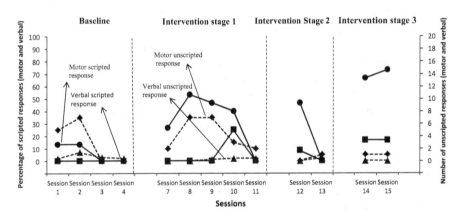

Fig. 18.7 Graphical representation of the percentage of responses (motor and verbal scripted) in the vertical y-axis (primary axis) and horizontal x-axis indicating the sessions. The secondary y-axis indicates the number of responses (motor and verbal unscripted) of participant 3

It was found that *participant 1* was able to perform most of the modelled scripted responses both motor and verbal with each session. Participant 1 achieved mastery of nearly 100% in both motor and verbal responses after few sessions without any other additional strategies. Thus, it can be concluded that following the introduction of the video modelling intervention, the percentage of modelled motor and verbal responses systematically increased from a stable baseline measure of average 23% of motor responses to an average of 84% responses. The range of scripted/modelled motor responses was 7.69–40% and 60–100% during the baseline and intervention sessions, respectively. The number of unscripted motor and verbal responses remained at a lower rate both in the baseline and intervention phase. Thus, participant 1 achieved 100% mastery of the target modelled/scripted responses both motor and verbal with the introduction of the first stage of the intervention, i.e. introduction of video modelling only without any other strategies without any experimenter-implemented contingencies or prompts. The range of number of unscripted motor responses ranged from 0 to 3 and for verbal responses from 0 to 1 for both baseline and intervention stages.

Participant 2 was able to achieve 80–100% mastery in the scripted/modelled target responses with the first stage of intervention but was unable to achieve the verbal responses. However, with the introduction of little instruction and demonstration in the second stage of intervention, participant 2 was also able to achieve 100% mastery in both verbal and motor responses. No other strategy apart from this was required for achieving mastery of the target behaviour. The number of unscripted motor responses also decreased from the baseline (range = 4–9) to (range = 1–3) intervention phase. Number of verbal responses remained 0 in both baseline and intervention phases.

Participant 3 showed 13.33% rate of motor responses and 0% motor responses in the baseline phase. Though the introduction of the video modelling intervention increased the scripted responses from 13.33% in the baseline to 53.33% in the first stage of intervention but then the data remained stable and no increasing trend was noted. The introduction of instruction and demonstration in the third stage of intervention showed further increase in the subject's performance but no further progress could be located. Thus, the introduction of the third stage of intervention was necessary where reinforcement (token) was introduced as an additional strategy. Token which already was the most preferred reinforcement for participant 3 was introduced along with all other strategies of the earlier stages of intervention in the third stage of intervention. With few sessions in the third stage of intervention, participant 3 showed increased rate of responses both in the motor and verbal scripted/motor responses. The number of unscripted motor and verbal responses also kept on decreasing subsequently.

The study shows the effectiveness of video modelling for all the three participants under study, strengthening earlier findings and researches. The study depicted how a long sequence of behaviour can be achieved with ease by students with autism through video modelling. This study can be a good model for various other complex behaviours/responses that can be targeted to be achieved by the children with developmental delays including autism. The study also depicts the necessity and significance of individualized educational intervention for children with autism based on the nature of their special needs, ability and challenges. The present study also establishes the effectiveness of video modelling to enhance/increase verbal and communicative responses among children with autism. It reconfirms that with the implementation of little modification based on the function of the behaviour, mastery can be achieved and performance can be enhanced in all children. The study can also be extended by introducing more complex play situations/play initiations and interactions among two or more children with autism/developmental delays.

Critical Comments

The chapter depicts three different interventions completely individualized to suit the individual needs to target the problem behaviour and showed the effectiveness for bringing about positive behaviour in the individuals.

The first case shows how through implementation and effectiveness of trial-based functional analyses (FA) the function of the problem behaviour is determined and then a completely individualized function-based intervention is sought to target the problem behaviour in different phases as per the progress of the subject shown clearly through graphical representations.

The second case documents the effectiveness of the behavioural intervention through echoic and exemplar training to target children having phonological disorders. Here the single-subject design research shows how the mastery of the target sounds is achieved in the two participants with diverse special needs. The intervention also shows how the articulation needs are met in both the subjects in varied pace based on the child's needs and also how the same is generalized for the target words in the set.

The third experiment clearly brings out the importance of video modelling as an intervention strategy for children having diverse special needs to teach play skills including both verbal and motor responses. The experiment also brings out how in a most scientific way the same strategy can be personalized to bring about progress in all the subjects with diverse characteristics. The experiment very well depicts not only the effectiveness of video modelling to achieve socially approved scripted but also unscripted motor and verbal play skills among the subjects which should be considered a remarkable achievement among children with developmental delays and more specifically ASD where one of the foremost challenges of the child is how to develop social skills.

Conclusion

Inclusion of children with special needs is one of the foremost objectives of the international and national legislations and the stakeholders all over the world. The practical implementation of the same, however, is faced with multiple challenges on both the levels: individual needs and the context. Policy makers, stakeholders, special educators are struggling hard to ameliorate the most suitable strategy to include children with diverse needs in an inclusive setting. When it comes to children with developmental delays including ASD due to the diversities in the individual needs and characteristics, it becomes even more of a challenge and a concern for the special educator teachers to best cater their needs in a heterogeneous class. How the strategies/interventions can be scientifically tailor-made/personalized to best suit the individual needs within a common setting is a necessary skill which needs analytical understanding of the problem behaviour and then targeting with a function-based intervention in a personalized way. The chapter provides few snap shots of some of those significant strategies much needed for the special educators/practitioners for an inclusive setting.

Note Treatment integrity and inter-observer agreement was done in keeping with the guidelines of BCBA. Informed consent was undertaken from the family and/or the subject as per the ethical consideration and requirement. All raw data and any related documents are kept confidential.

Acknowledgement I would like to acknowledge the contribution of the BCBA mentor, Julliane Bell, BCBA, who provided all guidance throughout the experiments. I would also like to acknowledge the scope and assistance provided by Behaviour Momentum India (BMI) and the Autism centre, Kolkata for allowing to conduct the research work leading to generalization of findings.

References

American Psychiatric Association (APA). (2013, April). *DSM-5 proposed revisions include new category of autism spectrum disorders* [Online]. Available: http://www.dsm5.org/Newsroom/Documents/Autism%20Release%20FINAL%202.05.pdf

Axelrod, S. & Kates-McElrath, K. (2008, March). Applied behavior analysis: Autism and beyond. Paper presented at the meeting of the Pennsylvania Association for Behavior Analysis, Hershey.

Bellini, S., Akullian, J., & Hopf, A. (2007). Increasing social engagement in young children with autism spectrum disorders using video self-modeling. *School Psychology Review, 36*, 80–90.

Bloom, S. E., Iwata, B. A., Fritz, J. N., Roscoe, E. M., & Carreau, A. B. (2011). Classroom application of a trial-based functional analysis. *Journal of Applied Behavior Analysis, 44*(1), 19–31.

Boutot, E. A., & Myles, B. S. (2011). *Autism spectrum disorders: Foundations, characteristics, and effective strategies.* Upper Saddle River: Pearson Education, Inc..

Centers for Disease Control (CDC). (2014). Autism and developmental disabilities monitoring network surveillance (2010). Prevalence of autism spectrum disorder among children aged 8 years-autism and developmental disabilities monitoring network, 11 sites, United States, 2010. *MMWR. CDC Surveillance Summaries, 63*, 1.

Council for Exceptional Children. (2009). *What every special educator should know: Ethics, standards, and guidelines* (6th ed.). Arlington: Author. Retrieved from http://www.cec.sped.org/content/navigationmenu/professionaldevelopment/professionalstandards/.

Crone, D. A., & Horner, R. H. (2003). *Building positive behavior support systems in schools.* New York: Guilford Press.

Delano, M. E. (2007). Improving written language performance of adolescents with asperger syndrome. *Journal of Applied Behavior Analysis, 40*, 345–351. doi:10.1901/jaba.2007.50-06.

Eikeseth, S., & Nesset, R. (2003). Behavioral treatment of children with phonological disorder: The efficacy of vocal imitation and sufficient-response-exemplar training. *Journal of Applied Behavior Analysis, 36*(3), 325–337. doi:10.1901/jaba.2003.36-325.

Ganaie, S., & Bashir, A. (2014). Global Autism: Autism, Autism etiology, perceptions, epistemology, prevalence and action. *International Journal of Clinical Therapeutics and Diagnosis (IJCTD), 2*(2), 39–47.

Government of India. (1996). The Persons with Disabilities (Equal Opportunities, Protection of Rights and Full Participation) Act 1995. New Delhi: Government of India. United Nations Enable Convention on the Rights of Persons with Disabilities, http://www.un.org/disabilities/default.asp?id

Horne, P. J., & Lowe, C. F. (1996). On the origins of naming and other symbolic behaviour. *Journal of the Experimental Analysis of Behavior, 65*(1), 185–241. doi:10.1901/jeab.1996.65-185.

Individuals with Disabilities Education Act Amendments of 1997 [IDEA]. (1997). Retrieved from http://thomas.loc.gov/home/thomas.php

Iwata, B. A., & Dozier, C. I. (2008). Clinical application of functional analysis methodology. *Behavior Analysis in Practice, 1*, 1–9. 35

Iwata, B. A., Dorsey, M. F., Slifer, K. J., Bauman, K. E., & Richman, G. S. (1982/1994). Towards a functional analysis of self-injury. *Journal of Applied Behavior Analysis, 27*, 197–209.

Johnson, C. P. (2004). Early clinical characteristics of children with autism. In V. B. Gupta (Ed.), *Autistic spectrum disorders in children* (pp. 96–134). New York: Marcel Dekker.

Krantz, P., & McGlannahan, L. (1993). Teaching children with autism to initiate to peers: Effects of a script-fading procedure. *Journal of Applied Behavior Analysis, 26*, 121–132. doi:10.1901/jaba.1993.26-121.

Krantz, P. J., & McGlannahan, L. E. (1998). Social interaction skills for children with autism: A script-fading procedure for beginning readers. *Journal of Applied Behavior Analysis, 31*, 191–202. doi:10.1901/jaba.l998.31-191.

Mayton, M. R., Wheeler, J. J., Menendez, A. L., & Zhang, J. (2010). An analysis of evidence-based practices in the education and treatment of learners with autism spectrum disorders. *Education and Training in Autism and Developmental Disabilities, 45*, 539–551.

Mesibov, G. B., & Shea, V. (2011). Evidence-based practices and autism. *Autism, 15*, 114–133.

Miranda, P. (2003). Toward functional augmentative and alternative communication for students with autism: Manual signs, graphic symbols, and voice output communication aids. *Language, Speech, and Hearing Services in Schools, 34*, 203–216.

National Institutes of Health & National Institute on Deafness and Other Communication Disorders. (2010, April 13–14). NIH workshop on nonverbal school-aged children with autism. Retrieved from http://www.nidcd.nih.gov/funding/programs/10autism/pages/detail.aspx

Nikopoulos, C. K., & Keenan, M. (2004). Effects of video modeling on social initiations by children with autism. *Journal of Applied Behavior Analysis, 37*(1), 93–96.

No Child Left Behind Act of 2001, 20 U.S.C. 70 § 6301 *et seq.* (2002). Retrieved from http://www2.ed.gov/policy/elsec/leg/esea02/107-110.pdf

Odom, S. L., Collet-Klingenberg, L., Rogers, S. J., & Hatton, D. D. (2010). Evidence-based practices in interventions for children and youth with autism spectrum disorders. *Preventing School Failure, 54*, 275–282.

Peeters, T. (1997). *Autism: From theoretical understanding to educational intervention San Diego.* CA: Singula Pub. Group.

Quill, K. A. (1995). *Teaching children with autism: Strategies to enhance communication and socialization.* Albany: Delmar.

Quill, K. A. (1997). Instructional considerations for young children with autism: The rationale for visually cued instruction. *Journal of Autism and Developmental Disorders, 27*, 697–714. doi:1 0.1023/A:1025806900162.

Quill, K. (1998). Environmental supports to enhance social-communication. *Seminars in Speech and Language, 19*, 407–422. doi:10.1055/s-2008-1064057.

Sigafoos, J., O'Reilly, M., & de la Cruz, B. (2007). *How to use video modeling and video prompting.* Austin: Pro-Ed.

Simpson, A., Langone, J., & Ayres, K. M. (2004). Embedded video and computer based instruction to improve social skills for students with autism. *Education and Training in Developmental Disabilities, 39*(3), 240–252.

Smith, T. (1998). Outcome of early intervention for children with autism. *Clinical Psychology: Science and Practice, 6*, 33–49.

Stansberry-Brusnahan, L. L., & Collet-Klingenberg, L. L. (2010). Evidence-based practices for young children with autism spectrum disorders: Guidelines and recommendations from the National Resource Council and National Professional Development Center on Autism Spectrum Disorders. *International Journal of Early Childhood Special Education, 2*, 45–56.

Thompson, R. H., & Iwata, B. A. A. (2007). Comparison of outcomes from descriptive and functional analyses of problem behavior. *Journal of Applied Behavior Analysis, 40*, 333–338.

Tiger, J. H., Hanley, G. P., & Bruzek, J. (2008). Functional communication training: A review and practical guide. *Behavior Analysis in Practice, 1*, 16–23.

United Nations. (2006). *Convention on the rights of person's with disabilities and optional protocol, office of the high commissioner*. Geneva: United Nations.

Resources

National Autism Center. http://www.nationalautismcenter.org/

This website contains information regarding the National Standards Project, a free downloadable Educator's manual, resource articles and guides, and answers to frequently asked questions.

Chapter 19
Employment and Living with Autism: Personal, Social and Economic Impact

Darren Hedley, Mirko Uljarević, and David F.E. Hedley

Abstract Individuals with autism are often faced with significant barriers to entering the workforce, irrespective of their individual level of functioning or capabilities. Research suggests that even in the developed countries adults with autism experience higher rates of unemployment than almost all other disability groups. These findings are concerning if we have in mind the known positive effects of employment on the individual, the family system, and as a means of offsetting the economic costs of autism. Furthermore, unemployment can have devastating impacts on the mental and physical health of the unemployed individual. Despite the importance of improving employment outcomes for individuals with autism, there is a marked lack of research regarding employment supports or interventions for adults with autism. In this chapter we first review the existing literature with regard to what we know about employment and employment programs in individuals with autism. Next we draw attention to the high rate of co-morbid disorders in adults with autism, in particular depression and suicidal ideation, anxiety and the potential impact of sleep disorders. Consistent with the theme of this book, personal narratives are provided in the form of case studies from people affected by autism. Our first case study describes the life of a young man who participates in supported employment and who is actively engaged with his community. We then describe an innovative employment program operating in Australia that has been effective in providing meaningful employment opportunities in the information technology sector to adults with autism. The benefits of employment for the individual and the family unit are then set in the broader context of the net economic gains for society. For a successful transition into employment the economic gains and productivity improvement over the lifetime of the individual are positive and significant, far outweighing the costs of the intervention.

Darren Hedley and Mirko Uljarević are equally contributed.

D. Hedley (✉) • M. Uljarević
Olga Tennison Autism Research Centre, La Trobe University, Melbourne, Australia
e-mail: d.hedley@latrobe.edu.au

D.F.E. Hedley
Independent Economic Consultant, Melbourne, Australia

© Springer International Publishing AG 2017
S. Halder, L.C. Assaf (eds.), *Inclusion, Disability and Culture*, Inclusive
Learning and Educational Equity 3, DOI 10.1007/978-3-319-55224-8_19

Introduction

Autoethnography describes 'people in the process of figuring out what to do, how to live, and the meaning of their struggles' (Bochner and Ellis 2006, p. 111). Perhaps in no other realm do these elements feature as predominantly as in employment. Employment meets not only the most basic economic needs of individuals and of their families, but is also associated with a sense of achievement and self-realisation, as well as providing opportunities for widening social networks (Linn et al. 1985). Social interaction in the workplace also creates the building blocks for successful engagement in a wider community. Conversely, unemployment and job loss have been found to lead to a number of negative mental and physical health effects, including decreased perceived competence, life satisfaction and activity, and increased sense of loneliness and isolation, depressive symptoms, somatisation and anxiety, physical symptoms, medication use, and days in bed sick (Feather and O'Brien 1986; Linn et al. 1985). With this in mind, it is particularly concerning that individuals with disabilities or other physical or mental health conditions face significant barriers entering the workforce and establishing careers, placing them at increased risk of suffering from the negative effects of unemployment.

Autism spectrum disorder (ASD)[1] is a cluster of a neurodevelopmental disorders characterised by impairments in social interaction, communication and restricted and repetitive behaviours and interests (DSM-5; American Psychiatric Association 2013). Adults with autism, including those with and without accompanying intellectual impairment, are at particular risk, experiencing exceptionally high rates of unemployment worldwide when compared to individuals with other disabilities or those without a disability (Baldwin et al. 2014; Eaves and Ho 2008; Holwerda et al. 2012; Howlin et al. 2004; Roux et al. 2015; Shattuck et al. 2012; for a recent review of the literature, see Hedley et al. 2016). In Australia, employment participation rates for people with disabilities (52.8% in 2012) are well below the OECD average suggesting there is much scope for improvement by moving towards international best practice (Australian Bureau of Statistics 2014; OECD 2009). For Australians with autism, employment participation rates are even lower (42% in 2012; Australian Bureau of Statistics 2014). The economic costs of not moving to best practice employment interventions, particularly for people with autism, are significant, even for interventions that target relatively small numbers of individuals. For example, data analysed by PricewaterhouseCoopers for the Dandelion Program (described below), an employment intervention for adults with autism, indicated that if 101 individuals could maintain a 20-year career from this type of intervention, the total benefits are in the order of AUD$167 million for government, and around AUD$425 million in additional gross domestic product (GDP; PricewaterhouseCoopers 2015).

---

[1] Some advocates prefer the term 'autistic'. However, and consistent with the Disability Rights Movement, we retain the use of person-first language (Snow 2010). The term 'disorder' may also be construed as disabling. We thus use the term 'person with autism' when referring to people who identify as autistic, along with those who have a diagnosis of an autism spectrum disorder or diagnosis that predates DSM-5 criteria (e.g., Autistic Disorder, Asperger's Disorder/Syndrome).

If employment intervention can be scaled up, the total benefits to society are truly significant as the benefits of employment go far beyond a simple GDP estimation. The Survey of Disability, Ageing and Carers estimated that in 2012 around 114,400 people with autism were living in Australia (Australian Bureau of Statistics 2013). Given the positive contribution of meaningful employment to mental and physical health (Feather and O'Brien 1986; Linn et al. 1985), increasing rates of employment in individuals with autism and other disability groups are likely to impact not only the individual and the family unit, but also the society by way of net economic gains resulting from, amongst other things, reduced costs of health care.

A significant portion of individuals with autism have co-morbid intellectual disability and are either non- or minimally verbal. Even individuals with autism who have average or high intelligence quotients (IQ) and are highly verbal (often referred to as high-functioning, although this term can be misleading as it also implies good adaptive skills, which is often not the case) present with specific social and communication atypicalities including an overly formal and pedantic manner of speaking, literal interpretation of language, flat, emotionless tone of voice, lack of gestures, as well as either lack of, or too intense and prolonged, eye contact. In addition to this, people with autism tend to have very strict and inflexible adherence to certain rules and routines, poorly developed theory of mind (the ability to attribute mental states to oneself and to others) and sometimes a lack of ability to interpret or understand other people's emotions and what is expected of them in particular situations and contexts.

Characteristics of the disorder, such as the ones just described, may contribute uniquely to the way people with autism perceive and experience work. For example, a strict sense of duty and a feeling that it is the 'right thing to do' may motivate individuals to seek employment. In the following transcript a young unemployed man with autism describes work as a 'duty to society' and a 'logical' consequence of being part of a society. For him, work is not about personal economic gain, in fact he describes being willing to work for less than the disability pension he receives from the government.

> "What is important isn't the money, it's giving something back to society that's important. I can get by on a little bit of money, I'm ok, that's not important. Without a job, I feel like I'm a drain on society... I feel like I'm not giving anything back, I feel it's my duty – it's the right thing to do... we have an understanding of how society works, even if we don't fit in. Logically we understand how it works, this is something we do understand, even if we don't understand people's emotions we do understand how society functions" (personal communication 2016).

While this young man seems to have 'worked out' what he should do, and in addition to receiving job-seeking support with a government funded employment agency, he has been unsuccessful in gaining suitable employment. This is despite his strong motivation and willingness to do so. It is likely that rejection and possibly not understanding the cause of this rejection will also have a significant psychological impact. This, in turn, may affect his motivation and ability to secure a job in the future. In the next section we provide a brief review of the current literature concerning adult outcomes, in particular regarding co-morbidities, education and employment, as well as social integration outcomes for adults with autism, as a way of illustrating some of the difficulties that people with autism face in their everyday lives.

Autism in Adulthood

Despite the fact that autism is a lifelong condition, the main focus of research till relatively recently has been on understanding, diagnosing and treating this disorder during early childhood, with research on autism during adolescence and adulthood being relatively neglected. Although outcomes in adulthood can be conceptualised and measured in different ways, regardless of the approach, it can be said that outcomes are poor. For example, several studies (as reviewed by Howlin et al. 2013) have used global indicators of outcomes ranging from very poor to good or very good. Results across different studies suggest that at least 50% of individuals have very poor or poor outcomes and that only 20% or less can be characterised as having good outcomes. Other studies have explored more specific outcomes, ranging from core autism traits to co-morbid symptoms, education and employment and social integration. Although reviewing the findings on the outcomes in terms of core autism traits and cognitive (IQ) outcomes is beyond the scope of this chapter (for systematic overviews please refer to Levy and Perry 2011; Magiati et al. 2014), it is important to note that, on the whole, core symptoms and IQ tend to either remain stable over time or slightly improve. However, significant individual variability is notable.

Co-morbidities

The presence of at least one, and usually multiple, co-morbid symptoms can be considered a rule rather than an exception in autism. Reported rates vary widely from study to study (e.g., ranging from 4 to 81%), but it is has been reported that almost all individuals with autism have, at some point in their life, experienced significant co-morbid symptoms, and the rates of co-morbid symptomatology in autism have been found to be significantly higher than amongst individuals with other neurodevelopmental or neuropsychiatric diagnoses (Eaves and Ho 2008; Hofvander et al. 2009; Lainhart 1999; Leyfer et al. 2006; Simonoff et al. 2008). Attention deficit hyperactivity disorder (ADHD) is one of the most commonly reported co-morbid diagnoses during early to mid-childhood and although it tends to be less prevalent during adulthood, prevalence is nevertheless quite substantial with, for example, Hofvander et al. (2009) reporting that 43% of their sample met the diagnostic criteria for ADHD. Other disorders such as obsessive compulsive disorder (OCD), schizophrenia and substance abuse are much less common. We provide below a more detailed overview of three of the most common problems in autism, not only in adulthood but throughout the lifespan. We focus on anxiety, depression and sleep problems due to the high prevalence of these conditions in autism, and also due to their potential to impact negatively on employment if not managed appropriately.

The presence of anxiety symptoms has been noted in individuals with autism ever since Leo Kanner and Hans Asperger first described this disorder seven decades ago. Individuals with autism are found to exhibit significantly higher presence of anxiety symptoms when compared to both typically developing (Bellini 2006; Gadow et al. 2005; Lopata et al. 2010) and individuals with other disorders, ranging from Down syndrome (Evans et al. 2005) and Williams syndrome (Rodgers et al. 2012) to conduct disorder (Green et al. 2000). Although reported rates of anxiety in autism vary widely (e.g., from 13 to 84%; van Steensel et al. 2011) the majority of studies suggest figures of 40 to 50% as the most realistic estimation. This has been confirmed by a systematic review that calculated that 39.6% of 2121 included individuals met criteria for clinically elevated levels of anxiety (van Steensel et al. 2011).

Sleep problems have been reported to be one of the most frequent problems in the general population with at least 30% suffering from poor sleep at some point in their lives (Roth 2007). It is not surprising that individuals with autism are also faced with a range of sleep problems. It is estimated that up to 80% of individuals with autism, regardless of age or IQ, have significant sleep disturbance, with insomnia being the most common sleep complaint (Baker and Richdale 2015; Richdale and Schreck 2009).

Individuals with autism have been found to be prone to depressive symptoms and episodes, especially during late adolescence and adulthood (Hedley and Young 2006; Whitehouse et al. 2009). Data from studies that have explored clinic-referred individuals with autism suggest that depression is the most prevalent co-morbid psychiatric disorder with a lifetime rate of 53% (Hofvander et al. 2009). In trying to understand what might contribute to increased rates of depression in young individuals with autism, Hedley and Young (2006) found that, from a relatively young age, feelings of difference from others were associated with elevated levels of depressive symptoms. A desire to fit in, while at the same time lacking the necessary social skills, may therefore be one of the factors that contributes to increased rates of depression in this group.

Despite their prevalence, the underlying factors and mechanisms leading to such high rates of co-morbid problems in individuals with autism are unclear. Consequently, many therapeutic choices that are currently available are of limited efficacy and, in cases where psychopharmacological agents are used, with sometimes significant side effects. This is particularly concerning as anxiety, depression and sleep problems have a pronounced negative impact on individuals with autism, sometimes even more so than core traits, significantly limiting their ability to function independently and lead a fulfilling life. For example, sleep disturbances in autism have been found to be associated with behaviour difficulties, internalising and externalising behaviours, and poorer cognitive function (Richdale and Schreck 2009). A particularly worrying consequence of anxiety and depression in this population is the potential risk of suicide, especially if we consider the finding from the general population that of people who attempt or commit suicide, 90% suffer from clinically significant depression (Baraclough et al. 1974). Only a few studies have explored the presence of suicidal ideation and rates of suicide attempts in individuals with autism. Although, with an exception of a relatively recent study by Cassidy et al. (2014), other studies have been limited by small participant numbers (Mayes et al. 2013; Raja et al. 2011; Storch et al. 2013), it seems clear that at least 30% of individuals with autism have experienced suicidal ideation and attempted suicide at some point during their life. This fact makes the task of understanding and treating co-morbid symptoms in this population even more important and urgent.

In summary, individuals with autism experience a number of co-morbid symptoms and disorders, with anxiety, sleep problems and depression being the most prevalent, and these problems cause significant additional impairments in this population, and most importantly increase risk for suicide, which is significantly higher in individuals with autism compared to other clinical groups (apart from depression).

Educational, Employment and Social Integration Outcomes

Both educational and employment outcomes in adults with autism have been found to be poor. At least 50% of young people with autism leave school without any qualifications and less than 40% attend post-secondary education, with even lower percentages completing their degree (Levy and Perry 2011; Shattuck et al. 2012). As noted earlier, it is particularly discouraging, for both these young people and their families, but also for the wider society, that even after individuals with autism obtain degrees which should allow them to be competitive in gaining employment, less than half are likely to secure employment (Baldwin et al. 2014; Eaves and Ho 2008; Holwerda et al. 2012; Howlin et al. 2004; Roux et al. 2015; Shattuck et al. 2012). Even in cases where employment has been secured, the meaningfulness of employment is questionable as, in a majority of cases, these individuals tend to work in low paid jobs that are often well below their qualification level – it should come as no surprise that job retention rates are also low (Henninger and Taylor 2013; Shattuck et al. 2012).

Finally, at least 60% of individuals with autism continue to live with their parents, with minimal active societal participation (Levy and Perry 2011). A majority of people with autism report feelings of loneliness, isolation, and very few have active and sustained friendships or social supports beyond the immediate family, with only 5 to 10% being in a long-term romantic relationship (Eaves and Ho 2008; Howlin et al. 2004; Jobe and White 2007; Mazurek 2014; Orsmond et al. 2004).

In summary, both quantitative and qualitative research studies highlight poor outcomes for people with autism when they reach adulthood. In the following sections we will extend these findings by providing narratives from individuals affected by autism. We also describe an example of an employment program that supports people with autism in finding a place in the workforce and indirectly, in enriching and bringing meaning into their lives and the lives of their families.

Case Example: MH

The following case study provides a description of the life of MH who, despite significant expression of autism which affects his ability to live independently, lives a meaningful and fulfilling life. He is actively engaged in his community, is involved in many recreational activities, is an avid follower of the Collingwood Australian Rules football club, and is an established artist. The following case study was developed in conjunction with MH's mother.

MH was born in Melbourne, Australia, in 1979. He is 37 years old and was diagnosed with autism when aged four. He required extra help in his education and still needs assistance in the everyday things most others take for granted. MH lives semi-independently in a self-contained bungalow in the family backyard. He is dependent on his family to facilitate his social and recreational life, provide emotional support and help with basic needs like shopping and banking. It has been a long journey for him to reach the skills and standards that have seen his artwork exhibited in many galleries and in private and corporate collections around Australia, but MH's creativity has shone through and his work and dedication to his art have led to acclaim and financial gain.

MH attended schools with specialised programs for children with autism, supplemented with integration in both local primary and secondary schools. MH's mother says that she only realised that MH was interested in art after he left school and 'can't remember much of his early work'. During his teenage years MH held various jobs including working in a supermarket, a nursery, gardening and doing odd jobs until, at 20, he was offered to attend a community art program for individuals with disabilities. The artist in residence encouraged MH to continue with his art and, according to his mother, MH 'has never looked back'. MH was urged to take a painting class at a community college. He continued with life drawing which helped develop his style.

MH works in supported employment as a ceramics worker and also attends a supported art program. His mother describes him as very capable with household chores and he uses public transport effectively to navigate the city. His independence is enhanced by his mobile phone. Although he does not make phone calls to people outside the family he lets them know where he is or if he will be late for a pre-arranged appointment. Like many individuals with autism, MH can experience significant levels of anxiety when routines are disrupted or when there are unexpected changes. Because of their awareness of these triggers, MH's family aim to plan ahead and provide plenty of notice of forthcoming changes. Nonetheless, there are times when prior warning is impossible. In these instances, the mobile phone has proved indispensable in managing his anxiety and behaviour. MH leads a full life and is active in athletics and ten-pin bowling with Special Olympics, railway excursions, bushwalking, movies and music. He is a keen environmentalist and recycler and is passionate about sharks and marine life, which often figure in his paintings. MH is aware of his autism but identifies as 'artistic' more than 'autistic'.

MH works in an art studio run by a not-for-profit business that also promotes his work. The studio provides a supportive environment for MH. On other days MH travels independently by public transport to a ceramics workshop which supports over 20 artists. MH has developed his own line of ceramic bowls and platters with a theme of Australian flora and fauna, and marine creatures. A former support worker noted that (his) 'attention to detail is outstanding - he surprises us with his constant improvements and his eagerness to try new subject matter... his eye for detail is exceptional, he loves to put birds in amongst foliage. No two works are the same'.

MH's activities and varied interests add to his sense of self-worth and enjoyment of life. In spite of his symptoms, MH has found meaningfulness through a combination of his own determination and abilities, the support of committed family members and the support of his community and the services available to him.

Case Example: Dandelion Employment Program

Dandelion is the name given to a supported work program designed to provide individuals with autism employment in Science, Technology, Engineering and Math (STEM) occupations, and a pathway to competitive employment (Austin and Sonne 2014; Austin et al. 2008). Individuals are employed at competitive rates of pay, and are also provided with significant workplace supports, particularly in the first year of the program. The program is driven largely by the principle that, along with being a disability where individuals have specific needs and often benefit from supports, autism also represents a difference that needs to be acknowledged and embraced and individuals can make significant contributions to a society that values diversity (Austin et al. 2008).

The Australian implementation of Dandelion is a collaboration between a Danish company Specialisterne, the information technology company Hewlett Packard Enterprise and the Australian Government Department of Human Services. The program was launched in 2015 and had been in operation for just over a year at the time of writing. Specialisterne's founder, Thorkil Sonne, provides the following analogy regarding the origin of the term 'Dandelion':

> A Dandelion is seen as a weed if in an unwanted place. But if you take that plant to a wanted place you'll see it as an herb and as one of the most valuable plants in nature. That's what we're doing. We're putting people in places where they are welcomed and where they can excel.

Specialisterne is part of a growing movement that aims to acknowledge the strengths of many individuals with autism, such as an attention to detail, and their potential match for jobs that, for example, require good focus (Austin and Sonne 2014; Austin et al. 2008). Specialisterne operates worldwide to assess and train individuals with autism to meet the requirements of business customers. The company also contracts out individuals with autism who provide information technology-based services. In Australia the business model is unique. Applicants participate in a 4-week assessment conducted by Specialisterne following an initial screening process. Those who successfully complete the assessment and who are considered to have the necessary skills for the positions are offered employment with Hewlett Packard Enterprise. Employees start a 3-year training program (which requires successful completion of a 6-month probationary period). Positions are initially part-time with opportunities to increase to full-time depending on progress. Individuals operate in teams that are contracted out to the Department of Human Services. Job tasks include software test analysis, data analytics and monitoring and automation. While individuals do not require experience or education in information technology or STEM fields to apply, a background or interest in computing (e.g., programming, hardware, and development) is advantageous. Candidates' employment history and curriculum vitae only play a minor role in selection. Instead, candidates are assessed under a variety of conditions that simulate the work environment during the 4-week assessment. Skills assessed include social skills, ability to work within a team and job-specific skills.

In the workplace each group is provided with a support team (please refer to Fig. 19.1) consisting of a full-time consultant with experience working with individuals with autism who mentors and provides supports such as one-to-one counselling, a manager who oversees the workload and training, and experienced co-workers who are able to provide support and job-based training. Support can also extend to include adaptive skills, such as nutrition, navigation of public transport, and budget management. To encourage acceptance of the teams in the workplace, co-workers

Fig. 19.1 Example support model provided to the Dandelion teams

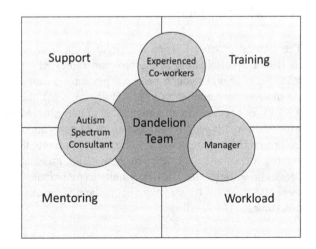

participate in an autism awareness session and managers who work directly with the individuals participate in diversity training. Hewlett Packard Enterprise report a positive effect of the program on the company:

> We're very grateful to the Dandelion program for broadening our perspective. We've been thrilled to play a part in demonstrating the value for employers and giving these talented people the opportunities they deserve. (M. Fieldhouse, Director, Emerging Businesses & Federal Government, Hewlett Packard Enterprise).

At the time of writing, 37 individuals had participated in the program. Twenty-two were full-time employees and 14 were in the probation period. One individual was not retained following probation, suggesting a preliminary retention rate of 97%. While this is encouraging, an appreciation of the psychosocial impact of the program on individuals and their family members is required. Furthermore, although Hewlett Packard Enterprise offer some assistance (e.g., job-seeking counselling) to those individuals who apply but are unsuccessful in their job applications, it is not clear what the impact on individuals who apply but are rejected, or who complete the 4-week assessment period but are then not successful in gaining a position, is.

The program is an example of a private and government collaboration that provides employment opportunities to select individuals who are able to complete specific job tasks that, in turn, can provide a revenue resource which offsets some of the extra costs. For those willing to provide the necessary support and training, to modify the work environment, and to challenge the perceptions of managers and co-workers who may not be familiar with working alongside individuals with an autism, both the direct (e.g., different perspectives to the job task brought by the individuals themselves) and indirect (e.g., improving management styles which benefit the organisation more broadly) benefits can offset costs and make significant contributions to the business (Austin and Sonne 2014).

Economic Benefit of Increasing Employment Through Intervention

The figures produced from the small sample Dandelion trial are compelling. Individuals participating in the program represent a range of attributes similar in many ways to other young people. They have a range of educational backgrounds (from secondary education to university degrees), they also have a range of prior work experience; predominantly casual or part time. Most are living with family. As with other young people there is a range of goals and objectives for participating in the program. Their personal needs are also similar to that of the broader population: earning a regular salary, learning new skills, meeting people, and building confidence and self-esteem. The opportunity to participate in work that can lead to a real career is important for all young people and represents an important and significant milestone.

The key results from Dandelion provide a window into the long-term economic costs and benefits at stake for this group of people if action is not taken to maximise their opportunities to participate in meaningful employment. The value of these types of interventions is broad: benefits to the individual and their extended support networks, benefits to the community and benefits to society in the form of contributing to tax bases, higher productivity and ultimately higher national income and GDP. Looking at the direct benefit, the most important change is the switch from welfare dependency to employment. PricewaterhouseCoopers estimate that the net benefit from a successful intervention in Dandelion (assuming a move from welfare dependence to work) can be expected to generate a net benefit to the individual of just under AUD$29,000 per annum, while the net benefit to the government was estimated to be just over AUD$26,000 per annum (PricewaterhouseCoopers 2015). This is considered an underestimate of the total benefit as it does not consider the benefit to carers (e.g., Deloitte Access Economics has estimated the benefit of home carers being able to pick up extra hours of work; Economics 2015); the reduced cost of medical and other health interventions associated with employment is also an important consideration. Lower rates of general practitioner (GP) visits or other medical visits, and generally better health outcomes have been proven to reduce the likelihood of co-morbidities. Over a lifetime these can represent significant savings for the health system, greatly reducing the burden of disease on both the individual and the cost borne by the broader society. There are also contributions to the community to be considered, for example, through other forms of engagement (e.g., through additional volunteer work as participants become fully functioning members of their local communities and seek to assist others). All of these outcomes need to be considered and fully costed to accurately capture the true benefit of a career for the individual, society and the economy. PricewaterhouseCoopers estimated the broader economic and fiscal impacts of the program grossed up for 101 participants attaining average career length of 20 years (PricewaterhouseCoopers 2015). In this analysis, indicated total benefits are in the order of AUD$167 million for government, and around AUD$425 million in economic benefits creating additional GDP over the 20 years. As is outlined in the case studies here, creating career opportunities for individuals with specialised skills, as is evident in some adults with autism, is generating a win-win-win compact that generates significant value. A win for the individual and their carer support network, a win for employers, and a win for the economy and government in terms of lower health costs and greater income.

Case Example: RT

This next case study was provided by RT who was asked to write about the personal impact participation in the Dandelion program had on him, and on his family. RT's story is presented here to highlight the challenges in finding meaningful employment experienced by an otherwise independent and, in many other ways, accomplished young man. Although RT had made significant achievements in his academic and personal life, and despite being well qualified for work in his chosen occupation, he faced incredible difficulties finding employment; evidenced by a history of unemployment or jobs well below his level of education. At the time of writing RT had been employed for over 15 months in Dandelion and had developed exceptional leadership skills in the workplace.

RT received a Bachelor of Engineering with Honours at one of Australia's most prestigious universities, but nevertheless struggled to find work, even following his graduation. He received a diagnosis of Asperger's syndrome when he was in middle school. Since finishing his studies he worked in several jobs, including a full-time position as a salesperson. However, he found it difficult to engage with customers and thus experienced great difficulty selling products. As a result, RT found it a challenge to make a living and relied largely on government payments to survive. After applying for a position with Dandelion, RT reported being 'ecstatic' when he discovered that he had been accepted into the 4-week training and assessment program. For him, the process removed the stress of a traditional interview and provided 'an excellent environment (for me) to learn about the job, develop new skills related to software testing and show the abilities (I) already had'. RT not only met and became friends with others who shared his gifts, but who also shared the challenges that he experienced. Following over a year's employment as a system test analyst, RT has made new friends with his work colleagues and no longer relies on government payments. He and his wife have also moved into better housing and have some certainty about their future. RT looks forward to learning about other roles in the information technology sector and further developing his skills.

While it seems inconceivable that someone with RT's skills and education would be effectively unable to achieve appropriate employment, his lived experience proved otherwise and, at best, his employment options were restricted to jobs that were poorly matched to his strengths and were well below his qualification level. This resulted in him functioning poorly, earning significantly less than others with similar qualifications and being (unwillingly) overly reliant on the welfare system. When provided an opportunity to work in a more suitable environment, RT is able to contribute to society, the economy and support his family. Although not specifically identified in his narrative, it seems reasonable to speculate that (and consistent with research findings; c.f., Feather and O'Brien 1986; Linn et al. 1985) in addition to improved quality of life, appropriate and meaningful employment would be likely to have a positive impact on his psychological health and wellbeing.

Case Example: CM

Next, we provide the story of CM as narrated by his mother. Like RT, CM is currently employed with Dandelion. His mother relates the significant challenges faced by CM growing up, and how his involvement with the program has provided him with his first opportunity to engage in the workforce. This last case study provides a different perspective to those above yet the message remains clear – there are many broad benefits of employment but many individuals with autism face overwhelming barriers getting there.

CM was diagnosed at 9 years of age with Asperger syndrome and a severe behaviour disorder. He is now 26 years old. He struggled throughout his school years, finding it difficult to cope with the confusion and noise within the school environment. Similarly, his teachers had difficulty accommodating his learning style which differed from that of other children. Nonetheless, CM attended school every day as his parents believed social engagement was important for his development. His attendance at school varied from a few minutes to a couple of hours a day from year two until he completed year 12 of high school. His parents encouraged learning at home and also promoted social engagement by introducing him to the 'Warhammer' gaming community. CM found it difficult to make friends – his mother recalls only two friendships throughout this period of his life.

CM has suffered from depression most of his life. When he completed college, he undertook a year of university studies. While he was successful in his studies he found the university environment overwhelming and he experienced a lack of appropriate support services. As a recipient of a disability pension, CM was not required to seek work, but he persevered for three years searching for work through job placement companies who cater to individuals with disabilities. He applied for jobs several times a week but was only successful in one interview, and eventually the support agencies discontinued support due to lack of a successful outcome. This rejection led to CM retreating from society and becoming a recluse for several years. His hygiene was very poor and his appearance degraded substantially. He began to engage in self-harm and would regularly cut himself, particularly his feet. He became suicidal and was committed to a hospital mental health unit on several occasions.

Following one of his stays in the mental health unit, CM's brother encouraged him to study to become an electrician. To achieve the fitness level required of the job and despite not having ridden a pushbike previously, he began cycling three hours a day. He became fit and gained his electrical certificate but was then unable to secure an apprenticeship. This led to another bout of depression. It was at this point that CM was invited to apply for a position with Dandelion through a local autism support organisation. According to his mother his symptoms of depression reduced and his attitude and appearance improved significantly. CM also began to participate in social activities including cycling to gaming events and volunteering to set up local matches. At work he pays close attention to his appearance, his work hours and behaviour. He is more confident, for example, he is no longer intimidated when required to provide verbal reports. While CM remains somewhat removed from his colleagues at work and tends to talk about his own interests, he has already established one friendship at work.

For the first time CM has a real opportunity to develop a career. He is motivated and determined to succeed. He has immersed himself in learning and is developing solutions to problems he identifies in work systems. He has received positive feedback at work which motivates him further. CM's mother describes her son as being 'a highly intelligent person with a deep and broad range of knowledge, an inquisitive mind, a logical approach and a lot to offer'. She no longer sees his future as limited and is encouraged when he applies himself and strives to achieve his goals. Most of all, meaningful, appropriate employment has given CM control over his own destiny: 'the empowerment of my son was all achieved through this inclusive program of work that brings hope where there was none'.

Summary

In this chapter we have provided evidence from both quantitative and qualitative research, and from subjective, lived experience accounts, that all strongly show significant difficulties and struggles that people with autism and their families face in their everyday lives. These struggles are partly a consequence of the condition itself, but also a consequence of the lack of understanding and support from society and employers. However, vivid and eloquent accounts from individuals with autism and their families also show that, with proper support and understanding, their lives can be indeed active, meaningful and rewarding. We have also shown that building understanding with employers and working closely with government can not only lead to greater employment opportunities for individuals with autism (and also other disabilities or mental and physical health conditions) but can greatly enhance outcomes for families, society and also the economy. Moreover, and consistent with the theme of this book, our intention was not only to provide evidence of the importance and relevance of inclusive practice (and the personal and economic cost of not being inclusive), but also to provide stories from individuals who *have* successfully traversed the challenges posed by a society not adept at enabling success in those perceived as somehow 'different' or 'less able'. Inclusion of people with disabilities in all facets of society demands innovation, not only in terms of practical supports, services, and politics, but also in terms of social perception and bias.

Acknowledgements We acknowledge the intellectual contribution of Professor Cheryl Dissanayake, Associate Professor Amanda Richdale, Professor Timothy Bartram, Dr. Simon Moss and Dr. Jenifer Spoor to the ideas and themes presented here, and thank the many individuals at Hewlett Packard Enterprise and the Department of Human Services who have also contributed to our research endeavours and attempts to document the Dandelion process. We would like to especially thank the contributors to the case studies presented in this chapter for so freely sharing their very personal stories.

Funding Sources Dr. Hedley is funded by Hewlett Packard Enterprise and the Australian Government Department of Human Services. Dr. Uljarević is funded by an Autism CRC Postdoctoral Research Fellowship.

References

American Psychiatric Association. (2013). *Diagnostic and statistical manual of mental disorders* (5th ed.). Washington, DC: American Psychiatric Publishing.

Austin, R. D., & Sonne, T. (2014). The dandelion principle: Redesigning work for the innovation economy. *MIT Sloan Management Review, 55*, 67–72.

Austin, R. D., Wareham, J., & Busquets, J. (2008). *Specialisterne: Sense and details*. Boston: Harvard Business School.

Australian Bureau of Statistics. (2013). *4430.0 - Disability, ageing and carers*. Australia: Summary of Findings, 2012 [Press release]. Retrieved from http://www.abs.gov.au/ausstats/abs@.nsf/lookup/A813E50F4C45A338CA257C21000E4F36?opendocument

Australian Bureau of Statistics. (2014). *4428.0: Autism in Australia, 2012* [Press release]. Retrieved from http://www.abs.gov.au/ausstats/abs@.nsf/Latestproducts/4428.0Main%20Features62012?opendocument&tabname=Summary&prodno=4428.0&issue=2012&num=&view

Baker, E. K., & Richdale, A. L. (2015). Sleep patterns in adults with a diagnosis of high-functioning autism spectrum disorder. *Sleep, 38*, 1765–1774.

Baldwin, S., Costley, D., & Warren, A. (2014). Employment activities and experiences of adults with high-functioning autism and Asperger's disorder. *Journal of Autism and Developmental Disorders, 44*, 2440–2449.

Baraclough, B., Bunch, J., Nelson, B., & Sainsbury, P. (1974). A hundred cases of suicide: Clinicial aspects. *British Journal of Psychiatry, 125*, 355–373.

Bellini, S. (2006). The development of social anxiety in high functioning adolescents with autism spectrum disorders. *Focus on Autism and Other Developmental Disabilities, 2*, 138–145.

Bochner, A. P., & Ellis, C. S. (2006). Communication as autoethnography. In G. J. Shepherd, J. S. John, & T. Striphas (Eds.), *Communication as...: Perspectives on theory* (pp. 110–122). Thousand Oaks: Sage.

Cassidy, S., Bradley, P., Robinson, J., Allison, C., McHugh, M., & Baron-Cohen, S. (2014). Suicidal ideation and suicide plans or attempts in adults with Asperger's syndrome attending a specialist diagnostic clinic: A clinical cohort study. *Lancet Psychiatry, 1*, 142–147.

Eaves, L. C., & Ho, H. H. (2008). Young adult outcome of autism spectrum disorders. *Journal of Autism and Developmental Disorders, 38*, 739–747.

Economics, D. A. (2015). *The economic value of informal care in Australia in 2015*. Australia: Deloitte Access Economics, Carers Australia.

Evans, D. W., Canavera, K., Klinepeter, F. L., Taga, K., & Maccubbin, E. (2005). The fears, phobias and anxieties of children with autism spectrum disorders and Down syndrome: Comparisons with developmentally and chronologically age matched children. *Child Psychiatry and Human Development, 36*, 3–26.

Feather, N. T., & O'Brien, G. E. (1986). A longitudinal study of the effects of employment and unemployment on school-leavers. *Journal of Occupational Psychology, 59*, 121–144.

Gadow, K. D., DeVincent, C. J., Pomeroy, J., & Azizian, A. (2005). Comparison of DSM-IV symptoms in elementary school-age children with PDD versus clinic and community samples. *Autism, 9*, 392–415.

Green, J., Gilchrist, A., & Cox, A. (2000). Social and psychiatric functioning in adolescents with Asperger syndrome compared with conduct disorder. *Journal of Autism and Developmental Disorders, 30*, 279–293.

Hedley, D., & Young, R. (2006). Social comparison processes and depressive symptoms in children and adolescents with Asperger syndrome. *Autism, 10*, 137–151.

Hedley, D., Uljarević, M., Cameron, L., Halder, S., Richdale, A., Dissanayake, C. (2016). Employment programs and interventions targeting adults with autism spectrum disorder: A systematic review of the literature. *Autism. Advance online publication.* doi:10.1177/1362361316661855

Henninger, N. A., & Taylor, J. L. (2013). Outcomes in adults with autism spectrum disorders: A historical perspective. *Autism, 17*, 103–116.

Hofvander, B., Delorme, R., Chaste, P., Nydén, A., Wentz, E., Ståhlberg, O., et al. (2009). Psychiatric and psychosocial problems in adults with normal-intelligence autism spectrum disorders. *BMC Psychiatry, 9*, 1–9.

Holwerda, A., van der Klink, J. J. L., Groothoff, J. W., & Brouwer, S. (2012). Predictors for work participation in individuals with an autism spectrum disorder: A systematic review. *Journal of Occupational Rehabilitation, 22*, 333–352.

Howlin, P., Goode, S., Hutton, J., & Rutter, M. (2004). Adult outcome for children with autism. *Journal of Child Psychology and Psychiatry, and Allied Disciplines, 45*, 212–229.

Howlin, P., Moss, P., Savage, S., & Rutter, M. (2013). Social outcomes in mid- to later adulthood among individuals diagnosed with autism and average nonverbal IQ as children. *Journal of the American Academy of Child and Adolescent Psychiatry, 52*, 572–581.

Jobe, L. E., & White, S. W. (2007). Loneliness, social relationships, and a broader autism phenotype in college students. *Personality and Individual Differences, 42*, 1479–1489.

Lainhart, J. E. (1999). Psychiatric problems in individuals with autism, their parents and siblings. *International Review of Psychiatry, 11*, 278–298.

Levy, A., & Perry, A. (2011). Outcomes in adolescents and adults with autism: A review of the literature. *Research in Autism Spectrum Disorders, 5*, 1271–1282.

Leyfer, O. T., Folstein, S. E., Bacalman, S., Davis, N. O., Dinh, E., Morgan, J., et al. (2006). Comorbid psychiatric disorders in children with autism: Interview development and rates of disorders. *Journal of Autism and Developmental Disorders, 36*, 849–861.

Linn, M. W., Sandifer, R., & Stein, S. (1985). Effects of unemployment on mental and physical health. *American Journal of Public Health, 75*, 502–506.

Lopata, C., Toomey, J. A., Fox, J. D., Volker, M. A., Chow, S. Y., Thomeer, M. L., et al. (2010). Anxiety and depression in children with HFASDs: Symptom levels and source differences. *Journal of Abnormal Child Psychology, 38*, 765–776.

Magiati, I., Tay, X. W., & Howlin, P. (2014). Cognitive, language, social and behavioural outcomes in adults with autism spectrum disorders: A systematic review of longitudinal follow-up studies in adulthood. *Clinical Psychology Review, 34*, 73–86.

Mayes, S. D., Gorman, A. A., Hillwig-Garcia, J., & Syed, E. (2013). Suicide ideation and attempts in children with autism. *Research in Autism Spectrum Disorders, 7*, 109–119.

Mazurek, M. O. (2014). Loneliness, friendship, and well-being in adults with autism spectrum disorders. *Autism, 18*, 223–232.

OECD. (2009). *Sickness, disability and work: Keeping on track in the economic downturn – Background paper.* Stockholm: Organisation for Economic Co-operation and Development, Directorate for Employment, Labour and Social Affairs.

Orsmond, G. I., Krauss, M. W., & Seltzer, M. M. (2004). Peer relationships and social and recreational activities among adolescents and adults with autism. *Journal of Autism and Developmental Disorders, 34*, 245–256.

PricewaterhouseCoopers. (2015). *Realising potential: Australian government corporate and NGO partnerships establish the dandelion program to deliver social and economic benefits for workers with autism Spectrum disorder and all Australians.* Australia: PricewaterhouseCoopers.

Raja, M., Azzoni, A., & Frustaci, A. (2011). Autism spectrum disorders and suicidality. *Clinical Practice and Epidemiology in Mental Health, 7*, 97–105.

Richdale, A. L., & Schreck, K. A. (2009). Sleep problems in autism spectrum disorders: Prevalence, nature, & possible biopsychosocial aetiologies. *Sleep Medicine Reviews, 13*, 403–411.

Rodgers, J., Riby, D. M., Janes, E., Connolly, B., & McConachie, H. (2012). Anxiety and repetitive behaviours in autism spectrum disorders and Williams syndrome: A cross-syndrome comparison. *Journal of Autism and Developmental Disorders, 42*, 175–180.

Roth, T. (2007). Insomnia: Definition, prevalence, etiology, and consequences. *Journal of Clinical Sleep Medicine, 3*, S7–S10.

Roux, A. M., Shattuck, P. T., Rast, J. E., Rava, J. A., & Anderson, K. A. (2015). *National Autism indicators report: Transition into young adulthood.* Philadelphia: Life Course Outcomes Research Program, A.J. Drexel Autism Institute, Drexel University.

Shattuck, P. T., Narendorf, S. C., Cooper, B., Sterzing, P. R., Wagner, M., & Taylor, J. L. (2012). Postsecondary education and employment among youth with an autism spectrum disorder. *Pediatrics, 129*, 1042–1049.

Simonoff, E., Pickles, A., Charman, T., Chandler, S., Loucas, T., & Baird, G. (2008). Psychiatric disorders in children with autism spectrum disorders: Prevalence, comorbidity, and associated factors in a population-derived sample. *Journal of the American Academy of Child and Adolescent Psychiatry, 47*, 921–929.

Snow, K. (2010). *To ensure inclusion, freedom, and respect for all, it's time to embrace people first language*. Retrieved June 1, 2016, from https://www.disabilityisnatural.com/pfl-articles.html

van Steensel, F. J., Bogels, S. M., & Perrin, S. (2011). Anxiety disorders in children and adolescents with autistic spectrum disorders: A meta-analysis. *Clinical Child and Family Psychology Review, 14*, 302–317.

Storch, E. A., Sulkowski, M. L., Nadeau, J., Lewin, A. B., Arnold, E. B., Mutch, P. J., et al. (2013). The phenomenology and clinical correlates of suicidal thoughts and behaviors in youth with autism spectrum disorders. *Journal of Autism and Developmental Disorders, 43*, 2450–2459.

Whitehouse, A. J., Durkin, K., Jaquet, E., & Ziatas, K. (2009). Friendship, loneliness and depression in adolescents with Asperger's syndrome. *Journal of Adolescents, 32*, 309–322.

Chapter 20
Legislation, Case Law and Current Issues in Inclusion for the United States, Australia and India

Mary Keeffe and Rittika Ghosh

Abstract This chapter examines the emergent legislative frameworks that protect the rights of people with disabilities and inform inclusive practices in schools. We explore the nature of disability discrimination legislation in the United States, Australia and India. Trends in how legislation is developed and reviewed indicate problems and processes in the governance of inclusion in schools. In general trends, the United States has articulated access and participation rights, but these rights are constantly contested in litigation. Australia has a broad definition of who may have a disability, but their appeal mechanisms are limited and costly, and long court cases interfere with the continuity of student learning. India has the context of a large population, poverty and a diverse range of needs for people with disabilities, so the focus in schools remains on access rather than the quality of the learning experience, and so compliance is not enforced. The hurdles for inclusive education, although unique to each country, are also globally consistent as issues of access, participation and pedagogical quality impinge on learning and the quality of life outcomes for all students with disabilities.

Introduction

Parent, civil rights, education and advocacy groups initiated a socio-political movement towards inclusive education in the 1960s by challenging education authorities to include students with disabilities in regular school settings. They argued from a 'rights-based platform' that reflected the ideals of equity and social justice expressed in a number of international statements, including the Universal Declaration of

M. Keeffe (✉)
Department of Education, La Trobe University, Melbourne, VIC, Australia
e-mail: m.keeffe@latrobe.edu.au

R. Ghosh
La Trobe University, Melbourne, Australia
e-mail: rittikaghosh@gmail.com

© Springer International Publishing AG 2017
S. Halder, L.C. Assaf (eds.), *Inclusion, Disability and Culture*, Inclusive Learning and Educational Equity 3, DOI 10.1007/978-3-319-55224-8_20

313

Human Rights (1948) and the United Nations Convention on the Rights of the Child (1972). It was not until legislative changes were made in the United States, however, that schools were required to educate students with disabilities alongside their non-disabled peers to the maximum extent possible. Since then, special education and the management of inclusion in schools have become public and accountable through the law, and the pace of litigation over issues that relate to inclusion, student rights, disability and discrimination significantly increased each year (Rioux 2013).

This chapter analyses and compares legislation and appeal processes that relate to disability discrimination and the management of inclusion in schools in common law countries including the United States, Australia and India. We take an historic perspective to show the progression of how case law has informed inclusive practices in schools and educational settings. Specific laws in the United States and the rights of appeal against administrative decisions and school actions that relate to inclusion are identified. Following this description, the Australian disability discrimination legislation is described and analysed through the interpretation of case law. In particular, the concepts of 'reasonable adjustment' and 'unjustifiable hardship' are discussed in relation to the way that principals manage inclusion in Australian schools. The chapter then moves to an explanation of how schools in India respond to their legal obligations to provide educational services for students with disabilities.

The description of the law and appeal processes used in the United States provides an international, contextual basis for both the analysis of the Australian legislation, particularly the *Disability Discrimination Act*, 1992 (Cth.), and the emergence of Indian rights and responsibilities. Australia's relatively low level of litigation in the area of special education belies the fact that the number of cases progressing to full court hearings is increasing and that the cases are becoming more complex. While the notion of treating a person with a disability less favourably is relatively consistent in the United States, in Australia and India, it is the unique interpretations in each context that inform service delivery. The single issue of communication impairment, for example, is complicated by numerous definitional, diagnostic and service parameters that differ in each country (McLeod et al. 2010). This chapter aims to track the history of some of those developments and interpretations so that we can step beyond rights and access and move towards responsive schools, effective policies and quality in educational service provision.

The authors of this chapter have worked in schools, higher education and organisations to advocate for the needs of students with disabilities in India and Australia. They recognise that legislative requirements are sometimes nebulous and that the terms of disability discrimination are difficult to argue in a court of law, yet disability discrimination legislation provides a framework of expectations that inform social values as well as policies and processes in the community, schools and organisations. To a great extent, this creates a reliance on case law to test the parameters of the obligations established so that clear and unambiguous policies may be developed by all education authorities and service providers.

Legislation, Case Law and Current Issues in Inclusion for Schools in the United States

A Review of the Legislation

In the United States, Section 504 of the Rehabilitation Act (1973), the Education of All Handicapped Children Act or EAHCA, PL 94-124 (1975), and the Individuals with Disabilities Education Act or IDEA (1990, 1991 and 1997) are the most important statutes that are used to challenge procedural issues or resolve claims of discrimination on the grounds of disability (Barton 2009). In this section, examples from case law are analysed to provide an historical perspective of the way the law has shaped educational decision-making towards full inclusion. Current, recurring legal issues identify specific areas of concern in the interpretation of the law. Consequently, the way the courts analyse and interpret these issues has a significant impact on the provision of educational services for students with disabilities in schools.

Parents have regularly used litigation to challenge and appeal decisions made about the provision of educational services for students with disabilities, and as a consequence, the parameters of inclusive education are clarified, defined and redefined as a result of decisions reached in the courts. In this way, comprehensive case histories have developed to set precedents in many aspects of the management of educational services for students with disabilities.

Although the landmark decision of Brown v. Board of Education (1954) did not relate to a case about disability, it established the right to access regular schools rather than segregated settings for students from racial minority groups. This case has been identified as important in initiating the relationship between education and the law, and it was in this case that Warren, then Chief Justice gave judicial recognition to the importance of equal access to education for all students. He claimed, 'in the field of public education, the doctrine of "separate but equal" has no place. Separate educational facilities are inherently unequal'.

The right to access education in regular school settings was not generally extended to students with disabilities, however, until the parents of children with an intellectual impairment from Pennsylvania successfully contested a class action against the state education authority. Known as the PARC[1] case (Pennsylvania Association for Retarded Children v. Pennsylvania, 1972) the parents convinced the court that their children were being undereducated in segregated settings and that their opportunities to succeed in learning and in society were, consequently, significantly reduced.

Section 504 of the Rehabilitation Act of 1973 followed quickly after the findings from the PARC case. Under this statute, discrimination against a person with a disability is prohibited in any programme or activity that receives federal financial

---

[1] The Pennsylvania Association for Retarded Children v. The Commonwealth of Pennsylvania 334 F. Supp.1257 (U.S. District Court, E.D. Pennsylvania 1972.

assistance (Section 104.1). The broad terms of the Act require education systems to protect and advocate for the needs of individuals with disabilities, proactively manage programmes and services by establishing a rationale and priorities for the provision of services, establish grievance procedures, and ensure that extra funds are available to promote discrimination-free services.[2] Similar provisions were introduced into the private sector through the Americans with Disabilities Act (A.D.A.) in 1990.

Two years after the *Rehabilitation Act* (1973) was passed, more comprehensive legislation that was specifically related to schools and inclusive education was introduced in *the Education for All Handicapped Children Act* (1975) *or PL 94-124*. In this legislation, two important principles were introduced that would have an impact on inclusive education throughout the world. The first principle of the least restrictive environment (LRE) states that students with disabilities should be educated beside their non-disabled peers to the maximum extent possible. The second principle insists that a free and appropriate education for all students (FAPE) should include special education and related services and be provided at public expense to meet the same standards as the state education agency. These principles were comprehensively debated in numerous court cases in the United States in the 1970s and 1980s.[3] Parents of students with disabilities and school or education authorities argued on the interpretations, expectations and legislative intentions of what constitutes the least restrictive environment (LRE) and what may be regarded as free or appropriate education (FAPE) for each student.

Contentions in case law also surround the definition of who has a disability. The *Rehabilitation Act* (1973) defines a handicapped person as any person who 'has a physical or mental impairment which substantially limits one or more major life activities'.[4] Major life activities are regarded as caring for one's self, performing manual tasks, walking, seeing, hearing, speaking, breathing, learning and working. Clearly, the more effectively a person is able to accommodate or compensate for a disability, the less will be the protection granted by the law.

This subjective interpretation of disability in the *Rehabilitation Act* (1973) does not extend to the IDEA legislation. There are now 14 categories of disability in the IDEA that rely on a diagnosis from a medical practitioner. The categories determine a student's right to access special education services, and they include autism, deaf-blindness, deafness, developmental delay, emotional disturbance, hearing impairment, intellectual disability, multiple disabilities, orthopaedic impairment, other health impairment, specific learning disability, speech or language impairment, traumatic brain injury and visual impairment. Unlike the rarely contested Australian Commonwealth definition of disability, Osborne (1999) claimed that questions

---

[2] Rehabilitation Act, 1973 # 794d (f).

[3] For example, Mills v. D.C. Board of Education 384 F. Supp. 866 (District Court of Colombia, 1972) and Honig, California Superintendent of Public Instruction, v. Doe 484 U.S. 305, 108 S. Ct.592, 98 L. Ed. 2d 686 (1988).

[4] Section 504, Rehabilitation Act of 1973. Subpart A. Reg. Sec.104.3 (j).

regularly emerge in the courts regarding the definition and subsequent eligibility for a student to receive special education services.

Eventually, the inclusive principles of the LRE and the FAPE were clarified, developed, expanded and incorporated into the renamed *Individuals with Disabilities Education Act* (IDEA) of 1990. The PL94-142 and IDEA have been regularly reviewed by Congress (1978, 1986, 1990 and 1997) to reflect interpretations from the courts. While there is still no single definition for what may be the 'least restrictive environment', several authors have determined processes that may inform school and parent/carer/student negotiations to make lawful decisions in this area. The IDEA legislation is now regarded as the most important statute that promotes inclusion and provides protection for students with disabilities in educational settings (Lipsky and Gartner 1997; Osborne 2000; Russo 2001).

Reauthorisations of the IDEA occurred in 1997 and 2004 and are currently under review to reflect recent case law interpretations. The aim of future reauthorisations has been to reduce acrimony between parents/carers and students and the school decision-making authorities. Areas that have been upgraded and those that have been subject to Congressional research for consideration in any future reauthorisations include:

1. Strengthening parental participation in the educational process by protecting the rights of parents through the implementation of procedural due process hearings or mediation services in all states;
2. Increasing the accountability for student participation and success in the general education curriculum through the mastery of individualised education plan (IEP) goals/objectives and the inclusion of the general education teacher in the IEP team;
3. Implementing a continuum of educational possibilities that will provide the most appropriate educational environment for students, particularly those with challenging behaviours.
4. Reducing the incidence of inappropriate use of restraints and seclusion
5. Due process in all decision-making
6. Expanded authority to local decision-making (school boards)
7. Teacher quality, professional development and career pathways

Clearly, the United States Congress regards the current issues of increased parental participation in educational processes, greater educational accountability in educational outcomes, behavioural management strategies for students with disabilities and qualified teachers as priorities for the reduction of discrimination against students with disabilities in educational settings. The IDEA sets out comprehensive, procedural steps to achieve each of these outcomes and provides financial incentives as the motivation to comply. Unlike the *Rehabilitation Act* (1973) where funding is withdrawn if compliance is not achieved, the IDEA ensures federal funding when the state can guarantee that all public schools comply with the procedures and requirements of the Act (McKinney and Mead 1996).

To increase parental participation in the educational process, for example, the IDEA requires that either mediation services or independent Due Process Hearing

Officers should be available in each state so that appeals against decisions made in the field of special education and inclusion may be negotiated through mediation or an independent appeals process rather than litigation. It is important to note that these measures were also introduced in an attempt to address educational issues promptly so that disruption to schooling for a student with a disability who is waiting for the outcome of a trial is minimised.

To promote the protection of students with disabilities who have challenging behaviours that are a manifestation of their disability, the IDEA specifies a range of requirements that include an assessment of the student's needs, a contextual analysis of the student's behaviour from the IEP team and the development of individualized behaviour management plans. Regulations for the suspension of a student are also clearly defined in what is now referred to as 'the ten day stay put rule'". Briefly, the student may be suspended for up to 10 days, an educational service must be provided for the student during the suspension and the student must be returned to the school of origin (Rutherford-Turnbull et al. 2001). Only in exceptional circumstances (usually involving drugs, guns and the safety of students and teachers) can the suspension be extended (to a maximum of 45 days) or the placement changed, and this requires a court hearing.

In summary, the requirements of the IDEA in the United States are specific and have been changed and modified to become more responsive to student, parent and school needs in a climate of rapid social and educational change. Broad issues that have emerged in a study of case law in the United States also recur in our analysis of Australian case law. Issues that relate to national predispositions of inclusion and exclusion (Slee 2010), the complex nature of disabilities (see McLeod et al. 2010), expanding definitions of disability to include young people with socio-emotional differences (Holt 2016), and the contentious notions of students with challenging behaviours and their exclusion from regular schools (Graham et al. 2010).

Legislation and Disability Discrimination Case Law in Australia

A Review of the Legislation

Unlike the United States, Australia does not have a Bill of Rights to establish fundamental human rights expectations for all citizens and from which legislation such as the IDEA is drawn. Consequently, before anti-discrimination legislation was introduced into state, territory and federal jurisdictions, Australian education authorities did not have any immediate or binding obligation for inclusive education. Instead, Australia's commitment to inclusion, at least theoretically, was formalized when Australia became a signatory to international conventions and conferences[5] that endorsed inclusive schooling for students with disabilities. Through these commitments, the United Nations called on the international community to recognise the importance of providing education for all children within the regular education system and encouraged countries such as Australia to adopt the principles of inclusive education as a matter of law or policy.

Australia relies entirely on the anti-discrimination statutes to eliminate disability discrimination by educational authorities, and inclusive education practices, though recommended, are left to the goodwill and expertise of the principal of the school or the teacher in the classroom. Innes (December 2000b) has claimed that 'complaints based on general non-discrimination provisions alone would not be sufficient to achieve widespread elimination of disability discrimination' (p3); however, other attempts to clarify or administer the legislation more effectively such as Disability Standards for Education (2005), Public Inquiries or Exemption Powers have not been successful to date.

Parents of students with a disability in Australia, therefore, have to rely on the long, expensive, stressful and at times unsuccessful conciliation, and personal complaint processes to redress a claim of discrimination (Flynn 1997). Teachers, schools and education authorities, on the other hand, have to rely on interpretations made from case law to clarify the expectations of the anti-discrimination provisions. Legislative requirements are analysed in this chapter to determine how discrimination may be reduced and inclusive practices promoted in schools. Finally, the benefits of a broad definition of disability are discussed, as are the limitations that broad interpretations of the objectives of the anti-discrimination acts have.

Disability Discrimination Legislation in Australia

The Commonwealth *Disability Discrimination Act* (DDA) of 1992 and the anti-discrimination legislation or equal opportunity legislation from each state and territory (except Tasmania) are the specific pieces of legislation that impact most significantly on the provision of discrimination-free educational services for students with disabilities in Australian schools.

Ramsay and Shorten (1996) describe three main areas in which the legislation prohibits discrimination in education:

- Admission of a student may include the refusal to accept an enrolment or negotiating differential terms upon which an applicant may be admitted
- Access to educational benefits may encompass such matters as subject offerings, attendance at school camps or excursions and course choices

---

[5] See, for example, the Universal Declaration of Human Rights, 1948; the United Nations Declaration on the Rights of Mentally Retarded Persons, 1972; the United Nations Convention of the Rights of the Child, 1989; the World Conference on Education for All, 1990; the United Nations Standard Rules for the Equalisation of Opportunities for Persons with Disabilities, 1993; and the Salamanca Statement, 1994.

- Expulsion or exclusion in which educational authorities are prohibited from expelling students on any of the grounds of a disability, even though these decisions are likely to arise out of a complex factual matrix.

Even though there are minor differences between the State, Territory and Commonwealth legislation, this chapter focuses on the Commonwealth *Disability Discrimination Act* or DDA (1992); however, reference is also made to the *Queensland Anti-Discrimination Act* or QADA (1991) in the analysis of the definition of disability as well as the discussion of case law.

A Broad Definition of Disability

For the purposes of the legislation, a person has a disability under the Commonwealth law (DDA) if there is:

- Total or partial loss of the person's bodily or mental functions
- Total or partial loss of a part of the body
- Presence of organisms causing disease or illness in the body
- Presence of organisms capable of causing disease or illness in the body
- A malfunction, malformation or disfigurement of a part of the person's body
- A disorder or malfunction that results in the person learning differently from a person without the disorder or malfunction
- A disorder, illness or disease that affects a person's thought processes, perception of reality, emotions or judgement or that results in disturbed behaviour
- Includes a disability that
- Presently exists
- Previously existed but no longer exists
- May exist in the future
- Is imputed to a person

In the above definition, the Commonwealth legislation makes provision for those students in schools, for example, who may have HIV/AIDS, social and emotional difficulties, brain injury, medical conditions or psychiatric illness and also students who 'learn differently'.

In Australia, the right to disclose or not to disclose if or when a student has a disability has featured in more tribunal hearings than any discussion from the definition of disability. Parents who choose not to disclose may be fearful of the possibilities that the student is rejected at enrolment or that disclosure may result in prejudice from the school through stereotypical behaviours or attitudes (Flynn 1997). There are currently no legal obligations for parents or students to disclose a disability; however, the Human Rights and Equal Opportunity Commission has identified the importance that disclosure has for the identification of educational needs, the planning of appropriate programmes and the provision of appropriate support services. Commissioner Innes, for example, has claimed that this was a shared responsibility, and schools had an obligation to collaborate with parents, medical, therapeutic, educational and behaviour experts for each student to get the information needed to develop sound educational programmes.[6] The process of identifying, assessing and addressing the educational needs of students with disabilities in schools has not been developed or formalized to the same extent as the IDEA in the United States, and this continues to remain a contentious area of concern for parents, students, education authorities, principals, guidance officers and teachers in Australian schools.

The Objectives of the Disability Discrimination Act (Cth.) (1992) and the Disability Standards for Education (2005)

The Objectives of the DDA Are Clearly Defined

1. To eliminate discrimination, as far as possible, against people with disabilities
2. To ensure, as far as practicable, that people with disabilities have the same rights to equality before the law as the rest of the community
3. To promote recognition and acceptance within the community of the principle that persons with disabilities have the same fundamental rights as the rest of the community

Disability discrimination statutes state that it is unlawful to directly or indirectly treat someone with a disability less favourably than a person without the disability would be treated in circumstances that are materially the same. In *Finney*,[7] for example, a school treated a young girl with spina bifida less favourably when they rejected her application for enrolment. The school admitted that they had discriminated against the student because of her disability, and they appealed to the Human Rights and Equal Opportunity Commission to make the discrimination lawful on the grounds of unjustifiable hardship. In another case,[8] a young boy was treated less favourably when he was suspended five times before being excluded from a school. The tribunal hearing found that a causal nexus existed between the student's disability and his behaviour and that he was, consequently, discriminated against because of his disability.

In some circumstances, positive discrimination may be needed for people with a disability to experience substantive equality or equality of opportunity. In schools for example, the provision of medical, therapeutic or technological support services and teacher aide assistance may be required before a student with a disability is able

---

[6] See Alex Purvis on behalf of Daniel Hoggan v. the State of New South Wales (Department of Education) 2000 [HREOC].

[7] Finney v. the Hills Grammar School [1999] HREOC (20 July 1999).

[8] See Alex Purvis on behalf of Daniel Hoggan v. the State of New South Wales (Department of Education) 2000 [HREOC].

to participate equally in an educational programme. These services are provided to minimise barriers to learning and to focus on student independence, learning and the achievement of educational goals. An example of ensuring that a student with a disability has equal access to educational experiences may include changing room allocations to ground level rooms for a student with a hip complaint who experiences difficulty when climbing stairs.[9]

The third objective identifies the important educational role that schools have not only for student learning and educational outcomes but also as role models in the community for discrimination-free behaviours and attitudes. Consequently, the Human Rights and Equal Opportunity Commission has a high regard for school compliance with the objectives of the *DDA* (1992), and this important community leadership role is considered when determining consequences for non-compliance. In *Finney*, for example, the hearing Commissioner found that the level of hardship that the school was expected to undergo by enrolling a child with a disability did not warrant a claim of unjustifiable hardship. In weighing up the benefit and detriment for all concerned in the case, the Commissioner found that the school personnel had based their decisions on flawed assumptions about the student's disability and the modifications she required. Moreover, he argued that the student and the entire school community would benefit significantly from her attendance at the school. It was held that Scarlett Finney and her parents were entitled to relief in the form of compensation for the discrimination that had been experienced.

Teachers are also inextricably linked to the role model responsibilities of schools, and stereotypical attitudes or behaviours identified in discrimination cases are not tolerated. In *Hoggan v. The State of New South Wales* for example, it was held that the education authority be fined $40,000 for the suspension and exclusion of a student with a disability. An important component of the decision in this case was that the principal and/or the education authority had failed to provide teachers with professional development or disability discrimination awareness programmes to reduce stereotypical assumptions made about the student. The findings in this case were eventually overturned in a High Court appeal.

In a comprehensive Australian study of 784 people and 30 key organizations, Flynn (1997) identified a complex and pervasive culture of direct disability discrimination in Australian schools. As a qualitative study, Flynn's research reveals a vivid portrayal of the manipulation involved in discrimination by schools, the frustration that parents and carers experience, and the ostracizing impact that discrimination has on the student with the disability. A report from the Disability Standards Task Force from the Department of Education, Training and Youth Affairs (2000) used discrimination reports, case law and conciliated settlements to identify enrolment, participation, curriculum development, student support services and harassment as major areas of consideration for the development of standards in education to reduce discrimination.

---

[9] See Mrs. J, on behalf of herself and AJ v. a School [1998] HREOC (23 March 1998).

Indirect Discrimination from Unfair Rules and Expectations

Indirect discrimination arises when rules, expectations, traditions, policies, admission criteria, practices or requirements are applied to everyone, but they have a disproportionate impact on a person with a disability and are not reasonable in the circumstances. Indirect discrimination is defined in Act[10] as a requirement or condition:

1. With which a substantially higher proportion of persons without the disability comply or are able to comply
2. Which is not reasonable with regards to the circumstances of the case
3. With which the aggrieved person does not or is not able to comply

In *Grahl*,[11] Commissioner Carter identified circumstances that resulted in indirect discrimination. Sian was born on 10 March 1991. She has a severe disabling physical condition known as spinal muscular atrophy, which is a degenerative neuromuscular genetic disorder. Sian experienced a rapid deterioration in her condition after she enrolled at the local primary school in February 1996. By the beginning of the next year, she could only sit for a maximum of 30 minutes in an upright position before requiring assistance; she was easily fatigued and had difficulty holding a pen or pencil. She does not have an intellectual disability. Eventually, Sian needed a wheelchair, and her mother would walk with her to school every day and access the school via a convenient side entrance. After storm damage to the access, the principal of the school decided to lock the gate to the side entrance. As a consequence Sian and her mother had to travel a longer distance to the front of the school to gain access. Commissioner Carter stated,

> I am satisfied that the gate closure and the denial of access was treatment of Sian which was less favourable than the treatment afforded able bodied children who had a variety of alternatives provided for them so that they could access the school.

In this situation, the school was not able to provide the evidence that the requirement or expectation that Sian and her mother should use the front gate of the school was not discriminatory because:

- A substantially higher proportion of the students without the disability were able to comply with the access requirements of going through the front gate
- It was not reasonable to require the extended journey when minor repairs to the driveway would have allowed continued access and for many reasons including safety, comfort and convenience. Sian and her mother habitually used this entrance
- The decision to close the gate was taken on account of Sian's disability

---

[10] Section 7, DDA, 1992.

[11] Marita Murphy and Burkhard Grahl on behalf of themselves and Sian Grahl v. the State of New South Wales (NSW Department of Education) and Wayne Houston (2000) HREOC (27 March 2000).

The Parameters of Reasonable Adjustments and Unjustifiable Hardship

A reasonable adjustment may include any appropriate action or decision that considers all the relevant factors of the situation. Factors that have been recommended for consideration in the Disability Standards for Education (p3) include:

- The effect of student' disabilities on their education or training
- The effectiveness of the actions or adjustments in achieving substantive equality for students with disabilities
- The impact of the appropriate actions or adjustments on other students and staff

Before an adjustment may be determined, a comprehensive analysis of the situation is necessary. This may involve obtaining information from those who are informed about the needs of the student including parents, carers and classroom teachers or from experts in the field such as doctors, specialists, psychologists, education advisors, and special education or behaviour management specialists. This is usually a collaborative process in which the parents and/or the student and the school identify barriers to learning, and the least intrusive adjustments that minimize these barriers are recommended.

A number of tribunal hearings relate to the different interpretations of what parents, schools and education authorities believe may or may not be a reasonable adjustment. Schools and education authorities regularly contest the value of what may be considered reasonable when parents' perspectives differ (Denman 2014). In *Finney*, for example, the hearing Commissioner admitted that the borders between a reasonable adjustment and an unjustifiable hardship were not clear and required a comprehensive process of weighing 'indeterminate and largely imponderable factors and making value judgements... which requires a balancing exercise between the benefits and detriment to all parties'. He continued to clarify the difference when he explained that the contextual analysis of the entire case was important rather than specific issues or discrepancies from different points of view.

In *Hoggan*, Commissioner Innes applied a test of reasonableness that was referred to in *Secretary Department of Foreign Affairs and Trade v. Styles* (1989). The test defined reasonableness as,

> ...less demanding than one of necessity, but more demanding than one of convenience... The criterion is an objective one which requires the court to weigh the nature and extent of the discriminatory effect on the one hand against the reasons advanced in favour of the requirement or condition on the other. All the circumstances of the case must be taken into account.

In this case, the nature of the discriminatory effect of excluding the student from the educational experience of attending school was more significant than the reasons given for requiring the student to comply with the expectations outlined in behaviour management plans. The extent of the discriminatory effect was also a significant consideration because the student was unable to return to the school and had effectively been denied his secondary years of schooling.

Currently, the unjustifiable hardship clause in the Australian Commonwealth legislation (DDA) only applies to enrolment. Section 22 (4) provides,

> This section does not render it unlawful to refuse or fail to accept a person's application for admission as a student at an educational institution where the person it admits as a student by the educational authority, would require services or facilities that are not required by students who do not have a disability and the provision of which would impose unjustifiable hardship on the educational authority.

This means that the unjustifiable hardship exemption clause cannot be applied if there is a significant deterioration in the student's condition or if a student becomes disabled after the enrolment had been accepted. In *Finney,* the school claimed that they would have to accommodate Scarlett's needs for the full 13 years of her possible attendance at the school and that this would include extensive renovations to the school buildings and pathways.

In summary, the school estimated that renovations to the school would exceed one million dollars, that the school fees would have to be increased for all students, that Scarlett required support for catheterisation that was currently unavailable at the school, that the curriculum would have to be changed, that alternative schools could accommodate her needs and that her attendance at the school was not in her best interests. The hearing Commissioner then considered the evidence provided by medical specialists who suggested that Scarlett's support needs were minimal. After an inspection of the school, the Commissioner found an unused toilet that would be suitable for Scarlett's requirements for catheterisation. In this case, a comprehensive amount of data was collected and analysed according to Section 11 of the DDA that states that all relevant circumstances of the particular case are to be taken into account including:

1. The nature of the benefit or detriment likely to accrue or be suffered by any persons concerned
2. The effect of the disability on a person concerned
3. The financial circumstances and the estimated amount of expenditure required to be made by the person claiming unjustifiable hardship
4. In the case of the provision of services or the making available of facilities, an action plan given to the Commission under Section 64

Commissioner Innes found that the estimations made by the school were fundamentally flawed because no professional or educational assessment had been carried out to specifically identify Scarlett's needs. He found that Scarlett, her parents, the teachers, other students and community in general would benefit from the inclusion of a student with spina bifida in the regular school. He analysed the debt and the economic structures of the school in conjunction with the proposed estimate for the cost of the renovations and found that the school had grossly exaggerated Scarlett's needs and that the school could afford the minimal changes required for the more realistic time estimation of 6 years. The application for exemption on the grounds of unjustifiable hardship was, consequently, rejected by the Human Rights and Equal Opportunity Commission and again on appeal by the Federal Court of Australia.

There are currently no clear guidelines that will ensure a baseline of consistency for parental expectations or for schools to feel confident about the decisions they make about adjustment that may or may not be reasonable. The process of negotiating adjustment may also be emotive, contentious and complex. At the very least, this will require a high level of communication skills from the principal, a comprehensive understanding of the principles of due process and a framework for decision-making that reflects the objectives of the legislation.[12] Unlike the government and education authorities from the United States, which have legislation for due process and mediation, there are currently no similar services, procedures or policies in Australian schools that ensure natural justice principles are followed and positive and productive communications are maintained.

In a report from the disability sector's response to the draft Disability Discrimination Standards for Education, the unjustifiable hardship clause is identified as a "core tool of discrimination" (p5). The Queensland submission from Parents of People with a Disability also claims that the clause legitimises discrimination. Their argument is that the claimant may be successful and prove a case where discrimination has occurred only to find that an appeal on the grounds of unjustifiable hardship may determine that the discriminatory practice is lawful.

In *Hoggan*, Commissioner Innes clarified the parameters of the unjustifiable hardship clause further when he suggested that it would be difficult for an education authority with a multi-million dollar budget to justify an exemption on the basis of unjustifiable hardship (p77). In all cases,[13] the educational experience for the student with a disability is highly valued and is the most important consideration in determining whether the costs of any adjustment is reasonable or whether it may cause unjustifiable hardship.

Litigation Trends and the Management of Inclusion in Australia

At this point in time, Australia has not experienced the same 'flood' of special education litigations that is prominent in the United Kingdom and the United States. A complex complaint-based appeal process, unwanted expense and publicity, the exemption clause of 'unjustifiable hardship', and the increased level of stress associated with lengthy court cases (Flynn 1997) are some of the factors that make

---

[12] "I" v. O'Rourke and Corinda State High School and Minister for Education for Queensland (2000) provides a good example of the complexity of this process.
[13] See, for example, Finney v. the Hills Grammar School [1999] HREOC (20 July 1999) and "P" v. the Director-General, Department of Education, Townsville. [1997] Queensland Anti-Discrimination Tribunal (13 March 1997).

Australia's historical trend of reduced litigation in special education unique amongst other common law countries.

Anti-Discrimination Commissions in each state and territory and the Human Rights and Equal Opportunity Commission at the Commonwealth level all rely on the personal complaints method of appeal. A comprehensive conciliation process is usually initiated after a student or a parent who feels that they have been discriminated against makes a formal complaint. The Commission is then obliged to collect a significant bulk of data so that interpretations may be lawful, decisive and fair. Consequently, it is not uncommon to have a time delay of 18 months to 2 years before a hearing may be determined. This causes extreme stress for both the parents and the school representatives, and disruptions in communications are not uncommon (Flynn 1997).

In an attempt to address the inadequacies of the complaint-based system used in Australia, Innes (December 2000a) has suggested that consideration must be given to faster resolutions if the objects of the Disability Discrimination Act are to be achieved. He raises the possibility of 'regulatory relief', in which the educational authority may be granted a specific amount of time to systematically address the issue of discrimination raised by a complaint. The education authority would remain accountable to the Human Rights and Equal Opportunity Commission while due processes may be formalized or educational programmes implemented that effectively reduce discrimination in schools.

The broadly inclusive statements included in the Education Acts in each state proactively promote the principles of inclusive education, but they do not translate easily into lawful and effective school management practices. Lindsay (1997) has claimed that there is a discrepancy between the inclusive ideals stated in the legislation and the level of commitment required for the lawful management of inclusion. This discrepancy creates a tension for principals who then have to rely heavily on good management practices rather than policy documents to prevent litigation. A limited knowledge of the law (Stewart and McCann 1999), inexperience as a principal (Stewart 1998), challenges from changing educational priorities such as educational accountability and competition for the educational dollar (Barton and Slee 1999; Parrish 2001; Pullin 1999), discriminatory attitudes and undervalued relationships with parents (Flynn 1997) are all factors that contribute to discriminatory practices and behaviours in schools and, consequently, litigation.

There is a growing body of evidence to suggest, however, that the Australian trend of minimal litigation is changing. Parents, students, teachers, political and advocacy groups have raised the awareness of discriminatory practices in schools, workplaces and the community. A spike in hearing applications in the 1999–2000 Annual Report for the Human Rights and Equal Opportunity Commission has levelled in 2015. There may be many reasons for this including a collaborative approach to problem solving or clearer policies and less discrimination in schools. Some researchers (see for example, Slee 2013; Cumming and Dickson 2012; Graham et al. 2010) would suggest that the reduction in case law has more to do with the acceptance in Australian society that exclusion is a reasonable adjustment, the unlikely chance that litigation will be successful, the expensive costs of litigation and the unfortunate length of time that a student may be excluded from school while a case is being heard. Clearly, the legislated need for principals to provide discrimination-free educational services and manage inclusion effectively is weak, and a soundly based pedagogical approach to inclusion may be more effective.

India and the Persons with Disabilities Act (1995)

A Review of the Legislation

India is a country steeped in a multitude of cultures and religions, which temper the beliefs and behaviours of its people. The predominant religious communities of India have so far held the belief that disability was a Karmic punishment for sins committed in the previous life of the child with disability or that of his mother, or that it was God's punishment, or that the individual with a disability was possessed by unfriendly spirits. These beliefs often led to the isolation, ostracism and abuse of those with disabilities.

It is within this context that legislation to guide inclusive practices in India has been developed and implemented with varying degrees of success. India at present has four different laws regarding people with disabilities: they are – the Mental Health Act of 1987, the Rehabilitation Council of India Act of 1992, the Persons with Disability Act of 1995, and the National Trust for Welfare of Persons with Autism, Cerebral Palsy, Mental Retardation, and Multiple Disabilities Act of 1999. This section will briefly examine how international programmes of action regarding people with disabilities influence the introduction of Indian legislation aimed at supporting those with disabilities and their families and how that legislation has emerged to meet complex social demands.

According to the 1948 United Nations Declaration of Human Rights, the rights of all people including those with disabilities were to be upheld around the world. Since the Human Rights Declaration was not legally binding, it has not been maintained in many parts of the world. As a result, people with disabilities and others less fortunate in society have experienced discrimination through neglect, ostracisation, and denial of basic human rights.

To begin efforts to improve the situation for those with disabilities and ensure their rights, the United Nations International Year of Disabled Persons was declared in 1981, followed by the World Programme of Action Concerning Disabled Persons in 1982. To ensure a workable timeframe within which actions decided in the World Programme of Action Concerning Disabled Persons could be implemented, the United Nations General Assembly proclaimed 1983–1992 the United Nations Decade of Disabled Persons.

The Mental Health Act of 1987 was originally meant for the protection of the general community from patients with mental illnesses who were considered 'dangerous' by isolating them. The Act addresses the need for a shift from custodial to community care of those people with mental illnesses as well as focus on the rights and welfare of those individuals with mental illnesses. The Act also ensures that individuals are not isolated in institutions without sufficient cause.

The Rehabilitation Council of India Act of 1992 constituted the Rehabilitation Council of India, which was responsible for the regulation of the training of professionals in the field of rehabilitation. The Council was also made responsible for the Central Rehabilitation Register and all other matters related to rehabilitation professions. At this stage in India, the focus on disability came from a medically based, curative, rehabilitation approach where people with disabilities could be 'fixed' and returned to the community. Neither the Mental Health Act nor the Rehabilitation Council of India Act was dedicated to the rights and treatment of people with disabilities and their families. The first such Act was the Persons with Disability Act (1995), which was as a result of programmes by The United Nation focusing on the rights and involvement of people with disabilities rather than the medically driven rehabilitative models used previously.

Following the United Nations Decade of Disabled Persons, the Economic and Social Commission for Asian and Pacific made a unique initiative in the December of 1992 to implement actions concerning people with disabilities in their own regions. They declared the Asian and Pacific Decade of Disabled Persons from 1993 to 2002. One of the achievements of the Asian and Pacific Decade of Disabled Persons was the Agenda for Action, a framework that laid out 12 key policy areas based on which Government and Non-Government organizations can develop policies and methods of implementation. As one of the signatories to the 'Proclamation on the Full Participation and Equality of the People with Disabilities in the Asian and Pacific Region' adopted in the beginning of the Asian and Pacific Decade of Disabled Persons, the Indian Government took a positive step by enacting the Persons with Disabilities (Equal Opportunities, Protection of Rights and Full Participation) Act in 1995.

The Persons with Disabilities (Equal Opportunities, Protection of Rights and Full Participation) Act of 1995 (reviewed in 2000), also known simply as the Persons with Disability Act (PWD), covers a number of important points regarding the support and rights of persons with disabilities. The Act begins by defining disability. The Act covers a number of disabilities, all of which are categorically defined, and they include blindness, low vision, leprosy-cured, hearing impairment, locomotor disability, mental retardation and mental illness. The Act goes on to call for the formation of two central committees (Governments) and two state committees (Local Authorities), that is, the central coordination committee and the central executive committee as well as the state coordination committee and the state executive committee. These committees are responsible for ensuring that the necessary changes in policy and programmes are made regarding people with disabilities. The executive committees are responsible for the implementation of the decisions made by the respective coordination committees.

The PWD requires the government to take steps to prevent and reduce cases of disability. Studies were undertaken to determine the risk factors that may lead to various disabilities, and steps were taken to protect children from contracting diseases and disabilities during the pre-natal to early childhood stages. Steps were also taken to ensure early intervention in all possible cases.

The Persons with Disability Act also specified provisions regarding education for those with disabilities. According to the Act, the government would provide free education for children with disabilities. The Act encourages the integration of children with disabilities into regular schools while also providing opportunity for the development of special education institutes where the specific needs of children with disabilities may be met. The Act requires children with disabilities to be provided a well-rounded education that includes basic academics as well as vocational training and provisions for non-formal education and school supplies when necessary. The PWD also includes policies for the training of teachers, especially for teaching children with disabilities and for the availability of aids for those with visual impairment.

As per the Persons with Disability Act, the government of India is responsible for making the buildings, parks and public spaces accessible for those with disabilities. This includes modifications such as construction of ramps, availability of elevators, inclusion of signs and buttons in braille, modified pathways and pavements, auditory signals and announcements, and various other modifications to make the general environment more accessible. Although guidelines were planned as to how government building codes could conform with the standards identified in the act, little progress has been made, and a lack of enforcement means that physical access to buildings and public spaces remains hypothetical for people with disabilities. Mehrotra (2011) claims the PWD emerged more from international pressure than from an informed commitment to respond to the complex needs of persons with disabilities in India.

The PWD also calls for the appointment of a Chief Commissioner who is responsible for hearing complaints regarding discrimination against those with disabilities and regarding the deprivation of their rights. The Act also makes the government economically responsible for individuals with disabilities who have no family support system and are unable to provide for themselves.

The PWD includes rules for obtaining a 'Certificate of Disability'. The certificate is issued by a medical board at the state or district level upon thorough examination of the individual applying for the certificate. If the individual is found to have 40% or more disability, he is issued a certificate of disability that allows him access to all the benefits provided by the Act. The Act also includes provisions regarding penalties for people who avail the benefits meant for those with disabilities while not having a disability themselves. In 1996, a number of amendments were made to the PWD regarding the definitions of disability, application for the Certificate of Disability, issue and refusal of the certificate, various rules concerning the Chief Commissioner and forms regarding the issue of disability certificates (Ministry of Social Justice and Empowerment, 2009).

Various amendments were made to encourage positive discrimination and give those with disabilities opportunities to be a contributing member of the community. Provisions were allowed to encourage private and public sectors to reserve a percentage of positions among their staff for those with disabilities. Amendments were made to ensure the people with disabilities had their rights upheld.

Further efforts were made to uphold the rights of those with disabilities through amendments made to other Acts such as the Transfer of Property Act, Contract Act of 1872, The Hindu Succession Act, Aircraft Act, Airport Authority of India Act, Right to Information Act, Special Marriage Act, Hindu Marriage Act, Muslim Dissolution of Marriage Act, Hindu Adoption and Maintenance Act, Indian Divorce Act, Right to Education Act and various other Acts.

The National Trust for the Welfare of Persons with Autism, Cerebral Palsy, Mental Retardation and Multiple Disabilities Act (1999) was set up to provide a national body for the welfare of individuals with disabilities. The Act aimed to enable and empower individuals with disabilities to live as independently as possible while participating in their community as much as possible. The Act provides support for individuals with disabilities living with family members including need-based support in times of crisis. The Act also provides for support to help persons with disabilities who do not have family support, which includes care and support in the case of death of the parents or guardians of the individual with disability. The Act includes procedures to appoint suitable guardians or trustees for individuals with disabilities who may need the support. Therefore, the National Trust Act provides all the necessary support for the facilitation of equal opportunities, protection of rights and full participation of persons with disabilities. The provisions of this important Act are relevant to every part of India except Jammu and Kashmir.

Currently, the Rights of Persons with Disabilities bill of 2014 is still being processed, and it seeks to replace the Persons with Disabilities Act of 1995. Whereas the PWD specified only seven disabilities, the Rights of Persons with Disability bill covers 19 conditions. The Bill provides for benefits such as reservations in education and employment, preference in government schemes, and other benefits for those individuals with a minimum of 40% disability. The Bill also provides people with disabilities the right to accessible public spaces including but not limited to public transport, public buildings, and polling booths. The Bill also requires the district courts to provide two types of guardians, as and when either is necessary. Guardianship may be limited guardianship where decisions for the individual with disability are taken jointly with the individual and Plenary Guardianship where decisions for the individual with disability are taken without consulting him at all. The Bill also mandates strict penalty for those who violate any provisions of the Act (PRS Legislative Research).

Though these legislations all aim to uphold the rights of people with disabilities and provide them with opportunities to be included in the community, there is only limited progress. Among the various reasons for the limited progress, three are pertinent. The first is the general societal attitude, which among the lower socio-economic and rural population still views disability as a result of karmic punishment, the displeasure of some wrathful Gods, or possession by an evil spirit. These beliefs have led to the continuing abuse, ostracism, and neglect of people with disabilities in various parts of India. The second is the overwhelmingly large and diverse population of India. Disability legislation and issues must cross caste, race, religion, gender, and economic and geographic boundaries. With a population of over a billion and growing, trying to increase awareness and education regarding disability as well as provide those with disabilities with adequate care becomes extremely challenging. The third is inadequate financial support due to the extreme size of the Indian population. The models for disability support that underpin the rhetoric are based on medical, charity and religious models that can disempower people with disabilities and reduce the Government initiatives required for full participation. We concur with Mehrotra (2011) that as long as beliefs that surround karma, family ideologies, charity and pity inform government legislation, policies and practices, the rate of inclusion in society for people with disabilities will remain marginalized.

In summary, this chapter has identified the fact that different legislation in the United States, Australia and India have not changed the nature of the issues that each of these countries has to manage to provide safe and effective educational services for students with disabilities. Aspects of the IDEA (United States), the DDA (Australia) and the PWD (India) have been analysed, and although the expectations for the management of inclusion in schools is much clearer in the legislation, it has not resulted in a reduction in the number of court hearings, and there is no empirical evidence to suggest that discrimination is reduced. Issues of recurring concern for parents, schools and students with disabilities in the United States, Australia and India have changed in focus from access and enrolment to more complex management issues that relate to the provision of quality educational experiences, medical services, behaviour management, suspension and exclusion. The increasing autonomy of schools through school-based management and the increasing complexity of the management of inclusion raise the level of urgency that issues associated with the provision of educational services for students with disabilities deserves careful and considered legal and educational attention from a global perspective.

This chapter has analysed the various processes and contributions that disability discrimination legislation have made in the United States, Australia and India. The historic examination of case law has provided a template for the resolution of issues related to inclusive practices in schools. It seems that while the rhetoric of the legislation as it relates to access and participation is largely accepted and understood in developed countries, it is still the detail of improved pedagogies, listening to the voice of people with disabilities and understanding the complex nature of disability that will challenge schools. Clear and lawful policies that guide best practice, a willingness to share decision-making, and building teacher capacity to address learner diversity will help schools to become more responsive to the unique needs of students with disabilities.

References

Barton, B. (2009). Dreams deferred: Disability definitions, data, models, and perspectives. *The Journal of Sociology and Social Welfare, 36*(4), 13–24.

Barton, L., & Slee, R. (1999). Competition, selection and inclusive education: Some observations. International Journal of Inclusive Education, 3(1), 3–12. http://doi.org/10.1080/136031199285147

Cumming, J., & Dickson, E. (2012). Educational accountability tests, social and legal inclusion approaches to discrimination for students with disability: A National case study from Australia. Assessment in Education: Principles, Policy and Practice, 20(2), 221–239.

Department of Education, T. a. Y. A. (2000). Disability standards for education – Draft. Canberra: Department of Education, Training and Youth Affairs.

Flynn, C. (1997). Disability discrimination in schools. London: National Children's and Youth Law Centre.

Graham, L., Sweller, N., & Van Bergen, P. (2010). Detaining the usual suspects: Charting the use of segregated settings in New South Wales government schools. Contemporary Issues in Early Childhood, 11(3), 234–248. doi:10.2304/ciec.2010.11.3.234.

Holt, L. (2016). Young people with socio-emotional differences: Theorising disabilty and destabilising socio-emotional norms. In V. Chouinard, E. Hall, & R. Wilton (Eds.), Towards enabling geographies: 'Disabled' bodies and minds in society and space (pp. 145–160). New York: Routledge.

Innes, G. (2000a, December 6). The disability discrimination act seven years on: Have we had the good years or are they still to come. Paper presented at the Pathways Conference, Canberra.

Innes, G. (2000b, December 4). The role of public enquiries and exemption powers in eliminating disability discrimination. Paper presented at the Constructing law and disability conference, Australian National University.

Lindsay, K. (1997). Discrimination law and special education. Paper presented at the legal and accounting management seminar on school law, Sydney.

Lipsky, D. K., & Gartner, A. (1997). Inclusion and school reform: Transforming America's classrooms. Baltimore: Brookes.

McKinney, J. R., & Mead, J. F. (1996). Law and policy in conflict: Including students with disabilities in parental choice programmes. Educational Administration Quarterly, 32(1), 107.

McLeod, S., Press, F., & Phelan, C. (2010). The (In)visibility of children with communication impairment in Audtralian health, education and disability legislation and politics. Asia Pacific Journal of Speech, Language and Hearing, 13(1), 67–75.

Mehrotra, N. (2011). Disability rights movements in India: Politics and practice. Economic and Political Weekly, XLVI(6), 65–72.

Osborne, J. A. G. (1999). Students with disabilities. In C. J. Russo (Ed.), The yearbook of education law (pp. 141–179). Daytona: Education Law Association.

Osborne, J. A. G. (2000). Students with disabilities. In C. J. Russo (Ed.), The yearbook of education law 2000 (pp. 167–195). Dayton: Education Law Association.

Parrish, T. B. (2001). Who's paying the rising cost of special education. Centre for Special Education Finance.

Pullin, D. (1999). Whose schools are these and what are they for? The role of the rule of law in defining educational opportunity in American public education. In G. J. Cizek (Ed.), Handbook of educational policy (pp. 3–29). Toledo: Academic Press.

Ramsay, I. M., & Shorten, A. R. (1996). Education and the law. Sydney: Butterworths.

Rioux, M. (2013). Disability rights in education. In L. Florian (Ed.), The sage handbook of special education (pp. 131–147). Los Angeles: Sage.

Russo, C. J. (2001). Disciplining students with disabilities. Paper presented at the canadian association for the practical study of law in education. Vancouver.

Rutherford-Turnbull, H., Wilcox, B. L., Stowe, M., & Turnbull, A. P. (2001). IDEA requirements for the use of PBS (Positive behavioural interventions and supports): Guidelines for responsible agencies. Journal of Positive Behavior Interventions, 3(1), 11.

Slee, R. (2013). How do we make inclusive education happen when exclusion is a political predisposition? International Journal of Inclusive Education, 17(8), 895–907. doi:10.1080/1360311 6.2011.602534.

Stewart, D. J. (1998). Legalisation of education: Implications for principals' professional knowledge. *Journal of Educational Administration, 36*(2), 129–145.

Stewart, D. J., & McCann, P. (1999). Educators and the law: Implications for the professional development of school administrators and teachers. *Journal of In-Service Education, 25*(1), 135–150.

Part IV
Insights from Caregivers

Chapter 21
Better Understanding the Complex Academic, Mental Health and Health Needs of Children in the United States

Elizabeth M. Anderson

Abstract Using socio-cultural theory and an ecological perspective, this study utilized a case study format to explore how families and teachers understand children with complex academic, mental health, and health needs in the United States. These case studies were developed based on home and school observations and semi-structured interviews with the parents and teachers of two children with complex needs attending a primary school in the United States. Data analysis revealed that parents and teachers may understand a child's development differently because they become conscious of it at different times and construct meaning out of it in unique ways. For parents, the contexts and interactions surrounding their child's evaluation process greatly influenced their emotional response to, and understanding of, their child's development, primarily in terms of one developmental area. As a result, subtle yet important changes in other developmental areas went unnoticed or diminished in potential importance, making it difficult for parents to optimize potential outcomes through advocacy. For teachers, understandings of a child's development were framed by an existing personal teaching philosophy. The stronger and more complimentary the understandings of a child's development by both teachers and parents, the greater was the likelihood of developmental opportunities for the child. As the parent of a child with complex needs, this chapter also includes my own narrative as the lens through which I analyze the data.

The Changing Ecology of Childhood in the United States

I remember with both clarity and intensity the day my daughter was diagnosed with a mental health disorder at 12 years of age. I can easily recall her words as she described in detail how she felt during periods of frantic elation and deep despair. The implied responsibility that came with her diagnosis weighed so heavily on me that I could hardly stand to leave the room. As I walked to our car, parked in the

E.M. Anderson (✉)
Graduate School of Education, Binghamton University, Binghamton, NY, USA
e-mail: eanders@binghamton.edu

© Springer International Publishing AG 2017   337
S. Halder, L.C. Assaf (eds.), *Inclusion, Disability and Culture*, Inclusive
Learning and Educational Equity 3, DOI 10.1007/978-3-319-55224-8_21

looming shadow of a former psychiatric institution in the Northeast United States, I felt completely distraught. Ten years earlier, my daughter had been identified as a young child with a developmental delay. Several years later, she would be diagnosed with a chronic illness. Somewhere in the span between these diagnoses, the essence of who she was and the context of our lives was somehow forgotten.

My experience with children with complex academic, mental health, and health needs is both personal and professional. As a mother and a teacher, I often lay awake at night thinking about the complex needs of my own child and my students. Over the years, some of the families I knew sought help for their child, with limited success. The professionals consulted were often knowledgeable about child development but not mental health. Alternatively, they were mental health specialists who were less knowledgeable about child development. Unfortunately, the complex and highly individual nature of children's strengths and areas of concern remained largely unaddressed in the well-intentioned programs and services available in this region of the United States.

As our children got older, concerns about language, cognitive, or motor development eventually became overshadowed by the increasingly complex relationship among their academic, mental health, and health needs. Some families, including my own family, had the resources to access further evaluation, attend meetings, and search for specialists. There were times when we felt empowered such as when an education, mental health, or health professional who understood a child's complex needs provided us with the hope that symptoms could be better managed. Still, there were times when even the most resourceful of us became disempowered.

According to Turnbull and Turnbull (2001), empowerment is considered critical for families to develop the motivation, knowledge, and skills necessary to take positive action on the part of their child. Empowerment occurs when there is a transaction between one or more individuals and the context in which we are taking action. Components include self-efficacy, perceived control, great expectations, energy, and persistence (Turnbull and Turnbull 2001). However, each component is informed by how each of us understands a child's unique development. This understanding influences, directly and/or indirectly, our transactions and contexts and provides a critical link to connect us with each other and the contexts in which supports and services may be provided. My experience has been that many families and teachers in the United States are often initially motivated to translate their understanding of a child's unique development into effective supports. However, when we do not have the resources, knowledge, or skills, either individually or collectively, to address a child's needs or if the home or school context is constraining, we can become overwhelmed (Turnbull and Turnbull 2001).

The challenges I faced were never just about my daughter. They were never just about my students. They were never just about my family or my students' families. No child, parent, or teacher exists in isolation. These challenges were, and continue to be, about the many subtleties and complexities of living and working with a child with complex needs while navigating the waters of the often highly fragmented and imposing education, mental health, and/or healthcare systems in the United States. The challenges that I faced, as well as those faced by other families and teachers, were also impacted by a broader social context where understandings of children's academic, mental health, and health strengths and needs were created and where our children will "sink" or "swim" (Garbarino and Gaboury 1992).

Exploring Child Development in Context

Exploring the development of children with complex academic, mental health, and health needs in the United States, and how it can be impacted by different contexts, is fundamental to an ecological orientation. This orientation is supported by the ecological theory (Bronfenbrenner 1979; Garbarino and Abramowitz 1992) as well as the theories of developmental contextualism (Lerner 1992), risk and resilience (Sameroff et al. 2000; Jenson and Fraser 2006), and developmental psychopathology (Sroufe 1997; Zeanah 2000). Although this "child in environment" perspective should lie at the heart of the "helping" professions in the United States, it can be difficult to realize.

It is estimated that one billion people have a disability, making this population the world's largest minority (United Nations 2014). In the United States, the number of children with disabilities represents 13% percent of the total school enrollment (NCES 2013). Recent estimates in the United States are that one in every five children is experiencing significant social and emotional difficulties (NIMHCM Foundation 2005) and that 30% of children have a chronic illness (Allen and Vessey 2004). These complex academic, mental health, and health needs can invariably interfere with a child's ability to succeed in US schools (Bronstein et al. 2012).

Significant discrepancies exist in the United States between the growing number of children with complex academic, mental health, and health needs that require additional supports and services and those that actually receive them (Lynn et al. 2003). The stakes appear to only get higher as children get older. In the United States, children with significant emotional and behavioral difficulties have the lowest grade point average and the highest dropout rates of all student demographics, including all disability categories (Wagner and Cameto 2004). When their health care needs are not adequately met, these children are also more likely to miss school because of illness (Grant and Brito 2010). As a mother and a teacher, I conducted this autoethnographic research to provide a rich description of some of the complexities such children and their families may face currently in the United States.

Viewing children with complex needs in the United States as part of the people and environments affecting them *is* complicated. To say a child *has* complex academic, mental health, and health needs places the problem primarily *within* the child. When we explore how a child *is* an individual *and* part of relationships *and* environments, responsibility for supporting development belongs to everyone. To explore how families and teachers in the United States may come to understand children with complex needs, I asked them the following questions: How do you understand a child's complex academic, mental health, and health needs? How does this understanding inform your parenting and/or teaching practices? What do you think are some of the contexts and interactions that can influence a child's development?

The Community

My study was conducted in a small, economically depressed city in the Northeast United States. At the time of this study, the primary school in this community served approximately 600 students from diverse socio-economic, racial, ethnic, religious, and linguistic backgrounds.

The Children

Matt Matt is a 6-year-old boy who lives with his mother, Karen, and his 10-year-old sister, Jackie. Karen and their father, Steve, divorced several years ago. Both Karen and Steve have extended family living in this community. Matt was classified by his school as multiply disabled. His educational supports include special education services; occupational, physical, and speech therapy; adaptive physical education; a paraprofessional; and services from a teacher for the visually impaired. Matt also receives aqua therapy and hippotherapy outside the school. He utilizes the following adaptive equipment: wheelchair, walker, augmentative communication device, leg splints, adaptive scissors, gait trainer, and a "sippy" cup. Matt has been diagnosed with cerebral palsy, septo-optic dysplasia, and schizencephaly. Matt is considered to have complex needs because of his disability, chronic health issues, and periodic episodes of self-injurious behavior and "shutting down" in over-stimulating environments.

Timmy Timmy is a 7-year-old boy who lives with his mother, Sue, step-father, Don, and younger brothers, David and Billy. Timmy has not seen his biological father in over 2 years. There is a family history of domestic violence. Timmy is in a special education classroom for students with significant emotional and behavioral issues. Timmy receives speech/language therapy and adaptive physical education services. He spends mornings in another classroom with his non-disabled peers. Over the years, Timmy has been diagnosed with attention deficit disorder, pervasive developmental disorder, oppositional defiant disorder, and bipolar disorder. He takes three psychotropic medications daily. Timmy is considered to have complex needs because of his disability, chronic dental health issues, and aggressive and non-compliant behaviors.

Overview of the Study

This chapter is based on the extensive time that I spent with Matt's and Timmy's parents and teachers in both home and school settings. This autoethnography aims to highlight my role as a complete member researcher (Adler and Adler 1987). In this role, I was fully committed to, and immersed in, the groups I was studying as a member of mothers of children with complex academic, mental health, and health needs.

Following 5 months of home and school observations and multiple interviews with Matt's and Timmy's parents and teachers, I developed descriptive case studies as a first level of analysis. During a second level of data analysis, I engaged in the coding and interpretation of categories using an open and axial coding process adapted from Strauss and Corbin and based on the original process by Glaser & Strauss (Shank 2002). Using my own personal narrative to guide the data analysis process, two primary themes emerged.

Understandings of Children with Complex Needs Differ Based on the Context and Interaction

One reason parents and teachers in the United States may come to understand a child with complex academic, mental health, and health needs differently, particularly when a child has complex academic, mental health, and health needs, is that they become conscious of it at different times and construct meaning out of it in different ways. For Matt's and Timmy's mothers, interactions with professionals during their evaluation process greatly influenced understandings of their child's development. For Matt's and Timmy's teachers, these understandings were greatly influenced by an existing teaching philosophy.

Parents' Understandings

In the United States, when parents have concerns about their child's development, they may have their child evaluated by a professional to determine if he or she has a disability. Typically, professionals in the United States identify children with severe disabilities, like Matt, during infancy. Other children, like my daughter and Timmy, may be identified later due to milder exceptionalities or later onset. However, in the United States, regardless of the age of the child, an evaluation process is the gateway to special education supports and services (Turnbull et al. 2006). When families in the United States are told their child has a disability, they often enter the "world" of special education that has its own terminology, rules, settings, and people. This can be a highly emotional process that also greatly informs their understandings (Graungaard and Skov 2007).

Matt's Mother Born with congenital disabilities, Matt's evaluation process began in this community in the United States shortly after his birth. Matt received three medical diagnoses and had two surgeries before he was a year old. The first surgery, which opened his skull to decrease pressure on his brain, was life threatening. Whether or not to have this surgery was very traumatic for Karen because Matt's life was at risk either way. Most of his early years were spent in one of nine doctor's offices or receiving physical and occupational therapy services. While doctors closely monitored Matt's medical conditions, therapists intensively supported his physical development, including muscle tone, strengthening and coordination. These services later expanded to include speech therapy and special education services.

Matt's evaluation process was highly emotional for his mother Karen. The baby she thought would be born healthy had a severe disability and needed life-threatening surgery. Karen was also in the early stages of a divorce. Through his evaluation process, Karen came to understand the primary cause of Matt's disability as medical/physical. This understanding was further shaped by Matt's physical and occupational therapists with whom she developed very close relationships. Karen described,

> I mean I trusted these people. They came into my home. They were just really nice. They just basically helped me through it, like getting his wheelchair, his orthotics, his hand splint. I mean they guided me through all of it.

Karen's understanding of Matt's development primarily in medical/physical terms also influenced the allocation of family resources. For example, Karen purchased a different vehicle specifically so she could transport Matt's wheelchair. Recently, she also began the time-consuming process of transferring Matt's out-of-school therapy services from one program for children with developmental disabilities in the United States to another so that he could receive additional services. Maintaining Matt's intensive therapy schedule also consumed much of Karen's time and energy. Her understandings also influenced how she set goals for him and viewed progress. Karen believed Matt was making great progress in his motor skills. She hoped that someday he would walk.

Timmy's Mother During the first few years of his life, Timmy moved several times within this region in the United States with his mother; had two step-fathers, several step-sisters, and two brothers; witnessed domestic violence; and was the victim of sexual abuse. Timmy's initial evaluations revealed severe emotional and behavioral needs, and he attended a special education preschool specifically for young children with challenging behaviors.

Timmy's evaluation process was highly emotional for his mother. Sue was coping with her own trauma, coping with Timmy's challenging behaviors, and caring for her three young children. Through this evaluation process, she came to understand his development as emotionally and behaviorally disordered. This understanding was further shaped by a psychiatrist who diagnosed Timmy with Bipolar

Disorder at age five. Sue explained, "I don't care what anybody says, there is no fixing him. He is Bipolar."

Sue's current understandings of Timmy's development also influenced the allocation of family resources. Replacing the household items that were broken during Timmy's behavioral outbursts and filling three psychiatric medications for him was expensive. Although it created financial hardship, Sue had a cell phone so his teacher could easily contact her and kept a well-maintained car in case she had to get to his school quickly. Coping with Timmy's behavior and communicating with school personnel consumed much of Sue's time and energy.

Sue's understanding of Timmy's needs as primarily emotional and behavioral also influenced how she set goals for him and viewed progress. Sue thought that Timmy was becoming less aggressive. She hoped his behavior would stabilize enough that he could continue living in her home and eventually graduate from school.

My daughter's evaluation process was a highly emotional time for me. I had four children under the age of 5 years. My daughter had difficulties eating and sleeping. She cried a great deal of the time and reacted negatively when touched. The evaluation process indicated that she had significant sensory processing issues. My understanding was further shaped by the occupational therapist that conducted her evaluation and suggested sensory activities as a way to help regulate her behavior. My understandings of my daughter's needs as primarily sensory also influenced the allocation of family resources. I purchased books on sensory processing and sensory toys and joined a support group for parents of children with sensory processing disorders.

Teachers' Understandings

When a child with a disability in the United States receives special education services, an individualized education program (IEP) is developed around their educational performance and goals, appropriate programs and/or services, and how progress will be measured (IDEA 2004). For teachers, this program was greatly informed by an existing teaching philosophy.

Matt's Classroom Teacher: Mrs. Williams Mrs. Williams' teaching philosophy was that children in schools in the United States are unique and bring different strengths to school. Her role is to open the door for learning and model the acceptance of all students' backgrounds and abilities. Mrs. Williams believed Matt benefited from being included in her classroom. She explained,

> The students were fighting over who got to ride in the elevator in the school with him and push his wheelchair, so I had to come up with a system for the children to take turns using our class list of names.

Mrs. Williams believed that opportunities for her students to participate in classroom activities are very important. She described, "I try to have at least two classroom learning centers a day that Matt can do like computers because he loves that." Mrs. Williams also thought it was important to have high expectations. She explained, "Maybe because I have high expectations for his learning is why Matt is blossoming so." Mrs. Williams believed Matt was making great progress this year at school from being with peers. "Seeing what his peers are doing, he wants to do it too."

Matt's Special Education Teacher: Ms. Stone Mrs. Stone's philosophy was that children in schools in the United States should not be expected to do things in the same way, time, or pace. When she worked with Matt, she presented him with different activities such as identifying numbers 1–5, the letters in his name, colored blocks, and books.

Mrs. Stone thought it was important to provide clear expectations and try different strategies. She believed Matt's challenging behavior of biting his thumb was purposeful. When Matt started biting his thumb, she and Mrs. Williams ignored it. Next, they put him in the classroom "think chair" as a time out. Lastly, they went back to ignoring it. Mrs. Stone explained, "He wants a reaction from me; he knows." Mrs. Stone believed Matt had come "leaps and bounds" since the beginning of the school year.

Timmy's Special Education Teacher: Mrs. Connelly Mrs. Connelly believed that students in schools in the United States with emotional and behavioral disorders need consistency. She believed it was important to offer students an educational program where they learned appropriate behavior. Mrs. Connelly believed that the lives of her students were often unpredictable, and they cycled through difficult times. She explained,

> They can do fabulous work, and they can completely bottom out, whether it is something going on within them, a genetic kind of thing, or something going on at home. For whatever reason, these kids bottom out, and when they do, they need a supportive environment.

> Mrs. Connelly thought she had a clear idea of what each of her students needed to be successful. She described being aware of educational theories suggesting that school programs should become more fluid but didn't see that as realistic for her students, many of whom had been in abusive situations.

Mrs. Connelly believed that Timmy had the skills but just didn't use them. She believed he knew how to interact with peers but was reluctant to do so. She thought his language skills were good when he chose to exhibit them. She believed he comprehended what she was saying but just didn't want to put in the effort. Mrs. Connelly recognized that Timmy's past experiences created challenges for him but felt he w⌐ ⌐responsible for his behavior. She believed Timmy had made a lot of pr⌐   vear.

⌐ral Education Classroom Teacher: Mrs. Gaston** Timmy spent
'. Gaston's classroom with his non-disabled peers. She described
⌐sophy as strongly guided by her experiences as a parent in the
'wo sons with Autism. Mrs. Gaston explained,

> I see children with disabilities in my classroom a little differently than somebody who hasn't had that experience. By watching my own children develop, the biggest thing I have learned is to look for what precipitated the behavior.

> Mrs. Gaston structured students' mornings into different learning centers where they were expected to work quietly and independently. It was also important for her to have center activities done in a certain order and fashion.

Mrs. Gaston understood Timmy's behaviors as attention seeking because when she ignored his early attempts to get her attention, he eventually stopped the behavior. In spite of her efforts to ignore his behaviors, however, Mrs. Gaston believed Timmy detracted from other students' learning. She described, I will be honest with you. It is work reading with Timmy every day. I have had to change who he comes to reading group with because he is a detriment to the other kids in the group.

Like Timmy and Matt's teachers, my daughter's teacher, Ms. Masterson's, philosophy framed her understanding of her development. This teaching philosophy was based on the belief that children in schools in the United States need to work at their own pace. Ms. Masterson believed that my daughter had all of the necessary skills to be successful in her school; they were just delayed. She felt her classroom was just the right environment to support my daughter's development. It was her belief that, in time, my daughter would outgrow her developmental needs and no longer need special education or related services.

The Contexts and Interactions in Which a Child Develops in the United States Can Create Risks and/or Opportunities

Some children with complex academic, mental health, and health needs in the United States may be provided with more developmental opportunities than others. Although few children in the United States escape risk completely, the accumulation of risk can jeopardize development particularly in the absence of enough compensatory forces (Garbarino and Abramowitz 1992). By exploring the people and places in these children's lives in the United States, we can begin to view the impact on their development, depending on the degree to which each child was offered material, emotional, and social encouragement compatible with their needs and capacities in this context (Garbarino and Abramowitz 1992).

Matt Matt's developmental risk was more the result of his own biology than his immediate environment in the United States. For the most part, Matt's home life was very stable. He also developed positive reciprocal relationships with extended family. However, as a single mother working in customer service in the United States, Karen couldn't financially meet Matt's needs without additional support from a federally funded government program for children with developmental disabilities. This program provided funding for Matt's equipment such as his wheelchair, assistive technology, and augmentative communication and to pay for medical appointments. As a result, this program played an integral role in creating developmental opportunities for children such as Matt in the United States.

Development is also enhanced when children in the United States are able to observe differences in their own dyadic experiences because a third party is present (Garbarino and Abramowitz 1992). Jackie support Matt's development as a third party to the mother–son dyad through a positive reciprocal relationship that expanded his capacity to play, work and love (Bronfenbrenner 1979). Additionally, Matt's relationships with his extended family, teachers, and therapists also created additional developmental opportunities by providing him with a more comprehensive support system. His mother, Karen, was an effective advocate for Matt not only in her ability to obtain supports and services to meet his unique academic, mental health, and health needs but by closely monitoring his providers to ensure he was given a level of material, emotional, and social encouragement that was compatible with these needs in this context. To be an effective advocate for Matt, however, Karen expended a tremendous amount of time and energy meeting his needs. As a result, there were times when Karen was physically and emotionally vulnerable, which also created developmental risk for him.

As a customer service representative in the United States, Karen was able to flex her work hours to be compatible with Matt's therapy schedule, and this created developmental opportunities for him. Karen's work schedule, however, was set by her employer in advance and could not accommodate any last minute schedule changes for her. In order to flex her work hours to match Matt's therapy schedule, Karen worked some evenings and Sundays. This provided fewer opportunities for her to focus on Matt and Jackie's schoolwork and Matt's therapeutic activities, potentially increasing their developmental risk. A customer service position in the United States provided Karen with little or no job security and few opportunities for economic advancement. Any reduction in government funding at the federal or state level, under consideration at the time of this study, could lead to a decrease in the number and/or quality of Matt's programs and services and increase his developmental risk.

It was also through a federally funded government program that Karen had access to an individual that provided on-going coordination for Matt's special education supports and services. Karen described Matt's service coordinator as an integral component in her ability to effectively advocate for Matt. As Matt ages, he will need different equipment and activities. If Karen continues to receive support in her advocacy efforts, Matt should experience developmental opportunities. If Karen does not receive enough support or if she is unable to maintain strong relationships between contexts (due to, e.g., illness), she could be at risk for exhaustion. The long-term neglect of Karen's own needs may eventually create risk for Matt.

Timmy Timmy experienced several different family contexts in the United States as a young child, at least two of which were abusive. He also faced biological vulnerability due to a family history of bipolar disorder. This created additional developmental risk for him. Unlike Matt, Timmy experienced an accumulation of risk in this community without adequate compensatory forces. One reason why was that his mother, Sue, was also the victim of physical and emotional abuse. As a result, her decreased sense of empowerment diminished her ability to offer Timmy the material, emotional, or social supports compatible with his developmental needs and capacities in this context. For example, Timmy was very active yet lived in what is considered in this community in the United Sates as a small home that was shared with four other family members. His mother, Sue, had an authoritarian parenting style that provided few opportunities for positive reciprocal interactions in the mother–son dyad. Timmy and his brothers also had to compete for limited family resources. In addition, Timmy did not receive any special education supports or services outside of the school setting.

Timmy experienced a great deal of developmental risk. Like many young children who live with poverty in the United States, Timmy often had limited access to what would be considered in his community to be safe environments that supported exploration, stimulated his learning, and provided opportunities for warm, responsive interactions with adults (Erwin 1996). As a mother and a full-time college student in the United States, Sue had no personal income and a busy schedule that allowed for little flexibility. When there was an unexpected expense or when she had to change her schedule to meet the needs of her family, Sue experienced increased stress that usually resulted in increased conflict with Timmy. Sue considered herself an advocate for Timmy, but the effectiveness of her advocacy was periodically compromised by feelings of powerlessness that started long before Timmy but continued to limit her ability to effect change in either Timmy's home or school setting in this community.

My daughter experienced both developmental opportunity and risk. As a young child in the United States, she lived in a neighborhood where she had access to safe environments and positive reciprocal relationships with both peers and adults. For the first 5 years of her life, I was her full-time caregiver. As a result, I was able to flex my time to be compatible with her therapy schedule, provide therapeutic activities in our home, and attend meetings with professionals at school. This created a developmental opportunity for her. When I became a full-time teacher and a graduate student at a university in this same community, there were times when I was unable to maintain strong relationships between these contexts. Like Karen and Sue, I expended a tremendous amount of time and energy meeting my daughter's complex academic, mental health, and health needs. As a result, there were times when I was physically and emotionally vulnerable, which also created developmental risks for her.

A Child's Evaluation Process Can Be a Very Emotional Experience for Parents

As mothers in the United States, Sue, Karen, and I were greatly influenced by the contexts and interactions that surrounded our children's evaluations. While the reason for the referral, timing, and location of each child's evaluation was different, it was a highly emotional experience for all of us. Whether the reason for referral was a speech, motor, or social and emotional concerns or the child was preschool age, an infant, or a toddler, part of what made this experience emotional was our level of vulnerability. For Karen, this vulnerability stemmed from being a single mother of a medically fragile child and having little knowledge of congenital disabilities. For Sue, this vulnerability stemmed from being the victim of domestic violence, a single mother of three children, and having little knowledge of mental health disorders. For me, this vulnerability stemmed from being the mother of four young children with very little knowledge of sensory processing disorders. Although access to resources may provide a buffer for a parent's level of vulnerability, the evaluation process for children with complex academic, mental health, and health needs remains a highly emotional and influential time for families in the United States.

As mothers of children with complex academic, mental health, and health needs, our interactions with professionals during their evaluation process also varied, based primarily on our level of participation. Karen and I had high degrees of participation in our children's evaluations and questioned neither the process nor the outcome. We observed all their evaluations, completed forms and questionnaires, and spoke directly with evaluators. Sue also participated in Timmy's evaluation process but did not directly observe all evaluations, completed most forms, and had fewer opportunities to speak with evaluators. She did, however, privately question both the evaluation process and its outcome. In contrast to Karen and me, who believed our participation could positively impact our children's experiences during the evaluation process, Sue believed her potential impact was limited. This limited her participation, possibly in response to the stigma attached to Timmy's psychiatric diagnosis and the severity of his externalizing behaviors. Through a unique set of contexts and interactions involved in the evaluation process, each of us came to understand our child's development as delayed, primarily in terms of one developmental area.

For young children with disabilities in the United States, clinical approaches based on diagnostic/prescriptive and behavioral models of intervention continue to be dominant. Based on these models, discrete areas of deficit are identified for remediation guided by a set of distinct professional competencies for therapeutic intervention (Erwin 1996). For example, in the United States, speech therapists typically evaluate and remediate speech–language difficulties, occupational therapists evaluate and remediate fine motor and sensory difficulties, physical therapists evaluate and remediate gross motor difficulties, and special education teachers and psychologists evaluate and remediate cognitive difficulties and challenging behaviors. Based on these diagnostic/prescriptive and behavioral models, evaluations are the gateway to special education services in the United States. For our children, such evaluations drove decisions about the type, number, and frequency of special education services, parent priorities, and educational placement. Periodic reviews of each child's strengths and needs informed this decision-making process but not with the same degree of impact.

According to Graungaard and Skov (2007), it is critical that professionals in the United States offer possibilities for taking action to parents of children with complex academic, mental health, and health needs. For Karen, the professionals in this community provided her with viable options for taking action to support Matt's academics and health but not necessarily his mental health. For Sue, the professionals in this community provided her with one viable option for taking action to support his mental health needs but not necessarily to address his unique academic and health needs. The professionals in this community provided me with viable options to address my daughter's sensory processing issues but not necessarily to address her unique academic, mental health, or health needs.

For the professionals involved in our children's evaluations, the context of the evaluation process framed their interactions. In contrast, as mothers of children with complex academic, mental health, and health needs, the interactions during the evaluation process framed our context. As mothers of children with complex needs, not only were our interactions with the professionals in this community disability-specific, but we were greatly impacted by the degree to which these individuals helped us identify possibilities for taking positive action on our children's behalf. When a child's disability was identified in a cognitive, speech–language, sensory, or motor developmental domain, possibilities for taking positive action were evident, and our interactions with professionals were viewed as supportive. For example, when my daughter exhibited sensory issues, I viewed her occupational therapist as supportive when she provided ideas for specific sensory activities that we could do at home. When Matt exhibited difficulties with motor development, Karen viewed the physical therapist as supportive when she provided muscle strengthening exercises they could do at home and a hand splint to wear while doing them. It is important to note, however, that neither therapist considered in their assessment framework the possibility of a mental health component to our children's behavior. When Timmy exhibited significant social and emotional difficulties, Sue did not find the mental health professionals in this community very supportive. It is also important to note that these professionals did not appear to have considered the potential of an academic or chronic health component to his behavior.

Implications for Parent Advocacy

Using an ecological perspective, as parents of children with complex academic, mental health, and health needs in the United States, it is important that we are able to understand their unique development and note specific developmental changes and how they occur (Benn and Garbarino 1992). If we understand our children's development primarily in terms of one developmental area, we may not fully recognize the inherent complexities necessary to optimize their potential outcomes (Benn and Garbarino 1992). As a result, subtle yet important changes in other developmental areas may go unnoticed or diminished in potential importance and may impact our advocacy. So, although children such as ours may have very different complex needs, we might miss subtle, yet important, changes in our children's development that can impact both individual and collective parent advocacy efforts in the United States.

If Karen understands Matt's development primarily in terms of his physical development, she may not recognize subtle, yet important, changes in his social, emotional, or language development. As a result, she may not advocate for additional strategies or services such as re-programming his augmentative communication device to increase his opportunities for social interaction or positive behavior supports, which could optimize Matt's potential outcomes.

If Sue understands Timmy's development primarily in terms of his social and emotional development, she may not recognize subtle, yet important, changes in his fine motor skills or academics. As a result, she may not advocate for additional strategies or services, such as those provided by the school's occupational therapist or reading specialist, which may help optimize Timmy's potential outcomes.

If I understand my daughter's development primarily in terms of her sensory processing, I may not recognize subtle, yet important, changes in her academics, mental health, or health. As a result, I may not advocate for additional strategies or services that might help optimize my daughter's potential outcomes.

Implications for Home–School Partnerships

Through different experiences and interactions, parents and teachers in the United States develop an understanding of children with complex academic, mental health, and health needs. How such children's development is understood can either strengthen or weaken the relationship between the home and school setting, further impacting each child's development.

Some parents of children with complex academic, mental health, and health needs in the United States may not develop close relationships with teachers who understand their child's development in substantially different ways than they do. In addition, some teachers of such children may not develop close relationships with parents who have a different understanding than they do. In the United States, when understandings of a child's development are similar, as they were for Matt and my daughter, the home–school partnership can be strengthened. When these understandings are different, as they were for Timmy, the home–school partnership can be weakened. The stronger and more complementary the linkages between home and school in communities in the United States, the more powerful is the influence on a child's development (Garbarino and Abramowitz 1992). For Matt and my daughter, a strong and complimentary home–school link created additional developmental opportunities. As a child whose link between home and school was neither solid nor complementary, this link created additional developmental risk for Timmy.

Conclusion

Families and teachers of children with complex academic, mental health, and health needs in the United States are often initially motivated to translate their understanding of a child's development into effective supports. Some families, however, have access to more resources than others, and some home and school settings have more constraints than others. When parents do not have the knowledge, resources, or skills to access effective supports or if the home or community context is constraining, they can feel overwhelmed or disempowered.

In the United States, when a child's disability is identified as cognitive, speech/language, sensory, or motor, possibilities for taking action may be more evident, and parents might consider their interactions with professionals supportive. Karen and I were overwhelmed at times, but the possibility of taking positive action on behalf of our children offered us hope. When a child's disability is identified as primarily as a mental health issue and there are aggressive behaviors, the possibility of taking action may be less evident and interactions with professionals deemed less supportive. Sue was overwhelmed at times and, without the possibility of taking positive action, was not offered hope.

Ultimately, we must ask ourselves whether we are offering all parents and teachers of children with complex academic, mental health, and health needs in the United States possibilities for taking positive action on behalf of such children and, in turn, offering them hope. Among the most dynamic aspects of a parent–teacher relationship is the ability to move beyond our individual and collective limitations, see the possibilities for taking positive action, and offer each other hope. As a parent and a teacher of children with complex academic, mental health, and health needs, I believe that it is only when we are offered possibilities for taking positive action and hope that we are able to offer them to our children and students and provide them what may be their most important developmental opportunities.

Lessons Learned and Next Steps

This study fills a gap in the literature on young children with complex academic, mental health, and health needs by exploring the experiences of families and teachers in the United States. First, we learned that understandings of a child's development can be constructed very differently, depending on the person and the context. This has important implications for the ways in which observation and evaluation can be used to better capture the complex interactions among developmental domains by including multiple settings and interactions. Secondly, we learned that family, teacher, and caregiver relationships greatly impact a child's learning and development. This has important implications for closer examination of the current emphasis on academics in the broader context of an interrelationship of care that fosters interprofessional collaboration and strengthens home–school partnerships for children with complex academic, mental health, and health needs. Since many families and other school professionals may not be aware of, or are unsure how to respond to, a child's complex academic, mental health, or health needs, we also learned that there is an urgent need for more targeted family training and professional development for school staff. Lastly, we learned about the importance of gaining a much clearer picture of the number of young children with complex academic, mental health, and health needs and the nature of them. This has important implications for the types of supports and services that will help children with complex needs achieve optimal outcomes in inclusive settings.

References

Adler, P. A., & Adler, P. (1987). The past and the future of ethnography. *Journal of Contemporary Ethnography, 16*(1), 4–24.

Allen, P. J., & Vessey, J. A. (2004). Does family involvement and psychosocial support influence coping in teenage patients who have congenital disease. *Pediatric Nursing*. Retrieved from goliath.ecnext.com, 4 Apr 2014.

Benn, J., & Garbarino, J. (1992). The developing child in a changing environment. In J. Garbarino (Ed.), *Children and families in the social environment* (pp. 99–130). New York: Aldine De Gruyer.

Bronfenbrenner, U. (1979). *The ecology of human development.* Cambridge, MA: Harvard University Press.

Bronstein, L., Anderson, E., Terwilliger, S., & Sager, M. (2012). Evaluating a model of school-based health and social services: An interdisciplinary community-university collaboration. *Children & Schools, 34*(3), 155–166.

Erwin, E. J. (1996). *Putting children first.* Baltimore: Paul H. Brookes Publishing.

Garbarino, J., & Abramowitz, R. (1992). The ecology of human development. In J. Garbarino (Ed.), *Children and families in the social environment* (pp. 11–33). New York: Aldine De Gruyer.

Garbarino, J., & Gaboury, M. T. (1992). An introduction. In J. Garbarino (Ed.), *Children and families in the social environment* (pp. 1–10). New York: Aldine De Gruyer.

Grant, R., & Brito, A. (2010). *Chronic illness and school performance: A literature review focusing on asthma and mental health conditions.* New York: A Children's Health Fund Monograph.

Graungaard, A. H., & Skov, L. (2007). Why do we need a diagnosis? A qualitative study of parents' experiences, coping and needs, when the newborn child is severely disabled. *Child: Care, Health and Development, 33*(3), 296–307.

Individuals with Disabilities Education Improvement Act. (2004). Washington, DC: U.S. Government Printing Office.

Jenson, J. M., & Fraser, M. W. (2006). *Social policy for children and families.* Thousand Oaks: Sage Publications.

Lerner, R. (1992). *Developmental systems theory: An integrative approach.* Thousand Oaks: Sage Publications.

Lynn, C. J., McKay, M. M., & Atkins, M. S. (2003). School social work: Meeting the mental health needs of students through collaboration with teachers. *Children & Schools, 25*(4), 197–209.

National Center for Education Statistics. (2013). Retrieved on September 30, 2014, from http://nces.ed.gov/fastfacts/display.asp?id=64

National Institute for Mental Health Care Management. (2005). *Mental health: An overview of key considerations for health system stakeholders.* Washington, DC: National Institute for Healthcare Management Foundation.

Sameroff, A., Lewis, M., & Miller, S. (2000). *Handbook of developmental psychopathology.* New York: Plenum.

Shank, G. (2002). *Qualitative research: A personal skills approach.* Columbus: Merrill Prentice Hall.

Sroufe, L. A. (1997). Psychopathology as outcome of development. *Development and Psychopathology, 9,* 251–268.

Turnbull, A. P., & Turnbull, H. R. (2001). *Families, professionals and exceptionality: A special partnership for collaborating for empowerment.* Upper Saddle River: Prentice Hall.

Turnbull, A. P., Turnbull, H. P., Erwin, E., & Soodak, L. (2006). *Families, professionals, and exceptionality.* Upper Saddle River: Pearson Education, Inc.

United Nations Enable. (2014). Retrieved on September 30, 2014, from http://www.un.org/disabilities/default.asp?id=18

Wagner, M., & Cameto, R. (2004). *The characteristics, experiences, and outcomes of youth with emotional disturbances.* Minneapolis: National Center on Secondary Education and Transition NLTS2 Data Brief. Retrieved April 1, 2008, from http://www.ncset.org/publications/printsource.asp?id+1687

Zeanah, C. H. (2000). *Handbook of infant mental health.* New York: The Guilford Press.

Chapter 22
Great Expectations for the Modern-Day Dispossessed: A Personal Journey

Natalya Panteleyeva

Abstract This is an account of one's experience of taking care of a child with a diagnosis of a rare congenital genetic abnormality resulting in multiple developmental disabilities in the moderate to severe range. It provides a glimpse into how an individual cultural and socioeconomic background as well as personal preferences in conjunction with available societal services in three locales in the US led to choices, decisions, and planning for a single family. Life experiences shaped opinions that are intended to help providers and policymakers address issues that are not limited to disability but are related to the success of the existing support structures and quality of life of everyone directly involved.

Dreams Shattered

My eldest daughter was born after an uneventful pregnancy during which no testing was performed because there was no family history of genetic disorders and I was young. Lack of experience and exposure to non-neuro-typical individuals delayed diagnosis until she was 15 months old. Developmental pediatrician and genetic counselors were able to provide a label for the found genetic difference and even attribute it to an error in chromosomal orientation in a step in the cell division process. However, for a parent, this information is not useful compared to a prognosis of the impact the difference will have on the child's life. Because of the extreme rarity of the condition, at the time, no one knew about it. The single article in the scientific literature that the developmental pediatrician managed to find described a single case of a child who was still very young. The short-term prognosis was not good, and the long-term prognosis did not exist.

In retrospect, the range of emotions was mindboggling and overwhelming to the point I neither could articulate nor feel most of them. It was easier to shut them down and get busy fixing the kid in the denial stage of a shock reaction. How was I

N. Panteleyeva (✉)
Mother (Parent) Greater Denver Area, Denver, CO, USA

Chromosome 18 Registry, San Antonio, TX, USA
e-mail: natalya.panteleyeva@gmail.com

© Springer International Publishing AG 2017   355
S. Halder, L.C. Assaf (eds.), *Inclusion, Disability and Culture*, Inclusive
Learning and Educational Equity 3, DOI 10.1007/978-3-319-55224-8_22

fixing her? First of all by deciding that she was not sitting by herself because we've always propped her up for support, denying her the opportunity. If I removed support, she'd sit. This seemed logical to me at the time. So, I sat her down on the carpet in our tiny efficiency apartment and let go of her, catching her whenever she lost balance before she hit the floor. Strangely, this worked, and rather quickly. At 15 months, she began sitting and at 18 months walking. I recall her estimating the distance between herself and a sturdy object nearby, such as a table or a chair and then taking a few quick steps before falling onto it for support. Almost immediately her balance improved to the point where a few steps turned into unsteady running, especially outdoors. I still remember the bewildered look on her face. It was like she just woke up and realized that there was an entire world out there that she did not have a clue how to deal with. It looked like she was trying to run away from it all… Luckily, as tiny as she was, I could still catch her. She became petrified of many things – cried on a swing, then in a pool. Rather than not exposing her to the stress of being there, I persisted. I did not have to decide how long to keep trying because she quickly adapted to both these settings – stopped crying, got stronger, and moved better. Shortly after I began taking her to the pool, her physical therapist noted that she gained about a year in gross motor skill development.

This rapid progress fueled all kinds of dreams, beliefs, and hopes that clashed with my increasing awareness about the lack of progress in other areas of development and remaining apparent of physical differences between her and other kids her age. I was stunned when I observed my daughter next to a friends' kid almost exactly her age. Their girl had noodle legs: she'd round them up when sitting with muscles completely relaxed. My daughter's muscles and joints were always so tight that one could not straighten her arms completely. When we tried extending her arms over her head, they remained locked at her shoulder level, bent at the elbow. She also could not open her legs to sit. She sat on one side with both legs together on the opposite side with her spine twisted. When I tried to correct her sitting, I managed to open her stiff legs by a notch in front of her. She clearly was not comfortable in this position. Her movements were jerky and uncoordinated, like Tin Man's from the *Wizard of Oz* (The Wonderful Wizard of Oz, 1990) whose oilcan went missing. Occasionally, her eye turned in. She made sounds resembling words but did not speak as expected- in one- and two-word sentences. She rocked a lot, flapped her arms when excited, and sucked her thumb. Instead of moving her fingers in front of her eyes, now she found strings to run her fingers endlessly. Later she replaced the strings with less pliable crayons and markers. She fed herself but often bolted food down in pieces so large that I wondered how she did not choke as she barely chewed her bites before swallowing. She put simple puzzles together and learned to stack blocks and a set of toy cups of graduating sizes.

Another peculiarity of my daughter's, this time rather helpful, was her health. After a couple of bouts of particularly persistent high fevers early in life that took a strong antibiotic to take down, she had no serious illnesses. I cannot recall her ever being out of school for a routine cold or flu, although she had a couple of ear infections early in her life. It is possible that she had a decreased sensitivity to pain and discomfort or could not express it so we didn't notice. In fact, she really has been

extremely healthy in the traditional sense of the word. My understanding is ti
robust health is considered highly unusual for individuals with a genetic disor

How Am I Supposed to Parent Now?

I have seen slogans in support of diversity in our college town, which did not prepare me for the differences I began perceiving between my daughter and her typically developing peers. As long as intellectual and communication similarities
existed, differences were indeed less important, although noted. With her patterns of
behavior that were ritualistic and seldom communicative, it was impossible to avoid
the conclusion that our future has irrevocably changed.

What opportunities for growth and development existed for us to pursue or create
to ensure a reasonable outcome for my daughter, like integration into society with a
high quality of life? Being in a college town, I audited a class on special needs children for future special needs teachers. This attempt to obtain knowledge and guidance as a parent turned out to be a mixed experience.

At the time, examples of special needs children were drawn from diagnoses of
down syndrome, cerebral palsy, and mental retardation in the underprivileged population. The teacher's job was essentially to analyze the tasks typically developing
children pick up intuitively without difficulties, break them down into smaller parts,
and drill those parts individually for them to be able to grasp them. If they did not,
the parts were not simple enough and needed to be broken down further. This gives
one an idea that as long as the teacher is clever enough to break any task into sufficiently small parts, the student will learn them, although slowly. This expectation in
practice added to my and my daughter's frustration when I tried helping her with
different self-help tasks, some of which she has yet to master. I expect this strategy
to be more productive when an individual can communicate their problems, which
stem from their way of processing the world that does not match our expectations.

As one may conclude from this brief description, teachers educated predominantly in this framework (about half of all teachers through her entire school experience) were unsuccessful in helping my daughter learn. Her best successes came
from those with training and experience in visual support, sensory processing, and
other areas helpful with autism.

Interventions and Specialists

At the age when kids are not expected to do much, the specialists diagnosed my
daughter with "mild developmental delays" based mostly on her overall gross motor
skills. The specialists were physical, occupational, and speech therapists through
the First Steps program that began working with her in our home soon after diagnosis. First Steps is a government-funded program for children of low-income families

from birth to age three. Intervention frequency was lim-
specialist maximum, regardless of the diagnosis and
not recall significant changes in any area of develop-
intervention. Her physical therapist fitted her with plastic
intent to stabilize her ankles and, consequently, her gait. I have
an opinion from more than one specialist that this intervention
en more harmful than helpful to her development, possibly contribut-
ufficient rotation out in her feet and current abnormal gait.

ing attended college-level classes for speech therapists and special education
chers, I found a singular view of the instructor to dominate over other approaches often deemed to be insufficiently scientific and unworthy of attention. Their proponents were treated as modern equivalents of charlatans whose purpose is to part the fools, or desperate parents of special needs children, and their money. However, studies evaluating the efficacy of any form of therapy are necessarily limited in their scope by our incomplete knowledge and limited understanding of complex developmental conditions. The same diagnostic label presupposes sufficient similarities in individuals that share it, which may not be the case. With my daughter's condition label, the common set of symptoms and their severity vary widely among the affected individuals to expect similar underlying brain architecture, wiring, and processing, suggesting a possibility of finer underlying genetic differences yet to be uncovered.

In our experience, the effectiveness of methods of treatment approved by the insurance was very limited. If there was any measurable progress, it took a very long time to see it. When the range and degree of symptoms are significant for a given label, as is the case in the autism spectrum disorder, a single therapy method that science and insurance qualify as successful will be difficult to produce. Even more unlikely, there will be methods specific to and approved for a rare (and even more common) genetic disorder. Studies in congenital genetic disorders do not get government funding due to perceived low need as defined by affected population size. In recent years, a link between Down's syndrome and Alzheimer's disease in the elderly raised a possibility of viable genetic conditions providing insight into and potential treatment for common ailments in the general population. The research, however, continues to be funded privately for the most part and thus progresses slowly.

When a child failed to make progress in therapy, by default, the child was viewed as a patient, not a provider failure, because the provider is the one presenting reports to the insurance company. It became the grounds for dismissal from therapy to not waste money rather than a referral to another specialist. An occupational therapist dismissed my daughter at the onset of puberty for the lack of demonstrable progress on goals despite the fact that she still does not tie her shoes, engage her zipper, or write her name legibly, although she has made great progress in all of these tasks since then. She plateaued at the time with that trained professional, on that professional's schedule of reasonable progress. Similarly, a physical therapist dismissed her even earlier despite her gross motor movement, skills, and balance not being on a level comparable to her peers.

These were professionals engaged privately through a hospital. Disabled children in the US may qualify for therapy through the school setting. By law, the school therapy is limited to the skills essential to school success rather than approximating age-appropriate level of development to the extent possible. Because my daughter walked, moved her arms, and held her head independently, she never received direct physical therapy through the school, only consult. She received occupational therapy, limited to an hour a month despite more significant deficits, which included inability to move a writing utensil in a purposeful way, cut with scissors, tie shoes, button clothes, or brush teeth and hair. Work on these skills was delegated to special needs teachers, who in turn passed it onto the paraprofessionals who are not required to have training beyond high school. The only type of therapy my daughter received through the school system consistently throughout her school years (ages 3 through 21) was speech therapy due to her profound delays in this area vital for success in life. She worked directly with a school speech therapist in three different states and school systems, with quality of the services I can rate as above those received in an average private setting.

Available programming and options significantly depend on one's place of residence. A small rural area will predictably have reduced choices compared to those provided in an area with a sizable urban population. We lived in a small town in the Midwest with a big university, and private services received in the academic setting were hands down the best available to us.

For many years, my daughter was lucky to have speech therapy through the university Speech and Hearing Clinic. Service providers were graduate students under the supervision of a faculty member. Their practice has not become routine yet, and they were highly motivated, enthusiastic, creative, and playful, which was very appropriate for my daughter's age and development level. When she began attending the clinic at the age of six, she was saying five to seven single words. If she began using a new word, she'd stop using the one she was able to say before. She could not pronounce many sounds, especially vowels. In addition to her extreme difficulties with speech production, she struggled with focus and attention. She received services on schedules that varied from three times a week for half an hour to twice a week for 45 min. Often she worked with two therapists at a time, which helped her focus better and provided them with the experience of servicing a difficult case. They structured and sequenced all activities, allowing her to become successful in tasks in a span of one semester. They also kept detailed and meticulous notes that we never encountered in another setting. Their records were able to demonstrate the progress required for insurance to continue covering the sessions for as long as she was attending therapy there. Over the years with them, my daughter progressed to simple individual sentences with sufficient intelligibility for us, although she still prefers to keep to a few familiar patterns in her communicative attempts.

Another example of services in an academic setting was a lab in a course for the future teachers of adaptive physical education in the kinesiology department. Under the supervision of the course instructor, a single student planned and implemented gross motor activities for the entire semester for one or more participants. They met once a week for an hour. My daughter worked with them on improving balance, posture, and developing movement patterns outside her limited rigid repertoire (for years, she would throw a ball only down to the ground from the overhead position and swing a bat or a racket also only downward). We received short summary notes updating us on her progress on goals specific for this semester. Her participation contributed to an increase both in the variety of the movement patterns she was able to acquire as well as in the speed of learning new gross motor skills that continue to be her strength and the most significant contributors to her quality of life at the present time.

The specialists and approaches to which she responded better had a less mechanistic view of human development and were not covered by insurance. Over the years, we encountered two speech therapists out of state who not only had exceptional rapport with my daughter but also used techniques that we did not encounter in our settings; one worked on oral muscles and the other used whole body to build phonemic memory. The distance and out-of-pocket costs were prohibitive to regular face-to-face sessions, and local providers in Indiana at the time showed no interest in learning about what we found as working better for us allegedly because of the lack of scientific support of positive impact of oral musculature exercises on speech production.

In Colorado, we found support through speech therapy with assistive communication technology at the level appropriate for my daughter's current communicative needs and challenges, where she loves sharing stories of events in her life documented with ubiquitous cameras. With a sizably low and non-verbal population, both the speech therapy and the technology including technical support are covered by insurance. In addition, our large urban locale has specialists in therapies that provide diverse brain stimuli through differentiable body movement and hands-on manipulation for those unable to follow verbal instructions. Having experienced the effects of these movements personally in a workshop, I attest to their efficacy as demonstrated by my increased focus and attention and decreased reaction time to stimuli. Adequate brain stimulation is necessary to normal development, and other providers, such as chiropractors, also espouse a similar philosophy where improvement in physical movement yields improvement in cognitive functioning. They treat the muscle tightness affecting ligaments and bones, which also over time produces small but important positive behavioral changes, including improved communication and thought processing.

Decisions, Decisions, Decisions… Doctors' Advice Regarding Genetic Disorders

Inclusion means love, support, and respect that start in the smallest relevant unit before a child is born – a family. With the divorce rates significantly higher in families with special needs children than in the general population, one can see that inclusion is not easy to embrace in practice. As any parent of a special needs child knows all too well, the limitations extend to the entire family that leads a life many do not experience. I understand those who choose not to go through pregnancy after receiving a prenatal diagnosis of a genetic disorder. Having seen the effects of having a child with a disability on the lives of different people, I also support recommending genetic testing covered by insurance across the board for all women regardless of whether they are considered medically to be high risk. It would give them time to decide what they want to do without any pressure. It is necessary that the expecting parents receive accurate and complete available information regarding the diagnosed condition in words they understand. It is not uncommon for them to deal with the worst-case scenario based on very limited academic knowledge. This worst-case scenario boils down to a list of conditions associated with the underlying cause, as in the following report: "The phenotypic consequence of these abnormalities will be primarily due to the 1q deletion. The 1q42-q44 deletion syndrome shows variable features and may include: moderate to severe intellectual disability, limited or absent speech, characteristic facial features, hand and foot anomalies, microcephaly, abnormalities of the corpus callosum (agenesis/hypogenesis), and seizures." (Personal communication via social media, 2014) Not only do the specialized terminologies require a translation but also they are not always obtained from a qualified physician. It is nearly impossible to imagine any quality of life in a person who may not speak and has a small head with parts of the brain missing. The report does not specify how many actual cases went into building the horror list, which feature combinations were common among them, and how they affected different individuals in their daily lives.

Certainly, exceptional specialists with adequate experience and wonderful bedside manners exist, as well as practitioners who realize the limitations of their knowledge, training, and experience and honestly and clearly communicate the limited scope of their understanding of the reported cases they read about before talking to the parents. Typical physician training, in my experience, does not adequately prepare doctors to talk to the parents facing a diagnosis of their baby's genetic disorder. Most, if not all, of their knowledge of genetic differences comes from medical textbooks that aim at objectively presenting the condition. This objectivity consists of presenting phenotypes as in the excerpt quoted above, occasionally accompanied by pictures of naked affected individuals, some of them with an eye block placed on their faces to preserve anonymity. Rarity of conditions makes them even more confusing and scary for physicians who are expected to provide qualified professional advice. This lack of knowledge permeates not only prenatal counseling but the entire life, with recommendations often interpreting "best interests" as in what is the least likely to incur any liability for the advice given. Today parents facing any prenatal diagnosis can turn to the Internet and social media for more subjective and often humane views of other parents and caregivers of the children and adults with the same or a similar condition. This will give them a different first-hand perspective on the upcoming changes in their lives to assist in arriving at a decision that works for them. Needless to say, no information sufficiently prepares people electing to keep the baby for the road ahead of them.

Free Appropriate Public Education (FAPE)

The law makes provisions for educating children with a disability from birth through 21 years in public schools. Efficacy is not considered – I am not aware of exclusions based on severity of conditions or a possibility of gainful employment upon graduation. While the law is all encompassing, its primary target can be seen in extending graduation age until 21. It is 4 years, or approximately 1/3 of the 13 years it takes most students to complete secondary education. Since the level of intellectual impairment of the majority of the students with disabilities is mild, defined as IQ 70, in theory, in 4 years, these students with mild intellectual disabilities will catch up to their normally developing peers who graduate at 18.

Disabilities are not limited to cognitive impairments, and the schools need to address them to the extent they interfere with education. The law does not mandate schools to provide optimal development environment having the students work up to their full potential, just assure academic success defined as passing courses. Schools in conjunction with families are tasked with determining the course of education for each student, and the more significant challenges the student faces, the more difficult it becomes to plan for their education in the sense of helping them prepare for their lives as adults regardless of academic success.

We found that school districts vary in how they serve students with disabilities. Most of our personal experience comes from a small south central Indiana community with a small school district of around ten elementary schools. It centralized services where the most involved students with extensive medical needs that required constant attention from medically trained staff attended a single school. At the next level were schools that had self-contained classrooms with small number of students with significant educational needs. They allow the curriculum and delivery be tailored to their level, which is considerably behind that of their peers. Inclusion was an option for a wide variety of students in every school.

My daughter's cognition is affected by atypical neurological and sensory processing that was not well understood or successfully addressed at that time. We received reports of her high energy being a safety issue during recess when she did not remain on the playground with the other children. Attention deficit disorder and hyperactivity are diagnosed with a questionnaire and treated with medication, which temporary alleviated concerns. While speech therapists reported improvements during sessions, we did not observe dramatic changes in her performance in any area. Over time, she began looking overmedicated, and we discontinued her medication after trying unsuccessfully to find one without side effects. She attended a self-contained classroom beginning in elementary school, with some inclusion.

Usually parents perceive and report highest success at the elementary school level, and we were no exception. The academic skills are in the inception stage for most typically developing students, with inclusion being the easiest to support in most settings. The curriculum encompasses basic academic skills like reading, counting, and writing, which are practical and useful throughout life and therefore appropriate for a very wide variety of students with most levels of impairment. By middle school, however, the curriculum and the skills required to master it begin to diverge more dramatically for students with moderate degrees of impairments. They join a non-academic track, where they do not participate in standardized testing at their grade level but instead engage mostly in community and everyday life activities of which shopping, eating out and bowling are popular ones. Some programs support limited simplified cooking. Academic focus fades and may be eliminated entirely. My daughter worked on reading and mathematics in the context of cooking and shopping with very limited success. Teaching math through concepts like rounding to the nearest dollar amount (legacy of outdated teacher training) was neither appropriate for her comprehension level at the time nor practical for her situation in today's world. By high school, the focus is on post-secondary adult life, including finding a potential work place in the community fitting to existing skills, interests, and strengths. My daughter tried a variety of traditional vocations in a simulated environment, from bussing tables to stacking bathrooms with supplies. She was welcomed at a home inspection agency where she shredded reports. The agency extended a part-time employment offer for her after school. However, the state of Indiana limited disability support by the time my daughter turned 18. I was informed that the state will not allocate money for her in the form of the Developmental Disability waiver, and the funds through the Supported Living Services waiver were insufficient to provide for her programming after her part-time work. This meant I could not work full-time and keep her at home. To continue living in Indiana and be able to support my family financially, I would have had to place her in an institution. This news was the decisive factor in severing ties with the state where she was born and we spent most of our lives.

High school services in Colorado were similar to those in Indiana but different in one important aspect; they did not address post-secondary employment. The teachers believed it did not exist for my daughter. They also lacked knowledge of options for her after school, which made planning for and transitioning to her post-secondary life less successful for us than Indiana, where the school system was actively involved in on-site job skill training in high school. I had state assistance in the form of a Medicaid waiver more appropriate for individuals who become disabled later in life because the waiver for the developmental disabilities had a waiting list. Not having access to services available for children with developmental disabilities until the last semester of high school complicated the planning for transition for her after high school and my employment. Services targeting developmental disabilities were available in the area, but my daughter was on a wait-list until her last semester of high school. This complicated my employment and her transition out of high school. Unable to plan for her life after high school while in high school, I succeeded in obtaining support for the development of her academic skills. She excelled at sight reading in early elementary school and has been maintaining basic reading skills since that time. Her teacher provided reading materials from the general elementary curriculum on which we worked daily. It was difficult to find content that was appropriate to her developmental level, both challenging and meaningful. However, after much effort, often quite painful, one of the most rewarding recent developments is my daughter initiating reading books for pleasure and fun. While they are very simple, she reads them with a high degree of fluency and accuracy, building the foundation for future progress.

Another fond memory from the last years of high school was participation in Special Olympics basketball in a mixed team environment where regular students assist specials needs students. They structured my daughter's movement on court so that she was able to shoot a basket, providing excellent level of support. The degree of adaptation makes me question whether this was inclusion, but this was an experience done right in our book. It enabled meaningful participation for every participant, each with their own unique set of challenges. My daughter learned to throw the ball up into the hoop rather than slam it down as she did invariably for many years. She also had fun with her peer group.

Fun in Life : Independent Living

It is tempting to create an impression that family life with a person with a disability is centered on this person and consists of interventions and services. Nothing can be further from the truth. We have been extremely fortunate throughout my daughter's lifespan to find activities she could participate in with assistance. For the youngest children, they include typically listening and responding to music. They are inclusive, easy to locate, and participate in many locations. Later on, we added horseback riding. In Wyoming, a comprehensive Medicaid waiver covered hippo-therapy, which is an occupational and physical therapy with the participant being on a horse. In Indiana, we did not have this coverage and paid out of pocket for therapeutic horseback riding for 15 years. It provided similar benefits – improved posture and balance, decreased sensory processing difficulties including tactile defensiveness, and built a connection with the animals, which promotes an increased sense of competence, confidence, calm, and overall wellbeing. The horses are seasoned veterans, with personalities well suited to supporting riders with special needs and beginners. My daughter's younger siblings began their riding at a very young age through the same program, which instilled in them love for the horses as well as made them competent riders. We are extremely grateful to the program director for creating, sustaining, and extending this wonderful program in south central Indiana. There were several other sport programs by the city and the YMCA that had adaptive focus and were very affordable – a fraction of the costs of programming for the typically developing children, with scholarships supporting low-income families. Adaptive baseball, basketball, soccer, martial arts, swimming, and later dance were of high quality, with my daughter acquiring life-saving skill of being comfortable in water. In the summer, the city provided camps that included my daughter and provided an aid for no additional cost. These were both regular and specialized camps, where she went sailing on a nearby lake. She also attended overnight camps, with Riley Children's camp in Bradford woods as the best known in the state, and also a catholic camp around Nashville, Indiana, that supported inclusion and a camp near Kentucky. She enjoyed activities of a typical camp and learned from a young age to be separated from her family overnight, important for building her independence skills. I taught her to walk on ice independently – this is her version of ice-skating. She compared this experience to flying on several occasions.

A college town also supported love for the arts. Our family held season tickets to the opera, theater, and ballet, all of which my daughter appreciated from a very young age. She has learned to behave appropriately during performances that we can all attend anywhere as a family.

While as a young toddler she appeared least interested in her surroundings when we attended children's museums, zoos, or similar attractions, over time she began expressing interest in and appreciation of these places. She now loves to travel and has better stamina than her siblings in visiting places of interest.

We also befriended a local artist comfortable with special needs and spent several years learning working in clay as a family. I typically assisted my daughter with special needs, who at first would not touch the clay, avoiding both the texture and the mess it could create for her wardrobe. We gradually increased the time she handled the clay, allowing her to desensitize to the irritants. She tolerated touching but much preferred glazing and creating unique color combinations. In high school, her color combinations pleasantly surprised her art teacher. We are hoping to build on her existing skills in the near future in a business setting.

We miss dearly many of these activities after we moved to Colorado from Indiana. We did not find sufficient support for her in classes for individuals with a disability through the city parks and recreation. In addition, the costs are significantly higher for these classes in Colorado. However, we found great outlets for participation in great outdoors activities, specialized in providing services for the people with disabilities as well as those that supported the participation of our entire family. We went rock climbing, alpine skiing, and white water rafting. Cross-country skiing did not take my daughter a long time to learn with assistance first from an instructor, than from me. There are several camps in the beautiful mountain area that my daughter attends. We also found an organization that specializes in traveling with individuals with disabilities and promoting disability awareness in young adults. We travel to national parks and monuments in the area, including Yellowstone, and enjoy hikes and drives through beautiful nature. While it is impossible to gauge the developmental impact of life activities, they certainly contribute to a wonderful quality of life, which we would aim to preserve and enhance.

What Do We Want and How Do We Get There?

Despite communication difficulties, my daughter unequivocally expressed her desire for an adult life with choices and relationships that goes beyond the scope of the complacent behavior expected in an institution. We are hoping to find a setting and support system that will bring us closer to fulfilling our dreams for her. Limitations of social mobility are another combined effect of a disability and life choices. I am unable to move without making sure there are at least minimal support services available for my daughter that we can get within a reasonable time frame.

In Indiana we waited for over 12 years for her to get comprehensive support, with me employed in positions below my earning potential, straining the family financially, only to have the level of support we dreamt about and have been waiting for eliminated. In Indiana, her options would have been living with her family with a limited state support or being placed into a group home (eight or more individuals) somewhere in the state that has a spot open. Both settings have their downsides. Family typically provides care and life experiences superior to an institutional setting without the worry of possible abuse and neglect. The downsides are insufficient state support resulting in my underemployment and, equally importantly, more time to deepen her attachment and dependency on the family, which will make her adjustment to a different setting as an adult more difficult. In Colorado, she has more options regarding living arrangements including living with a family that signs up with the state to provide support services but no realistic employment options to date. Yet in another state, the options will undoubtedly differ, and I will not know enough about them until after we move to that state. To decrease competition for limited resources, service agencies limit positive information to out of state residents seeking services for their loved ones. A reliable source of information would be caregivers of adults with disabilities who are living the lifestyle we seek and are willing to share their experiences with services. In the end, my decisions for the foreseeable future will have to be based on less than optimal information.

Acknowledgments Author's Note: With deep gratitude, I wish to thank my family, friends, and providers whose love, support, and sharing of resources have always made the difference in our lives and circumstances.

Chapter 23
A Journey in the Spectrum

Lily Chakraborty

Abstract Lily Chakraborty is a special educator and mother of Zico, a child with autism. This chapter draws on her experience as a mother and takes the reader into the world of those parents who experience the pains and joys of bringing up their child with autism. It provides a unique perspective on both autism in India and the UK from the viewpoint of a concerned parent.

Introduction

An eight-year old boy, anxious, standing in a long queue along with his mother for 20 long minutes, was coping with the stress caused by the surrounding environment. Finally, when they reached the booth for security check at the airport, the lady in charge told the mother: "He is such a grown-up boy! Send him to the men's booth." The poor mother tried to convince her by stating: "Actually he is a special child: he is autistic and has difficulty in understanding verbal instructions, and he needs help. Please allow him to be with me." The lady looked at the boy, observed him thoroughly from head to toe and then shared: "What is his problem? He looks so normal. Send him to the other security booth." The lady did not believe the mother and was not ready to listen to her either. The poor mother was trying to make her understand the difficulties the child was having. By then, people standing behind the mother and the child in the queue started getting furious. Everyone was in a hurry! No one had the patience to support or cooperate with the mother – humanity failed!!!

Finally, the desperate mother switched over to English to advocate for her child. (By the way, till then, the communication had been in Bengali, her native tongue.) The scenario changed immediately! Thank God, the British ruled us for 200 years and injected Western culture and English language in our soul, which has become the measure for class in our society!! Out of respect, the lady in-charge of the security now immediately allowed the child to accompany the mother (without of course understanding a single word spoken to her by the mother)! This incident made the

L. Chakraborty (✉)
Aarohan Welfare Society for Differently Abled Children,
Kolkata 700 033, West Bengal, India
e-mail: rumpa_c@hotmail.com

© Springer International Publishing AG 2017   367
S. Halder, L.C. Assaf (eds.), *Inclusion, Disability and Culture*, Inclusive
Learning and Educational Equity 3, DOI 10.1007/978-3-319-55224-8_23

mother more confident to manage her son under various circumstances in our so-called "rule-based" society. That mother is none other than me, Lily Chakraborty, the narrator of this story.

Let us look back a few years down the line. I married my childhood friend and went to the UK. We lived in Ipswich, a small town, and 4 years passed by happily. It was 3 June 2004. I was blessed with a baby boy, fully termed, healthy, like any other child. My husband (he was a huge soccer fan) named him "Zico" which was happily approved by us all. Zico was born in Kolkata, India and we went back to the UK when he was 6 months old. He traveled ten long hours but did not disturb any-one in the flight. My husband and I were amazed to see such a well-behaved baby boy. The three of us started to bond well gradually.

Zico started growing up, developing all necessary motor skills. I was very happy to have such a beautiful living and breathing doll and was never worried whether he was achieving all developmental milestones or not. Zico was always happy and so was I. The only times I used to feel bad was when he did not appear to be sad if I had to leave him to go somewhere or did not show much joy when he saw me back after a period of absence. Zico never crawled. Instead he started walking when he was 15 months old (little delayed compared to normal milestone). However, he never pointed at things for drawing attention or for asking for things he wanted. Neither did he ever track objects pointed at. The concept of "object permanence" was not in place. "Pretend play" was also missing. There were very few echoic and intraverbal responses, and he showed lots of stereotyped motor movements, like flapping of hands and spinning.

Diagnosis: Two Scenarios

Early diagnosis is very important for any developmental abnormality. As the brain's plasticity remains the same till the age of 6–7, the more stimulation is given, the more positive outcomes occur. In a country like UK, doctors' predictions were absolutely correct along with intervention whereas in India knowledge about devel-opmental abnormalities is still lagging behind. I still wonder if I could have accepted the fact early and had educated myself simultaneously at that early stage, Zico would have moved ahead in a much better way. Most of the doctors including pedia-tricians in India don't know the varied behaviors of the child under the spectrum. Mostly they know only its severe syndrome.

So, for doctors in India, it was difficult to diagnose a child who was happy, was capable of giving a social smile and able to enjoy listening to music to be autistic. When I think back, I remember he never waved "bye," never pointed to things which he wanted including a noticeable lack of name call response which could have been easily diagnosed before the age of one. In the UK I saw different playgroups: teachers used to organize different activities for different developmental purposes for kids aged 6 months to 3 years. I remember they used to organize what they called "messy play" where children played with lots of messy substances like wet sand, dry sand, baked beans, water, water color, paints, foam, glue, slime, etc. Teachers observed the behavior of each and every child during this activity. Some children avoided a few things and some enjoyed the experience. However, there was always a fine line between enjoyment and seeking. Zico fell under the second category. He was a tactile seeker. He used to seek rubbing and mouthing almost all the time, which showed some sort of not-"normal" (or abnormal) behavior that was absent in neurotypical children. Lack of motivation in play and social communication are the core indicators which helped the teachers to convey the probability of difficulties of the children to the parents so that early diagnosis could be identified.

At the age of one and a half, the National Health Service (NHS) health visitor first mentioned the probability of Zico being autistic. There was obvious denial by my husband and me, but I developed a suppressed fear. I started surfing the Internet, looking for information and found that Zico had lots of autistic characteristics. A portage worker (who provides home-visiting service for preschool children with developmental or learning difficulties or other special needs) started to come to our home with lots of attractive toys with different functions (visual tracking toys, toys with cause and effect), but Zico was not at all motivated to play with these toys in a meaningful manner. If he was offered a car, he would prefer to spin the wheel. He roamed around when we went to other children's birthday parties, had no sustained attention span, no sitting tolerance, no parallel play. His hearing was tested; the report identified no hearing loss, and we became even more anxious.

Meanwhile we came to India to spend our holidays and met some of the renowned doctors in the city. Surprisingly, all of them (except one), said: "He is absolutely fine, such a lovely child. 'You' must have some problem (pointing towards me), don't worry. There is only a slight delay in speech, he will speak soon. Enjoy motherhood." I wanted to hear exactly that and was very happy. After our visit to India, I went back to the UK happy. Finally, at the age of two and a half, Zico was officially diagnosed with autism spectrum disorder. Anyone familiar with autism knows that such individuals are full of paradoxes; obsession and complete indifference, bouts of extreme focus and bouts of extreme distraction, grave deficits and strong talents. Because of this complexity, the challenge of developing a treatment program for people with autism has been quite a conundrum for clinicians and researchers for over 50 years. Professionals and parents have attempted various treatments to maximize the happiness, productivity and cognitive abilities of these complex people despite an inability to fully understand the disorder they are addressing.

At the age of 4, other children with "normal" theory of mind learn empathy. They can watch puppets on real actors performing different roles and experience different sequences of a plot or story, and can imagine what a particular puppet or actor who missed a part of the story would think or know or do. Children with autism, like Zico, at the age of five behave like younger children who are unable to put themselves into another person's shoes and are known to be unable to work out the deficits, true or false of others, desires or emotions. He never detected deception.

Impact on Family

The diagnosis not only affected me and my husband; there was an impact on Zico. As in most of the other similar cases, I tended to jump in with both feet and get overly involved with the situation, thinking that everything will become alright. My husband supported me immensely. However, he still had the opportunity to withdraw himself from the situation daily during his office hours. For me, lacking any kind of break resulted in burn out, no matter how much I loved my child. At times I started to feel hopeless, numb, restless and angry at the same time. I knew a mother with a child with disability who ran away from her share of responsibilities, away from her marriage, even away from her child. This incident shocked me but at the same time I felt like doing it at times.

Resentment was an ever-present emotion in our family, affected by Zico's diagnosis. It was hard not to feel resentment when diagnosis took away many things from our lives which are taken for granted usually such as undisturbed sleep, quiet meal times and many others. I should thank God we did not have the typical family problems which often get compounded by "genetic blame" wondering whose genes carried the disorder. But yes, I had mild depression at times. I always felt blessed that I had full support from the family right from day one. But withdrawn from public life, my depression was amplified, as there was obvious denial about the diagnosis from my side in the initial days.

After the diagnosis, NHS arranged a postdiagnostic workshop for parents. My husband and I attended the one-day workshop. It was quite good, informative and educative. But still our mind was stuck at the same place. By this time I had come to know of various world-renowned personalities like Einstein, Bill Gates and Alfred Hitchcock et al. who had autism but I never wanted to understand the various degrees of autism or their cognition level. I started to believe that one day my son would also be like Einstein. Even my in-laws, who always stood by me, from the time of diagnosis till now, said: "A genius has been born in our family." Actually, we all wanted to keep ourselves happy and stress free. Few months passed with this myth still persisting.

Therapeutic Journey: Disparity Between Countries

There is no medicine that can cure autism. Therapy is the only remedy to get the best results, hence Zico's therapy started. A competent team of pediatricians, a child psychologist, Speech and Language Pathologist (SLP), portage, health visitors, coordinator, neurologist and special educator developed Zico's Individualized Education Program (IEP), and thus his therapeutic journey started. I did not have to pay a single penny for it in the UK. It was good to see that the government valued children with special needs and took care of them in such a way that the parents did not have to worry. But at the same time, I found that there was a huge disparity with respect to socio-cultural matters. I remember, my first teaching goal was toilet training, but Zico's team opposed the idea. They said: "Do not put stress on the child right now, let us focus on his eating skills (with spoon)." I was confused. Now I realize they were right in their own way.

In the UK, there were a lot of playgroups for children with autism. Volunteers used to take care of the children going to the playgroups and parents/caregivers would be given some respite during that time. Children enjoyed playing on the playground equipment and parents enjoyed themselves with refreshments. I came across a few families with children with autism. I was the only Asian and was constantly anxious about Zico. I also had difficulty following their accent during our conversations. It took me a few months to get used to the environment. However, Zico was happy as always. I was always surprised to see that the other parents were stress free, relaxed and not at all worried about teaching new skills or managing the challenging behavior of their children. They showed much more interest in different government schemes where they could collect disability allowance for their children.

As I was a middle-class Indian woman, I became judgmental due to my values about their characteristics and culture and used to think: "How can a parent collect money in the name of his/her disabled child?" Along with Zico's health visitor, many of these parents also tried to convince me to apply for disability allowance for Zico. I would get mad whenever I heard their suggestions. I had my own explanation and they had their own. Now I understand what a fool I was. They were much more practical than I was. Two important things – acceptance and understanding the needs of the children, were totally missing for me.

Around this same time, I planned to visit India along with Zico but was scared to travel alone. One parent suggested I create one identity card for Zico with a caption – "I am autistic, please help." I could not digest the suggestion, as I was still not ready to accept the reality in my mind. I kept telling everyone that Zico was absolutely fine; his speech was just a little bit delayed, which was absolutely normal. But now I am happy with myself that I have won over all my inhibitions, and I can suggest the same things to parents of special children in India just as those in the UK used to advise me.

When Zico was 2 years and 10 months old, I came back to Bengaluru, India and got a second opinion and diagnosis at National Institute of Mental Health and Neurosciences. And yes, the earlier diagnosis was absolutely correct. While the disorder is not rare, a multitude of people with autism in India have not been diagnosed, and more critically, there is a tremendous lack of awareness and misunderstanding about autism among medical professionals, who may either misdiagnose or underdiagnose the condition. One of the major difficulties faced by parents of autistic children in India is obtaining an accurate diagnosis. A parent may take their child because he is just "slow." Unsatisfied, they visit a psychologist, to be told their child is "mentally subnormal." Convinced that their child does not fit the typical picture of mental retardation, they may visit a psychiatrist, to be told that their child has attention deficit disorder and must be put on medication to control hyperactivity. After that they may again start the cycle of searching for a correct name for their child's problem. Fortunately, the process of obtaining a diagnosis of autism in India is improving in the major cities, as more and more pediatricians are becoming aware of the condition, Still some doctors may feel that nothing can be gained by a diagnosis of autism if the services are nonexistent. Yet as more and more children are diagnosed as autistic and awareness of the disorder spreads, there will be a demand for services.

Many people want to know: What is autism in India like? Does it look the same as for children in other places? What kinds of services are available? What do families do? Is the prevalence the same? These are all very intriguing and important questions. Some of these can be answered from the experience of working with hundreds of families. However, without empirical research, there are many questions about autism in India (and other places in the world) that remain unanswered. Data released from Centers for Disease Control and Prevention USA in April 2014 placed the prevalence of autism in the US at approximately 1 in 68 children (www. autismspeaks.org). There are no data available from India to provide an India-specific estimate of the prevalence, and it is unknown whether there are variations in this rate worldwide.

I was supposed to stay in India for a few months as I wanted to try a different approach for Zico. He got admitted to an early intervention center. I found that the mothers there were very much dedicated and motivated to work with their children to bring some difference to their lives. I was touched. Actually, there are lots of challenges in life in our country to fit into the society we belong. At the end of the day, the government wasn't there to care for people like us. In this condition, inclusion is nothing but a fancy word to parents like me. So, I made up my mind and told myself: "Keep your motivation high and work hard to make your child as independent as possible." I decided to stay in Bengaluru.

Undiagnosed Associative Condition

As I mentioned earlier, Zico showed obsessive behavior towards texture and swinging and did not show much potential in motor activities which were signs of sensory integration dysfunction – the inability to process certain information received through the senses. Scientists say the neurological disorganization can occur in different manners. One effect is when the brain does not receive messages because of a disconnection in the neuron cells. A second effect is when sensory messages are received inconsistently. The third way is when sensory messages are received consistently, but do not connect properly with other sensory messages (Kranowitz and Stock 1998). I feel the third reason is enough to explain the weird emotional responses of a person with autism along with sensory processing disorder (SPD). For example, sometimes when Zico gets hurt, instead of crying he laughs!

Though we all have some sensory processing difficulties, we can cope with that through our executive functional capabilities which are mostly missing in children with autism. Our brain constantly needs mechanisms like modulation, inhibition, habituation and facilitation. In the process of modulation, the brain turns neural switches on or off to regulate its activity. The brain reduces connections between sensory intake and behavioral output when certain sensory information is not needed to perform a particular task in the process of inhibition. In habituation, we become accustomed to familiar messages. In facilitation, the brain promotes connections between sensory intake and behavioral output by sending messages of displeasure or pleasure. Children with autism mostly have difficulties in the above neurological process. The outcome of these difficulties shows behaviors like rigidity, sudden emotional outburst, inappropriate language etc. Though all these types of behaviors were present in Zico, he remained undiagnosed in the UK as SPD along with autism. What was totally undiagnosed in the UK was that Zico had severe sensory issues along with hypotonia. So, teaching him any skill became more and more challenging. Various occupational therapists helped me develop knowledge in this field.

Along with sensory processing disorder, Zico received added diagnosis of somatodyspraxia because he often exhibited poor tactile and proprioceptive processing like clumsiness, frequent tripping, falling and bumping into objects, difficulty in fine motor and manipulation skills and poor organization (Cermak and Larkin 1991). Occupational therapy suggested we focus more on heavy work, deep pressure and light touch experiences. At the age of three, I started to make Zico carry shopping bags. People used to feel pity on him and perhaps cursed me for my cruelty but I continued that practice of heavy work for betterment of his praxis issues. I was determined towards inclusion for my son in the mainstream education system as well as in society.

Since autism is a spectrum disorder, all children emerge different from each other. But most of them have difficulty in bilateral motor coordination, which involves clapping, jumping, hopping, skipping etc. along with bilateral self-care skills such as fastening and tying shoes, buttoning etc. Zico had right-left confusion as well. He avoided midline crossing and had difficulty developing hand preference. Till the age of six, we could not make out which was his preferred hand. Additionally, he appeared to have vestibular and proprioceptive difficulties. A sensory diet was planned and scheduled activity program implemented by an occupational therapist that was designed and developed to meet the specific needs of Zico's nervous system. I was happy about my decision to stay in India because all of these activities improved Zico's diagnosis, treatment and eventual progress.

Slowly, my home was turning into a kind of a therapeutic center! We did not have a sofa set but we had bean bags which we used for Zico to jump down from height. We had a huge mirror which acted as an extra stimulus for Zico to learn imitation skills. Kilograms and kilograms of different pulses became sources of tactile input, not for cooking!!

Through intensive occupational therapy, Zico was improving in terms of motor skills. The therapist was quite stubborn to get the work done by hook or crook. Sometimes the therapist would hit him; I don't know how I managed to bear all these! Since he was showing progress, I ignored the therapist's cruelty. Later on, when we started Applied Behavior Analysis (ABA), I realized how unscientific all those strategies were. ABA taught me how to teach every skill in a scientific way where we could see the progress on a graph from baseline to its mastery along with increasing motivation towards learning new skills. My thought process had changed completely by now. Though behavior analysts don't believe in sensory integration therapy as such, I believe if a child has lots of sensory issues, it can be managed by sensory integration process to a certain extent using ABA principles.

Education, Inclusion: The Reality

Currently, the needs of autistic children are not being met in either the regular or special education systems. With an understanding teacher or possibly an aid, a more able autistic child can function very well in a regular school and learn valuable social skills from his peers. However, even children with very high IQs are often not permitted in regular classes. Also, the rigidity and pressure of schools in India can make it difficult for an autistic child to cope without special allowances. Some children with higher support needs, who form the majority of autistic children, may attend special schools, but these schools often lack in understanding of effective methods of handling the challenging behaviors of autistic children. Children with autism are frequently refused admission in special schools because officials protest that they are not equipped to handle autistic children, who are sometimes more challenging than children with other disabilities. This happened with me too. When Zico was 6 years old, I decided to put him in a regular school with a shadow teacher. I went to a primary school with him. After observing Zico, the principal told me: "I am really very sorry that we cannot admit your child as other children may be scared when they see his stereotype behavior. But we do admit special children, we have a few with intellectual disability, but as you can understand an autistic child is difficult to handle." At that moment, I decided I would not go anywhere else and beg for my child. I would create my own school where my son will learn with full right and pride! So, we started Blossom – our own school, with three other mothers with special children. We got ourselves formally trained and we started our journey with the very best school in the world. Hence my dream of mainstream inclusion was ruptured. I was upset, though not broken.

In India, parents of special children run from one therapist to another to get best possible help for our children but due to lack of a collaborative approach, the therapies cannot reflect the optimum progress. In special education, multidisciplinary approach is a must. Though there are lots of professionals in this field available in India, due to lack of collaboration, the child suffers the most and as end result, inclusion in regular schools becomes near to impossible. Even in special schools or therapeutic clinics, there are disparities between therapists in different fields and this affects the child the most.

When the Persons with Disability Act was passed, initially autism was not considered as a disability as it was considered as a hidden disability. After lots of debate and conflict in 1999 the National Trust Act included autism with other disabilities. Now schools cannot deny admission based on this disability. But in practice, the denial process is still going on. Most schools rationalize not accepting autistic children because of lack of special educators and resource rooms.

A very few percentage of children under the spectrum with high cognition and no behavior issues are getting a chance to enter the mainstream classroom. Central Board of Secondary Education has given lot of exemptions in the examination process for these children in terms of giving additional time to answer questions. But the question is: What happens with the children with low cognition or behavioral problems? They are literally nowhere. For them, the word "inclusion" is a myth. Parents literally try to exclude them from the society. Middle-class or upper-middle-class families try to continue therapies mostly till the age of 15–16. After that the teenagers stay at home only. Earlier, there was the concept of a joint family, when all family members used to stay together. If a child had a disability, there were many people around to take care of the child. But now as families have become nuclear, the support system has been affected. Actually right now, we stand at the crossroads of Eastern and Western culture which has confused us even further.

In many other countries, inclusion is a major part of the education system. From a very early age, other neurotypical children are taught to be empathic towards children with special needs. Hence the whole society is aware of persons with disabilities. Ideally, social stigma gets eradicated. But in countries like India it is a major problem in our society. We, as parents feel scared to have our children evaluated. Sometimes I feel is it really necessary to label the child as autistic, mentally retarded, or slow learner? After assessment, if we find that the developmental criteria are not matching with the "neurotypical" parameters we can work on the deficits, without discussing the name of the disability. Unfortunately, that is the common practice in our society. But definitely from a legal perspective, the labeling is important to specify the rights of a person with any type of disability.

In my journey, I have heard "I'm sorry" many times. People were always empathic. But they made me feel worse, not better. I never wanted people to be sorry for me or my child. My life and my child might be different, but, these are not the things I feel sorry for. No one else should either. From these interactions, I realized I needed to learn more about autism and the need for formal training and education drove me towards special education which gave me enormous opportunity to understand the biological and psychological perspective of autism. Now when I see a child just after diagnosis, I never console the parents saying: "He or she will be fine". In fact, nobody knows whether he or she will be "fine." I don't know what the next 20 or 30 years will look like for the child and the family. If he does not overcome his disabilities, if he does not get into the mainstream, if he does not progress as he matures, does that mean I have failed? We should never compare our journey with others who have children with autism. Autism spectrum disorder is a very complex disorder and no two journeys are the same.

The most commonly debated question that arises is inclusion. There is no point in discussing inclusion if a regular school is not equipped to provide accommodation for a student with autism. What can we gain, then, in larger settings? Individuals with autism are often recognized by their inability to socialize with others. Some of them have no speech or they speak things which are inappropriate. If a student remains in a regular classroom with limited interaction with mainstream peers, he/ she will undoubtedly experience little or no social growth. Teaching individuals with autism on how to form relationships and effective communication skills is more important than academic learning while considering the future potential of such students. Since this is the greatest area of weakness, schools have an important responsibility to include this in the curriculum, irrespective of the fact whether the student with autism is a part of a regular educational setting or a special education classroom. Schools do not always recognize this responsibility.

Teaching skills in both regular educational settings as well as the special setting has proved to be effective. In order to do this, lessons may need to be modified as per the student's capability. Concepts can be taught differently due to their lack of ability to learn in the traditional way. Individuals with autism are mostly visual learners. They perceive things visually. Hence, every concept or lesson can be taught through various visual aids. These adaptations may affect the success of a student with autism. Due to the fact that very few institutions feel the need to train their professionals and paraprofessionals to accommodate the needs of disabled students, differentiated instruction and effective inclusion is more often a desire than a reality. Too often, in India, a classroom full of 40 or 50 students, with different abilities, are entrusted with one teacher for their care and learning. Practically it is difficult for a single teacher to use differentiated instruction which is believed to be one of the most effective parameters in the academic growth of a student with special needs in a regular educational setting.

Successful inclusion of a student with autism in regular school setting depends on the severity of the disability, effective training and knowledge of the educators and collaboration with other professionals and parents. Inclusion is the best possible condition for many students with autism, but not always productive for all students. Even for high-functioning students with major sitting intolerance due to sensory dysfunction, inclusion is nearly impossible, in spite of huge potential in academics.

Future: Is There Any Scope?

Enhancing employment opportunities for people with disabilities is one of the main concerns of the disability sector in India. The employment rate of disabled people has actually fallen from 42.7% in 1991 down to 37.6% in 2002 (http://infochangein-dia.org/other/books-a-reports/as-indian-economy-booms-the-disabled-fall-behind-world-bank.html). There are several employment exchange offices in India. People with various disabilities are getting jobs but it is rare in the case of autism. People with high functional autism or Asperger's syndrome are getting some amount of opportunities in terms of employment, but the rest, the average population with autism, are jobless which is very unfortunate. The software company SAP has taken initiative to give employment to the persons with autism based on their unique talents. Again here we are talking about high functional or Asperger's population. They are taking them as software tester and programmers.

Around 700,000 people in the UK have autism – that's more than 1 in 100 (www.autism.org.uk/teacherpack). It was shown that 17% of children with autism have been suspended from school, 48% of these had been suspended three or more times, and 4% had been expelled from one or more schools (Reid 2011). About 70% of adults with autism say that they are not getting the help they need from social services. The same percentage of adults with autism also told that with more support they would feel less isolated (Özmen 2013).

At least one in three adults with autism is experiencing severe mental difficulties due to a lack of support. Only 15% of adults with autism in the UK are in full-time, paid employment, (Redman et al. 2009) but the best thing about this country is social security. If a person is disabled mentally or physically, the government supports their basic needs, which is not the case in India. Hence parents' initiatives, community living, and supported employment are the ultimate options in India for a secured future for people with autism.

Hoping for all these positive outcomes, we came back to Kolkata, our hometown. In the last few years, a lot of awareness has spread across the society. For example, one day we went for a swim in our residential apartment complex's swimming pool. Since Zico is still not fully independent, I took him to the women's changing room. A little girl, not more than 4 years old, asked me: "Aunty, there is another changing room for boys. Could you (pointing towards Zico) ask him to go there?" I replied: "Dear, he is a special child with autism, he needs help." At once the little one said: "Oh, sorry Aunty, special child? Okay. Okay." It felt good. God knows how much the little girl understands about autism but at least she is aware of the word "Special Child" and knows the meaning of it! These small incidents helped to change my mind-set and made me realize that people are mostly good.

Nowadays many Non-Government Organizations (NGOs) are developing various facilities for persons with special needs in India. As the government is not able to take the initiative, they are encouraging NGOs to build different setups for the betterment of individuals with autism. The main concern for parents is what would happen to their children after the parents die? As these children cannot speak out about the quality of services they are getting, abuse becomes a very common practice in this field. There is an urgent need to begin planning residences and centers for these children when they become adults. People with autism have a normal life span and many will require considerable support after their parents' death.

In the last 8 years, I have found a purpose in my life. I have learned to become strong enough to fight this extreme battle. My little prince, who could not even walk properly when he should have been running, can now skate, swim, play in the park, and also ride a bicycle. He is now able to organize himself to visit a crowded place and can wait for small shopping trips and restaurant visits. He can communicate his basic needs with little speech and gesture and can manage Activities of Daily Living (ADL). I have taught myself to compare him with only him and no one else. There have been changes in the grandparents' attitudes as well. They have become more understanding and have acknowledged my efforts. All these changes have given me more confidence to move on.

Theoretically inclusion in the mainstream educational setting can bring best possible outcome for children with autism. But till date it has been near to impossible to establish a suitable modified environment in India. Most of the autistic children demonstrate manipulative behavior due to sensory overload. So, pushing them towards an unstructured setup against their natural system for the sake of social integration is objectionable to me. A child can learn various skills without mainstream educational setup, which can be ignored at this time, but we cannot ignore the environment, the society and the people around – as he/she has to face these challenges on a regular basis. To me, creating awareness is the key to develop inclusion in India at present. Parents and professionals can make this happen. Even entertainment media can play a major role in this regard. If we can make people around us understand autism, social training would no longer be difficult for children with autism.

Being a professional in this field, my main focus is to empower parents of children with special needs and to create awareness within the society. It's a journey, a long journey… When I look back on the therapies, sleepless nights, tears, and struggles, all I can say with absolute certainty is "It was absolutely worth it!"

References

Autism A resource pack for school staff Compiled and edited by the Autism Information Team, The National Autistic Society. (2015). Retrieved from www.autism.org.uk/teacherpack

Centers for Disease Control and Prevention's (CDC) Surveillance Study. (2014, March 27). Retrieved from https://www.autismspeaks.org/what-autism/prevalence

Cermak, S. A., & Larkin, D. (1991). *Developmental coordination disorder*. Quebec City: Delmar.

Kranowitz, A., & Stock, C. (1998). *Out of sync child*. New York: Berkley Publication.

Özmen, A. (2013). *Push for action we need to turn the autism act into action*. London: The National Autistic Society.

'*People with Disabilities in India: From Commitments to Outcomes' report released by the World Bank Commissioned by the Indian government.* (2004). Retrieved from http://infochangeindia. org/other/books-a-reports/as-indian-economy-booms-the-disabled-fall-behind-world-bank. html

Redman, S., Downie, M., Rennison, R., & Batten, A. (2009). *Don't write me off: Make the system fair for people with autism*. London: The National Autistic Society.

Reid, B. (2011). *We've got great expectations*. London: The National Autistic Society.

Chapter 24
Global Diversity and Inclusion: Critical Reflections and Future Directions

Santoshi Halder and Lori Czop Assaf

Abstract Following the developed countries, an increasing number of countries including the developing ones have shown their agreeableness to adapt to changes in legislations, administration and practice, aiming participation of individuals with disabilities for an inclusive environment. Unfortunately, agreeableness does not necessarily ensure full participation or social acceptance or inclusion. This chapter summarizes the diversities of culture and inclusion as brought forward by various authors across countries, cultures and disciplines with critical reflections bridging the gap of diversities and inclusion building a universal model of inclusion from the learnings derived from each chapter. In this text, we share our understandings of disability and the global nature of the cultural features that impinge on quality of life to help establish what is universally true about disability and what may be unique to specific cultures or countries and individuals. The future directions lies in exploring the positive practices from various countries and cultures as exposed by the authors through their own lived experiences which may provide models for more universal approaches to disability so that a strategic cross-cultural, interdisciplinary and holistic approach may result in a valued positioning of people with disabilities transforming the world into a global inclusive community in the real sense of the term.

Introduction

Inclusion, a fundamental principle underlying diversity in society, highlights the importance of a cohesive community which accepts and respects differences and is responsible to individual needs ensuring that people feel they belong, are engaged and connected. It is a universal human right which aims at embracing all people

S. Halder (✉)
Department of Education, University of Calcutta,
Alipore Campus, Kolkata, West Bengal, India
e-mail: santoshi_halder@yahoo.com

L.C. Assaf
Department of Curriculum and Instruction, Texas State University, San Marcos, TX, USA

© Springer International Publishing AG 2017   379
S. Halder, L.C. Assaf (eds.), *Inclusion, Disability and Culture*, Inclusive
Learning and Educational Equity 3, DOI 10.1007/978-3-319-55224-8_24

irrespective of race, gender, disability or other attributes which can be perceived as different (UNESCO 2005). Miller and Katz (2002) defined inclusion as: "… a sense of belonging; feeling respected, valued; feeling a level of supportive energy and commitment from others so that you can do your best". Inclusion is more than simply placing individuals with and without disabilities together with proper and timely identification assessment, intervention, accessibility, rehabilitation and independent living. Rather, inclusion includes allocating services, changing attitudes and developing a sense of responsibility. Inclusion is also about how a society and its people get ready for individuals with a disability. The developments over the past few decades have led to a series of changes at the societal level reflecting a global trend of inclusion envisaged by numerous legal instruments at the national and international levels to ensure equal opportunity for all (Pijl et al. 1997). Following initiatives led by developed countries, an increasing number of other countries have shown their agreeableness to adapt to the changes in legislations, administration and practice, aiming at participation of individuals with disabilities with the objective of creating an inclusive environment. Unfortunately, agreeableness does not necessarily ensure implementation, full participation or social acceptance. In spite of various legislative measures, several studies have documented the exclusion of individuals with disabilities from meaningful participation in the economic, social, political and cultural life of communities as one of the greatest problems facing individuals with disabilities today.

The various authors of this book, from a range of professions, cultures, countries and disciplines, uncover significant aspects of inclusion. The case studies, ethnographic perspectives, snapshots exposed from the authors' own lives or experiences capture essential aspects of inclusion either prevalent or necessary for developing a global inclusive environment for all. These studies and personal narratives describe important topics that help us bridge the gap between global diversities and inclusion and expose the reader to great insights. The authors' insights provide important information to help create inclusive principles and practical ideas to guide the transition towards implementation of inclusion policies for effective implementation across cultural contexts and countries.

Disability and Identities

The authors carefully situate their own identities and disabilities through their auto-ethnographic experiences to explain and critically reflect on how their lives have been shaped through negative and positive experiences. Some authors have provided a comparative analysis across various countries. As Christopher and colleagues discuss the complexity of how disability is conceptualized in the United States and India, they also describe the influence of cultural and historical backgrounds on one's identity and disability. Christopher and colleagues conclude by highlighting common and explanatory themes across the two countries. Identity intersects with a wide variety of contextual factors including (but not limited to) national context. Further, agencies that aim to support persons with disabilities approach identity in different ways. Through this exploration of theory, preliminary empirical work and self, we understand that personal identity is dynamic as each person has a way of thinking about disability and how he or she is affected by personal traits, life experiences and attitudes from a society. If a positive self-identity is the goal for an individual with and without disabilities, a careful approach to disentangling the societal barriers that promote exclusion, and also seeking personal services such as counselling, building the self-concept and vocational supports appear to be the most appropriate path forward.

Delving deep into literature and theosophy, the chapter by Samidha Shikha unravels the complexity of identity with renewed vigour and understanding and brings forth a new perspective to disability. Of course it's too hard to imagine how a drooping eyelid, called 'Ptosis', could cause so much pain and inferiority complex that has been so hard to shrug off and so complicated to share. Insensitivity towards others and the harm it perpetrates in a society is not easy to gauge. The family, culture and society is all the cause and answer to the entire incompetency rampant in the so-called able society. This write-up is an attempt to think about the nameless prodigies and 'would be' achievers that may appear normal but actually need tender concern to return to normalcy. In other words, the apparently 'able' people may be suffering from unrecognized disabilities or mental handicaps which establish themselves on the physique and personality of an individual. One needs a discerning attitude to fathom the scale of cultural ostracism that leads to conquerable incapacities.

Satendra Singh reflects on the shaping of identity and disability through his narrative. He explains his personal perspectives from the point of view of a medical doctor, a teacher, a family person and a disability rights activist in India. He reflects on his experiences through an auto-ethnographic lens that brings the reader into his life, his struggles, and his eventual insights and inspirations. He exposes his transition from a sufferer to an activist - offering an understanding into the larger political, social and cultural scenario of living with a disability in Indian context. His journey was surely long but he believes in the importance of passion, pertinacity and perseverance.

Anjali Forber-Pratt, an assistant professor at Vanderbilt University, USA, presents an auto-ethnographic account of her experiences as a disabled adopted woman of colour. She describes two stories – one of her travels to India, her birthplace, and the other to Ghana as a Paralympic athlete who advocates for disability rights in the context of education and work. This auto-ethnography captures how one person interrogated, challenged and survived obstacles faced by many individuals with disabilities. Yet, she believes experiencing oppression and challenging stereotypes can actually strengthen and enhance one's development of identity, rather than jeopardize it. At the same time, Forber-Pratt points out the positive side of these experiences. Today she is able to connect to others and give them hope by encouraging them to embrace their experiences and allowing them to shape their identity rather than destroying it, so they too can develop a strong sense of self and find their purpose in life.

Similarly Simon Hayhoe argues that impairments are subjective and that context must always be considered when evaluating and judging disabilities. He examines his experience of late deafness and describes his experiences in becoming deaf, being diagnosed and living with his new impairment in England. His analysis considers his experience of becoming deaf from the point of view of subjective and objective disability. It does not matter whether we see or hear, touch or smell as everyone else does, we can still engage culturally and emotionally in any subject matter uniquely according to our personal histories as these emotions come from different life experiences. Therefore, the different experiences of educational, medical, governmental or cultural institutionalization, and the exclusion that is derived from this institutionalization, in relation to the congenitally and early disabled person must be considered when communicating or developing policies and support for them.

Truly a cross-cultural and cross-disciplinary encounter is extremely necessary to enhance the debate about disability and inclusion. Oliveira shares the story of her life growing up with a disability from childhood to adulthood while living in Brazil and the United States. She describes how she came to accept herself and her disability as a child and how she moved through the education system all the way to earn her doctorate despite many barriers. She concludes with an honest portrayal of how difficult it was to write about her life but believes it is her responsibility to speak out and fight against inequities that prevent people with disabilities from living a normal life. Her writing provides great insight and a new understanding of the stigma around disability as she argues that a democratic society is reached only through an inclusive education, a frequent dialogue between different and diverse.

Besides the gaze of society on individuals with disabilities, it is also important to consider the way stigma influences one's self-perception regarding individual abilities. The lack of access to information makes this population even more vulnerable to this kind of misconstruction, contributing to the stigmata resonate in social learning. Although the social movements for accessibility are built upon a rights-based model, the medical model continues to hold the most prominent position in most societies. The medical model continues because most societies, including Brazil, focus on what a disability prevents the impaired from doing, instead of concentrating on their capabilities or the community's accountability. Flávia Affonso Mayer addresses how visually impaired individuals can be influenced by misleading ideas about their impairment that those stigmatized viewpoints become entrenched in their own experiences. She shares her own experiences by describing the scenarios of social mobilization and accessibility rights in Brazil and in the United States, and argues for how social barriers and the lack of information can reinforce the stigma on people with disabilities. This is a very difficult perspective to change, but it is urgent for democratic societies.

Inclusion means having unlimited opportunities to engage the individual in personal and professional endeavours, despite functional limitations, in ways that celebrate differences. Thus, professionals with different abilities are called upon to lead the identity and civil rights movement of the differently abled community. The experiences of being a female with a disability bring additional challenges and barriers including the strength to overcome those challenges. Caroline Muster redefines the term disability as different ability and describes her own story of how individuals with different abilities must persevere through the life-long process of reconsidering their personal views of themselves when faced with negative perceptions and societal prejudices. She highlights the specific struggles differently abled females must face such as intersexuality and sexual oppression. Individuals belonging to a differently abled community, having identification with the community, can be a source of pride for others. Daily challenges help them become resilient contributing to a sense of identity. The physical scars serving as reminders of the pain, the moments of rejection fostering more authentic relationships with the allies and the encounters with barriers to personal and political freedom engendering creativity and perseverance.

Complexities of Communication and the Differently Abled

Communication is important with differently abled individuals as it is with the neuro-typical persons. An important prerequisite for inclusion is barrier-free communication, or knowledge about differently abled. Communication is a complex phenomenon. Ivana applies theories and her own research to understand how people with and without disabilities communicate in any context. She presents attitudes towards communication from different perspectives unravelling the basis of her own empirical research experiences that individuals are prejudiced regarding communication with differently abled. Too often they lack knowledge about that population in their societies. Equal treatment of differently abled in communication does not exist according to the research results, and people approach communication without basic knowledge about it. From Ivana's writings it becomes evident that there is need to invest more time in formal and informal education about differently abled so as to establish prerequisites for complete inclusion of differently abled in societies around the globe.

As we move towards more inclusive societies, our awareness of emotional understanding and acceptance of others play a significant role in promoting authentic communication with people with disabilities. The chapter by Erna Alant highlights the importance of self-other awareness as part of the inter-subjective process of meaning-making to facilitate inclusion of people with disabilities in our society. With exhaustive cross-cultural empirical experiences of working in close proximity with individuals with special needs in countries like South Africa and the United States, Erna Alant and colleagues bring out an entirely new concept of empathetic communication and its relevance in facilitating communication between people with communication disabilities and typical communicators as described. She discussed different examples of interaction between a caregiver and an adult with disabilities as well as a cross-cultural interaction between a therapist and a mother of a child with disabilities. She identifies issues that impact the process of empathetic communication; the level of task-orientedness or purposeful structure imposed on the interaction, and the experiential and conceptual differences between communication partners. Alant establishes how the ability to communicate empathetically is at the basis of promoting inclusion of people with disabilities in our society. Communication is not just a cognitive process that requires exchanging messages with someone, it is also a process based on emotional resonance with another. Only by understanding the need for self-other awareness as part of the communication process can we move towards sustainable intervention processes.

The complexity of communication is also not beyond the complexities as Shakila Dada and colleagues summarize the barriers and enablers to inclusion through their research with severe communication disabilities in a South African context. The social model of disability reminds us that a person is often made to feel more or less disabled by environmental factors such as poverty, unequal societies, the view from which Augmentative and Alternative Communication (AAC) systems are developed, communication partners, multilingual and multicultural contexts, people and resources. Augmentative and Alternative Communication (AAC) as an intervention is one method used to increase levels of engagement and participation for needs of the individuals with diverse needs. Shakila and her colleagues highlight context-relevant practices and considerations. This chapter is written from a point of accepting diversity and promoting social inclusion within society. The role of rehabilitation professionals as advocates for change and for empowering individuals with significant communication disabilities and their families cannot be overlooked. The chapter highlights the importance of accessible communication through AAC as a key strategy for inclusion of persons with communication disability and promotes at the outset an integrated approach across disciplines and stakeholders to create an inclusive society for persons that use AAC. The solutions to providing inclusive environments should be pursued from the views of the marginalized rather than only from the perspective of the empowered.

Communication of information and making that information accessible through the application of new technologies is an important prerequisite for an inclusive environment. Alison explores how the application of principles used for communication of information to disabled visitors can enhance the experiences of all museum visitors. Within this chapter Alison explored related research and practitioner perspectives on audio description (AD), multisensory learning and museum experience to create an argument for the extensive use of AD in museums for blind and sighted audiences. By maintaining separate strategies for different disabilities, we reinforce exclusion. The evidence from practitioners, as well as the evidence on multisensory memory and imagery suggests that the use of a rich range of multisensory imagery and metaphors would create a richer experience for the listener. Henceforth, AD becomes a crucial step towards creating a shared museum experience for those with and without sight, within which people of all levels of visual experience and visual ability can gain an enhanced experience of 'seeing', and perhaps also of 'touching', 'hearing', even 'smelling' and 'tasting'. At the same time, while AD may prove to be a valuable tool in the enhancement of a museum visit for all visitors, irrespective of their level of vision, museums have to be responsible for inclusive and accessible communication. They must consider whether accessible resources are of little worth without marketing and audience development to encourage attendance, and training staff. Future research on the impact of multisensory AD on engagement, learning and memorability should consider its use for an audience who 'sees' in a variety of ways. Nevertheless, taking AD from the niche audience of visual impairment and projecting it onto the mass market of the 'sighted' could have a revolutionary impact on the museum experience and our understanding of access and difference. Access stops being a sidelined addition for a small group of visitors, and becomes a shared inclusive approach which considers the needs of all visitors.

Inclusive Policies and Practices

National and international legislation, laws and policies for successful inclusion, is paramount to the discussion of disability and inclusion. However, the implementation of the status quo has led to questionable outcomes and often limited access. Mary in her chapter has identified the fact that different legislation in the United States, Australia and India has not changed the nature of the issues and that each country has to provide safe, effective educational services for students with disabilities. Mary analysed the various processes and contributions that disability discrimination legislation has made in the United States, Australia and India. The historic examination of case law provides a template for the resolution of issues related to inclusive practices in schools. It seems that while the rhetoric of the legislation as it relates to access and participation is largely accepted and understood in developed countries, it is in need of improved pedagogies by listening to the voice of people with disabilities and understanding the complex nature of disability that will challenge schools. Clear and lawful policies that guide effective practices, a willingness to share decision making and building teacher capacity to address learner diversity will help schools become more responsive to the unique needs of students with disabilities.

There is indeed a glaring need for a total transformation in our professional attitudes towards the manner in which our future generations are going to be educated. Implementing policies in classrooms with learners is important for inclusion. Poulomee, originally from India, and her colleagues from Australia in their chapter portray the concept of inclusive education within the Australian context through case studies in mainstream classrooms across different states of Australia. The total education plan provides deep insights into the inclusive practices undertaken for successful inclusion in Southern Australia. These authors bring forth a critical reflections derived from the various case studies provided within the Australian context in relation to achieving inclusion in mainstream classes as an important consideration towards inclusion.

Inclusion of children with special needs is one of the foremost objectives of international and national legislations and the stakeholders all over the world (United Nations 2006). The practical implementation of the same, however, is faced with multiple challenges on both levels: individual needs and the context. Policy makers, stakeholders and special educators are struggling to ameliorate the most suitable strategy to include children with diverse needs in an inclusive setting. When it comes to children with developmental delays including Autism Spectrum Disorder (ASD) due to the diversities in their needs and characteristics, it becomes even more of a challenge and a concern for special education teachers to best cater their needs in a heterogeneous class. Customizing the strategies/interventions scientifically to best suit the individual needs within a common setting is a necessary skill which needs analytical understanding of the problem behaviour and then targeting with a function-based intervention in a personalized way. The chapter provides a few significant strategies needed for special education practioners in order to provide an inclusive setting. Dr. Halder reveals that the foremost challenge for the professionals and practioners is to design the most suitable intervention programme to ameliorate the skill deficits in individuals with developmental disabilities including Autism Spectrum Disorder (ASD). The significance of a need-based intervention strategy for socially approved behaviour has been well published worldwide. However, the acceptance and implementation of the same in various countries and cultures are with mixed results quite specifically in the low socioeconomic and less affluent countries. The author depicts and explores the significance of various strategies designed to cater to individual needs in an Indian context. The findings of these three single-subject design studies conducted on different subjects in different contexts establish the effectiveness of need-based individualized behaviour modification approaches to target the skill deficits in children with disabilities.

Among the various categories of disabilities, the gifted population is often neglected by teachers. Author Partha Pratim Roy explored the meaning, characteristics and successful interventions for gifted students through case studies and snapshots from his experiences as a teacher of more than 20 years in one of the most reputed higher secondary school in an Indian context and brings out some common generalizations on the line. Recipient of the distinguished Fulbright Teacher award by the United States India Education Foundation (USIEF) for exploring his research potentials in United States in 2011, he guided, assisted and nurtured numerous students in his own school through 'discovery teaching and learning' and helped to identify the gifted minds and nurture their abilities. Roy has shown with practical instances how even the most 'ordinary' student can turn creative to win accolades in prestigious science competitions across the globe. He strongly argues through his own practical experiences as a teacher with passion for his role as a torch bearer that the concept of the giftedness is a social construct of questionable validity. In a country like India where we are still far away from making education available to all children, any demand for special provisions for a few because they are termed 'gifted' by some parameters is untenable. Partha revealed that if discovery learning method is adopted in teaching science for all students at the school level, the identification and nurturing of the 'gifted' students will be done automatically. His auto-ethnographic account of dealing with a large number of high school children ($N \approx 62,500$) can provide teachers and researchers issues for further investigation and application. The triangular interaction of the conceptual primitive, epistemology and metacognition becomes conspicuously visible in a discovery learning situation, and this interaction is key to unleash the hidden abilities in a student. His account may provide important directions in identifying problems for newer research not only in the field of 'gifted and talented education', but also in 'inclusive education' and 'education' in general. Finally he stresses on the role of the teachers and educators to identify and nourish those abilities so that the students can flourish at some point in life.

The impact of culture and context on individuals with disability has been an important aspect well written and argued from time to time in various literatures. As against context-specific characteristics, disability defines merely a physical or intellectual impairment of a person from a charity perspective where the ideology of karma plays a crucial role by providing a justification for the existence of inequality among human beings. Chandani Liyanage from Srilanka, explores socio-cultural construction of disability in Sri Lanka and its impact on the everyday lives of persons with disabilities. While acknowledging the strengths of the social mode, the chapter brings forth the existing gaps and argues that disability demands an integrated approach towards empowering persons with disabilities and to mobilize the entire society to create an environment with reasonable adjustments for an inclusive society that accepts disability as part of the diversity. The findings suggest that not only the masses but also professional and different service providers have an unfavourable attitude towards moving from a charity perspective to a rights-based approach. She insists on the need to have a higher authority to deal with issues related to disability where legal aspect should be further strengthened.

Author Norma acknowledges the strengths of the social model in her chapter arguing that disability demands an integrated approach towards empowering persons with disabilities to mobilize the entire society to create an environment with reasonable accommodation for an inclusive society that accepts disability as part of the diversity. Coming from an architectural background, Norma clearly and quite interestingly stresses the need for accessibility and architectural design tracing down the history of the evolution of necessity while simultaneously strengthening the beauty of an accessible environment and the benefit of it for all.

Inclusion includes identification, assessment, intervention including the successful rehabilitation of the individuals in society and independent living. Darren brings forth experiences from Australia and points out that despite the importance of improving employment opportunities for individuals with ASD, there is a marked lack of research regarding employment supports or interventions for adults with ASD. The chapter reviews the existing literature with regard to employment and employment programmes available for individuals with ASD including co-morbidity. Not much literature can be found on this aspect in the developing countries where the struggle still revolves around the initial aspects of inclusion like identification and assessment. The chapter provides evidence from quantitative and qualitative research and from subjective, lived experience accounts that people with autism and their families face significant difficulties and struggles in their everyday lives. The author describes that building understanding with employers and working closely with the government can not only lead to greater employment opportunities for individuals with autism but can greatly enhance outcomes for families, society and also the economy. The writing provides evidence of the importance and relevance of inclusive practice (and the personal and economic cost of not being inclusive), and also provides stories from individuals who *have* successfully traversed the challenges posed by a society not adept at enabling success in those perceived as somehow 'different' or 'less able'. Inclusion of people with disabilities in all facets of society demands innovation not only in terms of practical supports, services and politics but also in terms of social perception and bias.

Perspectives of Caregivers

Perspectives of the parents and caregivers who are the ones struggling with providing for their children with special needs is an important consideration for designing inclusive practices. A family typically provides care and life experiences superior to an institutional setting without the worry of possible abuse and neglect. The author reflects on their child rearing practices and experiences in various countries and directly or indirectly brings in many valuable points for consideration of inclusive approach. Elizabeth from United States as a parent of a child with special needs in her chapter uses socio-cultural theories, an ecological perspective and a case-study format to explore how families and teachers understand children with complex academic, mental health and health needs in the United States. Anderson stresses that the more understanding parents and teachers have about a child's development, the greater the likelihood of developmental opportunities for that child. This study fills a gap in the literature on young children with complex academic, mental health and health needs by exploring the experiences of families and teachers in the United States. This has important implications for closer examination of the current emphasis on academics in the broader context of an interrelationship of care that fosters inter-professional collaboration and strengthens home–school partnerships for children with complex academic, mental health and health needs. Since many families and other school professionals may not be aware of, or are unsure how to respond to, a child's complex academic, mental health or health needs, we also learned that there is an urgent need for more targeted family training and professional development for school staff. Lastly, we learned about the importance of gaining a much clearer picture of the number of young children with complex academic, mental health and health needs, and the nature of those needs. This has important implications for the type of support and services that will help children with complex needs achieve optimal outcomes in inclusive settings.

Natalaya gave a personal and detailed account and describes her experiences as a mother of a child with a congenital rare genetic abnormality and multiple developmental disabilities. She highlights her responses and adjustments over time to her daughter's diagnosis and provides a glimpse into how an individual's cultural and socioeconomic background as well as her personal preferences in conjunction with available societal services in three locales in the United States led to choices, decisions and planning for a single family. Limitations of social mobility is another combined effect of a disability and life choices.

Another parent Lily Chakraborty from India, a special educator and mother of a child with autism, unravels her own struggles, challenges and joys through a comparative analysis of her own experience of living in a developed and developing country. This chapter draws on her experience as a mother and takes the reader into the world of those parents who experience the pains and joys of raising a child with autism. It provides a unique perspective on autism both in India and in the UK from the viewpoint of a concerned parent. Theoretically, inclusion in mainstream educational setting can bring the best possible outcome for children with autism. She brings in the contrasting challenges of both the contexts as a caregiver. She stresses the role of empowering parents and professionals for inclusion specifically in an Indian context.

Future Directions

Inclusion is seen as a process of addressing and responding to the diverse needs of all through increasing participation among cultures and communities and reducing exclusion by providing appropriate responses to the broad spectrum of needs. It involves changes and modifications in content, approaches, structures and strategies, with a shared vision to transform the environment in order to respond to all kinds of diversities. It aims towards enabling all concerned to feel comfortable with diversity and to see it as a challenge and enrichment of the learning environment, rather than a problem (UNESCO 2005; UNICEF 2013).

From an ethical point of view, human rights are fundamental to overcoming disabling barriers and promoting inclusion. A human rights approach should ensure positive processes and outcomes for disabled people, including treating people with dignity and respect and ensuring that society no longer disables its citizens. It is argued that in developing human rights-based approaches to inclusion, cognizance should ensure that all individuals with disabilities are able to access the basic rights and appropriate services regardless of the circumstances in which they find themselves (UNICEF 2013).

The discussions and discourses in each chapter identify the indicators of quality-of-life for people with disabilities with respect to support services available in their own context and capacity as they are provided by each country with implications for disability policy, practice and future research. The chapters provide an important contribution to the knowledge of the association between one's living arrangement, choice and quality of life for individuals with disabilities. The text engages various authors from a number of countries who take us with them on their journeys depicting the struggles, successes, conflicts, barriers, abilities and challenges they faced due to disabilities. The ideas and experiences shared provide important suggestions and future directions for how we can create adequate community-based networks of social and health services. It also informs how we can develop consensually valid criteria for quality of care and appropriateness. In the developing world, however, there is a lack of globally reliable epidemiological data on Quality of Life (QOL) with respect to various subjective and objective factors. This text lays the framework for necessary comparisons in this regard. It is important for practitioners and related service personnel to have an understanding of the evidence base and to partner with various countries to transmit sound information on research-based strategies for proper rehabilitation and independent living of the people with disabilities in society.

Conclusion

Inclusion is a dynamic approach of responding positively to pupil diversity and seeing individual differences not as problems, but as opportunities for enriching learning. Therefore, the move towards inclusion is not simply a technical or organizational change but a philosophical shift (UNESCO 2005).

The perspectives of various professionals, parents, self-advocates, researchers, self-educators, experts and specialists identify the gaps in policy frameworks and implications in the everyday life of people with disabilities on a global front. These identified variables will be of enormous help to assist the policy makers in getting an insight for modification of the resources and technology to suit individual needs for the implementation of needs-based culture-specific realistic, functional and accessible support services and provisions for the people with disabilities.

References

Miller, F. A., & Katz, J. H. (2002). Unleashing the real power of diversity. In *The inclusion break-through*. San Francisco: Berrett-Koehler Publishers.

Pijl, S. J., Meijer, C. J., & Hegarty, S. (1997). *Inclusive education: A global agenda*. London: Routledge.

UNESCO. (2005). Guidelines for inclusion: Ensuring access to education for all published in 2005 by the United Nations Educational, Scientific and Cultural Organization 7, place de Fontenoy, 75352 PARIS 07 SP Composed and printed in the workshops of UNESCO.

UNICEF. (2013, May). *The state of the World's children 2013 executive summary children with disabilities*. United Nations Children's Fund (UNICEF), New York, USA.

United Nations. (2006). *Convention on the rights of person's with disabilities and optional proto-col, office of the high commissioner*. Geneva: United Nations.